THE BIOLOGY OF SEA SNAKES

THE BIOLOGY OF
SEA SNAKES

edited by
William A. Dunson, Ph.D.
The Pennsylvania State University

University Park Press
Baltimore · London · Tokyo

UNIVERSITY PARK PRESS
International Publishers in Science and Medicine
Chamber of Commerce Building
Baltimore, Maryland 21202

Typeset by The Composing Room of Michigan, Inc.

Printed in the United States of America by Universal Lithographers, Inc.

Library of Congress Cataloging in Publication Data
Main entry under title:

The biology of sea snakes.

Includes index.
1. Sea snakes. I. Dunson, William A.
QL666.0645B56   598.1'2'0492   75-11790
ISBN 0-8391-0819-2

Contents

Ecological Relationships

Physiology

Venomous Nature of Sea Snakes

Relationships to Man

Contributors

Dr. Jurgen von Bredow, Experimental Medicine Department, Medical Research Laboratory, Edgewood Arsenal, Aberdeen Proving Ground, Maryland 21010

Dr. Harold G. Cogger, Curator of Reptiles, The Australian Museum, 6–8 College Street, P.O. Box A285, Sydney South, NSW 2000, Australia

Mr. Milton S. da Costa, Department of Microbiology, Indiana University, Medical Center, Indianapolis, Indiana 46202

Dr. Roger J. Cuffey, Associate Professor of Geosciences, Pennsylvania State University, University Park, Pennsylvania 16802

Dr. William A. Dunson, Professor of Biology, Pennsylvania State University, University Park, Pennsylvania 16802

Ms. Marie M. Grenan, Division of Medicinal Chemistry, Walter Reed Army Institute of Research, Washington, D.C. 20012

Dr. Harold F. Heatwole, Associate Professor of Zoology, University of New England, Armidale, NSW 2351, Australia

Dr. Emerson Hibbard, Professor of Biology, Pennsylvania State University, University Park, Pennsylvania 16802

Dr. Chaim Kropach, Steinitz Laboratory of Marine Biology, Hebrew University in Jerusalem, Elat, Israel

Mr. Colin Limpus, National Parks Section, Department of Forestry, Evans Road, Salisbury, Queensland 4107, Australia

Dr. John E. McCosker, Director, Steinhart Aquarium, California Academy of Sciences, San Francisco, California 94118

Dr. Sherman A. Minton, Professor of Microbiology, Indiana University, Medical Center, Indianapolis, Indiana 46202

Dr. George V. Pickwell, Biosystems Research Department, Naval Undersea Center, San Diego, California 92132

Mr. Emmanuel Y. Punay, General Manager, The Sea Snakes Company of the Philippines, Room 401 Doña Amparo Building, España Boulevard, Cor. Cataluña Street, Sampaloc, Manila, Philippines

Dr. H. Alistair Reid, O.B.E., School of Tropical Medicine, Liverpool L3 5QA, England

Dr. Roger E. Seymour, Department of Zoology, Monash University, Clayton, Victoria 3168, Australia

Dr. Nobuo Tamiya, Professor of Chemistry, Tohoku University, Sendai, Japan

Dr. James A. Vick, Experimental Medicine Department, Medical Research Laboratory, Edgewood Arsenal, Aberdeen Proving Ground, Maryland 21010

Dr. Leon P. Zann, School of Biological Sciences, James Cook University, Townsville, Queensland 4810, Australia

Preface

Sea snakes are extremely abundant in many tropical areas of the world. They have been highly successful in the sea, which is a rigorous habitat for reptiles and difficult to colonize. The highly venomous nature of sea snakes and their association with the mythical sea serpents of sailors' yarns have given them an aura of dangerous mystery. Until very recently, few scientific data were available to dispel the cloud of anecdotes that has built up around this unique group of serpents. The awakening of scientific interest in the sea and the financial support given to oceanographic ships and shore laboratories in the tropics have allowed biologists to gain first-hand experience in the study of sea snakes. No longer is the sea snake merely a shriveled specimen in the pickle jar. Now we think of it as a living entity coexisting with other animals and plants on a coral reef, along a rocky coast, or perhaps in a mangrove swamp. My first personal encounter with sea snakes was a thrilling experience. The element of personal danger is, of course, a factor, but it was fascinating to watch sea snakes and directly observe details of feeding, reproduction, and other aspects of their life.

The only book published in this century on sea snakes was the *Monograph of the Sea-Snakes* by Malcolm Smith. Even today, this classic 1926 taxonomic account is the standard reference for identification. A reader interested in other aspects of sea snake biology has to search out a widely scattered body of literature. Our hope, in the present volume, is to summarize the aspects of sea snake biology which are sufficiently researched to warrant coverage and for which qualified authors could be found. Thus, several areas of importance, such as natural history of Asian species, reproduction (endocrinology), and functional morphology, unfortunately could not be included. This book, then, represents the present state of our knowledge, and I hope any deficiencies in coverage will stimulate others into taking up the study of sea snake biology.

The most difficult aspect of these investigations has been the procurement of healthy snakes and their maintenance in the laboratory. One oceanographic vessel, the R/V *Alpha Helix,* operated by the Scripps Institution of Oceanography, has played an important role in this work. On two cruises, a two-week transit from San Diego to Panama in 1970, and a longer six-week expedition to the Australian Timor Sea (Ashmore Reef) in 1972–1973, an international group of scientists was given the opportunity to carry out detailed experimental studies on sea snakes. Ten of the authors of this volume participated in at least one of these two cruises which I organized. Their interest and enthusiasm have been the major impetus behind the publication of this volume. Many of these studies were supported by grants from the National Science Foundation, and this assistance is separately noted in each contribution. Any opinions, findings, conclusions, or recommendations expressed in this volume are solely those of the authors and do not necessarily reflect the views of the National Science Foundation.

A Diver's Prayer

Snake, snake in the sea
Please don't put the bite on me,
Friend we are—not anemone
Please don't try to envenom me!

Jerry Robinson
Peter Richards
R/V *Alpha Helix*
Ashmore Reef Expedition
January, 1973

INTRODUCTION

one

Adaptations of Sea Snakes

William A. Dunson

In this chapter, important aspects of the adaptations that sea snakes have made to a life at sea are briefly discussed. Contemporary discoveries of major interest are emphasized to orient the reader to recent trends in research. Reference should be made to the individual chapters cited for detailed discussions of each point.

COLONIZATION OF THE SEA

Sea snakes are especially interesting because they represent the end result of millions of years of specialization for life under very stringent conditions. The high concentration of salts in sea water (about 3.5% NaCl) makes it difficult for reptiles to retain water in their bodies and keep the salt concentration low. The total concentration of the body fluids of vertebrates is usually only about one third that of sea water. Only a few animals, like the peculiar hagfish, can tolerate blood salt concentrations as high as sea water. Marine mammals keep a low blood salt level by excreting a very concentrated urine and in most instances by obtaining their water from their food rather than by drinking sea water. This procedure is modified somewhat in sea birds, where the kidney is less efficient, and a powerful salt-excreting gland is found. This salt gland, whose true function was only discovered in 1958 by Dr. Knut Schmidt-Nielsen of Duke University (Schmidt-Nielsen and Fangë, 1958), is present in all marine birds and in certain terrestrial forms where access to drinking water is limited. Since the reptilian kidney is unable to produce urine more concentrated than the blood, it is perhaps not surprising to find that all marine reptiles have salt glands (see Chapter 16).

The reptilian group is a very ancient one, and the three major living evolutionary groups, (1) the turtles, (2) the crocodilians, and (3) the lizards and snakes, diverged from one another rather early in time. A recent estimate places the age of the reptiles at about 300 million years (Bellairs, 1970). The turtles are probably the most ancient group and have changed little in external form since the Triassic period. Later, the crocodiles and the alligators developed, and some of their descendents gave rise to the birds. The lizards and snakes are by far the most abundant of modern reptiles and developed along a third evolutionary line after the turtles had become established. Snakes and lizards are very closely related, and it is suspected that burrowing forms of lizards gave rise to the first serpents. This would explain some of the peculiarities of snakes, the loss of limbs, the loss of external ear openings, the protection of the eye by a transparent spectacle, and the strange anatomy of the visual cells of the eye.

The snake shape seems ideally suited for a wide variety of habitats, including the sea. Some of the sea snakes are the only living reptiles that live and breed completely at sea without returning to land. Other sea snakes (*Laticauda*) and the sea turtles must return to land to lay eggs (Figure 1). The only lizard which has the slightest claim to be labeled marine, the Galápagos marine iguana, lives on seaside rocks and goes into the sea to feed on algae. One form of Pacific crocodile (*Crocodylus porosus*) is sometimes seen far at sea, but it is mainly a coastal or estuarine species, as is *Crocodylus acutus.* Large crocodiles can withstand sea water for considerable periods of time because their large bodies have a relatively small surface to volume ratio. However, the sea snakes, 50 kinds in all, are by far the most successful marine reptiles. This may be attributable in part to the advantage their shape gives them in swimming, to their development of efficient mechanisms of osmoregulation, or to the fact that all of them are quite venomous. The venom not only protects them against potential predators but makes it easier for them to secure prey.

The divergent evolutionary paths taken by the ancestors of marine reptiles on their way to the sea are revealed in a striking fashion by the kinds of salt glands developed (see Chapter 16). The salt gland seems to be an absolute necessity for colonization of the sea by reptiles, but in the turtles, lizards, and snakes we find three completely different types of glands developed. In the turtles salty "tears" are secreted around the eye by a lachrymal gland behind the eye. In the marine iguana a very large nasal gland secretes a fluid which is sneezed out the nostrils. In the sea snakes a third type of salt gland located under the tongue and secreting into the mouth was recently discovered.

DISTRIBUTION

The sea snakes (Family Hydrophiidae), like their close relatives the elapids (cobras and kraits), have fixed fangs and a potent venom. They can be

Figure 1. The amphibious banded sea snake *Laticauda* sp. from Fiji. This genus of sea snakes retains the ability to move about on land and is usually found on rocky reefs (A) or coiled on land in crevices or under bushes. Although *Laticauda* retains many features more typical of terrestrial forms, it does have the flattened tail (B) characteristic of all sea snakes.

subdivided into two subfamilies by differences in the width of the ventral scales and by certain skull characteristics. There is also a difference in habits between these two groups, representatives of one being more adapted for a life completely at sea (Figure 2) whereas the other types may be more often encountered on the shore (Figure 1). Sea snakes as a family are widely distributed, being found between South Africa and Japan in the western Pacific and Indian Oceans, eastward to a zone between Mexico and Ecuador. There are no sea snakes in the Atlantic Ocean, the Mediterranean Sea, or the Red Sea. The Atlantic Ocean has only narrowly escaped being a home for these successful reptiles since they apparently migrated to the New World sometime after the Central American land bridge rose out of the sea for the last time, about 4 million years ago. Prevented from taking the easy route into the Caribbean, these tropical serpents were then faced with a journey around the southern tips of Africa or South America if new habitats were to be colonized. This has proved to be impossible because of the cold southern currents in these regions (see Chapter 23). On occasion, sea snakes are found just inside the South Atlantic Ocean at Cape Town, but they are as rare and as out of place as the doomed sea turtles swept to the British Isles by the Gulf Stream. Thus, we find that the sea snakes are only rarely found outside the tropical zone or the transition zone between the tropics and the temperate

Figure 2. An example of the highly specialized sea snake genus *Hydrophis*. This is *Hydrophis elegans*, which has the elongate body and relatively narrow neck and head characteristic of snakes that feed on elongate hole-dwelling fish. This specimen was trawled off Townsville, Queensland, Australia, and is usually found in waters less than 10 fathoms in depth (see Chapter 7).

zone. Even the most widespread form, the yellow-bellied sea snake, *Pelamis*, is usually found at water temperatures above 20°C (Dunson and Ehlert, 1971). This particular snake, by means of its ability to feed at the surface and to float with ocean currents, has by far the greatest range of any sea snake. Other kinds, represented by *Laticauda,* are much more restricted in range. However, there are unconfirmed reports that this latter snake has been found in the New World in Nicaragua (Villa, 1962) and in Mexico (del Toro, 1972). The Indo-Australian area is probably the ancestral home of the sea snakes, and it is here that we find the greatest number of species. The Straits of Malacca, between the Malay peninsula and Sumatra, harbor as many as 27 different kinds. Unfortunately, we know very little about how so many species can live in the same area without competing with one another. In large part, this lack of information may be blamed on the fact that sea snakes are tropical and biologists are not. In addition, there are few scientists dedicated enough to work on an animal whose bite may kill them. At the present time, the only commercial antivenin is prepared by using the venom of a single species of sea snake.

FEEDING

The bits of information and anecdotes available about the life history and ecology of sea snakes reveal many interesting adaptations for life at sea. These snakes are, of course, air breathers and must come to the surface to get air. The flattened tail and laterally compressed body make them very efficient swimmers, although most remain in relatively shallow water. Dives of 20 to 90 feet or even possibly 500 feet are recorded, but no one knows the maximal depth to which these snakes can dive (see Chapter 15). Since many species feed on eels and other fish found on the bottom (Figure 3) they cannot venture into water too deep for their feeding dives. Pickwell (1972) has observed *Laticauda* trap small fish in rock crevices with folds of its body and then grasp the fish with its mouth. I have made similar observations on this snake in a small aquarium where coils of the body are used to immobilize a fish before it is seized and swallowed. This feeding response may explain how sea snakes can catch fish would could easily outswim them. Shrimp or prawns have been found in the stomachs of certain sea snakes; they may be caught while buried in bottom sand or mud. A completely different mode of feeding is found in the yellow-bellied sea snake (*Pelamis*) which is entirely a surface feeder (see Chapter 10). This snake floats at the surface, perhaps simulating a stick, and fish are attracted to it as to any floating object. These snakes have been observed many times with a group of small fish swimming underneath; a backward motion, a swift sideways strike, and the snake has an easy meal. Yet if the fish is dropped, *Pelamis* is unable to find it even if it is lying on the bottom of an aquarium a few centimeters away. This curiously

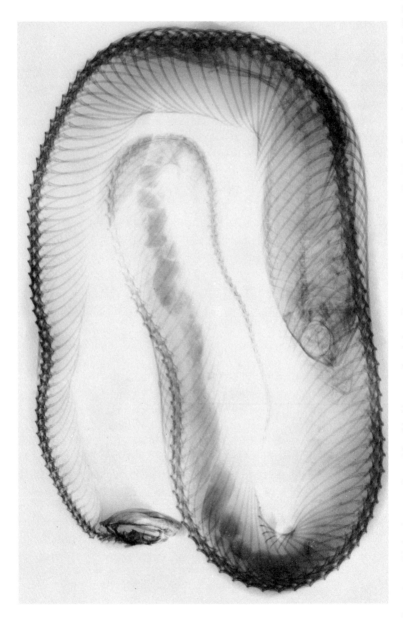

Figure 3.   A large fish has been swallowed by this *Aipysurus laevis* from Townsville, Queens, Australia. The radiograph was made by Dr. H. G. Cogger.

stereotyped feeding behavior is apparently related to the structure of the retina (see Chapter 17). Probably the most peculiar feeding habits of any snake are found in sea snakes of the genus *Emydocephalus* in Australia and Formosa (Figure 4). Voris (1966) found that these snakes have very few teeth and their stomachs contain only fish eggs; because of the reduction of teeth, they probably cannot catch and eat fish. *Aipysurus eydouxii* also seems to be solely an egg eater (see Chapter 11).

DIVING AND RESPIRATION

Respiration in sea snakes is an interesting area of study, since some snakes reportedly are capable of staying submerged for as long as 2 to 8 hr. The metabolism of snakes is, of course, much slower than that of mammals, but this only partially explains dives of this length. The suggestion has been made that these snakes might remove oxygen directly from the water, as fish or certain aquatic turtles do (i.e., the softshell turtle) (see Chapter 15). The lung of the sea snake is greatly enlarged, extending all the way to the base of the tail. As in other snakes, the left lung is very small and the right lung is highly developed. Even the trachea, the windpipe connecting with the lung, has been modified to provide an area for exchange of gases. Certain areas of the lung in the rear of the body may serve no respiratory function but rather function as a hydrostatic organ. In this way, the snake might be able to regulate its

Figure 4. A melanistic *Emydocephalus annulatus* from Ashmore Reef. Various reef species have a tendency toward melanism. This egg-eating species has several other color phases and is very abundant on certain coral reefs.

buoyancy as fish do with their swim bladder. It might also be expected that sea snakes have an increased tolerance for anoxia, or lack of oxygen, which allows them to pay off an "oxygen debt" after they return to the surface. Pickwell (1972) reported that one yellow-bellied sea snake left undisturbed in its tank only breathed once in a 90-min period. The amphibious sea snake *Laticauda* comes to the surface as often as once every half hour. Some sea snakes in the Philippines which feed only on bottom-dwelling eels have been observed diving down out of sight in clear water of a maximal depth of 500 feet (Herre, 1942). Man is able to dive only to about 250 feet when holding his breath. The increase in pressure with each additional 33 feet of depth is 1 atmosphere and causes a proportional decrease in lung volume. Beyond a certain point, blood and body fluids will enter the lungs with possibly fatal results. We just do not know how the sea snakes avoid the effects of this lung "squeeze" and other effects of great pressure at these depths (see Chapter 15). It is interesting that the types of sea snakes which must dive to the bottom for their food are confined mainly to waters well within the 100 fathom line. Thus they may not be able to dive to depths as great as this.

REPRODUCTION

The timing of breeding or reproduction is not well understood in most sea snakes (see Chapters 4–10). In the Philippine Islands there is a commercial fishery based on islets where *Laticauda* apparently congregate for breeding (see Chapter 21). It has been estimated that in a single year more than 10,000 snakes are killed for their skins on Gato Islet (Herre and Rabor, 1949). Others are taken alive, spitted on a pointed bamboo stick, and then roasted or smoked before being eaten. The gall bladders are eaten to strengthen the eyes. The shore-breeding sea snakes of this type lay eggs in crevices or the sand and leave them to hatch. The yellow-bellied sea snake, as has already been mentioned, never comes ashore even at breeding time. Mating or copulation takes place at sea and the young are born alive in the water (Figure 5). Some attempts have been made to define the breeding season of sea snakes, but it is by no means certain that reproduction is limited to a particular time of year. However, young sea snakes have been found to be extremely numerous at certain seasons (Pickwell, 1972; Barme, 1968), and it is quite possible that the pregnant females resort en masse to protected bays to bear their young.

SEA SNAKES IN LAKES

At the time of the monsoon season, sea snakes become very abundant along the coasts and estuaries of Southeast Asia (Barme, 1968). It is at this time

Figure 5. A dissection of a gravid female yellow-bellied sea snake (*Pelamis platurus*) which was nearly ready to give birth to six babies.

that fishermen encounter the snakes as they pull in their nets. The snakes may move into river mouths where the salinity is quite low and on occasion continue up the rivers. In one case a sea snake was caught in a fresh-water lake (Grand Lac) in Cambodia after having ascended the Mekong River (Bourret, 1934). Among some species these occurrences may not be too unusual. Movements of this type may account for the presence of a species of sea snake in fresh-water Lake Taal in the Philippines. The lake is connected to the sea, about 10 km away, by the Pansipit River. The snakes in this lake now seem to be thoroughly land locked since they are distinct from a closely related species found in nearby Balayan Bay (Smith, 1926).

An even more peculiar example of lake-dwelling sea snakes is found in Rennell Island in the Solomon Group (Wolff, 1969). The most surprising aspect of these lake-dwelling sea snakes is their tolerance of very low salinities. In fact, this may turn out to be characteristic of all sea snakes, even those forms normally found only in the sea (see Chapter 16). Yellow-bellied sea snakes have been kept in fresh water for 6 months (Dunson and Ehlert, 1971). From what little we know, this is one of the species which is never found in coastal regions of low salinity. These snakes may, like certain other marine animals, choose to remain in water of a high salt content even though lower salinity water is not physiologically detrimental to them. Perhaps the unique adaptations which fit them so well for a life at sea are not advantageous in smaller bodies of water.

We know almost nothing about the ability of sea snakes to survive changes in salinity in the opposite direction, towards a higher salt content. Sea snakes have not succeeded in colonizing the Red Sea, which is about 3.8%

to 4.1% salt (compared to 3.5% for the open ocean). However, high sea surface temperatures in the Red Sea may be responsible for this. There is an upper limit to the ability of the sea snake salt gland to excrete salts taken in from the water (see Chapter 16). Thus, it seems only likely that research eventually will show that sea snakes cannot live indefinitely in water above a certain salinity.

EFFECTS OF TEMPERATURE

In trying to understand why sea snakes live in certain places and not in others, we must consider temperature as a major factor since sea snakes are primarily tropical. One way to study the effect of temperature on an animal is to compare worldwide seasonal temperature patterns with the animal's distribution. The yellow-bellied sea snake is rarely found in areas where there is a single month in which the average temperature of the sea surface is less than 20°C. This is true even of equatorial regions (Galápagos Islands, Peruvian coast) where the sea is relatively cool (Dunson and Ehlert, 1971). On the warmer Ecuadorian coast, in nearshore waters, sea snakes are extremely numerous. Another useful zoogeographic example is found in South Africa. Migrants from the warm waters of the Indian Ocean are sometimes carried as far as Cape Town on the southwestern tip of Africa, but they soon die if they drift any farther. Cool waters would probably also prevent the yellow-bellied sea snake from invading the Mediterranean Sea, even if it could cross the barrier posed by the warm, salty waters of the Red Sea.

The yellow-bellied sea snake is very sensitive to high temperatures; the upper lethal limit for indefinite survival is about 33°C (Dunson and Ehlert, 1971). Since the surface temperature of the tropical seas where these snakes live is as high as 31°C, they may have a problem in keeping cool. When the body temperature of *Pelamis*, floating at the surface off the coast of Panama, was measured, it was found that some snakes were cooler than the water that surrounded them. The only plausible explanation is that the snakes are diving into the cool water below. Because of the presence of a thermocline, an area of rapidly changing temperatures, the water at 30 m is quite cool (about 25°C) compared with the surface. Even at shallower depths the water is usually at least a little cooler than the surface. If the purpose of diving is only to escape the hot rays of the sun, then shallow dives would be effective because even an inch of water would protect the snakes (Dunson and Ehlert, 1971). Even in tropical areas there are often pronounced seasonal changes in sea temperature. The mean monthly sea surface temperature in coastal Queensland (Townsville) varied between 21.8°C (in July) and 31.2°C (in January) (Kenny, 1974). These changes require compensatory acclimation if rates of physiological activity are to be regulated at a constant level. Although little is known about this process in snakes, I have observed that Queensland *Lapemis* in July ("winter") die at 30°C. They easily tolerate this temperature in the southern hemisphere during summer (Dunson and Dunson, 1974). It seems likely that this species is capable of seasonal adjustments in the upper lethal temperature. However, Graham, Rubinoff, and Hecht (1971) reported no acclimation effects after a 10-day exposure of *Pelamis* at 17°C.

PREDATION

The yellow-bellied sea snake is very conspicuous when not floating in drift lines containing assorted debris from the land. The startlingly marked tail is especially noticeable. Some interesting experiments carried out by Rubinoff and Kropach (1970) indicate that predatory fish recognize this snake. In the eastern Pacific it has no known enemies. Voracious Pacific predatory fish such as snappers refuse even to nibble at this snake unless it is completely camouflaged inside a piece of squid, and then they reject the morsel as soon as they taste it. The reason for this aversion becomes obvious when the snakes are offered to Atlantic predatory fish. These fish, which have never encountered a sea snake before, will eat them, and in about one out of 12 meals will be bitten by the snake and die. Thus, it seems rather likely that there has been a selective pressure against those Pacific fish with a taste for sea snakes. It is quite interesing that both sight and taste seem to be involved in the recognition of the snake by Pacific fish. Viewed in this light, the coloration of the yellow-bellied sea snake might be considered to be a warning signal.

A host of perplexing problems are raised by these findings. How is it that fish are endowed with this apparently instinctive knowledge? How do the predatory fish recognize the snakes when they vary in color from a rare completely yellow form, to blotched varieties, to the more typical yellow-bellied, black-backed type? What is the nature of the taste substance recognized by the fish? Perhaps the most important question has to do with the generality of this phenomenon. Do all sea snakes have this relationship to predators? There have been isolated reports of eagles and sea birds eating sea snakes (see Chapter 12), and sea snakes have also been taken from the stomachs of Philippine moray eels (Herre, 1942) and sharks (Chapter 12).

MOVEMENTS

The question of the abilities of sea snakes to move or to migrate is an interesting one since the various species differ greatly among themselves in this trait. We have already mentioned the possible movements of snakes into shallow water during the stormy monsoon season and the return to deeper water during the dry season. These movements are essentially perpendicular to the coast and do not generally involve travel over any great distances. The large breeding aggregations of *Laticauda* in the Philippines may involve travel of thousands of snakes to a locality particularly favorable for reproduction. We know nothing of the extent of these journeys. They may or may not be anything like the navigational feats performed by sea turtles or salmon homing to their hatching grounds. One of the most astounding observations ever made on massed sea snakes was reported by W. P. Lowe (1932, pp. 43–44) in the Straits of Malacca:

> Leaving Colombo we departed for Penang, and the voyage from now on became more interesting, as there was a good deal to be seen, such as rocks covered with sea-birds, chiefly Gannets and Shearwaters. To starboard lay the beautiful green island of Sumatra, and to the port the Malay Peninsula. The water now became very calm and oily in appearance. After luncheon on 4th May I came on deck and was talking to some passengers when, looking landward, I saw a long line running parallel with our course. None of us could imagine what it could be. It must have been four or five miles off. We smoked and chatted, had a siesta, and went down to tea. On returning to the deck we still saw the curious line along which we had been steaming for four hours, but now it lay across our course, and we were still very curious as to what it was. As we drew nearer we were amazed to find that it was composed of a solid mass of sea-snakes, twisted thickly together. They were orange-red and black, a very poisonous and rare variety known as *Astrotia stokessii*. Some were paler in colour and as thick as one's wrist, but the most conspicuous were as thick as a man's leg above the knee. Along this line there must have been millions; when I say millions I consider it no exaggeration, for the line was quite ten feet wide and we followed its course for some sixty miles. I can only presume it was either a migration or the breeding season. I have on various occasions looked in vain in these same waters, and also inquired from officers of ships navigating this region, but have failed to hear of a similar occurrence. Many people have seen snakes of this description but never in such massed formation.
>
> It certainly was a wonderful sight. As the ship cut the line in two, we still watched the extending file of foam and snakes until it was eventually lost to sight.

Note that Lowe emphasizes the calmness of the sea and mentions that the snakes were mixed with foam, which he subsequently attributes incorrectly to the breeding process. From our present knowledge of sea surface phenomena, this is a classic description of a slick or drift line, albeit an unusually long one. Slicks are formed by the convergence of surface water currents. Anything floating at the surface, a few molecules of organic material, a sea snake, or a tree truck, may be concentrated into slicks by the horizontal convergence of flow. In fact, the reason that we can see the slick is that the organic surface film of the oceans, concentrated in a narrow line several feet wide, lowers the surface tension of the water like a detergent, and calms the waves, giving the sea a smooth, silky appearance. Foam may be present in slicks as I myself have often observed. I am convinced that this aggregation of sea snakes occurred in a large slick because the same phenomenon has been observed on a smaller scale in the eastern Pacific (Dunson and Ehlert, 1971; Kropach, 1971). The yellow-bellied sea snake is a passive drifter most of the time and it is at the mercy of surface water movements. On days with little wind, slicks are formed off the coasts of Mexico and Central America, and they often contain hundreds and even thousands of snakes. In about 2 hrs, scientists from the R/V *Alpha Helix* collected almost 300 snakes from a slick about two miles long in the mouth of a bay in Costa Rica.

The association of yellow-bellied sea snakes with slicks and drift lines has been noted many times by fishermen. Previously, no one realized the impor- tance of this fact. It means that this sea snake probably spends most of its time at the surface in a passive, motionless state. Oceanographers would term such an animal planktonic, but there are few vertebrates of this size that fit the description. Most of them swim actively and resist the action of surface currents. The giant ocean sunfish, the Mola, is a well known example of a very weakly swimming or planktonic vertebrate. Some will doubt that the yellow-bellied sea snake can be so passive. However, this conclusion is consistent with all observations made of the habits of this snake. It is rarely if ever seen swimming actively unless disturbed or diving vertically. It is com- monly observed in association with drifting debris in slicks, where current convergence carries all floating objects. On windy or choppy days this snake is widely dispersed and is difficult to find at all. The yellow-bellied sea snake is also commonly found stranded on beaches, where it perishes because it is unable to crawl back to the water. These same observations could be made for the planktonic Portuguese Man-of-War (*Physalia*), the stinging colonial coelenterate with which this sea snake is often found associated in slicks. The ability of the yellow-bellied sea snake to drift in this fashion undoubtedly contributes to its success as a world traveler. It can cross vast expanses of open ocean wafted by currents and feeding occasionally on fish which seek cover in its shadow. It does not habitually live in pelagic or open ocean areas, probably because these areas are relatively sterile and low in productivity. The coastal zones provide a much more abundant source of fish. However, the open ocean is no barrier to its movements, as it definitely is to many species of sea snakes in the Indo-Australian region which feed on the bottom and whose movements are thereby limited by their diving ability.

MAINTENANCE IN CAPTIVITY

If some of the peculiar habits of the sea snakes are taken into account and the snakes are healthy when obtained (Figure 6), it seems that they are not difficult to keep alive in captivity. The amphibious forms like *Laticauda* seem

Figure 6. The author demonstrating a method of capture of sea snakes (in this case *Emdydocephalus annulatus* on Ashmore Reef) with snake "tongs." If minimal pressure is applied with the tongs and a boat is nearby for a pickup, little or no damage to the snake occurs, and it may be kept alive in an aquarium for a considerable time.

to prefer an aquarium with rocks in which to seek their food. The open water forms such as the yellow-bellied sea snake will feed readily enough on small fish offered with forceps, but special precautions must be taken to prevent injuries to the head from bumping into the sides of the tank. One method I have found successful is to use a circular container lined with a plastic bag to prevent the snakes from pushing against the sides. Since this species apparently never touches solid objects, it seems to be psychologically deranged by confinement and can rarely if ever accept the concept that its world is bounded by walls. The result is that in a square aquarium the snake may spend all day swimming futilely against the wall and end up with a fatally infected mouth. Agitation of the water by circulation seems to partially convince the snake that it really is in the ocean after all and can relax. Another trick is to put only a few or at best only one snake in a single tank.

Yellow-bellied sea snakes go into a frenzy when feeding and will not hesitate to bite anything within reach, including the body of their neighbor. While these bites do not seem to be fatal, the scratches made by the teeth often become infected or inflamed in sea water. The San Diego Zoo has been notably successful with this species, having established records of more than two years in captivity.

It is only by keeping snakes under observation for such long periods of time that important questions can be answered about growth, reproduction, and behavior. For example, it has often been said that sea snakes are unusual among snakes because they shed their skins in pieces. The snakes in captivity have been found to shed their skins in one piece like other snakes, and to do so with amazing frequency (as often as every 12 days). This is probably necessary to avoid the growth of fouling organisms which trouble ships by infecting the hulls, The yellow-bellied sea snake also frequently goes through coiling motions, a process that must be to clean adhering objects from the skin between the shedding times (see Chapters 10–14).

VENOM

In the early stages of their evolution for a life in the sea, sea snakes probably derived a considerable advantage from their venom. All of the sea snakes are poisonous, and it is significant that the other major group of estuarine snakes, the homalopsines of Southeast Asia, are rear-fanged and mildly poisonous. The original purpose of the venom may have been to subdue large prey and perhaps secondarily to protect against predators. Some sea snakes, for example *Laticauda,* are famous for their docile nature. Children in Fiji pick them up and bites are very rare. On the other hand, certain sea snakes are easily aggravated and may bite readily if provoked by being stepped on or handled roughly (see Chapter 22). Only a small percentage of people bitten by sea snakes ever show signs of poisoning. However, there is no doubt that the venom is extremely potent (Figure 7) (see Chapters 18–20). Although no accurate statistics are available, the fatality rate in cases of bites where venom is injected and medical treatment is carried out is estimated to be about 3% (Chapter 19). There is still some dispute over the exact nature of the toxic effect of the venom. In animal experiments, sea snake venom seems to have a paralyzing effect on the junction between nerves and muscles, leading to a paralysis of the diaphragm and death from suffocation. In humans, Reid has concluded that direct damage to the muscles occurs. The appearance of the dark colored muscle protein myoglobin in the urine of poisoned patients is evidence for this muscular damage. It is very roughly estimated that at least 40,000 people die every year from snake bite, both terrestrial and marine. The proportion of these bites that is attributable to sea snakes is not known.

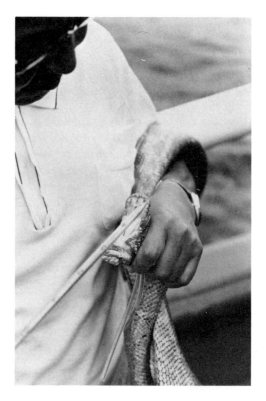

Figure 7. The "milking" of venom from a large *Astrotia stokesii* by Dr. N. Tamiya for subsequent toxicity testing.

Reid's studies show that in a 4-year period, 21 persons drowned in the waters around Penang Island, Malaysia, but only two died from sea snake bites.

SUMMARY

Sea snakes (Hydrophiidae) are the most successful marine reptiles, yet more has been written about legendary sea monsters than about these fascinating serpents. The sea snakes are poisonous relatives of the cobras and kraits (Elapidae), but most species are inoffensive and are certainly not dangerous unless provoked. The center of distribution for this mainly tropical family is the Indo-Australian region, but one species (*Pelamis*) occurs along the west coast of North America. No sea snakes live in the Atlantic Ocean, although the proposed Atlantic–Pacific sea level canal could allow migration from the Gulf of Panama into the Caribbean. The recent increased availability of tropical research facilities (both ship and shore based) has stimulated a great deal of interest in this unique group of reptiles. As a result, several major

discoveries on diving ability, venom toxicity, salt balance, temperature tolerance, and ecology have been made.

REFERENCES

Barme, M. 1968. Venomous sea snakes (Hydrophiidae). In W. Bücherl, E. E.
Buckley, and V. Deulofeu (eds.), Venomous Animals and Their Venoms.
Vol. 1: Venomous Vertebrates, pp. 285–308. Academic Press, New York.

Bellairs, A. 1970. The Life of Reptiles. Vol. 1. Universe Books, New York.

Bourret, R. 1934. Les Serpents marins de l'Indochine Française. Gouvernement Général de l'Indochine, Hanoi.

Dunson, W. A., and M. K. Dunson. 1974. Interspecific differences in fluid
concentration and secretion rate of sea snake salt glands. Amer. J. Physiol.
227:430–438.

Dunson, W. A., and G. W. Ehlert. 1971. Effects of temperature, salinity, and
surface water flow on distribution of the sea snake Pelamis. Limnol.
Oceanogr. 16:845–853.

Graham, J. B., I. Rubinoff, and M. K. Hecht. 1971. Temperature physiology
of the sea snake Pelamis platurus. An index of its colonization potential in
the Atlantic Ocean. Proc. Natl. Acad. Sci. 68:1360–1363.

Herre, A. W. C. T. 1942. Notes on Philippine sea snakes. Copeia 1942:7–9.

Herre, A. W. C. T., and D. S. Rabor. 1949. Notes on Philippine sea snakes of
the genus Laticauda. Copeia 1949:282–284.

Kenny, R. 1974. In shore surface sea temperatures at Townsville. Aust. J.
Mar. Fresw. Res. 25:1–5.

Kropach, C. 1971. Sea snake (Pelamis platurus) aggregations on slicks in
Panama. Herpetologica 1971:131–135.

Lowe, W. P. 1932. The Trail That Is Always New. Gurney and Jackson,
London. pp. 43–44.

Pickwell, G. 1972. The venomous sea snakes. Fauna July/August (no. 4):17–
32.

Rubinoff, I., and C. Kropach. 1970. Differential reactions of Atlantic and
Pacific predators to sea snakes. Nature 228:1288–1290.

Schmidt-Nielsen, K., and R. Fänge. 1958. Salt glands in marine reptiles.
Nature 182:783–785.

Smith, M. 1926. Monograph of the Sea Snakes (Hydrophiidae). British
Museum of Natural History, London.

del Toro, 1972. Los Reptiles de Chiapas. Instituto de Historia Natural, Tuxtla
Gutierrez, Chiapas, Mexico. 178 p.

Villa, J. R. 1962. Las Serpientes Venenosas de Nicaragua. Novedades,
Managua.

Voris, H. 1966. Fish eggs are the apparent sole food item for a genus of sea
snake, Emydocephalus (Krefft). Ecology 47:152–154.

Wolff, T. 1969. The fauna of Rennell and Bellona, Solomon Islands. Philos.
Trans. R. Soc. Lond. B 255:321–343.

two

Geographic Distribution of Sea Snakes

Sherman A. Minton

Recent summaries of sea snake distribution (Barme, 1968; U.S. Navy, 1968) have been chiefly limited to a tabulation of known records. An analysis of biogeography on a world-wide basis is handicapped by inadequate knowledge of the systematics and biology of many species. Factors limiting sea snake distribution seem to be unique to the group, and analogies with terrestrial snakes or other groups of marine vertebrates must be drawn with caution. In keeping with their elapid lineage, sea snakes tend to be mechanically versatile but physiologically limited, especially with respect to adjusting their reproductive cycles to temperate conditions. Breeding populations much beyond the limits of the tropics are unknown for most sea snakes, although adults of several species may be found sporadically in cool temperate waters. A distinctive aspect of sea snake biology involves seasonal shifts of populations coincident with winds, currents, and possibly food supplies. This has been documented for the Gulf of Carpentaria (Shuntov, 1971) and the east coast of Australia (Cogger, Chapter 4). There are suggestions that it also occurs in the Gulf of Siam, Tonkin Gulf, and the region around Karachi. Salinity gradients may influence the distribution of certain sea snakes (Shuntov, 1966), and a few species have secondarily invaded fresh or brackish water. Observations on sea snake stomach contents and feeding behavior indicate most species capture prey on or near the bottom in relatively shallow water (50 m or less). Moreover, a strong tendency toward feeding specialization is evident, especially where numerous species occur together. Limited observations indicate sea snake species differ widely in their swimming and diving ability. There is evidence that some species conserve energy and avoid predation by remaining quiet on the bottom for considerable periods.

When the above ecological requirements are considered, it is obvious that the broad continental shelves of northern Australia and southeast Asia provide an optimal sea snake habitat (see Table 1), with great expanses of shallow, warm water showing little seasonal variation in temperature. The geologic variability of the region, with the presence of peninsulas, islands, reefs, trenches, and former land bridges, favors speciation by providing isolation and habitat diversity. The biogeography of the Australian sea snakes has been treated by Cogger (Chapter 4). A distinctive feature of the Australian fauna is the presence of several endemic and primitive genera. *Hydrelaps* and *Ephalophis,* with one and two species respectively, are known only from the Aru Islands and a few localities on the north coast of Australia west of Torres Straits. Burger and Natsuno (in press) consider the differences between *Ephalophis greyi* and *E. mertoni* sufficiently great to warrent erection of a new genus, *Parhydrophis,* for *mertoni.* The present distribution of these species is probably relictual, but the range of the group was evidently never very extensive. Although very little is known of the ecology of these snakes, they are small reptiles, apparently weak swimmers, and confined to shallow, inshore waters, where they occupy a niche comparable to that of certain small homalopsine snakes such as *Cerberus, Bitia,* and *Myron. Aipysurus* is another characteristically Australian genus of presumably primitive sea snakes. All of the seven species occur today in the region between the Sahul Shelf and the Gulf of Carpentaria, and this may have been the site of origin for the genus. From this region *A. duboisii, A. laevis,* and *A. eydouxii* evidently dispersed eastward into the Coral Sea following the opening of the Torres Strait seaway, while *A. eydouxii* also spread northward as far as the Gulf of Siam and South China Sea, being the only member of the genus to invade the Indo-Malayan region. *Emydocephalus* is derived from *Aipysurus,* although serological evidence (Minton and da Costa, Chapter 3) indicates it may have branched off quite early. *E. annulatus* ranges from the Sahul Shelf to the Loyalty Islands, while *E. ijimae* occurs off northern Taiwan and the southern Ryukyu chain. Morphological differences between the species are slight, and the range disjunction may not be so great as now believed.

The monotypic genus *Acalyptophis* is also predominantly Australian in distribution, but occurs north to the Gulf of Siam and Strait of Formosa (Tu and Stringer, 1973). It is a species of relatively deep water, not often found close to shore. Its affinities appear to be with the *Aturia* subsection of the genus *Hydrophis* and hence with the more highly evolved sea snakes (McDowell, 1972). *Disteira,* as redefined by McDowell (1972) and further restricted by Cogger (Chapter 4), contains two strictly Australian species, *kingii* and *major,* with a third, *nigrocincta,* in the Bay of Bengal. It remains to be demonstrated if *Disteira* in any sense is a natural assemblage of species. The large and taxonomically chaotic genus *Hydrophis* is represented in the Australian region by 10 species. As presently understood, only one, *H. elegans,* is continued

Species	Persian Gulf	West Coast of India, Arabian Sea	Bay of Bengal	Burma; W. Coast Malay Peninsula; Strait of Malacca	Gulf of Siam	S. China Sea to Formosa Strait	Ryukyu Islands	Yellow Sea	Philippine Region	Java Sea; Great Sunda Islands	Banda Sea	Molucca Region	Celebes Sea	Polynesian and Micronesian Islands	Solomons and Bismarck Archipelago	New Caledonia, New Hebrides, Loyalty Is.	Australia and New Guinea[b]	West Coast Middle America
Acalyptophis peronii					X	X										R	X	
Aipysurus apraefrontalis																	X	
Aipysurus duboisii																X	X	
Aipysurus eydouxii					X	X			X	X							X	
Aipysurus foliosquama																	X	
Aipysurus fuscus											R	P	R				X	
Aipysurus laevis											?	P	R				X	
Aipysurus tenuis											X						X	
Astrotia stokesii		X		X	X	X				X	X						X	
Disteira kingii			X	X													X	
Disteira major																	X	
Disteira nigrocincta			X	X														

Table 1. *cont.*

Species	Persian Gulf	West Coast of India Arabian Sea	Bay of Bengal	Burma; W. Coast Malay Peninsula; Strait of Malacca	Gulf of Siam	S. China Sea to Formosa Strait	Ryukyu Islands	Yellow Sea	Philippine Region	Java Sea; Great Sunda Islands	Banda Sea	Molucca Region	Celebes Sea	Polynesian and Micronesian Islands	Solomons and Bismarck Archipelago	New Caledonia, New Hebrides, Loyalty Is.	Australia and New Guinea[b]	West Coast Middle America
Emdocephalus annulatus																X	X	
Emydocephalus ijimae							X											
Enhydrina schistosa	R	X	X	X	X	X				X	X	X					X	
Ephalophis greyi											X	X					X	
Ephalophis mertoni																	X	
Hydrelaps darwinensis																	X	
Hydrophis belcheri									X	X	P	X	X	X	X		X	
Hydrophis bituberculatus		Single known specimen allegedly from Colombo, Ceylon																
Hydrophis brookii		X	X	X	X	X				X							X	
Hydrophis caerulescens		X	X	X	X	X		R	P	X	P	X					?	
Hydrophis cantoris		X	X	X														
Hydrophis cyanocinctus	X	X	R	X	X	X	X	X	X	X								

24

continued

Species	Persian Gulf	West Coast of India; Arabian Sea	Bay of Bengal	Burma; W. Coast Malay Peninsula; Strait of Malacca	Gulf of Siam	S. China Sea to Formosa Strait	Ryukyu Islands	Yellow Sea	Philippine Region	Java Sea; Great Sunda Islands	Banda Sea	Molucca Region	Celebes Sea	Polynesian and Micronesian Islands	Solomons and Bismarck Archipelago	New Caledonia, New Hebrides, Loyalty Is.	Australia and New Guinea[b]	West Coast Middle America
Hydrophis elegans		R	X														X	
Hydrophis fasciatus		X	X	X	X	X			X	X							X	
Hydrophis gracilis	X	X	X	X	X	X				X							X	
Hydrophis inornatus						P			X	X							X	
Hydrophis klossi				X	X													
Hydrophis lapemoides	X	X	R															
Hydrophis mamillaris		X	X	P	?													
Hydrophis melanocephalus						X	X	R	X	X			P				X	
Hydrophis melanosoma				P		X											X	
Hydrophis obscurus[c]		X	X	X											X		?	
Hydrophis ornatus	R	R	X	X	X	X	X	X	X	X				X	X	X	X	
Hydrophis parviceps[d]						X												

Table 1. cont.

Species	Persian Gulf	West Coast of India, Arabian Sea	Bay of Bengal	Burma; W. Coast Malay Peninsula; Strait of Malacca	Gulf of Siam	S. China Sea to Formosa Strait	Ryukyu Islands	Yellow Sea	Philippine Region	Java Sea; Great Sunda Islands	Banda Sea	Molucca Region	Celebes Sea	Polynesian and Micronesian Islands	Solomons and Bismarck Archipelago	New Caledonia, New Hebrides, Loyalty Is.	Australia and New Guinea[b]	West Coast Middle America
Hydrophis semperi (Lake Taal, Luzon, Philippines only)																		
Hydrophis spiralis	X	X	X	X	P	X			R	X			P					
Hydrophis stricticollis			X	X														
Hydrophis torquatus				X	X	X				X								
Kerilia jerdoni			X	X	X	X												
Kolpophis annandalei				P	X	X				R								
Lapemis curtus	X	X	R															
Lapemis hardwickii				X	X	X		R	X	X	X	P	P		P		X	
Laticauda colubrina			R	X	X	X	X		X	X	X	X	X	X	X	X	X	
Laticauda crockeri (Lake Tegano, Rennell Island, Solomons only)																		
Laticauda																		?

26

Species	Persion Gulf	West Coast of India; Arabian Sea	Bay of Bengal	Burma; W. Coast Malay Peninsula; Strait of Malacca	Gulf of Siam	S. China Sea to Formosa Strait	Ryukyu Island	Yellow Sea	Philippine Region	Java Sea; Great Sunda Island	Banda Sea	Molucca Region	Celebes Sea	Polynesian and Micronesian Island	Solomons and Bismarck Archipelago	New Caledonia, New Hebrides, Loyalty Is.	Australia and New Guinea[b]	West Coast Middle America
Laticauda semifasciata						X	X	X	X	X	X	X	X					
Laticauda schistorhynchus														X	X	X		
Pelamis platurus[e]	R	X	X	X	X	X	X	X	X	X	X	X	X	X	X	X	X	X
Praescutata viperina	X	X	X	X	X	X				X								
Thalassophis anomalus					X	X				X		X						

[a]The symbol X indicates widespread distribution of the species within the area in suitable habitats; R indicates an isolated record or a very few records possibly based on strays or waifs; P indicates probable presence of the species without a definite record; ? indicates a record questionable as to provenance or identity of the specimen.

[b]For detailed distribution of species within the Austrialian region, see Cogger, Chapter 4, Table 3.

[c]Species largely confined to brackish water.

[d]Known only from coast of South Vietnam.

[e]For additional records of this species see text.

exclusively Australian; however, Australian populations now referred to such species as *H. caerulescens, H. belcheri,* and *H. obscurus* may well represent undescribed taxa. Other species seem to represent penetration of the Australian region by Indo-Malaysian elements.

The other great area of sea snake diversity extends from the Ganges delta southward to the edge of the Sunda Shelf and thence northward along the peninsulas of Malaya and Indochina to the Tonkin Gulf and east to the northwest coast of Borneo. Much of the region lies within the 50-m isobath. Coral reefs are less extensive here than in the Australian region. The sea snake fauna of this region includes two distinctive and specialized endemic genera, *Kerilia* and *Thalassophis,* and a third, *Kolpophis,* which is questionably distinct from *Lapemis. Hydrophis* is represented by 17 species, of which six are endemic or virtually so. An additional 10 species represent wide-ranging genera or elements of the Australian fauna. To the north of Hainan the fauna decreases in diversity, although 13 species are reported from waters around Taiwan. Eight species including the endemic *Emydocephalus ijimae* are known from the Ryukyu Islands, and five species reach Tsingtao at the southern end of the Shantung Peninsula in the Yellow Sea.

Although dense sea snake populations exist in Philippine waters, diversity is rather low with only 12 species reported. One, *Hydrophis semperi,* is endemic, being confined to a freshwater lake on Luzon near the coast. Similarly diminished faunas are reported for the Banda Sea (about 11 species) and Celebes Sea (about nine species). Tu and Tu (1970) have provided a summary of sea snake distribution in southeast Asian waters.

Few sea snake species range eastward into the tropical Pacific beyond the continental shelves. Seven species are known from New Caledonia and the Loyalty Islands. Three of these are Australian; the others are wide-ranging species probably of Asian origin. Four species reach Fiji, and an endemic form of *Laticauda* occurs in the Tonga Islands and western Samoa. Two species of *Hydrophis* reach Micronesia, *H. belcheri* being known from the Carolines and *H. ornatus* from the Gilbert Islands. The exceptionally wide-ranging *Pelamis platurus* and at least one species of *Laticauda* also occur in western Micronesia.

Sea snakes records are virtually lacking from the eastern Pacific until the western coasts of Middle America are reached. Here dense populations of *Pelamis* occur from the southern end of the Gulf of California almost to the Galápagos. There is an unconfirmed report of *Laticauda colubrina* from the Pacific coast of Nicaragua (Villa, 1962).

From the western coasts of the Indian peninsula to the head of the Persian Gulf, there occurs a moderately diverse sea snake fauna of 14 species, nine of which have been recorded west of the Strait of Hormuz. The majority of these are extraordinarily wide-ranging species; however, *Hydrophis lapemoides, H. mamillaris,* and *Lapemis curtus* are characteristic of this fauna, although not restricted to it.

The most widely distributed sea snake, indeed the most widely distributed to all snakes, is *Pelamis platurus*. Peripheral records of this species extend from Possiet Bay in southern Siberia to coasts of New Zealand and Tasmania. It is the only sea snake of the western Indian Ocean, where it occurs south to the Cape of Good Hope, and is the only sea snake in American Pacific waters. Its wide dispersal is undoubtedly related to its ability, unique among sea snakes, to adapt to a pelagic way of life. The extent of its breeding range is unknown, but it is believed to be confirmed to virtually tropical waters. No subspecies are currently recognized; this may indicate that its dispersal has been relatively rapid.

Perhaps the second most widely distributed sea snake is *Hydrophis ornatus*, which has been recorded from the Persian Gulf to the Gilbert Islands, north to the Yellow Sea and south along much of the east coast of Australia, with a record of the subspecies *ocellatus* for Scamander Bay, Tasmania (Kinghorn, 1956). Other widely distributed species of *Hydrophis* are *H. cyanocinctus* (Persian Gulf to Sea of Japan, mostly north of the equator), *H. caerulescens* (vicinity of Karachi to Yellow Sea and possibly south to Gulf of Carpentaria), *H. fasciatus* (vicinity of Karachi to Arafura Sea), *H. spiralis* (Persian Gulf to Strait of Macassar and Philippines), and *H. gracilis* (Persian Gulf to Hong Kong and south to Coral Sea). The difficulty in defining species within this genus introduces a problem in evaluating distribution records of all these forms. There seems to be no particular feature that sets the widely distributed species of *Hydrophis* apart from other members of the genus. *H. ornatus* is an unspecialized and possibly rather primitive species of moderate size and rather stocky build. *H. spiralis* and *H. cyanocinctus* are both very large sea snakes, regularly reaching a length of 1.8 m or more, but *H. caerulescens* is one of the smallest members of the genus. *H. fasciatus* and *H. gracilis* are among the species characterized by long, slender necks and tiny heads, a specialization associated with a diet of burrowing eels.

Enhydrina schistosa, representing an easily recognized monotypic genus, occurs from the Persian Gulf to Vietnam and south to Queensland; and *Astrotia stokesii*, representing another monotypic genus, has a similar distribution, being known from the Gulf of Oman to the Gulf of Siam and southeastward well into the Coral Sea and along the east coast of Australia. In most of the Indo-Malayan region, *Enhydrina* is by far the more abundant of the two, while in Australian waters, *Astrotia* is relatively common and *Enhydrina* quite rare. *Praescutata*, a third monotypic genus recognized by many workers but recently combined with *Lapemis* by McDowell, is recorded from the Persian Gulf to the Java Sea and northward to the Strait of Formosa. All these snakes are to some degree specialized. *Astrotia* is very large and deep-bodied; *Enhydrina* has markedly extensile jaws, a strongly decurved rostral, and well developed venom apparatus; *Praescutata* has enlarged ventrals on the anterior part of the body. *Astrotia's* large size and presumably strong swimming ability would facilitate its crossing deepwater barriers. *Enhydrina* is also a strong swimmer and may be particularly adept at preying on a variety of food items. *Praescutata* seems to be a species of shallow, turbid water, and I can find no factor to account for its wide distribution.

The laticaudine sea snakes present an interesting distributional picture. Their anatomical characteristics and amphibious habits indicate a closer relationship to Asian terrestrial elapids than to other sea snakes (McDowell, 1967). If Sundaland is considered a likely site of origin for the group, dispersal to the east has been more successful than to the west. Both *Laticauda colubrina* and *L. laticaudata* are known from Fiji as well as from New Caledonia, New Hebrides, and the Solomons; *L. colubrina* reaches the Carolines. *L. schistorhynchus* is restricted to Tonga and Samoa. The genus has also been more successful than most sea snakes in temperate waters. *L. semifasciata, L. colubrina,* and *L. laticaudata* all occur most of the length of the Ryukyu chain, where they are abundant enough in places to support a commercial fishery; *L. semifasciata* is recorded off the main islands of Japan occasionally. Along the east coast of Australia there are sporadic records of *L. colubrina* and *L. laticaudata* south to the Tasman Sea. The genus is rare in Indo-Burmese waters, although both *L. colubrina* and *L. laticaudata* are recorded from the Bay of Bengal.

Although seemingly possessing no exceptional swimming or diving ability and, insofar as known, doing their feeding on the bottom, the laticaudine snakes have shown surprising ability to cross deep water barriers and establish populations in such island groups as Fiji and Tonga. It is also of some interest that *Laticauda colubrina* and *L. laticaudata,* of much the same size and general appearance, are macrogeographically sympatric over an immense range while two other quite similar species, *semifasciata* and *schistorhynchus,* are widely separated. A final small distributional anomaly is afforded by *L. crockeri,* which is confined to a brackish lake on Rennell Island in the Solomons.

REFERENCES

Barme, M. 1968. Venomous sea snakes (Hydrophiidae). In Venomous Animals and their Venoms (W. Bucherl, E. E. Buckley, and V. Deulofeu, eds), Academic Press, New York. pp. 285–308.

Burger, W. L., and T. Natsuno. A new genus for the Arafura smooth sea snake and redefinitions of other sea snake genera. The Snake (in press).

Kinghorn, J. R. 1956. The Snakes of Australia. 2nd ed. Angus and Robertson, Sydney.

McDowell, S. B. 1967. *Aspidomorphus,* a genus of New Guinea snakes of the family Elapidae with notes on related genera. J. Zool. Soc. London 151:497–543.

McDowell, S. B. 1972. The genera of sea-snakes of the Hydrophis group (Serpentes: Elapidae). Trans. Zool. Soc. London 32:195–247.

Shuntov, V. P., 1966. Distribution of sea snakes in the South China Sea and east Indian Ocean. Zool. Zhur. 45:1882–1886. (Translation by U.S. Naval Oceanographic Office)

Shuntov, V. P. 1971. Sea snakes of the north Australian shelf. Ekologiya, 4:65–72. (Translation by Pacific Ocean Scientific Research Institute for Fisheries and Oceanography)

Tu, Anthony T., and J. M. Stringer. 1973. Three species of sea snake not previously reported in the Strait of Formosa. Jour. Herp., 7:384–386.

Tu, Anthony T. and T. Tu. 1970. Sea snakes from southeast Asia and Far East and their venoms. In Poisonous and Venomous Marine Animals of the World by Bruce Halstead. Washington, D.C., Government Printing Office, vol. III, pp. 885:903.

U.S. Navy Bureau of Medicine and Surgery, 1968. Poisonous Snakes of the World. Washington, D. C. Government Printing Office, pp. 157–167.

Villa, Jaime. 1962. Serpientes Venenosas de Nicaragua, Managua.

ACKNOWLEDGMENTS

Observations vital to the development of this paper were made on the *Alpha Helix* Ashmore Reef expedition supported by the National Science Foundation and Scripps Institution of Oceanography. Drs. William A. Dunson and W. Leslie Burger helpfully supplied literature and unpublished data.

three

Serological Relationships
of Sea Snakes and Their
Evolutionary Implication

Sherman A. Minton
and Milton S. da Costa

Sea snakes form a readily recognized group anatomically and physiologically adapted to a marine or estuarine habitat. Their affinity with the Elapidae has never been seriously questioned; the recent tendency has been to accord them subfamilial status (Underwood, 1967). The features separating them from elapids are largely adaptations to marine life. They evidently represent a radiation into the marine environment which has otherwise been only marginally exploited by other groups of recent snakes (*Acrochordus,* some homalopsids, a few natricids). Whether these differences are sufficiently extensive and fundamental to warrant familial status for some or all species is largely a matter of opinion.

Regardless of the group rank accorded them, the sea snakes show a high degree of diversity. Smith (1926) recognized two subfamilies, the Laticaudinae with three genera and the Hydrophiinae with 12. Nine of the genera as then recognized were monotypic, and only two were represented by more than five species. He considered *Laticauda* the most primitive genus but otherwise hazarded little speculation on the origin and phylogeny of the group. In a subsequent paper (Smith, 1931), he described the monotypic genus *Ephalophis,* which he considered primitive and intermediate between the two subfamilies.

McDowell (1967) proposed that *Laticauda* be dissociated from the other sea snakes and presented evidence showing its closer affinity to terrestrial

Asian elapids of the *Calliophis-Maticora* group. In a later paper (McDowell, 1969), he transferred *Hydrophis mertoni* to *Ephalophis* and associated this genus with *Aipysurus* and *Emydocephalus*, suggesting that these genera and probably all other sea snakes except *Laticauda* were derived from Australian elapids of the *Demansia* group, more specifically those close to the genus (or subgenus) *Drepanodontis*. In a recent comprehensive revision of the sea snake genera (McDowell, 1972), this thesis was further elaborated, with *Hydrelaps* and *Ephalophis* considered the most primitive sea snake genera and *Rhinoplocephalus* of western Australia another possible terrestrial ancestor. Within the group, Lacepede's genus *Disteira* was revived to include *Hydrophis major*, *H. kingi*, *H. nigrocinctus*, *Enhydrina schistosa*, and *Astrotia stokesii*. The two species of *Microcephalophis* were transferred to *Hydrophis* and this genus partitioned into three subgenera. The genus *Lapemis* was expanded to include the monotypic genera *Kolpophis* and *Praescutata*. Accordingly, the elapid subfamily Hydrophiinae (*sensu* McDowell) contains 11 genera, of which eight contain fewer than five species.

Being specialized, without a fossil record, and showing considerable adaptive radiation as well as probably convergence and parallelism, the marine snakes are a group where serological and other nonmorphological taxonomic criteria may be expected to be particularly helpful in determing the phylogeny of the group, as well as its probable site of origin. The *Alpha Helix* Ashmore Reef expedition provided the opportunity to obtain serum samples from a number of sea snake species, as well as a few samples from Australian elapids and snakes of other groups.

MATERIALS AND METHODS

Most of the sea snake serum samples were collected during the course of the *Alpha Helix* Ashmore Reef Expedition in December 1972 and January 1973. Anesthetized snakes were bled by cardiac puncture, using aseptic precautions. Serum was separated and stored in sterile containers under refrigeration, except for brief periods, until brought to our laboratory. At this time, about half the sample was stored in the refrigerator, with sodium azide (final concentration 1:15,000) added as a preservative. The remainder was divided into aliquots of about 0.5 ml, which were frozen at $-20°C$. Other snake serum samples were obtained from reptiles kept in our laboratory. The serum was collected as described above and generally used soon after collection.

Antisera against the sera of the sea snakes *Lapemis hardwickii*, *Hydrophis melanocephalus*, a terrestrial elapid *Denisonia superba*, and the natricine *Natrix sipedon* were prepared by injecting rabbits with 2.5 ml of snake serum in complete Freund's adjuvant, administered by multiple routes. One month after initial immunization, a 1-ml booster dose of the same material was administered subcutaneously. A trial bleeding was done about a week later, and if the antiserum gave an immunoelectrophoresis pattern similar to Figure 1-A, with homologous antigen, the rabbit was exsanguinated. Its serum was separated, and aliquots were stored at −20° C and thawed as needed. If a satisfactory pattern was not obtained, the rabbit was given an additional booster injection.

Immunoelectrophoresis of the serum samples was carried out at room temperature on agar-coated slides made up in barbital buffer, pH 8.6, 0.025

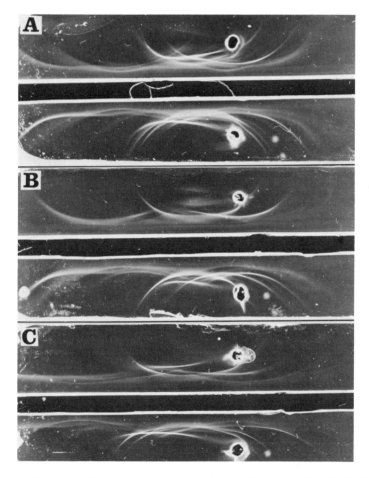

Figure 1. Immunoelectrophoresis preparations of sea snake sera developed with *Hydrophis melanocephalus* antiserum. In this and all subsequent figures, the anode is to the left. A. *Hydrophis melanocephalus* (upper) and *H. ornatus* (lower). B. *Aipysurus laevis* (upper) and *Astrotia stokesii* (lower) C. *Pelamis platurus* (upper) and *Hydrophis ornatus* (lower).

ionic strength. Each set of slides was run for about 60 min at 7.4 v/cm and developed with antiserum for approximately 24 hrs at room temperature. Slides were photographed, and the preparations dried and stained with amidoschwarz for permanent record. Ouchterlony reactions were done in Immuno-plates, pattern B (Hyland Lab.).

Absorption was carried out by adding 0.1 ml of snake serum to 0.4 ml of rabbit antiserum, mixing, and allowing the mixture to remain in the refrigerator 72 hrs. Tubes were then centrifuged and the supernatent pipetted off. If the antiserum still reacted in a capillary precipitin test with the serum used for absorption, an additional 0.05 ml of snake serum was added and the procedure repeated. The absorbed antisera contained a slight excess of the absorbing antigens. Absorbed antisera were stored in the refrigerator with sodium azide as a preservative.

Common serum-venom antigens were detected by carrying out Ouchterlony or immunoelectrophoresis reactions between the snake sera and recently outdated commercial antivenins, or between venom samples frozen immediately after collection and the rabbit antisera produced against snake sera.

RESULTS

In immunoelectrophoresis preparations, snake serum developed with homologous antiserum shows a basic pattern of six arcs, three on the anode side and three largely on the cathode side (Figures 1A, 2C, and 3C; see also Minton and Salanitro, 1972, Figure 1). There are three to six additional arcs, most of them near the origin. In this paper these are referred to as minor arcs. The two rapid anodally migrating fractions have arbitrarily been designated A-1 and A-2, the fraction giving a strongly developed arc just to the anodal side of the origin is designated 0, and the three cathodally migrating fractions designated C-1, C-2, and C-3. The C-3 fraction has been identified as a γ-globulin (Salanitro and Minton, 1973).

Fifteen sea snake sera developed with *Hydrophis* and *Lapemis* antisera show well developed basic patterns, usually with two or more minor arcs (Tables 1 and 2). *Denisonia* antiserum likewise develops strong patterns with all sea snake sera, although with most the A-1 and A-2 arcs are faint or absent (Table 3; Figures 3 and 4). Most sea snake sera show surprisingly strong reactions with *Natrix* antiserum; however, there is consistently only one A arc, and there are usually no minor arcs; 0, C-1 and C-2 arcs are usually well developed (Table 4; Figure 5).

Aipysurus sera show more characteristic patterns with more minor arcs when developed with *Lapemis* antiserum than when developed with *Hydrophis* antiserum (Figures 6B-D, 7B, and 7C). Reactions of *Aipysurus laevis* and

Table 1. Sea snake sera developed with antiserum against the
sea snake *Hydrophis melanocephalus*[a]

	A–1	A–2	O	C–1	C–2	C–3	MA
Acalyptophis peronii	++	+	++	++	+	+	3
Aipysurus apraefrontalis	+	++	++	++	+	0	0
Aipysurus duboisii	++	?	++	++	+	0	0
Aipysurus foliosquama	+	++	++	++	+	0	2
Aipysurus fuscus	++	?	++	++	0	0	2
Aipysurus laevis	++	+	++	++	+	0	0
Astrotia stokesii	++	+	++	++	++	+	3
Emydocephalus annulatus	0	?	?	++	0	0	2
Hydrophis melanocephalus[b]	++	++	++	++	+	+	5
Hydrophis elegans	++	++	++	+	++	0	3
Hydrophis ornatus	++	+	++	++	+	+	6
Lapemis hardwickii	++	++	++	+	+	+	4
Laticauda laticaudata	++	++	++	++	+	0	1
Laticauda semifasciata	++	++	++	?	+	+	0
Pelamis platurus	++	+	++	++	+	+	2

[a]See text for identification of A–1, A–2, O, C–1, C–2, and C–3
arcs. MA: Minor arcs. ++Well defined arc; +Faint arc; ?Identity of arc
uncertain.
[b]Caught on Ashmore Reef and tentatively identified by H. G.
Cogger, Subsequent revision of the status of these specimens is likely.

Table 2. Sea snake sera developed with antiserum against the sea snake *Lapemis hardwickii*

	A–1	A–2	O	C–1	C–2	C–3	MA
Acalyptophis peronii	++	++	++	+	++	++	4
Aipysurus apraefrontalis	++	0	++	0	0	0	0
Aipysurus duboisii	++	++	++	+	+	+	3
Aipysurus foliosquama	++	0	++	++	++	0	3
Aipysurus fuscus	++	++	++	++	+	+	0
Aipysurus laevis	++	++	++	++	++	0	5
Astrotia stokesii	++	++	++	?	++	++	2
Emydocephalus annulatus	++	?	++	+	+	0	0
Hydrophis melanocephalus	++	++	++	+	++	++	3
Hydrophis elegans	++	++	++	++	+	0	1
Hydrophis ornatus	++	++	++	++	++	++	3
Lapemis hardwickii	++	++	++	++	++	++	5
Laticauda laticaudata	++	0	++	++	0	+	1
Laticauda semifasciata	++	0	++	?	0	+	1
Pelamis platurus	++	++	++	+	++	++	2

A. foliosquama with *Denisonia* antiserum show about twice as many arcs as those of *A. apraefrontalis* and *A. duboisii.*

Emydocephalus is aberrant in showing a more typical pattern of basic arcs when developed with *Natrix* antiserum (Figure 5A), than when developed with *Lapemis* antiserum (Figure 2A) or *Hydrophis* antiserum.

Sera of *Laticauda semifasciata* and *L. laticaudata* show a better developed pattern of basic arcs when developed with *Hydrophis* antiserum than when developed with *Lapemis* or *Denisonia;* however, minor arcs are better devel-

Table 3. Sea snake sera developed with antiserum against the terrestrial elapid *Denisonia superba*

	A1	A2	O	C1	C2	C3	MA
Acalyptophis peronii	++	+	++	++	++	++	4
Aipysurus apraefrontalis	+	?	++	0	++	0	1
Aipysurus duboisii	+	0	++	++	0	0	1
Aipysurus foliosquama	+	++	++	++	++	0	2
Aipysurus fuscus	−	−	−	−	−	−	−
Aipysurus laevis	++	+	++	++	+	+	2
Astrotia stokesii	++	+	++	++	+	+	4
Emydocephalus annulatus	+	+	++	++	+	?	1
Hydrophis melanocephalus	++	+	++	0	0	0	4
Hydrophis elegans	++	0	++	++	+	?	1
Hydrophis ornatus	++	+	++	++	?	+	3
Lapemis hardwickii	+	+	++	++	++	?	2
Laticauda laticaudata	+	+	++	+	?	0	1
Laticauda semifasciata	++	+	++	?	?	0	2
Pelamis platurus	++	+	++	0	?	?	2
Denisonia superba	+	++	++	++	+	+	3

oped by *Denisonia* antiserum (Figure 8). There seems to be no significant difference between the two species of *Laticauda*.

Of the three species of *Hydrophis* studied, *H. melanocephalus* and *H. ornatus* give virtually identical immunoelectrophoretic patterns; *H. elegans* differ slightly but probably significantly (Figures 1A, 1C, and 6D). *Acalyptophis peronii* and *Astrotia stokesii* show immunoelectrophoretic patterns that are similar to each other and to those of *Hydrophis* and *Lapemis* (Figures 1B, 6A, and 7A). *Pelamis platurus* also belongs in this group, being somewhat

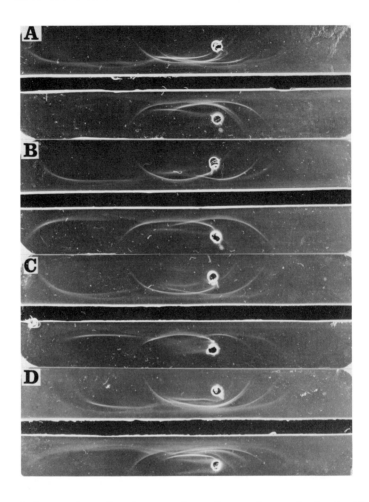

Figure 2. Immunoelectrophoresis preparations of sea snake sera developed with *Hydrophis melanocephalus* antiserum. A. *Acalyptophis peronii* (upper) and *Emydocephalus annulatus* (lower). B. *Aipysurus duboisii* (upper) and *A. fuscus* (lower). C. *A. laevis* (upper) and *A. apraefrontalis* (lower). D. *A. foliosquama* (upper) and *Hydrophis elegans* (lower).

better developed by *Lapemis* antiserum than by *Hydrophis* (Figures 1C and 2B). Reaction with *Denisonia* antiserum is comparatively weak (Figure 4C).

Reactions of sera of snakes of other groups are shown in Table 5. Sera of *Denisonia* and *Notechis* show strong reactions with *Hydrophis* and *Lapemis* (Figure 7A), but in no case is a complete pattern of basic arcs seen. Sera of *Crotalus horridus*, *Thamnophis sirtalis*, and *Masticophis flagellum* show moderate reactivity with *Hydrophis, Lapemis,* and *Denisonia* antisera, with *Thamnophis* serum generally giving the fewest arcs. However, absorption of these antisera with *Masticophis* generally eliminates reactivity with sera other than those of hydrophids and elapids, while absorption with *Thamnophis* or *Crotalus* does not eliminate reactivity with *Masticophis, Elaphe obsoleta, Liasis childreni, Boa constrictor,* and, in the case of *Lapemis* antiserum absorbed with *Crotalus* serum, with *Acrochordus granulatus.*

Serum of the file snake, *Acrochordus granulatus,* gives a faint two or three arc pattern with the four antisera (Figures 4C, and 5D, 7B). Serum of the carpet python, *Morelia spilotes,* shows three arcs when developed with

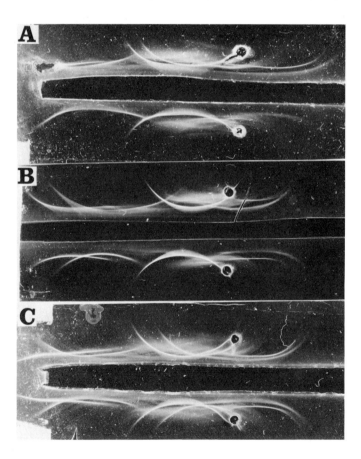

Figure 3. Immunoelectrophoresis preparations of sea snake sera developed with *Lapemis hardwickii* antiserum. A. *Hydrophis ornatus* (upper) and *Emydocephalus annulatus* (lower). B. *Hydrophis melanocephalus* (upper) and *Pelamis platurus* (lower). C. *Lapemis hardwickii* (upper and lower).

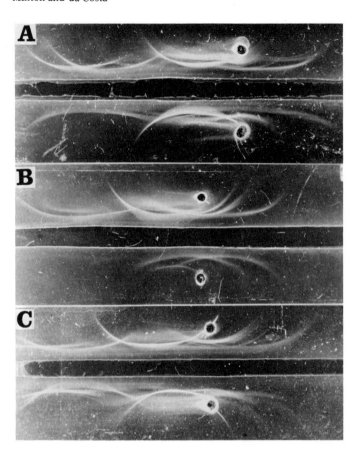

Figure 4. Immunoelectrophoresis preparations of snake sera developed with *Lapemis hardwickii* antiserum. A. *Acalypotophis peronii* (upper) and *Notechis scutatus* (lower). B. *Aipysurus foliosquama* (upper) and *Acrochordus granulatus* (lower). C. *Aipysurus duboisii* (upper) and *A. fuscus* (lower).

Hydrophis or *Denisonia* antiserum; and one arc with *Lapemis* or *Natrix* (Figure 9). A characteristic feature of both *Acrochordus* and *Morelia* patterns is the absence of very weak development of the 0 arc, which is very distinct in nearly all other serum-antiserum combinations.

At least some antigens of sea snake serum are quite stable on storage. Samples of *Hydrophis cyanocinctus* and *Hydrophis cantoris* sera collected in July, 1961, stored almost three years in the refrigerator, and then lyophilized, were restored in a concentration of 50 mg per ml more than 12 years later. When developed with *Hydrophis* antiserum, they showed fairly characteristic patterns of 6 and 5 arcs respectively (Figure 9A). Reactions with *Lapemis* antiserum were similar but fainter. A sample of *Lapemis* serum stored 10 months in the refrigerator showed little change in pattern, compared with serum stored three months, when developed with homologous antiserum.

In preliminary Ouchterlony preparations, seven sea snake sera gave moderate to strong reactions with sea snake antivenin and four elapid antivenins, and very weak or no reaction with three additional elapid antivenins and seven viperid antivenins (Table 6). Six sea snake sera were then used in immunoelectrophoresis preparations developed with sea snake, tiger snake, Iran cobra, and coral snake antivenins. With sea snake antivenin, strong

Table 4. Sea snake sera developed with antiserum against the North American watersnake, *Natrix sipedon*.

	A–1	A–2	O	C–1	C–2	C–3	MA
Acalyptophis peronii	0	++	++	++	++	+	0
Aipysurus apraefrontalis	0	0	+	0	+	0	0
Aipysurus duboisii	0	0	++	+	+	0	0
Aipysurus foliosquama	0	0	+	0	+	0	0
Aipysurus laevis	0	++	++	+	+	+	0
Astrotia stokesii	0	++	++	+	+	+	0
Emydocephalus annulatus	0	++	++	++	++	0	1
Hydrophis melanocephalus	0	++	++	++	++	+	0
Hydrophis elegans	0	0	++	+	+	0	0
Hydrophis ornatus	0	++	++	+	+	+	1
Lapemis hardwickii	0	++	++	++	++	+	1
Laticauda laticaudata	0	++	++	?	?	0	0
Laticauda semifasciata	0	++	++	?	++	0	0
Pelamis platurus	0	++	++	+	+	0	0
Natrix sipedon	+	++	++	++	++	++	2

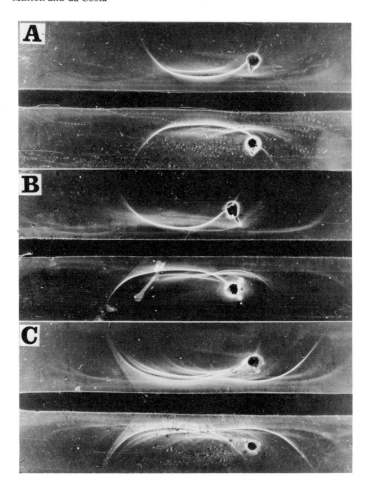

Figure 5. Immunoelectrophoresis preparations of snake sera developed with *Denisonia superba* antiserum. A. *Acalypotophis peronii* (upper) and *Emydocephalus annulatus* (lower). B. *Lapemis hardwickii* (upper) and *Hydrophis elegans* (lower). C. *Denisonia superba* (upper and lower).

patterns were obtained with all sera except *Laticauda* and *Lapemis*. Most patterns consisted of a faint A arc, a distinct 0 arc and C-1 arc, and one or two minor arcs (Figure 10). Tiger snake antivenin gave similar patterns except that A arcs were absent or very faint. 0 arcs were absent in *Laticauda* and *Lapemis* patterns. Coral snake antivenin gave strong 0 arcs with all sera, and fainter C-1 arcs with all but *Emydocephalus* (Figure 11). Cobra antivenin gave weak patterns, with the best defined arcs in the C-1 position.

Adequate samples of sea snake venoms were not available; however, freshly collected or frozen samples of *Notechis scutatus, Denisonia superba, Naja naja,* and *Crotalus horridus* venoms were used in immunoelectrophoresis preparations developed with *Hydrophis, Lapemis,* and *Denisonia* antisera. A well developed arc in the C-1 position was observed when *Naja* venom was developed with *Denisonia* antiserum (Figure 12). Less well developed arcs were observed when *Naja* and *Denisonia* venoms were developed with *Hydrophis* antiserum. An Ouchterlony preparation indicated different antigens were involved.

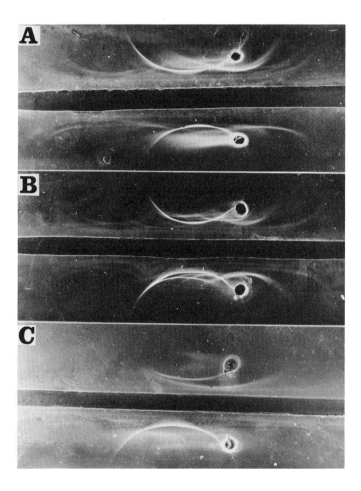

Figure 6. Immunoelectrophoresis preparations of snake sera developed with *Denisonia superba* antiserum. A. *Aipysurus laevis* (upper) and *A. apraefrontalis* (lower). B. *Astrotia stokesii* (upper) and *Hydrophis ornatus* (lower). C. *Acrochordus granulatus* (upper) and *Pelamis platurus* (lower).

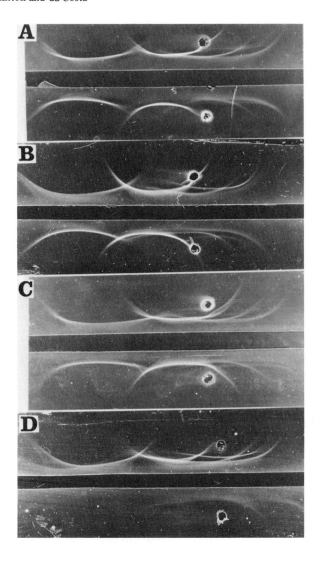

Figure 7. Immunoelectrophoresis preparations of snake sera developed with *Natrix sipedon* antiserum. A. *Emydocephalus annulatus* (upper) and *Pelamis platurus* (lower). B. *Hydrophis melanocephalus* (upper) and *Aipysurus laevis* (lower). C. *Acalyptophis peronii* (upper) and *Astrotia stokesii* (lower). D. *Thamnophis sirtalis* (upper) and *Acrochordus granulatus* (lower).

DISCUSSION

Information from serological study of sea snakes largely confirms relationships established by morphological criteria. Close affinity with Australian elapids is shown by well developed patterns when sea snake sera are developed with *Denisonia* antiserum, and when *Denisonia* and *Notechis* sera are developed with *Lapemis* and *Hydrophis* antisera. Absorption of *Lapemis* and *Hydrophis* antisera with *Notechis* serum markedly reduces their reactivity toward sea snake sera, and completely abolishes it for *Lapemis* and *Aipysurus*

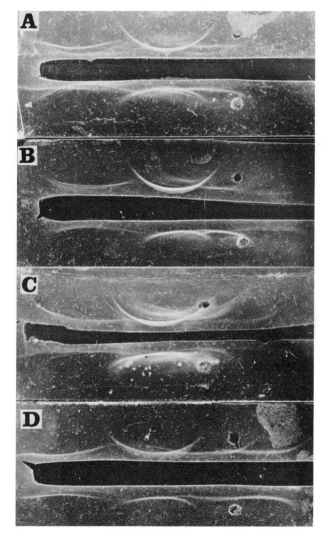

Figure 8. Immunoelectrophoresis preparations of *Laticauda laticaudata* serum (upper wells) and *L. semifasciata* serum (lower wells) developed with A. *Hydrophis melanocephalus* antiserum; B. *Lapemis hardwickii* antiserum; C. *Denisonia superba* antiserum; and D. *Natrix sipedon* antiserum.

Table 5. Reactions of sera from various snake species (other than sea snakes) and antisera prepared against sera of *Hydrophis, Lapemis, Denisonia* and *Natrix,*[a]

| | Snake Antiserum | | | | | | | |
| | *Hydrophis* | | *Lapemis* | | *Denisonia* | | *Natrix* | |
	BA	MA	BA	MA	BA	MA	BA	MA
Denisonia superba	3	3	5	0	6	3	4	0
Notechis scutatus	5	2	4	0	6	3	3	1
Crotalus horridus	3	1	3	2	2	3	3	0
Thamnophis sirtalis	2	1	2	1	1	2	6	0
Masticophis flagellum	2	1	2	3	3	1	3	1
Acrochordus granulatus	0	2	2	1	2	0	2	0
Morelia spilotes	2	1	0	1	2	1	1	0

[a]Figures show the number of arcs of the basic pattern (BA) and the number of minor arcs (MA) developed.

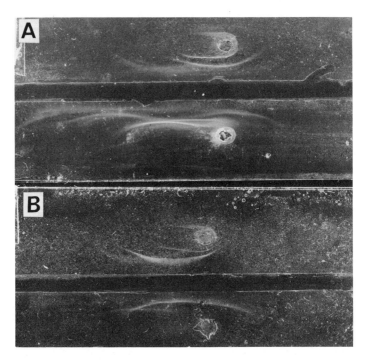

Figure 9. Immunoelectrophoresis preparations of A. *Morelia spilotes* serum (upper) and *Hydrophis cantoris* serum (lower) developed with *Hydrophis melanocephalus* antiserum; and B. *Morelia spilotes* serum (upper) and *Acrochordus granulatus* serum (lower) developed with *Denisonia superba* antiserum.

Sea snake serum

Antivenin	Hydrophis ornatus	Lapemis hardwickii	Acalyptophis peronii	Astrotia stokesii	Aipysurus laevis	Emydocephalus annulatus	Laticauda semifasciata
Commonwealth Sea Snake	3	3	2		4	3	2
Pasteur Dendroaspis	3	2	1		2	1	1
Butantan Coral Snake	4	3	2		2	3	2
Razi Inst. Naja naja	3	2	2		2	2	2
Pasteur Naja	0	0	0		0	0	0
Bangkok Bungarus	0	0	0		0	0	0
Commonwealth Tiger Snake	2	2	1		3	3	1
Commonwealth Taipan	0	1?	0		0	0	0
Razi Inst. Echis	0	0	0		0	0	0
Pasteur Bitis	0	0	0		0	0	0
Razi Inst. Vipera lebetina	0	0	0		0	0	0
Tokyo Habu	0	1?	0		1	1?	0
Pasteur Ancistrodon	0	0	0		0	0	0
Butantan Lachesis	0	0	0		0	0	0
Wyeth Crotalid	0	1?	0		0	0	0

[a] 1. One faint precipitin band; 2. One distinct precipitin band; 3. Two precipitin bands, one or both indistinct; 4. Two or more distinct precipitin bands.

49

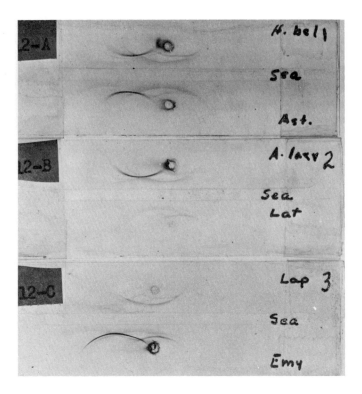

Figure 10. Immunoelectrophoresis preparations of sea snake sera developed with sea snake antivenin (Commonwealth Serum Laboratories). From top to bottom: *Hydrophis melanocephalus, Astrotia stokesii, Aipysurus laevis, Laticauda semifasciata, Lapemis hardwickii*, and *Emydocephalus annulatus*.

laevis. Denisonia antiserum absorbed with *Lapemis, Aipysurus laevis,* or *Laticauda semifasciata* sera failed to react with any of the five sea snake sera tested against it, or against 10 sera from snakes of other groups.

Subgroups within the sea snakes are difficult to define serologically. The aberrant patterns given by *Emydocephalus* serum indicate that this genus is more distinct from *Aipysurus* and from other sea snakes serologically than it is morphologically. Moreover, *Emydocephalus* serum reacts with *Hydrophis* and *Lapemis* antisera after both have been absorbed with *Aipysurus laevis* and *Laticauda semifasciata* (Figure 13). The slightly greater reactivity of *Laticauda* sera with *Denisonia* antiserum, rather than with *Lapemis* or *Hydrophis* antiserum, is at least compatible with McDowell's hypothesis that this genus is more closely allied to terrestrial elapids than to other sea snakes. However, its serological divergence from *Hydrophis* is no greater than that of

Aipysurus or *Emydocephalus.* Lack of close relationship between *Aipysurus* and *Laticauda* is indicated by the observation that absorption of *Hydrophis* or *Lapemis* antiserum with *Aipysurus laevis* serum does not abolish reactivity toward *Laticauda semifasciata;* nor does absorption of *Hydrophis* or *Lapemis* antiserum with *L. semifasciata* abolish reactivity toward *A. laevis. Aipysurus* sera show considerable variation within the genus, with each of the five species showing different patterns with *Hydrophis, Lapemis,* and *Denisonia* antisera. These serological differences are observed between members of the species pairs, *A. apraefrontalis–A. foliosquama* and *A. duboisii–A. fuscus.* Unfortunately, most of the *A. fuscus* serum was lost by leakage during transport, and the small sample from *A. apraefrontalis* may have become somewhat denatured. *A. duboisii* and *A. foliosquama* show markedly different patterns when developed with *Denisonia* antiserum.

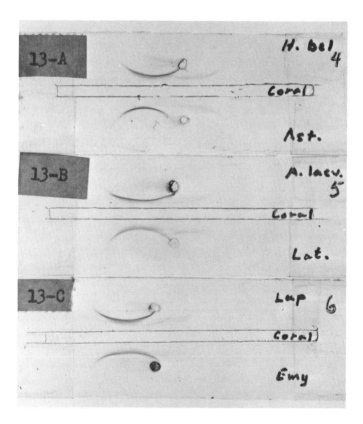

Figure 11. Immunoelectrophoresis preparations of sea snake sera shown in Figure 10, developed with coral snake antivenin (Instituto Butantan).

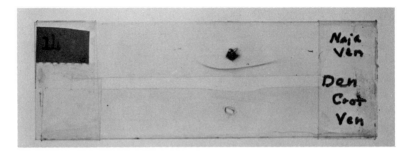

Figure 12. Immunoelectrophoresis preparation of *Naja naja* venom (upper well) and *Crotalus horridus* venom (lower well) developed with *Denisonia superba* antiserum.

Lapemis hardwickii, Acalyptophis, Astrotia, and the three species of *Hydrophis* form a rather closely related group, based on similarity of electrophoretic patterns and complete loss of reactivity when *Hydrophis* antiserum is absorbed with *Lapemis,* or *Lapemis* antiserum absorbed with *Hydrophis melanocephalus* or *H. ornatus. Pelamis* also appears to belong here, showing a pattern which is best developed with *Lapemis* antiserum and poorly developed with *Denisonia* antiserum.

The well developed patterns seen when sea snake sera are developed with *Natrix* antiserum indicate an unexpected affinity between hydrophids and natricids. Some observations, not reported in detail at this time, indicate much weaker reactions between *Elaphe vulpina* and *Coluber constrictor* antisera and sea snake sera, and moderately strong reactions between sea snake sera and *Crotalus horridus* antiserum. However, these antisera were prepared by a different method than the *Natrix* antiserum, and it would be premature to speculate at this time on serological relationship between the sea snakes and other Caenophidian groups.

The weak reactions seen between the antisera used here and the sera of *Morelia spilotes, Liasis childreni,* and *Boa constrictor* confirm the existence of a rather fundamental serological difference between the Boidae and the Caenophidia, as suggested by earlier observations (Kendall and Minton, 1969; Domergue et al., 1970; Minton and Salanitro, 1972). Similar weak reactions with the serum of *Acrochordus granulatus* support anatomical evidence that this genus belongs to the Henophidia and probably deserves family status (Underwood, 1967). The observation that *Lapemis* antiserum absorbed with *Boa constrictor* serum reacts with *Acrochordus* serum, indicates that at least one antigen shared by *Lapemis* and *Acrochordus* is not shared with *Boa.* The lack of close serological relationship between *Acrochordus* and hydrophids is of interest, since *Acrochordus* has several of the anatomical and physiological adaptations of sea snakes, and *A. granulatus,* at least, occurs with sea snakes in estuarine and shallow water marine habitats (Dunson and Dunson, 1973). The observation that snake sera of most groups react with antivenins, especially those prepared against elapid venoms, was verified for seven of the sea snake sera studied and is probably true of the others. Reaction of *Hydrophis cyanocinctus* serum with cobra, coral snake, tiger snake, and two pit viper antivenins has been previously reported (Minton, 1973). A reciprocal experiment using sea snake venoms and antisera prepared against sea snake sera could not be carried out because of a lack of sea snake venoms in sufficient quantities. However reactions were obtained between *Naja naja* and *Denisonia superba* venoms and antisera against *Hydrophis* and *Denisonia* sera. This clearly indicates presence of common antigens in two elapid venoms and the serum of *Hydrophis melanocephalus*. By implication, these antigens are also probably present in *Hydrophis* venom. It is worth mentioning in passing that venoms of *Denisonia superba* and *Notechis* did not react with *Lapemis* antiserum, nor did *Notechis* venom react with *Denisonia* antiserum or

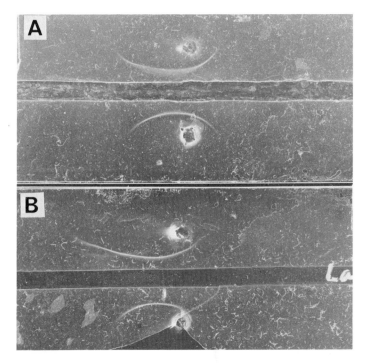

Figure 13. Immunoelectrophoresis preparations of *Lapemis hardwickii* serum (upper wells) and *Emydocephalus annulatus* serum (lower wells) A. Developed with *Lapemis hardwickii* antiserum absorbed with *Laticauda semifasciata* serum; and B. Developed with *Lapemis hardwickii* antiserum absorbed with *Aipysurus laevis* serum.

Hydrophis antiserum, despite reactions between *Notechis* serum and sea snake and elapid antivenins. While the presence of common antigens in the serum and venom of elapids and hydrophids appears to be established, an earlier hypothesis (Minton, 1973), that the reactions between antivenins and snake sera can be accounted for by contamination of venom used for antivenin production with snake blood or tissue fluid, is not completely refuted, and may still account for some of the reactions observed.

CONCLUSIONS

Serological data from this investigation indicate that sea snakes are a relatively homogenous group closely related to Australian elapids and probably to other members of the Elapidae. It appears that *Acalyptophis, Astrotia, Pelamis, Lapemis hardwickii,* and three species of *Hydrophis* studied have similar immunoelectrophoretic patterns and may represent a group which has undergone recent adaptive radiation. If serum proteins are considered relatively conservative taxonomic characters, then the divergence and variation in serum protein pattern seen in *Aipysurus* and *Emydocephalus* indicate that they may represent an older marine radiation, although one that is still largely confined to coral reef habitats in the Australian region. *Laticauda* shows no closer serological relationship to *Aipysurus* than to *Hydrophis* and associated genera. This study throws no light on its possible Asian rather than Australian origin or on its position in the Family Elapidae.

Sea snakes show a moderately close serological affinity to natricids and probably to some other Caenophidian groups, but are remote from the Henophidia as represented by *Acrochordus* and three genera of boids.

Evidence was obtained for the presence of common antigens in sea snake sera and venoms. Some of these antigens are also present in elapid venoms.

ACKNOWLEDGMENTS

Acknowledgment is made to the National Science Foundation and Scripps Institution of Oceanography which supported the *Alpha Helix* Ashmore Reef Expedition. Dr. Nobuo Tamiya generously supplied samples of *Laticauda* sera, and H. W. Peterson donated a live specimen of *Pelamis*. For photographs, advice, and use of equipment, we are indebted to Frank Padgett, D. C. Bauer, and the Illustration Department of Indiana University Medical Center. James B. Murphy of the Dallas Zoo generously donated the antivenins used.

REFERENCES

Domergue, C. A., J. Richaud, and E. R. Brygoo. 1970. Application des techniques serologiques a l'etude de la systematique des serpents de Madagascar. *Compt. Rend. Seances Soc. Biol.* 164:2690–2692.

Dunson, W. A., and M. K. Dunson. 1973. Convergent evolution of sublingual salt glands in the marine file snake and the true sea snakes. J. Comp. Physiol. 86:193–208.

Kendall, S. H., and S. A. Minton. 1969. The serum profiles of certain reptile sera and preliminary observations of antibody formation in snakes. Proc. Indiana Acad. Sci., 78:113–114.

McDowell, S. B. 1967. *Aspidomorphus*, a genus of New Guinea snakes of the Family Elapidae with notes on related genera. J. Zool. 151:497–543.

McDowell, S. B. 1969. Notes on the Australian sea-snake *Ephalophis greyi* M. Smith (Serpentes, Elapidae, Hydrophiinae) and the origin and classification of sea-snakes. Zool. J. Linn. Soc. 48:333–349.

McDowell, S. B. 1972. The genera of sea-snakes of the *Hydrophis* group (Serpentes, Elapidae). Trans. Zool. Soc. Lond. 32(pt. 2):189–247.

Minton, S. A. 1973. Common antigens in snake sera and venoms. In A. deVries and E. Kochva (eds.), Toxins of Animal and Plant Origin, pp. 905–917. Vol. 3. Gordon and Breach, New York.

Minton, S. A., and S. K. Salanitro. 1972. Serological relationships among some colubrid snakes. Copeia 2:245–252.

Salanitro, S. K., and S. A. Minton. 1973. Immune response of snakes. Copeia 3:504–515.

Smith, M. A. 1926. A Monograph of the Sea Snakes. Taylor and Francis, London.

Smith, M. A. 1931. Description of a new genus of sea snake from the coast of Australia with a note on structures providing for complete closure of the mouth in aquatic snakes. Proc. Zool. Soc. Lond. 397–398.

Underwood, G. 1967. A Contribution to the Classification of Snakes. British Museum of Natural History, London.

NATURAL HISTORY OF AUSTRALIAN SPECIES

four

Sea Snakes
of Australia
and New Guinea

Harold G. Cogger

The seas of tropical Australia support a rich sea snake fauna, with a strong endemic component and with a greater species diversity than any other region. Some 32 species (out of a world total of approximately 55 species) are currently recorded from this region, of which nearly 50% are endemic.

The reasons for this high species diversity seem fairly obvious: a tropical coastline of some 10,000 kilometers, combined with an extensive northern continental shelf and the rich and complex trophic systems of the Great Barrier Reef present many opportunities for niche specialization. However, despite the richness of the sea snake fauna, little is known of the status or distribution of the majority of species.

The high order of endemicity is more difficult to explain. Most other groups of tropical non-sessile marine organisms display relatively little endemism in the Australian region, and consist largely of faunal elements common throughout the entire tropical Indo-Pacific region. Sea snakes, though often more specialized in their habits and habitat requirements than is usually acknowledged, are nonetheless well adapted to survive long sea journeys; one would therefore expect accidental dispersal by storms and strong currents to result in higher levels of gene flow between adjacent geographic populations throughout the tropics than appears to occur.

Typically, knowledge of the taxonomy of a group precedes the study of its broader biological characteristics. In many sea snakes, however, the biochemical characteristics of the venom or the physiological responses to diving are better known and understood than systematic relationships or the factors influencing distribution.

In recent years the intensive collecting efforts of such workers as F. Parker in Papua New Guinea, and W. Dunson and H. Heatwole in Australia, have resulted in a wealth of new knowledge of the distribution of Australian sea snake species. A single voyage of the Scripps Institution of Oceanography's research vessel *Alpha Helix,* in December 1972 to January 1973, resulted in the collection of nearly 500 specimens of 16 species from the waters of northwestern Australia and West Irian. Australian commercial and research prawning vessels have taken large numbers of sea snakes opportunistically while trawling in the Gulf of Carpentaria and the Arafura Sea, while research vessels of the U.S.S.R. have also taken large hauls of sea snakes from northern Australian waters (Shuntov, 1971). Unfortunately many of these opportunistic collections lack accurate geographical information. However, despite this rapid increase in collecting effort, taxonomic studies still lag behind research into other aspects of sea snake biology.

The principal aim of this chapter is to review current knowledge of the taxonomy and distribution of the sea snakes known to occur in Australian waters, and to present a brief diagnostic guide to their identification. Many taxonomic problems, especially in one species-group in the genus *Hydrophis,* remain unresolved at the present time and will be the subjects of future papers. Nevertheless some major problems must await further collecting before they can be re-examined fruitfully, and it is hoped that this paper may serve to bring these problems to the attention of non-taxonomists.

Sea snakes are highly specialized reptiles with some remarkable adaptations to a marine existence. These adaptations are becoming the subject of considerable research. Sea snakes are also venomous, the venoms of some species being among the most powerful animal toxins known to man. For these reasons there is a need to provide accurate identifications of those sea snakes used in toxicological and other research, and, more especially, of specimens involved in cases of snake bite.

An attempt is also made to review the biogeography of Australian sea snakes. It is hoped that this will complement the detailed distributional information given for particular subregions in other chapters of this book.

MATERIALS AND METHODS

Some 1200 specimens were examined for the survey here reported. Of these, the majority are in the collection of the Australian Museum and when cited have the prefix AM; other specimens were examined from the collections of the Northern Territory Museum and Art Gallery (prefix NT), and the Museum of Comparative Zoology (prefix MCZ).

All specimens have been used in constructing the distribution maps, together with literature records where applicable. Morphological, meristic, and scutellation characteristics have been taken from most specimens, except that in the case of common species, samples have been selected from different geographic regions. The statistical breakdown of these data is presented elsewhere. Where scale counts fall entirely within the ranges cited in the literature, the extremes quoted are those found therein.

Because of their tenuous nature, subgenera and subspecies are omitted from the taxonomic accounts.

TAXONOMIC BACKGROUND

As early as 1869, Krefft was able to list 15 species of sea snakes from Australian seas; Boulenger (1896) had increased the number to 17 (plus seven from generalized adjacent areas), while M. Smith (1926), in his classic monograph on sea snakes, recorded 25 Australian species. Since Smith's monograph, seven additional species have been added to the Australian fauna: one new species and six range extensions into this region. Voris (1969), using a variety of analytical techniques, studied the relationships of sea snakes and proposed only minor modifications of the generic and species categories proposed by Smith. McDowell in a series of papers (1967, 1969, 1972, 1974) has proposed major changes to Smith's familial and generic classifications on the basis of detailed morphological and anatomical studies. McDowell placed special emphasis on venom gland musculature, dental characteristics, hemi-penial structure and the relative positions of particular organs within the body; he made few taxonomic changes at the species level.

Table 1 lists the sea snakes currently recorded from the Australasian region; the particular genus/species combinations proposed by Smith (1926), Voris (1969), McDowell (1969, 1972) and the present study are compared. Although specific taxa will be discussed in detail in the following accounts, some general comments are appropriate in considering the validity of the various classifications presented in Table 1.

McDowell has convincingly demonstrated the separate origins of the laticaudine sea snakes, which group he regards as no more than a divergent line within the terrestrial elapids, and whose morphological resemblance to the true sea snake he implies is the result of convergence. Like others before him, he has stressed the obvious close affinities between the terrestrial Elapidae and the strictly marine Hydrophiidae, and in regarding them as confamilial he implies only a subtle shift in the traditional view of their relationships.

Voris (1969), on the other hand, supports Smith's (1926) view that *Laticauda* is the most primitive genus of sea snakes and that it shares a common origin with the more specialized sea snakes. He postulates that

Table 1. The species of sea snakes currently recorded from Australia and their generic dispositions

Classification adopted in this paper	Genera in which species cited have previously been disposed		
	M. Smith, 1926	Voris, 1969	McDowell, 1972
Laticauda colubrina	*Laticauda*	*Laticauda*	*Laticauda*
Laticauda laticaudata	*Laticauda*	*Laticauda*	*Laticauda*
Acalyptophis peronii	*Acalyptophis*	*Acalyptophis*	*Acalyptophis*
Aipysurus apraefrontalis	*Aipysurus*	*Aipysurus*	*Aipysurus*
Aipysurus duboisii	*Aipysurus*	*Aipysurus*	*Aipysurus*
Aipysurus eydouxii	*Aipysurus*	*Aipysurus*	*Aipysurus*
Aipysurus foliosquama	*Aipysurus*	*Aipysurus*	*Aipysurus*
Aipysurus fuscus	*Aipysurus*	*Aipysurus*	*Aipysurus*
Aipysurus laevis	*Aipysurus*	*Aipysurus*	*Aipysurus*
Aipysurus tenuis	*Aipysurus*	*Aipysurus*	*Aipysurus*
Astrotia stokesii	*Astrotia*	*Astrotia*	*Disteira*
Disteira kingii	*Hydrophis*	*Hydrophis*	*Disteira*
Disteira major	*Hydrophis*	*Hydrophis*	*Disteira*
Emydocephalus annulatus	*Emydocephalus*	*Emydocephalus*	*Emydocephalus*
Enhydrina schistosa	*Enhydrina*	*Enhydrina*	*Disteira*
Ephalophis greyi	—	*Ephalophis*	*Ephalophis*
Ephalophis mertoni	*Hydrophis*	gen. nov.	*Ephalophis*
Hydrelaps darwiniensis	*Hydrelaps*	*Hydrelaps*	*Hydrelaps*
Hydrophis belcheri	*Hydrophis*	*Hydrophis*	*Hydrophis (Aturia)*
Hydrophis sp.	*Hydrophis*	*Hydrophis*	*Hydrophis (Hydrophis)*
Hydrophis caerulescens	*Hydrophis*	*Hydrophis*	*Hydrophis (Aturia)*
Hydrophis elegans	*Hydrophis*	*Hydrophis*	*Hydrophis (Leioselasma)*
Hydrophis fasciatus	*Hydrophis*	*Hydrophis*	*Hydrophis (Hydrophis)*
Hydrophis gracilis	*Microcephalophis*	*Microcephalophis*	*Hydrophis (Hydrophis)*
Hydrophis inornatus	*Hydrophis*	*Hydrophis*	*Hydrophis (Aturia)*
Hydrophis melanocephalus	*Hydrophis*	*Hydrophis*	*Hydrophis (Leioselasma)*
Hydrophis melanosoma	*Hydrophis*	*Hydrophis*	*Hydrophis (Hydrophis)*
Hydrophis obscurus	*Hydrophis*	*Hydrophis*	*Hydrophis (Hydrophis)*
Hydrophis ornatus	*Hydrophis*	*Hydrophis*	*Hydrophis (Aturia)*
Hydrophis pacificus	*Hydrophis*	*Hydrophis*	*Hydrophis (Leioselasma)*
Lapemis hardwickii	*Lapemis*	*Lapemis*	*Lapemis*

Laticauda might have evolved in an Australian or Asian mangrove swamp/estuarine environment, but his comparison of *Laticauda* with the terrestrial Australian elapid snakes of the genus *Hoplocephalus* is based on erroneous data concerning the latter's ecology and habitat preferenda. McDowell (1972) has pointed out that many of the morphological and other characters on which traditional sea snake classification has been based are of dubious reliability or validity, being subject to excessive individual or geographic variation. However, in utilizing a particular suite of myological and anatomical features, McDowell has assumed that these characters are more conservative than those previously used. His interpretation of elapid-hydrophid phyletics, is, I believe, somewhat unconvincing and tautological. Indeed, the fact that his classification contrasts so strongly with the one by Voris, based on the multivariate analysis of some 153 characters, suggests that broader relationships should be interpreted with caution.

McDowell's subgeneric divisions within *Hydrophis* appear to be natural ones. However, the group of species which he assigns to the genus *Disteira* appears to be an assemblage of divergent species with only a small suite of common features, but which in most respects represent several distinct phyletic lines, a view taken by Smith (1926) and Voris (1969) and supported by the present study. *Enhydrina schistosa,* in particular, has diverged strongly from other sea snakes, and its many distinctive features and wide distribution together suggest a long, independent period of specialization.

In removing *schistosa* and *stokesii* from *Disteira,* I have seriously weakened the genus as redefined by McDowell. Although the relationship between the two remaining Australian species—*major* (the type species of the genus) and *kingii*—is far from clear, I have retained them in *Disteira* pending a reassessment of their affinities.

It can be seen from the preceding discussion that I have adopted the more conservative view and have largely retained the older Smith classification. Only the application of a variety of new approaches, including biochemical and karyological studies, can determine which classification most accurately reflects the phylogenetic history of the sea snakes.

THE BIOGEOGRAPHY OF AUSTRALIAN SEA SNAKES

That sea snakes are derived either directly from terrestrial elapid snakes or as an offshoot of a group of pre-elapid terrestrial snakes is generally accepted (Underwood, 1967). McDowell (1969, 1972, 1974) has commented at length on hydrophiid/elapid affinities and has postulated that sea snakes in the *Hydrelaps/Ephalophis* group display many features which are intermediate between the generalized elapid and hydrophiid conditions. If McDowell's hypotheses are correct, Australia is probably at or near the geographic origin of the true sea snakes. Certainly there is little doubt that Australia represents an area of one or more major radiations within the group, and the *Aipysurus/Emydocephalus/Hydrelaps/Ephalophis* complex clearly represents an old endemic Australian element. Underwood (1957, 1967) has postulated that the Australian elapid snake fauna may be derived secondarily from early sea snakes.

The marine benthic fauna of the tropical Indo-Pacific region is probably the richest in the world. In terms of the geographical distribution of this fauna, small pockets of local endemism tend to be overshadowed by the high proportion of widespread faunal elements, which extend from the central and western Pacific to the Indian Ocean.

It appears surprising, therefore, that despite common elements throughout the region, many sea snakes are ecologically and geographically localized, with major components of the sea snake fauna (e.g., members of the genus *Aipysurus*) virtually confined to the Australian region. Indeed, although about 60% of the known species of sea snakes are found in Australian waters, less than 40% of the Australian sea snake fauna is common to that of the adjacent Indo-Malayan Archipelago; the deep water troughs delineating the western boundary of the Sahul Shelf appear to have been an effective barrier to the interchange of sea snakes between Australia and the seas around and to the west of the Lesser Sunda Islands. That the limits of the continental shelf should mark a clear delineation of a regional sea snake fauna is scarcely surprising, given the shallow benthic feeding patterns of most sea snakes.

Perhaps more surprising is the marked subregional variation in species composition within the Australian region; available data are summarized in Table 2. It is possible that the regional differences in species composition indicated in Table 2 might reflect no more than differences in collecting effort in each area. However, this explanation appears unlikely, as several species which are abundant and widely distributed (e.g., *Lapemis hardwickii* and *Hydrophis elegans*) make up a substantial segment of collections from all localities; furthermore, some of these common elements, such as *H. elegans* and *D. major,* are confined to the Australian region, and confirm that the break between the sea snake faunas of Indonesia on one hand, and Australia/New Guinea on the other, is a real one in biogeographic terms.

What, then, are some of the factors which might have contributed to the high species diversity in the Australian sea snake fauna, and to the development of regional differences in the species composition of that fauna?

The seas surrounding Australia can be conveniently divided into two main water masses—a northern tropical and a southern cold/temperate.

Typically, each of these is characterized by a distinctive biotic assemblage, with mixing of the two along the eastern and western seaboards. The zone of overlap varies with season, being displaced southwards by up to 1000 km at the end of summer. At this time, many tropical species (including sea

Table 2. Regional distribution of the sea snakes recorded from Australian waters

Species	Indo-Malaysia	Timor Sea	North-west Shelf	Arafura Sea	Gulf of Carpentaria	Gulf of Papua	Coral Sea
Laticauda colubrina						+	+
Laticauda laticaudata	+					+	+
Hydrophis melanocephalus					?	+	+
Hydrophis obscurus						+	?
Hydrophis gracilis	+	?	?	?	?	+	?
Hydrophis inornatus	+	?	?	?	+	?	?
Hydrophis pacificus				+	+	+	
Hydrophis melanosoma			*			+	
Hydrophis caerulescens	+	?	?	?	+	?	
Disteira kingii		?	?	*	+	+	+
Enhydrina schistosa	+	?	?	+	+	+	+
Aipysurus eydouxii	+	?	?	+	+	+	+
Hydrophis elegans			+	+	+	+	+
Disteira major		?	+	+	+	+	+
Hydrophis belcheri	?	?	?	?	?	?	?
Hydrophis ornatus	+	+	+	+	+	+	+
Aipysurus laevis		+	+	+	+	+	+
Aipysurus duboisii		+	+	+	+	+	+
Emydocephalus annulatus		+	+	+	+	+	+
Acalyptophis peronii		+	+	+	+	+	+
Lapemis hardwickii	+	+	+	+	+	+	+
Pelamis platurus	+	+	+	+	+	+	+
Astrotia stokesii		+	+	+	+	+	+
Hydrophis sp.			+·	+	+	+	+
Ephalophis mertoni				+	+		
Ephalophis greyi			+		+		
Hydrelaps darwiniensis			+	+	+		
Aipysurus tenuis		?	+	*			
Hydrophis fasciatus	+	+		+			
Aipysurus apraefrontalis		+	+	*			
Aipysurus foliosquama		+	+	*			
Aipysurus fuscus		+	?				

*Literature record; +, specimen(s) examined; ?, unverified record and/or presumed occurrence.

snakes) temporarily extend their ranges southward. This is especially marked along the eastern coast where the summer notonectian or East Australian Current sweeps southward along the central and southern coast, bringing some tropical forms almost to the Victorian border, although the majority drop out at about the latitude of Jervis Bay. However, the southern limits of the resident tropical faunas are generally determined by the winter isothermal patterns, and sea snakes, with the exception of the pelagic species *Pelamis platurus,* are virtually absent from the cold/temperate fauna of southern Australia.

The tropical seas of Australia are characterized by marked seasonal changes in temperature patterns, current movements, and nutrient content. The winter months are generally characterized by a stable water mass, in which prevailing winds and currents are easterly or southeasterly; at this time there is an upwelling of nutrient-rich water from the ocean depths, which extends across the benthic layer of the continental shelf.

The summer monsoons result in a virtual reversal of the winter pattern, especially west of Torres Strait. Currents are mostly westerly in western and northern Australia, and northeasterly in eastern Australia (sweeping southwards as they meet the coast), while tropical cyclones disrupt the normal pattern of the southeast trade winds and produce considerable instability in the waters of the continental shelf.

Broad seasonal changes in currents and water temperature are shown in the upper two charts in Figure 1. Shuntov (1972) reports significantly higher summer temperatures than indicated here in the lower part of the Gulf of Carpentaria; this is not unexpected in a region with such shallow seas and in which thermal exchanges with cooler water masses are not possible.

If one considers that the Torres Strait seaway has probably existed only since middle to late Pleistocene times, and that until then it was probably closed almost continuously since the Carboniferous era (Doutch, 1973), the order of differentiation between the sea snake faunas on either side of Torres Strait, especially given the major differences in the benthic ecology of the two regions, is perhaps even less than might have been anticipated.

The high vagility of the marine fauna of the tropical Indo-Pacific is generally ascribed to the fact that the majority of marine invertebrates and most fishes have pelagic eggs. This permits dispersal over vast distances and maximizes gene flow even between widely separated shallow benthic biotas.

Sea snakes, on the other hand, produce living young, which at birth have ecological restraints placed upon them which are more or less identical to those of their parents. Contrary to Shuntov's (1972) contention that feeding specialization is rare in sea snakes, most species have highly specialized feeding habits, so that there is relatively little exchange of individuals between populations which are isolated by extensive tracts of unsuitable habitats. Hence, in many respects sea snake populations exhibit many of the characteristics of terrestrial faunas, and less closely resemble the other components of the marine biotas of which they are a part.

As pointed out above, the Torres Strait seaway is a relatively recent phenomenon dating from the middle to late Pleistocene, so that a major land barrier separating the marine faunas of the Coral Sea and of the Sahul Shelf

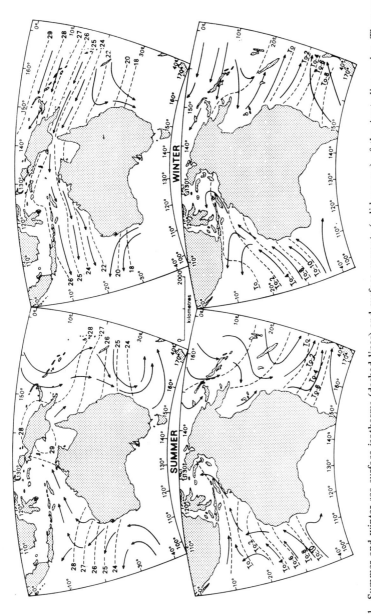

Figure 1. Summer and winter sea surface isotherms (dashed lines) and surface currents (solid arrows) of the Australian region. The upper charts refer to the present distributions, while the lower charts indicate a tentative construction of the distributions during the maximum of the last glaciation. Reproduced with permission from Webster and Streten, 1973.

has probably existed since the early Miocene, and may even date back to the end of Cretaceous times.

If the presently accepted palaeogeographic history of northern Australia is correct, and it is supported by the high order of endemism (compared with other marine groups) in the Australasian sea snake fauna, then it would be reasonable to expect some measurable differences between the sea snake fauna of the Australian continental shelf east and west of Torres Strait. Unfortunately, the situation is complicated by the fact that the shelf benthos east of Torres Strait is very different from that of the Gulf of Carpentaria and the Sahul Shelf. The former is characterized by the numerous offshore reef complexes of the Great Barrier Reef, with only a narrow fringe of turbid onshore waters, except for the more extensive shoals of the Gulf of Papua. West of Torres Strait, however, the shallow waters of the Gulf of Carpentaria and the Arafura Sea have relatively impoverished reefs and extensive mud and silt deposits. Not until the clearer waters of the Indian Ocean are encountered, along the northwest shelf of Western Australia and along the eastern edge of the Timor Sea, do rich silt-free reef complexes again appear.

Hence, the regional differences in species composition which are apparent in Table 2 probably reflect differences in benthic ecology superimposed on broader biogeographic patterns.

Table 2 also analyzes the distribution of Australian sea snakes in terms of east-west range limits. This shows that the seas east and west of Torres Strait, though having a substantial common sea snake fauna, nevertheless demonstrate significant regional endemism.

The apparent absence of members of the genus *Laticauda* from the western fauna may be no more than an artifact of collecting, or it may indicate that *Laticauda* has reached the Indo-Malayan Archipelago via a route to the north of New Guinea.

Unfortunately, records of several species of sea snakes (e.g., *Hydrophis belcheri, H. inornatus*) are too scattered to provide data of use in zoogeographic analysis.

A further potentially important factor in limiting sea snake distribution and contributing to a reduction in gene flow between the sea snake populations of Australia and Indonesia is shown in the lower pair of charts in Figure 1. Van Andel et al. (1967) have postulated that during the Pleistocene glacials (and by extrapolation during the prolonged earlier closure of the Torres Strait seaway), the sea surface temperatures in the Timor Sea would have been substantially lower, especially in winter, due to the blockage of the warmer Torres Strait current (by the Torres Strait land bridge) and the incursion of cooler southern waters. Thus, sea surface temperatures off northwestern Australia would have been markedly lower than surface water temperatures in similar latitudes of eastern Australia. "To" in Figure 1 represents the reference isotherm; its value can only be guessed at, but Webster and Streten (1973) estimated that the most likely value of To is 20–22°C.

Temperatures of this order would mean that summer surface temperatures in the Timor Sea during the Pleistocene glacials would have been roughly equivalent to those which today appear to limit the dispersal of sea snakes farther south. Hence, the effectiveness of deep sea trenches bordering the Sahul Shelf in isolating the sea snake faunas of Australia and Indonesia appears to have been reinforced by past sea surface thermal barriers.

Few of the sea snakes examined in the course of this study have sufficient accompanying ecological or geographic data to permit any meaningful assessment of the factors influencing their distribution and abundance. Sea snakes are usually collected opportunistically as an adjunct to commercial or research trawling operations for other marine organisms; they are generally much feared by fishermen, and sea snakes from different trawls are usually lumped together without regard for accurate locality data. These factors discourage the accumulation of quantitative data. However, most commercial prawn trawling operations take place in depths of less than 30 m, providing a rough indication of the local distribution of the snakes collected.

Apart from results presented elsewhere in this book, the only attempt to analyze species diversity, relative abundance, and seasonal movements of sea snakes in Australian waters is that of Shuntov (1972), who reported the results of extensive trawling operations in northern Australian waters between 1967 and 1970.

Shuntov (1972) reports that few sea snakes occur beyond the 100 m isobath, and that species of *Hydrophis* (s.l.) tend not to extend beyond the 50 m isobath. However, most observations would indicate that benthic feeding sea snakes are found in depths rarely exceeding 30 m. Of special significance is Shuntov's finding that the distribution of sea snakes varies markedly with season in the area of his study. Although his data are not quantified, he reports that most species are widely distributed over the shallower parts of the continental shelf in winter, but that they migrate to coastal waters in summer. The dispersal of snakes in winter he attributes partly to prevailing winds and currents, partly to lowered temperatures in the southern part of the Gulf of Carpentaria, and partly to an abundance of food fishes in offshore waters at this time.

Shuntov also reports that migration of sea snakes to inshore waters corresponds with an inshore shift of plankton and food fishes, but that active migration takes place against prevailing currents in spring, in anticipation of summer feeding patterns.

He also relates the summer inshore migration to breeding habits, stating that the adults move inshore to breed, the newborn young remaining near the coast. This hypothesis appears to be based on the small proportion of young snakes in offshore samples, but must be suspect until inshore summer samples confirm a high percentage of young sea snakes. Indeed, there is some evidence to suggest that there are high postnatal mortality rates in sea snakes, and that the percentage of small individuals in Shuntov's samples (5–6%) may represent maximal values even in the breeding season.

Shuntov's results clearly demonstrate the need for further quantified studies of the distribution and abundance of Australian sea snakes, especially in relation to annual activity (including dietary changes) and migration patterns.

ANNOTATED LIST OF THE SEA SNAKES RECORDED FROM AUSTRALIA, WITH ARTIFICIAL KEYS TO THEIR IDENTIFICATION

The present paper is the result of a preliminary survey of some 1200 specimens of sea snakes from most parts of the Australian region. In the course of this survey, several major taxonomic problems have been encountered which, for their solution, will require the examination of further material from adjacent geographic regions. New taxa have been encountered which will be the subjects of future papers. In the meantime, this chapter is intended to provide for fieldworkers brief diagnostic descriptions of the sea snakes recorded from Australian waters. For this reason, emphasis has been placed on those characters which can be fairly readily examined in the field, while the genera and their contained species are treated alphabetically. Detailed descriptions of most species are readily available in the literature, and it would be unnecessarily repetitive to include them here. However, references to such descriptions are provided for each species.

The abbreviated diagnostic descriptions provided in this section are intended to be applied only to specimens from Australian seas, while the diagnoses are hierarchical, i.e., are valid only in relation to other species within the same genus.

The keys have been somewhat oversimplified for use by non-specialists. Reference should be made to the detailed keys provided by Smith (1926) and McDowell (1969, 1972) for more comprehensive diagnoses.

The "average total length" in each description is not a statistical mean, but simply an approximation to indicate to a fieldworker whether a specimen is at or near adult size.

Sea snakes display greater intraspecific and ontogenetic variation than most other reptilian groups, features which have led to considerable confusion in identification. Traditionally, they have been difficult to collect, and frequently their extensive ranges are represented only by isolated individual records. All of these factors have discouraged accurate identification by non-specialists, with a consequent low reliability of literature citations.

The status of several species within the genus *Hydrophis* is still uncertain, and although such uncertainty is indicated in the individual accounts, it should be born in mind when using the keys.

Key to the Genera of Australian Sea Snakes

1. Ventrals large, at least three times as
    wide as the adjacent body scales 2
    Ventrals small, scarcely more than twice
    as wide as the adjacent body scales 6
2. Nasals in contact 3
    Nasals separated by internasals . . . . *Laticauda*
3. Six or more supralabials 4
    Three supralabials . . . . *Emydocephalus*
4. Posterior chin shields not reduced, and
    separated by a mental groove; portion of
    rostral scale bearing median valve-like
    fold continuous with remainder of scale 5
    Posterior chin shields usually reduced
    and separated by one or more small scales;
    portion of rostral scale bearing median
    valve-like fold sometimes separated from
    remainder of scale by a suture . . . . *Aipysurus*
5. No preocular scale; rostral with a median
    lobe at its anterior-most end, this lobe
    fitting into a median notch in the mental
    and completely dividing the lingual fossa
    of the rostral into separate left and
    right grooves . . . . *Hydrelaps*
    Preocular scale present; rostral with a
    median sharp fold located within the
    mouth, behind the median and undivided
    lingual fossa, this fold formed from the
    posterior edge of the portion of the
    keratinized scute extending within the
    lining of the lip . . . . *Ephalophis*
6. Head scutes enlarged, regular, symmetrical;
    supraoculars without projecting tubercles
    or spines 7
    Head scutes broken up into small,
    irregular and asymmetrical scales;
    supraoculars with projecting
    tubercles or spines . . . . *Acalyptophis*
7. A distinct mental groove 8
    No distinct mental groove . . . .*Pelamis*
8. Mental normal, triangular, broader
    than long and not partially hidden in
    the shallow mental groove 9
    Mental narrow, splint- or dagger-shaped,
    much longer than broad and partially
    hidden in the deep mental groove . . . . *Enhydrina*

9. Either fewer than four solid maxillary
teeth or, if four or more, anterior
chin shields reduced and not or scarcely
contacting the mental groove, from which
they are separated by the elongate first
infralabials 10
Four or more solid maxillary teeth;
anterior chin shields large and mostly
bordering the mental groove .... *Hydrophis*

10. Ventrals single or divided, but
usually distinct posteriorly 11
Ventrals not distinct posteriorly ....*Lapemis*

11. Ventrals, except on throat, divided
into pairs of foliform scales which in
most specimens form a mid-ventral keel .... *Astrotia*
Ventrals mostly undivided, never foliform
and never with a mid-ventral keel ....*Disteira*

Genus *Aipysurus* (Lacépède)

Recognition: Ventral scales large, at least three times as wide as the adjacent body scales; nasal scales in contact; six or more supralabials; posterior chin shields (postgenials) usually reduced and separated by one or more small scales; preocular scale present.

Remarks: A group of seven species of strictly marine snakes. Some are rarely seen, but others sometimes congregate in large numbers on particular reefs. Skindivers have reported that such congregations occur seasonally on certain reefs in the Great Barrier Reef complex. Smith (1926) and McDowell (1969) have provided expanded generic descriptions. The number of young produced per female is small, usually < 4, and the young are large (see species accounts) at birth. In those species with cross-bands, the bands are more conspicuous and clearly defined in the young. The brown color which predominates in snakes of the genus becomes pale blue-grey when the skin becomes dry. This feature should be taken into account in the species descriptions, which are mostly based on wet skin colors.

Distribution: With the exception of one species (*A. eydouxii*), all species are confined to the waters of the continental shelf of Australia/New Guinea and to the islands of the extreme southwest Pacific Ocean.

Key to the Species of *Aipysurus*

1. Ventrals with or without a slight median
notch on the hind edge 2
Ventrals with a deep median notch on the
hind edge 6

2. Most head shields, but at least the

parietals, broken up into a series of
smaller scales 3
Head shields (including parietals), normal,
enlarged, symmetrical..........................*eydouxii*
3. Head shields more or less regular and
symmetrical, larger than scales on the
neck 4
Head covered with small irregular scales
more or less equal in size to those on
the neck .... *duboisii*
4. Ventrals fewer than 180 5
Ventrals more than 180 ....*tenuis*
5. Scales normally in 19 rows at mid-body;
ventrals more than 155 ....*fuscus*
Scales normally in 21 or 23 rows at
mid-body; ventrals fewer than 155 .... *laevis*
6. Prefrontals present; scales in 19 rows .... *foliosquama*
Prefrontals absent; scales in 17 rows .... *apraefrontalis*

Aipysurus apraefrontalis (Smith) (Figure 2)

Recognition: A small, rather slender snake with a small head and a somewhat
pointed snout. Dark olive-brown or purplish-brown above, with either very
faint olive-brown cross-bands (which are most conspicuous on the lower
sides) or, in some specimens, with more conspicuous pale brown cross-bands
and scattered cream-colored scales (with olive-brown tips) which are mostly
confined to the lateral and lower lateral scale rows. Throat with small scales
which are creamy-white anteriorly and dark brown posteriorly. Ventral sur-

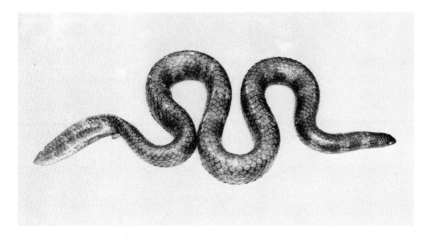

Figure 2. *Aipysurus apraefrontalis* (Ashmore Reef).

face more or less uniform grey-brown, with occasional white or white-blotched scales. The concealed part of each ventral scale is creamy white. The eye has a distinct small, round black pupil (in daylight) in the center of a large, pale, cream-colored iris. Head shields mostly large and symmetrical but with some fragmentation, the *parietal shields divided* but larger than scales on neck; *prefrontal scales absent,* the nasals in direct contact with the frontal shield. Body scales smooth or each with a low tubercle or short keel posteriorly, imbricate, the hind edge of each scale extensively free and somewhat pointed or bifid, *in 17 rows* at mid-body. Ventrals 140–155, *deeply notched behind and often with ragged hind margins.* Anal divided. Subcaudals 18–25, all single. Average total length about 0.5 m.

Remarks: On Ashmore Reef (the type locality) this species is largely an inhabitant of the reef flat and reef edge. Some species were found (with *A. foliosquama* and *A. fuscus*) in cavities under dead coral debris fully exposed at low tide.

Distribution (Figure 3): Until recently known only from the vicinity of the type locality, but Shuntov (1972) cites this species as constituting 7% of

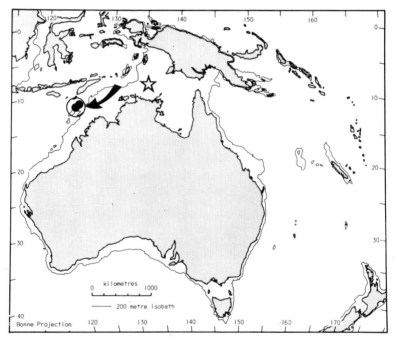

Figure 3. Distribution of *Aipysurus apraefrontalis.* ✩, generalized literature records, i.e., Shuntov's "Arafura Sea;" •, specimens examined; ○, literature record; and ◉, three or more specimens examined from the same locality.

Figure 4. *Aipysurus duboisii* (Ashmore Reef).

species trawled in the Timor Sea. The distribution of his percentages, however, suggests that the actual number of snakes taken may have been small. Smith (1974) has recently described the *Aipysurus* of Western Australia.

Aipysurus duboisii (Bavay) (Figure 4)

Recognition: A moderately built snake, highly variable in color. Typically dark purplish-brown above, the concealed surface of each scale pale cream and sufficiently visible to form a reticulated pattern over the dorsal surface; some specimens are more or less uniform brown, but more typically the scales of the lower flanks are creamy-white or white spotted, forming wedge-shaped pale areas which extend upward toward the dorsum as a series of pale bands alternating with darker ones which are formed by downwards extensions of the dorsal color; in some specimens the dark brown is confined to spots on the individual scales, so that the ground color is pale cream or salmon with obscure darker crossbands. Scales of throat white, tipped with brown. Ventral surface ranges from cream to uniform dark brown. Eye as in *A. apraefrontalis. All head shields except rostral and nasals fragmented into small, irregular scales,* the individual fragments not or scarcely larger than the scales on the neck. Scales usually smooth, occasionally with a slight central keel or series of tubercles, imbricate, in 19 rows at mid-body. Ventrals 150–165, slightly notched behind. Anal divided. Subcaudals 23–35, all single. Average total length 0.7 m.

Remarks: The darker forms described above are usually found in the areas west of Torres Strait, whereas paler and larger specimens predominate on the Great Barrier Reef.

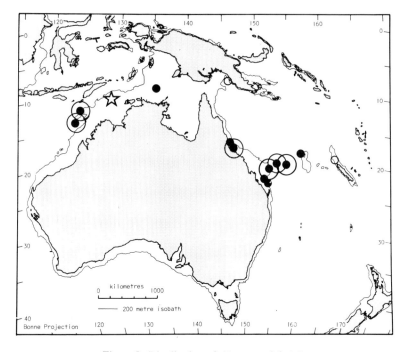

Figure 5. Distribution of *Aipysurus duboisii.*

Distribution (Figure 5): Apparently confined to the waters of the Austral-ian-southern New Guinea continental shelf, and the islands east to New Caledonia (the type locality).

Aipysurus eydouxii (Gray)

Recognition: A moderately built snake. Cream- to salmon-colored above, with a series of broad, often very irregular blackish cross-bands, which may taper and terminate on the sides or extend to the ventral surface. The scales of the paler interspaces usually with dark margins, while the interspaces may contain secondary darker bars or blotches, especially on the lower sides. Ventrals vary from entirely blackish to pale with a dark median zone. Head uniform brown or flecked with darker. *Head shields enlarged, regular and symmetrical, without any indication of fragmentation.* Scales smooth, imbri-cate, in 17 rows at mid-body. Ventrals 124–150, not or scarcely notched behind. Anal divided. Subcaudals 23–35, all single. Average total length 1 m.

Remarks: This is the most widely distributed of all *Aipysurus*, being the only species ranging westward through the Indo-Malayan Archipelago to the Indo-Chinese coast. McDowell (1969) has pointed out that this species tends to bridge the gap between *Aipysurus* and *Emydocephalus,* on which basis he retains the latter genus only with reservations. The similarity between *A. eydouxii* and *E. annulatus* is real, and the only ready external feature clearly separating the two is the number of supralabials, three in *Emydocephalus,* six or more in *A. eydouxii.* All of the records cited below are of trawled specimens taken in deeper water, suggesting that the species does not inhabit clear reef waters.

Distribution (Figure 6): Apparently widely distributed in tropical Australian waters. Extra-limital through the Indo-Malayan Archipelago to the coastal waters of Southeast Asia.

Aipysurus foliosquama (Smith) (Figure 7)

Recognition: A small moderately sized snake similar in most respects to *A. apraefrontalis,* including its distinctive eye. Rich brown to dark blackish-brown or purplish-brown above, usually with obscure paler brown cross-bands (which are most conspicuous on the lower sides) and scattered white or cream-colored scales. Ventral surface as in *A. apraefrontalis.* Head shields

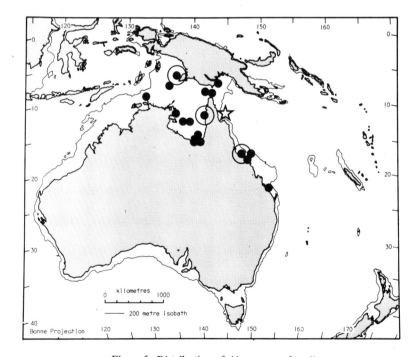

Figure 6. Distribution of *Aipysurus eydouxii.*

Figure 7. *Aipysurus foliosquama* (Ashmore Reef).

mostly large and regular, but with *some fragmentation of the parietals* and with *paired prefrontal scales* separating the frontal from the nasals. Scales smooth or each with a low tubercle or short keel posteriorly, imbricate, the hind edge of each scale extensively free, and somewhat pointed or bifid, in 19–21 rows at mid-body. *Ventrals 135–155, each deeply notched behind.* Anal divided. Subcaudals 20–30, all single. Average total length 0.6 m.

Remarks: Habits and distribution similar to those of *A. apraefrontalis,* but much more abundant than the latter; from the details of specimens examined, it can be seen that nearly six times as many *foliosquama* were collected as *apraefrontalis,* a proportional distribution confirmed by underwater observations.

Distribution (Figure 8): Presently recorded only from a small area of the northwestern shelf of Australia.

Aipysurus fuscus (Tschudi) (Figure 9)

Recognition: A small, moderately built snake superficially resembling *Aipysurus foliosquama.* Brown, blackish-brown or purplish-brown above, more or less uniform but often with faint indications of paler cross-bands on the lower sides; in some specimens the center of each lateral scale is darker, resulting in faint dark longitudinal striations. Head shields, especially the *parietals, partly fragmented,* but major shields more or less regular. Scales smooth, imbricate, *usually in 19 rows* (rarely 21) at mid-body. Ventrals 155–180, *slightly notched behind.* Anal divided. Subcaudals 20–40, all single. Average total length 0.6 m.

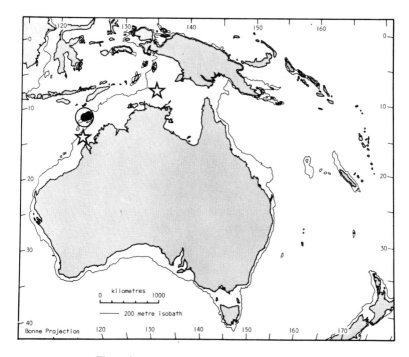

Figure 8. Distribution of *Aipysurus foliosquama.*

Figure 9. *Aipysurus fuscus* (Ashmore Reef).

Remarks: Smith (1926) inadvertently referred to an Ashmore Reef specimen as the type, despite the fact that he correctly cited the type specimen on
the following page. Like Smith, I have seen specimens only from the Ashmore
Reef region, but cannot confirm that these are conspecific with the type
specimen from 'Celebes.' Shuntov (1972) failed to record this species in any
of his trawls over a 3-year period, suggesting that the species represented by
the Ashmore Reef specimens may indeed be endemic to the northwest
Australian shelf.

Distribution (Figure 10): As pointed out above, the type specimen is
from 'Celebes,' but all other records are from the complex of reefs whose
extremes are represented by Hibernia, Ashmore, and Cartier Reefs, between
Australia and Timor.

Aipysurus laevis (Lacépède) (Figure 11)

Recognition: A large, rather heavily built snake. Highly variable in color
and pattern: some specimens are uniform rich dark brown or purplish-brown
above, gradually fading into a paler brown on the ventral surface, but more

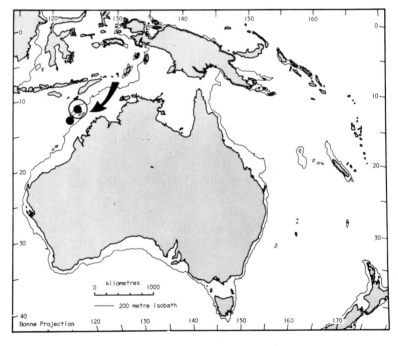

Figure 10. Distribution of *Aipysurus fuscus.*

Figure 11. *Aipysurus laevis* (Ashmore Reef).

often there are numerous creamy-white scales, or spotted scales, scattered irregularly over the body; in some paler specimens the ventral and lateral scales are entirely creamy-white; the brown scales on the body often have darker centers which form faint darker longitudinal striations. Tail uniform brown to almost pure white, except for a dark brown dorsal ridge. Head shields mostly large and symmetrical, with only *partial fragmentation, especially of the parietals.* Scales smooth, imbricate, in *21–25 rows at midbody. Ventrals 135–155,* rarely more, and *slightly notched behind.* Anal divided. Subcaudals 25–35, all single. Average total length about 1.2 m, but commonly reaches nearly two m.

Remarks: This is the largest and bulkiest member of the genus, and is one of the most abundant species on coral reefs throughout its range. There have been many reports by divers of aggressive behavior by this species, and there is little doubt that this is one of the most curious sea snakes. Repeatedly, this species has been observed to make swiftly for a diver when first made aware of his presence, often entwining itself around the diver's arms or legs. However, all observations suggest that bites do not occur spontaneously, but only when the snake is roughly grasped.

Distribution (Figure 12): Waters of the continental shelf of northern Australia and New Guinea, with eastern outliers on the reefs of the Coral Sea as far as New Caledonia.

Aipysurus tenuis (Lönnberg and Andersson)

Recognition: "Light brown with dark brown spots on the tips of the scales forming longitudinal lines on the back and more or less distinct cross-bars

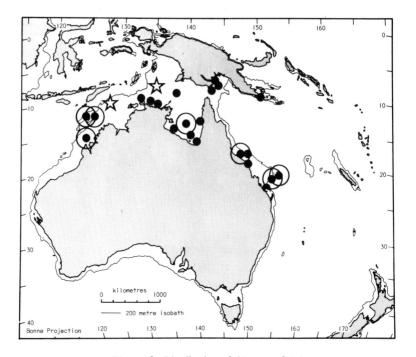

Figure 12. Distribution of *Aipysurus laevis.*

on the sides. Head above dark brown" (Smith, 1926). Head shields more or less regular and symmetrical, the parietals and frontal partially fragmented, but the fragments much larger than the scales on the neck. Scales imbricate, smooth or outer rows with a small tubercle, in 19 rows at mid-body. *Ventrals 185–195,* each with, at most, a slight median notch behind, and each with a small median keel and a series of tubercles along the hind edge. Anal divided. Subcaudals 35–40, single. Maximum known length 1.02 m.

Remarks: No specimens were examined in the course of the present survey, despite the fact that Shuntov cites this species as constituting 4% of sea snakes trawled in the Arafura Sea. However, as Shuntov does not provide any details of the actual numbers of snakes trawled, it is not known whether significant numbers of specimens of this species were taken. It is also pertinent that Shuntov records no specimens from the shoal waters of the northwest coast of Australia, despite the fact that the type specimens were taken near Broome, Western Australia.

Distribution (Figure 13): Known only from the vicinity of Broome, Western Australia (Lönnberg and Andersson, 1913) and the Arafura Sea (Shuntov. 1972).

Genus *Acalyptophis* (Boulenger)

Recognition: A monotypic genus characterized by the following combination of characters: parietal and frontal shields irregularly divided into smaller scales; prefrontal scales absent; supra- and post-ocular scales with tubercles (young) or projecting spines (adults).

Remarks: Smith (1926) and McDowell (1972) provide expanded generic descriptions. The latter appears to have recognized *Acalyptophis* as distinct from *Hydrophis* with reservations—"only on the basis of its peculiar external appearance and must dissected head scutellation." There seems little doubt that these features reflect real and important biological differences; similarities in internal anatomy should not necessarily override other indicators of phyletic divergence.

Distribution: From West Irian (Joes Island, near Salawati, vide Brongersma, 1956) throughout the tropical waters of Australia and southern New Guinea eastward to "west of New Caledonia" (McDowell, 1972).

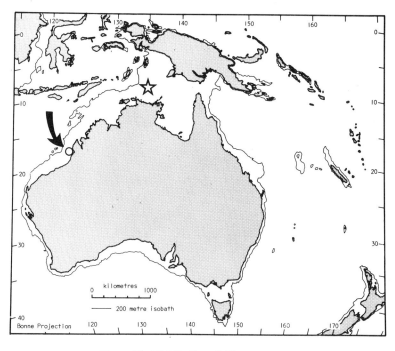

Figure 13. Distribution of *Aipysurus tenuis*.

Acalyptophis peronii (Dumeril) (Figure 14)

Recognition: A moderately built snake, the head and neck only moderately thinner than the rest of the body. Cream, grey, or pale brown above, the body with a series of about 25–30 dark brown cross-bands which are widest dorsally (nearly as wide as the paler interspaces) and taper on the sides. Sometimes a series of incomplete secondary dark bands between the primary ones, while many of the scales on the paler parts of the body are dark-centered. The banding may become obscure in older adults, but in all ages the head is pale while the bands on the tail are more obscure than those on the body. *Head shields irregular, fragmented; many, but especially those around the eye, raised posteriorly to form projections or spines;* this condition is best developed in older adults. *Prefrontal scales absent.* Scales moderately imbricate (anteriorly) to almost juxtaposed (posteriorly), each with a short central (and often darker) keel, and in 23–31 rows at mid-body. Ventrals 140–210, about as wide as adjacent body scales. Anal divided. 5–8 maxillary teeth following the fang. Average total length about 1.0 m.

Remarks: Poorly known; often seen on the surface in reef waters, especially at night. Feeds on a variety of fishes. A gravid female (MCZ R142383) with a snout-vent length of 112 cm contained eight well-developed embryos.

Distribution (Figure 15): As for genus.

Genus *Astrotia* (Fischer)

Recognition: Nasals in contact; ventral scales, except on the throat, divided into pairs of foliform scales each of which is scarcely larger than an

Figure 14. *Acalyptophis peronii* (Ashmore Reef).

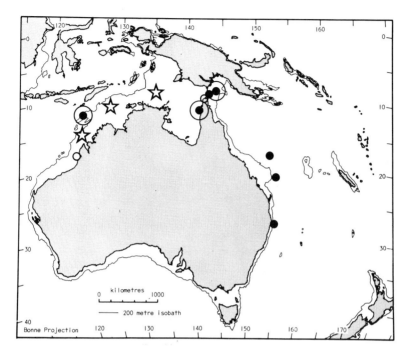

Figure 15. Distribution of *Acalyptophis peronii.*

adjacent body scale, and which in all but juveniles form a high median ventral keel.

Remarks: McDowell (1972) placed this genus in the synonymy of *Disteira,* defining the latter almost solely on the basis of the superficial head musculature, and including within it a diverse group of species which earlier workers had placed in several different genera. The resemblance between juvenile and subadult *A. stokesii* and *D. major* is sometimes quite striking, but should not obscure the very real differences upon which Smith (1926) has commented, and on which his recognition of *Astrotia* is based.

Distribution: Found throughout the waters of tropical Australia and New Guinea. Extra-limital in Indo-Malaya. Apparently does not extend eastward as far as New Caledonia.

Astrotia stokesii (Gray) (Figure 16)

Recognition: A large, heavily built snake with a broad and massive head in the adult. Adults range from almost uniform creamy-white to leaden gray or almost black (Figure 16a), sometimes with obscure dark ocelli or a paler reticulate pattern on the lower half of the body. Half-grown specimens with

Figure 16. *Astrotia stokesii* (Ashmore Reef).

some obscure transverse dark-centered pale blotches along the vertebral line and below with two series of dark spots or blotches—one on the lower lateral surface alternating with the second series along the mid-ventral line. The distinctive pattern of the newborn young is shown in Figure 16b.

Head shields large, symmetrical. Nasals in contact. Body scales imbricate, each with a median keel or series of tubercles, in 45–63 rows at mid-body. *Ventrals 226–286, those on the throat single but the remainder divided into pairs of elongate, foliform or pointed scales which form a strongly raised ventral keel except in juvenile specimens.* Enlarged anal (=preanal) scales. Average total length about 1.2 m. A small number of large young produced in a brood; one female from Darwin contained 5 full-term embryos.

Distribution (Figure 17): As for genus.

Genus *Disteira (Lacépède)*

Recognition: Ventrals small, scarcely wider than adjacent body scales and mostly distinct and undivided; fewer than four solid maxillary teeth behind the fang, or if more than four, the anterior chin shields are reduced and at most in only narrow contact along the mental groove; head shields enlarged, regular; mental triangular, broader than long.

Remarks: This genus was resurrected from the synonymy of *Hydrophis* by McDowell (1972) to accommodate a polyglot assemblage of species. For reasons outlined above, I regard two of the four Australian species in McDowell's *Disteira* to be but distantly related to the others; indeed, retention of the remaining two species (*kingii* and *major*) is largely by default; their unique common possession of an adductor mandibulae externus superficialis muscle which completely conceals the adductor externus medialis (McDowell, *loc. cit.*) should not obscure the significance of the major differences between the component species.

   Distribution: As here restricted (artificially), the members of the genus are found from the Persian Gulf to Australia.

Key to the Australian Species of Disteira

       Anterior chin shields not or scarcely
       contacting the mental groove from which
       they are separated by the elongated first
       infralabials; six or more maxillary teeth
       following the fang .... *major*
       Anterior chin shields large and mostly
       bordering the mental groove; fewer than
       four maxillary teeth following the fang .... *kingii*

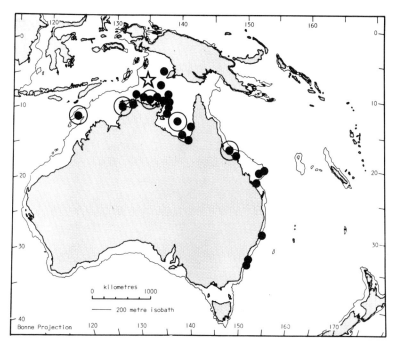

Figure 17. Distribution of *Astrotia stokesii*.

Disteira kingii (Boulenger)

Recognition: A distinctive elongated and slender sea snake. *Head and throat black.* Dorsal half of body grey, on which is superimposed a series of 45–50 darker grey rhombs or blotches extending lower on the sides than the grey dorsal color. Lower half of body cream or pale brown except for a blackish mid-ventral stripe and usually a series of dark mid-lateral triangular blotches below the paler grey interspaces (which may join with the darker blotches to leave a single longitudinal series of pale oval upper lateral blotches) and a series of much smaller lower lateral dark spots. The dorsal blotches may form incomplete black rings on the neck, often with narrow white or yellow interspaces. Dorsal pattern continues on to tail. Head shields enlarged, regular, symmetrical. Anterior chin shields large and mostly bordering the mental groove; two or three solid maxillary teeth following the fang. Scales imbricate, keeled, in 37–39 rows at mid-body. Ventrals 324–342, markedly wider than adjacent body scales. Anal scales not enlarged. Average total length 1.5 m.

Remarks: Little is known of the ecology of this species. All of the specimens examined were taken in trawls, suggesting that it occurs in deep waters (30–50 m), but the locality records would indicate that the species is found on a variety of benthic types.

Distribution (Figure 18): Confined to Australian seas, where it occurs around the tropical northern coastline from northwestern Australia to the east coast of Queensland.

Disteira major (Shaw) (Figure 19)

Recognition: Head olive or brown above with darker flecks. Body pale grey above with a series of 25–30 dark dorsal blotches or cross-bars (the first on the nape), each slightly narrower than the intervening paler areas, and each extending about halfway down each side of the body into the cream or yellowish lower half of the body. A narrow dark bar, usually no more than one scale in width, in the middle of each pale dorsal inter-blotch zone. A series of large, dark and lateral blotches, each below the narrow inter-blotch bar, and a series of smaller lower lateral blotches, each tending to lie below a large dorsal blotch. Most ventral scales dark grey or tipped with darker. Juvenile specimens (Figure 19) with a more conspicuous and better-defined pattern than the adults. Head shields enlarged, regular, symmetrical. *Anterior chin shields not or scarcely contacting the mental groove, from which they are largely separated by the elongated first infralabials.* Scales imbricate, each with a low, blunt keel, in 37–43 rows at mid-body. Ventrals 230–266, scarcely wider than the adjacent body scales. Anal scales enlarged. *Fang followed by 6–8 solid maxillary teeth.* Average total length 1.3 m.

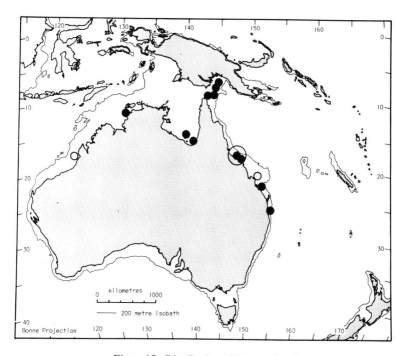

Figure 18. Distribution of *Disteira kingii.*

Figure 19. *Disteira major* (near Melville Island, Northern Territory).

Remarks: McDowell (1972) has commented on the strong general resemblance of *D. major* to *A. stokesii,* but this resemblance is largely due to similarities of color pattern rather than of general morphology. Nevertheless, the resemblance is real, so that reference to the ventral condition may be necessary to distinguish the two species on external features.

Not usually seen by divers, the species is apparently found in deeper, more turbid waters throughout its range.

Distribution (Figure 20): Apparently confined to Australian seas, where it occurs along the tropical coast of Australia, from northwestern Australia to eastern Queensland, and from the Arafura Sea and the southern coast of New Guinea.

Genus *Emydocephalus* (Krefft)

Recognition: Unique in possessing three supralabials, the second very long and subocular; ventral scales large, at least three times as wide as the adjacent body scales; nasal scales in contact; posterior chin shields usually reduced and separated by one or more small scales; preocular scale present; a conspicuous rostral spine in adult males.

Remarks: The genus currently includes two closely allied species, *E. annulatus* and *E. ijimae,* only the former occurring in Australasian waters. McDowell (1969) has commented upon the close relationship between *Emydocephalus* and *Aipysurus,* and had reservations about recognizing the former as a distinct genus. This close affinity is apparent in living specimens of *E. annulatus,* which in the field may be difficult to distinguish from some specimens of *Aipysurus fuscus, A. apraefrontalis* and *A. foliosquama* without reference to the labial condition.

Distribution: Seas of the Australian/New Guinea region (*annulatus*) and the seas of Taiwan and the Ryukyu Archipelago (*ijimae*).

Emydocephalus annulatus (Krefft) (Figure 21)

Description: A small, slender snake, highly variable in color and pattern. Ranges from uniform black, dark brown or dark grey above and below, through various degrees of banding in which more or less complete rings of creamy-white scales alternate with slightly wider complete darker rings, 3–4 scales in width. Usually the light-colored rings contain some brown or brown-blotched scales, while the black rings may contain some white-flecked scales. In banded forms the head is usually creamy-white or yellow above, speckled and blotched with dark brown, and with a dark brown band extending from behind each eye (and sometimes continued in front) which joins the first dark body ring on the nape. Head shields large and regular, not fragmented. The rostral shield usually bears a conical projection, which in

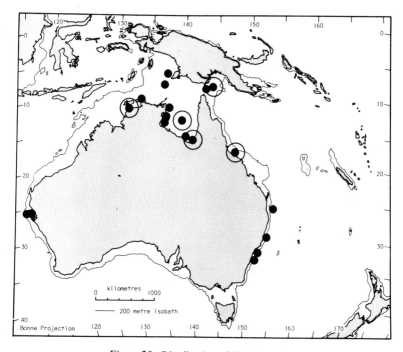

Figure 20. Distribution of *Disteira major*.

Figure 21. *Emydocephalus annulatus* (Ashmore Reef).

adult males is a conspicuous blunt spine. *Three supralabials.* Scales smooth or with several longitudinal series of low tubercles, imbricate, in 15–17 rows at mid-body. Ventrals 125–145, with small tubercles and usually a median keel. Anal usually single. Subcaudals 20–40, all single. Average length 0.75 m.

Remarks: Usually encountered in clear shallow reef waters, where it sometimes occurs in large numbers on individual reefs. Appears to feed exclusively on fish eggs (Voris, 1966; McCosker, Chapter 11). The species is subject to marked polychromatism, but no geographic or sexual trends were observed in the specimens examined.

Distribution (Figure 22): Waters of tropical Australia, from the Timor Sea to the southwest Pacific Ocean.

Genus *Enhydrina* (Gray)

Recognition: Mental shield greatly elongated and much longer than broad, dagger-like, its posterior part lying within the mental groove; head shields enlarged, regular; ventrals scarcely wider than the adjacent body scales.

Remarks: McDowell (1972) synonymized *Enhydrina* with *Disteira,* an action with which I cannot agree. This monotypic genus possesses many distinctive morphological features (Smith, 1926), which I believe overshadow those on which McDowell characterized his *Disteira* assemblage.

Distribution: Smith (1926) records this genus from the Persian Gulf to the coast of Indo-China, the Indo-Malayan Archipelago and the coast of Australia. In Australian waters it is known from only a few specimens from widely scattered localities (Figure 23).

Enhydrina schistosa (Daudin)

Recognition: Smith (1926) records the young as having dark grey or black annuli, but Australian juveniles possess from 45–55 transverse bars which scarcely extend more than half-way down the flanks, the lower half of the body whitish, without pattern. Adults more or less uniform grey above, whitish below. Dark bars from as wide as to much wider than paler interspaces. Head dark grey above, pale below. Head shields enlarged, regular, symmetrical. Mental shield greatly elongated, dagger- or splinter-shaped, partly hidden in a deep mental groove formed by elongate anterior infralabials joined by highly extensile skin which forms a concertina-like anterior throat region. Scales more or less imbricate, each with a short, low keel, in 49–66 rows at mid-body. Ventrals 239–322, scarcely wider than the adjacent body scales. Anal scales only slightly enlarged. Fang followed by 3–4 solid maxillary teeth. Average total length 1.2 m.

Remarks: One of the most widely distributed and abundant sea snakes; its status in Australian waters is uncertain. Smith (1926) recorded only two

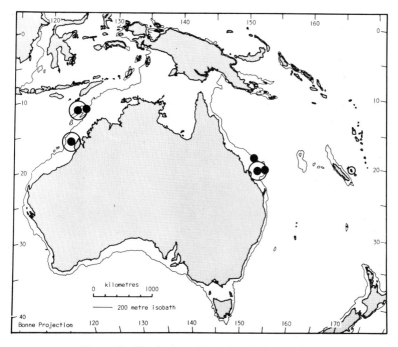

Figure 22. Distribution of *Emydocephalus annulatus.*

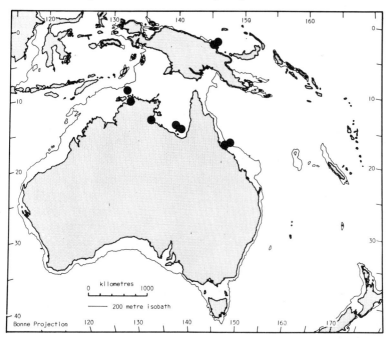

Figure 23. Distribution of *Enhydrina schistosa.*

specimens from Australia, while McDowell (1972) had only one male from the north coast of New Guinea which he doubtfully assigned to *schistosa*. This individual differed from Asian specimens in possessing a weakly bilobate hemipenis and the preocular scale fused to the prefrontal.

Several of the specimens examined were taken in rivers, suggesting that in Australia the species prefers estuarine conditions.

Distribution (Figure 23): Apparently occurs throughout the waters of New Guinea and northern Australia. No records are known from the Pacific Islands and east of Australia.

Genus *Ephalophis* (Smith)

Recognition: Small sea snakes characterized by large ventral scales, at least three times as wide as the adjacent body scales; large posterior chin shields bordering the mental groove or separated by a small scale; preocular scale present.

Remarks: Originally described as a monotypic genus (type species *Ephalophis greyi*), McDowell (1969, 1974) has redefined and expanded the genus to include *Disteira mertoni* (Roux, 1910) from the Aru Islands. However, Burger and Natsuno (in press) have erected a new monotypic genus to accommodate *mertoni*. The material available to me is inadequate to assess either viewpoint, and I have here followed McDowell's proposals despite major differences in morphology between the two species.

Key to the Species of *Ephalophis*

> Posterior dorsal scales smooth; scales in
> more than 30 rows at mid-body .... *mertoni*
> Posterior dorsal scales with spine-like
> keels; scales in fewer than 30 rows at
> mid-body .... *greyi*

Ephalophis greyi (Smith) (Figure 24)

Recognition: McDowell (1969, 1974) has provided detailed descriptions of the known specimens of this species. Following is a brief summary of its salient external features: cream or pale olive-brown above, the head blotched or mottled with dark grey and with 25–40 dark grey dorsal blotches which are often more or less fused along the vertebral zone to form an irregular and interrupted zig-zag vertebral stripe; tail with 7–8 dark rings. Head shields enlarged, regular and symmetrical. *Body scales imbricate, in 19–21 rows at mid-body,* the lateral scales smooth but the *dorsal scales (at least posteriorly) with blunt keels.*   Ventrals 159–169, nearly as broad as the body. Anal

Figure 24. *Ephalophis greyi* (Broome, Western Australia). (Photograph by G. Gow.)

divided. Subcaudals 28–33, undivided. Fang followed by 7–8 maxillary teeth. Tail shallow, not noticeably deeper than body. Average total length 0.5 m.

Remarks: McDowell (1974) has suggested that *Ephalophis greyi* is the most primitive sea snake, with features linking it with the elapid snakes *Drepanodontis* and *Rhinoplocephalus.* McDowell states that the "swamp-living" habits of at least the former are ". . . . what might be expected in a sea-snake ancestor." Although the resemblance between these taxa is striking, such a broad conclusion is based on quite erroneous interpretation of the published habits of these Australian elapids, which, though preferring well-watered habitats, are typical terrestrial snakes. The utilization of the ecological preferenda of contemporary *species* in defining familial phylogenies, especially where divergent ecologies are found *within* the families under discussion, is biologically simplistic. One of the rarest species in collections, McDowell (1974) has described the four known specimens, while a fifth specimen (NTM 457) was used in compiling the above description.

Distribution (Figure 25): All known specimens have been found in the vicinity of Broome, Western Australia.

Ephalophis mertoni (Roux) (Figure 26)

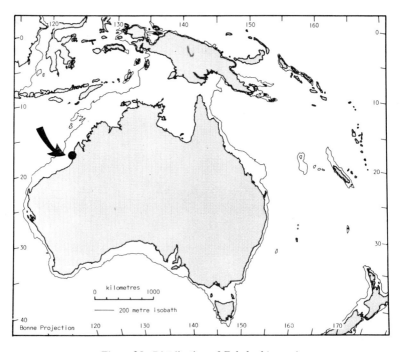

Figure 25. Distribution of *Ephalophis greyi.*

Figure 26. *Ephalophis mertoni* (Roper River, Northern Territory). (Photograph by G. Gow.)

Recognition: Blue-grey or grey-brown above with 40–50 irregular blackish crossbands or rings, often confluent on the mid-line, each slightly narrower or broader than the paler interspaces, broadest vertebrally and tapering on the sides, and broken only by the ventrals; the dark dorsal bands may sometimes have paler centers. Head above brown with blackish variegations; snout and sides of head blackish. Ventrals brown anteriorly, paler posteriorly; subcaudals often blackish, linking the 6–8 dark bands on the tail. Head shields enlarged, regular and symmetrical. *Body scales smooth, imbricate, in 36–39 rows at mid-body.* Ventrals 158–160. Anal divided. Subcaudals 29–35, all single except for one or two divided anterior scales. Fang followed by 5–8 maxillary teeth. Average total length approximately 0.5 m.

Distribution (Figure 27): Known only from the Aru Islands, the lower Gulf of Carpentaria and the Roper River, Northern Territory. G. Gowe (in lit.) reports a specimen from the vicinity of Darwin.

Genus *Hydrelaps* (Boulenger)

Recognition: No preocular scale; ventrals large, at least three times as wide as the adjacent body scales; nasal scales in broad contact; six or more supra-

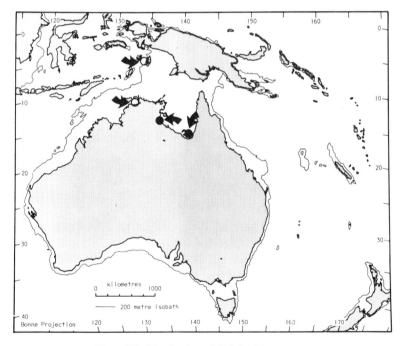

Figure 27. Distribution of *Ephalophis mertoni.*

labials; posterior chin shields at least as large as anterior chin shields, separated by the mental groove.

Remarks: This monotypic genus has been fully redescribed by McDowell (1972), who regarded it as one of the most primitive of sea snakes. It is apparently confined to shallow coastal waters, including tidal mud flats and mangrove swamps.

Distribution: Confined to the shallow coastal water of northern Australia and southern New Guinea, west of Torres Strait.

Hydrelaps darwiniensis (Boulenger) (Figure 28)

Recognition: In view of McDowell's (1972) very complete redescription of this species, only the major external features are summarized in the following description: cream or yellowish above, the body with 32–48 dark rings or crossbands, each about twice as broad as the paler interspaces, and usually complete on the belly; occasionally bands continuous on the vertebral line but displaced on either side so that they fail to make complete rings; 5–8 complete dark rings on the tail, the subcaudals sometimes all black. Head dark with yellow or cream variegations. Head shields enlarged, regular, symmetrical; preocular scale absent, the prefrontal bordering the eye anteriorly. Body scales imbricate, smooth, in 25–29 rows at mid-body. Ventrals 163–172, relatively narrow, only about three times as broad as the adjacent body scales. Anal divided. Subcaudals 27–39, usually single but occasionally with a few divided anteriorly. Fang followed by 3–6 maxillary teeth. Average total length 0.5 m.

Distribution (Figure 29): As for genus.

Genus *Hydrophis* (Latreille)

Recognition: Ventrals small, scarcely wider than adjacent body scales and mostly undivided except in one species, in which they are all divided posteriorly, but never foliform; four or more solid maxillary teeth behind the fang; anterior chin shields large and mostly bordering the mental groove; head shields enlarged, regular; mental triangular, broader than long.

Remarks: The largest genus of sea snakes with approximately 25 species. McDowell (1972) has removed a number of species from the genus as defined by Smith (1926) and has allocated the remaining 21 species to three subgenera—*Hydrophis* (eight species), *Aturia* (nine species), and *Leioselasma* (four species). I believe that McDowell's subgenera represent natural groups.

Twelve species have been recorded from Australian seas, including several species which are known only from isolated individual records. Members of the genus are subject to marked ontogenetic variation in color, pattern, morphology and allometry, all of which complicate the taxonomy of the

Figure 28.   *Hydrelaps darwinienis* (Darwin, Northern Territory). (Photograph by G. Gow.)

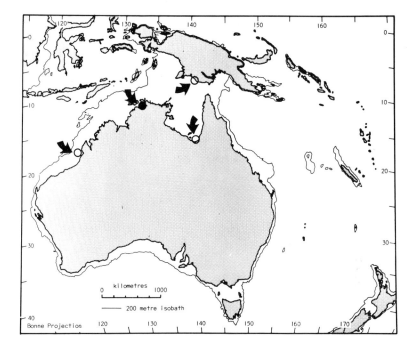

Figure 29. Distribution of *Hydrelaps darwiniensis.*

group when samples are small and geographically widely dispersed. The taxonomy of the small-headed *Hydrophis,* especially, is poorly known and in need of study.

The members of the genus *Hydrophis* are found in a wide variety of situations, although the habitat specificity of particular species is poorly known. Many species are specialized feeders, suggesting that those feeding on benthic organisms (such as eels) may live within rather more narrowly defined habitats than those species feeding on surface or mid-water fishes.

Distribution: Found throughout the tropical seas of the Australian region, with some species making regular incursions into southern waters during the summer months. Extra-limital throughout the Indo-Malayan Archipelago and the coastal waters of Asia.

Key to the Australian Species of *Hydrophis*

1. Posterior ventrals distinct and mostly undivided 2
    Posterior ventrals all divided . . . . *gracilis*
2. Fewer than 10 solid maxillary teeth behind
    the fang 3
    10 or more solid maxillary teeth behind the fang 10

3. Anterior part of maxilla not arched upwards,
    the tip of the fang projecting conspicuously
    below a line connecting the tips of the solid
    maxillary teeth 4
    Anterior part of maxilla arched upward, so that
    the tip of the longer fang is nearly or quite
    on a line with the tips of the solid maxillary
    teeth 7
4. Normally two or more supralabials contacting
    the eye 5
    Normally a single supralabial contacting
    the eye . . . . *belcheri*
5. Tip of tail and most or all of the ventral
    side of the tail black at all ages; dark
    cross-banding of adults more or less of equal
    intensity along length of body, without
    secondary bands or blotches between the main
    bands . . . . *melanocephalus*
    Tip of tail greyish, paler than darker cross-
    bands when the latter are present; dark
    cross-banding of adults more intense anteriorly,
    often with secondary bands or blotches between
    the main bands 6
6. Usually only third and fourth supralabials
    contacting the orbit; some indication, at least
    posteriorly, of dark scales, spots or blotches
    in the pale interspaces between the dark bands . . . . *elegans*
    Usually the third, fourth and fifth supralabials
    contacting the orbit; no indication of dark
    scales, spots or blotches in the pale interspaces
    between the dark bands . . . . *pacificus*
7. Usually 25 or more scale rows on the neck;
    scales on neck as well as posterior part
    of body, with central tubercle or short keel 8
    Fewer than 25 scale rows on the neck;
    scales on neck smooth but keeled
    posteriorly . . . . *obscurus*
8. Head small; body very slender anteriorly;
    parietal bone not contacting prefrontal 9
    Head moderate; body not noticeably slender
    anteriorly; parietal bone contacting the
    prefrontal . . . . *melanosoma*
9. Head black, even in adults, sometimes with
    a yellow spot behind the eye and/or nostril;
    rostral normal, triangular, broader than
    high; first infralabial normal, about as
    long as pregenial . . . . *fasciatus*
    Head black in young, with conspicuous yellow
    marking on the crown, but becoming much paler
    in adults; rostral large, oval, at least as
    high as broad; first infralabial large, strap-
    like, much longer than pregenial . . . . sp.

10. 14 or fewer solid maxillary teeth;
dentary teeth usually fewer than 23;
heart just behind anterior third of
body 11
12 or more solid maxillary teeth;
dentary teeth 22 or more; heart about
mid-way along body . . . . *caerulescens*
11. Width of head between the eyes at least
half the distance from tip of snout to
rear edge of parietal scales; adults
with dark dorsal blotches . . . .*ornatus*
Width of head at level of eyes
less than half the distance from tip of
snout to rear edge of parietal scales;
adults without dorsal blotches . . . . *inornatus*

Hydrophis belcheri (Gray) (Figure 30)

Recognition: About 60 dark cross-bands on body, broadest dorsally, almost fading on belly; posterior ventrals undivided; fewer than 10 maxillary teeth following the fang; anterior part of maxilla not arched upward, the tip of the fang projecting well below a line connecting the tips of the solid maxillary teeth; usually *a single supralabial contacting the eye.*

The holotype (together with an additional specimen from the Java Sea) has been very fully redescribed by McDowell (1972). As I have no material which would require any amendment of McDowell's description, reference should be made to McDowell's paper for a full description of this species. As there is no published figure of *H. belcheri,* a photograph of the holotype is reproduced here (Figure 30).

Remarks: I have not examined any specimens during the present study (other than the holotype) which I could refer to this species with confidence, and Shuntov (1972) did not record it from any of his sampling areas west of Torres Strait.

McDowell (1972) has shown that *"H. belcheri"* of Smith (1926) was composite, and redefined the species on the basis of the type and a specimen from the Java Sea. Other Australasian specimens which Smith had later identified as *belcheri* (from the Coral Sea and from the Fiji Islands), Mc-Dowell has referred to *H. melanocephalus* (q.v.). The characters defining *belcheri* above and its key characters are therefore derived from McDowell (1972).

Hydrophis pacificus, which was placed in the synonymy of *H. belcheri* by Smith, was transferred to the synonymy of *H. elegans* by McDowell (1972). I believe that *H. pacificus* is a valid species and I have resurrected it below.

Distribution: The only specimen recorded from the Australian region is the holotype, from "New Guinea." Extra-limital in Indo-Malayan waters.

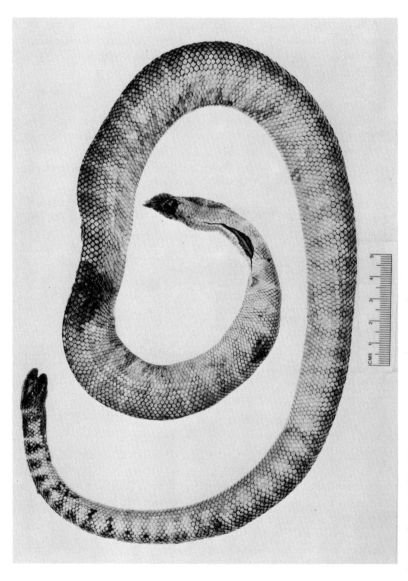

Figure 30. *Hydrophis belcheri* holotype, British Museum (N.H.). (Photograph courtesy of the British Museum (Natural History).)

Hydrophis caerulescens (Shaw)

Recognition: McDowell (1972) has fully described the only two specimens then known from the Australian region, to which I have been able to add a third (gutted) specimen from precisely the same locality (Karumba, Queensland) as McDowell's two specimens. Salient features of the Australian specimens are *head blackish, body with 41–43 blackish blotches or transverse bands* which may be divided or alternating on either side of the vertebral line; whitish below; tail with 7–9 dark bands (or black with four pale blotches on its dorsal edge, vide McDowell, 1972). Head shields enlarged, regular, symmetrical. Third and fourth supralabials contacting orbit. *12 or more solid maxillary teeth following the fang; 22 or more dentary teeth; heart about mid-way along body.* Body scales imbricate, in 37–39 rows at mid-body. Ventrals 266–287, scarcely wider than adjacent body scales except anteriorly and mostly undivided. Average total length 0.6 m.

Remarks: Previously known only from the region extending from India and China to the Moluccas, this species has previously been recorded from Australian waters only by McDowell (1972). I have assigned a further specimen to this species largely on its possession of 22 dentary teeth and its relatively small and narrow head. The relative position of the heart (a diagnostic feature used by McDowell) could not be ascertained in my specimen, which had been largely eviscerated by the collector. In scalation this specimen falls within the range of variation described for the species by McDowell (1972).

Distribution (Figure 31): All known Australian specimens are from Karumba, at the mouth of the Norman River, lower Gulf of Carpentaria.

Hydrophis elegans (Gray) (Figure 32)

Recognition: A highly variable species in which the young may differ markedly from the adults. Young with black heads and strongly banded bodies, the 35–55 bands widest on the mid-dorsal and mid-ventral lines, narrowest laterally where all or some may be broken. *Usually at least some indication of spots or narrow bands in the paler interspaces between the primary bands,* at least on the neck and tail. Adults with bands reduced to a series of vertebral transverse bars or blotches, and two series of spots on the sides: a mid-lateral series in which each spot lies below a pale interspace and a lower lateral series in which each spot lies below a dark dorsal bar. In addition, there may be narrow secondary cross-bars or rows of dark scales. Ventrals usually blackish on the throat and forepart of the body. Head shields enlarged, regular, symmetrical. *Third and fourth supralabials usually contacting orbit. Fewer than 9 solid maxillary teeth following the fang; anterior part of maxilla not*

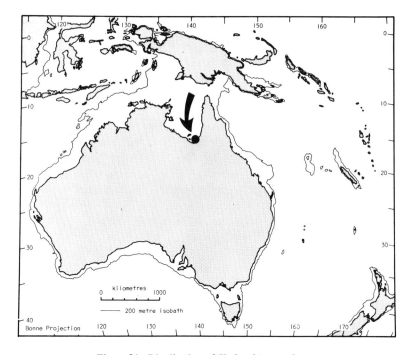

Figure 31. Distribution of *Hydrophis caerulescens.*

Figure 32. *Hydrophis elegans* (MacCluer Gulf, West Irian).

arched upwards, the tip of the fang usually distinctly projecting below a line connecting the tips of the solid maxillary teeth. Body scales imbricate, in 37–49 rows at mid-body. Ventrals 345–432, scarcely wider than adjacent body scales except anteriorly and mostly undivided. Average total length 1.7 m.

Remarks: A widespread and abundant species characterized by its greatly elongated body and great bulk with age. Highly variable in color pattern and scalation, as presently constituted it may well represent a complex of two or more species. Newborn and juvenile specimens, especially, may represent major difficulties in identification.

The only record of the related *H. cyanocinctus* from Australian waters is based on the two juvenile syntypes of *Disteira macfarlani* (Boulenger), a species which Smith (1926) placed in the synonymy of *cyanocinctus*. Mc-Dowell (1972) has since referred *D. macfarlani* to the synonymy of *H. elegans.*

McDowell has placed *elegans* in the subgenus *Leioselasma*, which he characterizes as possessing a maxilla which is not arched anteriorly, so that the tip of the fang projects well below a line joining the tips of the solid maxillary teeth. However, although the maxillary is not arched in *elegans*, it possesses relatively short fangs which at times barely project below the line of the maxillary teeth.

As here recognized, *H. elegans* may be almost always distinguished by the presence of darker scales, spots or blotches in the paler interspaces between the dark body bands; in juvenile specimens these markings may be small or restricted to the neck or posterior body and tail. The high ventral count will usually distinguish this species from all others in the region except *H. pacificus, H. fasciatus* and *Hydrophis* sp.; from the latter two it may be distinguished by the characters cited in the key. Juveniles have frequently been misidentified as *Disteira kingii*, but the number of maxillary teeth following the fang (5–8 in *elegans*, 2–3 in *kingii*) will readily distinguish between them.

H. elegans is rarely seen by divers except in deeper water and most specimens are trawled in depths > 30 m (shallower near Townsville; see Chapter 7). Except for the types of *Disteira grandis* from the Malay Archipelago (which species Smith placed in the synonymy of *elegans*), all known specimens are from Australian waters.

Five gravid females contained 17, 19, 20, 20, and 23 embryos respectively.

Distribution (Figure 33): Found throughout the waters of northern Australia and southern New Guinea. Individuals are commonly encountered in higher latitudes during the summer months.

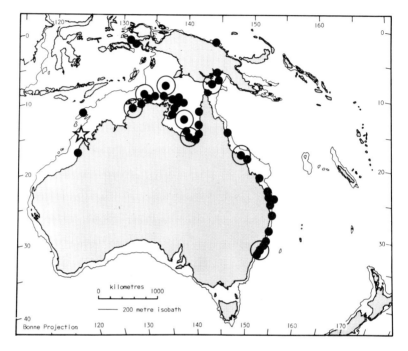

Figure 33. Distribution of *Hydrophis elegans.*

Hydrophis fasciatus (Schneider)

Recognition: Head very small, body very slender anteriorly, very deep and greatly compressed posteriorly. Young with 50–70 black cross-bands which may form complete rings. In adults the bands may be reduced to a series of dorsal blotches. Head black in both young and adults. Ventrals blackish, at least anteriorly. Head shields large, regular, symmetrical. Third and fourth supralabials contacting the orbit. *Anterior part of maxilla arched upwards, so that the tip of the fang is more or less on a line with the tips of the solid maxillary teeth. 25 or more rows of keeled scales on the neck. Rostral more or less triangular, broader than high. Suture between first infralabials about as long as suture between anterior chin shields.* Body scales imbricate, in 35–49 rows at mid-body. Ventrals 323–514 (vide Smith, 1926), approximately 484 (mean count) in single Australian specimen examined, mostly undivided. Average total length about 1.0 m.

Remarks: Records of this species from Australian waters are few and of doubtful status. Apart from Kinghorn's (1929) record from 'Sydney' (New South Wales), a record which I have been unable to confirm from a specimen, all other literature records appear to be based on AM 6715 from 'Australian

Seas' and a Basle specimen reported from the 'Aru Islands' by Smith (1926) but not seen by him, and Shuntov's (1972) report that this species constituted 1% of sea snakes trawled in the Arafura Sea.

AM 6715 appears to be correctly assigned to *H. fasciatus atriceps,* but its provenance is much less certain. Collected by Captain Creed prior to 1869 (see comments under *H. gracilis*), there is a strong possibility that this specimen was collected in Asian waters.

Only one specimen (AM R14022), a juvenile from Darwin, has been tentatively assigned to this species. With its high ventral count it would fall into the nominate subspecies rather than *fasciatus atriceps,* the only subspecies recorded from Australia by Smith (1926).

Distribution (Figure 34): The only specimen seen by me is from Darwin, Northern Territory. See *Remarks* for literature records. Extra-limital in Indo-Malaysia and East Asia.

Hydrophis gracilis (Shaw)

Recognition: A very small-headed species with very slender body anteriorly contrasting with the very deep and strongly compressed posterior part of the

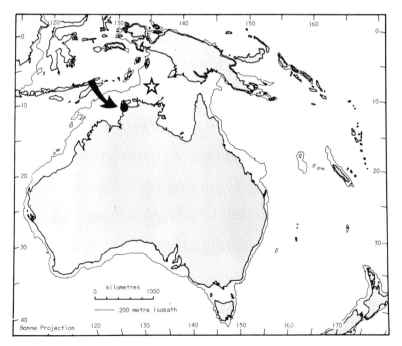

Figure 34. Distribution of *Hydrophis fasciatus.*

body. Young "black with a series of whitish dorsal bands or oval lateral spots on the slender part of the body, and more or less complete bands posteriorly, altogether from 40 to 60 in number" (Smith, 1926). Adults usually with indistinct bars, more or less uniform grey above, whitish below. The keels or tubercles on the lower lateral scales often darker than the scales themselves. Head shields large, regular, symmetrical. Third and fourth supralabials contacting the orbit. Body scales juxtaposed, in 30–36 rows on the body, *the lower lateral scales usually larger than the dorsals, juxtaposed and either tubercular or with prominent high keels.* Ventrals 220–287 (257 in single Australian specimen examined), *more or less all divided* posterior to the neck. Average total length about 0.7 m.

Remarks: McDowell (1972) relegated the genus *Microcephalophis* to the synonymy of *Hydrophis,* and placed *gracilis* in his subgenus *Hydrophis.*

Until the present time the occurrence of this species in the Australian region appears to have been based on a single specimen (AM 6719) from 'Australian Seas.' This specimen, which was acquired from Captain Creed sometime prior to 1869, is of doubtful provenance. However, a further specimen (MCZ R142375) from the Gulf of Papua confirms the occurrence of this species in Australian waters, where it appears to be rare. Cranial scalation is virtually identical to that for *Hydrophis* sp. described below.

Distribution (Figure 35): The only Australasian specimen with known provenance is from the Gulf of Papua. Extra-limital in the region extending from the Persian Gulf to Indonesia.

Hydrophis inornatus (Gray)

Recognition: A relatively small, moderately built snake, the body more or less uniform and undifferentiated throughout its length. Bluish-grey above, the young with 50–65 blackish bars or cross-bands which sometimes form complete rings, and which disappear or are reduced to obscure dorsal blotches in the adult; lower half of body otherwise whitish. Head shields large, regular, symmetrical. Third and fourth supralabials contacting the orbit. *10–13 solid maxillary teeth following the fang; dentary teeth fewer than 21; heart situated just behind anterior third of body: width of head at level of eyes less than half the distance from tip of snout to rear edge of parietal scales.* Body scales imbricate, in 35–48 rows at mid-body. Ventrals 195–293, mostly undivided. Average total length about 0.7 m.

Remarks: McDowell (1972) has commented on the close affinity between *H. ornatus* and *H. inornatus,* and has suggested that they may be either races of the one species (*ornatus,* vide Klemmer, 1963) or that they may together form a superspecies and be geographically exclusive. In his treatment of this form, Klemmer followed Mittleman (1947), who confined the race *inornatus* to the Philippines.

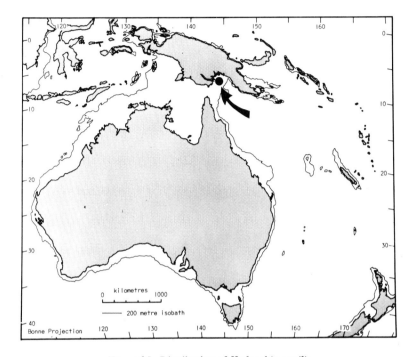

Figure 35. Distribution of *Hydrophis gracilis.*

Shuntov (1972) records that *H. inornatus* constituted 6% of sea snakes trawled in the Arafura Sea, although the species was absent from catches in the Timor Sea and on the northwest coast.

Only two juvenile specimens have been tentatively assigned to this species in the course of the present study, one from the Arafura Sea off Coburg Peninsula and the other from the Northern Territory coast. AM 6717 was referred to *H. inornatus* by Smith (1926) from 'Australian Seas'; even this generalized locality is doubtful. The above specimens extend the range of ventrals for the species. Smith (1926) noted marked sexual dimorphism in body and ventral scale counts.

Distribution (Figure 36): see *Remarks* above.

Hydrophis sp.

Recognition: Head very small; body extremely slender anteriorly, very deep and strongly compressed posteriorly. Head dark olive or black. Throat and anterior ventrals dark grey to black. Body cream above, tending to become pale yellowish ventrally. A series of dark grey or blackish dorsal blotches along the vertebral line, each blotch extending about one-third of the way

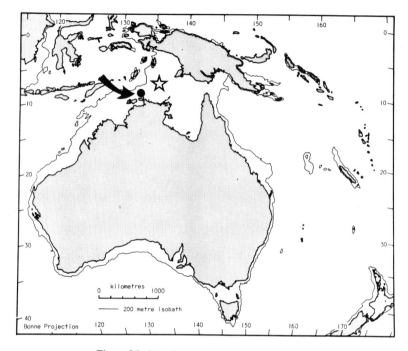

Figure 36. Distribution of *Hydrophis inornatus.*

down the body. On the sides are usually three series of dark grey, sometimes black-edged, markings: an upper lateral series of inverted triangles or elongated rhombs, each lying below the pale interspace between the vertebral blotches; a smaller lower lateral series of irregular blotches, each lying below a vertebral blotch; an even smaller series of lower lateral spots or irregular vertical bars, each below a pale vertebral interspace. In addition, narrow, sometimes disrupted secondary dorsal bars may be present in the pale interspaces. Tail with four or five obscure grey bands, usually with a narrow disrupted band in the paler interspaces. Third and fourth supralabials contacting the orbit. *Anterior part of maxilla arched upwards so that the tip of the fang is more or less on a line with the tips of the solid maxillary teeth; 23 or more rows of keeled scales on the neck; rostral large and oval, at least as high as broad; suture between first infralabials about twice as long as the suture between the anterior chin shields.* Body scales imbricate in 35–39 rows at mid-body. Ventrals 252–274, mostly undivided. Average total length about 1.0 m.

    Remarks: McDowell (1972) assigned a specimen from the Norman River at Normanton, Queensland to *Hydrophis* cf. *brookii,* a species otherwise known from Java to the coast of southeast Asia. McDowell suggested that his specimen, which he described in considerable detail, might represent an undescribed species.

Having examined a series of specimens from various parts of Australia, I can confirm McDowell's suggestion. They differ in a number of major respects from both *brookii* and *fasciatus,* and represent an undescribed species. This species will be formally named and described elsewhere.

It should be noted that AM 8300, which Smith (1926) assigned as an aberrant *H. elegans* and which McDowell (1972) suggested might be an example of his *H.* cf. *brookii,* is indeed a specimen of this new species and has been included in the paratype series.

A gravid female (AM R41993) with snout vent length of 750 mm contains two full term embryos which display an identical color pattern to that of the adults.

Distribution (Figure 37): The seas surrounding the north coast of Australia and the southern coast of New Guinea.

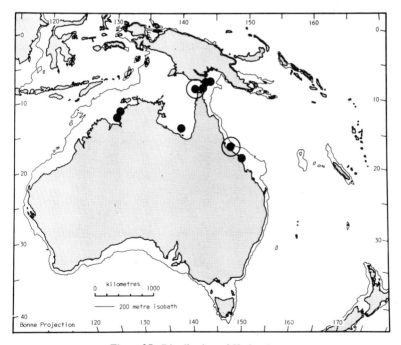

Figure 37. Distribution of *Hydrophis* sp.

Figure 38. *Hydrophis melanocephalus* (Ashmore Reef).

Hydrophis melanocephalus (Gray) (Figure 38)

Recognition: A slightly built snake, the adults with small head, body slender anteriorly and moderately deep and compressed posteriorly. Head black with conspicuous snout and postocular yellow markings in the young, olive-grey with darker flecks in adults. 32–38 (in Australo-Pacific specimens), 40–55 (in Japanese/Taiwanese specimens) dark cross-bands on the body and tail, each band expanded dorsally and ventrally and more or less equal in width to the pale yellowish (in young) or olive-grey (in adults) interspaces. End of tail and usually most of its lower half black. Anterior body bands usually confluent ventrally. Anterior part of maxilla not arched upward, the tip of the fang distinctly projecting below a line connecting the tips of the solid maxillary teeth. Fewer than 10 solid maxillary teeth following the fang. Usually only third and fourth supralabials contacting the orbit. Body scales imbricate, in 29–34 rows at mid-body. Ventrals 289–358 (Smith, 1926, for Japanese/Taiwanese specimens), but 278–317, mean 295, for a sample of 30 Australian specimens, scarcely wider than adjacent body scales except anteriorly and mostly undivided. Average total length 1.0 m.

Remarks: Although the holotype of this species was said to come from the 'Indian Ocean,' Stejneger (1907) and Smith (1926) each doubted its provenance. The latter regarded the species as being confined to the Ryukyu Archipelago and the seas around Taiwan. McDowell (1972) referred to this species two specimens which Smith had identified as *H. belcheri.* These specimens (from the Coral Sea and the Fiji Islands) differed from typical *melanocephalus* in adult head color and the number of dark bands on the body. On the basis of these differences, McDowell suggested that the relationship between *H. spiralis* and *H. melanocephalus* might be closer than previously suspected. Klemmer (1963) regarded *melanocephalus* as a race of *Hydrophis spiralis.*

I have not examined McDowell's specimens, but have tentatively referred to *melanocephalus* a large series of specimens from the Ashmore Reef region of the Timor Sea. These specimens key out fairly readily to *melanocephalus* on the basis of McDowell's diagnostic characters, but differ markedly from both typical *melanocephalus* and McDowell's specimens (vide Table 3). They are almost certainly not conspecific with *H. semperi,* which species McDowell places in the synonymy of *H. melanocephalus.*

As I have seen no other material from the Australian region, it remains to be seen whether the Ashmore Reef specimens are conspecific with Mc-Dowell's Australian specimens. They are almost certainly distinct from typical *melanocephalus* and probably represent an undescribed taxon. They are so abundant in the area where they were taken that their apparent absence from Shuntov's Timor Sea samples is difficult to explain.

Distribution (Figure 39): See *Remarks* above.

Hydrophis melanosoma (Günther)

Recognition (characters of single Australian specimen examined given in parentheses): A moderately built snake, the head and anterior body moderate, posterior part of body only moderately compressed. Head black, body and tail cream or yellowish, with 50–70 (53) black cross-bands, each about twice as broad as the paler interspaces. Anterior part of maxilla arched

Table 3. Geographic variation in scale counts for *Hydrophis melanocephalus*[a]

	East China Sea (Smith, 1926) n=34	Coral Sea, Fiji (McDowell, 1972) n=2	Ashmore Reef n=30
Ventrals	289–358 (324.6)	312–322	278–317 (295.8)
Scale rows on neck	23–27 (25.6)	28	22–26 (23.9)
Mid-body scale rows	–	35	29–34 (30.9)
Scale rows on thickest part of body	33–41 (35.7)	–	31–36 (33.0)
Scale rows near vent	–	33	27–31 (28.6)
Dark cross-bands on body	40–55	31	33–41 (36.5)

[a]Means in parentheses.

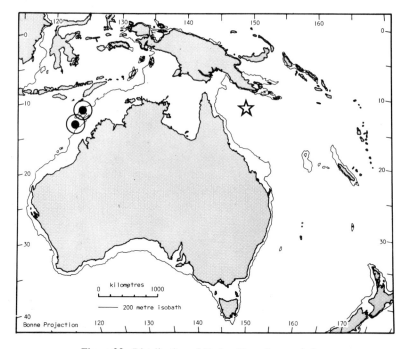

Figure 39. Distribution of *Hydrophis melanocephalus.*

upward (vide McDowell, 1972) but scarcely so in single specimen examined. Fewer than 10 solid maxillary teeth following the fang (6). Third and fourth supralabials contacting orbit. Body scales imbricate, in 37–43 (43) rows at mid-body. Ventrals 266–368 (mean of 369 for several counts), scarcely wider than adjacent body scales and mostly undivided. Average total length about 1.0 m.

Remarks: The only record of this species from Australian waters is that of Shuntov (1972), who reported that it constituted 19% of snakes trawled in the shoal waters of the northwest coast of Australia, being the second most abundant species (after *Hydrophis ornatus*) taken in that region.

I tentatively refer one specimen (MCZ R141278) from Orangerie Bay, Papua, New Guinea, to this species, largely by default. In this specimen the maxilla is not arched anteriorly (as defined by McDowell for the subgenus *Hydrophis,* in which he places *melanosoma*), but in most other respects it fits his definition of this species.

Distribution (Figure 40): See *Remarks* above. Extra-limital in the waters of Malaya and Indonesia.

Hydrophis ?obscurus (Daudin)

Recognition: Head very small; body very elongated, very slender anteriorly, only moderately deep and compressed posteriorly. A series of 73—74 dark cross-bands along the length of the body and tail, each band broadest dorsally, narrowest laterally, where each band is about as wide as the whitish interspaces, and completely encircling the body. Occasional dark bands divided or displaced on either side of the vertebral line. Normally no indication of secondary markings in the pale interspaces, except on the extreme hind part of the body and tail. Anterior portion of maxilla distinctly arched upward, the tip of the fang more or less on a level with the tips of the solid maxillary teeth. Six solid maxillary teeth following the fang. Third and fourth supralabials contacting the orbit. Body scales imbricate in 29—35 rows at mid-body. Ventrals 331—345, scarcely wider than adjacent body scales except anteriorly, and mostly undivided. Length of only specimen examined: 0.51 m.

Remarks: Until the present time, the only record from the Australian region has been McDowell (1972), who tentatively assigned a young female

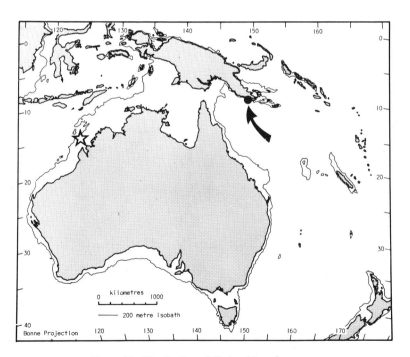

Figure 40. Distribution of *Hydrophis melanosoma.*

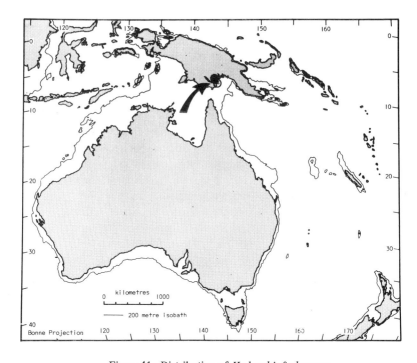

Figure 41. Distribution of *Hydrophis ? obscurus*

specimen from the Fly River, Papua, New Guinea to this species. A further specimen, MCZ R141279 from Balimo, Aramia River, Papua, New Guinea, appears to be conspecific with McDowell's specimen. These specimens are probably incorrectly assigned to the Indian species *obscurus*, but I have followed McDowell's determination in view of the inadequacy of the material available to me. McDowell (1972) includes the species represented by these specimens in his subgenus *Hydrophis*.

Distribution (Figure 41): See *Remarks* above. Otherwise known only from the seas of India and Burma.

Hydrophis ornatus (Gray) (Figure 42)

Recognition: A moderate to heavily built snake, the body more or less undifferentiated. Grey or bluish-gray above, with 30–60 broad blackish transverse bars or blotches, and a lateral series of dark-edged ocellate markings and smaller dark blotches. Otherwise pale cream or whitish on the lower half of the body. In older specimens the dorsal markings may become obscure and reduced to a uniform blue-grey dorsum. Heart just behind anterior third of body. 10–14 solid maxillary teeth following the fang. Usually fewer than 23 dentary teeth. Usually only third and fourth supralabials contacting the orbit. Body scales imbricate, in 39–59 rows at mid-body. Ventrals 246–336, about twice as broad as adjacent body scales, mostly undivided. Average total length about 1.0 m.

Remarks: Shuntov (1972) records this species as being by far the most abundant in trawls in the Arafura Sea (36%), Timor Sea (58%) and shoal waters of the northwest coast of Australia (66%). This abundance is not reflected in any of the samples available to me, including trawls from the Arafura Sea and the Gulf of Carpentaria. Smith (1926) relegated all Australian examples to the subspecies *ocellatus,* together with specimens from the Aru Islands and West Irian. Other specimens from the south coast of New Guinea and from the Bismarck Archipelago he assigned to the nominate subspecies. Mittleman (1948) referred these latter specimens to the race *ocellatus.*

On the basis of scalation the Australian specimens examined for this review fall within the range of variation described by Smith (*loc. cit.*) for *Hydrophis ornatus ocellatus.* The color pattern of most Australian specimens is that described by Smith (1926) and Mittleman (1947) for *H. ornatus ocellatus.*

Distribution (Figure 43): Widely distributed throughout the coastal waters of northern Australia. Individuals are often encountered in higher latitudes during the summer months, and this is one of only three species recorded from Tasmania by Scott (1931). Extra-limital in the regions extending from the Persian Gulf to Indonesia.

Figure 42. *Hydrophis ornatus* (McCluer Gulf).

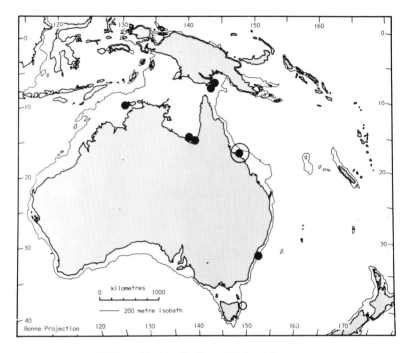

Figure 43. Distribution of *Hydrophis ornatus.*

Hydrophis pacificus (Boulenger)

Recognition: A large snake with moderately large head, body relatively slender anteriorly, rather deep and compressed posteriorly. Adults dark grey above, whitish below, the two colors merging along a distinct midlateral zone; a series of 49–72 dark transverse bands, expanded as (sometimes well-defined) blackish blotches dorsally, but continuing around the body as obscure grey bands, expanded again ventrally. The bands on the neck are usually connected along the ventral line, while some of the body bands may be divided or displaced on either side of the vertebral line. Dorsally the dark bands are much wider than the paler interspaces, but the reverse is true on the flanks. Head dark grey above, with obscure paler flecks. Young with well-defined black bands encircling the body, the bands on the neck connected by a broad black ventral region to the black throat; head black above, with one or two pale yellow spots behind each eye and some small pale spots on the fronto-nasal region. Anterior part of maxilla not noticeably arched upward, the tip of the fang projecting below a line connecting the tips of the 5–8 solid maxillary teeth following the fang. *Third, fourth, and fifth supralabials contacting the orbit.* Body scales imbricate, in 45–49 rows at mid-body.

Ventrals 324–421, not much broader than adjacent body scales, mostly undivided. Average total length 1.4 m.

Remarks: Smith (1926) placed this species in the synonymy of *Hydrophis belcheri,* and it should be noted that the upper limit of 324 ventral scales in Smith's description of *H. belcheri* is derived from the type of *H. pacificus.* McDowell (1972) showed that Smith's *belcheri* description was composite, and removed *H. pacificus* to the synonymy of *H. elegans.* In the latter species the third and fourth supralabials are usually in contact with the orbit (100% of 50 specimens examined); whereas in *H. pacificus* the third, fourth, fifth supralabials contact the orbit (all specimens examined).

I have resurrected *Hydrophis pacificus* to accommodate those specimens whose chief diagnostic features are described above. These include specimens which on the basis of Smith's (1926) and McDowell's (1972) data would otherwise fall within the range of variation of *H. elegans.* A series of newborn young (or possibly full term embryos) have much larger heads than newborn *H. elegans.* A gravid female, MCZ 137962, of snout-vent length 186 cm contained 17 embryos.

McDowell (*loc. cit.*) has commented on the close affinity between *H. elegans* and *H. cyanocinctus,* and it is possible that *H. pacificus* is more closely allied to the latter than the former.

This species falls within the subgenus *Leioselasma* of McDowell (1972).

Distribution (Figure 44): Gulf of Papua, along the New Guinea coast to the eastern Arafura Sea. The type specimen is from New Britain.

Genus *Lapemis* (Gray)

Recognition: Ventral scales small, no larger than adjacent body scales and rarely distinct posteriorly; head shields enlarged, regular, symmetrical, without projecting tubercles or spines; anterior chin shields reduced, only narrowly contacting the mental groove and more or less separated by the first infralabials; body scales juxtaposed, hexagonal or square, the lower laterals much larger than the remainder (all specimens) and with grossly enlarged tubercles in adult males.

Remarks: Voris (1969) relegated one of the two species (*curtus*) recognized by Smith (1926) to the synonymy of *hardwickii,* whereas McDowell (1972) recognized *curtus* with reservations. However, McDowell (*loc. cit.*) expanded the genus to include *Kolpophis annandalei* (Laidlaw) and *Thalassophina viperina* (Schmidt).

Only one species (*hardwickii*) is found in the Australian region.

Lapemis hardwickii (Gray) (Figure 45)

Recognition: as for genus. Australian specimens are typically pale to dark olive-grey above, uniform cream or pale yellowish below, the two colors

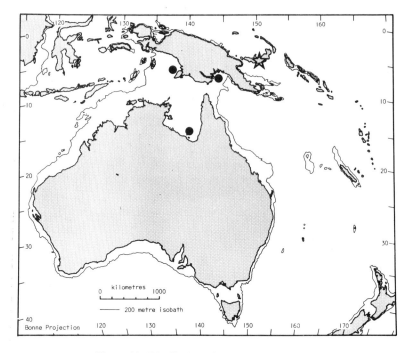

Figure 44. Distribution of *Hydrophis pacificus.*

Figure 45. *Lapemis hardwickii* (McCluer Gulf, West Irian).

meeting along an obscure zig-zag line along the side of the body and tending to intergrade in the apical portion of each triangular lateral section. In juveniles and some adults the pattern is more conspicuous, with a series of 30–55 mid-dorsal blotches which are usually confluent on the vertebral line. Smith (1926) records that the dorsal bars may continue around the body as complete bands, but I have not observed this pattern in any specimens from the Australian region, where the species displays little variation throughout its range. Head shields enlarged, regular, symmetrical. Scales juxtaposed, hexagonal or squarish, in 23–45 rows at mid-body, the lower laterals in adult males with greatly enlarged tubercles or blunt spines. Ventrals 114–235, virtually unrecognizable posteriorly. Anal (=preanal) scales scarcely enlarged. Average total length 1.0 m.

Remarks: McDowell (1974), in recording a specimen of *Ephalophis greyi* from Broome, Western Australia which had been erroneously identified as *Lapemis hardwickii,* commented that the latter was "... not otherwise known from northwestern Australia or the Timor Sea region," while Smith (1926) regarded the species as rare in Australian waters. As can be seen from Figure 46, this species is one of the most common and widely distributed of Australian sea snakes. It appears to be an inhabitant of turbid waters, being the dominant species in most trawls made west of Torres Strait.

Distribution (Figure 46): Found throughout the tropical waters of the Australia/New Guinea continental shelf and its outliers in the Coral Sea.

Genus *Laticauda* (Laurenti)

Recognition: A group of sea snakes characterized by the following combination of characters: nostrils lateral; nasal scales separated by two or more internasal scales; body scales smooth, imbricate; ventral scales broad, more than half the width of the body; body banded with a series of complete black rings or bands.

Remarks: Smith (1926) and McDowell (1967) provided expanded generic descriptions. Smith (1926) placed this genus with *Emydocephalus* and *Aipysurus* in the subfamily *Laticaudinae,* but this relationship has since been rejected by McDowell (1969, 1972) as artificial. McDowell (*loc. cit.*) suggested that *Laticauda* represents an independent marine invasion by a group of terrestrial elapids (and consequently includes it in the subfamily *Elapinae*), whereas *Emydocephalus* and *Aipysurus* belong with remaining sea snakes in a probable monophyletic assemblage represented by his subfamily *Hydrophiinae.* However, Voris (1969), as pointed out above, has supported Smith's original suggestion that *Laticauda* represents a primitive genus of true hydrophiid sea snakes. Mostly nocturnal, but sometimes found foraging on reefs or mud flats during the day. Although the venom is very toxic, these snakes are inoffensive and rarely attempt to bite even when freshly captured.

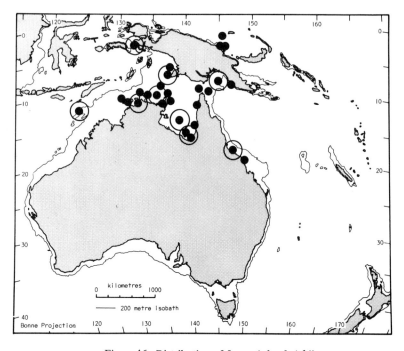

Figure 46. Distribution of *Lapemis hardwickii.*

Partly terrestrial, members of this genus are oviparous and are often 'found in rocky or coral crevices along the shore, or in mangrove swamps, sometimes considerable distances from the sea. Although three species have been recorded from the Australian region, one of them (*Schistrohynchus*) appears to be endemic to the Tongan/Samoan region and a single record from Bertrand Island (= Tendanye Island, near Wewak), New Guinea, has not been confirmed. For this reason *L. schistorhynchus* is omitted from the following accounts, although it is included in the key. Also omitted are *Laticauda laticaudata wolffi* and *Laticauda crockeri,* forms endemic to Lake Tegano, Rennell Island, Solomon Group. The status of these snakes is uncertain, and Voris (1969) has suggested that *wolffi* may represent the product of recent hybridization between *crockeri* and immigrant *laticaudata.*

Distribution: Widely distributed from the islands of the western Pacific through the·Indo-Malayan Archipelago and the Philippines to Japan and the Bay of Bengal.

Key to the Australian Species of Laticauda

    1. Scales in 21 or more rows at mid-body 2

Scales in 19 rows at mid-body .... *laticaudata*
2. Rostral divided horizontally; fewer
than 200 ventrals .... *schistorhynchus*
Rostral not divided; more than 200
ventrals .... *colubrina*

Laticauda colubrina (Schneider) (Figure 47)

Recognition: A moderately built snake, blue or blue-grey above with 20–65 black cross-bands, each of which completely encircles the body. Snout and upper lips yellow, the remainder of the head black except for a bar of yellow extending back above the eye to the temporal region; belly cream or yellow. Usually a large azygous shield between the prefrontals. *Rostral undivided. Body scales smooth, in 21–25 rows at mid-body. Ventrals 210–250.* Anal divided. Subcaudals divided, 29–35 in females, 37–47 in males (vide Smith, 1926). Average total length about 1 m.

Distribution (Figure 48): Coast of New Guinea and most islands of the Western Pacific, but rarely encountered in Australian waters. One of only two species of sea snakes recorded from New Zealand (McCann, 1966). Extralimital through the Indo-Malayan Archipelago to the Indian coast.

Laticauda laticaudata (Linnaeus)

Recognition: Similar in most respects to *L. colubrina.* Blue or blue-grey above, with 25–70 black cross-bands, some or all of which completely

Figure 47. *Laticauda colubrina* (Kadavu, Fiji).

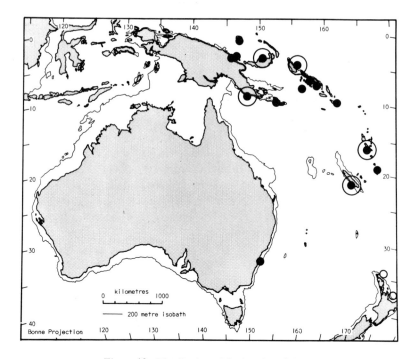

Figure 48. Distribution of *Laticauda colubrina*.

encircle the body. Head black above, except for a yellow bar above the eye and sometimes a yellow snout continuous with this supraocular bar. Upper lips brown. Belly cream or yellow. No azygous shield between the prefrontal scales. *Rostral undivided. Body scales smooth, in 19 rows at mid-body.* Ventrals 225–245. Anal divided. Subcaudals divided, 30–35 in females, 38–47 in males (vide Smith, 1926). Average total length 1 m.

Distribution (Figure 49): As for *L. colubrina.*

Genus *Pelamis* (Daudin) (Figure 50)

Recognition: A monotypic genus with a unique color pattern, in which a black or dark brown upper half of the body contrasts with a cream, yellow or paler brown lower half; these colors are sharply disjunct along a mid-lateral line. Tail yellowish, with black bars or spots. Scales small, juxtaposed, more or less hexagonal or rectangular in shape, in 49–67 rows at mid-body. The ventrals are small, usually divided, and scarcely wider than the adjacent body scales, 264–406. Head shields enlarged, symmetrical, unfragmented. Mental groove absent. Average total length 0.7 m.

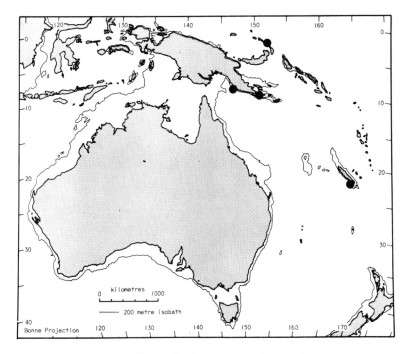

Figure 49. Distribution of *Laticauda laticaudata.*

Distribution (Figure 51): Tropical and warm-temperate waters of the Indo-Pacific region, from the east coast of Africa to the west coast of the Americas. Individuals frequently stray into higher latitudes. One of three species recorded from Tasmania, and one of two species known as waifs from New Zealand.

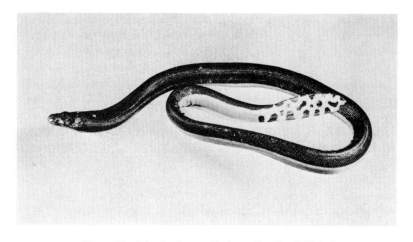

Figure 50. *Pelamis platurus* (Sydney, New South Wales).

127

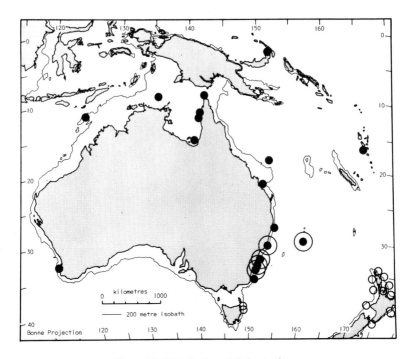

Figure 51. Distribution of *Pelamis platurus.*

Pelamis platurus (Linnaeus)

Recognition: As for genus. Smith (1926) analyzes the variety of color patterns found in this wide-ranging species.

Remarks: The most widely distributed of all sea snakes and, because it is the only species occurring in the New World, has been more thoroughly investigated than any member of its family. A pelagic species, its latitudinal distribution is greater than any other sea snake and the status of populations in higher latitudes is disputed. Dunson (1971) and Dunson and Ehlert (1971) have suggested that a minimum sea temperature of 20°C is needed to maintain permanent (feeding, breeding) populations, a view similar to that held by Graham et al. (1971). Although it would be unwise to extrapolate from one population or region to another, there is little doubt that the population living off the central coast of New South Wales is both permanent and breeding. Figure 52 indicates the seasonal distribution of 93 *Pelamis* taken from waters of the central coastal region of New South Wales, based on specimens received by the Australian Museum since the beginning of this century. Results from all years are pooled, as records clearly indicate that virtually all specimens have been washed ashore during heavy coastal storms,

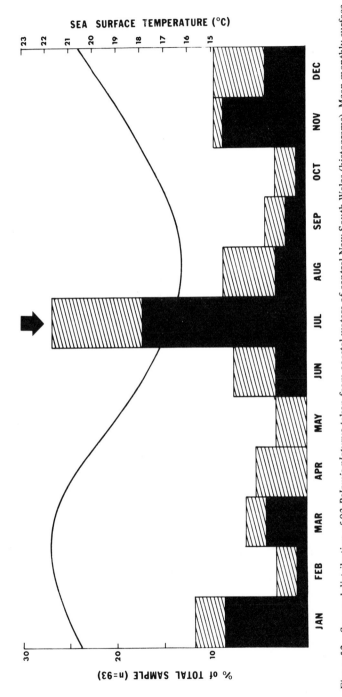

Figure 52. Seasonal distribution of 93 *Pelamis platurus* taken from coastal waters of central New South Wales (histograms). Mean monthly surface temperatures (1943–1972, CSIRO) at a recording station over 50 m of water off Port Hacking, New South Wales are also indicated. Arrows indicate those months in which gravid females have been found. Solid parts of histogram indicate specimens with precise collecting dates; shaded parts indicate specimens with only approximate collection dates.

which have no marked seasonal occurrence. Months in which gravid females have been recorded are indicated in Figure 52, while mean sea surface temperatures for a 50 m (depth) recording station off Port Hacking are superimposed on the snake distribution histogram. The highest number of snakes has been taken in midwinter (July) when sea-surface temperature is at its annual minimum; at this time gravid females are present. A second (but much lower or conversely more highly dispersed) peak occurs in early summer (November–January).

ACKNOWLEDGMENTS

For the loan of specimens under their charge, I am grateful to E. E. Williams, G. Gow, and R. G. Zweifel. Mr. Gow also generously provided me with Figures 24, 26, and 28.

Specimens were provided for the present study by W. Dunson, H. Heatwole, D. Lindner, F. Parker, and J. Wombey. N. A. Streten and the Department of Biogeography and Geomorphology, Australian National University, kindly permitted me to reproduce Figure 1 from a paper by P. J. Webster and N. A. Streten. F. Davies of the C.S.I.R.O. Division of Fisheries and Oceanography provided data on sea temperatures off Sydney.

I gratefully acknowledge the support of the National Science Foundation under grant NSF GA35835 to the Pennsylvania State University and grants NSF GA34948 and NSF GD34462 to the Scripps Institution of Oceanography for operation of the *Alpha Helix* Research Program. To my colleagues on the 1972 *Alpha Helix* Ashmore Reef Expedition I am especially indebted, with particular thanks due to W. Dunson, H. Heatwole, and S. Minton for subsequent help and advice. P. Webber and Mrs. A. Young assisted in the examination of specimens and the preparation of the typescript.

REFERENCES

Boulenger, G. A. 1896. Catalogue of the Snakes in the British Museum (Natural History), Vol. 3. British Museum, London. pp. 266–309.

Brongersma, L. D. 1956. Notes on New Guinean reptiles and amphibians. V Proc. Ned. Akad. Wet. 59C(5):599–610.

Burger, W. L., and T. Natsuno. A new genus for the Arafura smooth sea snake and redefinitions of other sea snake genera. The Snake (in press).

Doutch, H. F. 1973. The palaeogeography of northern Australia and New Guinea and its relevance to the Torres Strait area. *In* Bridge and Barrier: The Natural and Cultural History of Torres Strait (D. Walker, ed.). Publication BG/3 (1972), Department of Biogeography and Geomorphology, Research School of Pacific Studies, Australian National University, Canberra. pp. 1–10.

Dunson, W. 1971. The sea snakes are coming. Natural History 80(9):52–60.

Dunson, W. A. and G. W. Ehlert. 1971. Effects of temperature, salinity, and surface water flow on distribution of the sea snake *Pelamis*. Limnol. and Oceanog. 16:845–853.

Graham, J. B., I. Rubinoff, and M. K. Hecht. 1971. Temperature physiology of the sea snake *Pelamis platurus:* an index of its colonization potential in the Atlantic Ocean. Proc. Nat. Acad. Sci. USA 68:1360–1363.

Kinghorn, J. R. 1929. Snakes of Australia. Angus and Robertson, Sydney. pp. 1–198.

Klemmer, K. 1963. Liste der rezenten Giftschlangen *In* Der Giftschlangen der Erde. N. G. Elwert, Marburg/Lahn, pp. 255–464.

Krefft, G. 1869. The Snakes of Australia; an illustrated and descriptive catalogue of all the known species. Government Printer, Sydney. pp. i–xxv, 1–100.

Lönnberg, E., and L. G. Andersson. 1913. Results of Dr. E. Mjöbergs Swedish Scientific Expeditions to Australia 1910–1913. III. Reptiles. Kungl. Svenska Vetensk.-akad Handl. 52(3):1–17.

McCann, C. 1966. The marine turtles and snakes occurring in New Zealand. Rec. Dominion Mus. 5(21):201–215.

McDowell, S. B. 1967. *Aspidomorphus,* a genus of New Guinea snakes of the Family Elapidae, with notes on related genera. J. Zool. Lond. 151:497–543.

McDowell, S. B. 1969. Notes on the Australian sea snake *Ephalophis greyi* M. Smith (Serpentes: Elapidae, Hydrophiinae) and the origin and classification of sea snakes. Zool. J. Linn. Soc. 48:333–349.

McDowell, S. B. 1972. The genera of sea snakes of the *Hydrophis* group (Serpentes:Elapidae). Trans. Zool. Soc. Lond. 32:189–247.

McDowell, S. B. 1974. Additional notes on the rare and primitive sea snake, *Ephalophis greyi.* J. Herpetology, 8(2):123–128.

Mittleman, M. B. 1947. Geographic variation in the sea snake, *Hydrophis ornatus* (Gray). Proc. Biol. Soc. Wash. 60:1–8.

Roux, J. 1910. Reptilien und amphibien der Aru- und Kei- Inseln. Abh. Senckenberg. naturf. Ges. 33:210–247.

Scott, E. O. G. 1931. On the occurrence in Tasmania of *Hydrophis ornatus,* variety *ocellatus,* with a note on *Pelamis platurus* (=*Hydrus platurus*). Pap. Roy. Soc. Tas. 1931:111.

Shuntov, V. P. 1972. Sea snakes of the North Australian Shelf. Translation of 1971 paper in Ekologiya 4:65–72, by Consultants Bureau, New York.

Smith, L. A. 1974. The sea snakes of Western Australia (Serpentes: Elapidae, Hydrophiinae) with a description of a new subspecies. Rec. West. Aust. Mus. 3(2):93–110.

Smith, M. 1926. Monograph of the Sea Snakes (Hydrophiidae). British Museum of Natural History, London. pp. i–xix, 1–130.

Stejneger, L. 1907. Herpetology of Japan and Adjacent Territory. Bulletin 58, United States National Museum, Washington. pp. i–xx, 1–577.

Underwood, G. 1957. On lizards of the family Pygopodidae: a contribution to the morphology and phylogeny of the Squamata. J. Morph. 100:207–268.

Underwood, G. 1967. A Contribution to the Classification of Snakes. Publication No. 653, British Museum of Natural History, London. pp. i–x, 1–179.

Van Andel, T. H., G. R. Heath, T. C. Moore, and D. F. R. McGeary. 1967. Late Quaternary history, climate, and oceanography of the Timor Sea, northwestern Australia. Am. J. Sci. 265:737–758.

Voris, H. K. 1966. Fish eggs as the apparent sole food item for a genus of sea snake, *Emydocephalus* (Krefft). Ecology 47(1):152–154.

Voris, H. K. 1969. The evolution of the Hydrophiidae with a critique on methods of approach. PhD thesis. University of Chicago.

Webster, P. J., and N. A. Streten. 1973. Aspects of late Quaternary climate in tropical Australasia. *In* Bridge and Barrier: The Natural and Cultural History of Torres Strait (D. Walker, ed.). Publication BG/3 (1972), Department of Biogeography and Geomorphology, Research School of Pacific Studies, Australian National University, Canberra, pp. 39–60.

APPENDIX

The majority of specimens examined in the course of preparing this chapter, and on which the distribution maps are based, are listed below. Omitted are those without, or with imprecise, locality data, and a few specimens whose identities are still regarded as indeterminate. These latter specimens will be dealt with elsewhere at a later date.

Genera and species are listed in alphabetical order.

Aipysurus apraefrontalis

Ashmore Reef, Timor Sea (AM R37141, R40493, R42711, R44475, R44616, R44878).

Aipysurus duboisii

Great Barrier Reef, Qld. (AM R8641); Arafura Sea, (AM R14427); Heron Island, Qld. (AM R15088); Hinchinbroke Island, Qld. (AM R17743); Chesterfield Reefs, Coral Sea (AM R20779); Townsville, Qld. (AM R41005, R41057, R41059, R41060-5); Ashmore Reef (AM R37139, R40497, R41511, R41520, R42024, R44428, R44457, R44459, R44552, R44611, R44631, R44861, R44903); Outer Barrier Reef (AM R44398, R44408, R44410, R44412-3); Observatory Key, Kenn Reef (AM R44401); Frederick Reef (AM R44402, 44404); Fairfax Island, Qld. (AM R42102) Saumerez Reef (AM R44399, R44407, R44496, R44502); Scott Reef (AM R44430, 44617, 44863, 44895).

Aipysurus eydouxii

Torres Strait (MCZ R142385); Mawatta, Western District, Papua (MCZ R142377); Bundaberg Qld. (AM R45822); Gulf of Carpentaria (AM R44524, R44969, R45790, USNM AG308); 50 m north of Kaap Valsch, West Irian (AM R44975, R44982, R44984); junction of Embley and Hay Rivers, Weipa,

Qld. (AM R44424); Karumba, Qld. (AM R44564); Weipa, Qld. (AM R17623, R44415-7, R44419-20); Townsville, Qld. (AM R41030-3, R41058); Arafura Sea (AM R33244, R33246, R33249, R33251, R33278); Port Denison, Qld. (AM R6703, R8301).

Aipysurus foliosquama

Ashmore Reef (AM R37134, R37137, R37140, R37143, R40483, R40488, R40489, R40492, R40496, R40499, R41508, R41521-2, R41526, R41537, R41542, R42701, R44443, R44446, R44456, R44576, R44592, R44597, R44619, R44646, R44872, R44877, R44890, R44896, R44899, R44902, R44906, R45797); Hibernia Reef (AM R41516).

Aipysurus fuscus

Ashmore Reef (AM R37135, R37142, R40481, R40482, R40487, R40498, R41054-6, R41531, R41533-5, R41538, R42697, R42708, R44431, R44441, R44445, R44462, R44469, R44484, R44580, R44586, R44588, R44603, R44862, R44865, R44869, R44879-80, R44886-7, R44914, R44916); Scott Reef (AM R44893).

Aipysurus laevis

Karumba, Qld. (USNM AJ722); Scott Reef (AM R42699, R44442, R44568, R44606, R44629, R44633); Swain Reef (USNM AJ740-5, AJ747, AJ749, AM R19137, R21450-1, R21453-4, R42030, R42032-3, R44497-8, R44500-1, R44510, R44525-6, R44529, R44531-2, R44534, R44536, R44541, R44549-50, R44561); Gulf of Carpentaria (USNM AJ750, AM R42038, R44523); Cleveland Bay, Qld. (AM R6804); Port Denison, Qld. (AM R7740); Great Barrier Reef (AM R8642-3); Hayman Island, Qld. (AM R11327); Samarai Island, New Guinea (AM R15089); Weipa, Qld. (AM R18254); Masthead Island, Capricorn Group, Qld. (AM R33282); Sir Edward Pellew Islands, Gulf of Carpentaria (AM R33208); Arafura Sea (AM R33247, R33272, R33274); Cartier Island, (AM R44572, R44584, R44644, R44864, R44868); Ashmore Reef (AM R33353-5, R37138, R40490-1, R40501, R41507, R41510, R41514, R41523-5, R41527-30, R41532, R41539, R42698, R42703, R42709, R44439, R44452, R44460, R44571, R44587, R44595-6, R44620, R44627, R44643, R44860, R44866, R44898, R44904, R45055); Townsville, Qld (AM R41004-14, R41034-5, R41043, R41048-52); Saumerez Reef (AM R 44397, R44503-5, R44508, R44539); Hibernia Reef (AM R44429, R44455); Bathurst Island to Groote Island (AM R45012, R45042); Parama Island, New Guinea (MCZ R137242); Gulf of Papua (MCZ R137507); Bobo Island, New Guinea (MCZ R137508, R137695, R137958);

Dagagota Reef, Gulf of Papua (MCZ R137509); Mornington Island, Gulf of Carpentaria (MCZ R137524-5).

Acalyptophis peronii

Weipa, Qld. (AM R18253, R44421); Ashmore Reef (AM R33356-7, R41069, R41068, R42028, R42705, R42710, R44434, R44569, R44581, R44589, R44602, R44640, R44881, R44888, R44917, R44919); Torres Strait (AM R40685, R40687, MCZ R142383); Evans' Head estuary, NSW (AM R42713); Marion Reef (AM R44403); Saumerez Reef (AM R44405).

Astrotia stokesii

Gulf of Carpentaria (USNM AG291, AG310, AG719, AG727, AJ751); Bathurst Island to Groote Island (AM R44999, 45006-9, R45011, R45015, R45044, R45046-7, R45049); 50 m north of Kaap Valsch, West Irian (AM R44979); Port Essington area (AM R45022); Swain Reefs (USNM AJ748); Shellharbour NSW (AM R3162); Port Essington (AM R45022); Darwin (AM R3390, R17626, R44461, R44579); Vernon Island (AM R9186-7); Sydney District NSW (AM R9286); Arafura Sea (AM R14432, R33242, R33256, R33274, R33351-2, R42007-9); Heron Island, Qld. (AM R17042); Urunga, NSW (AM R18833); Karumba, Qld. (AM R42041-3, R42695-6); Ashmore Reef (AM R42700, R44393-4, R44593-4, R44598, R44630, R44892, R44907, R45054); Saumerez Reef (AM R44506); Yeppoon, Qld. (AM R44547).

Disteira kingii

Gladstone, Qld. (AM R8933); Bathurst Island, NT (AM R14429); Moreton Bay, Qld. (AM R20727); Gulf of Papua (AM R40683, R40693); Townsville, Qld. (AM R41988-9); Karumba, Qld. (AM R44535); Mornington Island, Gulf of Carpentaria (MCZ R137520-1); Torres Strait (MCZ R137685, R142384).

Disteira major

Morton Bay, Qld., 70 m off coast; Gulf of Carpentaria (USNM AG278, AG284, AG286, AG289-90, AG304, AG307, AJ720, AJ721, AJ&33, AM R42040, R44521); Karumba, Qld. (USNM AJ724, AM R33144, R44513-4, R44517-8); Darwin (AM 1/AMF 4967, 2/AMF4968, 6/AMF4969); Sydney district, NSW (AM R9107); Arafura Sea (AM R33269, R44851, R44857); 50 m north of Kaap Valsch, West Irian (AM R44976); Fairfax Island (AM R40177); Newcastle (AM R40663); Gulf of Papua (AM R40695, MCZ R137243-4, R137683, R142382, R142387); Port Essington NT (AM R45021); Bathurst Island to Groote Island (AM R45031, R45033); Townsville, Qld. (AM R42012-4, R42016, R42020-1); Gove Peninsula, NT (AM R45823); Clarence Strait mear Fenton Patches (AM R44450, R44473, R44613); Sawtell, NSW (AM R44511); 30 m south of Carnarvon, WA (AM R45824-5).

Emydocephalus annulatus

Saumerez Reef, Qld. (USNM AJ746, AM R44396, R44489-90, R44492-5, R44507, R44509, R44537, R44540, R44540, R44554-5); Frederick Reef, Qld. (AM R16793); Swain Reefs, Qld. (AM R21452); Ashmore Reef (AM R3358-9, R40484-6, R40494-5, R40500, R40502-3, R41512-3, R41515, R41517, R41536, R41540-1, R42025-6, R44432-3, R44451, R44466-8, R44470-2, R44474, R44487, R44573, R44585, R44590-1, R44600, R44604, R44608, R44615, R44621, R44645, R44874, R44876, R44882, R44884, R44912, R45050, R45053); Scott Reef (AM R42702, R44622, R44624, R44889); Hibernia Reef (AM R42704, R44485, R44641, R45051); Outer Barrier Reef (AM R44400), R44406, R44409, R44543); Swains Reef (AM R44414).

Enhydrina schistosa

Darwin (17/AMF4975); Roper River, NT (AM R9936); mouth of Sepik River New Guinea (AM R25824-31); Arafura Sea (AM R33279); Forsyth River, NT (AM R41037-8); Ayr, Qld. (AM R41053); Repulse Bay (AM R42017); Gulf of Carpentaria (AM R42035, R44542, R44544); 50 m north of Kaap Valsch, West Irian (AM R44973, R44985, R44987-8).

Ephalophis mertoni

Gulf of Carpentaria (AM R44565).

Hydrelaps darwiniensis

Kiamari, Papua (AM R8051); Van Diemens Gulf (AM R8934); Forest River East Kimberley (AM R9993).

Hydrophis caerulescens

Karumba, Qld. (AM R44516).

Hydrophis elegans

Gulf of Carpentaria (USNM AG275, AG282-3, AG294, A302-3, AG307, AJ723, AM R44512, R44546, R44562, R44972, MCZ R137485); Mornington Island, Gulf of Carpentaria (MCZ R137486, R137522, R137960-1); Manly, Qld. (AM R1791); Sydney district NSW (AM R5392, R6252, R13127); Moreton Bay, Qld. (AM R3421); Yamba, NSW (AM 4564); Darwin, NT (12/AMF4971, 13/AMF4972, 14/AMF4973, 19/AMF4974, 20/AMF4977); Farquahar Inlet, Manning River, NSW (AM R6783); Broome, WA (AM R10559); Burnett River, Qld. (AM R11515); Bundaberg, Qld. (AM R11628); Lindeman Island, Qld. (AM R11705); Karumba, Qld. (AM R20781, R33145-6, R44558); Taree NSW (AM R40675); Forster, NSW (AM R21257); mouth of Sepik River, New Guinea (AM R25835); Hawkesbury River, NSW (AM R26365); Arafura Sea (AM R33245, R33253, R33266, R33268, R33270, R33273, R33275); Ashmore Reef (AM R33361, R44635); Gulf of Papua (AM R40684, R40692, R40694, MCZ R137239, R137241, R137686, R142388-93); Torres Strait (AM R40691, MCZ R137692, R137694, R137751); McCluer Gulf (AM R44642); Port Hacking, NSW (AM R44949); 50 m north Kaap Valsch, West Irian, (AM R44978); Kalamai Creek, Ayr, Qld. (AM R41015); Townsville, Qld. (AM R41016-7, R41028-9, R42058-61, R42687-9, R42690-4); Weipa, Qld. (AM R42031); 4 m. up Gilbert River Qld. (AM R44522); Cairns, Qld. (AM R44527-8); Deception Bay, Papua (AM R44548); Cape van Diemen to Groote Island (AM R44997-8); Bathurst Island to Groote Island (AM R45002, R45004, R45013-4, R45016-9, R45032, R45034, R45039-40, R45043, R45045); Port Essington (AM R45020, R45024-5, R45028, R45030); McCluer Gulf, West Irian (AM R45796).

Hydrophis fasciatus

Darwin, NT (AM R14022).

Hydrophis gracilis

Gulf of Papua (MCZ R142375).

Hydrophis inornatus

Arafura Sea (NTM 897).

Hydrophis sp.

Port Denison, Qld. (AM R8300); northeast of Peron Island, NT (AM R14425); 60 m west of Port Keats, NT (AM R14428); Torres Strait, near Darnley Island (AM R40688, R40689, R40690); Townsville District, Qld. (AM R41991, R41992, R41993); Gulf of Papua, 40–50 m east of Daru (MCZ R135376, R137512); Torres Strait (MCZ R137487); Mornington Island, Gulf of Carpentaria (MCZ R142386).

Hydrophis melanocephalus

Ashmore Reef (AM R33335-50, R39019-20, R42002-3, R42006, R42027, R42706-7, R42712, R44425, R44436-7, R44444, R44449, R44458, R44463-5, R44476-83, R44486, R44570, R44575, R44577, R44582-3, R44605, R44607, R44623, R44625-6, R44628, R44632, R44636-8, R44873, R44875, R44883, R44885, R44891, R44897, R44900-1, R44905, R44908-9, R44911, R44913, R44918); Scott Reef (AM R44435, R44566, R44610).

Hydrophis melanosoma

Orangerie Bay, New Guinea (MCZ R141278).

Hydrophis obscurus

Balimo, Aramia River, Papua New Guinea (MCZ R141279).

Hydrophis ornatus

Gulf of Carpentaria (USNM AG299); Hawkesbury, NSW (AM R8020); Bathurst Island, NT (AM R14424); Karumba, Qld. (AM R20778); Townsville, Qld. (AM R42010, R42022-3), Gulf of Papua (MCZ R137560-1).

Hydrophis pacificus

50 m north of Kaap Valsch, West Irian (AM R44983, R45092); Mornington Island, Gulf of Carpentaria (MCZ R137962); Gulf of Papua (MCZ R142394-403); Orokolo Bay, Papua New Guinea (AM R45092).

Lapemis hardwickii

Gulf of Carpentaria (USNM AG279, AG301, AJ725-6, AJ728-32, AJ734-9, AJ799, AJ800, AM R42036, R42039, R44491, R44499, R44538, R44556, R44563, R44970-1); Bathurst to Groote Island (AM R45000, R45003, R45005, R45010, R45035-8, R45041, R45048); Java Cay (A 1821-2); Townsville, Qld. (AM R6945, R41018-26, R41066-7, R42044-57, R44379-92); Darwin, NT (AM R17625); NT coast east of Bathurst Island (AM R44995); Cape van Diemen to Groote Island (AM R44996); off coast between Mitchell and Nassau Rivers, Qld. (MCZ R137562-4); Arnhem Bay NT (AM R18267); 50 m north of Kaap Valsch, West Irian (AM R44974, R44977, R44980-1, R44986, R44990); Albatross Bay, Qld. (AM R19376-80); Karumba, Qld. (AM R20780, R33139-43, R44515, R44520, R44557);

Ashmore Reef (AM R44634); Weipa, Qld. (AM R44418, MCZ R142356-7); Port Moresby, Papua (AM R21206); Sepik River mouth, New Guinea (AM R25832-3); Arafura Sea (AM R33240-1, R33243, R33248, R33250, R33252, R33254-5, R33257-65, R33267, R33271, R33277, R44852-6); Gulf of Papua (AM R44647-9, R44850, MCZ R142295, R142404-7); Mc-Cluer Gulf (AM R37136, R44427, R44438, R44447, R44453-4, R44567, R44574, R44578, R44599, R44601, R44609, R44639, R44871, R44894, R44915); Torres Strait (AM R40686, MCZ R137687-8, R137690); Port Essington area (AM R45023, R45026-7); Morobe District Papua (MCZ R142376); near Proserpine Qld. (AM R41027); 1–2.5 m upstream Peter John River NT (AM R41036); Tjipripu River, Melville Island, NT. (AM R41040); Yeppoon, Qld. (AM R44545).

Laticauda colubrina

Fiji (AM R209-10, R8506, R45816-7, R45819-21); Solomon Islands (AM R1952, R2594, R3643, R7267, R8687-8, A9762, A17132); Tonga (AM R2345); New Britain (AM R3153, R11184, R45794); Port Moresby (AM R3424, R10913, R13727, R13791, R13849, R13851-2); New Hebrides (AM R3825, R7053, R7056); Suva (AM R5068); Bougainville Island (AM R7002, R20591, R45793); Maldeula, Fiji (AM R7181); Eitape District, New Guinea (AM R8886) New Caledonia (AM R9113, B9150, R13531); Malekula (AM R10177); Tana, New Hebrides (AM R10185); Manus Island, Papua (AM R10548); Samoa (AM R13009); Finschaven (AM R13756); Saidor, 60 m east of Madang (AM R14319); Sydney district, NSW. (AM R20883); Louisade Archipelago, New Guinea (AM R44395).

Laticauda laticaudata

Fiji (AM R6698); Port Moresby, Papua (AM R+0941); Tonga (AM R14932); Noumea, New Caledonia (AM R17951); New Ireland (AM R42765); Samarui, Papua New Guinea (AM R45795).

Pelamis platurus

Ashmore Reef, Timor Sea (AM R42005); Sydney district, NSW (AM R314, R1604, R3187, R3828, R4164, R6750, R7012, R7032, R7279, R7759, R8773, R8944, R9182, R9270, R9316, R9504, R9688, R10365, R10386, R10552, R11254, R11622, R11734, R12447, R13008, R13139, R13272, R13760-1, R13766, R13785, R13811, R14803, R15028, R15205, R15421, R15444, R15599, R15601, R16020-1, R16898, R16935, R17624, R17865, R19101, R20414, R20752, R25773, R26084, R26268, R26276, R27317-20, R29920, R39058-9, R39062, R39065-6, R39508, R39921-2, R40668,

R40925, R41105-8, R45812, R45814-5); New Hebrides (AM R1150); Tonga (AM R14931); Bird Island, Rockhampton, Qld. (AM R2506); New Britain (AM R3154); Lord Howe Island, NSW (AM R3291, R7200, R8138); Ulladulla, NSW (AM R3791); Wreck Bay, NSW (AM R4283); Betiv Mele Bay (AM R6092); Madras, India (AM R6727); Marshall Islands (AM R7027); Wollongong, NSW (AM R7433, R10502, R44378); Port Stephens, NSW (AM R7993); Tuggerah, NSW (AM R7994); Ballina, NSW (AM R8979); Milton, NSW (AM R9213); Norah Head, Newcastle, NSW (AM R9420, R13040, R13075); Hunter River, NSW (AM R9507); Port Hacking, NSW (AM R10385, R11578, R12448, R14825); Port Macquarie (AM R13445); Toronto, NSW. (AM R14379); Bunbury, WA (AM R15446); Arafura Sea (AM R14426); Lake Illawarra, NSW (AM R16862); Burning Palms, NSW. (AM R17173); North Haven, NSW (AM R17976); Jervis Bay (AM R18260); Karumba, Qld. (AM R21243); Sussex Inlet, NSW (AM R26269); Seal Rocks, NSW (AM R7186); Thursday Island, Qld. (AM R37362); Ashmore Reef (AM R39018); Gordon's Bay, NSW (AM R39057); The Entrance, NSW (AM R39060-1); Masters Beach, NSW (AM R39067); Queenscliff, NSW (AM R40926); Ramsgate, NSW. (AM R41104); Bateman's Bay, NSW (AM R41194); Bulli, NSW. (AM R44377); Woolgoolga, NSW. (AM R44530); Gulf of Carpentaria (AM R44551, R44553); Coral Sea (AM R44559); Montague Island, NSW (AM R45485); Hawkesbury River (AM R45811); Garie Beach NSW (AM R45813); Weipa, Qld. (MCZ R142378-9).

Note (to paragraph 1 of Materials and Methods)
added in proof: AG and AJ numbers, prefixed by USNM, refer to field tags on specimens collected by H. Heatwole and to be deposited in the U.S. National Museum.

five

Sea Snakes from three Reefs of the Sahul Shelf

Sherman A. Minton
and Harold Heatwole

Ashmore Reef (12° 12′ S; 123° 5′ E) is located on the Sahul Shelf in the Timor Sea, about 500 km north of Derby, Western Australia (Figure 1). This reef and the nearby Cartier (12° 32′ S; 123° 33′ E), Scotts (14° 5′ S; 121° 50′ E), and Hibernia (12° 0′ S; 123° 23′ E) reefs were visited during the *Alpha Helix* expedition. Most observations were made at Ashmore Reef with supplementary ones on the other reefs mentioned. Teichert and Fairbridge (1948) provide a general description of the reefs on the Sahul Shelf.

Observations were made from 31 December 1972 through 13 January 1973. Submerged snakes were observed by snorkeling and with scuba gear. A transect of about 0.8 km was made between the ship and the reef edge from a depth of about 25 m to 2 m. Snakes at the surface were captured whenever possible. A total of 420 snakes was collected and numerous others observed (Table 1).

Two species, *Aipysurus foliosquama* and *Aipysurus apraefrontalis,* seem largely confined to shallow water and were not found at depths greater than 10 m. Although occasionally found together, *A. apraefrontalis* seems to prefer a sandy bottom with sparse coral, whereas *A. foliosquama* prefers areas heavily grown with coral. *A. foliosquama* seems to be the more abundant, with 36 specimens collected as opposed to seven of *A. apraefrontalis.*

Emydocephalus annulatus, Aipysurus duboisii, and *A. fuscus* occur in shallow water but are also found in the 12- to 25-m zone. All were found in areas of moderate to heavy coral growth but were not confined there. All

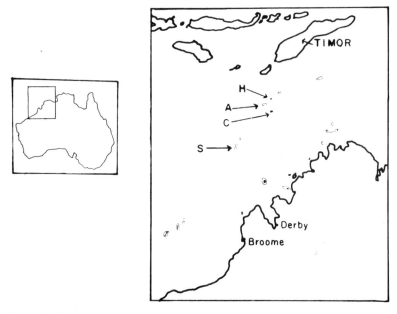

Figure 1. Map of part of the Sahul Shelf (right) showing the locations of the reefs studied. H = Hibernia Reef. A = Ashmore Reef. C = Cartier Reef. S = Scott Reef. Left: map of Australia showing location of inset map.

Table 1. Sea snakes caught on reefs of the Sahul Shelf by the R/V Alpha Helix Ashmore Reef Expedition[a]

Species	Ashmore Reef	Scott Reef	Cartier Island	Hibernia Reef
Acalyptophis peronii	10	5	–	–
Aipysurus apraefrontalis	2	–	–	–
Aipysurus duboisii	5	24	–	9
Aipysurus foliosquama	10	–	–	9
Aipysurus fuscus	10	13	–	–
Aipysurus laevis	12	34	75	27
Astrotia stokesii	5	–	–	–
Emydocephalus annulatus	16	8	25	55
Hydrophis melanocephalus[b]	30	16	–	–
Lapemis hardwickii	0.3	–	–	–
Pelamis platurus	0.5	–	–	–
Total catch for each reef	367	38	4	11

[a]Figures are presented as the percent of total catch for each reef. Total catch in bottom row refers to number of individuals.
[b]Snakes tentatively identified by H. G. Cogger. Subsequent revision of the status of these specimens is likely.

three species, but especially *E. annulatus,* tended to congregate along gullies and channels with sandy bottoms. *Emydocephalus* was the most frequently observed species along the transect and at most of the dive sites.

Aipysurus laevis was most often noted on the reefs at depths of 5–8 m, but was also seen on numerous occasions around the ship when anchored in water 25–45 m deep. It and *Emydocephalus* were the only species collected at all reefs visited on the Sahul Shelf. *Astrotia stokesii* showed a similar depth distribution but was present in smaller numbers than *A. laevis.*

Hydrophis melanocephalus and *Acalyptophis peronii* were never observed in the shallow water coral habitat, but both were obtained in good numbers at the surface in water 12 m or more in depth. An individual of *H. melanocephalus* was observed foraging on the bottom at a depth of 44 m. This species is almost entirely nocturnal in its surface activity; *Acalyptophis* shows nocturnal tendencies but is also seen on the surface by day.

The pelagic *Pelamis platurus* was recorded on the basis of two juveniles collected and a third observed. All were in relatively deep water. A single *Lapemis hardwickii* was netted from the ship while at anchor. Although generally abundant in north Australian and New Guinea waters, the latter species is probably not a part of the regular Ashmore Reef fauna. It seems to prefer a mud or sand bottom and avoids coral, and the captured individual was probably a stray.

A. apraefrontalis was caught only on Ashmore Reef and *A. foliosquama* only on Ashmore and Hibernia reefs (Table 1). Recently these two species have been found to have a wider distribution (Chapter 4). Except for the type specimen allegedly from Celebes, *A. fuscus* is known only from Ashmore and Scott reefs. *A. laevis, A. duboisii,* and *Acalyptophis* are largely restricted to tropical Australian waters and approach the northwest limit of their ranges in the Timor Sea. *Aipysurus eydouxii,* with some of its range in common with these species, was not observed at Ashmore and may be excluded by the presence of large populations of other small *Aipysurus* and *Emydocephalus. Emydocephalus* has an Australian and a western Pacific population. The genus appears to be a specialized derivative of *Aipysurus* that presumably evolved in Australian reef habitat. Its dispersal may be related to its ability to exploit a specialized feeding niche by subsisting entirely on fish spawn. *A. stokesii* is a wide-ranging Indo-Pacific species with apparent ability to cross deep water barriers and utilize a variety of habitats. *H. melanocephalus* has a northwest Pacific distribution, but the status of the Ashmore Reef population requires further taxonomic study and possible revision. It is the only representative of the long-necked, small-headed sea snakes found in the area.

In summary, the sea snake fauna of the Sahul Shelf consists of five shallow water species closely associated with coral formations, two species found in deeper water and not closely associated with coral, and two species occurring frequently in both types of habitat. In addition, there is one pelagic species and one represented by one presumed stray individual. The vertical distribution of species at Ashmore Reef is diagrammatically depicted in Figure 1 of Chapter 11. A generalized classification of sea snakes by diving depths appears in Chapter 15.

ACKNOWLEDGMENTS

This work was supported by the National Science Foundation under grant NSF GA 35835 to the Pennsylvania State University and grants NSF GA 34948, and NSF GD 34462 to The Scripps Institution of Oceanography for operation of the *Alpha Helix* Research Program.

REFERENCES

Teichert, C., and R. W. Fairbridge. 1948. Some coral reefs on the Sahul Shelf. Geogr. Review 38:222–249.

six

Sea Snakes of the Gulf of Carpentaria

Harold Heatwole

The Gulf of Carpentaria is shallow (depth about 65 m; see Galloway and Löffler, 1972) with a rather smoothly contoured bottom. The many rivers tributary to it (Figure 1) discharge large amounts of silt washed into them by the monsoonal rains; consequently, the substrate is mostly mud or a mixture of mud and sand. Very little coral is present, although there are some local patches (e.g., around some of the islands such as Bountiful, Bentinck, and Wellesley Islands and around the Sir Edward Pelew group; see Fairbridge, 1950). Because of the muddy water and correspondingly low visibility, conditions are often unsuitable for underwater observation of snakes, and data were obtained by (1) accompanying prawn trawlers and collecting the snakes they captured in their nets; (2) using a light pontoon aircraft to pull a small trawl while taxiing on the surface of rivers flowing into the Gulf; and (3) opportunistic collecting by myself, my colleagues and personnel of the trawlers. Locality records thus obtained are indicated in Figure 1. In addition, literature records and specimens collected by others are discussed in the text.

SPECIES COMPOSITION OF THE SNAKE FAUNA

Shuntov (1971) presents the data on sea snakes obtained from Russian trawlers on the northern Australian Shelf, including the Gulf of Carpentaria. The density of snakes was greater in the Gulf of Carpentaria than anywhere else, except within the narrow band of coastal waters fringing the shores of northern Australia (Figure 2). He found that sea snakes as a group were distributed throughout the Gulf, rather evenly during the periods of the

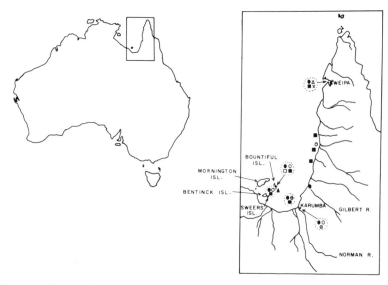

Figure 1. Map of the eastern part of the Gulf of Carpentaria (right) with locations at which sea snakes were caught: dots (*Hydrophis elegans*); circles (*Disteira major*); circles with a central dot (*Hydrophis inornatus*); + (*Hydrophis ornatus*); open triangles (*Aipysurus eydouxii);* closed triangles (*Aipysurus laevis*); open squares (*Astrotia stokesii*); closed squares (*Lapemis hardwickii*); and x's (*Acalyptophis peronii*). Specimens with only a general locality designation are excluded, as are literature records (see text). Left: Map of Australia showing location of inset.

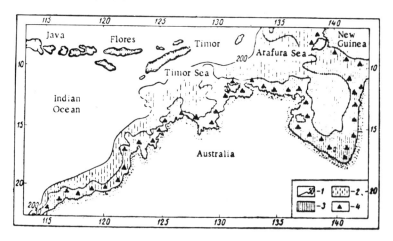

Figure 2. The distribution of sea snakes on the north Australian coast: (1) isobaths, (2) distributional range of sea snakes, (3) areas with highest numbers of snakes, and (4) distributional range of the genus *Aipysurus*. From Shuntov (1972); reprinted by permission.

southeast trade winds (winter), but becoming much more concentrated in the shallower coastal waters during the monsoon (summer). Unfortunately, his distributional data are not presented at the species level. Although he lists 16 species from the Arafura Sea (apparently including within this designation the Gulf of Carpentaria), it is not possible to tell which of these actually were found in the Gulf proper. The only detailed information one can extract is that the genus *Aipysurus* occurs in the Gulf (he provides a distributional map of this genus separately) and that he obtained a specimen of *Pelamis platurus* from the northeastern part of the Gulf of Carpentaria.

I obtained nine species from the Gulf. These were *Hydrophis elegans, Disteira major, Hydrophis ornatus, Hydrophis inornatus, Lapemis hardwickii, Astrotia stokesii, Aipysurus eydouxii, Aipysurus laevis,* and *Acalyptophis peronii.* I also had opportunity to examine a small collection of sea snakes made in 1961 and kept in Karumba until I obtained them in 1967. In this collection there were, in addition to some of the species listed above, two specimens of *Pelamis platurus.* Their locality was listed only as "Gulf of Carpentaria." *A. laevis* is usually found in the vicinity of coral reefs. There are small local reefs around some of the islands. The single specimen of this species that I captured in the Gulf was about 40 km from the nearest known patch of reef and may have been a stray. There was also a specimen of *A. laevis* in the Karumba collection but only "Gulf of Carpentaria" was given as the locality. McDowell (1969, 1974) mentions *Hydrelaps (darwiniensis)* and *Ephalophis mertoni,* both from "Karumba;" the latter species is rare and the specimen to which he referred is the only one in existence besides the type. Thus the total known sea snake fauna of the Gulf of Carpentaria is 12 species, with the possibility that some of the species Shuntov (1971) listed from the Arafura Sea may also have come from the Gulf.

In addition to the true sea snakes, the estuarine colubrid, *Cerberus rynchops australis,* occurs in the Gulf region; my collection contains one taken at Karumba (3 km upstream from the mouth of the Norman River).

ABUNDANCES

The most abundant species in the Gulf is *H. elegans.* Most of the specimens collected in trawls or sighted from boats are of this species. The second most abundant one is *D. major,* followed by *L. hardwickii. Astrotia* is only occasionally encountered, and *H. inornatus* is represented in my collection by only two individuals, one trawled off Karumba and the other hand-netted from the Norman River at Karumba. *Hydrophis ornatus* is known only from one specimen trawled southeast of Bountiful Island. *A. eydouxii* and *A.*

Table 1. Results of trawls in the waters between Karumba, Queensland, and Sweers and Bountiful Islands, Gulf of Carpentaria (see Figure 1)[a]

Species	No. of snakes	Percent of total catch
Hydrophis elegans	31	54
Disteira major	14	25
Hydrophis inornatus	1	2
Hydrophis ornatus	1	2
Lapemis hardwickii	7	12
Astrotia stokesii	3	5
Total	57	100

[a]Trawls made at night from December 1970 to January 1971 and in January, 1972, and in the daytime in May 1967.

peronii are known only from the Weipa area, except for specimens with only general locality data.

The relative numerical importance of *H. elegans, D. major,* and *L. hardwickii* is evidenced by the trawl data (Table 1). These three species collectively accounted for about 94% of the snakes captured in trawls.

LOCAL DISTRIBUTION

The prawn trawlers sampled only one habitat type, albeit the most common one in the Gulf; all trawls were in 20–30 m of water where the bottom was either mud or a mixture of mud and sand. This appears to be favorable habitat for *H. elegans, D. major,* and *L. hardwickii,* since they were abundant there. Shuntov (1962) lists *L. hardwickii* as a littoral species. *A. stokesii,* though occurring with the above species, is also found on coral reefs.

The trawled species are not widely separated spatially, as combinations of several or even all three of the most common species have been captured in the same areas (Figure 1). However, at least some of the species also tolerate brackish water and penetrate the mouths of rivers. All species of *Hydrophis* (except *H. ornatus*) were taken in the Norman River at Karumba in water 4 m deep, where the bottom was muddy; *H. elegans* was trawled by airplane 6.5 km upstream from the mouth of the Gilbert River in water 6 m deep (muddy bottom). *L. hardwickii* has been recorded from the Norman River at Normanton (about 40 km upstream from Karumba) (McDowell, 1974). *A. eydouxii* was taken from the junction of the Embly and Hey Rivers, near Weipa, Queensland, in water 2–3 m deep.

In summary, the sea snake fauna of the Gulf of Carpentaria consists of at least 11 bottom-foraging species, most of which occupy a habitat of water ranging in depth from 2 m to about 20–30 m. Many of the species also penetrate the rivers tributary of the Gulf. All of these species live in areas characterized by muddy bottoms and some may be restricted to such sites; others also are found in other types of habitat (e.g., *A. stokesii*) and one, *A. laevis,* is usually found elsewhere (coral reefs). In addition, there is one pelagic species, giving a total known fauna of 12 species.

REFERENCES

Fairbridge, R. W. 1950. Recent and Pleistocene coral reefs of Australia. J. Geol. 58:330–401.
Galloway, R. W., and E. Löffler. 1972. Aspects of geomorphology and soils in the Torres Straits region. *In* Bridge and Barrier: the Natural and Cultural History of Torres Strait (D. Walker, ed). Publ. BG13 of the Research School of Pacific Studies, Aust. National Univ., Canberra, pp. 11–28.
McDowell, S. B. 1969. Notes on the Australian sea-snake *Ephalophis greyi* M. Smith (Serpentes: Elapidae, Hydrophiidae) and the origin and classification of sea-snakes. Zool. J. Linn. Soc. 48:333–349.
McDowell, S. B. 1974. Additional notes on the rare and primitive sea-snake, *Ephalophis greyi.* J. Herpetol. 8:123–128.
Shuntov, V. P. 1962. Sea snakes (Hydrophiidae) of the Tonking Bay (Northern Viet-Nam). Zool. Zhur. 41:1203–1209. (In Russian).
Shuntov, V. P. 1971. Sea snakes of the north Australian Shelf. Ékologiya 4:65–72. English translation by Consultants Bureau (1972).

seven

Sea Snakes of Tropical Queensland between 18° and 20° South Latitude

William A. Dunson

These observations on sea snake distribution and ecology in the region around Townsville, Queensland, were made between January 1972, and February 1973. The area lies approximately between 18° and 20° south latitude (Figure 1). It is characterized by a series of bays along the shore, lined by sandy beaches interspersed between mangrove swamps. Although the climate of this area is definitely tropical, there are pronounced seasonal temperature changes. Surface sea water temperatures near the coast decrease by about 9°C between February and July (Kenny, 1974). Further offshore near Keeper Reef, the change is only about 6°C. Temperature differences between the surface and the bottom are minor near the coast but can be as much as 4°C off Keeper Reef in February (austral summer). In July (austral winter), there were no temperature changes with depth near the reef (Kenchington, unpublished observations).

Rainfall is fairly low in the Townsville area (111 cm/year) but increases both to the North and to the South. Many rivers flow only in the wet season (January to March) and are tidal salt water in the dry season. In areas of higher rainfall, such as in Hinchinbrook channel, mangrove forests are very extensive. Near Townsville, mangroves form only a narrow band along the tidal creeks. Coastal waters are turbid and there are few rocky habitats found except around the mainland islands in the Palm Group, and Magnetic Island. Although there are coral reefs around these islands, much greater reef devel-

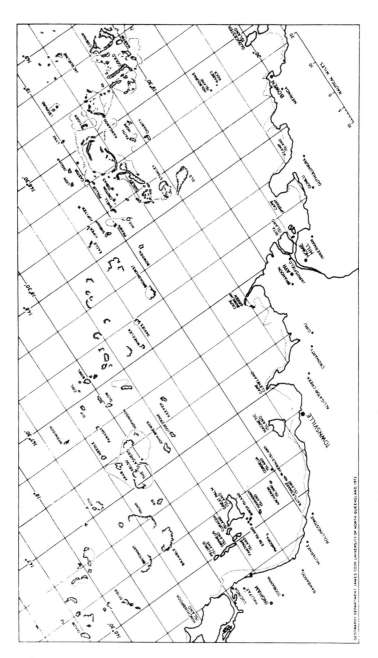

Figure 1.   A map of the general area of the tropical Queensland coast along which sea snakes were collected.

opment occurs in the "barrier" itself, 20 to 30 nautical miles (37–55 km) offshore. The barrier is, of course, not a single structure, but is composed of thousands of individual reefs. The sea floor between the barrier reef and the mainland is very flat and gently sloping to 25 fm on the inner side of the reef. Little coral development occurs in this plain-like area inside the reef, but it is here that most of the sea snakes are found. The barrier reef is poorly charted and little known biologically. However, it does appear, contrary to intuition, that the highly productive reef area harbors few snakes. There is one exception, Otter Reef, which has numerous snakes, but divers on the other reefs rarely report seeing any. As one continues seaward through the reef, individual reefs change in character (Maxwell, 1968) and finally disappear at the edge of the continental shelf (about 60 nautical miles, or 110 km, offshore). Very few reefs are found arising from water deeper than 40 fm in the barrier itself. However, at a greater distance from the coast (about 100 nautical miles or 185 km), complexes such as Flinders Reef rise from depths in excess of 500 fm. Almost nothing is known of these oceanic areas, primarily due to the difficulty and expense of reaching them. The purposes of this study were to determine the diversity and distribution of sea snakes along a seaward transect in tropical Queensland, and to attempt to identify factors which seem to be important in restricting certain species to specific habitats.

MATERIALS AND METHODS

The most economical way to collect sea snakes is to accompany local prawn trawlers or to pay them to bring in snakes. In the Townsville area, trawlers concentrate on the banana prawn, a shallow water (3–6 fm) daytime feeder, and the tiger prawn, a nocturnal feeder found in slightly deeper water (10–12 fm). Trawling is discontinued in the wet season (January to March), so that there is a seasonal and a depth discrimination to this collecting technique. The most serious disadvantage to obtaining snakes from prawn trawlers is that the ships often cover a large area of the coast and cannot be expected to give reliable information on capture localities. To provide some perspective on this problem, personal collections were made by dip net from a 15 foot aluminum boat fitted with a 40-hp outboard motor. On calm days, trips 20 to 35 nautical miles offshore could be safely made. Since sea snakes apparently do not spend a great deal of time at the surface, this technique did not yield a large number of specimens. Another means of collection was use of the research vessel of the James Cook University, the *James Kirby*. This ship was used on six occasions to systematically trawl in the coastal zone between the mainland and the barrier reef. Trawling in the vicinity of reefs was difficult since the net was sometimes torn. An otter trawl approximately 12 m wide and 3 m deep was towed at 3.7 km/h for 30 min at 48 different sites. These collecting sites were located in Bowling Green Bay, west of Magnetic Island, and along a transect between Townsville and Keeper Reef. Positions of each locality were determined by shoreline bearings taken by radar or by sextant. Occasional specimens were obtained when they were washed up on the beach, seined in bait nets, or caught by local hook and line fishermen. Dr. Harold Cogger identified the specimens and the entire collection has been deposited in the Australian Museum (Sydney).

RESULTS AND DISCUSSION

Species Diversity

The total number of specimens of each of the 11 species collected are listed in Table 1. Three species, *Lapemis, H. elegans,* and *A. laevis* represented almost 80% of the total. The former two were commonly caught in very shallow water over sandy bottoms, areas frequented by banana prawns. Fewer *A. laevis* were caught by prawn trawlers; those that were captured were found in tiger prawn habitat in 10–12 fm. Since 60% of the total snake sample came from commercial trawlers, shallow water species are disproportionately represented. This shows up very clearly if frequency of occurrence of the species is compared for each of the three main collecting techniques (Table 2). Prawn trawlers operating in shallow water caught mainly *Lapemis* and *H. elegans.* Use of the *James Kirby* in deeper water led to an increase in the catch of *A. laevis,* but a decline in *Lapemis* and especially in *H. elegans.* Most of the snakes caught by dip netting were *A. laevis.*

Density

A rough calculation of density can be derived from the known dimensions of the otter trawl (it fishes about 8 m wide), the speed of the ship (about 2 knots), the time (0.5 hr), and the number of snakes caught. A total of 27 snakes were caught in 48 trawls. This averages out to one snake/1.77 trawls and is equivalent to about one snake in each 160 m^2 of bottom. This figure is likely to be an overestimate of certain areas, and an underestimate of others, since 27 of the 48 trawls yielded no snakes at all, 15 had one snake each, and 6 had two snakes each. Thus it appears that bottom distribution is patchy and that certain habitats are more favorable than others. Nearshore distribution of fish and prawns seems to follow a similar pattern and there is some qualitative evidence that the snakes are found with concentrations of other forms of life. Prawn fishermen report that snakes are generally caught one or two at a time; on rare occasions dozens or even hundreds of snakes may be caught on the prawning grounds. Data from the *James Kirby* trawling in deeper water indicate that the distribution of sea snakes may be more homogeneous in

Table 1. Frequency of occurrence of the 11 species of sea snakes found along the tropical Queensland coast between 18° and 20° south latitude

Species	Code	Specimens caught	Percent of total
Lapemis hardwickii	L	73	41
Hydrophis elegans	HE	40	23
Aipysurus laevis	A	26	15
Aipysurus duboisii	AD	10	6
Disteira major	DM	7	4
Astrotia stokesii	AS	5	3
Aipysurus eydouxii	AE	4	2
Hydrophis ornatus	HO	3	2
Disteira kingii	DK	3	2
Hydrophis sp.	H	3	2
Enhydrina schistosa	E	2	1
Total		176	101

Table 2. Relative species frequencies for each group of snakes obtained by prawn trawler (108 snakes), trawling with the *James Kirby* (27 snakes) or dip netting (14 snakes)[a]

	Species as percent of each catch		
Species	Prawn trawler	*James Kirby* trawling	Dip netting
L	49	37	14
HE	30	7	0
A	9	15	57
DM	5	4	0
AD	1	15	14
AS	3	0	7
AE	3	0	0
HO	0	7	7
DK	1	4	0
H	0	11	0
Total	101	100	99

[a]Species are listed in order of decreasing pooled abundance. See Table 1 for a species key.

these areas. Fewer trawls come up empty and there is a substantial number with two snakes each. The latter case corresponds to a maximum density of about one snake per 90 m^2. The efficiency of the net in catching all those snakes of sufficient size to be trapped on the bottom is unlikely to be more than 25%. There must also be many smaller snakes that escape through the mesh and snakes swimming above the catching area of the net that never become entrapped. The greatest density in 15–30 fm waters can thus be estimated at 10 times the highest measured value of two snakes/trawl. This corresponds to an upper limit of about one snake per 30 m^2.

Distribution in Relation of Depth

The difference in species composition obtained from prawn trawlers and from trawling with the *James Kirby* (Table 2) suggested that sea snakes were restricted to certain depths. This can be examined more precisely by plotting the collecting localities on a hydrographic chart (Figure 2). The depths at which snakes were caught in Bowling Green Bay and north and west of Magnetic Island are also favored for prawn fishing. *Lapemis, H. elegans,* and *D. major* were all caught in 6 fm or less. One *D. major* was even caught several kilometers from the mouth of tidal Crocodile Creek (full strength sea water, 554 mM Cl at high tide). The two *E. schistosa* also came from tidal "creeks," one from Groper Creek near Ayr and one from the O'Connell River south of Proserpine (just to the south of the study area). *E. schistosa* may be restricted to saline creeks. Only one specimen of any other species was reported from a tidal creek, in this instance, *H. elegans* from Kalamia Creek just north of Ayr. *H. elegans* was also trawled as far out as the 10-fm line. The little file snake (*Acrochordus granulatus*) was also caught in coastal tidal creeks and in shallow nearshore waters. This snake (Acrochordidae) is not a member of the family Hydrophiidae (the true sea snakes), but has many similar habits (Dunson and Dunson, 1973).

Lapemis was found from very near the beach all the way out to 15 fm (Figures 2 and 3). In the McCluer Gulf, *Lapemis* was caught at the surface in water more than 30 fm deep. The failure to utilize areas of comparable depth in the Townsville area may be related to a difference in the benthic communities, rather than water depth itself.

Beyond the 10-fm line, but in less than 30 fm, four new species appeared: *H.* sp., *A. laevis, A. duboisii,* and *H. ornatus* (Figure 2). Only one species (*D. kingii*) seemed to be restricted to the 20 to 30 fm depth zone (one specimen only). The relationship between depth and species diversity is summarized in Table 3. These data are based on 41 specimens of eight different species collected by trawling with the *James Kirby* and by dip netting. Further sampling will be necessary to confirm the definite patterns of zonation

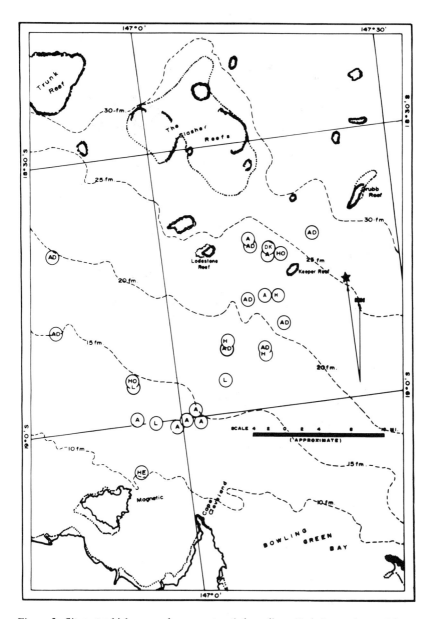

Figure 2. Sites at which sea snakes were trawled or dip netted along a transect from Townsville to the vicinity of Keeper and Lodestone Reefs. Scale in nautical miles. A, *Aipysurus laevis;* AD, *Aipysurus duboisii;* HE, *Hydrophis elegans;* DK, *Disteira kingii;* H, *Hydrophis* sp.; HO, *Hydrophis ornatus;* and L, *Lapemis hardwickii.*

Figure 3. The author with a large *Lapemis* trawled at 15 fm. This was the deepest record for this species near Townsville.

Table 3. The relationship between depth, diversity, and species composition in *James Kirby* trawl or dip net samples along a transect between Townsville and the Barrier Reef

		Species present[a]							
Depth (fm)	Total no. of species	DM	HE	L	H	A	AD	HO	DK
0–10	3	X	X	X					
10–20	5			X	X	X	X	X	
20–30	5				X	X	X	X	X

[a]See Table 1 for a species key.

observed. It does seem likely that the species are associated with particular bottom communities characteristic of various depths.

The collection of three *H.* sp. between 18 and 22 fm leaves little doubt that this is a resident species. Cogger (Chapter 4) considers it likely that these specimens represent a new species. He has other records from the Northern Territory, Torres Strait, and the Gulf of Papua. This species has a minute head, by far the smallest of any sea snake in this area (Figure 4).

Figure 4. *Hydrophis* sp. (on the right) and *A. duboisii* caught by the author in a trawl at 19 fm. Crinoids and sea cucumbers were numerous and the benthic fauna was diverse. Note the extremely small head of *Hydrophis* sp. This is the first record of this undescribed species from eastern Australia.

Habitat Preferences

In the immediate area of Townsville and along a transect to Keeper Reef, eight species of snakes were collected. Two additional species, *A. eydouxii* and *Astrotia,* were caught in localities nearby. Specimens of *A. eydouxii* came from the Cape Upstart and Dunk Island areas. *Astrotia* were trawled on the west side of Orpheus Island (near Lucinda), at Cairns, and one was caught while diving on Otter Reef. All five *Astrotia* were melanistic, in contrast to all of the other species in this area.

The relative insignificance of depth itself in directly controlling the distribution of sea snakes in coastal areas is illustrated by a single collection made on Otter Reef (northeast of Hinchinbrook Island). This platform reef has a back reef apron with depths of 2–7 fm. *A. laevis* (normally found in 10–30 fm water) were numerous in this shallow area, even though they were not present in water of similar depth on the adjacent coast. Extensive questioning of divers with local knowledge of most of the reefs in the area leads to the conclusion that, with rare exceptions, sea snakes are not found on reefs. Otter Reef is one of the exceptions and a major unanswered question concerns the apparent unsuitability of most reefs as sea snake habitat. Another important question deals with the benthic shore to reef faunal gradient and the precise ecological requirements of each snake species. Extensive information is needed on the biological zonation along a transect from the mainland to the outer edge of the continental shelf.

Aside from *A. eydouxii* and *Emydocephalus,* which feed only on fish eggs, most other sea snakes feed on fish or possibly some invertebrates. Since some snakes are very specialized feeders, prey distribution may be one of the most important factors in determining distribution.

A crude estimate of the changes in bottom fauna has been gained from the contents of each Otter trawl. Along the 6-fm line, no sessile invertebrates appear in the trawl; large catches of fish and prawns are occasionally made. Between 10 and 20 fm there is a great diversity of benthonic invertebrate and vertebrate life; crinoids, sea cucumbers, many fish, sea urchins, and scallops are caught (Figure 4). Nearer the reef, coral boulders appear on the flat, gently sloping bottom and there are areas where little else but scallops and perhaps a snake (*A. dubiosii*) are found (Figure 5). Little is known of the bottom quite close to the reefs since trawling is impossible.

At Ashmore Reef the depth gradient is fairly steep and about 11 species of sea snakes were found within a horizontal distance of less than 2 km. On the coast of Queensland near Townsville, 11 species were found over a 55-km distance from the coast. Habitat diversity is probably involved in this difference, as well as the tendency for species diversity in sea snakes to increase towards the Indonesian region. An additional factor is that several potential sea snake habitats in Queensland have not been adequately sampled. The reef

Figure 5. *A. duboisii* and associated benthic invertebrates (scallops, crinoids, sea cucumber) trawled in 23 fm near Keeper Reef. Note the preponderance of scallops and the low faunal diversity compared to Figure 4.

proper is difficult to census except by diving in as many areas as possible. The outer edge of the continental shelf and the outer reefs are little visited and very poorly known. The widespread yellow-bellied sea snake (*Pelamis*) is definitely not found inside the reef, so it must be present further offshore, if it breeds in this latitude at all. Another widespread genus (*Laticauda*), which is found commonly in New Guinea to the north and New Caledonia to the east, seems to be completely absent. These amphibious snakes prefer small offshore islands with crevices, caves or vegetation in which they can hide during the day. This type of habitat is not abundant along the tropical Queensland coast, but even on islands such as the Palm Group, which appear suitable, no *Laticauda* were ever found.

SUMMARY

Eleven species of sea snakes (*L. hardwickii, H. elegans, H. ornatus, Hydrophis* sp., *D. major, D. kingii, A. laevis, A. duboisii, A. eydouxii, A. stokesii, E. schistosa*) were collected along the Queensland coast between 18° and 20° south latitude. *H.* sp. is a new species which is to be described by H. Cogger. Several genera that were not collected are present, at least occasionally, along the sub-tropical and temperate coast to the south. These are *Pelamis, Emydo-*

cephalus, H. gracilis, Acalyptophis and *Laticauda* (a common genus in New Caledonia and New Guinea). A definite effect of depth on distribution was noted. *D. major, H. elegans* and *E. schistosa* are nearshore species found in less than 10 fm and, in some instances, actually in tidal creeks. Between 10 and 20 fm, five species were found, of which *L. hardwickii* and *A. laevis* were the most common representatives. Sea snakes continue to be commonly found at bottom depths of 30 fm, but are not often seen on reefs. A notable exception to this rule was Otter Reef, lying to the NE of Hinchinbrook Island. Along the back reef apron, sea snakes often were seen foraging on the bottom. Between the mainland and the reef, sampling was carried out mainly by otter trawling. The maximum observed density (two snakes caught per 0.5-h trawl) corresponds roughly to a bottom density of one snake per 90 m^2 (not corrected for efficiency of the net). The observed patchiness of sea snake distribution was quite striking, especially in the reef habitat. The relationship between preferred habitat type and depth needs further investigation, especially in little studied areas at the outer edge of the barrier reef.

ACKNOWLEDGMENTS

This study was carried out during the tenure of an Australian Queens Fellowship in Marine Science. Dr. C. Burdon-Jones and his staff at the James Cook University were very helpful. My special thanks are extended to the crews of the prawn trawlers *Mary Jay, Duroon, Fantine,* and *Dorothy Dune* and to Albert Hansen, Arnold Gaunt, and especially Alan Fitzmaurice, for taking me to Otter Reef. Supported by National Science Foundation Grants GB16653 and GA-35835.

REFERENCES

Dunson, W. A., and M. K. Dunson. 1973. Convergent evolution of sublingual salt glands in the marine file snake and the true sea snakes. J. Comp. Physiol. 86:193–208.

Kenny, R. 1974. Inshore surface sea temperatures at Townsville. Aust. J. Mar. Freshwat. Res. 25:1–5.

Maxwell, W. G. H. 1968. Atlas of the Great Barrier Reef. Elsevier Publishing Co., New York. 258 pp.

Smith, M. 1926. Monograph of the sea snakes (*Hydrophiidae*). British Museum of Natural History, Weldon & Wesley, London.

eight

Sea Snakes Found on Reefs in the Southern Coral Sea (Saumarez, Swains, Cato Island)

Harold Heatwole

Three localities in the southern Coral Sea have been observed underwater with sufficient intensity for some tentative generalizations to be made about local distribution and abundance of sea snakes. These are Cato Island, Saumarez Reef, and the Swain's Reefs (Figure 1). They are treated in turn.

CATO ISLAND

Cato Island, lying about 445 km east of Gladstone, Queensland (latitude 23° 15' S; longitude 155° 32' E), is a sparsely vegetated sand cay abundantly inhabited by nesting sea birds. A reef flat surrounds the island and impounds a lagoon of relatively calm water about 7–8 m deep. This lagoon has a white sand bottom interspersed with patches of coral, largely of the staghorn type, although there are also extensive areas of other types. The reef flat consists primarily of dead coral rubble reaching to, or nearly to, the surface.

Only four species were observed at this locality during the study period (May 1968). One was represented by a single, unidentified individual of the small-headed type, seen at the surface in deep water off the eastern part of

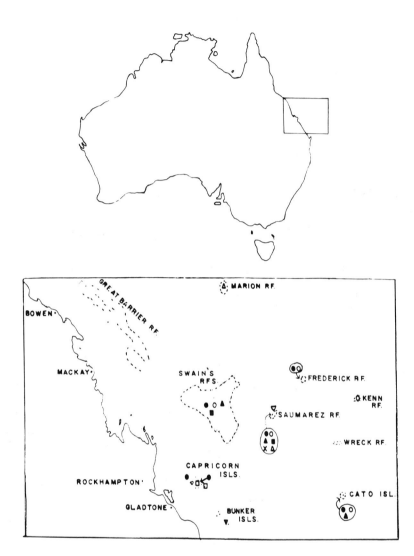

Figure 1. Map of Australia (upper) showing location of inset (lower) of the offshore islands in the Coral Sea at the southern end of the Great Barrier Reef. Dots indicate locality records of *Aipysurus laevis*, circles those of *Aipysurus duboisii*, closed squares those of *Astrotia stokesii*, x's those of *Microcephalophis gracilis*, closed triangles those of *Emydocephalus annulatus*, open squares those of *Pelamis platurus*, open triangles those of *Acalyptophis peronii*, closed up side down triangles those of *Disteria major*, and open up side down triangles those of *Disteira kingii*. Several symbols enclosed in a circle indicate that all the enclosed species were taken from the locality to which the arrow points.

the island. The other three species, *Aipysurus laevis, Aipysurus duboisii,* and *Emydocephalus annulatus,* were in the lagoon or on the reef flat, and were all very abundant.

There seemed to be some spatial separation of species (Figure 2). *A. laevis* was found only in the lagoon where water was more than 6 m deep; it was never found over the reef flat in shallow water, although a number of hours were spent there searching for snakes. By contrast, *A. duboisii* was primarily in shallower water. Only four individuals were observed in water deeper than 1.5 m, and these were at the edge of the reef flat where it dropped off into the lagoon. On a number of occasions, this species was observed foraging in water 2–15 cm deep. Sometimes the water was too shallow to permit active swimming and the snakes had to crawl in order to continue foraging.

E. annulatus occupied depths similar to those of *A. laevis,* with all observed individuals except two being found in the lagoon; one of the exceptions was over the reef flat and the other at its edge.

Thus there appear to be one shallow-water (reef flat) species and two species occurring at greater depths (lagoon, and probably also outside the lagoon in deeper water, although this habitat was not adequately checked). Even though the two lagoon species were not spatially separated, they are known to be ecologically segregated on the basis of food habits, *E. annulatus* feeding upon fish eggs and *A. laevis* preying upon fish (see Chapter 11). I examined the guts of 15 recently captured individuals of *E. annulatus* (various localities in the Coral Sea) and all, except one that was empty, had the stomach and/or intestine packed with sand, sometimes accompanied by fish eggs. Consequently, the patches of sand probably would be of utmost importance to this species as a feeding area, but would be of little significance to *A. laevis,* which preys on fish among the coral (Chapter 11). In a mosaic of the two substrates, such as occurs at Cato Lagoon, this subtle difference in habitat requirement would not be obvious, but it did become evident at Saumarez Reef (see below). At Cato, both species utilized similar resting sites during inactivity, primarily coiling among staghorn corals, less commonly among other types, and occasionally resting on the sandy bottom at the edge of corals. *A. duboisii* usually rested in dead coral rubble, perhaps because this was the most common substrate on the reef flat, rather than because it was preferred to live clumps. In other localities I have observed it resting in a variety of live corals.

SAUMAREZ REEF

Saumarez Reef lies about 325 km east of the Queensland coast (latitude 21° 52′ S; longitude 153° 40′ E). It is a narrow reef about 30 km long. The reef flat is emergent, or nearly so, at low water, dropping sharply into deep water

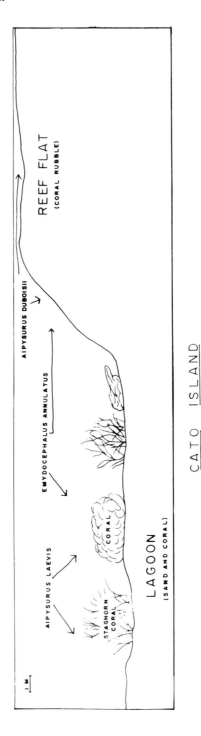

Figure 2.   Diagrammatic summary of the local distribution of sea snakes at Cato Island.

on the eastern side, but sloping more gradually on the western side. The area in which sea snakes were observed was just west of the southern end of the emergent reef, in relatively calm water 10–15 m in depth. The bottom was of white sand with scattered coral patches and large, flat-topped, steep-sided coral bommies reaching close to the surface. The observations summarized here were made primarily in July 1971, with supplementary ones in July 1968.

The fauna at Saumarez was richer than at Cato Island and consisted of *A. laevis, E. annulatus, A duboisii, Astrotia stokesii, Microcephalophis gracilis,* and *Acalpytophis peronii.* The first three were very abundant, the next two occasionally observed but much less common, and the last represented by only one individual, taken at the surface near a ship some distance from the reef.

Despite the different structure of the reef at Saumarez, the three common species showed spatial relations similar to those at Cato Island. *A. laevis* was at deeper levels (10–15 m in the study area but down to at least 30 m elsewhere on the reef), occurring either on coral patches or at the bases of bommies. *A. duboisii* was associated with the tops and upper edges of bommies, seldom occurring more than 5 m down the sides; only one was observed on the bottom (10 m depth). Depth measurements were made on 14 *A. duboisii* around several bommies; mean depth (excluding one animal first seen surfacing for air) was 3.5 m (range 1–5 m). At the same site the mean depth of nine *A. laevis* was 10.1 m (range 5–15 m).

The habitat differences between *A. laevis* and *E. annulatus* were more evident at Saumarez than at Cato, because of the more extensive areas of sand at the former site (Figure 3). Like *A. laevis, E. annulatus* occurred on the bottom rather than at the tops or sides of bommies. However, all *E. annulatus* observed foraging were doing so over the open sand plain or at the junction of sand and bommie, whereas *A. laevis* foraged among coral, only occasionally crossing large sandy areas and then only in moving to another coral patch; they did not stop to investigate the sand. *M. gracilis* foraged on the sand and, like *E. annulatus,* eats fish eggs (see MacLeish, 1971). Both of the latter were found together in the same places. Too few *M. gracilis* were observed to detect any possible ecological differences between it and *E. annulatus.* However, *M. gracilis* is probably eurytopic since Minton (1966) records it from a mangrove swamp near Karachi. *A. stokesii* was observed foraging among corals and swimming over sandy areas. Too few were observed to appreciate nuances of their local distribution or habitat preferences.

In summary, it appears that there is one shallow water species (*A. duboisii*) that is associated with the tops and sides of bommies and feeds on fish (see Chapter 11); a deeper water species that also forages among coral and eats fish (*A. laevis*); a third fish eater that forages widely (*A. stokesii*) and perhaps overlaps with *A. laevis*; and two sand-foraging fish egg eaters (*E.*

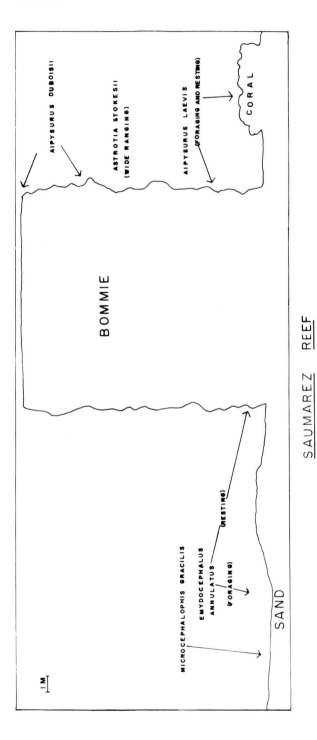

Figure 3.   Diagrammatic summary of the local distribution of sea snakes at Saumarez Reef.

annulatus and *M. gracilis*), both of which, of course, are associated with the bottom. The fauna is thus richer and ecologically more complex than at Cato Lagoon, although the three most abundant species are common to both areas and show similar ecological relations at both localities.

SWAIN'S REEFS

The Swain's Reefs lie about 240 km off the Queensland coast (center of reef complex, latitude 21° 45′ S, longitude 152° 12′ E). They make up a highly complex system of reefs about 160 km long by 80 km wide (Figure 1). Within this system there is an intricate interdigitation of patch reefs, bommies, open sandy areas, channels, reef flats, and sand cays. Local distribution of sea snakes is correspondingly mosaic in nature, some local areas having exceedingly dense snake populations; whereas, less than 1 km away, a reef may be entirely devoid of snakes, even though no gross differences are apparent to the investigator. In company with several other divers, I spent 2 days vainly searching for snakes in one area, only to move a short distance away and encounter one of the densest multi-species populations I've found anywhere. The factors influencing local distribution in the Swain's Reefs complex remain largely a mystery. However, intensive study of this area should be rewarding since it might provide a key to larger scale patterns in distribution. It is characteristic of sea snake distribution that, within the known geographic range of a species, some localities will support very dense populations, whereas other, seemingly similar ones have none.

The observations reported here were made on several visits to the Swain's Reefs (November 1967, June 1971, and October 1972). Sea snakes were found in abundance at four different localities on the reefs. No attempt was made to survey the reef as a whole; instead, effort was concentrated in making behavioral observations in those areas known to contain large numbers of snakes. The areas studied were (1) near Hixon Cay, (2) Sanctuary Reef, (3) Sweetlip Reef, and (4) Surprise Reef. Snakes were also seen at Zodiac Cay, but were not investigated in detail.

Species known from the Swain's Reefs are *A. laevis, E. annulatus, A. duboisii,* and *A. stokesii. A. laevis* is by far the most common species in these localities, the number observed being far greater than all other species combined. The more complex reef structure in the Swain's seemed to permit a greater proximity of individuals of the various species than the previously mentioned sites. However, observations on habitat preference and spatial relations of *A. laevis, E. annulatus,* and *A. duboisii* supported the conclusions based on studies at Cato Island and Saumarez, where depth gradients were steeper and/or habitat types more sharply delimited.

OTHER REEF LOCALITIES

No other localities in the area under consideration received as much attention as did those discussed above, although snakes were widely distributed throughout the area (Figure 1). On two occasions I found a live individual of *A. duboisii* active at the edge of a beach (Observatory Cay, Kenn Reef, and at an unnamed cay on Frederick Reef). I found a third one in a shallow, brackish pond in the center of North Reef Cay, Frederick Reef. These observations support the conclusion that *A. duboisii* inhabits very shallow water and may even come out on land briefly.

SUMMARY

It appears that the snake fauna of the reefs of the southern Coral Sea and southern Great Barrier Reef is dominated by three species that are locally abundant (*A. laevis, A. duboisii,* and *E. annulatus*). The local distribution of these three and other less common species on a particular reef is influenced by vertical (water depth) and horizontal (substrate type) factors. Among the common fish eaters are *A. duboisii,* a shallow water form; *A. laevis* from deeper water; and *Astrotia stokesii,* which appears to be quite eurytopic (see sections on Gulf of Carpentaria and Ashmore Reef), but overlapping in habitat to some extent with *A. laevis.* In addition there are two sand-foraging fish egg eaters, one abundant (*E. annulatus*) and the other rare (*M. gracilis*). Most of the observations were made in water of 15 m or less in depth. It is probable that in deeper water different species and/or ecological interactions might occur. For example, *Acalyptophis peronii* (probably an intermediate form; see Chapter 15) and *Disteira kingii* (one specimen from shallow water at Northeast Cay, Saumarez Reef) have also been recorded from the area under consideration, but not in sufficient numbers to evaluate habitat preferences or relations with other species.

The records from the Capricorn and Bunker groups may also be misleading. *Pelamis platurus* is a pelagic species which is frequently washed into coastal areas and onto beaches by storms, and records of it in the channel between Heron Island and Wistari Reef and near One Tree Island probably represent accidental occurrences. The records of *A. laevis* from Douglas Shoals and from between Heron and Wreck Islands are probably *bona fide.* However, populations of this species in the Capricorn group are very small in comparison to the reefs previously discussed. Many divers and snorkelers inhabit these waters year-round and yet only a few records are available (see Chapter 15). I cannot comment on the single record of *Disteira major* from nearby Fairfax Island, Bunker Group, since I have not dived in that region, and my only knowledge of the snake fauna there arises from my having examined a single specimen in the U.S. National Museum (Catalogue No. 160971).

REFERENCES

MacLeish, K. 1972. Diving with sea snakes. National Geographic 141:564–578.

Minton, S. A. Jr. 1966. A contribution to the herpetology of West Pakistan. Bull. Amer. Mus. Nat. Hist. 134:27–184.

nine

Coastal Sea Snakes of Subtropical Queensland Waters (23° to 28° South Latitude)

Colin J. Limpus

In subtropical Queensland waters, sea snakes are most often caught in prawn trawling operations in the estuaries, bays, and shallow continental shelf waters over mud or sand/mud substrata. Skindivers can expect to encounter sea snakes around the coral and rocky reefs along this coast. Apart from injured or sick snakes which occur as beach-washed specimens, they are rarely seen along the popular surfing beaches.

This discussion is restricted to the sea snake species of the coastal waters of Queensland from Gladstone (approx. 23° 30' S) to Gold Coast (28°S), the majority of the observations being made between 24° 30' and 28°S. See Figure 1 for localities. Included are a wide range of habitats, from mangrove-lined estuaries, shallow bays, sheltered and exposed offshore waters with substrata of sand and mud, to rocky and coral reefs. The southern end of the Great Barrier Reef is represented by the Capricorn and Bunker Groups. There is only minimal seine netting with small mesh nets in these waters, most net fishing being with otter trawls for prawns and scallops. A small amount of beam trawling for prawns occurs along the estuaries.

In presenting this information, I have relied not only on my own observations and collections made while sailing and skindiving widely in these waters during the past 5 years, but also on specimens and data provided by the fishermen in a number of the ports along the coast. This has been supplemented by data from the Queensland Museum's sea snake collection, which

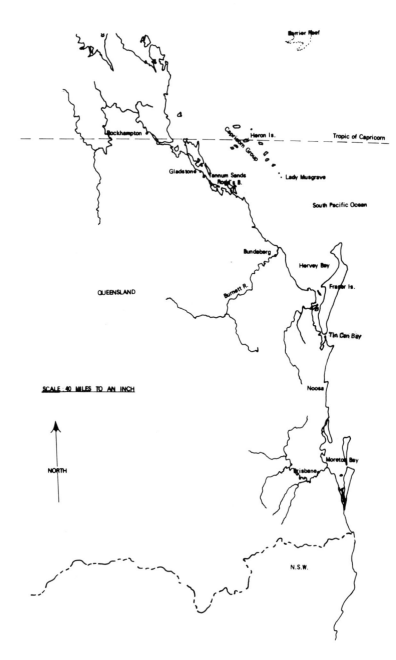

Figure 1. A map of southern Queensland, Australia, showing the collecting localities.

consisted principally of beach-washed specimens collected over some 60 years. In all, approximately 330 specimens were examined, and 12 species of sea snake have been recorded from these subtropical waters. The standard length measurement unless otherwise stated is the snout-vent length (SVL).

SPECIES

Aipysurus duboisii (Bavay)

Only four *A. duboisii* were available, all beach-washed specimens, snout-vent length (SVL) ranging from 78–106 cm. While these specimens were found as far south as Hervey Bay (25°S), they were probably waifs which drifted south from their preferred habitat. It is unlikely that *A. duboisii* breeds in subtropical Queensland waters.

Aipysurus eydouxii (Gray)

Over 100 specimens were examined. This species was common in estuaries and shallow bays from Fraser Island north and was most commonly associated with a mud substratum. In the Bundaberg area, *A. eydouxii* was most common in the Burnett River, where it regularly was seen surfacing for air around the wharves at the city, 12 km upstream from the mouth. In dry seasons, it has been seen by fishermen some 30 km upstream from the mouth. During the summer months, December and January, five to 10 specimens per night were regularly taken in the city reaches by the prawners using beam trawls. At other times, smaller catches occurred and prawners could work for perhaps a month without catching a snake. In spite of its abundance in the Burnett River, relatively few specimens were obtained over the sand/mud substrata off the coast from Bundaberg, where *Hydrophis elegans* was the most abundant species. Only one *A. eydouxii* was encountered during our skindiving over rock and coral bottoms. Specimens of what was reported as the most common species in Rodd's Bay (48 km south of Gladstone) were all *A. eydouxii,* collected in approximately 10 m of water over sand/mud substrata. Fishermen identified *A. eydouxii* from photographs as a common snake in Gladstone Harbour and in the straits between Fraser Island and the mainland.

In contrast with its abundance in beam trawl catches in the Burnett River, *A. eydouxii* was unknown to the fishermen using beam trawls in the Noosa River and associated estuarine lakes south of Fraser Island. Only one specimen in the collection was recorded south of 26°S.

In mid-April 1970, an exceptionally large aggregation of *A. eydouxii* was encountered on one night by a prawner on the Fairymead Reach of the

Burnett River, and "hundreds of sea snakes were caught, spilling out of the sorting tray and wriggling all over the deck." Other prawners several miles upstream in the city reaches on the same night caught no snakes. Fishermen who have fished these waters for some 40 years have no recollection of such a large number of snakes in one place before, and no similar aggregation was sighted in the Burnett River in the following 2 years. The function of this aggregation is unknown.

A. eydouxii appears to feed exclusively on benthic fish egg clumps (frequency of stomach contents examined: 38% clumps of fish eggs and sand/mud particles, 16% organic debris and sand/mud particles, 46% nil, N = 37). Young are born in May to August with SVL ranging 26–32 cm. Adults ranged up to 97.6 cm (total length = 114 cm).

Aipysurus laevis (Lacépède)

While only occasionally taken in prawn trawls over sand/mud substrata, *A. laevis* was the most common snake of the subtidal rocky coastline and coral reefs, where it was regularly encountered by skindivers from Hervey Bay northward. South of Hervey Bay, no records were obtained from numerous diving excursions in this area. Fifty specimens were examined.

Along the rocky coastline off Bundaberg, usually one *A. laevis* per hour was sighted by divers, but about 30 were seen there in 2 hrs of diving in February 1967. During this aggregation of *A. laevis,* the snakes were foraging independently among the coral, rocks, and algae in about 1–7 m of water. Only one snake was seen in the same area at the same time the following day. The species has been observed to at least 20-m depth on other reefs.

While *A. laevis* was common on the coastal rocky and coral reefs near Bundaberg and Gladstone, and on Polmaise Reef (westernmost reef of the Capricorn Group), it was rarely seen by skindivers on the coral reefs of the rest of the Capricorn and Bunker Groups of the Barrier Reef. Indeed, sea snakes of any species were uncommon in the waters of the Capricorn and Bunker Group, but *A. laevis* accounted for the majority of sightings.

A. laevis is an opportunistic, generalized, benthic feeding carnivore, probably taking most of its food while foraging beneath the boulders and coral among which it was most frequently found. Of 18 stomach contents specifically examined, the following occurred with the indicated frequency: prawns 3 times, crabs 4 times, fish 4 times, fish egg mass 1 time, nil 6 times. No one type of fish was favored. Coral trout (*Plectropomus maculatus,* Fam. Serranidae), tusk fish (*Choerodon sp.,* Fam. Labridae), and juvenile diamond trevally (*Alectis indica,* Fam. Carangidae) were among the fish identified. Fishermen in Hervey Bay have identified *A. laevis* as having been caught on lines baited with polychaete worms and the Decapod crustacean *Callianassa* sp. What appeared to be courting pairs of this species were often reported by skindivers in May and June. No births have been recorded for the area, but females carrying advanced embryos were caught between January and May. SVL of captured specimens ranged from 42–122 cm. Longest total length was 144 cm.

Emydocephalus annulatus (Krefft)

Only one specimen of *E. annulatus* is known from this area: a beach-washed melanistic female, SVL 68.5 cm, not pregnant. This specimen, found on the beach near Noosa, was probably a waif, and the paucity of data for this species suggests that it is an uncommon species in subtropical Queensland waters.

Acalyptophis peronii (Dumeril)

The two specimens of *A. peronii* known from this area were beach-washed specimens, SVL 70 and 101 cm, from near Noosa and Moreton Bay, respectively. Like *E. annulatus* above, they were probably carried into the area by currents from the north and the species can be regarded as uncommon in subtropical Queensland waters.

Astrotia stokesii (Gray)

Of four specimens examined, collection data were available for three. One was a beach-washed specimen from just south of Moreton Bay, while the other two were trawled off a sand subtratum in 10 m of water off Tannum Sands, and north of Bundaberg respectively. The latter specimen, a pregnant female with an embryo 12.5 cm in length, was collected in January. The specimen from Tannum Sands was collected in May. If *A. stokesii* is one of the species of sea snakes breeding in subtropical Queensland waters, it is present in low density.

A. *stokesii* can be regarded as a benthic feeding piscivore. Three specimens had eaten fish, one of which was identified as a banded frogfish (*Halophryne diemensis*, Fam. Batrachoididae).

Enhydrina schistosa (Daudin)

While *E. schistosa* was found to be common in areas to the north, only two were found in subtropical Queensland waters, both beach-washed adult male specimens. *E. schistosa* would appear to be uncommon in these subtropical waters, the above specimens probably being waifs.

In Repulse Bay (20.5°S) to the north, *E. schistosa* was commonly taken in seine netting over shallow mud and sand substrata. Two of three Repulse

Bay specimens examined for stomach content contained catfish (*Hexane-matichthyes* sp., Fam. Tachysuridae). *E. schistosa* would appear also to be a benthic feeding piscivore.

Hydrophis elegans (Gray)

H. elegans was the most common species of sea snake taken in otter trawls over the sand to sand/mud substrata off shore from Bundaberg south. Though common in the trawling catches, it was rarely seen on the surface. Most of the trawling occurred in 10–35 m depth.

The frequency of capture of *H. elegans* in these prawning nets decreased on moving south from Bundaberg to Tin Can Bay and Moreton Bay. Whereas up to a dozen large *H. elegans* per 4-day trip were reported by Bundaberg based trawlers, prawners operating out of Moreton Bay expect to catch less than 10 per year. Only one *H. elegans* was observed while skindiving. It was foraging on a sand substratum in less than 2-m depth, just outside the breaker line of a surfing beach. Several were identified surfacing for air and then diving in water approximately 80 m deep and 32 km offshore from Bundaberg. One was also brought up in a prawn trawl off Moreton Bay from approximately 80 m. The fisherman concerned was confident that the snake had been trawled on the bottom.

H. elegans was also taken in estuaries, some being captured at least 12 km upstream from the mouth of the Burnett River. Each December and January, one or two per week were taken in the beam trawls operating along the intertidal banks of the Bundaberg reaches of the Burnett River. At other times of the year, this species was rarely caught in that part of the river. In the Noosa estuary, 200 km to the south, similar beam trawling occurs and *H. elegans* was a rare catch at any time.

Of seven stomach contents examined, three were empty and four contained fish remains. The prey species identified were whiting (*Sillago* sp., Fam. Sillaginidae), the eel-like catfish (*Euristmus* sp., Fam Plotosidae), and eel (*Leiuranus semicinctus*, Fam. Ophicthyidae). This small headed snake is a benthic feeding piscivore, preferring elongated fish species.

Live young were born from March to May (five litters observed) and SVL ranged from 38.6–49.1 cm. All other *H. elegans* specimens ranged from 92–196 cm, the largest being a female that produced a litter of 16, and she measured a total length of 211 cm.

Disteira kingii (Boulenger)

Though apparently uncommon in subtropical Queensland waters, uncon-firmed reports indicate that *D. kingii* may be common and breeding some 80 km north of Gladstone. Some were taken in prawn trawls off Gladstone and a very small specimen (SVL 46.3 cm) was found on the beach there. Mature, beach-washed specimens were found near Bundaberg and as far south as Moreton Bay. *D. kingii* would appear to be a breeding species in the northern part of subtropical Queensland waters, but probably should be regarded as a tropical species. No stomach contents were available from the seven specimens examined. SVL ranged from 46–173 cm. The total length of the largest specimen was 186 cm.

Disteira major (Shaw)

D. major was at times a common species off Bundaberg and in Hervey Bay. It has been recorded occasionally in Moreton Bay. Off Bundaberg, the trawled specimens were taken on a sand/mud substratum in 10 m of water. The only specimen observed while skindiving was seen on a mud substratum in about 3 m depth. Of 20 specimens examined from Fraser Island to Bundaberg, all were obtained from August to January, and some pregnant females were included. The nine specimens from south of Fraser Island were all beach-washed. SVL of all specimens ranged from 84–137 cm. No direct evidence of breeding by *D. major* in subtropical Queensland waters was obtained. However, the regularity with which this species can be taken off Bundaberg towards the end of each year, and the fact that it is fourth in abundance in the collection of species on which this study is based, would justify the inclusion of *D. major* in the main sea snake fauna of subtropical Queensland waters.

Lapemis hardwickii (Gray)

Although a common species from coastal areas off Mackay to Townsville to the north of the study area, only five specimens were obtained from subtropical waters; all from prawn trawling on a sand substratum in 10 m depth off Tannum Sands. SVL ranged from 70–101 cm, and neither of the two females was pregnant. The one stomach content examined was unidentifiable fish remains. The complete absence of this species from a collection of over 300 specimens of sea snakes from Bundaberg south indicates that *L. hardwickii* has a very restricted distribution in subtropical Queensland.

Pelamis platurus (Linnaeus)

No *Pelamis* were recorded from any of the netting activity and none were observed while skindiving. All used in collection data were collected as beach-washed specimens, with SVL ranging from 32–91 cm, and were uniformly distributed along the coast. Kropach (1971) shows *Pelamis* to be a pelagic species frequenting surface waters. The complete absence of sightings in surface waters and in bottom-sampled collections suggests that *Pelamis* is not abundant in the coastal waters of subtropical Queensland. Although sufficient data are not yet available, I have the impression that this species is most frequently found following strong onshore winds. However, the presence of the very small specimens indicates that they may not have been drifting for long. Presumably, if *Pelamis* is not breeding in subtropical Queensland waters, it is breeding not far distant.

DISCUSSION

Sea snakes are regularly encountered in a number of habitats from approximately 26°S northward to Tin Can Bay. South of Tin Can Bay they were infrequently encountered; the majority recorded were beach-washed specimens. *A. eydouxii. A. laevis* and *H. elegans* decrease greatly in abundance south of the Hervey Bay–Tin Can Bay waters. However, other species appear to have the southern limit of their main distribution to the north of Gladstone or near by (approx. 23° 30'S), e.g., *D. kingii, Lapemis hardwickii.* The catches by prawn fishermen illustrate the decreasing abundance of sea snakes with increasing latitude. Prawners working out of Bundaberg expect to catch several hundred sea snakes annually; prawners working out of Tin Can Bay expect to catch 50–100 annually; and those prawning from Moreton Bay expect to catch less than 10 annually. The sea snake catch, then, in otter trawls offshore from Bundaberg was usually 0–3 per day but catches of more than 10 per day occurred, the largest offshore catches being expected in August to October, while the largest Burnett River catches occurred in December and January. The seasonal variation in abundance of snakes such as *A. eydouxii, H. elegans,* and *D. major* in the Bundaberg area is probably typical of all species for these waters. Although no quantitative study of the factors associated with sea snake abundance was made, it would appear that sea snakes are only regularly taken in the otter and beam trawls when there are reasonable catches of prawns. The fishermen often say that when there are no prawns there will be no snakes, even if there are large catches of fish. Yet the most frequently caught species, *H. elegans* and *A. eydouxii,* do not seem to feed on prawns. No snakes were obtained from the scallop fishing off Bundaberg. Scallops are trawled in deeper water than prawns, with larger mesh nets. The mesh size is the most likely reason for lack of snakes, but a lower abundance of sea snakes in deeper water must not be ruled out.

Of the 12 species, only three exist in large numbers and are definitely breeding in these subtropical waters, at least as far south as 26°S. These are *A. eydouxii, A. laevis,* and *H. elegans.* Two other species, *A. stokesii* and *D. major,* also could be breeding here. The southern end of the main distribution of *D. kingii* and *L. hardwickii* appears to extend just into subtropical waters. Until more data are available, the remaining five species, *A. duboisii, E. annulatus, A. peronii, E. schistosa* and *P. platurus,* are best regarded not as regular inhabitants of subtropical Queensland waters, but as only isolated specimens being carried in on currents from the north.

H. ocellata (=*H. ornatus*) was recorded as common in the Burnett River, Bundaberg, by Gray (1930), but it was not found in my collection of some 200 sea snakes from the Bundaberg coast and Burnett River.

Kinghorn (1956) records seven species as occurring in the temperate waters of New South Wales to Tasmania. Four of these, *Laticauda laticaudata, L. colubrina, Hydrophis fasciatus,* and *H. ornatus,* were not recorded during this survey of subtropical Queensland waters. None of these species recorded from waters south of Queensland is indicated to be common there. There is thus, in the sea snake fauna, not only decreasing abundance but also decreasing diversity with increasing latitude.

In the Bundaberg area, the three common species which occur all the year round can be separated fairly well into different niches. *A. eydouxii* is a benthic fish-egg-eating species, usually associated with the mud substratum of the estuary and the area immediately off the mouth of the river. *A. laevis* is a generalized bottom-feeding carnivore, usually associated with coral or rocky reefs. *H. elegans* is a bottom-feeding piscivore favoring elongated fish species. It is usually found associated with offshore sand/mud substrata, but does enter estuarine areas.

The niches occupied by the other species are not yet clear, but all except *P. platurus* can be regarded as bottom feeders. If they do occupy the same habitat, piscivorous species such as *A. stokesii* and *L. hardwickii* should utilize different fish species from those preferred by the smaller headed *H. elegans*. The dentition of *A. duboisii* resembles closely that of *A. eydouxii* in smallness and orientation of fangs and maxillary teeth (Limpus, unpublished). *A. eydouxii* is a fish-egg eater as is *E. annulatus* (Voris, 1966), which has even more reduced dentition. The similarity in dentition suggests *A. duboisii* may also be an egg-eating species, presumably from a different habitat, such as the coral reefs further north. Species such as *H. elegans* and *D. kingii,* which appear to be similar in habitat and food preferences, are probably being kept apart in this area by different climatic requirements.

CONCLUSIONS

1. Twelve species of sea snakes are recorded from subtropical Queensland waters. The diversity and abundance of the sea snake fauna decrease with increasing latitude.

2. *A. eydouxii, A. laevis,* and *H. elegans* are the most common, each in its

preferred habitat over mud, rocky and coral reefs, and offshore sand/mud substrata respectively.

3. *A. eydouxii* feeds exclusively on benthic fish egg clumps, while *A. laevis* is an opportunistic, generalized benthic feeding carnivore. *H. elegans* feeds on elongated benthic fish.

4. The three above, together with *D. major* and *A. stokesii*, are probably the only species breeding in these waters, although the breeding distributions of *D. kingii* and *L. hardwickii* may extend just into subtropical waters.

5. *A. duboisii, E. annulatus, A. peronii, E. schistosa,* and *P. platurus* occur infrequently, probably drifting in on currents from the north.

ACKNOWLEDGMENTS

The information presented here was collected as part of an investigation of the toxicology of subtropical Queensland sea snakes for an M.Sc. thesis, in preparation, University of Queensland. I thank Dr. Endean for his encouragement and advice. I am indebted to M. Helmuth, E. Modrow, V. Langford, and the other fishermen who collected so many specimens for me. I thank Miss J. Covacevich, Curator of Reptiles, Queensland Museum, for the use of the Museum's collection.

REFERENCES

Gray, M. E. 1930. Notes on sea snakes. Aust. Nat. 8:88.

Kinghorn, J. R. 1956. The Snakes of Australia. Angus and Robertson, Sydney.

Kropach, C. 1971. Sea snake (*Pelamis platurus*) aggregations on slicks in Panama. Herpetologica. 27(2):131–135.

Voris, H. K. 1966. Fish eggs as the apparent sole food item for a genus of sea snake, *Emydocephalus* (Krefft). Ecology. 47:152–153.

PELAMIS

ten

The Yellow-bellied Sea Snake, Pelamis, in the Eastern Pacific

Chaim Kropach

Pelamis platurus, the only truly pelagic sea snake, is of great interest to the zoogeographer and ecologist. It is the only species found well beyond the Indo-Malayan and Australian centers of distribution of the sea snakes, and the only one which has reached the eastern Pacific. This chapter deals with several aspects of the biology and natural history of *Pelamis* in the Eastern Pacific, and is a result of my field study in that area, particularly in the Gulf of Panama, during 1969–1970.

DISTRIBUTION

The Range of *Pelamis* in the Eastern Pacific

From writers such as G. Fernandez de Ovideo y Valdes in 1519 and Rananau de Lussan in 1693, we know that the occurrence of *Pelamis* in the Eastern Pacific predates the appearance of white men in this region, and excludes the possibility of human transport (Taylor, 1953). However, the absence of *Pelamis* from the Caribbean testifies to a post-Isthmian and, therefore, a recent colonization of the Eastern Pacific, a colonization which has been taking place in the past 4 million years. The means of colonization are not known, but, as is customary among zoogeographers, it may be inferred from what is known today of its biology. This reveals a close association with surface currents. It is suggested (Kropach, 1973) that *Pelamis* migrated to the

Table 1. The distribution of *Pelamis* in the eastern Pacific

Locality	Reference
Clipperton Island	Sachet, 1962
Galapagos Islands[a]	Krefft, 1953
Ecuadorian Coast	Boulenger, 1890; Orces, 1948; Peters, 1960; Klawe, 1964
Colombia	Daniel, 1955
Panama	
Gulf of Panama	Cope, 1887; Smith, 1935; Smith, 1958
Chiriqui Coast	Ambrose, 1956
Bahia Honda	Myers, 1945
Costa Rica	Strauch, 1974; Cope, 1887; Taylor, 1951
Nicaragua	Villa, 1962
Guatemala	Rodas, 1938
Mexico	
Acapulco, Guerrero	Dunson and Ehlert, 1971
Chiapas	Toro and Smith, 1956
Salina Cruz, Oaxaca	Smith, 1926; Dunson and Ehlert, 1971
Michoacán	Duellman, 1961
Tres Marias	Zweifel, 1960
Banderas Bay	Pickwell, 1971
Sinaloa	Hardy and McDiarmid, 1969
Guaymas	Cope, 1887
Los Angeles Bay (Gulf of California)	Shaw, 1961
San Felipe (Gulf of California)	Pickwell (pers. comm.)

[a]Waifs only; see Dunson and Ehlert (1971).

eastern Pacific via the Equatorial Countercurrent of the Pacific Ocean, and that this migration may still be taking place. This current is known for its steadiness and speed, and it averages 50 cm/sec most of the year; only in March and April does the speed drop to 20 cm/sec or less (Neumann and Pierson, 1966). An alternative but unlikely hypothesis of colonization by *Pelamis* of the eastern Pacific was proposed by Neill (1964). It rejects the possibility of *Pelamis* crossing open ocean, and suggests colonization during a past warm climate, when the snakes could have migrated through the shallow waters south of the Bering Bridge, and from there, south.

The distribution of *Pelamis* in the eastern Pacific is well documented from Ecuador to the Gulf of California (Table 1). The southern and northern limits seem to be determined mainly by the presence of cold surface waters (Graham et al., 1971; Dunson and Ehlert, 1971). Taylor's reference (1951) to *Pelamis* from Chile is interesting, but is not supported by others or by records from Peru. It is questionable that *Pelamis* could live in the cold coastal waters of Peru and Chile, which do not exceed 22°C and may be as cold as 15°C (Sverdrup et al., 1942). The actual southern limit probably is near the Gulf of Guayaquil at 3–5°S. *Pelamis* are not resident in the Galápagos area (Dunson and Ehlert, 1971). In the north, records of *Pelamis* are known from the Gulf of California, as far north as San Felipe (Pickwell, pers. comm.). Shaw (1961) reported the finding of *Pelamis* in Los Angeles Bay, approximately 30°N Lat., 114°W Long., and its subsequent preservation in a bottle of tequila. Recently there have been several occurrences of *Pelamis* along the coast of California, where they must have been swept by currents (Pickwell, pers. comm.). One well-publicized case was that of *Pelamis* washed onto a San Clemente beach (Anon., 1972). These northern records obviously represent a waif distribution which does not reflect the breeding range of the species. The northernmost locality in the Eastern Pacific where a *Pelamis* population is known to exist and breed is Bahia Banderas, Mexico (Pickwell, pers. comm.; *Alpha Helix* records, 1970).

Distribution in the Gulf of Panama

The notion that *Pelamis* is a deep-water species which does not come close to shore is widespread, both among the lay public and biologists. It was used in the sea level canal controversy as an argument that sea snakes would not be able to reach the Caribbean Sea when the new canal is constructed (e.g., Miami Herald, June 5, 1970). The distribution of *Pelamis* in the Gulf of Panama is patchy and unpredictable with respect to locality and time. Snakes in large numbers can be observed in places varying in depth and distance from the shore. These snake groupings are met with the year around, and are not seasonal (Kropach, 1973). They occur in shallow waters of 10 m or less, among the Pearl Islands, or close to the mainland, at the southern entrance to the Canal, or within several hundred yards of Panama City. Snakes, in fact, are often washed up on local beaches because of their occurrence near the shore.

If one were to look for a single, most important factor in determining the distribution of sea snakes in the Gulf of Panama, this factor would have to be the ocean slick, a zone of convergence of currents. Upwelling and cooling of water in the Gulf of Panama during the dry season may influence the distribution of *Pelamis* in this area, but this was not apparent during the 1970 season. Duellman (1961) concluded that in Michoacán, Mexico, the abundance of *Pelamis* depended on the season. There was no evidence for such seasonal effect on the distribution or abundance of *Pelamis* in the Gulf of Panama, where the sole factor seemed to be the surface currents. Perhaps the longshore surface currents in Mexico have seasonal patterns, thus giving *Pelamis* a seasonal distribution.

THE HABITAT OF *PELAMIS* IN THE GULF OF PANAMA

Slicks as Surface Phenomena

Sea snakes were commonly found in large aggregations along ocean slicks, usually accompanied by an impressive faunal concentration. Slicks are smooth, narrow, long lines on the ocean surface (see Figure 1). They have been known to men traveling on the high seas for a long time, and were recorded in Captain James Cook's account of his first voyage around the world. Often various floating objects, vegetation, and debris accumulate along slicks, hence the commonly used term "drift lines." Many different factors are involved in the formation of surface lines which are referred to as slicks, drift lines, streaks, wind rows, or fronts (Dietz and LaFond, 1950; Langmuir, 1938; Assaf et al., 1971; Ewing, 1950a, b; Cromwell and Reid, 1956; Amos et al., 1972). All these surface features share the essential property of marking the places where surface currents converge. Therefore, the biological effect of bringing together oceanic fauna is similar, and differences are mainly of size and duration. Fronts are sometimes permanent oceanic features of great magnitude, while slicks have a more localized effect of limited duration, although repetitive.

Figure 1. A narrow slick with foam compacted into sheets and without flotsam.

Association of *Pelamis* with Slicks

The common occurrence of *Pelamis* in groups along slicks was noted early in my study (Kropach, 1971) and by Dunson and Ehlert (1971). Snake aggregations (Allee, 1931) ranged in size from several individuals (probably when an aggregation was just beginning to build up) to thousands of snakes. They included adult and juvenile *Pelamis*. These groupings of snakes were not seasonal although calm weather favored their formation. The most prominent drift lines usually occurred after heavy rains, when debris washed out from rivers and eventually collected along slicks. However, snakes were regularly observed along slicks without drifting objects. Some of the aggregations appeared overnight, indicating that aggregation may occur rapidly. Drifting objects placed on either side of a slick moved toward it at varying speeds (3–25 cm/sec).

Dietz and LaFond (1950) found the waters of slicks to be warmer than those of the surroundings, but my own repeated measurements of surface temperatures on either side of and within slicks showed no clear trend. Most of the slicks observed had no temperature differences. On three occasions the slick was warmer than the waters beside it by 0.1–0.2°C. Twice the slick was found to be cooler than the water on one of its sides by 0.2 and 0.6°C. Finally, on two occasions larger differences between the two sides were observed, one of 1.0°C and the other of 3.0°C. In both cases, the appearance of the slicks (as lines separating water masses of different colors, great accumulations of flotsam, and agitated water at the line of convergence) indicated oceanic fronts as described by Cromwell and Reid (1956) and Amos et al. (1972). In the front described by Beebe (1926), the temperature difference between the two sides was 4°C. Dunson and Ehlert (1971) observed no differences in temperature or salinity across three fronts in Mexico and Costa Rica.

No apparent correlation between the existence of a temperature gradient (or temperature discontinuity) and the presence of snakes on a slick could be established. Therefore, attraction of the snakes to slicks by some thermal gradient should be ruled out. Similarly, ample evidence from the field and laboratory excludes attraction to floating wood or debris. The possibility that the snakes find the slicks through their random search for food and stay on them, thus collecting into a large aggregation, is unlikely since *Pelamis* swim very little at the surface. The mechanism most likely to be responsible for the gathering of snakes into large groupings is surface currents. Often *Pelamis* were observed being swept along by surface currents in the Gulf of Panama. Many authors have also noted that snakes are swept by currents onto beaches.

The activities of *Pelamis* while the snakes were on a slick were observed from a boat whenever aggregations were encountered. The main activity of

Pelamis while on a slick was feeding, which took place at the surface and at a depth of 1–6 feet. Many snakes were followed to 60 feet. Occasionally snakes were seen to go through sequences of knotting. Snakes were not seen shedding at sea, but a number of shed snake skins were seen in some of the aggregations. Even when much driftwood was present, not once was a snake seen to bask on a floating log or otherwise to be interested in it. No matings were witnessed in the aggregations, although such situations would present excellent opportunity for reproductive activity. No other social interaction among the snakes was apparent. Interaction with other species was restricted to feeding. Predation on *Pelamis* was never observed in spite of the presence of large marine predators among slicks.

Although most of these observations were made in the Gulf of Panama, they seem to describe correctly the behavior of *Pelamis* in other parts of the Eastern Pacific (Dunson and Ehlert, 1971; pers. obs.). It is quite astonishing that the association of *Pelamis* with slicks had not been noted earlier. Several authors (Klauber, 1935; Myers, 1945; Paulson, 1967), although describing *Pelamis* in slick conditions, apparently failed to realize its association with this environmental condition. One explanation is that in open oceanic water slicks may be more difficult to detect, since there might be too little material for "drift lines," as compared with an enclosed gulf into which many rivers drain and where productivity is high. Sea snakes aggregations have been known, however, for a long time (Cantor, 1841). The possibility that they are not a phenomenon restricted to *Pelamis* is suggested by the widely-quoted account of a huge aggregation of the sea snake *Astrotia stokesii* in the Indian Ocean (Lowe, 1932).

Biological Significance of Slicks

The organisms observed on slicks represent a considerable sample of the marine fauna of the Eastern Pacific. These include dense concentrations of planktonic organisms and fishes of all sizes. Porpoises, sea turtles, and elasmobranchs also were observed along slicks commonly, and marine birds in large flocks usually were feeding on the surface. These slicks have been known among local fishermen for a long time as good fishing grounds. Similarly rich in fauna were the "fronts" seen by Beebe (1926) and Amos et al. (1972). To Japanese fishermen they are known as "Siome" (Uda, 1938). The faunal buildups along a convergence start with the accumulation of organic molecules (Dietz and LaFond, 1950) and plankton. Weakly swimming organisms such as *Pelamis* are carried by currents in the same manner that land-based flotsam is brought there. The more powerful swimmers are able to reach these food-rich zones actively. The role that convergences play in oceanic ecology is therefore important. They provide a mechanism by which organic matter and nutrients are gathered, around which faunal concentrations build up and a food web is established. This may be of particular importance in areas of poor productivity.

The advantages that *Pelamis* derives from congregating on slicks are twofold. First, this facilitates the search for food, which consists of small fish (Klawe, 1964; pers. obs.). On slicks the chance of encountering a school of fish is greatly increased, and snakes were seen to feed there on a variety of fish (Hunter and Mitchell, 1967; pers. obs.). Second, in an aggregation, the finding of a mate is easier than by random search in open waters. There may be several disadvantages in coming to slicks. The first is increased competition with other snakes and other marine organisms; but in view of the super-abundance of food, this must be of minor importance. Second, slicks probably provide a situation in which harmful commensals can more easily find *Pelamis* and settle on them. The third theoretical disadvantage is the presence of potential predators. Predation, however, is minimized by *Pelamis'* anti-predator adaptations.

MOVEMENT AND RANGE

Locomotion

Pelamis swims by producing alternating lateral undulations. In forward swimming those lateral undulations progress caudad, thus exerting pressure posteriolaterally on the surrounding medium. In this respect, the movement of *Pelamis* is similar to that of many terrestrial snakes. *Pelamis* also exhibits characteristic backward swimming. Although the snakes are usually observed swimming slowly or lying motionless at the surface, rapid movement, reaching 1 m/sec, can be generated in the manner described above. Such speeds were maintained, however, for short distances only. Bursts of rapid swimming were observed when the snakes were disturbed, during dives, and while feeding. The snakes were not seen to swim against currents and were not able to overcome near-shore waves.

Several morphological adaptations exhibited by *Pelamis* enable this species to move in the water with greater ease than other species of snakes. The snakes are laterally compressed and thus are able to present a large lateral surface area to the surrounding medium. To increase this effect, the lower part of the body is often compressed in the form of a keel. The lateral compression of the body is brought about, in part, by the lengthening of the neural and haemal spines of the vertebrae. Also, the absence of the ventral plates and true ventral surface gives the snake a noticeably compressed shape. Some other vertebral modifications in sea snakes are discussed by Johnson (1955). The thin, flat tail aids in swimming, but it lacks the skeletal support for becoming a propulsion organ such as a fin. The head is small, and this, too, helps in swimming. In rapid swimming, the snakes often raise the head above the water in the same manner that water snakes (*Natrix*) do in rapid movement. Wall (1921) thought that this was the snakes' way of "looking around," but this behavior may have hydrodynamic significance.

On land, *Pelamis* is completely helpless, and cannot progress in spite of vigorous attempts to do so. This is another indication that the snake progresses in water by exerting force on the medium laterally. This snake cannot use the irregularities of a flat surface as points where pressure can be applied by ventral plates (as some terrestrial snakes do). In fact, not having a flattened ventral surface causes *Pelamis* to roll laterally when on land.

Range

During the period of the study, 961 snakes were marked and released in the Gulf of Panama. The marking program was initiated in order to arrive at population-size estimates and to obtain data on the activity range of *Pelamis;* that is, the range covered by the snakes in their daily activities. It was also hoped that it would be possible to discover whether movement of *Pelamis* into and out of the Gulf took place. The snakes were marked by notching their tails. The technique (Kropach, 1973) did not cause differential mortality in the snakes. Of the marked snakes, one was recaptured almost a year after release in the Gulf of Panama north of the release point. Three others were subsequently found 13 to 14 months later off Mexico by Pickwell.

There may be an outward movement of snakes from the Gulf. Surface currents move into the Gulf from the southeast, describe a counterclockwise arc, and move out in the southwest (Hydrographic Office, Publ. 106, 1963). There is a possibility that the snakes are continuously swept out of the Gulf, while new individuals are brought in by currents. However, the large number of snakes in the Gulf and their unpredictable location make the testing of this hypothesis very difficult.

FOOD HABITS

Feeding Behavior

Pelamis was fed in the laboratory by shaking a freshly killed fish in front of the snake. The snake would then bite at the fish and maneuver it into a position where it could be swallowed head first. Feeding in *Pelamis* was also elicited by rubbing the food fish on the ventral or rostral surfaces of the snake, on the sides of the jaws, or on the anterior portion of the trunk. The same method was also used by Shaw (1962). Two typical approaches to food capture were exhibited. One type of response is a slight bending of the head and a slow movement toward the source of vibrations, sometimes with an open mouth; capture then follows in a rapid sideways lunge. A second common response to the presence of fish or to tactile stimulation is backward swimming, which is often a component of the feeding sequence. This characteristic backward movement is observed either as a distinct action of alertness, followed by a pause, and then a rapid lunge at the food, or as a part of a continuous movement in which the food capture follows without a pause. *Pelamis* showed little ability to capture a single freely swimming fish in a tank, nor was it able to retrieve a fish it had dropped accidentally from its mouth. When a group of fish was placed in the tank, *Pelamis* reacted in a remarkably different way. The snakes would then start swimming rapidly in a "frenzy," accompanied by indiscriminate biting of any object in their path. In this way, many fish would be captured and mutual biting between snakes would take place.

The feeding of snakes in their natural habitat was observed many times in this study. It takes place along slicks, where schools of small fish abound and tend to aggregate under the snakes, as if under twigs and logs. Capture of food was in the manner described above. Such behavior was also described by other authors (Klauber, 1935; Hunter and Mitchell, 1967; Paulson, 1967). This feeding behavior is entirely different from the one described for *Laticauda* (Klemmer, 1967; Pickwell, 1971). While *Laticauda* actively pursues its prey, *Pelamis* relies on deception of the prey and on a slow, stealthy approach to capture.

Food Species

Hundreds of sea snakes were examined for their stomach contents. The diet of these snakes consisted entirely of fish, which included the following species:
Engraulidae: *Anchoviella* sp., *Engraulis* sp.
Atherinidae: *Melanorhinus cyanellus*
Fistulariidae: *Fistularia corneta*
Serranidae: *Lobotes pacificus*
Carangidae: *Caranx caballus, C. marginatus, Chloroscombrus orqueta, Vomer declivifrons*
Coryphaenidae: *Coryphaena hippurus*
Lutjanidae: *Lutjanus* sp.
Kyphosidae: *Kyphosus* sp.
Mullidae: *Mulloidichthys rathbuni*
Chaetodontidae: *Chaetodon humeralis*
Pomacentridae: *Abudefduf troschelli*
Stromateidae: *Peprilus medius*

Mugilidae: *Mugil cephalus, M. durema*
Sphyraenidae: *Sphyraena* sp.
Polynemidae: *Polydactylus approximans*
Blenniidae: *Blenniolus brevipinnis, Hypsoblennius* sp.
Acanthuridae: *Acanthurus xanthopterus*
Scombridae: (Not identified to genus).
Tetraodontidae: *Sphoeroides* sp.

This variety of food species could be found even in a small sample of snakes (30–50 individuals) and, therefore, is not an artifact resulting from the large sample. Many fish which were normally encountered on slicks in this study (i.e., *Engraulis, Fistularia, Abudefduf, Mugil, Acanthurus*) and by Hunter and Mitchell (1967) were also found in sea snakes. Of the fish found in *Pelamis*, mullets were by far the most common (Table 2). Also common were jacks (*Carangidae*), anchovies, *Abudefduf*, and juvenile dolphins (*Coryphaena*). In the snakes whose digestive contents could not be identified, it was still possible to verify that they consisted of fish remains from the many fish bones that usually were found in the rectum. From data gathered in this study, as well as in others (Klawe, 1964; Hunter and Mitchell, 1967), it is clear that *Pelamis* feeds on any available species which is of a size that can be ingested. This includes elongate fish such as *Fistularia,* pisciform species such as *Mugil, Caranx,* and *Coryphaena,* and very compressed, deep fish such as *Chaetodon* sp. and *Vomer* sp. Occasionally, even twigs were found in the snakes' stomachs. Some of the species (*Lutjanus, Chaetodon*) are certainly not common slick fish, but their juveniles might be swept in by currents (*Chaetodon* is a very unusual food for *Pelamis*). Of the more common fish it appears that the more abundant species are preyed upon more heavily, a conclusion also reached by Klawe (1964). Preference for food size was not shown by the snakes. Small fish (5–10 mm long) were found in large numbers within large *Pelamis,* while relatively large fish (40–50 mm) were found in the stomachs of juveniles. That *Pelamis* feeds on fish schools is evident from finding that many fish of a single species, often of the same size, were taken in one feeding.

POPULATION-LIMITING FACTORS

Predation

Field Observations Aggregations of *Pelamis* would present special opportunities for predation on the snakes. Therefore, to discover to what extent predation took place and whether any predator habitually fed on the sea snakes, many hours were spent observing the aggregations. Another approach

Table 2. Frequency of fish families as food for *Pelamis* in the Gulf of Panama

Stomach contents	No. snakes	Percent
No food	31	19.50
Food cannot be identified, but definitely fish	33	20.75
Mugilidae	19	11.95
Carangidae	13	8.18
Coryphaenidae	11	6.92
Serranidae (*Lobotes*)	11	6.92
Pomacentridae	8	5.03
Engraulidae	8	5.03
Polynemidae	6	3.77
Atherinidae	4	2.52
Acanthuridae	4	2.52
Blenniidae	2	1.26
9 other families[a] (1 fish each)	9	5.66
Total	159	

[a]Fistularidae, Lutjanidae, Kyphosidae, Stromateidae, Mullidae, Chaetodontidae, Sphyraenidae, Scombridae, Tetraodontidae.

was to examine the stomach contents of potential predators. A potential predator was any active pelagic predator large enough to ingest *Pelamis* (as determined by laboratory experiments).

Of the birds typical to slicks (brown booby, *Sula leucogaster;* brown pelican, *Pelecanus occidentalis;* man-of-war, *Fregata magnificens;* and occasionally gulls), none was ever observed to pick up *Pelamis,* or to show the slightest interest in the snakes. *Pelamis* normally did not react to disturbances at or above the surface. This suggests that predation pressure from this direction did not exist or the snakes would be more sensitive to disturbances and escape by diving.

A total of 457 potential fish predators belonging to 25 species was examined. These include 59 sharks of 14 species, 112 *Katsuwonus* sp., 139 *Coryphaena hippurus,* 77 scombrids, and 23 carangids (Kropach, 1973). All were collected at the area where *Pelamis* occurred, and 28% were collected from slicks at the same time that sea snakes were seen in large numbers, when there was no question of availability of *Pelamis* as potential food. About 60% had food in their stomachs, usually showing a rich and varied diet, but no sea snake remains were found. Examination of the stomach contents of a possible mammalian predator, the dolphin (169 *Stenella graffmani,* and 45 *S. longirostris*), also did not reveal sea snake remains, although the animals were caught where *Pelamis* were plentiful (Perrin, unpubl. obser.) Of about 1,000 Eastern Pacific sharks examined, most of which had been collected within the range of *Pelamis,* none contained the remains of sea snakes (Kato, 1970).

Although it is doubtful that there exists a predator-free species, it appears that predation on *Pelamis* in the Eastern Pacific is minimal and cannot be a serious population-limiting factor. It is possible that predation on sea snakes takes place in some parts of their range, but does not occur in the Eastern Pacific. This predator-free situation may in part be responsible for the large concentration of *Pelamis* in the Eastern Pacific. If sea snakes have a specialized predator in the Western Pacific such as the sea eagle *Haliaetus* (Cantor, 1841; Wall, 1921), it is possible that this predator was not able to migrate across the ocean and follow *Pelamis* to the Eastern Pacific. Wetmore (1965) reported that twice he sighted a man-of-war bird (*Fregata*) picking up *Pelamis,* then dropping it. This, as well as other accounts of predation by birds or sharks, may testify to an occasional loss of *Pelamis,* but not to a major limiting factor. Most apparent predation on sea snakes is probably by scavenging on the dying or dead animals after they have been washed ashore. These may be dragged into crab holes (Duellman, 1961) or taken by birds onto buoys (Smith, 1926). The source of injuries found occasionally on tails of *Pelamis* (see Chapter 12) is not known.

Laboratory Experiments The laboratory experiments conceived by Dr. Ira Rubinoff of the Smithsonian Tropical Research Institution, were designed in order to compare the reaction of Pacific and Atlantic predatory fishes to *Pelamis* offered as food (Rubinoff and Kropach, 1970). These experiments showed that Pacific fishes, even when they were starved, avoided *Pelamis,* while closely-related Atlantic species attacked the sea snakes. Of 383 trials with Atlantic fish, 35 resulted in successful attacks on *Pelamis*, while three fish died from bites by sea snakes. Of 316 trials with Pacific fish, there was one attack on *Pelamis,* followed by an immediate regurgitation, and no snake bites. Pacific fish did not attack *Pelamis* even when, mixed with Atlantic fish, their interest in *Pelamis* was increased due to social facilitation. After inspection of the snakes, the Pacific fish avoided them (Rubinoff and Kropach, 1970). A Pacific turtle, *Eretmochelys imbricata,* which had become used to feeding by hand on fish and squid, also refused pieces of *Pelamis.*

In some predatory fish (such as *Lutjanus*), species recognition of *Pelamis* seems to be visual. In others, such as *Ginglymostoma,* it may be primarily olfactory. Since ophichtid (*Myrichtys tigris*) and muraenid (*Priodonophis equatorialis*) eels were attacked and ingested by Pacific fish immediately upon contact, it can be concluded that serpentine shape alone is not sufficient to produce the avoidance reaction.

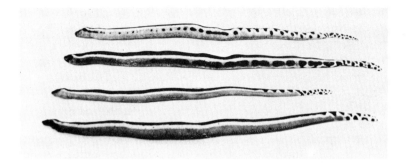

Figure 2. Some color variations in *Pelamis* from the Gulf of Panama. From bottom to top: a uniform pattern, 25% broken pattern, 50% broken, and a completely broken pattern.

Coloration of* Pelamis *as a Warning Signal The coloration of *Pelamis* is conspicuous (Figure 2). Although a multitude of variations occur, all possess bright yellow color ventrolaterally which, except in a rare variety, comes in contact with black dorsal marking. This coloration is unusual among sea snakes (Halstead, 1970), most of the other species being banded, blotched, or uniformly colored. This pattern could be interpreted as another case of countershading, so common in marine vertebrates, or as an example of obliterative shading and disruptive coloration. The conspicuousness of *Pelamis,* both underwater and at the surface, fails to support these interpretations. An alternative is that *Pelamis* exhibits warning coloration. To justify the view that in *Pelamis* the specific function of this advertising is aposematic (Wickler, 1968), four conditions must be met: (1) the snakes are conspicuous in their natural habitat; (2) the snakes are protected (venomous, unpalatable, or both); (3) potential predators (fishes and birds) can see the colors or patterns; and (4) predators avoid *Pelamis.* Since all these conditions seem to be met (Kropach, 1973), aposematic function is the best explanation for the coloration of *Pelamis.* In some situations the snakes may be camouflaged (i.e., among floating vegetation), but aposematic coloration and camouflage need not be mutually exclusive. On the contrary, the selective value of this color combination may increase because of its adaptiveness for a variety of environmental situations.

The curious mottled pattern in the tail of *Pelamis* probably acts to deceive predators and attract them to bite at the spotted posterior end. In the laboratory, several fish which seized snakes by the tail were bitten and died, while those seizing *Pelamis* by the head succeeded in swallowing it unharmed. In the field, snakes were occasionally seen with tail wounds (48 of about 2000 snakes), probable marks of successful escapes from would-be predators.

Incidentally, when *Pelamis* lies on the water, the tail hangs somewhat below the surface; this also may serve as a lure for potential predators, guiding them to the tail.

Parasitism and Disease

In the laboratory, *Pelamis* was afflicted with infections in the cephalic region, especially in the mouth and around the eyes. In another type of infection, the snakes developed sores all over the skin. In some of these sores, polychaetes could be observed microscopically, but these might have settled there after the infection had started. None of these pathological conditions was seen on *Pelamis* in the natural habitat, and it is doubtful that this is a significant cause of mortality. One snake was found with an extensive cancerous growth in the esophagus. The growth completely blocked the passage of food, and undoubtedly would eventually have caused the death of the snake.

In comparison with other marine species of high trophic levels which were examined in this study, *Pelamis* is relatively a parasite-free animal. In 60 snakes which were examined closely, one had three proglottids of a platyhelminth in the large intestine. Two other snakes had nematodes, one on the wall of the stomach and one on the small intestine. These were not identified. Lung and liver parasites were not found in these snakes. Parasitism, then, is not likely to be a population-limiting factor. Fouling organisms living on the skin are discussed in Chapters 13 and 14.

Physical Limiting Factors

The only major cause of mortality of Pelamis found in this study was current-caused beach stranding. Specimens of *Pelamis* were washed onto local beaches five times during the period September to March. From local residents it was learned that this was a regular occurrence, year around. Since sea snakes were seen, occasionally, very close to the shore, it is not difficult to guess how they could be deposited on beaches in large numbers. This phenomenon was known to early naturalists (Cantor, 1841; Fayrer, 1872). It was noticed particularly after storms (Ditmars, 1933; Glauert, 1950; Sachet, 1962). The high incidence with which it occurs is attested to by the numerous records of snakes being cast ashore in different parts of the species' range. It is, indeed, one of the most widely observed facts of the life and death of *Pelamis,* and was reported from Australia (Glauert, 1950; Cogger, 1959), Pakistan (Minton, 1966), South Africa (Rose, 1962; others), and the Eastern Pacific (Zweifel, 1960; Duellman, 1961; Hardy and McDiarmid, 1969; Dunson and Ehlert, 1971; Pickwell, 1972). Once cast onto a beach, the snakes are helpless. They cannot move or struggle back into the ocean, and they are subject to dehydration, predation, or scavenging by terrestrial animals. Even when trapped in a tidal pool, their death is almost certain, if somewhat delayed, as evidenced by a badly injured *Pelamis* found in such circumstances. Since the strategy of *Pelamis* is based on passive utilization of surface currents, the species could hardly have evolved a mechanism for selectively avoiding certain currents. Loss of individuals stranded on beaches and carried by currents into areas of cold waters is the price the species pays for maintaining this strategy.

POPULATION STRUCTURE AND REPRODUCTION

Sex Recognition and Sex Ratio

There is no clear external distinction between the sexes in *Pelamis*. Statistical differences are discernable between the males and the females with respect to several characters. However, the wide range of overlap between males and females does not allow the use of these characters for identification of sex in most individuals. There are four sexually dimorphic characters in *Pelamis*. First, the tubercules on the males' scales are more prominent than on the females' scales. In both sexes they are larger on adults than on young snakes. This character cannot be objectively measured and for this reason alone may be regarded as a poor one. The function of the tubercules is not known, but they may help the male to hold on to the female during copulation. Second, caudal vertebrae, 32–45 in the males, are more numerous than in the females, where the range is 30–40. This difference is reflected in the tail length, which in the male is proportionally longer, on the average, than in the female (Table 3). Third, the females are larger than the males (Table 3), as seen when the 10 largest specimens of each sample are arranged in descending order of size (Table 4). Despite the usual 1:1 ratio in the population, males represent only 29% of this sample. Fourth, there are some differences in head scutellation. Comparisons of head-scale counts of 126 female and 114 male *Pelamis* were made. Within each sex group juveniles and adults were compared. The five characters compared were the numbers of upper and lower labials, preoculars, preoculars, postoculars, and anterior temporals. Within each sex group the differences in scale numbers are not significant, but the differences between male and females, both in juvenile and adult categories, are significant in four scale traits (Table 2). The only exception to this is in the number of anterior temporals, where no significant difference was detected. The degree of overlap in these characters is so great that only when large samples are available does the dimorphism become apparent.

Sex ratio in all collected samples was close to 1:1 (340 males out of 712 snakes) although in nine out of 14 samples the number of females exceeded that of males. When sex ratios within the different size classes were com-

Table 3. Sexual dimorphism in some *Pelamis* characters[a]

Character	Males				Females					t	P
	N	$\bar{X}$	S	$S_{\bar{X}}$	N	$\bar{X}$	S	$S_{\bar{X}}$			
Total length (cm)	359	51.43	10.92	0.58	391	54.22	13.56	0.69		3.080	<0.01
Snout-vent length (cm)	359	45.20	9.74	0.51	391	48.11	12.13	0.61		3.426	<0.001
Tail length as % of oral length (cm)	242	12.10	2.08	0.134	259	11.42	0.711	0.044		4.966	<0.001
Number of upper labials	77	8.12	0.74	0.060	74	8.36	0.84	0.069		2.630	<0.01
Number of lower labials	77	11.22	0.83	0.067	74	11.43	0.92	0.076		2.080	<0.05
Number of preorbitals	77	1.05	0.24	0.019	74	1.16	0.37	0.030		3.034	<0.01
Number of postorbitals	77	2.06	0.37	0.029	72	1.97	0.41	0.034		2.021	<0.05
Caudal vertebrae	74	38.86	5.04	0.586	53	35.51	4.96	0.682		3.718	<0.001

[a]N = sample size; $\bar{X}$ = mean; S = standard deviation; $S_{\bar{X}}$ = standard error. Scale characters refer to adult *Pelamis*.

Table 4. The 10 largest snakes of each of 10 samples, all collected in the Gulf of Panama in 1970, arranged in descending order[a]

May Sex	Size	June 11 Sex	Size	June 12 Sex	Size	June 13 Sex	Size	June 14 Sex	Size	Aug. 15 Sex	Size	Sept. 10 Sex	Size	Sept. 19 Sex	Size	Sept. 20 Sex	Size	Oct. 26 Sex	Size
♀	765	♀	754	♀	789	♀	833	♀	697	♀	811	♀	728	♂	684	♀	735	♀	786
♀	761	♀	731	♀	746	♀	773	♀	696	♀	755	♂	651	♀	684	♀	705	♀	782
♀	737	♀	684	♀	710	♀	766	♀	678	♀	738	♂	649	♂	683	♀	633	♀	764
♀	737	♀	670	♂	698	♀	727	♀	669	♀	725	♂	647	♀	673	♂	633	♀	760
♀	716	♀	647	♀	690	♀	710	♀	659	♀	718	♂	645	♀	667	♀	619	♀	750
♀	673	♂	617	♂	689	♀	708	♂	643	♀	717	♂	627	♀	664	♀	617	♀	731
♂	670	♀	617	♀	683	♂	707	♀	641	♀	697	♂	611	♂	657	♀	614	♀	731
♀	668	♀	615	♀	661	♀	703	♂	635	♀	693	♂	609	♀	656	♂	614	♀	717
♀	667	♂	591	♀	646	♀	690	♂	632	♀	693	♂	608	♂	630	♂	613	♀	696
♀	666	♂	590	♂	641	♂	670	♂	621	♀	689	♀	606	♂	629	♂	600	♀	677
N = 25		14		55		141		19		101		96		57		48		67	

[a]Size refers to total length in mm; N= sample size.

pared, an approximate 1:1 ratio was retained (with one exception). The exception is in the 50–60 cm size class, where there are more males than females (Table 5). Apparently, when the males reach the size of 50 cm, they mature and their growth rate slows down, while the females maintain their growth rate. From this size on, the longer body of the females becomes apparent. The available data, however, indicate that the sex ratio does not change with age, and that there is no differential survival of either sex.

Size Classes

The mean total length for each of the samples collected during the year of the study was determined separately for males and females (Table 6). Analysis of variance of these samples indicates that they are significantly different; this suggests that the age structure of the population changed during the year. In fact, examination of samples which were collected during the same month

Table 5. Sex ratio in different size classes of three samples of *Pelamis platurus* from the Gulf of Panama, 1970

Class size (mm)	Sample size	♂	♀	♂/♀	X^2	P
June						
300 – 399	52	21	31	0.68	1.922	>0.20
400 – 499	34	15	19	0.79	0.470	>0.50
500 – 599	80	51	29	1.76	6.05	>0.02
600 – 699	59	23	36	0.64	2.864	>0.10
700 – 799	16	5	11	0.45	2.250	>0.20
800 –	1		1			
August						
300 – 399	7	2	5	0.40	1.286	>0.30
400 – 499	20	8	12	0.67	0.800	>0.50
500 – 599	18	11	7	1.57	0.889	>0.50
600 – 699	45	20	25	0.80	0.556	>0.50
700 – 799	10	2	8	0.25	3.6	>0.10
800 –	1		1			
September						
200 – 299	3	3				
300 – 399	90	45	45	1.0		
400 – 499	39	19	20	0.95	0.025	>0.90
500 – 599	33	20	13	1.54	1.485	>0.30
600 – 699	33	18	15	1.20	0.273	>0.70
700 –	3		3			

Table 6. Mean total length of *Pelamis,* collected in the Gulf of Panama in 1970[a]

	Males				Females			
Sample	N	$\overline{X}$	S	$S_{\overline{x}}$	N	$\overline{X}$	S	$S_{\overline{x}}$
March 13	5	43.78	12.34	5.520	5	44.71	11.87	5.309
April 15	6	40.60	4.72	1.926	8	60.90	8.87	3.138
May 30	10	56.18	8.75	2.742	15	63.42	12.26	3.167
June 11	6	57.78	4.27	1.742	8	65.70	6.58	2.326
June 12	30	55.32	8.69	1.586	25	57.19	11.42	2.284
June 13	64	50.01	10.41	1.291	77	49.89	13.35	1.532
June 14	15	55.22	10.23	2.643	17	55.72	11.93	2.892
Aug. 15	43	57.09	9.04	1.379	58	58.65	12.62	1.657
Sept. 10	51	42.74	9.35	1.309	45	41.73	8.330	1.242
Sept. 19	26	53.70	11.16	2.190	31	50.61	12.07	2.167
Sept. 20	29	42.00	10.09	1.875	19	49.40	13.19	3.026
Oct. 26	37	55.67	7.99	1.390	36	61.80	11.34	1.944
Oct. 30	9	61.80	4.278	1.426	16	61.85	7.950	1.988
Jan. 26	9	54.9	5.014	1.671	12	61.70	5.73	1.654
F value:	10.090				10.044			

[a]N = sample size; X = mean total length in cm; S = standard deviation; $S_{\overline{x}}$ = standard error.

(i.e., June and September samples) shows them also to be significantly different. The frequencies of individuals in various size classes are given in Table 7. The divisions into size classes are arbitrary, as they must be when dealing with a continuous character. I believe, however, that individuals below 300 mm in total length are juveniles in their first year; those above 500 mm are adults, and the range 300–500 mm probably includes both juveniles and adults as well as the sub-adults.

There are several weaknesses in the assumption that size-class distribution reflects the population age structure (Kropach, 1973). However, with caution, population events can be deduced from a careful examination of this type of information. For example, when reproduction is seasonal, the sudden appearance of newborn in the population should be seen through a high proportion of the smallest size class. Newborn *Pelamis* can be recognized by the umbilical opening (which I call the umbilical slit, because of its shape). After the slit closes, an umbilical scar remains, which is apparent for a long time, sometimes in snakes past their first year. Therefore, the presence of a scar cannot be used for estimating age, nor can size, since growth rate in *Pelamis* is not known.

Table 7. Frequency of size-class distribution (percent) in *Pelamis* sampled at different times of the year

Total length (mm)	April 15		May 30		June 11		June 12		June 13		June 14	
	♂	♀	♂	♀	♂	♀	♂	♀	♂	♀	♂	♀
N	6	8	10	15	6	8	30	25	65	76	15	17
200–299												
300–399	33.33			6.7			10.0	8.0	26.15	32.89	13.33	17.65
400–499	66.67	25.0	30.0	13.3			10.0	16.0	16.92	18.42	6.67	5.88
500–599			20.0	6.7	66.67	25.0	56.67	24.0	38.46	21.05	33.33	29.41
600–699		62.5	50.0	40.0	33.33	50.0	23.33	40.0	16.92	18.42	46.67	47.06
700–799		12.5		33.3		25.0		12.0	1.54	7.89		
800–										1.32		

Total length (mm)	Aug. 15		Sept. 10		Sept. 19		Sept. 20		Oct. 26		Jan. 26	
	♂	♀	♂	♀	♂	♀	♂	♀	♂	♀	♂	♀
N	43	58	51	45	26	31	29	19	45	52	9	12
200–299												
300–399	4.6	8.6	2.0	58.6	3.84		3.4	42.1	2.2	5.8		
400–499	18.6	20.7	52.0	30.4	11.53	32.25	55.2	15.8	8.9	9.6		
500–599	25.6	12.1	26.0	4.3	7.69	9.67	13.79	5.26	4.4	28.8	22.2	8.3
600–699	46.5	43.1	6.0	4.3	46.15	32.25	17.24	26.3	48.9	36.5	66.7	16.7
700–799	4.7	13.7	14.0	2.2	30.76	25.8	10.34	10.52	35.6	19.2	11.1	66.7
800–		1.7										8.3

The data in Table 6 show significant shifts in the mean total lengths of the population samples. Even samples which were expected to be homogeneous, such as the June 11–14 samples, collected on 4 consecutive days in the same general area, were significantly different. Another phenomenon seems to be the lowering of sample mean length with increase of sample size (Table 6, i.e., the sample of June 13 as compared with others of June, and the sample of September 10 versus others of that month). Two groups of snakes which were marked in January (344 snakes) and February (108 snakes), 1970, had mean lengths of 44.4 and 41.1 cm, respectively. Although several factors complicate the evaluation of this data, they suggest that a different population is sampled each time, as it would be if the snakes move through the Gulf but do not remain in it. Another possibility is that the population is very large and is not homogeneously distributed in the habitat. The lower mean length in the larger samples shows that the population is truly represented only when a large concentration of snakes is present. This could be the case if large snakes reach ocean slicks earlier than small ones.

Reproduction

Pelamis are ovoviviparous, as are most sea snakes. Becoming live bearers was one of the most significant adaptations for pelagic life, because it allowed the snakes to break the link with the terrestrial habitat. Brood size observed in *Pelamis* in this study was two to six. The brood is divided between the two oviducts. Visser (1967) found brood size in this species to range from one to six embryos. For *Pelamis* a brood of six may be maximal, but larger broods are known in other, larger sea snakes (see Kropach, 1973). The exact length of gestation of *Pelamis* is not known, but from observing a gravid female in the laboratory, this period lasts a minimum of 5 months and, more likely, 6 or more. Cantor (1841) estimated the gestation in hydrophiids to last 7 months, and Pickwell (1972) estimated it to be in the order of 8 months.

At birth the young measure 220–260 mm. Snakes born in the laboratory were 254 mm long. A 230-mm *Pelamis* was found by Minton (1966) and a 220 mm snake by Myers (1945). The largest fetuses found in the study were 215 mm long; smaller fetuses, measuring 192 mm, did not seem near term. The estimate of minimum size at birth appears to be put correctly at 220 mm. The newborn snakes have a rich fat storage and they are capable of feeding in their first day of life.

The rate of growth of young *Pelamis,* though not known exactly, seems to be rapid, at least during the first year. The males become sexually mature when they are approximately 500 mm total length (Table 4 shows that at the 500–600 mm size class the male:female ratio increases abruptly). In snakes below 500 mm, there is a strong correlation (0.894) between the length of testes and body length (Figure 3). This correlation does not exist (drops to

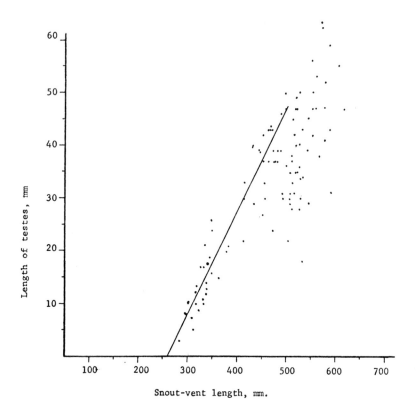

Figure 3. The relation between testes length and snout-vent length in 105 *Pelamis* collected in June 1970, in the Gulf of Panama. Line represents the regression for snakes less than 450 mm in length.

0.424) above this size class. The regression of testes length on body length drops from 0.196 to 0.095 as the snakes grow longer than 500 mm. This is interpreted as sexual maturation in snakes which have attained this size. The onset of reproductive activity in the females occurs when they are larger (645–765 in my samples; 623–758 mm in others) (Visser, 1967). Bergman (1943) assumed that at the onset of maturity both sexes were of equal size.

Pelamis was expected to have a seasonal mode of reproduction in the Gulf of Panama because of the ecological seasonality of this region (Forsbergh, 1969). Size-class data do not show an abrupt appearance of young in the population at any special period of the year. To the contrary, young were found throughout the year. The scattered occurrence of gravid females and the sizes of the fetuses also suggest non-seasonal breeding. Similar conclusions can be drawn from data presented by Visser (1967). Pickwell (1972) found a very extended breeding season for *Pelamis* in Mexico, with a peak in the late fall, but his data are also indicative of non-seasonal reproduction (pers. comm.). The fact that only seven gravid females were found out of a total of 372 snakes examined at various times of the year is remarkable. Preferential migration of pregnant females to areas other than those sampled may be occurring.

Other data, on the contrary, indicate that breeding of *Pelamis* in the Eastern Pacific is seasonal. A sample of 278 snakes, collected during the *Alpha Helix* Expedition, September 1970, in Golfo Dulce, Costa Rica, had 43% newborn! This suggests that females come to give birth in this gulf. Pickwell also found a large sample of gravid females in Bahia Banderas, Mexico. These, he concluded, came to the bay for parturition; upon examination, however, the fetuses were found to be at various stages of development (Pickwell, pers. comm.). Seasonal reproduction has been reported for some sea snakes (Cantor, 1841; Wall, 1921; Volsøe, 1939), and also for *Pelamis* (Cogger, 1959).

VARIATIONS IN THE POPULATIONS

Color Variations

Pelamis is known to occur in highly variable patterns. The variants differ in the relative abundance and specific configurations of their black, brown and yellow surfaces (Figure 2). A rare, all-yellow variety is known from the Gulf of Panama and Golfo Dulce, Costa Rica. The variations in the color of *Pelamis* are continuous; thus dividing a sample into color groups is difficult and often impossible. There are many intermediate forms among the color types, and sometimes patterns are superimposed on each other. Aging of the skin adds to the confusion of patterns—before shedding, yellow surfaces often appear dark brown. For a species whose coloration is aposematic, it presumably would be beneficial to have a uniform pattern in order to facilitate recognition by predators. To investigate whether there is selection for uniformity in *Pelamis,* juveniles and adults were compared with respect to their color variability. To measure this, the frequencies of snakes with uniform versus broken patterns (as in Figure 2) were observed. The fact that the frequency of broken patterns was no smaller in adults than in juveniles indicates that there is no apparent selection against color variability in *Pelamis.* To a predator, *Pelamis* may appear first as an array of contrasting black and yellow surfaces. It is possible that any such color combination acts aposematically and that there is no selection of one particular pattern.

Scale Variations

Studies of several reptile populations have shown that as juveniles grow, the degree of variability in a given population is reduced due to natural selection. Usually, the characters which are selected are of important functional value (Inger, 1943; Hecht, 1952). Dunn (1942) found almost a universal tendency, in snake populations, for decrease in variability of scales with older age. The decrease in such cases could be due to selection operating on somewhat less apparent characters. Because of the variations in the local scutellation of *Pelamis,* six scale characters were chosen for a comparison of variability in young and adults. In the "young" categories were fetuses and juveniles up to 350 mm total length. As shown in Table 3, significant differences were found between males and females, both in the young and adult groups. However, no significant differences between young and adults were found within each sex group (Table 8). Similarly, no significant difference was found between vertebral counts of young and adults.

SUMMARY

The sea snake *Pelamis platurus* was studied for a year in the eastern Pacific, primarily in the Gulf of Panama. Observations were made on the distribution, behavior, food habits and population parameters of the snakes.

First, the movement of *Pelamis* is determined by surface currents, their speed, direction, and persistence. As a consequence, *Pelamis* is often found in slicks.

Second, the poor recovery of marked snakes and the possibility of their moving by currents northward in the eastern Pacific indicate that the population of *Pelamis* in the Gulf of Panama may be transient.

Third, the only severe mortality factor for which there is substantial evidence is a physical one—that of being swept by currents onto the shore. Even heavier losses to the population may occur as snakes are carried by currents into areas of lethally cold water.

Fourth, several features allow *Pelamis* to be a successful colonizing species:

1. Complete independence from land by being ovoviviparous and by feeding at the surface.

2. *Pelamis* is a general feeder and thus is not restricted to the geographic range of a given food species.

3. *Pelamis* in the eastern Pacific is relatively predator-free. Experiments predict that when *Pelamis* reaches new areas it may initially be preyed upon heavily, but that selection against predation is intense. This selection may

Table 8. Comparison of variability in head scales between young and adult *Pelamis*[a]

Character	N	$\overline{X}$	S	CV	$S_{\overline{x}}$
Upper labials	53 YM	8.20	0.72	0.088	0.084
	77 AM	8.12	0.74	0.090	0.060
	52 YF	8.40	0.73	0.087	0.072
	74 AF	8.36	0.84	0.101	0.069
Lower labials	53 YM	11.09	0.86	0.078	0.100
	77 AM	11.22	0.83	0.074	0.067
	52 YF	11.26	1.01	0.089	0.099
	74 AF	11.43	0.92	0.080	0.076
Preorbitals	53 YM	1.05	0.23	0.216	0.026
	77 AM	1.05	0.24	0.228	0.019
	52 YF	1.18	0.41	0.349	0.040
	74 AF	1.16	0.37	0.318	0.030
Postorbitals	53 YM	2.07	0.25	0.122	0.029
	77 AM	2.06	0.37	0.178	0.029
	52 YF	1.90	0.41	0.214	0.040
	74 AF	1.97	0.41	0.209	0.034
Anterior temporals	53 YM	2.57	0.58	0.225	0.068
	77 AM	2.62	0.59	0.224	0.047
	54 YF	2.60	0.57	0.219	0.057
	74 AF	2.71	0.60	0.221	0.049

[a]N = sample size; $\overline{X}$ = mean; S = standard deviation; CV = coefficient of variation; $S_{\overline{x}}$ = standard error; Y = young; A = adult; M = male; F = female.

lead to evolution of predators which avoid *Pelamis*, and allow the undisturbed growth of a population.

4. *Pelamis* is capable of utilizing surface currents for transportation. This allows the snakes to arrive at food-rich areas with relatively little energy expenditure, to find mates and, ultimately, to expand the species range.

5. *Pelamis* breeds over an extended period, perhaps throughout the year.

6. From the study of several morphological characters it appears that varia-

bility in the population is maintained through time. The apparent lack of stabilizing selection (at least for some characters) helps maintain a diverse gene pool.

ACKNOWLEDGMENTS

I wish to thank Professor Max K. Hecht and Dr. Ira Rubinoff for their advice throughout the study. The Smithsonian Office of Academic Programs provided the funds for this study, and the Society of the Sigma Xi supported it with a grant-in-aid. Laboratory facilities were provided by the Smithsonian Tropical Research Institute, Balboa, Canal Zone. I also thank Dr. William Dunson and the Scripps Institution of Oceanography for the opportunity to work on board R/V *Alpha Helix*. The help of Drs. R. Rosenblatt and J. McCosker in the identification of fish is also gratefully acknowledged.

REFERENCES

Allee, W. C., 1931. Animal Aggregations. University of Chicago Press, Chicago. ix + 431 pp.

Ambrose, M. S. 1956. Snakebite in Central America. *In* Buckley, E. E., and N. Porges. Venoms. AAAS, Washington, D.C. Public. 44:323–329.

Amos, A. F., M. G. Lanseth, Jr., and R. G. Markel. 1972. Visible Oceanic Saline Fronts. *In* A tribute to George Wüst on his 80th birthday. Gordon and Breach, Science Publishers, New York. Vol. I:49–62.

Anon. 1972. Orange Coast Daily Pilot, San Clemente, Calif. Nov. 24–25, 1972.

Assaf, G., R. Gerard, and A. L. Gordon. 1971. Some mechanisms of oceanic mixing revealed in aerial photographs. J. of Geophys. Res. 76:6550–6572.

Beebe, W. 1926. The *Arcturus* Adventure. G. P. Putnam's Sons, New York. pp. 41–70.

Bergman, A. M. 1943. Breeding habits of sea snakes. Copeia 3:156–160.

Boulenger, G. A. 1890. The fauna of British India incl. Ceylon and Burma. Reptilia and Batrachia. Taylor and Francis, London. pp. 393–398.

Cantor, T. 1841. Observations upon pelagic serpents. Transac. Zool. Soc. London, 2:303–313.

Cogger, H. G. 1959. Sea-snakes. Aust. Mus. Mag. 13(2):37–41.

Cope, E. D. 1887. Catalogue of Batrachians and Reptiles of Central America and Mexico. Bull. U.S. Nat. Mus. Ser. 43(32):87.

Cromwell, T., and J. L. Reid, Jr. 1956. A study of oceanic fronts. Tellus 8:94–101.

Daniel, H. 1955. Algunos aspectos de la lucha biologica. IV. Los reptilias y la agricultura una serpiente bicefala. Como se han clasificado las serpientes. Rev. Fac. Nac. Agron. Medellin 16(48):3–168.

Dietz, R. S., and E. C. LaFond. 1950. Natural slicks on the ocean. J. Mar. Res. 9:69–76.

Ditmars, R. L. 1933. Reptiles of the World. Macmillan, New York. pp. 198–201.

Duellman, W. E. 1961. The amphibians and reptiles of Michoacán, Mexico. Univ. Kansas Public Mus. Nat. Hist. 15(1):1–148.

Dunn, E. R. 1942. Survival value of varietal characters in snakes. Amer. Nat. 76:104–109.

Dunson, W. A., and Ehlert, G. W. 1971. Effects of temperature, salinity, and surface water flow on distribution of the sea snake *Pelamis*. Limnol. Oceanog. 16:845–853.

Ewing, G. C. 1950a. Slicks, surface films and internal waves. J. Mar. Res. 9:161–187.

Ewing, G. C. 1950b. Relation between band slicks at the surface and internal waves in the sea. Science 111:91–94.

Fayrer, J. 1872. The Thanatophidia of India. Churchill, London. 156 pp.

Forsbergh, E. D. 1969. On the climatology, oceanography, and fisheries of the Panama Bight. Inter-Amer. Trop. Tuna Comm., Bull. 14(2):49–141.

Glauert, L. 1950. A Handbook of the Snakes of Western Australia. Western Australia Naturalists' Club, Perth. 50 pp.

Graham, J. B., I Rubinoff, and M. K. Hecht. 1971. Temperature physiology of the sea snake *Pelamis platurus:* An index of its colonization potential in the Atlantic Ocean. Proc. Natl. Acad. Sci. 68:1360–63.

Halstead, B. W. (Ed). 1970. Poisonous and Venomous Marine Animals of the World. Vol. III:626–755. U.S. Govt. Printing Office, Washington, D.C.

Hardy, L. M., and R. W. McDiarmid. 1969. The Amphibians and Reptiles of Sinaloa, Mexico. Univ. of Kansas Public Mus. Nat. Hist. 18(3):212.

Hecht, M. K. 1952. Natural selection in the lizard genus *Aristelliger*. Evolution 6:112–124.

Hunter, J. R., and C. T. Mitchell. 1967. Association of fishes with flotsam in the offshore waters of Central America. Fishery Bull. 66:13–29.

Inger, R. R. 1943. Further notes on differential selection of variant juvenile snakes. Amer. Natur. 77:87–90.

Johnson, R. G. 1955. The adaptive and phylogenetic significance of vertebral form in snakes. Evolution 9:367–388.

Kato, S. 1970. U.S. National Marine Fisheries Service, Tiburon Fisheries Laboratory, Tiburon, Calif. pers. comm.

Klauber, L. M. 1935. The feeding habits of a sea snake. Copeia 1935:182.

Klawe, W. L. 1964. Food of the black-and-yellow sea snake, *Pelamis platurus,* from Ecuadorian coastal waters. Copeia 1964:712–713.

Klemmer, K. 1967. Observations on the sea snake *Laticauda laticaudata* in captivity. Internat. Zoo Yearbook 7:229–231.

Krefft, G. 1953. Herpetologische eindrücke einer walfangreise. Aquar. Terrar. Zeit. 6:130–133.

Kropach, C. 1971. Sea snake (*Pelamis platurus*) aggregations on slicks in Panama. Herpetologica 27:131–135.

Kropach, C. 1973. A field study of the sea snake *Pelamis platurus* (Linnaeus) in the Gulf of Panama. Doctoral Dissertation, City University of New York. (Unpublished).

Langmuir, I. 1938. Surface motion of water induced by wind. Science 87:119–123.

Lowe, W. P. 1932. The Trail That is Always New. Gurney and Jackson, London. Chap. 2.

Minton, S. A., Jr. 1966. A contribution to the herpetology of West Pakistan. Bull. Amer. Mus. Nat. Hist. 134(2):27–184.

Myers, G. S. 1945. Nocturnal observations on sea-snakes in Bahia Honda, Panama. Herpetologica 3:22–23.

Neill, W. T. 1964. Viviparity in snakes: Some ecological and zoogeographical considerations. Amer. Nat. 98:35–55.

Neumann, G., and W. J. Pierson, Jr. 1966. Principles of Physical Oceanography. Prentice-Hall, Englewood Cliffs, N. J. xii + 545 pp.

Orces, G. V. 1948. Notas sobre los ofidios venenosos del Ecuador. Publicac. Escuela Politic. Nac., Quito. pp. 24. Revista Filosofia y Letras (3):231–250.

Paulson, D. R. 1967. Searching for sea serpents. Sea Frontiers 13:244–250.

Peters, J. 1960. The snakes of Ecuador: a checklist and key. Bull. Mus. Comp. Zool. Harvard 122:491–541.

Pickwell, G. V. 1971. Knotting and coiling behavior in the pelagic sea snake *Pelamis platurus* (L.) Copeia 2:348–350.

Pickwell, G. V. 1972. The venomous sea snakes. Fauna 1(4):17–32.

Rodas, T. J. C. 1938. Contribucion al estudio de las serpientes venenosas de Guatemala. Tipografia Nacional, Guatemala. pp. 73–75.

Rose, W. 1962. The Reptiles and Amphibians of Southern Africa. Maskew Miller, Cape Town. pp. 397–399.

Rubinoff, I., and C. Kropach. 1970. Differential reactions of Atlantic and Pacific predators to sea snakes. Nature 228:1288–1290.

Sachet, M. 1962. Monographie physique et biologique de l'Ille Clipperton. Ann. Inst. Oceanog. 40(1):1–108.

Shaw, C. E. 1961. Snakes of the sea. Zoonooz 34:3–5.

Shaw, C. E. 1962. Sea snakes at the San Diego Zoo. Internat. Zoo. Yearbook 4:49–52.

Smith, H. M. 1958. Handlist of the snakes of Panama. Herpetologica 14:222–224.

Smith, M. A. 1926. Monograph of the Sea Snakes (Hydrophiidae). British Museum, London. 130 pp.

Smith, M. A. 1935. The sea snakes (Hydrophiidae). Dana Report No. 8, 1935:3–6.

Strauch, A. 1874. Die schlangen des Russichen Reichs, in systematischer und zoogeographischer beziehung. Mem. l'Acad. Imper. Science St. Petersbourg, Ser. 7, 21:199–204.

Sverdrup, H. V., M. W. Johnson, and R. H. Fleming. 1942. The Oceans, Their Physics, Chemistry, and General Biology. Prentice-Hall, Englewood Cliffs, N.J. x + 1087 pp.

Taylor, E. H. 1951. A brief review of the snakes of Costa Rica. Univ. Kansas Sci. Bull. 34:12–13; 156–157.

Taylor, E. H. 1953. Early records of the sea snake *Pelamis platurus* in Latin America. Copeia 1953:121.

Toro, M. A. del, and H. M. Smith. 1956. Notulae herpetologicae Chiapasiae I. Herpetologica 12:3–17.

Uda, M. 1938. Researches on 'Siome' or current rip in the seas and oceans. Geophys. Mag. Tokyo 11:307–372.

Villa, J. 1962. Los Serpientes Venenosas de Nicaragua. Novedades, Managua. 94 pp.

Visser, J. 1967. Color varieties, brood size, and food of South African *Pelamis platurus* (Ophidia: Hydrophiidae). Copeia 1:219.

Volsφe, H. 1939. The sea snakes of the Iranian Gulf and the Gulf of Oman. Danish Scientific Investigations in Iran, Part I:9–45.

Wall, F. 1921. Ophidia Taprobanica or the Snakes of Ceylon. Cottle, Colombo. pp. 315—434.

Wetmore, A. 1965. The Birds of the Republic of Panama. Smithsonian Misc. Coll. 150:75.

Wickler, W. 1968. Mimicry in plants and animals. World University Library, McGraw-Hill, New York. 153 pp.

Zweifel, R. G. 1960. Results of the Puritan-American Museum of Natural History Expedition to Western Mexico. 9. Herpetology of the Tres Marias Islands. Bull. Amer. Mus. Nat. Hist. 119:111.

ECOLOGICAL RELATIONSHIPS

eleven

Feeding Behavior of Indo-Australian Hydrophiidae

John E. McCosker

Despite their abundance in the Indo-Australian reef fauna and importance as potentially lethal animals, little is known of sea snake behavior and ecology. The numerical abundance and species diversity of hydrophiids in the vicinity of Ashmore Reef, Australia, allowed a more extensive in situ examination of their resource utilization than has previously been reported. The presence at that locality of nine snake species, including four co-occurring species of *Aipysurus,* raises an interesting biological question; viz., what mechanisms have been evolved to exploit, without competition, the available resources?

As Smith (1926), Herre (1942), and others have observed, sea snakes feed almost entirely on fishes. References to the feeding behavior of hydrophiids were summarized by Volsøe (1939) and, more recently, by Voris (1972). Identification of gut contents is usually difficult, because of the partial digestion of prey before identification is possible. Previous identifications have generally been made only to the familial level, thus ruling out any analysis of dietary specialization. In my studies I have relied heavily upon in situ observations of feeding and rapid formalin preservation of snakes after collection, or forced regurgitation soon after their capture. Massive fish collections made with rotenone ichthyocides at various locations along the reef enabled prey identification to the specific level in many cases.

This paper comprises four sections: (a) comments on the diet and vertical zonation of each species encountered in the Ashmore Reef complex and the McCluer Gulf; (b) results of preliminary experiments of digestion rates; (c) an analysis of prey species diversity and redundance; and (d) general comments on the feeding strategies of hydrophiids.

METHODS

Reef-dwelling hydrophiids were collected by surface dipnetting or by divers in the vicinity of Ashmore, Hibernia, and Scotts reefs, northern Australia, during January 1973. Sand and mud-bottom associated snakes were collected by surface dipnetting in the McCluer Gulf, New Guinea, during December 1972.

Four hundred fifty-three specimens representing 12 species were collected; however, identifiable prey items were recovered from less than 10%. The specific identification of partially digested items was verified through comparison with intact fishes collected with Pronoxfish ichthyocide, quinaldine anaesthetic, otter trawls, 0.5-m net tows, and dipnetting. Since fish otolith digestion occurs quite slowly in the snakes, many fishes were identifiable to the species level solely on that basis. Fishes and otoliths are deposited at the Scripps Institution of Oceanography (San Diego), the California Academy of Sciences (San Francisco), and the Australian Museum (Sydney).

Approximately 60 hrs were spent by the author in the water observing and photographing sea snakes.

HYDROPHIID DIET AND ZONATION

The following section includes comments on the diet and zonation of all hydrophiids encountered in the Ashmore Reef area and McCluer Gulf. A generalized representation of Ashmore Reef species zonation is shown in Figure 1. All prey items are fishes unless otherwise noted. Refer to the Appendix for a total listing of prey species.

Acalyptophis peronii (Duméril)

Although rare in museum collections, 38 individuals of this species were collected at the Ashmore Reefs, generally over the deep sand bottom of the leeward reef. Gut contents included two species of *Cryptocentrus* (family Gobiidae), one of which was undeterminable, and the other a new species also found in northern Australia (to be described by J. E. Randall and D. F. Hoese). All prey were taken head first. These gobiids are fossorial fishes, generally found over sand and gravel bottoms in relatively shallow water. Males and females are dimorphic in tail length and often occupy the same burrow; two of the snakes which contained prey had both a male and a female in a similar state of digestion, suggesting that *A. peronii* captures its prey within the goby burrow.

Voris (1972) found another goby, *Oxyurichthys* sp., from an *A. peronii* from the west Pacific.

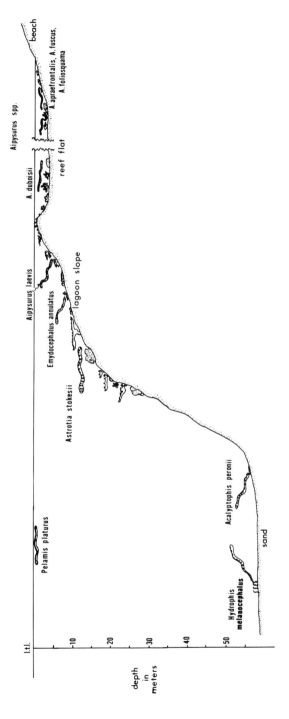

Figure 1. Diagrammatic representation of sea snake zonation along Ashmore Reef, leeward edge. The vertical dimension is exaggerated.

Aipysurus apraefrontalis (Smith)

Seven individuals of this species were collected over the shallow inner reef edge of Ashmore Reefs. None contained prey items. They were observed during daylight hours resting beneath small coral overhangs or coral heads in 1–2 m of water. Smith (1926) reported that the "stomach of one example contained a small eel."

Aipysurus duboisii (Bavay)

This species was generally observed over the protected platform reef top, along the inner reef to depths of 3–4 m, although infrequently it was seen just beyond the reef edge. Its diet was quite variable. The four prey items recovered from four Ashmore and Scotts reefs snakes included a small eel, a reef blenny, a surgeonfish, and a juvenile parrotfish. All fishes are reef-dwellers, either nocturnally or diurnally, and were taken head-first. The state of prey digestion would suggest that *A. duboisii* feeds crepuscularly.

A specimen of *A. duboisii* collected off Townsville, eastern Australia, by W. A. Dunson (no. 185), contained a scorpaenid fish, presumably *Richardson-ichthys leucogaster.*

Aipysurus foliosquama (Smith)

This species was collected over the shallow inner reef edge, along with *A. fuscus* and *A. apraefrontalis.* The only prey items found among the 35 *A. foliosquama* collected at Ashmore Reef were a set of wrasse (family Labridae) jaws and a neurocranium, presumably from a species of *Halichoeres.* Smith (1926) reported that three specimens contained *Platyglossus* (=*Halichoeres*) *trimaculatus.* This wrasse is an abundant shallow water, coral-associated species.

Voris (1972) reported two unidentified eleotrids and a tripterygiid (*Trypterygion*) from Ashmore Reef specimens.

Aipysurus fuscus (Tschudi)

Aipysurus fuscus, another inner reef species, also preys on labrid and gobiid fishes. A Scotts Reef specimen contained two *Eleotriodes longipinnis* (Gobiidae). Two East Ashmore specimens contained otoliths and neurocrania, identifiable as *Halichoeres* sp. (Labridae). Two other East Ashmore specimens contained two entire labrids, identified with the assistance of G. P. Whitley as *Cymolutes praetextatus,* previously unreported from Australian waters. Voris (1972) found an unidentified gobiid, fish eggs, and fish vertebrae in Ashmore Reef specimens.

Aipysurus laevis (Lacépède)

This species is an abundant and opportunistic predator along the lower reef edge and upper lagoon slope of the leeward reef. More than 60 prey items were taken from diver-caught and surface-dipnetted snakes. Little or no feeding preference was discovered. Snakes were observed feeding at dawn and throughout the day (Figure 2), and on several occasions aggressively chased divers from the water. Gut contents included both nocturnally (cardinal fishes and sweepers) and diurnally (groupers, juvenile parrotfishes, juvenile surgeonfishes, damselfishes, and six other prey types) active species, suggesting that *A. laevis* fed during periods of prey inactivity. This conjecture was confirmed by the state of prey digestion in relation to time of capture. A reef-dwelling shrimp and a file shell (*Lima* sp.) were also found.

A specimen of *A. laevis* collected off Townsville, eastern Australia, by W. A. Dunson (no. 182), contained a scorpaenid fish (*Minous* sp.).

Astrotia stokesii (Gray)

Ashmore Reef specimens of *A. stokesii* were found to have a specialized diet of a reef-dwelling batrachoidid, *Halophryne diemensis,* the "banded frogfish." Six of 19 specimens collected contained *H. diemensis,* and a seventh regurgitated a frogfish (field identified as *H. diemensis*) while being pursued by divers at a depth of 10 m. Batrachoidids possess pungent dorsal spines and opercular armature, and were always taken head first. *Astrotia* was observed in the field along the inner reef dropoff, generally between 7 and 10 m depth. This coincides with the general depth distribution of its prey, which hides beneath flat coral overhangs at the sand-reef interphase.

A single *Astrotia* was dipnetted over the sand and mud bottom of Darwin Harbor (depth ca. 10 m). It regurgitated the skeletal remains of an adult *Tandya* (family Opistognathidae). Species of *Tandya,* called jawfishes or smilers, are fossorial fishes which build permanent burrows over sand and mud bottoms, and retreat into their burrows when threatened. Presumably, they would be easily captured by a venomous predator such as a hydrophiid.

Emydocephalus annulatus (Krefft)

This minute-fanged species was found to eat only fish eggs. It was observed quite commonly along the upper lagoon slope in search of holes containing blenny or goby spawn. *E. annulatus* has apparently lost the ability to envenomate struggling prey. My identification of the eggs as being from blenniid and gobiid fishes agrees with the findings of Voris (1966). It is interesting that nearly one specimen in three possessed an abundance of eggs

Figure 2. Adult *Aipysurus laevis* searching for food along inner edge of West Ashmore Reef. Depth is 10 m.

in its mouth and gut, in contrast to the rarity of prey items in other captured snakes.

Hydrophis melanocephalus (Gray)

The diet of this species consisted entirely of burrowing eels of the families Ophichthidae, Congridae, and Moringuidae. This microcephalic, long-necked and highly venomous hydrophiid is well adapted to prey on eels. The half-banded snake eel, *Leiuranus semicinctus* (Figure 3), was the most abundant prey species, comprising 28 of the 47 identifiable items. *H. melanocephalus* was generally collected by dipnetting from the ship while at anchor, usually over the protected leeward reef flat in 30–40 m depth. While scuba diving beneath the ship's East Ashmore Reef anchorage, I observed an adult snake engaged in prey search behavior (time 1500–1515, depth −40 to −45 m). The snake, unaware of my presence, moved slowly over the sand and broken shell bottom and entered each hole it encountered. The eels it preyed

Figure 3. Adult half-banded snake eel, *Leiuranus semicinctus,* the most abundant prey of *Hydrophis melanocephalus.* Photo by John E. Randall.

upon make shallow permanent (*Taenioconger* sp.) or semi-permanent (certain ophichthids, moringuids, and other congrids) burrows, and rarely emerge completely from the substrate. The strikingly banded *Leiuranus semicinctus* may be exceptional in leaving the substrate nocturnally.

Several observations should be noted concerning this snake and its prey. *H. melanocephalus* often swallows its prey tail first (eight of 47 prey items) in contrast to other hydrophiids which always digest prey head first. This is apparently facilitated by the lack of spinous dorsal fin rays and cephalic armature among true eels. Young snakes preferred smaller and generally different eel prey than did the adults. Young snakes had eaten the much smaller, and generally weaker struggling, species of *Myrophis, Muraenichthys, Ariosoma,* and *Congrina,* whereas the adults preferred *Leiuranus, Callechelys* spp., and *Ophichthus cephalazona.*

Finally, it should be noted that among the eel prey of *H. melanocephalus* was discovered the first specimen of a "garden eel" from Australian waters (a new species of *Taenioconger*), as well as two snake eel species previously unrecorded from Australia, *Callechelys marmoratus* and *C. melanotaenia.*

Hydrophis elegans (Gray)

One specimen of *H. elegans* was dipnetted at a 6-fm anchorage in the McCluer Gulf. The trunk and tail of a moray eel, *Gymnothorax undulatus,* were regurgitated by the snake. This eel is an abundant and widely distributed shallow water reef associate. A single, partially digested specimen of an unidentifiable ophichthid eel, subfamily Ophichthinae, was regurgitated by another surface dipnetted snake from McCluer Gulf. The trunk and naked, hard-pointed tail of this eel were typically those of a mud- or sand-burrowing species. Denburgh and Thompson (1908) reported the sand-burrowing ophichthid *Muraenichthys thompsoni* (subfamily Myrophinae) as prey of *Hydrophis fasciatus.*

Disteira major (Shaw)

A single specimen of *D. major,* surface dipnetted beneath a nightlight at Clarence Strait, northern Australia, contained a "nettle-catfish," *Euristhmus nudiceps,* which measured 240 mm. The head of the fish had been digested. Species of *Euristhmus* are reported to have a venom apparatus associated with their pungent dorsal and anal spines.

Voris (1972) appropriately discovered a Cucumberfish, *Carapus* sp., in a Holothuria Bank specimen of *D. major.*

Lapemis hardwickii (Gray)

Many *Lapemis hardwickii* were collected by daylight surface dipnetting in the McCluer Gulf. Gut contents included a wide variety of species which inhabit several levels of the water column. *Lapemis* is apparently quite versatile in its feeding location, evidenced by pelagic prey items (young jacks and clupeids) as well as fishes from the sand-reef interphase (lizardfishes, wrasses, siganids, and snappers). The identification of prey was facilitated by otter trawl and meter net collections made at the same localities. Prey were identified with considerable assurance, using such fragmentary remains as jaw parts or otoliths.

The relatively undigested state and forward location within the snake's esophagus of cardinalfishes (*Apogon* spp.) suggest that nocturnal prey were captured during their diurnal period of inactivity.

A specimen of *L. hardwickii* collected off Townsville, eastern Australia, by W. A. Dunson (no. 178), had eaten a scorpaenid fish, *Minous* sp. Smith (1935) found specimens from Manila Harbor to contain a cornetfish (*Fistularia*) and a dragonette (Callionymidae). Voris (1972) found a similar variety of near reef and sand bottom prey from North Borneo specimens, including jacks, a scorpaenid, an ariid catfish (*Arius*), a tongue sole (*Cynoglossus?*), and an "amphipod."

Pelamis platurus (Linnaeus)

Neither of the two *Pelamis* which were dipnetted at the Ashmore Reefs contained prey. *Pelamis* typically feeds on juvenile fishes which shelter among surface drift material, often including fishes associated with medusae. *Pelamis* feeding has been discussed by Klauber (1935), Klawe (1964), Hunter and Mitchell (1967), and Kropach (in this volume).

DIGESTION RATE EXPERIMENTS

Experiments were carried out on shipboard to determine the digestion rate of prey species at $25°C$. These results must be considered preliminary in that too few experiments were run to allow precise measurements.

Six adult *Hydrophis melanocephalus* were force fed either intact moray eels (*Gymnothorax undulatus*) or wrasses (*Halichoeres nebulosus*) and sacrificed at measured time intervals. Snakes selected were captured by surface dipnetting and held for 24 hrs to insure that they had not fed during that period. Further determination of the absence of food was established by carefully feeling along the length of the digestive tract for prey items. Fishes were collected using rotenone ichthyocide along the exposed reef flat at low tide, carefully washed, and frozen immediately. Fishes were later thawed and, using 30-cm forceps, inserted head first into the snake's mouth. In most cases, the fishes were swallowed by the snakes after reaching the esophagus. Snakes were placed in covered plastic containers in a $25°C$ incubator and sacrificed by Nembutal injection and rapid freezing after 24 or 48 hrs had elapsed.

It was found that an adult snake (77 cm snout-vent length) required approximately 48 hrs to digest a 45-mm *Halichoeres* at $25°C$. An adult snake required 2 to 3 days to digest a juvenile moray eel (185 mm) at 25°C. From these experiments it was calculated that a typical *H. melanocephalus* prey item, e.g., an adult half-banded snake eel (*Leiuranus semicinctus*), would require 7 to 10 days for complete digestion. These findings are comparable to Klemmer's (1967) observations of adult *Laticauda laticaudata* in an aquarium, which ate "about three eels (medium-sized *Anguilla*) every 2 months."

Digestion occurs primarily in the stomach and lower intestine. A juvenile *Gymnothorax undulatus* (215 mm), removed after 48 hrs from an adult *H. melanocephalus,* displayed the constriction resulting from cardiac sphincter closure (Figure 4). The sharp contrast in the pre-digested hind portion is typical of most prey items regurgitated by hydrophiids.

FEEDING SPECIALIZATION

The co-occurrence of nine hydrophiids at Ashmore Reefs invited an analysis of their resource utilization and habitat specialization. This problem is particularly germane to this reef complex in that, of four sympatric species of *Aipysurus, A. foliosquama* and *A. apraefrontalis* are apparently endemic to that or nearby localities.

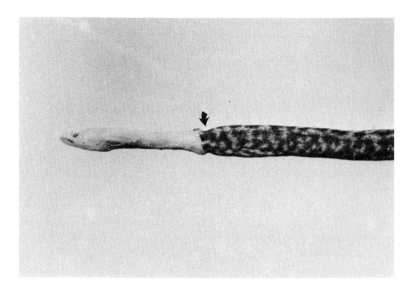

Figure 4. Young moray eel, *Gymnothorax undulatus,* removed from force-fed *Hydrophis melanocephalus* kept at 25°C for 24 hrs. Arrow indicates constriction of cardiac sphincter. Note contrast of digested and pre-digested portions of eel.

Indices of prey species diversity and redundancy from information theory were calculated to indicate the degree of feeding specialization and overlap of all Ashmore Reef hydrophiids. Combined data for McCluer Gulf and Ashmore Reef hydrophiids are summarized in Table 1. Prey were analyzed on a species-abundance basis, using a Shannon-Weaver (1949) diversity index as modified by Kohn (1966). It should be noted that prey biomass is not considered in this analysis. Prey species diversity (H) is derived using:

$$H = -\sum_{i=1}^{N} p_i \, {}^{ln}p_i$$

N is the number of species, p_i is the proportion of the ith species, relative diversity is H/H_{max} = $H/ln\ N$, and specialization, or redundancy (R) is $1-H/H_{max}$. Redundancy (Shannon and Weaver, 1949) is herein used as a direct measure of relative dietary specialization (Horn, 1966).

These indices are highly biased by the variability in prey/hydrophiid species examined; however, the relative specialization of several species (*A. stokesii, A. peronii, E. annulatus,* and *H. melanocephalus*), in contrast to the prey diversity of others (*A. fuscus* and *L. hardwickii*), is noteworthy. Overlap of prey "types," i.e., at the familial or generic level, is considerable, yet in no cases did prey overlap occur at the species level. The apparent absence or rarity of certain species of *Aipysurus* at Hibernia, Scotts, and within the Ashmore reefs did not appear related to the absence of suitable prey, but rather to the possible lack of specific shallow inner reef habitat at those locations.

COMMENTS ON FEEDING STRATEGIES

The inability of sea snakes to overcome their faster-swimming and more maneuverable prey has required the development of behavioral accommodations. Adaptation of behavioral strategies and prey specializations has made available to these elapid derivatives the extremely abundant food supply of the shallow tropical Indo-Pacific reefs. Specialized hydrophiid feeding strategies include: nocturnal feeding on diurnally active fishes, and, conversely, diurnal feeding on nocturnal fishes; surface feeding among accumulated surface drift, and on fishes in association with pelagic medusae; specialization to feed only on fish eggs; and feeding on fossorial fishes, and, in particular, eels.

The temporal feeding shift strategy utilized by shallow water species of *Aipysurus* takes advantage of the daily behavioral patterns of many fishes, including the wrasses (Labridae), parrotfishes (Scaridae), cardinalfishes (Apogonidae), bigeyes (Priacanthidae), and sweepers (Pempheridae). The

Table 1. Preferred habitat, prey diversity, and preferred prey items of several Hydrophiidae[a]

	Prey	R	H/H_{max}	Preferred habitat	Preferred prey
Acalyptophis peronii	8	0.667	0.323	OR	Eleotridae, Gobiidae
Aipysurus duboisii	4	0	1	IR,OR	Muraenidae, Blenniidae
Aipysurus foliosquama	4	1	0	OR	Labridae
Aipysurus fuscus	6	0.387	0.613	IR	Labridae
Aipysurus laevis	60	0.465	0.535	IR,OR	Apogonidae, Scaridae
Astrotia stokesii	7	0.449	0.551	OR	Batrachoididae
Emydocephalus annulatus	>20	"1"	"0"	IR,OR	Fish Eggs
Hydrophis melanocephalus[b]	47	0.599	0.401	OR	Ophichthidae, Congridae
Hydrophis elegans	2	0.500	0.500	G	Muraenidae, Ophichthidae
Disteira major	1	—	—	G	Clupeidae
Lapemis hardwickii	18	0.229	0.771	G,OR	Lutjanidae, Apogonidae
Pelamis platurus	—	—	—	P	—

[a]G, gulf; H/H_{max}, relative diversity; IR, inner reef; OR, outer reef; P, pelagic; R, redundancy.
[b]Identification is tentative, awaiting revision by H. C. Cogger.

wrasses and parrotfishes are diurnally active and return to the reef to "sleep" in the coral crevices or sand. Conversely, the large-eyed and generally red-colored nocturnally active cardinalfishes, bigeyes, and sweepers return to the reef crevices during daylight. While seeking refuge, these fishes are easy prey to the reef-searching predators. For example, the location of fang scars and necrotic sites on the regurgitated specimen of *Priacanthus cruentatus* (Figure 5) would suggest that it was bitten and envenomated while dormant and wedged horizontally in the reef.

The association of snakes with floating objects is well documented, particularly with reference to *Pelamis.* Surface convergences which result in extensive drift lines attract large populations of fishes. Juvenile jacks (Carangidae) and stromateoid fishes are very abundant in this habitat, as well as in association with pelagic medusae. The capture of young jacks, clupeids, and engraulids by *L. hardwickii* and *A. laevis* is probably accomplished through cautious stalking and rapid lunging behavior.

The particular fondness of hydrophiids for marine and freshwater eels as prey has been noted by numerous authors (Smith, 1926, 1935; Herre, 1942; Volsøe, 1933; Mahadaven and Nayar, 1965). Eels are ideal hydrophiid prey in that they are abundant on shallow reefs, scaleless, without spinous dorsal fins or cephalic armature, often cylindrical, elongate, and narrow in girth. Shallow water *A. duboisii* were observed, throughout the daylight hours, investigating

Figure 5. Intact specimen of *Priacanthus cruentatus* (above) collected at Ashmore Reef poison station. Compare to specimen (below) regurgitated by adult *Lapemis hardwickii.* Arrows indicate sites of envenomation and tissue necrosis.

the coral crevices and overhangs which are typical eel habitats. The deeper dwelling *H. melanocephalus* presumably behaves in a similar manner, entering its head in the sand and mud holes in search of congrid, ophichthid, or moringuid eels. Fossorial prey other than eels are selectively preyed upon by *A. peronii* and *A. stokesii.* Burrowing gobies are abundant along the reef edge and deeper sand bottoms. The microcephalic *Acalyptophis* was observed examining and often entering holes in the sand and broken coral bottom, apparently searching for gobies. Although the specimen of a hole-dwelling jawfish (Opistognathidae) eaten by an *A. stokesii* may represent an opportunistic catch, it does further illustrate this feeding behavior. The permanent burrows of jawfishes and other fossorial fishes make retreat impossible when discovered by a microcephalic sea snake.

I would suspect, based on the observations described above, that the highly toxic venom of sea snakes is more a feeding adaptation than a defense mechanism, in that, without it, feeding on large and struggling prey would be impossible. The eel feeding sequence of *Laticauda laticaudata* described by Klemmer (1967) may well fit the general pattern of hydrophiid feeding behavior. Upon contacting its prey, the snake bites, envenomates, withdraws, and then awaits prey death before swallowing it head first. This is particularly necessary when swallowing fishes with massive, pungent, and often venomous spines, such as the venomous catfishes, scorpionfishes, and batrachoidids. It should be noted that *H. melanocephalus* is the most venomous hydrophiid known (Chapter 18) and often feeds on eels of equal or greater girth than its own. My suggestion that sea snake venom is more important for feeding than defense is supported by the extensive reduction in dentition undergone by the egg-eating species *E. annulatus, E. ijimae,* and *Aipysurus eydouxii* (Voris, 1966). These species no longer possess a venom apparatus suitable to deter predation, and were often collected by barehanded expedition members. This hypothesis, however, is further complicated by the presence of other venomous sea snakes at each locality, which might act as Batesian models for the harmless mimics. This supposition would benefit from further observation and experimentation.

SUMMARY

Feeding selectivity and behavior of reef-dwelling hydrophiids are examined to explain the coexistence of the numerous snake species in the Ashmore Reefs complex. Prey items and habitat preferences are enumerated. Prey of each species are analyzed on a species-abundance basis using a modified Shannon-Weaver diversity index. No instances of prey species overlap were observed. Experiments to determine digestion rates of fish prey by *H. melanocephalus* are described. Feeding strategies of various hydrophiids include nocturnal feeding on diurnally active fishes, diurnal feeding on nocturnal fishes, and specialized diets of fish eggs or elongate fossorial fishes. The functions of hydrophiid venom as a feeding adaptation or defense mechanism are discussed.

ACKNOWLEDGMENTS

Many individuals have assisted in this study. Thanks are due to: William N. Eschmeyer (California Academy of Sciences), John E. Randall (Bernice P. Bishop Museum), Gerald Allen, Douglass F. Hoese, and Gilbert P. Whitley (Australian Museum) for aiding with fish identification; Maurice Giles for photographic assistance; Harold K. Voris for a pre-publication copy of his hydrophiid manuscript; William Dunson for help in various stages of this study; John E. Randall and Lillian Dempster for their comments on this manuscript; and the master and crew of the R/V *Alpha Helix* for assistance at sea.

REFERENCES

Denburgh, J. V., and I. C. Thompson. 1908. Description of a new species of sea snake from the Philippine Islands, with a note on the palatine teeth in the proteroglypha. Proceed. Calif. Acad. of Sci., 4th ser., 3:41–48.

Greenwood, P. H., D. E. Rosen, S. H. Weitzman, and G. S. Myers. 1966. Phyletic studies of teleostean fishes, with a provisional classification of living forms. Bull. Amer. Mus. Natl. His., 131(4):339–456.

Herre, A. W. C. T. 1942. Notes on Philippine sea-snakes. Copeia 1942:7–9.

Horn, H. S. 1966. Measurement of "overlap" in comparative ecological studies. Amer. Natur., 100:419–424.

Hunter, J. R., and C. T. Mitchell. 1966. Association of fishes with flotsam in the offshore waters of Central America. Fishery Bull., 66:13–29.

Klauber, L. M. 1935. Feeding habits of a sea snake. Copeia 1935:182.

Klawe, W. L. 1964. Food of the black-and-yellow sea snake, *Pelamis platurus*, from Ecuadorian coastal waters. Copeia 1964:712–713.

Klemmer, K. 1967. Observations on the sea snake *Laticauda laticaudata* in captivity. Internat. Zoo Yearbook 7:229–231.

Kohn, A. J. 1966. Food specialization in *Conus* in Hawaii and California. Ecology 47:1041–1043.

Mahadevan, S., and K. N. Nayar. 1965. Underwater ecological observations in the Gulf of Mannor off Tuticorin. J. Mar. Biol. Assoc. India 7:197–199.

Shannon, C. E., and W. Weaver. 1949. The Mathematical Theory of Communication. University of Illinois Press, Urbana.

Smith, M. 1926. Monograph of the Sea-Snakes (Hydrophiidae). British Museum of Natural History, London. 130 p.

Smith, M. 1935. The sea snakes (Hydrophiidae) Dana Report, no. 8, 6 pp.

Volsøe, H. 1939. The sea snakes of the Iranian Gulf and the Gulf of Oman. Danish Scientific Investigations in Iran, part 1:9–45.

Voris, H. K. 1966. Fish eggs as the apparent sole food item for a genus of sea snake, *Emydocephalus* (Krefft). Ecology 47:152–154.

Voris, H. K. 1972. The role of sea snakes (Hydrophiidae) in the trophic structure of coastal ocean communities. J. Mar. Biol. Assoc. India 13(no. 3–4).

APPENDIX: LIST OF HYDROPHIID GUT CONTENTS

This listing includes only those prey species identified as part of this study. Previous literature references are excluded. All species are teleost fishes unless otherwise noted. Family names follow the classification of Greenwood et al. (1966).

Acalyptophis peronii: 3 *Cryptocentrus* sp. a, 2 *Cryptocentrus* sp. b (Gobiidae).

Aipysurus apraefrontalis: none observed.

Aipysurus duboisii: 1 *Gymnothorax ?undulatus?* (Muraenidae); 1 *Salarias fasciatus* (Blennidae); 1 *Scarus* sp. (Scaridae); 1 *Acanthurus xanthopterus* (Acanthuridae).

Aipysurus foliosquama: 1 *Halichoeres* sp. (Labridae).

Aipysurus fuscus: 2 *Eleotriodes longipinnis* (Gobiidae); 1 *Halichoeres trimaculatus*, 1 *H. ?trimaculatus?*, 2 *Cymolutes praetextatus* (Labridae).

Aipysurus laevis: 1 *Pterocaesio diagramma*, 1 *Lutjanus* sp., 5 *Caesio ?chapozonas?* (Lutjanidae); 6 *Acanthurus* sp. (Acanthuridae); 31 *Apogon* spp. a, b, and c (Apogonidae); 2 *Abudefduf amabilis* (Pomacentridae); 1 *Epinephelus merra* (Serranidae); 1 *Parascorpaena* sp., 1 *Minous* sp. (Scorpaenidae); 4 *Scarus* sp. (Scaridae); 1 *Choerodon?* (Labridae); 14 *Parapriacanthus dispar* (Pempheridae); 1 *Engraulis australis* (Engraulidae); 1 *Dussumieria* sp. (Clupeidae); 1 benthic shrimp; 1 Pelecypod, *Lima* sp. (Limidae).

Astrotia stokesii: 7 *Halophryne diemensis* (Batrachoididae); 1 *Tandya* sp. (Opistognathidae).

Emydocephalus annulatus: More than 20 specimens collected containing fish eggs in their mouths and guts, apparently from Blenniidae and Gobiidae.

Hydrophis melanocephalus: 28 *Leiuranus semicinctus*, 2 *Callechelys melanotaenia*, 1 *C. marmoratus*, 3 *Ophichthus cephalazona*, 1 *Muraenicthys ?godeffroyi?*, 3 *Myrophis?* (Ophichthidae); 2 *Moringua ?macrocephalus?* (Moringuidae); 1 *Ariosoma* sp., 5 *Congrina* sp., 1 *Taenioconger* sp. (Congridae).

Hydrophis elegans: 1 *Gymnothorax undulatus* (Muraenidae); 1 unidentifiable Ophichthidae.

Disteira major: 1 *Euristhmus nudiceps* (Plotosidae).

Lapemis hardwickii: 1 *Minous* sp. (Scorpaenidae); 1 *Siganus* sp., 3 *S. nebulosus* (Siganidae); 1 *Apogon* sp., 1 *A. exostigma* (Apogonidae); 1 *Priacanthus cruentatus* (Priacanthidae); 1 *Saurida grandisquamma* (Synodontidae); 1 *Caranx?* (Carangidae); 3 *Nemipterus ?peronii?* (Lutjanidae); 1 *Choerodon?* (Labridae); 2 *Sardinella* sp. (Clupeidae); 3 unidentified clupeoids.

twelve

Predation on Sea Snakes

Harold Heatwole

Information on predation upon sea snakes is largely anecdotal and based on scattered chance observations, except for a few experiments on snake palatability to predatory fish. Neither the incidence of predation upon snake populations, interspecific differences in palatability, nor even the range of predators involved is known. However, some facts have emerged which warrant at least tentative conclusions.

Predation does occur. Known or suspected predators fall into five categories: (1) sharks and other predatory fish, (2) sea birds, (3) invertebrates, (4) other reptiles, and (5) humans. The last category is discussed in Chapter 21 and will not be treated here.

PREDATION BY FISH

Smith (1926) cites Günther as stating that sharks and other predatory fish prey extensively on sea snakes. Similarly, Cantor (1841) mentions observations suggesting sharks as natural enemies of pelagic serpents. In neither report are specific data provided. Heatwole et al. (1974) report two *Lapemis hardwickii* from the stomach of an estuary shark (*Carcharhinus lamia*) caught in the Gulf of Carpentaria, and a case of a tiger shark (*Galeocerda cuvieri*) being caught on a hook baited with a skinned *Aipysurus laevis*. McCormick et al. (1963) lists "poisonous sea snakes" from the stomachs of Phillippine tiger sharks.

The Department of Harbours and Marine of the Queensland Government, in response to shark attacks on bathers, initiated a long term netting program near selected bathing areas in late 1962. Many of the captured sharks were examined for stomach contents. Analysis of these data is now underway but is not yet complete for two localities, Mooloolaba and the Southport area. However, these are the southernmost two localities and, consequently, sea snakes are much less common there than further north where all data have been summarized. The locations of the study areas are indicated in Figure 1. A detailed treatment of the food habits of sharks will appear elsewhere (Heatwole et al., in prep.), and only the data relevant to sea snake predation are summarized here. Data are available now from a total of 7140 sharks, of which 3035 contained food. Of those, 223 contained sea snakes. Some individuals had more than one snake in the stomach; up to four were recorded. The minimum number of snakes involved was 263 or an average of 1.18 snakes per shark that had eaten snakes. Of the 19 species of sharks involved in the study, only six were found to eat sea snakes. These were the tiger shark (*Galeocerda cuvieri*), the common or black whaler (*Carcharhinus macrura*), the bronze whaler (*Carcharhinus ahenea*), the black-tipped shark (*Carcharhinus spallanzani*), the hammerhead (*Sphyrna lewini*), and the tawny shark (*Nebrius concolor*). Incidences of sea snakes in the stomachs of these species are presented by locality in Table 1.

It is clear that sea snakes are a relatively uncommon item in the diet of these sharks, except for the tiger shark. Tiger sharks from some areas contained large numbers of snakes (e.g., at Townsville almost half of the tiger shark stomachs containing food had at least one snake), and this species must be considered an important predator of sea snakes. Considering this species alone (and even more so when all sharks are evaluated collectively), shark predation on sea snakes cannot be looked upon as rare. It is clearly of sufficient magnitude to be ecologically important. Unfortunately, the contractors tending the shark nets do not retain the stomach contents and consequently the species identity of the snakes eaten is unknown; it is not possible to assess whether certain species are eaten more often than others.

The species of sharks in which sea snakes were not found were the leopard shark (*Stegostoma fasciatum*), the graceful shark (*Carcharhinus amblyrhynchoides*), coates shark (*Platypodon coatesi*), the grey nurse (*Carcharias arenarius*), the sharp-toothed shark (*Negaprion queenslandicus*), the school shark (*Galeorhinus australis*), the white pointer (*Carcharodon carcharias*), the blue pointer (*Isurus glaucus*), the "bull-nosed whaler" (species uncertain), the carpet shark (*Orectolobus ornatus*), the white-eye (*Protozygaena longmani*), the gummy shark (*Mustelus antarcticus*) and "unidentified species." These sharks collectively accounted for only 428 stomachs, of which only 76 contained food. Sample size for individual species ranged from one to 139. It is likely that at least some of these species may occasionally eat sea snakes, but it was not detected because of the small numbers of sharks caught.

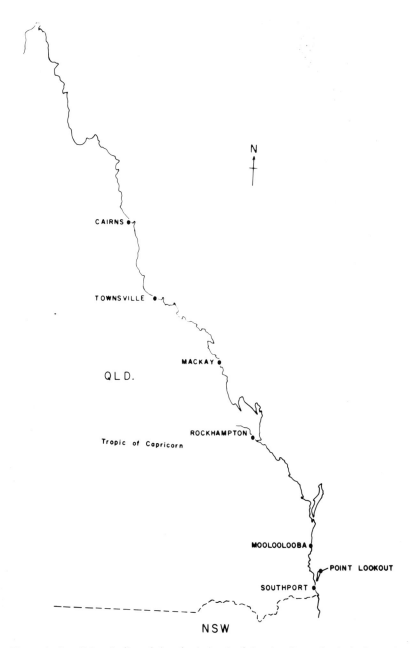

Figure 1. Localities (indicated by dots) involved in the Queensland shark netting program.

Table 1. Incidences of sea snakes in the stomachs of six species of sharks from Queensland, Australia

Species and locality	Total stomachs	Stomachs with food	Percent with food	Stomachs with snakes			Total snakes
				No.	Per cent of total	Per cent of those with food	
Tiger shark (*Galeocerda cuvieri*)							
Cairns	205	116	57	17	8.3	14.7	20
Townsville	291	209	72	97	33.2	46.4	123
Mackay	353	217	62	75	21.3	34.6	80
Rockhampton	61	19	31	3	4.9	15.8	6
Point Lookout	44	40	91	6	13.6	15.0	7
Mooloolaba	30	12	40	0	0	0	0
Southport	28	24	86	0	0	0	0
Total	1,012	637	—	198	—	—	236
Common whaler (*Carcharhinus macrura*)							
Cairns	153	33	22	3	2.0	9.1	3
Townsville	305	132	43	11	3.6	8.3	12
Mackay	115	62	54	0	0	0	0
Rockhampton	149	19	13	1	0.7	5.3	2
Point Lookout	25	25	100	0	0	0	0
Mooloolaba	30	9	30	0	0	0	0
Southport	16	14	88	0	0	0	0
Total	793	294	—	15	—	—	17
Bronze whaler (*Carcharhinus ahenea*)							
Cairns	472	305	65	1	0.2	0.3	1
Townsville	5	0	0	—	—	—	—
Mackay	66	17	26	2	3.0	11.8	2
Rockhampton	69	5	7	0	0	0	0

Total	625	333	—	3	—	—	3
Black-tipped shark (*Carcharhinus spaillanzani*)							
Cairns	221	58	26	2	0.9	3.5	2
Townsville	353	118	33	1	0.3	0.9	1
Mackay	342	91	27	0	0	0	0
Rockhampton	10	0	0	—	—	—	—
Point Lookout	10	10	100	0	0	0	0
Mooloolaba	71	10	14	0	0	0	0
Southport	20	14	70	0	0	0	0
Total	1,027	301	—	3	—	—	3
Hammerhead (*Sphyrna lewini*)							
Cairns	1,189	521	44	0	0	0	0
Townsville	808	481	60	3	0.4	0.6	3
Mackay	751	272	36	0	0	0	0
Rockhampton	257	46	18	0	0	0	0
Point Lookout	6	6	100	0	0	0	0
Mooloolaba	75	19	25	0	0	0	0
Southport	45	30	67	0	0	0	0
Total	3,131	1,375	—	3	—	—	3
Tawny shark (*Nebrius concolor*)							
Cairns	16	1	6	0	0	0	0
Townsville	52	16	31	1	1.9	6.3	1
Mackay	56	2	4	0	0	0	0
Rockhampton	0	—	—	—	—	—	—
Point Lookout	0	—	—	—	—	—	—
Mooloolaba	0	—	—	—	—	—	—
Southport	0	—	—	—	—	—	—
Total	124	19	—	1	—	—	1

Teleost fish also prey on sea snakes. Herre (1942) mentions moray eels as sea snake predators. Chacko (1949) found pieces of sea snake skin in a catfish (*Arius thalassinus*). Ben Cropp (pers. comm.) took an unidentified species of sea snake out of the stomach of a large grouper (*Promicrops lanceolatus*) speared at Swain's Reefs. He also reports an underwater observation of a Batfish coming up to a sea snake and nibbling at it, but not eating it. Some Queensland fishermen report that the Sweetlip (*Lethrinus chrysostomus*) eats sea snakes, but more specific information was not obtained. Thus at least some sharks and teleost fish occasionally eat at least some species of snake. Despite this fact, there is a widespread impression that sea snakes are relatively immune to predation. Prawn fishermen from the Gulf of Carpentaria report that unidentified species of sharks follow their ships and, although feeding on other "trash animals" discarded from the sorting trays, do not eat the sea snakes (chiefly *Hydrophis elegans*). Some field observations and experiments support the view that sea snakes are avoided and/or are unpalatable to a number of otherwise potential predators. Eva Cropp tamed a number of fish at a coral head on Heron Island Reef by feeding them by hand. Although readily accepting fish meat from her, most of the fish would not take dead sea snakes (*Aipysurus laevis* and *Aipysurus duboisii*). However, several fish rushed and bit a small individual, then dropped it. A blue cod (*Epinephalus flavocaerulens*) seized a snake attached to a piece of fish and retired to a hole in the coral, where it proceeded to swallow the entire snake. On another occasion, a blue cod half-swallowed an *A. laevis* and then spat it out. The snake was finally eaten by a moray eel. A coral trout ate skinned snake meat without subsequently spitting it out; similarly a maori cod and a blue cod both consumed and retained snake meat which had been wrapped in fish meat (E. Cropp, pers. comm.; see also MacLeish, 1972). It is probable that these fish would have been more discriminating in their food selection were it not for the fact that they were accustomed to being fed acceptable food by hand. Even so, the reluctance of many individuals to accept the food was more impressive than the few cases in which snakes were eaten.

The most extensive experimental work on sea snake predation has been carried out by Rubinoff and Kropach (1970) on *Pelamis platurus*. They have shown that a number of predatory fish on the Pacific side of the isthmus of Panama will not attack *P. platurus* (the only species of sea snake occurring there) and will not eat dead snakes, skinned or unskinned, or pieces of snake meat, fresh or frozen. If fed sea snake meat sandwiched between pieces of squid, sharks would eat the squid and expel the snake meat. Fish from the Atlantic side, where no sea snakes naturally occur, will attack *Pelamis* offered them; a behavior which sometimes results in their death by snake bite. It seems that *Pelamis* is relatively immune from attack by sympatric predatory fish.

PREDATION BY BIRDS

There are numerous published statements that both the red-backed (*Haliastur indus*) and white-breasted (*Haliaetus leucogaster*) sea eagles eat sea snakes (Campbell and White, 1910; Barrett, 1946, 1954; Roughley, 1961; Banfield, 1968). Dunson (pers. comm.) reports a sea eagle dropping an *A. laevis* at Esk Island (Palm Group), Australia. I have observed that remains of sea snakes are a common item in the material dropped by the white-breasted sea eagle around its nest and feeding perches. Jerdon (1877) mentions that the ground below nests of this species "is strewed and whitened with bones of sea snakes chiefly, but also of fish," and Cantor (1841) found sea snake remains in the stomachs of two sea eagles. Smith (1926) mentions a buoy covered with remains of sea snakes left from the meals of sea birds. Van der Meer Mohr (1927) repeatedly observed eagles returning from the sea with sea snakes in their claws. Barrett (1954) states that eagles catch snakes at the surface of the water; it is possible they may also pick up dead or moribund ones washed up on beaches.

Rubinoff and Kropach (1970) occasionally captured scarred snakes (*P. platurus*) (see Figure 2), and suggested that the origin of the wounds may have been predatory birds. Even if true, this does not necessarily indicate that

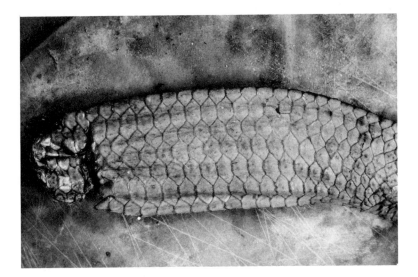

Figure 2. Recently healed laceration in the tail of an *Aipysurus laevis* of the type which, when complete, results in ends of the tail missing. It was at first considered that outboard motors might be the source of such an injury. However, injuries occurred in high frequencies in remote areas where power boats are rarely used.

birds actually consume this species, as Wetmore (1965) observed a frigate bird (*Fregata magnificens*) "pick up a sea snake [*Pelamis*] swimming at the surface and carry it, as it twisted and coiled, for a short distance with other frigates in close pursuit, and then finally let it drop." Smith (1926), Loveridge (1946) and Minton (1966) suggest that the occasional occurrence of sea snakes on land away from water can be explained by their having been dropped by predatory birds. The first author reports an eye-witness account of *Thalassophina viperina* falling over land from the claws of a sea eagle.

PREDATION BY OTHER REPTILES

Allen (1974) records unidentified species of sea snakes taken from the stomach of a salt water crocodile (*Crocodylus porosus*) from Palau.

PREDATION BY INVERTEBRATES

Van Bruggen (1961) reports an octopus feeding on a live *P. platurus* in a laboratory tank. Whether this also occurs in nature is unknown but probably would be rare. Duellman (1961) observed partially eaten *Pelamis* protruding from crab holes in a Mexican beach, and Kropach (1972) noted that dead *Pelamis* were mutilated by crabs and lobsters in a laboratory tank. These latter cases are scavenging rather than predation, but do indicate that dead sea snakes are acceptable as food to various crustaceans.

INCIDENCE OF WOUNDS ON SEA SNAKES

During field work on reef-inhabiting sea snakes, I was impressed with the frequency of individuals encountered which had either scars on the body or parts of the tail missing (in some instances the tail was completely gone) (Figures 2 and 3). Eventually I kept systematic records of such injuries (Tables 2 and 3). Wounds were separately listed as (1) large terminal portions of the tail missing as though sheared off; (2) curved chunks missing from some part of the tail (in a number of cases several "bites" had been taken out of the same animal); (3) small nicks in the tail; and (4) scars on the body (Figures 2 and 3). The first two categories I interpret as bite marks left by an unsuccessful predatory fish. The body scars were shaped more as one would expect from wounds left by talons or beak, and probably indicate an attack by a predatory bird. However, some may have arisen from other causes. The small nicks in the tail could result from injuries sustained by lashing the tail against sharp coral or, in the case of several species with irregularly arranged

Figure 3. The tails of a normal *Pelamis* (lower) and a bob-tailed *Pelamis* (upper) caught off Acapulco, Mexico, by W. Dunson.

scales on the caudal terminus, may be artifacts and not wounds at all. Consequently, although nicks are listed in a separate category in Table 2, they are included in the category "uninjured tails" in the summary of the data (Table 3). Thus, the incidences of wounds due to presumed predation are conservative in Table 3, since nicks which indeed may have resulted from predation attempts are not treated as injuries.

The specimens on which this report is based are those of my personal collection, and those readily accessible at the Australian Museum at the time of writing. The latter consisted of part of the specimens arising from the *Alpha Helix* expedition to the Ashmore Reef area, and a collection made by Dunson near Townsville. Specimens of uncertain taxonomic affinity and awaiting proper identification were not included in the analysis. No attempt was made to assemble specimens from other sources, since few museums have large series of sea snakes. In all, 593 specimens of 19 species were examined. Of these, 12 species (63%) had conspicuous wounds suggestive of predation by fish (tail nicks excluded). Of the seven species for which there were no records of large tail injuries, two (*Aipysurus apraefrontalis* and *Acalyptophis peronii*) had small tail nicks (which may have been caused by predators), and four (*Disteira kingii, Disteira major, Laticauda colubrina, Hydrophis gracilis;* not included in the tables) were represented either by one or by two specimens and therefore could not be considered a good sample. Only one species represented by large samples (*P. platurus*) lacked any suggestion of predation by fish (Tables 2 and 3). Similarly, nine (47%) of the species had

Table 2. Incidence of injuries in sea snakes from various localities.[a]

Species and locality	Uninjured tails		Tail with nicks		Bites on tail		Some or all of tail missing		N	Scars on body	
	No.	%	No.	%	No.	%	No.	%		No.	%
Acalyptophis peronii											
Ashmore Reef and vicinity	10	71.4	4	28.6	0	0	0	0	14	1	7.1
Saumarez Reef	0	—	1	—	0	—	0	—	1	0	—
Total	10	66.7	5	0	0	0	0	0	15	1	6.7
Aipysurus apraefrontalis											
Ashmore Reef and vicinity	0	—	1	—	0	—	0	—	1	0	1
Aipysurus duboisii											
Townsville	5	35.7	7	50.0	2	14.3	0	0	14	1	7.1
Arafura Sea	3	—	1	—	0	—	1	—	5	0	—
Cato Island	5	—	0	—	0	—	0	—	5	1	—
Saumarez Reef	10	90.9	1	9.1	0	0	0	0	11	0	0
Ashmore Reef and vicinity	6	40.0	5	33.3	1	6.7	3	20.0	15	0	0
Total	29	58.0	14	28.0	3	6.0	4	8.0	50	2	4.0
Aipysurus foliosquama											
Ashmore Reef and vicinity	14	45.2	10	32.3	5	16.1	2	6.5	31	0	0
Aipysurus fuscus											
Townsville	1	—	0	—	0	—	0	—	1	0	—
Ashmore Reef and vicinity	28	77.8	4	11.1	3	8.3	1	2.8	36	1	2.8
Total	29	78.4	4	10.8	3	8.1	1	2.7	37	1	2.7

Aipysurus laevis											
Townsville	11	61.1	1	5.6	5	27.8	1	5.6	18	0	0
Arafura Sea	1	—	0	—	2	—	1	—	4	0	—
Cato Island	3	—	0	—	0	—	0	—	3	0	—
Saumarez Reef	4	—	2	31.8	0	—	1	22.7	7	0	0
Swain's Reefs	9	40.9	7	21.3	1	4.5	5	4.3	22	0	0
Ashmore Reef and vicinity	32	68.1	10	—	3	6.4	2	—	47	1	0
Gulf of Carpentaria	0	—	1	—	1	—	0	—	2	1	—
Total	60	58.3	21	20.4	12	11.7	10	9.7	103	1	1.0
Astrotia stokesii											
Townsville	2	—	1	—	3	—	0	—	6	1	—
Arafura Sea	2	—	1	—	1	—	0	—	4	1	—
Saumarez Reef	0	—	0	—	1	—	0	—	1	0	—
Swain's Reefs	1	—	0	—	0	—	0	—	1	0	—
Ashmore Reef and vicinity	11	73.3	2	13.3	2	13.3	0	0	15	0	0
Gulf of Carpentaria	1	—	0	—	0	—	0	—	1	0	—
Misc. Localities	1	—	0	—	0	—	0	—	1	0	—
Total	18	62.1	4	13.8	7	24.1	0	0	29	2	6.9
Emydocephalus annulatus											
Cato Island	6	—	1	—	0	—	0	—	7	1	—
Saumarez Reef	17	100	0	0	0	0	0	0	17	0	0
Ashmore Reef and vicinity	38	79.2	4	8.3	5	10.4	1	2.1	48	1	2.1
Total	61	84.7	5	6.9	5	6.9	1	1.4	72	2	2.8
Enhydrina schistosa											
Gulf of Carpentaria	2	—	0	—	1	—	0	—	3	0	—
Hydrophis melanocephalus[b]											
Ashmore Reef and vicinity	48	75.0	8	12.5	5	7.8	3	4.7	64	1	1.6

Table 2. cont.

	N	%	N	%	N	%	N	%	N	N	%
Hydrophis elegans											
Townsville	16	80.0	2	10.0	2	10.0	0	0	20	0	0
Gulf of Carpentaria	29	80.6	3	8.3	4	11.1	0	0	36	1	2.8
Misc. localities	4	—	1	—	0	—	0	—	5	0	—
Total	49	80.3	6	9.8	6	9.8	0	0	61	1	1.6
Disteira kingii											
Townsville	0	—	0	—	1	—	0	—	1	0	—
Hydrophis ornatus											
Townsville	5	—	0	—	1	—	0	—	6	0	—
Lapemis hardwickii											
Townsville	29	80.6	3	8.3	1	2.8	3	8.3	36	1	2.8
Arafura Sea	19	79.2	4	16.7	1	4.2	0	0	24	1	4.2
McCluer Gulf	11	61.1	3	16.7	2	11.1	2	11.1	18	0	0
Gulf of Carpentaria	5	—	2	—	0	—	0	—	7	0	—
Misc. localities	1	—	0	—	0	—	0	—	1	0	—
Total	65	75.6	12	14.0	4	4.7	5	5.8	86	2	2.3
Pelamis platurus											
Various localities	28	100	0	0	0	0	0	0	28	0	0

[a]Tail injuries of various types tallied independently of body scars. Percentages not calculated for samples of less than 10 animals. N indicates sample size.
[b]Tentatively identified by H. G. Cogger, but subsequent revision likely.

Table 3. Incidences of conspicuous tail injuries and body scars on sea snakes

Species	Habitat	Percent with conspicuous tail injuries	Percent with scars	No. of specimens examined
Pelamis platurus	Sea surface, pelagic	0	0	28
Hydrophis melanocephalus	Deep water, reefs	12.5	1.6	64
Acalyptophis peronii	Medium depth, reefs	0	6.7	15
Lapemis hardwickii	Medium depth, not reef	10.5	2.3	86
Hydrophis elegans	Medium depth, not reef	9.8	1.6	61
Astrotia stokesii	Variable depths, eurytopic	24.1	6.9	29
Aipysurus laevis	Medium depth, reef	21.4	1.0	103
Aipysurus fuscus	Medium depth, reef	10.8	2.7	37
Aipysurus duboisii	Shallow to medium depth, reef	8.3	2.8	72
Aipysurus foliosquama	Shallow, reef	22.6	0	31

evidence of presumed avian attempts at predation. Of the 10 species lacking such injuries, eight were represented by inadequate samples (N = 6 or less; *Disteira kingii, Hydrophis ornatus, D. major, Hydrophis fasciatus, L. colubrina, H. gracilis, Aipysurus apraefrontalis, Enhydrina schistosa*), and only two (*P. platurus* and *Aipysurus foliosquama*) represented by large samples were free of body scars. The only species of those represented by adequate samples that had no injuries of any kind was *P. platurus.* The significance of this finding is discussed later.

In addition to the uncertainty as to whether the observed injuries actually did result from predators, there are several difficulties in interpreting the incidences of scars or damaged tails, even in the larger samples. One variable which might influence observed incidences is snake size. A small species may have a low incidence of injuries, not because it is not preyed upon, but because predation usually results in the entire snake being eaten, not just part of it. In this connection, it is interesting that the species with the highest incidence of both conspicuous tail injuries and body scars was *A. stokesii,* by far the bulkiest (though not the longest) species studied. Otherwise, however, there did not seem to be a consistent relationship between body size and incidence of injuries.

On an intraspecific basis also, body size could be important as larger (older) snakes would have lived longer and, therefore, would have a higher probability of having sustained an injury than a smaller (younger) one. Consequently, samples of a given species from different areas may show widely different incidences of injury, simply because of sampling at different stages of the annual cycle when population age structure is different. In the present analysis, no attempt was made to analyze adults and juveniles separately, or to separate the seasons; consequently some of the above bias may be inherent in the data. Until the population biology of sea snakes is better understood, a more refined analysis than the present crude one seems unwarranted. Keeping the above limitations in mind, several useful interpretations can be made. The most important one is that there was a relatively high incidence of injuries (presumably caused by would-be predators) sustained by most species in almost all localities from which reasonably large samples were available (Table 2). Most samples have roughly 10–25% of the population with conspicuous tail injuries and 1–3% with body scars. It therefore seems that most species are subjected to considerable predation pressure. The lower incidence of scars as compared to tail injuries may reflect lower numbers of avian as opposed to piscine predators, and/or the fact that most species of sea snakes spend most of their time underwater, where they are inaccessible to predatory birds. However, it should be noted that inter-locality differences in one species are not always paralleled in another. For example, incidence of total conspicuous tail injuries (bites plus tails with missing ends) in *A. laevis* from Ashmore Reef was about one third that at Townsville and Swain's Reefs, whereas, in *A. duboisii,* the incidence at Ashmore Reef was almost double that at Townsville. There was a high incidence of tail injuries for *L. hardwickii* at the McCluer Gulf, West Irian, compared to other localities. In *H. elegans,* the two areas sampled (Townsville, Gulf of Carpentaria) were almost identical.

On an ecological basis, one is tempted to postulate that the deep-water species have lower incidences of tail injury than those from shallower water, as two of the three deep-water species had no conspicuous tail injuries at all, whereas all other species had overall values between 8.3% and 24.1% (Table 3). However, within the shallower water there was no consistent relationship between tail injury and depth. Although the shallowest species (*A. folio-*

squama) had the second highest incidence, a species ranging through various depths (*A. stokesii*) had the highest. Also, there were no consistent differences between reef and non-reef species. Incidence of body scratches shows no consistent relationship to any of the above variables. Thus, if there are ecological correlates with incidence of injury, they are obscured by the operation of other variables.

In my samples, *P. platurus* was unique in not having injuries of any kind and would seem to be relatively free from attack by predators. This hypothesis is consistent with the experimental findings of Rubinoff and Kropach (1970) and with Kropach's (1972) field data. The latter examined 457 potential predators (sharks and large predatory teleosts) of 25 species collected in an area where *Pelamis* was known to occur, and often caught in the same place and at the same time that *Pelamis* were seen in large numbers. He also reported on the unpublished data of other investigators, who had examined 214 dolphins from areas where *Pelamis* were plentiful, and about 1000 eastern Pacific sharks. Neither in his study nor in those of the other investigators were any sea snakes found. In the area covered, *Pelamis* was the only species of sea snake present. Similarly, François (pers. comm.), in reply to a letter of inquiry, states regarding the New South Wales shark netting program: "There is no legal requirement for meshers to inspect the stomach contents of sharks. There has however been a tendency for some of them to investigate large sharks, but there appears to be no record of sea snakes being sighted in the contents." In contrast to the Queensland waters where a variety of species of sea snakes occur (and are eaten), only *Pelamis* is present in the area covered by the New South Wales shark netting program. All of the above types of data converge to suggest that *Pelamis* is relatively predation free. However, they are not completely so. Two stub-tailed individuals (out of 141 caught) have been found off Acapulco (Figure 3; Dunson, pers. comm.), and Rubinoff and Kropach (1970), Kropach (1972), Pickwell (pers. comm.) and Dunson (pers. comm.) have all observed individuals with scratches. The number of records of injured snakes of this species in nature is, however, very small. The only direct observation suggesting predation on *Pelamis* by fish is that of Paulson (1967). He states that "on two occasions we observed billfishes (sailfish or small marlins) striking sea snakes, knocking them completely out of the water and presumably swallowing them as they sank." In the absence of information as to whether the snakes were actually eaten, it is difficult to interpret the behavior of these fish, or to assess whether or not the snakes were accidentally involved in some surface activity of the fish other than predation.

P. platurus is also unusual among sea snakes in being conspicuously colored, and in spending much of the time at the surface where its coloration would be most visible (see Chapter 23). It is tempting to speculate that its coloration is aposematic, advertising the noxious qualities it is known to possess (at least in relation to many predatory fish). It is perhaps also noxious to predatory birds. Despite the fact that it spends a greater proportion of its time at the surface (where it would be exposed to bird attack) than do any of the other species, it was one of the two species completely lacking body scars in my sample. Selection against conspicuous coloration would be maintained as long as *any* common immune predator existed, since advertisement to such a species would almost certainly result in heavy mortality not counterbalanced by the value of warning other potential predators. It is suggested that only those species which have noxious qualities effective against *all* common predators can develop warning coloration, a combination of circumstances which seems to obtain in *Pelamis*. In all of the other species studied, predation seems to occur and consequently there is selection against conspicuous color patterns.

One other group of sea snakes, besides *Pelamis,* is conspicuously colored. The genus *Laticauda,* the sea kraits or banded sea snakes, have a bold pattern of alternating dark and light bands. There is some evidence that potential predators avoid them. Starck noted that, on Marion reef, sharks were reluctant to feed on them even during feeding frenzies and would not take baits tied to banded rods. They did take baits attached to plain colored rods (Allen and Paxton, 1974). Furthermore, sharks that approached divers clad in black suits would leave when a diver in a suit marked with a bold pattern of black and white bands entered the water. It appears that, despite its normally gentle temperament, *Laticauda* may be noxious to predators and its coloration may be aposematic.

SUMMARY

Although many predators seem to avoid feeding on sea snakes, some sharks, teleosts, and birds do eat some species. *Pelamis platurus* seems to be exceptionally free from predation; it is suggested that its uniquely conspicuous coloration is aposematic.

ACKNOWLEDGMENTS

This work was supported by the National Science Foundation under grant NSF GA 35835 to the Pennsylvania State University and grants NSF GA 34948 and NSF GD 34462 to The Scripps Institution of Oceanography for operation of the *Alpha Helix* Research Program.

REFERENCES

Allen, G. R. 1974. The marine crocodile, *Crocodylus porosus,* from Ponape, Eastern Caroline Islands, with notes on food habits of crocodiles from the Palau Archipelago. Copeia 1974:553.

Allen, G. R., and J. R. Paxton. 1974. A tropical outpost in the South Pacific. Austral. Nat. Hist. 18:50–55.

Banfield, E. J. 1968. The Confessions of a Beachcomber. Angus & Robertson, Sydney, 221 pp.

Barrett, C. 1946. Coast of Adventure. Robertson and Mullens Ltd., Melbourne, 216 pp.

Barrett, C. 1954. Wildlife of Australia and New Guinea. William Heinemann Ltd., Melbourne. 229 pp.

Campbell, A. J., and S. A. White. 1910. Birds identified on the Capricorn Group during expedition of R. A. O. U., 8th to 17th October, 1910. Emu 10:195–204.

Cantor, T. 1841. Observations upon pelagic serpents. Trans. Zool. Soc. London 2:303–313, plus 2 plates.

Chacko, P. I. 1949. Food and feeding habits of the fishes of the Gulf of Manaar. Proc. Indian Acad. Sci. 29:83–97.

Duellman, W. E. 1961. The amphibians and reptiles of Michoacán, México. Univ. Kansas Publ. Mus. Natl. Hist. 15:1–148.

Heatwole, H., E. Cameron, and T. Jones. Food habits of sharks from eastern Queensland with emphasis on their predation upon sea snakes. In preparation.

Heatwole, H., E. Heatwole, and C. R. Johnson. 1974. Shark predation on sea snakes. Copeia 1974:780–781.

Herre, A. W. C. T. 1942. Notes on Phillipine sea-snakes. Copeia 1942:7–9.

Jerdon, T. C. 1877. The Birds of India. Vol. 1. P. S. D'Rozario & Co., Calcutta. p. 85.

Kropach, C. 1972. A field study of the sea snake *Pelamis platurus* (Linnaeus) in the Gulf of Panama. Ph.D thesis, The City University of New York. pp. 115–122.

Loveridge, A. 1946. Reptiles of the Pacific World. The Macmillan Co., New York. 259 pp.

MacLeish, K. 1972. Diving with sea snakes. Natl. Geog. 141:564–578.

McCormick, H. W., T. Allen, and W. E. Young. 1963. Shadows in the Sea. Chilton Books, Philadelphia. 415 pp.

van der Meer Mohr, J. C. 1927. Notiz über Seeschlangen. Misc. Zool. Sumatrana 23:1–2.

Minton, S. A. Jr. 1966. A contribution to the herpetology of West Pakistan. Bull. Amer. Mus. Nat. Hist. 134:27–184.

Paulson, D. R. 1967. Searching for sea serpents. Sea Frontiers 13:244–250.

Roughley, T. C. 1961. Wonders of the Great Barrier Reef. Angus & Robertson, Sydney. 279 pp.

Rubinoff, I., and C. Kropach. 1970. Differential reactions of Atlantic and Pacific predators to sea snakes. Nature 228:1288–1290.

Smith, M. 1926. (1964 reprint). Monograph of the Sea Snakes (Hydrophiidae). Wheldon & Wesley Ltd., Codicote, Hertz. 130 pp., plus 2 plates.

Van Bruggen, A. C. 1961. *Pelamis platurus,* an unusual item of food of *Octopus* spec. Basteria 25:73–74.

Wetmore, A. 1965. The birds of the Republic of Panamá, Part 1: Tinamidae (Tinamous) to Rynchopidae (Skimmers). Smithsonian Misc. Collections 150:1–483.

thirteen

Fouling Organisms and Parasites Associated with the Skin of Sea Snakes

Leon P. Zann,
Roger J. Cuffey,
and Chaim Kropach

Marine reptiles and mammals are often colonized by a variety of unspecialized organisms normally found attached to objects drifting on the surface or, more rarely, to rocks on the sea floor. These are often the same species which foul vessels or other maritime installations at great inconvenience and cost to man. Such fouling organisms are opportunistic in their settlement because suitable substrates are limited in the open sea. It is not uncommon to find a small piece of stranded pummice or a bottle covered with stalked barnacles, bryozoans, hydrozoans, and algae, and teeming with polychaete worms, crabs, and other crustaceans.

The attachment of organisms to a mobile host is of interest to biologists, since the "hitch hikers" may widen their distribution in this way and their presence may indirectly interfere with the host's well being. Organisms fouling sea snakes may include very specialized ones found only on sea snakes. One of these, *Platylepas ophiophilus* Lanchester, a small barnacle, is discussed in Chapter 14. We will deal with those organisms found associated with sea snakes, the implications of the associations, the effects on the host, and the mechanisms by which the snakes endeavor to keep themselves free of fouling.

DIATOMS AND HIGHER ALGAE

Whales sometimes carry a film of diatoms on their skins. The species are typical epiphytic/epilithic forms, although certain are regularly occurring (Round, 1971). While diatoms were abundant on inanimate objects found drifting on the surface and on fouling panels placed in the waters off Townsville (Zann, in preparation), very few were found epibiotic on sea snakes. Their diminutive size (as small as 10 μ) might prevent their detection, but smears and scrapings from the skins of freshly collected snakes revealed very few diatoms or bacteria. Diatoms, probably epiphytic species, were more common on sea snakes which were fouled by higher algae. *Navicula* sp. was common on a *Disteira kingii* (Bouleng) fouled by an *Enteromorpha.*

Occasionally, higher algae have been reported on sea snakes. Smith (1926) mentioned that two Australian *Astrotia stokesii* (Grey) were covered by a dense growth, and that two species of *Enteromorpha* and two or three *Ulva* spp. were found on snakes from Ceylon. *Enteromorpha* sp. fouled two *D. kingii*, one of which had the diatom *Navicula* (above). Both snakes were stranded in a moribund condition, suggesting that the algae may have grown during prolonged periods on the surface or in shallow water. This species was trawled by Dunson near Keeper Reef and is considered by him to be a deep water form (see Chapter 7).

Algal fouling was more common on snakes collected from the clear shallow lagoon waters of Ashmore Reefs. Specimens of *Aipysurus foliosquama* (M. Smith), *A. fucus* (Tschudi), *A. laevis* Lacepede, *A. duboisii* (Bavay), and *A. apraefrontalis* (M. Smith) were fouled with algae, predominantly *Giffordia mitchellae* (Harvey) Hamel, with a few tufts of *Spyridia filamentosa* (Wulfen) Harvey and *Cladophora* sp. and an associated *Spyridia* sp. These algae had probably been grazed. Epiphytic diatoms were commonly found associated with the algae on these snakes.

It is probable that the snakes confined to the clear, shallow (2–6 m) lagoon waters of reefs accumulate algae because the high light intensity allows photosynthesis. Those snakes collected in coastal waters of North Queensland live in deeper waters (to 50 m), and the time spent breathing or basking on the surface may not be sufficient to enable algae to develop.

FORAMINIFERANS

Few protozoans were seen, possibly again because of their small size. Specimens of *Elphidium craticulatum* (Frichtel and Moll), *Amphistegina lessoni* d'Orbigny and *Operculina* sp. (cf. *O. complanata* [Defrance]) were seen adhering to adjacent scales of an *A. duboisii.* This snake also carried polychaetes and a bryozoan, and the presence of so many unspecialized forms suggests something unusual in this specimen's habits.

It is probable that these foraminiferans were not alive when the snake was collected, and it is doubtful that these normally benthonic species are symbiotic (Albani, pers. comm.).

HYDROZOANS

Tufty filaments of the hydrozoan *Dynamena quadridentata* (Ellis and Solander) were found on many of the characteristic spinous ventral scales of two specimens of *L. hardwickii* from North Queensland. Insufficient information on this relationship is available to draw conclusions on its regularity, but this hydrozoan does not normally have unusual substrate preferences (Pennycuik, 1959). Watson (pers. comm.) notes that the specimens examined do not conform exactly to the species description, possibly because of their unusual habitat. The spinous scales of male *L. hardwickii* were also a favored surface for symbiotic bryozoans (below).

Another hydrozoan, *Obelia longicatha* Allman, was found on an *H. elegans* and again on the spinous ventral scales of an *L. hardwickii* (Figure 1A), both collected from McCluer Gulf, West Irian. This species also does not normally have unusual substrate preferences.

Certain hydrozoan symbionts have an exclusive relationship with their hosts. Associations with bivalves and sand snails are well known, and hydrozoans have been reported as specific commensals of certain scorpaenid fish (Hand, 1961), but no records of associations with sea snakes are known. The peculiar association of hydrozoans with the spinous scales of *L. hardwickii* may be more regular than the others reported here.

SERPULID POLYCHAETES

Tubeworms of many species are common foulers of materials placed in the sea. Only one snake examined carried tubeworms, the *A. duboisii* which carried the foraminiferans and the bryozoan *Monoporella.* Two *Spirorbis* sp. tubes were found on adjacent scales. They were dead and slightly damaged, making identification difficult. Another serpulid, a juvenile *Pomatoleios krauseii* (Baird) (Figure 1B), also dead, was found associated with the *Spirorbis* sp. *P. krauseii* is a common fouler of vessels in North Queensland waters.

Although certain *Spirorbis* spp. have preferred substrates of algae, crustaceans, and molluscs, it is doubtful that the above have a regular association with sea snakes.

BIVALVE MOLLUSCS

Small specimens of a pearl oyster *Pinctada* sp. (Figure 1C) were collected from two *L. hardwickii.* One snake possessed one individual, the other

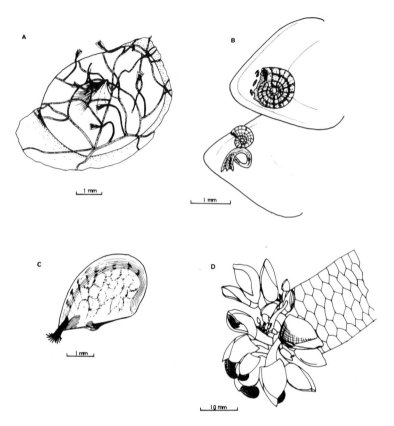

Figure 1. Fouling organisms on sea snakes.
  A. Hydrozoan *Obelia longicatha* covering a spinous scale of *L. hardwickii*. Dendritic
     hydrorhizae (stippled) cover scale and hydranths and hydrocauli (dark) are erect.
  B. Serpulids (two *Spirorbis* sp. and one *Pomatoleios krauseii*) on adjacent scales of *A.
     duboisii*.
  C. Pearl oyster (*Pinctada* sp.) from *L. hardwickii*. Note byssus for attachment.
  D. Cluster of *Lepas antifera* on tail of *E. annulatus*.

approximately 15. They were securely attached with the thread-like byssus
and their size (2–3 mm) indicated their young age. This species attained a
similar size after 2 weeks on fouling panels in Townsville harbor (unpublished
data). It is doubtful that they have a regular association with sea snakes.

BRYOZOANS

Bryozoan colonies usually attach to firm substrates, most fixed to the sea
bottom but a few drifting freely through surface waters. Many of the latter

are comparatively inert, such as brown algae, driftwood, debris, or ships. However, some are living, highly mobile animals, including sea snakes, turtles (Annandale, 1912), ammonites (Dunbar, 1928), and crustaceans (Sars, 1874).

The earliest report of bryozoans encrusting sea snakes involved a "zoophyte" termed *"Cellepora pertusa"* on *Hydrophis gracilis* off India (Cantor, 1840). Apparently, Harmer's (1931) comment that bryozoans encrust Indian Ocean sea snakes refers to this earliest report.

The next report concerning such associations was of *Electra angulata* on *Pelamis platurus* off Costa Rica (Cuffey, 1971). Shortly thereafter, Kropach and Soule (1973) noted *Membranipora tuberculata* on *P. platurus* off Panama. Meanwhile, Dunson and Zann obtained additional materials, discussed herein, off Australia—*Membranipora savartii* on *A. stokesii* and *L. hardwickii*, and *Monoporella?* sp. on *A. duboisii.*

Systematic treatment of bryozoans found thus far on sea snakes is greatly simplified by these species (all anascan cheilostomes; Bassler, 1953; Cuffey, 1973) having been extensively described elsewhere. Consequently, for each species, brief notes indicate morphologic peculiarities of the colonies taken from sea snakes (Figure 2), general ecologic and zoogeographic distribution, and circumstances of occurrences on sea snakes.

Membranipora savartii (Audouin, 1826) (Family Membraniporidae)

Colonies of this species (Canu and Bassler, 1929, p. 66–68; Cook, 1968, p. 129–130) taken from sea snakes are thin, encrusting, unilamellar sheets. The zooecial walls are somewhat elevated laterally and distally around the aperture/operculum to form a mural rim, the surface of which appears distinctly granulated or beaded. The proximal margin of the opesium generally lacks the

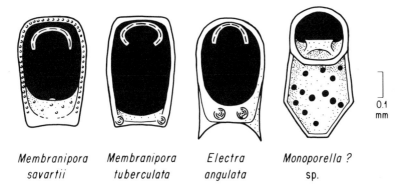

| *Membranipora* | *Membranipora* | *Electra* | *Monoporella ?* |
| savartii | tuberculata | angulata | sp. |

Figure 2. Schematic diagrams of representative zooecia in bryozoan colonies obtained from sea snakes.

prominent medium denticle developed on many previously figured specimens, although a minute rounded mound found there in a few zooecia probably represents the initial stages in formation of this denticle. Completely absent are the tiny spine-like spicules projecting into the opesium, and the low rounded tubercles at the zooecial angles, seen on some previously illustrated specimens. This species is found throughout tropical seas, in the Atlantic, Pacific, and Indian Oceans. Usually inhabiting normal marine waters, it is occasionally encountered in brackish water. Recorded specimens come from shallow depths, mostly 0–60 m, but a few down to about 120 m. This species is known as fossils back into the Eocene.

Membranipora savartii was obtained in 1972 by Dunson and Zann from sea snakes collected at several localities:

Off Dunk Island, Australia (at approximately 18° 00–30'S, 146° 10–20'E), bottom about 15 m; encrusting *L. hardwickii*

Off Orpheus Island, Australia (at 18° 38'S, 146° 26'E), bottom about 20 m; encrusting *A. stokesii*

Off Cape Upstart, Australia (at 19° 43'S, 147°43'E), bottom about 13 m; encrusting *L. hardwickii*

Membranipora tuberculata (Bosc, 1802) (Family Membraniporidae)

Encrusting, thin, sheet-like colonies of this species (Shier, 1964, p. 609–610) were recorded from a sea snake by Kropach and Soule (1973). Their photograph shows that the tubercles located at the zooecial angles are quite low or small, in contrast to the usual prominent development on many previously illustrated specimens. This species generally encrusts floating brown algae (especially *Sargassum*), on which it drifts throughout tropical and temperate Atlantic, Indian, and Pacific waters. It has been recorded also as an important fouling species (Ryland, 1972). Fossil representatives are known from Pleistocene strata.

Membranipora tuberculata has been noted on sea snakes at one locality (Kropach and Soule, 1973): off Isla Jicaron, Panama (at 7° 18'N, 81° 47'W), at surface of 24 m deep water; encrusting *P. platurus*.

Electra angulata (Levinsen, 1909) (Family Electridae)

Sea snakes have yielded unilamellar, thin, encrusting, sheet-like colonies of this species (Harmer, 1926, p. 207). Such specimens lack the tiny spines developed around the margin of the opesium in many previously figured materials. Seldom reported, this species is known only from tropical Indo-Pacific waters (off Thailand and Indonesia), and now also Costa Rica. Previously known specimens encrusted floating or sunken (at 275 m depth) driftwood. This species has not been found fossil.

Electra angulata was found by Dunson in 1970 on sea snakes at one locality (Cuffey, 1971): off Golfo Dulce, Costa Rica (at 8° 21'N, 83° 11'W), at surface of 180 m deep water; encrusting *P. platurus*.

Monoporella? sp. (Family Aspidostomatidae)

Two very small colonies taken from sea snakes represent a species similar to *Monoporella fimbriata* (Canu and Bassler, 1929, p. 156–158). However, the few intact zooecia available for study are insufficient for reliable identification. *Monoporella fimbriata* itself has been reported only from the tropical western Pacific, mostly at depths of about 50 m.

Monoporella? sp. was taken by Dunson and Zann in 1972 from sea snakes at one locality: off Lodestone Reef, Australia (at 18° 42'S, 147°11'E), on bottom 41 m deep; encrusting *A. duboisii*.

Hippodiplosia pertusa (Esper, 1796) (Family Schizoporellidae)

The earliest report of bryozoans on sea snakes was of this ascophoran cheilostome species (Canton, 1840, p. 309). The colonies have apparently been lost, which is particularly unfortunate because—as Cook and Hastings (1971, pers. comm.) also concluded—Cantor's illustration suggests that they were probably not *Hippodiplosia pertusa* (Shier, 1964, p. 632) and were possibly not even bryozoans.

Cantor's materials were obtained from sea snakes in the Indian Ocean: off the Ganges delta, India (at approximately 19–22°N, 88–92°E); encrusting *Hydrophis gracilis*.

Implications of Bryozoan Occurrences

None of the bryozoans encountered on sea snakes shows any morphologic adjustments to its unusual substrate. The zooecia are not stunted. Most specimens display some underdevelopment of features which develop gradually over the life-span of a long-lived colony; the sheet-like colonies are quite thin and not yet heavily calcified, and ornamental spines are atypically small or even absent. Such underdevelopment probably results from the short life-span permitted colonies settling on sea snakes.

Similarly, the small size (up to only 1 cm diameter personally observed) of the bryozoan colonies on sea snakes is also due to their being short-lived. Their size is much like that produced by other cheilostome species in comparably brief periods (Osburn, 1944). Apparently the species found on sea snakes do not exhibit accelerated growth rates as a special adaptation for encrusting them.

Bryozoans can occur on all parts of a sea snake body—on its tail, mid-section, and head; on its dorsal, lateral, and ventral surfaces—as illustrated well by one particular snake (Figure 3). Some snakes may bear as few as one colony. Other fouling organisms may accompany bryozoans on a snake; small pelecypods, barnacles, and other unidentified ectoparasites were found on the snakes from which the bryozoans discussed herein were taken. Each colony may cover the external surface of one to several adjacent scales; rarely, where barnacles such as *Platylepas ophiophilus* attach onto a sea snake, a single colony may encrust both the barnacle plates and the adjacent snake scales. In addition, bryozoans may occasionally be encountered on a sea snake's eye and nostril (Kropach and Soule, 1973). On *L. hardwickii*, bryozoans encrust the species' unique spinous ventral scales.

The small size of the bryozoan colonies compared to the snake body enables flexure while swimming to bend the colonies only slightly. Moreover, the thin and weakly calcified colonies retain slight flexibility, in comparison with longer-lived colonies of these same species. As a result, the bryozoan colonies on most sea-snake species are not irreparably broken up during life, even though they encrust a somewhat flexible substrate. On *A. stokesii*, however, the scales overlap or imbricate extensively, thus permitting considerable movement between adjacent ones; consequently, bryozoan colonies on this species are broken into separate adjacent sections, each restricted to a single scale (Figure 4).

Within local-population samples, relatively few of the sea snakes actually bear bryozoans (Kropach and Soule, 1973). Moreover, none of the bryozoan species involved is restricted to only sea snakes. Additionally, as mentioned previously, these bryozoans are not modified morphologically or physiologically for sea snake substrates. These facts strongly imply that the bryozoans are simply occasional accidental foulers on the sea snakes, rather than being exclusively or regularly associated with or specially adapted to the snakes. This accidental association between bryozoans and sea snakes could be of benefit to the former, inasmuch as a snake helps disperse its bryozoans

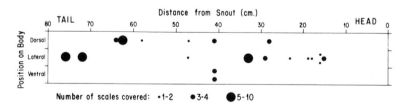

Figure 3. Distribution of bryozoan colonies (*Membranipora savartii*) upon one individual sea snake (*A. stokesii*).

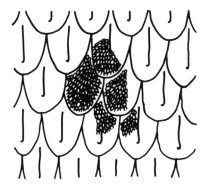

Figure 4. Bryozoan colony (*Membranipora savartii*) separated into single-scale sections due to imbricating scales of *A. stokesii.*

biogeographically, keeps them usually within the food- and oxygen-rich surface-water habitat, furnishes them with unoccupied substrate space, and carries them away from their normal benthonic predators. On occasion, the snake can carry the bryozoans into decidedly unfavorable environments in which they cannot survive, and their association then becomes an antagonistic or antibiotic one. The case of a bryozoan encrusting the eye and nostril of a sea snake (Kropach and Soule, 1973) suggests the possibility of such an association becoming synnecrotic by the bryozoan's preventing survival of the snake and, indirectly, its own survival.

FISH

A fish, probably a *Carangoides* (*Caranx*) *emburyi* (Whitley) juvenile, was seen on one occasion in very close association with an *L. hardwickii*, in open water 30 miles from Townsville. The fish would not leave the snake and was therefore easily caught with it (Veron, pers. comm.). It is probable that the solitary fish, usually a pelagic schooling species, used the drifting snake for protection from predators.

Juvenile *Caranx* spp. have been reported as sheltering under flotsam and a regular association has developed between a jelly fish and juvenile *C. trachurus* (Caullery, 1952). This protective association in which another organism is used for shelter is known as endoecism or inquilinism, and this behavior has been developed in the closely related pilot fish.

The cropped algae found on snakes from the Ashmore Reefs suggest that herbivorous fish were responsible, rather than grazing molluscs or other organisms.

PEDUNCULATE BARNACLES

The pedunculate or stalked barnacles are frequently found on objects floating in the sea and a number of species have adapted to living substrata. Less specialized species have been found on sea snakes (Cantor, 1840; Wall, 1921; Dean, 1938). Bennett (1971) mentions the occurrence of *Lepas anserifera* Linn. on the snake *Aipysurus laevis*. Darwin (1854) mentioned a small barnacle *Conchoderma hunteri* Owen from a *Pelamis* from the Indian or Pacific Ocean. *Dichelaspis grayii* Darwin and *D. pellucida* Darwin were both described from small specimens found on sea snakes but these species remain little known.

Lepas anatifera Linn., commonly attached to driftwood, drifting seaweed and vessels, was found on an *Emydocephalus annulatus* (Krefft) washed ashore in central New South Wales (Figure 1D). Associated with these barnacles was *Conchoderma virgata* Spengler. This snake had probably spent a considerable time drifting and was therefore susceptible to fouling by barnacles. *C. virgata* had previously been reported on sea snakes (Gotto, 1969) and the *C. hunteri* described by Darwin is closely related or even synonomous with this species. A very small *Conchoderma* sp. was found on an *L. hardwickii* from McCluer Gulf, West Irian. However, its small size (0.8 mm) prevented identification.

The genus *Conchoderma* has a close association with living substrates, being epizoic on whales. This association has been extended into parasitism in the closely related genus *Alepas* and may be quite complex. *C. indicum* Daniel, a little known species, was found attached to a sessile barnacle *Platylepas* sp., itself deeply embedded in a dugong (Daniel, 1963).

An *L. hardwickii* collected from the *East Indies* in 1898 carried large numbers of a pedunculate barnacle *Octolasmus* sp. The decalcification of the shell plates due to the specimens' age prevented further identification, but it is possible that they have a regular association with sea snakes, for Darwin (1854) described two species from sea snakes.

The specimens examined had a shell length of up to 1.6 mm, and a peduncule of the same size. The base of the peduncule was greatly expanded, with a diameter of 1.2 mm for the large specimens. This base was proportionally many times larger than those of the other pedunculate barnacles found on the *E. annulatus* and would indicate a specific modification to its unusual substrate. However, little is known of these barnacles and their host specificity.

In *Pelamis* from Panama, *Conchoderma virgatum* and *Lepas* sp. were rarely found (no more than 2% of the snakes). This is the first report of their occurrence on sea snakes in the Eastern Pacific. The barnacles were usually attached to *Pelamis* at the tail tip or side. An exception was a gravid female *Pelamis* from Mexico, now at the Kansas University Museum of Natural

History (KU 6342, courtesy of W. E. Duellman). This snake was covered with *C. virgatum* from neck to tail tip and, surprisingly, seemed to have been in good health at the time of capture.

Platylepas ophiophilus, a sessile barnacle found only on sea snakes, is the subject of the following paper.

ECTOPARASITIC ASSOCIATIONS

Sea snakes are relatively free of parasites. Ticks are commonly found on the semiterrestrial *Laticauda* spp., and one (*Amblyomma nitidum* Hirst and Hirst) is specific to these sea snakes (Wilson, 1970). Two species of chiggers (Trombiculidae) also parasitize *Laticauda; Vatacarus ipoides* Southcott and *V. kuntzi* Nadchatram and Radovsky are both found in the lungs of the sea snake. *Laticauda* apparently is the only genus hosting acarine parasites.

No ectoparasitics were found on the Australian snakes examined in this study. An unidentified turbellarian (platyhelmith) was found on one *Pelamis* from the Gulf of Panama. Heatwole (pers. comm.) found the host specific tick *Amblyomma nitidum* on a *Laticauda colubrina* from New Guinea. Another tick, *Aponomma* sp., was found on the same snake. This is the first report of an association with a sea snake, although this tick is characteristic of terrestrial reptiles and widespread in New Guinea (Wilson, pers. comm.). The semiterrestrial habit of *Laticauda* probably makes it prone to parasitism by acarines.

ANTIFOULING MECHANISMS OF SEA SNAKES

The general lack of fouling, except that by the highly specialized *P. ophiophilus,* suggests that some antifouling mechanisms are possessed by sea snakes. Fish and many marine invertebrates secrete a covering of mucus which discourages settling larvae. However, reptiles possess no such secretions and the skin is relatively inert, implying that no active antifouling mechanism exists.

Kropach and Soule (1973) comment on the lack of fouling in *Pelamis,* attributing it to the regular shedding of the skin and the habit of knotting. The average interval between sheddings was found, in a large group of *Pelamis* studied for a year, to be 19.5–25.4 days, with a minimum of 5 days and a maximum of 65 days. This is in general agreement with Shaw (1962) and Zeiller (1969), who reported on two snakes, and in great contrast with the report on *Laticauda* spp. (Klemmer, 1967; Mays and Nickerson, 1968), which shed at an interval averaging 90–99 days. High frequency of shedding as exhibited by *Pelamis* is presumably costly in energy, and must have evolved in response to stringent fouling pressures in the pelagic habitat. It is of interest to note that, in one field study, 14 days were required for *C. virgatum* and *Lepas* spp. to settle on floating logs (Hunter and Mitchell, 1967). No differences between shedding rates in adults and juveniles were discerned; thus the rate of shedding was not related to growth.

Knotting is a characteristic behavior of *Pelamis* both in the aquarium and in the natural habitat. It can be performed rapidly and vigorously and, at times, persistently for a period of hours. This behavior also appears in situations other than cleaning, such as shedding (Pickwell, 1971), or when the snakes are disturbed. When a piece of unshed skin remained on a snake because of barnacles attached at that point, the snake performed knots persistently for hours, until it removed both the barnacles and the skin. A beetle which accidentally landed on a snake was removed when the snake started knotting. Small pieces of tape placed on *Pelamis* also elicited knotting behavior which resulted in removal of the tape. The fact that barnacles are commonly found on the tail tip also suggests that knotting is primarily important in cleaning, because it is at the tail tip where knotting would be least effective as a cleaning method.

Test plates placed in Australian surface and bottom waters, adjacent to those from which many snakes were collected, accumulated a film of bacteria and diatoms within days, and developed a complex climax community within a month (Zann, in preparation). It is considered doubtful that knotting would remove so completely all the fouling, especially the microscopic organisms.

The flexibility of the skin may contribute to the antifouling and the snake's habit of diving, thereby changing the environment of the fouling organisms, may prevent development of many of these organisms.

Keratin, a material of low surface energy and, therefore, poor adhesiveness, and the presence of the surrounding water, may prevent the efficient bonding by cements, a problem in bioadhesive and dental research (Baier et al., 1968). Barnacles, notorious for the tenacity of their cement bond, rely heavily on mechanical penetration for the attachment of *P. ophiophilus*.

SUMMARY

The irregular occurrences of the majority of organisms (diatoms, higher algae, foraminifera, hydrozoa, sepulids, bryozoa, bivalves and pedunculate barnacles) associated with sea snakes suggest the adventitious settlement of larvae from the normally benthonic or flotsam-settling species. Possible exceptions are the peculiar relationship between the spinous ventral scales of *L. hardwickii* and hydrozoans and, to a lesser extent, bryozoans.

The implications of sea snake fouling are related to antifouling and bioadhesive research. The general lack of unspecialized fouling is attributed to the regular shedding of the skin, knotting behavior, the diving habit which involves changes in the fouling species' environment, and the poor adhesive properties of keratin.

ACKNOWLEDGMENTS

Dr. W. Dunson enthusiastically supplied most specimens of Australian sea snakes. Dr. H. Heatwole and Dr. H. Cogger supplied others. Help with the taxonomy was provided by Dr. I. Price (algae), Dr. A. Albani (foraminiferans), Miss Jeanette Watson (hydrozoa), E. Hokansson, A. H. Cheetham and S. S. Fonda (bryozoa), W. Dowd (fish), Dr. Nixon Wilson (parasites), and Miss Elizabeth Pope (barnacles). This work was supported by the National Science Foundation under grant NSF GA 35835 to The Pennsylvania State University and grants NSF GA 34948 and NSF GD 34462 to The Scripps Institution of Oceanography for operation of the *Alpha Helix* Research Program. The senior author performed much of the work while engaged in fouling research for the Australian Department of Supply at the James Cook University of North Queensland.

REFERENCES

Annandale, N. 1912. Polyzoa associated with certain Gangetic tortoises. Records Indian Mus. 7(2):147–150.

Audouin, V. 1826. Explication sommaire des planches de polypes de l'Egypte et de la Syrie. *In* Explications des Planches (Mollusques-Annelides-Crustacés-Arachnides-Insects-Echinodermes-Zoophytes-Ascidies-Polypes-Hydrophtes-Oiseaux) dont les Dessins ont été Fournis par M. J. C. Savigney; Description de l'Égypte–Histoire Naturelle. Commission d'Égypte, 1(4):1–339.

Baier, R. E., E. G. Shafrin, and W. A. Zisman, 1968. Adhesion: mechanisms that assist or impede it. Science N.Y. *162*:1360–1368.

Bassler, R. S. 1953. Bryozoa. *In* Treatise on Invertebrate Paleontology (R. C. Moore, ed.). University of Kansas Press, Lawrence. 253 pp.

Bennett, Isobel. 1971. The Great Barrier Reef. Lansdowne, Melbourne.

Bosc, L. A. G. 1802. Histoire Naturelle des Vers, 3.

Cantor, T. 1840. Observations upon pelagic serpents. Trans. Zool. Soc. London 2(4):303–13.

Canu, F., and R. S. Bassler. 1929. Bryozoa of the Philippine region. U. S. Nat. Mus. Bull. 100(9):1–685.

Caullery, M. 1952. Parasitism and Symbiosis. Sidgwick and Jackson, London.

Cook, P. L. 1968. Polyzoa from West Africa–The Malacostega, part I. Brit. Mus. (Nat. Hist.) Bull. 16:113–160.

Cuffey, R. J. 1971. Pacific sea snakes (*Pelamis platurus*)–a highly mobile substrate for bryozoans (*Electra angulata*) off Costa Rica. Presented at Int. Bryozool. Assoc. 2nd Int. Conf. (abs. 37).

Cuffey, R. J. 1973. An improved classification, based upon numerical-taxonomic analysis, for the higher taxa of entoproct and ectoproct bryozoans. *In* Living and Fossil Bryozoa (G. P. Larwood, ed.). Academic Press, London, pp. 549–564.

Daniel, A. 1953. *Conchoderma indicum* sp. nov. on *Platylepas* sp. embedded on a dugong from the Krusadi Islands. J. Zool. Soc. India 5:235–238.

Darwin, C. 1854. A Monograph on the Sub-class Cirripedia. Cramer, Weinheim.

Dean, B. 1938. Note on the sea-snake *Pelamis platurus* (Linnaeus). Science 88:144–5.

Dunbar, C. O. 1928. On an ammonite investing commensal Bryozoa. Amer. Jour. Sci. (5)16:164–165.

Esper, E. J. C. 1796 [1788–1850]. Die Pflanzenthiere in Abbildungen nach der Natur mit Farben erleuchtet nebst Beschreibungen. 5 Vols. Raspe, Nürnberg.

Gotto, R. V. 1969. Marine animals. Partnerships and other associations. English Universities Press. London.

Hand, C. 1961. A new species of athecate hydroid (*Podocoryne bella* Hydractiniidae) living on the pigfish *Congiopus leucopaccilus*. Trans. Roy Soc. N.Z. (Zool.) 1:91–94.

Harmer, S. F. 1926. The polyzoa of the siboga expedition; II, Cheliostomata Anasca. *In Siboga-Expeditie*. Brill, Leiden, 286. p. 183–501.

Harmer, S. F. 1931. Presidential address–Recent work on Polyzoa. Linn. Soc. London Proc. 143(8):113–168.

Hunter, J. R., and C. T. Mitchell. 1967. Association of fishes with flotsam in the offshore waters of Central America. U.S. Fish Wildl. Serv. Fish Bull. 66:13–29.

Klemmer, K. 1967. Observations on the sea snake *Laticauda laticaudata* in captivity. Internat. Zoo. Yearbook 7:229–31.

Kropach, C. and J. D. Soule, 1973. An unusual association between an ecoproct and a sea snake. Herpetologica 29:17–19.

Levinsen, G. M. R. 1909. Morphological and Systematic Studies on the Cheilostomatous Bryozoa. Bagge, Copenhagen.

Mays, C. E. and M. A. Nickerson. 1968. Notes on shedding in the sea snake *Laticauda semifasciata* (Reinwardt) in captivity. Copeia 1968:619.

Osburn, R. C. 1944. A survey of the Bryozoa of Chesapeake Bay. Md. Bd. Nat. Res. Chesap. Biol. Lab. Pub. 63:1–59.

Pennycuik, P. 1959. Marine and brackish water hydroids. *In* Faunistic Records from Queensland. Watson, Ferguson and Co., Brisbane. p. 141–210.

Pickwell, G. V. 1971. Knotting and coiling behavior in the pelagic sea snake *Pelamis platurus* (L.). Copeia 1971:348–350.

Round, F. E. 1971. Benthic marine diatoms. Oceanogr. Mar. Biol. Ann. Rev. 9:83–139.

Ryland, J. S. 1972. Bryozoa (Polyzoa) and marine fouling. *In* Marine Borers, Fungi and Fouling Organisms of Wood (E. B. Gareth-Jones and S. K. Eltringham, ed.). Organization for Economic Cooperation and Development, Paris, pp. 137–154.

Sars, G. O. 1874. Om en hidtil lidet kjendt maerkelig slaegstype of Polyzoer. Fordhandl. Vidensk. Selsk. Christiania for 1873.

Shaw, C. E. 1962. Sea snakes at the San Diego Zoo. Internat. Zoo. Yearbook 4:49–52.

Shier, D. E. 1964. Marine bryozoa from northwest Florida. Bull. Mar. Sci. Gulf Carib. 14:603–662.

Smith, M. 1926. Monograph of the Sea-Snakes (Hydrophiidae). British Museum of Natural History, London.

Wall, F. 1921. Ophidia Taprobanica or the snakes of Ceylon. Cottle, Colombo. p. 315–434.

Wilson, N. 1970. New distributional records of ticks from Southeast Asia and the Pacific (Metastigmata: Argasidae, Ixoidae). Oriental Insects 4:37–46.

Zann, L. P. (in preparation). Primary fouling in the surface waters of Cleveland Bay, North Queensland.

Zeiller, W. 1969. Maintenance of the yellowbellied sea snake *Pelamis platurus* in captivity. Copeia 1969:407–8.

fourteen

Biology of a Barnacle (*Platylepas ophiophilus Lanchester*) Symbiotic with Sea Snakes

Leon P. Zann

The skin of marine reptiles and mammals is often host to a variety of organisms. The associations may provide protection (inquilinism), transport (phoresis), attachment (epizoism, epibiontism), a share in the host's food (commensalism), or may involve a metabolic dependence (parasitism). All the relationships may be broadly termed 'symbiotic' (living together). Symbiosis has been used as a synonym of mutualism, an association of mutual benefit, but it is used here as a general term.

For filter-feeding animals such as barnacles, bryozoans, serpulid polychaetes, and others, a mobile substrate might provide protection from predators, beneficial feedings currents, a favorable environment (that of the host), or at least an unoccupied substratum for a searching larva. Competition for space is very intense in the sea and many larvae are opportunistic in their settlement.

Symbionts are often highly specialized for this niche and are often host specific. The related barnacles *Coronula, Tubicinella,* and *Xenobalanus* are found on cetaceans, *Chelonibia* on turtles and *Platylepas* on turtles, dugongs and sea snakes.

The occurrence of *Platylepas* on sea snakes was probably first noted by Darwin (1854), who mentioned, but did not name, a small species on a sea snake from Borneo. This barnacle was collected subsequently over a wide range of Southeast Asia, but was not described until 1902, by Lanchester. His specimens were embedded in an *"Enhydris curtus"* (*Lapemis hardwickii* Gray), also from Borneo. This species has received little attention subsequently. Pilsbry (1916) refers to a second species from Siam (Thailand) found on a *Hydrophis* sp. and a *Disteira* sp. Initially called *Cryptolepas ophiophilus* Krüger, Pilsbry renamed it *P. krügeri* and considered it a different species, although he acknowledged that it was incompletely described. Apart from infrequent observations, very little is known of the biology of *Platylepas* spp., or indeed, any other symbiotic barnacle.

The author recognized a unique opportunity to investigate the little known sea snake barnacle *P. ophiophilus* when, in 1972, Dunson drew his attention to the frequent occurrence of a small barnacle on sea snakes from North Queensland. The general biology and ecology of this barnacle, its relationships with the sea snake host, and the implications of its unusual substrate specificity were studied. It appeared that life would be particularly precarious for such a specialized organism. Sea snakes are not frequently encountered over much of its range and a barnacle larva must first find a snake, then settle near another barnacle to allow cross-fertilization, and grow to maturity during the life of the snake's skin. Evidence suggests they are shed with the old skin, an event occurring probably as often as every 3 or 4 weeks. Barnacles are rarely found in high densities on the snake, indicating a very small breeding population.

It was necessary initially to confirm that *P. ophiophilus* is specific to sea snakes. Likely hosts were examined but none carried this barnacle. Dolphins from Townsville were free of barnacles; green turtles (*Chelonia mydas*, Linn.) carried *Chelonibia testudinaria* (Linn.) on their shells and small *P. hexastylos* (O. Fabricus) on their flippers. Dugongs (*Dugong dugon* Muller) often carried large *P. hexastylos* on their backs and tail.

Before commencing the discussion of the specializations of *P. ophiophilus*, let us briefly examine a typical barnacle.

GENERAL BIOLOGY OF BARNACLES

Barnacles are sessile crustaceans enclosed in a shell of plates. They are filter feeders; small hairs (setae) are carried on the modified appendages (cirri) which beat the water, trapping plankton. Although hermaphroditic, cross-fertilization is the rule. The penis is protruded from the body and inserted into the mantle cavity of a neighbor, and the fertilized eggs are brooded until the nauplii larvae hatch and are liberated. They undergo a number of instars in the plankton until they reach the final stage, the cyprid, and then begin to search actively for a suitable substrate. They attach by cement glands in their antennae and metamorphose.

The cyprids can prolong their free living life, within limits, until a suitable area is found, mainly by physical and chemical investigation by sensors in the antennae. Proteins released by established barnacles are important stimuli, aiding gregariousness (Crisp, 1965).

BIOLOGY OF *PLATYLEPAS OPHIOPHILUS*

Platylepas Gray, 1825, is a small genus in the subfamily Coronulinae, Leach, 1825. It is characterized by six compartmental plates, each with an internal downward projecting rib, and has a membranous basis and large opercular valves. Its members live on turtles, dugongs, and sea snakes.

P. ophiophilus was originally described from Borneo but specimens from West Irian, Northern Australia, Malacca Strait, Manila, "East Indies," and the South China Sea were examined in this study. The geographic distribution probably reflects that of its sea snake hosts, although they appear to be absent from the *Aipysurus* spp. from Ashmore Reef and *Pelamis platurus*. It should be noted that many specimens examined possessed a small or vestigial sixth internal rib and the original specimen of Lanchester (1902) shows a reduced rib, not in strict accord with the generic definition. Other specimens, obviously of the same species, show more equal ribs.

The morphology of *P. ophiophilus* is basically similar to that of other sessile barnacles, but with certain modifications which will be outlined below.

Adhesion

The membranous basis is supported by six (or sometimes five) downward-extending ribs (Figure 1). These ribs penetrate the host's skin, giving mechanical attachment, and the three or four characteristic grooves on each side of the ribs also extend downwards into the host. The membranous basis secretes a cement characteristic of barnacles. Added adhesion may be achieved by the beads and growth lines on the exterior of the heavily ornamented shell, which is often embedded in the host.

The adhesion of the barnacles seen in this study varied. Figure 2 shows a densely fouled *Aipysurus laevis* with certain barnacles deeply embedded and others not. The smallest barnacles (0.6 mm) could be removed easily, but careful removal was necessary for the larger specimens; otherwise, they would fragment or tear the skin off the snake.

The shape of the barnacle as well as its attachment often varied from snake to snake. This phenomenon has complicated the taxonomy of the

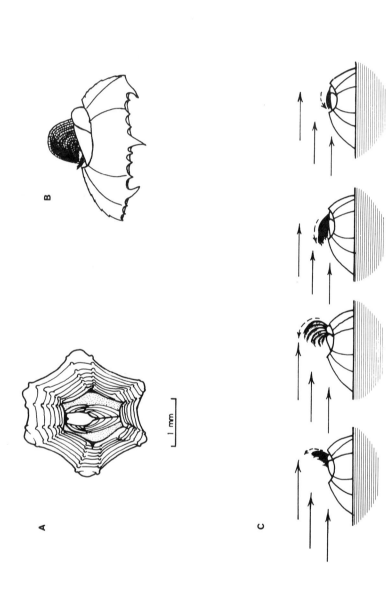

Figure 1. A, Shell and values of *P. ophiophilus* showing ornamentation (dorsal). B, Ribs and cirri (lateral). C, Orientation and direction of cirral beat.

Figure 2. *P. ophiophilus* around cloaca of *A. laevis.*

platylepads (Zullo, pers. comm.), but it is considered that the barnacles examined in this study represent a single species.

Snakes with strongly imbricate (overlapping) scales (e.g., *Aipysurus laevis, Astrotia stokesii*) generally carried barnacles with the typical inwardly produced large ribs (Figures 1 and 3). The ribs on many barnacles on *Lapemis hardwickii* extended outwards (Figure 4), and their ends were often bifurcated, probably to afford better anchorage. Certain specimens (Figure 5) show an extension of this trend with one or two of the six ribs extended to form a complex root structure embedded within the host's tissues.

Certain well attached barnacles may be retained when the snake sheds its skin. Sometimes, however, the barnacle is attached by only one or two ribs after the old skin is lost. These ribs then grow deeply into the host and the barnacle may survive subsequent sheddings. The "survivors" are sometimes apparent in size-frequency analysis of the population of a snake (below), and are often surrounded by younger barnacles. Certain *L. hardwickii* carried the more typically shaped *P. ophiophilus,* but these barnacles may have been younger.

It is thought that the great majority of barnacles remain attached to the old skin when it is shed. One *A. stokesii* and four *L. hardwickii* were captured in the process of shedding or shed shortly after capture. Only one barnacle, an average sized specimen from a relatively large population (75) on an *L.*

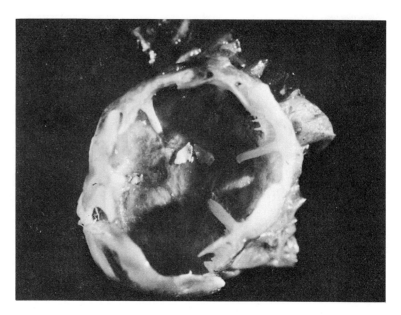

Figure 3. View through operculum of *P. ophiophilus* showing ribs and grooves penetrating host's skin (*H. elegans*). This large barnacle is probably a survivor of one or more sheddings (× 8).

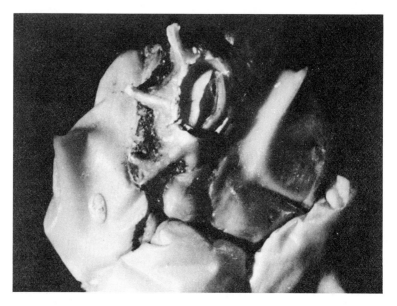

Figure 4. Outward extending ribs, a common growth form of *P. ophiophilus* on *L. hardwickii*. Note bifurcation of rib (× 8).

Figure 5. Dorsal (above) and ventral views of *P. ophiophilus* from *A. stokesii.* The ribs are heavily rooted and have been encysted by the host. The firm anchorage and large size indicate this barnacle probably survived sheddings (× 12).

hardwickii, was retained on the new skin. All other barnacles were shed, with the total number on the five snakes exceeding 1200. The survivor of the shedding had two or three ribs penetrating the new skin but was slightly lifted, and surrounding the embedded ribs was a small quantity of fresh blood.

The barnacles probably retained on other snakes include one found on the dorsal side, immediately before the tail, of a *Hydrophis elegans* (Figure 3), and one from the unique divided ventral scales of an *A. stokesii* (Figure 5).

The anatomical relationships between the barnacles and host were established by histological studies. Barnacles attached to a snake's skin were fixed in formalin, decalcified in Gooding and Stuart's fluid (formic acid and formalin) (Culling, 1963), and embedded and sectioned according to Madersons's (1965) method for snake skin. The severe nature of the decalcification process tended to cause some shrinkage, and the α- and β-layers of keratin were often separated in sectioning.

Barnacles attached to the shed skin were deeply embedded, with the snake's skin often reaching the operculum of the barnacle and partially enveloping it (Figure 6). A young barnacle included in this section is not deeply embedded, but appears to be surrounded by abnormally thickened keratin. This may have been achieved by the barnacle's growth splitting the α- and β-keratin layers of the skin, or by added production of keratin by the epidermis.

Whale barnacles often lie deep within their host's skin, probably more the result in the whale's skin growth than actual burrowing. However, certain types, e.g., *Tubicinella,* may actively grow into the host's skin, and normal barnacles are capable of exerting great pressure on their substrates and neighbors by growth. *P. ophiophilus* probably penetrates the host's skin by downward growth of the pointed ribs. Growth of the snake's skin and reaction by the snake's tissue may add to this embedding effect.

A cellular connective tissue was often seen surrounding the bases of barnacles (Figures 6 and 7), this probably being the "stratum intermedium" of Maderson (1965). This may indicate there is a cellular reaction by the snake to the invading barnacle shell, probably stimulating additional keratin production, since the keratin layers surrounding barnacles were abnormally thickened (Figures 6 and 8).

The barnacle surviving a skin shedding by an *L. hardwickii* was sectioned while attached to the new skin (Figure 8). Its ribs had penetrated deep into the dermis of the snake and a severe tissue reaction was taking place. A layer of heavily nucleated cells surrounded the ribs, probably representing the initial stage of an encystment process, which would isolate the barnacle from the snake's tissue but also enhance the anchorage of the barnacle.

Frequency of Occurrence, Density

Approximately half the snakes collected in North Queensland by Dunson between 18 and 20° S. Latitude hosted *P. ophiophilus* (see Chapter 7). All species except *Disteira kingii* (only two specimens were seen) carried barna-

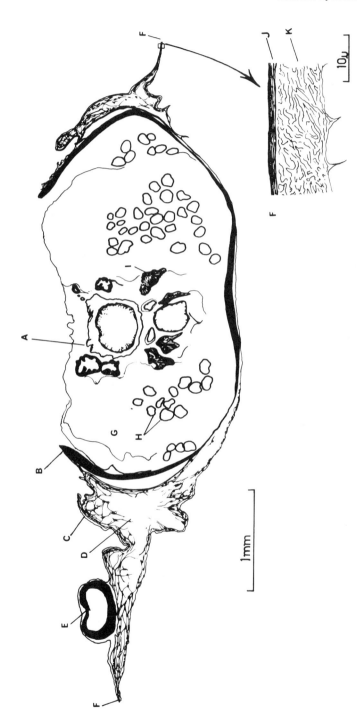

Figure 6. Section of barnacles attached to a shed skin. A, Barnacle soft parts (cirri, gut etc.); B, Shell; C, Keratin layer of snake's skin; D, Connective tissue surrounding barnacle; E, Small barnacle embedded in keratin; F, Normal structure of shed skin; G, Mantle cavity of barnacle; H, Eggs; and I, Testes. The structure of normal skin (F) is shown below): J, β-layer; and K, α-layer.

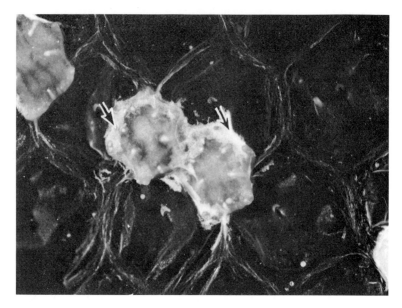

Figure 7. Underside of *P. ophiophilus* on a shed *L. hardwickii* skin. The aberrant connective tissue formations are indicated by arrows.

cles (Table 1). This frequency was high, considering that the skins of many snakes would be new and thus free from barnacles.

The number of barnacles per snake ranged from one to 585. Surface areas of snakes varied; some were slender, others thick, so direct comparisons of densities are not valid.

Figure 9 shows the number on all snakes examined. Many snakes had fewer than 10 barnacles. The average number of barnacles on the more heavily fouled snakes was calculated, regarding the snake as a cylinder. Densities reached one per $0.46/cm^2$ of skin, although observations showed that the distribution of barnacles on the snakes was not uniform.

Position on Snake

Distribution of barnacles on the snakes was almost invariably on the posterior two-thirds (Figure 10). The causes are unknown, but the distribution of the bryozoan *Membranipora savartii* was similar. Current may be more favorable on the latter half, since the snake propels itself with its flattened tail and undulates its body. In addition, the cleansing habit of knotting, mentioned by Kropach and Soule (1973) and in the previous chapter, may remove fouling from the anterior portion.

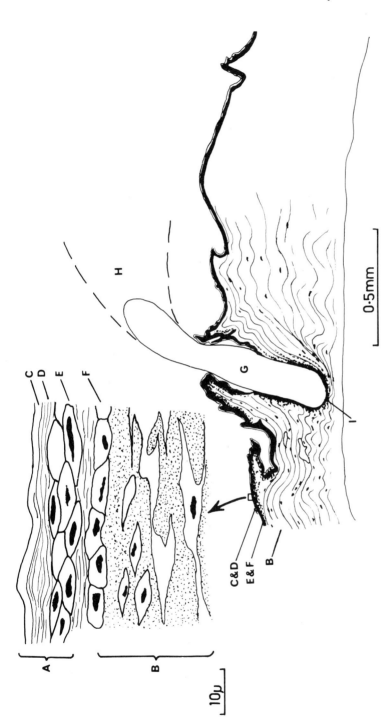

Figure 8. Rib of *P. ophiophilus* which had survived a shedding by the host (*L. hardwickii*), showing relationships with new skin. Structure of skin: A, Old generation epidermis; B, Dermis; C, β-keratin layer; D, α-keratin layer; E, Living epidermis; F, Substratum germinativum; G, Penetrating barnacle rib; H, Position of main part of barnacle (not shown on this section); I, Reaction by dermal tissue.

Table 1. Frequency of fouling on sea snakes by *P. ophiophilus*

Species	No. fouled	Total examined
Aipysurus laevis	9	14
Aipysurus duboisii	4	11
Aipysurus eydouxii	1	1
Hydrophis elegans	7	11
Disteira kingii	0	2
Disteira major	1	7
Astrotia stokesii	2	3
Lapemis hardwickii	22	41

Many snakes are banded or counter-shaded but, although many barnacles have color preferences in settlement (e.g., *Balanus amphitrite* in Townsville prefer black surfaces to white (Zann, in preparation), *P. ophiophilus* showed no obvious color preferences.

The position of larval attachment on the scales varied, but many young barnacles were found on the antèrior edge of the overlapping scales of *Aipysurus laevis,* apparently sheltered by the scale in the front. This may explain the presence of those few barnacles towards the anterior of an *A. laevis* (Figure 10).

The characteristic spinous scales of *L. hardwickii* were not unduly favored in settlement, unlike the marked preference shown by the hydrozoans and bryozoans.

Orientation

The longitudinal axes of the barnacles were usually parallel to those of the host, with the anterior of the barnacles facing the posterior of the snake (Figures 1 and 2). The cirral beat is towards the anterior of the snake and into the oncoming current when the snake is in motion. Briggs and Morejohn (1972) found that barnacles on the Californian grey whale were similarly orientated according to the direction of the current, and their orientation was used to establish the water-flow patterns over the surface of the whale.

Gregarious Behavior

P. ophiophilus are very gregarious, ensuring suitable habitat selection for the cyprid and cross-fertilization in the adults. Isolated barnacles usually do not

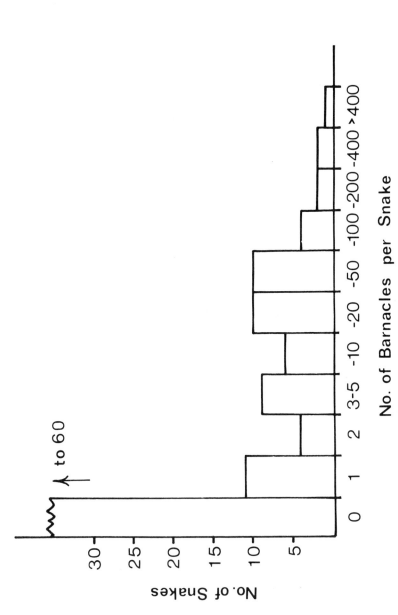

Figure 9. Frequency of occurrence of P. ophiophilus on a sample of sea snakes. Barnacle populations placed in arbitary categories.

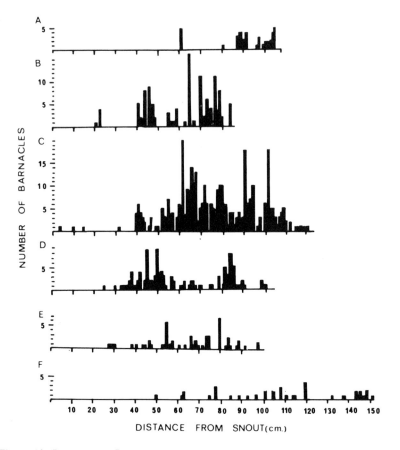

Figure 10. Positions of *P. ophiophilus* on a sample of heavily fouled snakes. A, *A. duboisii;* B, C, and D, *A. laevis;* E, *L. hardwickii;* F, *H. elegans.* Length of horizontal axes shows size of snake.

contribute to the breeding population, although self-fertilization may occur rarely in certain species (Barnes and Crisp, 1956).

Lanchester (1902) reported that the penis of *P. ophiophilus* is unusually long, up to twice the length of the shell. Isolated barnacles would not be cross-fertilized and, although highly gregarious, many barnacles on some of the less densely fouled snakes would not contribute to the breeding population. Even in densely fouled snakes a high proportion of barnacles would not be cross-fertilized. Figure 11 illustrates this proportion, assuming that the penis of an average-sized barnacle (3 mm) could protrude approximately 6 mm from the operculum. Considering the radii of the two barnacle neigh-

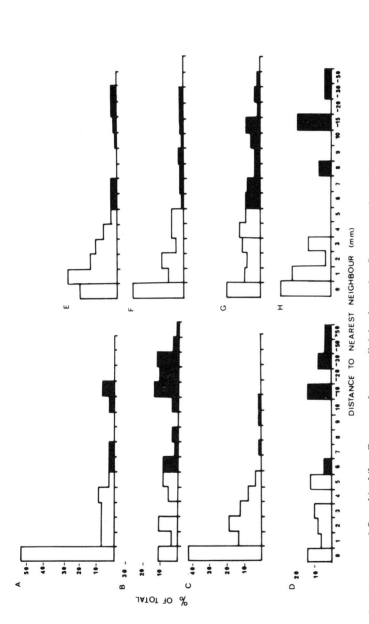

Figure 11. Gregariousness of *P. ophiophilus*. Zero mm denotes adjoining barnacles. Open areas show those barnacles probably cross-fertilizing; darkened areas show those too far apart for cross-fertilization. A, *A duboisii*; number of barnacles (n)=42; density (no. per cm^2 of skin) (D)=0.12. B, *L. hardwickii*; N=56; D=0.04. C, *L. hardwickii*; N=585; D=0.46. D, *H. elegans*; N=58; D=0.04. E, *A laevis*; N=141; D=0.38. F, *A. laevis*; N=342; D=0.15. G, *A laevis*; N=109; D=0.05. H, *A. duboissi*; N=34; D=0.07.

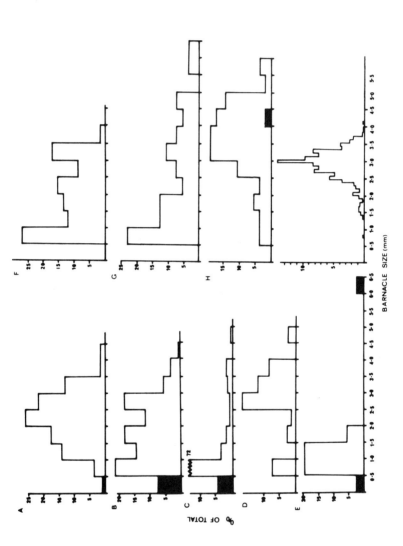

Figure 12. Size (maximum diameter) frequency distributions of barnacles on some densely fouled snakes. Darkened areas (0.5) denote newly settled barnacles. Horizontally shaded areas denote suspected (E) and observed (H) survivors of sheddings. A, *A. laevis*; number of barnacles (N)= 115. B, *A. laevis*; N=292. C, *A. laevis*; N=138. D, *A. duboisii*; N=41. E, *A. stokesii*; N=18. F, *H. elegans*; N=56. G, *L. hardwickii*; N=56. H, *L. hardwickii*; N=58. I, *L. hardwickii*; N=585.

bors' shells, barnacles much more than 3-6 mm apart could not be cross-fertilized.

Dissection of a sample of 50 barnacles from a shed skin showed one isolated specimen (130 mm from the nearest neighbor) was brooding fertile eggs, and six others at least 10 mm from their neighbors were also fertile. While it is possible that self-fertilization may occur, other factors must be considered; e.g., sperm retention or a neighbor subsequently lost may be responsible for fertilization. Self-fertilization would increase the potential breeding population in less dense populations by many times, but further research must be conducted in this field before conclusive evidence is obtained.

Life Cycle, Growth Rates, and Longevity

Dunson (pers. comm.) found that some Australian sea snakes in captivity shed at 2- to 6-week intervals. As most barnacles are shed with the skin and presumably die afterwards, the oldest barnacle in a normal population is approximately 6 weeks, unless survivors from a previous shedding are present. These survivors have been discussed above and may be seen in size-frequency analyses of populations (Figures 12E and H).

No cyprid larvae were seen; metamorphosis is probably very rapid as many barnacles of small size (0.45 mm) were seen.

The populations on shed skins (Figures 12H and I) are of maximum age, and the oldest individuals (presumed 4-5 weeks) reach a size of 4-5 mm in this time. This growth rate is rapid, but not unusual, as *Balanus amphitrite* in Townsville reach at least 10 mm within a month, and contain fertile eggs (unpublished data).

The size-frequency distributions show recruitment of the young is usually continuous during the life-cycle of the skin. However, occasional peaks (Figure 12C) indicate settlement over a short period. These data suggest that larval settlement is not synchronized with or dependent on the snake's skin condition.

The immature barnacles lost with the old skin would not contribute to the breeding population, a seemingly catastrophic event since the species has such a limited reproductive potential. Presumably, the older barnacles on a shed skin would have produced at least one brood before dying; and the small number of survivors of many sheddings would produce many broods as well as act as markers for the settling larvae. Although no studies have been made, it is thought that the larvae of symbiotic barnacles must have a specialized prolonged searching phase and precise mechanism for the chemical recognition of specific surfaces (Crisp, 1965).

Platylepas spp. and other symbiotic barnacles which settle on turtles and mammals would not be subjected to such a perilous existence as *P. ophio-*

philus, for their hosts do not shed their skins. However, certain barnacles living on other crustaceans which shed their exoskeletons are left attached to the old moult. The pedunculate barnacle *Trilasmis fissum hawaiense,* which is associated with lobsters, remains on the exoskeleton and is probably eaten by fish (Bowers, 1968).

Fecundity

Preliminary observations from a small sample (50) show that the eggs are of similar size (100 μ) and in similar numbers to other small barnacles. Egg production begins when the barnacles reach 2 mm in length and a large proportion (76%) of the sample (average size approximately 3 mm) carried advanced larvae (first nauplius), probably ready for hatching. The number of broods during the barnacle's life are unknown. Fecundity in *P. ophiophilus* and *P. hexastylos* will be the subject of a later paper (Zann and Harker, in preparation).

RELATIONSHIP WITH HOST

Gotto (1969) termed the relationship of *P. ophiophilus* with the sea snake "phoresis," a term describing a transport or "hitch-hiking" association. The currents set up by the swimming sea snake probably aid the barnacle's feeding, and the barnacle can exploit the diverse environments visited by its mobile host. It also gains protection from carnivorous gastropods and rasping fish. Because it occupies such a specialized niche, spatial competition is nonexistent. The host does not gain anything from the association.

Although the snake's scales may be damaged and there is tissue response to the penetrating ribs, the relationship cannot be considered parasitic. However, it does illustrate a trend in symbiotic barnacles towards parasitism. The profileration in certain individuals of the ribs and adjacent tissue may represent a step toward this way of life.

A barnacle, *Anelasma squalica,* found only on the fins of a certain shark is similarly modified, but, as well as feeding in the usual manner, the roots can extract nutrients from the host. The trend is extended in *Rhizolepas annelidicola,* which has ceased to feed normally, for its roots provide all its nourishment from the polychaete worm host. Finally, in the highly specialized *Sacculina carcani,* the roots ramify throughout the crab host's tissue and the adult bears no resemblance to other barnacles.

SUMMARY

The exclusive relationship between *Platylepas ophiophilus* and sea snakes necessitates morphological specializations promoting adhesion (penetrating ribs and associated grooves, ornamentation on the shell, ability to grow roots into the snake's tissue) and possibly others in its life cycle (self-fertilization, accelerated adult growth, a specialized cyprid larval stage).

The barnacles are distributed on the posterior areas, probably because of favorable currents and the cleansing knotting behavior of the snake. The anteriors of the barnacles almost invariably face towards the rear, and the cirral beat is towards the anterior of the snake and into the current.

The relationship of *P. ophiophilus* to its host is phoretic (i.e., for transport and currents), although slight damage to the snake may occur. Tissue reaction in the host takes place around the ribs, and if these penetrate the new skin they may be encysted. However, the association cannot be termed parasitic.

ACKNOWLEDGMENTS

Dr. W. Dunson, Dr. H. Heatwole, and Dr. H. Cogger supplied the sea snakes. Dr. Torben Wolff of Universitetets Zoologiske Museum, Denmark, supplied an interesting collection of *P. ophiophilus*. Advice and information were provided by Dr. V. Zullo, Miss Isobel Bennett, and Miss Elizabeth Pope. This work was supported by the National Science Foundation under grant NSF GA 35835 to the Pennsylvania State University and grants NSF GA 34948 and NSF GD 34462 to The Scripps Institution of Oceanography for operation of the *Alpha Helix* Research Program. The author wishes to acknowledge the assistance of Professor C. J. Burdon Jones and the staff of the James Cook University of North Queensland. Much of the work was conducted while on a fellowship provided by the Australian Department of Supply.

REFERENCES

Barnes, H., and D. J. Crisp. 1956. Evidence of self-fertilization in certain species of barnacles. J. Mar. Biol. Assoc. U.K. 35:631−639.

Briggs, K. T., and G. V. Morejohn. 1972. Barnacle orientation and waterflow characteristics in Californian gray whales. J. Zool. 167:287−292.

Bowers, R. L. 1968. Observations on the orientation and feeding behavior of barnacles associated with lobsters. J. Exp. Mar. Biol. Ecol. 2:105−112.

Crisp, D. J. 1965. Surface chemistry. A factor in settlement of marine invertebrate larvae. Botanica Gothoburgensia 3:51-65.

Culling, C. F. A. 1963. *Handbook of Histopathological Techniques*. Butterworths, London.

Darwin, C. 1854. A Monograph on the Sub-Class Cirripedia. Cramer, Weinheim.

Gotto, R. V. 1969. *Marine Animals. Partnerships and Other Associations*. English Universities Press, London.

Kropach, C., and J. D. Soule. 1973. An unusual association between an ecoproct and a sea snake. Herpetologica 29:17−19.

Lanchester, W. F. 1902. On the crustacea collected during the "Skeat Expedition" to the Malay Peninsula. Part II–Anomura, Cirripedia and Isopoda. Proc. Zool. Soc. London 2:371–372.

Maderson, P. F. A. 1965. Histological changes in the epidermis of snakes during the sloughing cycle. J. Zool. 146:98–113.

Pilsbry, H. A. 1916. The sessile barnacles (Cirripedia) contained in the collections of the U.S. National Museum. Bulletin 93, United States National Museum.

Zann, L. P. (in preparation). Primary fouling in the surface waters of Cleveland Bay, North Queensland.

Zann, L. P., and B. M. Harker. Egg numbers of the barnacles *Platylepas ophiophilus* Lanchester (from sea snakes), *Platylepas hexastylos* (O. Fabricus) (from dugongs), *Octolasmis warwicki* Gray (from bay lobsters) and *Lepas anatifera* Lin. (from pumice). In preparation.

PHYSIOLOGY

fifteen

Diving Physiology

Harold Heatwole
and Roger Seymour

Sea snakes are subjected to a variety of environmental influences that are not experienced by either terrestrial or semiaquatic snakes. Consequently, their behavior and ecology contrast markedly with those of their non-marine relatives and they are of special interest to students of comparative ecology and environmental physiology. Their almost total neglect by investigators in these fields, until recently, is understandable only in the context of the relative inaccessibility of live material and their venomous nature.

Some of the special eco-physiological problems faced by sea snakes are covered in other chapters (e.g., salt balance). In this chapter, those associated with diving are emphasized. Infrequent breathing would seem to demand some means of oxygen storage, reduction in the amount utilized, or basic modification in the ways it is exchanged with the environment or distributed among the various tissue components of the body. The elimination of CO_2 poses problems related to acid-base balance of the blood. Such phenomena directly involve cardiovascular function, the organs of gaseous exchange, and the properties of the gas transport system. In addition, the hydrostatic pressures to which sea snakes are subjected during diving complicate the problems of gas exchange and oxygen storage, and pose special problems in buoyancy regulation.

Sea snakes conceivably could have solved these problems either by developing entirely new adaptive systems not found in other snakes, or by accentuating and extending basic physiological properties of the general ophidian repertoire. The task of the comparative physiologist appears to be two-fold: (1) to ascertain the mechanisms underlying the respiratory and cardiovascular physiology of sea snakes and identify the stimuli setting them in motion; and (2) to compare sea snakes among themselves and with their non-marine relatives. This chapter reports on the progress which has been made so far.

In order to provide a proper perspective against which experimental data can be evaluated, it is necessary to examine first the depths to which sea snakes descend and, second, the lengths of time they remain submerged.

DIVING DEPTH

In only a few cases have divers directly observed sea snakes deeper than 30 m. *Hydrophis melanocephalus* was observed at 44 m near Ashmore Reef. Ron and Valerie Taylor (pers. comm.) have seen *Aipysurus laevis* and photographed *Hydrophis* sp. at about 43 m on the bottom of a channel between Heron Island and Wistari Reef, Queensland, and report snakes common at depths of 25–30 m at Swain's, Saumarez, Kenn, and Frederick Reefs in the Coral Sea, and around the Keppel Islands off Yepoon, Queensland. Three sightings have been made at 37 m: Steve Domm reported a snake he believed to be *Pelamis platurus* lying on the bottom in a channel near Heron Island; Ben Cropp reported an *A. laevis* at that depth near Southwest Cay, Saumarez Reef; and Dieter Omozik saw a snake similar in appearance to *Lapemis hardwickii* at 37 m near Heron Island (personal communications). These data almost certainly fail to delimit the maximal depth to which sea snakes are capable of diving. Indirect evidence suggests that snakes dive well below the depth to which divers normally descend and are thus out of range of direct observation. Observations of the habits of sea snakes at shallow depths (Chapters 5–9), analysis of stomach contents of snakes from deep water (Chapter 11), and anecdotal accounts of snakes diving down out of sight in clear, deep water (Herre, 1942), converge to suggest that, except for the pelagic *Pelamis platurus,* sea snakes normally dive to the bottom in waters in which they occur. Consequently, it is reasonable to consider the water depth in areas where snakes are seen on the surface as indicating the depth to which the species in question dives. Spurious values could be obtained in the case of individuals observed at the edge of a steep drop-off, swimming over narrow, deep channels, or in the process of migrating at the surface over areas of water deeper than that normally inhabited. Such a source of error can be reduced if rare values of exceptional depth are eliminated from consideration.

Shuntov (1962, 1966, 1971) summarized the sightings and trawl-catches of sea snakes from Russian research vessels. He found that *P. platurus* was the only species commonly found in deep water. Other species were associated with shelves and shallow bays. In the region of the Gulf of Siam and the

South China Sea generally, they were largely restricted to waters less than 90–100 m deep, with most occurring at 75 m or less. A more detailed study of the Tonkin Gulf of North Viet Nam gave similar results. Sea snakes ranged over the entire northern Australian shelf to a depth of 100 m; in fact, the 100 m isobath very closely outlined the distributional limits of non-pelagic sea snakes in that area.

It can be concluded that non-pelagic species seldom, if ever, dive deeper than 100 m. Although some species may indeed have capacities greater than this, there is at present no substantial body of data to suggest it. The 100-fathom (about 180 m) limit suggested by Herre (1942) seems excessive, and probably reflects less detailed and less accurate data on depth than was at Shuntov's disposal.

Within the above limit, individual species or genera may have much more restricted vertical ranges. For example, Shuntov (1971) suggests that *Acalyptophis peronii, Astrotia stokesii,* and the genus *Aipysurus* are restricted within the 50-m isobath. In the Tonkin Gulf, *L. hardwickii* occurs in littoral areas, with *Hydrophis fasciatus* in deeper water (Shuntov, 1962). Observations presented in Chapters 5–9 on local abundance and distribution also indicate that some species occur in a very narrow depth range. Those observations and the literature discussed above permit a rough classification of sea snakes, based on depth of diving, and a tentative assignment of a few taxa to the following categories.

Pelagic species

This category includes species which inhabit open water and feed at the surface. They are consequently not restricted to continental shelves or other shallow water and may be found long distances from land. The only example known is *P. platurus.*

Non-pelagic species

This category includes those sea snakes that dive to the bottom for feeding or other vital activities. They are consequently restricted to waters shallow enough to lie within their diving capacities.

Shallow Water Species These are species restricted to water 20 m or less in depth. Examples are *Aipysurus duboisii, Aipysurus apraefrontalis,* and *Aipysurus foliosquama.* The genus *Laticauda* may also belong here.

Intermediate Species These are species which sometimes occur in water deeper than 20 m, but which do not dive below 50 m. Examples are *A. laevis, A. stokesii, Emydocephalus annulatus,* and *A. peronii.*

Deep Water Species These are species which dive below 50 m. *Hydrophis melanocephalus* is an example and probably a number of other *Hydrophis* also belong here. Unfortunately, Shuntov (1971) does not provide sufficient detail to ascertain precise distributional patterns of all the various species he treated, and it is not certain which species he found deeper than 50 m.

Assignment of species to these broad categories does not imply that diving ability necessarily limits their vertical distribution to the designated depths (ecological factors such as food supply, substrate, or competing species may well be decisive), but does indicate the general conditions under which they carry out their daily activities.

VOLUNTARY SUBMERGENCE TIMES AND SURVIVAL TIME UNDER WATER

Submergence times of 6 hrs (Doughton, year unspecified) and 8 hrs (see Volsøe, 1939) have been reported. However, in neither case was there sufficient documentation to accept these values without question. Barme (1968) indicated that sea snakes "can remain for 10 min or more without breathing." Pickwell (1972) reports that inactive *Laticauda* in the laboratory surface for air about every 25–30 min and that one animal in nature remained submerged for 0.5 hr. Similarly, he found that *P. platurus* normally surfaces every 10–20 min in the laboratory although one resting animal remained submerged for 90 min. Webster (pers. comm.) has recorded voluntary submergence of *A. peronii* in the laboratory for 2.5 hrs. Heatwole (in press a) timed 855 submergences of nine species of sea snakes and file snakes under a variety of field and laboratory conditions. A number of variables affected duration of voluntary submergence. Active snakes usually submerged for shorter periods than did inactive ones under otherwise similar conditions. The extent to which activity reduced submergence time was highly variable although commonly active snakes were apneic only 20–40% as long as were inactive ones.

Increasing temperature within the range normally encountered by sea snakes resulted in a reduction of the submergence time.

Pough (1973b) has indicated that the Javan file snake (*Acrochordus javanicus*) was relatively inactive by day, breathing on the average every 22.5 min (range 8–32 min); at night the snakes moved actively about the tank and breathed at intervals of 20–175 sec depending on the degree of activity. Thus there was a diel change in submergence time undoubtedly mediated in part by activity differences. Heatwole (in press a) compared voluntary submergence times between day and night at given temperatures and levels of activity and found that diel differences were not significant either in *Acrochordus granulatus* or in two species of sea snake.

The conditions of captivity may impose stresses that alter voluntary submergence times; Heatwole (in press a) found a variable influence, not predictable as to whether submergence time would be lengthened or shortened. The most meaningful results will, consequently, be obtained from field observations. Laboratory measurements should employ snakes that appear to be accustomed to their artificial surroundings, but which have not been kept without food for prolonged periods.

In some respects, voluntary submergence time seems to show an inverse relation to metabolic rate. For example, the shortening of voluntary submergence time by increased activity and elevated temperature can reasonably be regarded as reflecting higher metabolic rates under those conditions. On the other hand, effect of the conditions of captivity do not necessarily bear any direct relationship to metabolism, and the lack of a consistent lengthening of submergence time during the night, when sea snake metabolic rates are lower (Heatwole and Seymour, 1975), suggests that voluntary submergence time is influenced by other factors in addition to metabolic rate.

It is clear from the foregoing that most species of marine snake commonly submerge for periods of up to 0.5 hr and that occasionally some may do so for 1.5–2.5 hrs without ill effect. However, there is little information on the maximum time they can endure submergence. Volsøe (1939), using a single lung volume and some general figures for reptilian metabolism, calculated that a sea snake should be able to survive a 2-hr submergence, a figure for which he later obtained empirical verification (Volsøe, 1956). Pickwell (1972) indicated that *Pelamis* tolerated 5 hrs of being restrained under water, and Dunson and Ehlert (1971) found that it endured forced submergence up to 5.5 hrs at 26–29°C and 4–24 hrs at 13°C. Graham (1974) found that, in the same species, survival time ranged from 113 to 300 min (1.9–5 hours) when held under water in wire cages. When oxygen tension was manipulated experimentally, survival times as low as 21 min (P_{O_2} less than 16 torr) and as high as 375 min (P_{O_2} 490 torr) could be obtained. In view of these experimental results, the maximum tolerance to submergence seems to be about 5 hrs under conditions normally encountered in nature, although unusual conditions (such as low temperature) may lead to longer survival times. Voluntary submergence times are usually well below the limits of danger from asphyxia.

GAS EXCHANGE

Lung

Morphology In some primitive snakes (e.g., boids and xenopeltids) the lungs are paired structures, whereas in other snakes there is a radical departure from this plan in that the left lung has been lost or is rudimentary, with the right one remaining as the sole or principal respiratory unit (Butler, 1895). Concomitant with this change have been a reduction and eventual loss of the left pulmonary artery (Bellairs and Underwood, 1951; Bellairs, 1969). Various degrees of reduction in the left lung and lung-vascular system occur in present-day snakes. In some species there are anastomoses between the left and right pulmonary arteries and consequently the pattern of blood supply to the lungs is complex. In some species with two well developed lungs, even when a left pulmonary artery is present, the right artery often sends branches to the left lung, supplying it as well as the right one. In extreme cases, the right pulmonary artery constitutes the sole supply of blood for the left lung, the left pulmonary artery being represented as a small diverticulum on the pulmonary trunk. These variations in the lungs and in the pulmonary circulation of snakes were documented in the early literature and have been summarized in a succinct review by Brongersma (1958). However, comparative studies on the functional morphology of a wide variety of snakes are badly needed before the ecological significance of these variations can be interpreted. Of immediate interest are the condition found in sea snakes and the radically different one found in file snakes.

The trachea of sea snakes is highly modified. The supporting cartilaginous elements do not form complete rings throughout, but rather, beginning from just behind the head to about halfway between the heart and head (McDowell, 1972), become semicircular in shape, with the ventral side of the trachea consisting of the base of the cartilage, from which dorsally directed horns project on either side. The dorsal part of the trachea is membranous and expanded so as to be several times the diameter of the tracheal cartilages (Figure 1). It is highly vascularized, and from the dorsal surface is practically indistinguishable in appearance from the lung proper. This organ is known as the tracheal lung. It is delimited anteriorly by the beginning of the enlarged areolar portion of the dorsal trachea, and posteriorly by the disappearance of the semicircular supporting cartilages. In most sea snakes it occupies the region from the neck to the heart, although in a few species tracheal cartilages are found considerably posterior to the heart. The primitive *Hydrelaps* is an exception in that it has a shorter lung with the tracheal part falling far short of the head (McDowell, 1969). In the cardiac region there is a constriction of the respiratory tube into which the heart fits. This constriction usually (though as indicated above, not always) marks the beginning of the true or bronchial lung. The latter is a tubular structure with a highly vascularized wall, but lacks cartilaginous supports (Figure 1); it is frequently of greater diameter than the tracheal lung, particularly just behind the heart. This represents the right lung (Butler, 1895). In most species of sea snake there are no vestiges of the left one. Exceptions are the hydrophid *Ephalophis greyi* (McDowell, 1974) and the sea krait *Laticauda* (Cope, 1894, erroneously listing the rudimentary lung as the right one instead of the left one). The bronchial lung extends posteriorly for a variable proportion of the body and leads directly into the posterior part of the lung known as the saccular lung. The latter is a cylindrical tube, smaller in diameter than either the tracheal or bronchial lung. It is poorly vascularized, possessing only a few nutritive

Figure 1. Internal surface of three sections of the lung of a 668-g *Aipysurus laevis*. In each case a section of the lung tube was incised longitudinally along the mid-dorsal surface and the cut edges pinned out and fixed in formalin; the center of each section, as viewed in the figure, is the mid-ventral line. Center: Anterior portion of the tracheal lung showing the semicircular cartilaginous supports in the mid-ventral line. Right: Transitional area between the tracheal and bronchial lung. Note the band of semicircular cartilages of the tracheal lung (top) giving way to the flat non-cartilaginous wall of the bronchial lung (bottom). Left: Section from the middle of the saccular lung. Note the network of connective or muscular tissue in the two sections of the vascular lung, and its absence from the saccular lung.

vessels. In some species, the anterior end of the saccular lung is marked by a small constriction and an abrupt termination of the pulmonary vascular bed; in others, the constriction is absent and the decrease in vascularity is more gradual, making the precise anterior limits of the saccular lung difficult to distinguish; there is individual variation within a species in this feature. Posteriorly, the saccular lung extends to the very end of the body cavity.

The tracheal and bronchial lungs are so similar in their vascularity that they can be referred to collectively as the vascular lung. The vascular lung is almost certainly the seat of direct respiratory gas exchange, whereas the saccular lung would seem to be incapable of functioning in this way.

In addition to the differences enumerated above, the internal walls of the vascular and saccular lungs differ greatly. The former has a network of non-striated muscle fibers on its inner surface forming shallow pockets, whereas the lining of the saccular lung is relatively smooth, although muscle fibers are present (Beddard, 1904; Varde, 1951; see also Figure 1). Despite the serial morphological and histological variation in the sea snake lung, the entire organ is one continuous tube; there are no large internal septa.

This type of lung is not peculiar to sea snakes, since tracheal lungs and saccular lungs occur in many non-aquatic snakes as well, including burrowers, terrestrial species and even arboreal ones, although in most the lung does not extend completely to the posterior end of the body as it does in sea snakes (Cope, 1900; George and Shah, 1956, 1965). Sea snake lungs are more muscular than those of land snakes (Beddard, 1904). This is especially true of the rear of the lung; sea snakes have smooth muscles in the wall of the saccular lung in contrast to the more membraneous nature of the air sac in most snakes (McDowell, 1969). Brattstrom (1959) has suggested the following functions of the saccular lung in snakes generally: (1) respiration, including air storage and a flow-through system permitting repassage of air over vascular areas during exhalation; (2) evaporative cooling including panting; (3) cooling of the gonads by bringing cool air internally; and (4) body support (both direct mechanical support and as a buoy in water). Numbers 2 and 3 seem highly unlikely for sea snakes, leaving respiratory and buoyancy functions to be considered, suggestions made as early as 1841 by Cantor.

McDonald (1959) has suggested a possible significance of the saccular lung overlooked by previous investigators. He points out that if a cylindrical sac is elongated but the surface area kept constant, its volume decreases. Thus lung elongation imposed by the ophidian body shape would limit the tidal volume (and hence amount of oxygen inspired), even though the total vascular surface area might be quite adequate for oxygen absorption by a snake of that size. He suggests that the saccular lung is a mechanism for increasing tidal volume and thereby compensating for the relative loss of lung volume in the elongated vascular lung. Vascularization of the saccular lung would be superfluous because the surface area involved in gas exchange is not limiting. These considerations would apply equally to terrestrial and sea snakes and would explain the presence of saccular lungs in a wide variety of non-diving species. The snake lung plan could also be generally adaptive in other ways. For example, a large food bolus in the stomach might occlude the posterior part of the lung and an anterior shift of vascularized tissue (tracheal lung) would seem advantageous. Also, many snakes ingest large prey which may occlude the trachea during swallowing, and a saccular lung used for oxygen storage can be construed as adaptive in any snake (George and Varde, 1941), particularly in view of the smooth muscle contractions observed in reptilian lungs that would permit intrapulmonary redistribution of gas (see Gans, 1970); Beddard (1904) has pointed out that sea snake lungs are unusually muscular and that contraction of muscles of the saccular lung would serve to expel air from it into the other parts of the lung. Such features may have merely pre-adapted sea snakes for apneic conditions of a different type. Other differences in sea snake lungs, such as the thicker wall of the saccular portion and the relative inelasticity of the lung in general, may be later modifications arising in response to selective pressures exerted by the marine habitat. There is also the possibility that structures like the saccular lung may have taken on new functions in a marine context. Certainly a saccular lung would not function in buoyancy control in a desert sand burrower (some of which have saccular lungs), whereas it might in sea snakes.

As mentioned above, the pulmonary circulation of snakes is highly modified in relation to the tendency toward reduction or loss of the left lung. In sea snakes only the right pulmonary circulation remains. The pulmonary arterial trunk emerges from the ventricle and continues anteriorly along the heart in close association with the two systemic arches. At the anterior end of the heart, it turns toward the lung and bifurcates into two major vessels. One, the pulmonary artery (or posterior pulmonary artery), turns posteriorly and runs along the edge of the bronchial lung, where it gives off numerous lateral branches which ramify into the vascular bed. The other branch, the tracheal artery (sometimes called the anterior pulmonary artery), continues anteriorly along the face of the tracheal lung, similarly giving rise to an extensive capillary bed in the tracheal lung. The venous system collects blood from the vascular bed of the tracheal lung and, via lateral branches, drains into the tracheal vein (anterior pulmonary vein), which courses in close proximity to the tracheal artery. Lateral veins drain the capillaries of the bronchial lung into the posterior pulmonary vein, which lies beside the posterior pulmonary artery. The posterior pulmonary vein and the tracheal vein join to form the common pulmonary vein, which empties into the left atrium. The relationship of the heart and its major vessels to the tracheal and bronchial lungs is illustrated in Figure 2.

It is clear that both of the vascular sections of the lung are directly supplied with blood from the heart, and that they return the oxygenated blood directly to the heart, where it can be distributed to the general system. It would therefore appear that both the tracheal and bronchial lungs are functional gas exchange organs.

The lung of the file snake differs from that of sea snakes in two important features: (1) the lung appears similar throughout with no well defined saccular region, and (2) the lung surface, particularly toward the anterior end, appears lobular. In contrast to the non-septate sea snake lungs which can be easily exhausted of their air content by mechanical pressure or filling with water, those of file snakes seem to have air trapped into small lobules which are almost impossible to evacuate without rupturing internal membranes. Brongersma (1958) has previously called attention to this unusual compartmentalization of the acrochordid lung in the following terms: "Le poumon-trachéal d'*Acrochordus* . . . . . .est des plus remarquables. La membrane dorsal de la trachée-artère a deux rangées de perforations; chaque pore conduit à un appendice. Ces appendices ont une structure alvéolaire, et chacun d'eux est un petit poumon accessoire." Cope (1894, 1900) figures these structures.

Lung Volumes As mentioned above, the lung of sea snakes and file snakes extends from near the neck to the posterior end of the body cavity. Thus a potentially great lung volume would be expected. Lung volume would deter-

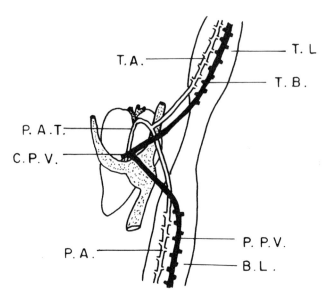

Figure 2. Pulmonary circulation of a sea snake (*Hydrophis caerulescens*) and its relation to the tracheal and bronchial sections of the lung. Note the constriction between the two parts of the lung. Stippled areas indicate systemic arterial trunks, systemic venous drainage and the sinus venosus. Black vessels are the pulmonary venous drainage and white ones the pulmonary arterial supply. P.A.T., pulmonary arterial trunk; P.A., pulmonary artery; T.V., tracheal vein; T.L., tracheal lung; T.A., tracheal artery; C.P.V., common pulmonary vein; P.P.V., posterior pulmonary vein; B.L., bronchial lung. Modified and redrawn from Bal and Navathe (1949).

mine the amount of air available to a snake during a dive, and relative volumes of the vascular and saccular sections may have a bearing on O_2 absorption rate and/or storage capacity. Certainly, lung volume would be important in any consideration of adjustment of buoyancy. Consequently, lung volumes were measured in a variety of sea snakes. The values obtained represent the maximum lung capacity, not necessarily the volume of air normally retained by live snakes.

The method of measuring maximum lung capacity involved removing the lung from a snake, inserting either a small funnel or a syringe (depending on the size of the snake) into the trachea, and pouring in water until the lung was full. Bubbles trapped in the network of the lung wall were released by gentle tapping. For comparative purposes the same method was applied to several species of land snake, but proved unsatisfactory because of the highly elastic nature of land snake lungs—they simply continued expanding as more water was added. This was not true of sea snakes. However, in order to check whether the weight of the water might be stretching the sea snake lung to an extent not visibly appreciated by the investigator, lungs were filled and the volume measured when all but the top of the trachea was submerged in a large water bath, and thus hydrostatic pressure was maintained on both sides of the lung wall. The volume was measured on the same lung suspended in air and the results compared with the submerged control (Table 1). In most species, total lung volume was larger by 7% or less in air than in water. In some, the difference was negligible, and attributable to measuring error (some had higher volumes in water). Two species were exceptions, *L. hardwickii* with a mean distensibility of 12.3% and *A. duboisii* with one of 14.4%. However, in both cases, most of the values were low and the means skewed as a result of one or a few exceptionally high values. In other experiments, we have observed that sea snake lungs begin to deteriorate soon after death and that there are concomitant increases in elasticity. It is probable that the few high distensibility values noted above were due to this effect. It can be concluded that volumetric measurements of maximum lung capacity in sea snakes give valid results if care is exercised in using only specimens in good condition; values obtained constitute slight overestimates (up to 7% too high).

Table 1. Comparison of lung volumes measured in air and in water

| Species | N[b] | Distensibility[a] | |
		Mean	Range
Aipysurus apraefrontalis	1	3.2	–
Aipysurus duboisii	2	14.4	0.5–28.7
Aipysurus fuscus	1	1.6	–
Aipysurus laevis	2	1.4	+1.6–4.4
Emydocephalus annulatus	5	5.7	0–9.8
Astrotia stokesii	1	+0.7	–
Hydrophis melanocephalus[c]	4	6.7	5.6–8.0
Hydrophis elegans	1	+2.2	–
Lapemis hardwickii	9	12.3	1.6–23.5

[a]Distensibility is expressed as the difference between "in air" and "in water" measurements in percent of the former value. Positive values indicate that the measurements in water were greater than those in air.

[b]N refers to number of individuals on which measurements were made.

[c]Tentatively identified by H. G. Cogger but subsequent revision likely.

Different species of sea snake are remarkably uniform in the relative proportions of their lungs which are vascularized. The volume of the vascularized part of the lung (tracheal lung plus bronchial lung) accounted, on the average, for about 85–98% of the total lung volume in all hydrophids tested. Thus, even though the saccular lung often occupies a considerable proportion of the total lung length (means of 16%, 19%, and 17% for 10 *E. annulatus,* six *A. duboisii* and 18 *A. laevis* respectively), it usually represents a relatively minor contribution to total lung volume (about 2–15%, see Table 2). *Laticauda* was an exception in having an exceptionally large proportion of total lung volume devoted to the saccular lung.

The relative sizes of the two components of the vascular lung vary widely among species, the tracheal part averaging from 11% to 43% of the total vascular volume (Table 3). Except for *L. hardwickii* most of the species with relatively large tracheal lungs are long, thin species, e.g., *H. elegans* and *H. melanocephalus*. This may have little direct significance to diving, but may be a morphological reflection of the general elongation of the pre-cardiac region in general.

Relative lung volume varies somewhat interspecifically. *A. apraefrontalis,* the shallowest diver, has the smallest lung volume per unit body weight of any species studied (0.19 ml/g body wt). Most species that dive to intermediate depths had mean values ranging from 0.25 to 0.37 ml/g (Table 2). Three species had larger mean lung volumes (0.42–0.55 ml/g). One of them is known to be a deep diver (*H. melanocephalus*). *A. stokesii* is an intermediate species. The diving depth of the third, *H. semperi,* is not known; it inhabits the fresh water of Lake Taal in the Phillipines and little is known of its ecology.

Relative lung volume does not seem to depend on body size, as a plot of these two variables against each other resulted in a general scatter with no consistent trends, nor did interspecific differences in relative lung volume seem related to body size (although *A. stokesii* is a large species with a relatively large lung).

Relative lung volumes have not been measured in lizards or land snakes. However, sea snakes have considerably greater values than do turtles. Patterson (1973) has reviewed relative lung volumes in 18 species of turtles from a variety of habitats, and found values ranging from 0.01 to 0.21 ml/g. Only two species of sea snakes had values low enough to overlap with those of turtles and these were near the upper limits of turtles (0.19 and 0.20 ml/g). This does not necessarily indicate that sea snakes are superior to turtles in the respiratory qualities of the lung, since the latter have internal septa which increase the surface area. In marine turtles there are secondary bronchi which subdivide the pulmonary surface, giving a compact lung of alveolar-lined tubes (Hughes, 1973). A greater proportion of chelonian body weight consists of bone (the shell), which is metabolically relatively inert. However, a greater

Table 2. Relative size of the vascular and saccular lungs and relative lung volume in some sea snakes and the file snake (measured in air)

Species	N[a]	Percent of total lung volume				Relative lung volume (ml/g body wt)	
		Vascular lung		Saccular lung			
		Mean	Range	Mean	Range	Mean	Range
Laticauda colubrina	2,2	28.7	26.9–30.5	71.3	69.5–73.1	0.32	0.32–0.32
Aipysurus apraefrontalis	1,1	92.7	–	7.3	–	0.19	–
Aipysurus duboisii	15,15	93.7	85.2–96.3	6.3	3.7–14.8	0.31	0.18–0.53
Aipysurus fuscus	1,1	93.3	–	6.7	–	0.26	–
Aipysurus laevis	35,20	94.5	90.4–98.7	5.5	1.3–9.4	0.26	0.10–0.38
Emydocephalus annulatus	21,21	96.1	90.2–98.8	3.9	1.2–9.8	0.36	0.15–0.52
Astrotia stokesii	1,3	92.3	–	7.7	–	0.55	0.29–0.89
Hydrophis melanocephalus	4,4	90.4	87.6–93.6	9.6	6.4–12.4	0.42	0.33–0.53
Hydrophis elegans	1,3	97.9	–	2.1	–	0.32	0.23–0.50
Hydrophis semperi	1,2	95.7	–	4.3	–	0.45	0.45–0.45
Lapemis hardwickii	3,9	85.0	80.2–90.7	15.0	9.3–19.8	0.36	0.25–0.44
Disteira kingii	2,2	100.0	100–100	0	0–0	0.20	0.17–0.22
Pelamis platurus	0,4	–	–	–	–	0.58	0.31–0.68
Acrochordus granulatus[b]	0,4	–	–	–	–	0.30	0.22–0.39

[a] The first N value refers to the sample size used in calculating volumes of the saccular and vascular lungs; the second N value is the sample size used in calculating relative lung volume. Sample sizes for the two types of measurement differ because (1) some measurements were made on board small, rocking vessels upon which accurate use of a balance to measure body weight was not possible, and (2) in the early part of the study, volumes of the different sections of the lung were not separately measured.

[b] *Acrochordus* values are approximate because of the difficulties involved in measuring lung volume in this species.

Table 3. Relative volumes of the two components of the vascular lung in some sea snakes

		Percent of total volume of vascular lung			
		Tracheal lung		Bronchial lung	
Species	N	Mean	Range	Mean	Range
Aipysurus apraefrontalis	1	11.8	–	88.2	–
Aipysurus duboisii	2	9.6	8.9–10.2	90.5	89.8–91.1
Aipysurus laevis	2	14.2	13.4–14.9	85.9	85.1–86.6
Aipysurus fuscus	1	14.7	–	85.3	–
Emydocephalus annulatus	5	5.0	2.2–7.1	95.1	92.9–97.8
Hydrophis melanocephalus	4	30.8	27.0–35.0	69.3	65.0–73.0
Hydrophis elegans	1	43.2	–	56.8	–
Lapemis hardwickii	2	32.9	32.0–33.8	67.1	66.2–68.0

potential buoyancy at maximum inhalation is indicated for sea snakes. *Chelonia mydas,* the only sea turtle mentioned in Patterson's study, was the species with the lowest relative lung volume (0.01 ml/g).

Graham (1974) measured the volume of air retained in the lungs of live *P. platurus.* The largest value he obtained was 0.13 ml/g body weight. This is slightly less than one fourth of the maximum relative lung volume measured in the species shown in Table 2. Thus it appears that snakes usually utilize only a small part of their available capacity. This will be discussed further in relation to buoyancy control.

Even smaller relative volumes of air are retained in other snakes. Using whole body plethysmography, Standaert and Johansen (1974) found *Acrochordus javanicus* had mean air volumes of 0.05 ml/g. If this species has the same relative maximum lung volume as the closely related *A. granulatus* (Table 2), it would be filling the lung only to about one sixth of its maximum capacity. *A. javanicus* has a mean tidal volume of 0.04 ml/g or about 80% of the volume of air retained in the lungs. The boa constrictor's tidal volume was only about 43% of the retained volume (Standaert and Johansen, 1974).

Pulmonary Oxygen Uptake Sea snakes intersperse their voluntary submergences with a trip to the surface where they breathe once (or sometimes several times) and then immediately return to the bottom. Thus breathing is quick and there would appear to be insufficient time to repay an extensive oxygen debt. On some occasions, sea snakes float or swim at the surface for a considerable time. It is doubtful, however, if even under these conditions the breathing pattern is altered, because in the laboratory such floating snakes undergo extensive periods of apnea interrupted by short intervals of breathing. The number of breaths taken at a given breathing event is usually one

(69% of the breathing periods), although two (25%) or even three (6%) breaths in quick succession sometimes occur (Heatwole and Seymour, 1975).

Resting oxygen consumption in sea snakes is similar to that of terrestrial snakes of similar size. *L. hardwickii* has values very near the metabolism-weight regression line calculated for land snakes by Dmi'el (1972). Other sea snakes are lower and lie outside the 95% confidence limits of the data he summarized. However, many recent studies have presented values also considerably below his confidence limits (Buikema and Armitage, 1969; Aleksiuk, 1971; Jacobson and Whitford, 1970, 1971). The sea snake data are comparable with the latter when effect of body size on metabolism is considered, and agree well with the oxygen consumption of the similarly sized *Pituophis catenifer* (Greenwald, 1971a). In contrast, file snakes have pulmonary oxyten consumption considerably lower than either sea snakes or terrestrial snakes (Standaert and Johansen, 1974; Heatwole and Seymour, 1975).

A number of variables affect the uptake of pulmonary oxygen in sea snakes. Animals in respirometers were categorized as "active" (swimming continuously and vigorously), "occasionally active" (leisurely swimming interspersed with periods of immobility), and "inactive" (immobile except when surfacing to breathe), and the oxygen consumption compared among the three categories. Pulmonary oxygen uptake was greater in active snakes than in inactive ones. Those showing occasional activity were intermediate although their lower range of values overlapped the upper range of inactive ones (Figure 3).

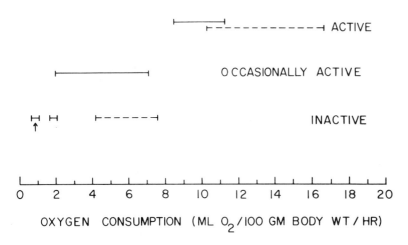

Figure 3. Relation of oxygen consumption to activity and time of day for six species of sea snakes collectively and for the file snake, *Acrochordus granulatus* (arrow). Solid lines indicate range of values obtained during the night; the dashed line is the range of those obtained during the day. Modified and redrawn from Heatwole and Seymour (1975).

Since the "active" sea snakes appeared to be exerting the maximum effort of which they were capable, and "inactive" ones only the locomotion required to surface for air, the difference in oxygen consumption between active and inactive animals can be considered a measure of the aerobic metabolic scope for activity. Few values of metabolic scope have been calculated for either terrestrial or marine snakes. Given the large variation among both groups in this small sample, generalizations about the relative values in sea snakes as compared to terrestrial ones must be tentative, especially since one cannot be completely certain in either case that the animals are exerting themselves maximally. However, of the species studied, the sea snakes have considerably lower metabolic scopes than do land snakes (Table 4).

Time of day is another important variable affecting oxygen consumption in sea snakes. Diel changes are independent of activity. For a given activity category and temperature, diurnal pulmonary uptake is higher than that at night (usually about twice as high for a given species) (Heatwole and Seymour, 1975; also see Figure 3).

The amount of oxygen consumed per breath varies greatly among sea snakes. Large individuals have greater uptakes per breath than do smaller ones. However, there is great variability even within a single individual for a given time of day and activity level. In most cases the largest values are 2–4 times the smallest ones, although 8–14-fold differences sometimes occur. The amount of oxygen consumed per breath does not seem to be related to the length of time the snake was previously submerged. When several breaths are taken during a breathing event, the average oxygen uptake per breath is lower than when only one breath is taken (Heatwole and Seymour, 1975).

Table 4. Metabolic scope of some sea snakes and terrestrial snakes

Species	Metabolic scope[a] ($ml\ O_2\ g^{-1}\ h^{-1}$)	Remarks and Authority
Sea snakes		
Hydrophis melanocephalus	0.125	One individual, daytime
	0.064	One individual, night
	0.078	Aggregate for 3 snakes, night
Lapemis hardwickii	0.042	One individual, daytime
Terrestrial snakes		
Pituophis catenifer	0.420	Peak value (at $30°C$); Greenwald (1971)
	0.350	$25°C$; Greenwald (1971)
Spalerosophis cliffordi	0.230	$25°C$; Dmi'el and Borut (1972)

[a]All values for sea snakes were measured at $25.2–27.0°C$.

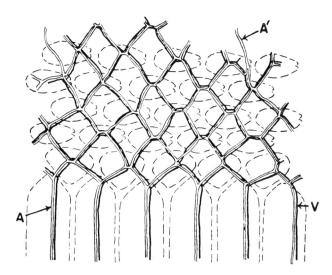

Figure 4., Arrangement of the integumentary blood vessels in snakes. A, integumental artery; A′, arterial derivative of intercostal artery; V, integumentary vein. Upper part of figure portrays dorsal skin, bottom part of figure shows gastrosteges. From White (1957); reprinted by permission.

Skin

Morphology Sea snake skin, because of its relative impermeability to sodium (Dunson, pers. comm.) and its heavy scutellation, does not appear to be a likely candidate for gaseous exchange. However, this is not the case and measurable amounts of oxygen and carbon dioxide traverse sea snake skin (see below).

White (1957) points out that in a variety of terrestrial snakes the integumentary vessels conform in pattern to the shape and arrangement of the scales. The integumentary arteries and veins are derivatives of the intercoastal arteries and veins. From their point of exit from the body wall the integumentary vessels course directly to the subcutaneous connective tissue, where they anastomose in such a manner as to form a network of diamond-shaped or hexagonal figures over the dorsum (Figure 4). The points of union of each adjacent diamond or hexagon are near the centers of the dorsal scales. In the ventral region the vessels run transversely beneath the centers of the gastrosteges (Figure 4). In both areas the pattern of the arteries is congruently superimposed upon that of the veins. From this mesh of vessels, small branches are sent to the skin proper. This arrangement of vessels was postulated by White to be an adaptation permitting considerable stretching of the skin (during swallowing of large prey) without injury to the cutaneous blood vessels. Whatever the function, this arrangement of blood vessels does not seem to be the most effective one possible in terms of cutaneous gas exchange. For example, if the blood vessels were to be within the interscalar spaces instead of anastomosing beneath the centers of scales, they would be in closer contact with the external medium.

Apparently, sea snakes have the above arrangement although they may depart from the general ophidian plan in some adaptive way (see Chapter 16). The number, distribution, and surface area of the small cutaneous branches arising from the integumentary network should be examined.

Cutaneous Respiration

Oxygen Uptake Some freshwater turtles undergo aquatic respiration, at least part of which occurs via the skin (Dunson, 1960), and in some cases the cutaneous component accounts for as much as 70% of the total aquatic oxygen uptake (Girgis, 1961; Belkin, 1968). However, only recently has any attention been focused on extrapulmonary respiration in aquatic snakes. Sea snakes are capable of cutaneous respiration, mean oxygen uptake in inactive individuals ranging up to 1.8 ml O_2 100 g^{-1} h^{-1} (Heatwole and Seymour, 1975; Graham, 1974). Interspecific differences may result from differences in body size and its concomitant alteration of surface area to volume ratios. Heatwole and Seymour (1975) studied five species of hydrophids and obtained mean cutaneous uptakes of 0–0.7 ml O_2 100 g^{-1} h^{-1} in inactive snakes. Graham (1974), working with *P. platurus,* obtained higher values (mean of 1.8 ml O_2 100 g^{-1} h^{-1}). He worked with smaller animals (7–116 g) than did Heatwole and Seymour (240–668 g). The mean cutaneous oxygen uptake in inactive *Acrochordus granulatus* and *A. javanicus* is 0.2 and 0.07 ml O_2 100 g^{-1} h^{-1}, respectively (Heatwole and Seymour, 1975; Standaert and Johansen, 1974). All of these values are higher than those obtained on the only terrestrial snake which has been studied (0.06 ml O_2 100 g^{-1} h^{-1} for the boa constrictor; Standaert and Johansen, 1974). Thus sea snakes have higher cutaneous oxygen uptake than file snakes, which in turn have higher uptake than the terrestrial boa. The one exception to this statement is *H. melanocephalus*, for which there was no measurable cutaneous uptake during inactivity. However, it did exhibit cutaneous respiration when active (see below).

The relative contribution of cutaneous oxygen uptake to total oxygen consumption also varies among the three types of snake. Excluding *H. melanocephalus,* cutaneous oxygen consumption on the average accounted for 5–22% of the total oxygen consumption in inactive sea snakes, whereas comparable values were 7% and 13% for the two species of file snakes and only 3% for the boa constrictor. Thus the terrestrial snake relies very little on cutaneous uptake, whereas a considerable proportion of the total oxygen exchange occurs through the skin in some of the aquatic snakes.

Although the relative proportion of pulmonary and cutaneous contributions to oxygen uptake is of the same order of magnitude in sea snakes and file snakes, the absolute levels of oxygen consumption, via both the lungs and the skin, are generally much lower in the latter. In terms of total oxygen consumption, sea snakes are not greatly different from terrestrial species (see previous section), and a reduced metabolic rate does not seem to be among their repertoire of diving adaptations. By contrast, the unusually low metabolic rates of file snakes may be an important factor contributing to their ability to submerge for long periods.

A variety of factors influence cutaneous oxygen uptake. The probable effect of body size has been mentioned above. Activity is also an important influence since active sea snakes had increases in cutaneous oxygen uptake of 14–120% above inactive levels, and *Acrochordus granulatus* had a corresponding figure of 100% (Table 5). None of the snakes, on which gaseous exchange through the skin was measured, engaged in activity sufficiently vigorous to be considered maximal. Consequently, the values in Table 5 are not representative of cutaneous aerobic metabolic scopes but would constitute underestimates.

Psychological factors may influence cutaneous uptake, since Heatwole and Seymour (1975) found that values were 10–18 times higher for an *A. granulatus* when restrained in a narrow glass tube, than for the same individual in a larger container.

Carbon Dioxide Elimination Carbon dioxide diffuses through animal tissues about 36 times faster than does oxygen (Krogh, 1919), and one would consequently expect the skin of aquatic snakes to be more effective in losing CO_2 than in taking up O_2. This view is consistent with the constancy of blood and lung P_{CO_2} during diving in sea snakes (Seymour and Webster, 1975) and has been empirically demonstrated in several snakes. *P. platurus*

Table 5. Effect of activity on mean aquatic oxygen uptake of sea snakes and the marine file snake[a]

Species	V O_2 (ml 100 g^{-1} h^{-1})		Increase in V O_2 caused by activity	
	Active	Inactive	ml O_2 100 g^{-1} h^{-1}	% of inactive value
Sea snakes				
Lapemis hardwickii	1.1	0.5	0.6	120
Hydrophis melanocephalus	1.0	0.0	0.0	–
Aipysurus duboisii	0.8	0.5	0.3	60
Aipysurus laevis	0.8	0.7	0.1	14
File snake				
Acrochordus granulatus	0.4	0.2	0.2	100

[a]Data from Heatwole and Seymour (1975).

cutaneously excreted CO_2 at rates of up to 94% of the total (pulmonary plus cutaneous) oxygen consumption (Graham, 1974), and in *A. javanicus* as much as 33% of the CO_2 elimination was via the skin (Standaert and Johansen, 1974). This ability is also found in terrestrial snakes, but to a more limited extent; 21% of the CO_2 exchange was aquatic in boa constrictors placed in water (Standaert and Johansen, 1974).

It would appear that aquatic snakes exhibit a high degree of bimodal gas exchange, whereby most of the O_2 requirements are met by the lung, and most CO_2 elimination occurs cutaneously.

GAS TRANSPORT

Heart

Structure; Mode of Functioning The reptilian heart is unique among vertebrates by virtue of having a dual aortic arch system, and right and left arches exiting separately from the heart. The right arch supplies the head region via the carotid arteries, and then courses posteriorly to unite with the left arch in the postcardiac dorsal midline and form the dorsal aorta, which carries blood to the posterior trunk. The left arch does not send major blood vessels to the head, but merely loops posteriorly to the junction with the right arch. All other vertebrates have a single systemic trunk, which leaves the heart and then branches into the various arteries supplying the head and trunk.

The heart of reptiles (excepting crocodilians) is a "three-chambered" one; i.e., there is no complete interventricular septum. Instead, there are two partial septa, the vertical septum and the Muskelleiste (muscle ridge), which tend to partially compartmentalize the ventricle and aid in functionally maintaining separate flow patterns for the systemic and pulmonary returns (Webb et al., 1971, 1974; Webb, 1972) (Figure 5). The vertical septum, in conjunction with the septal atrioventricular valves, keeps the blood from the right and left atria separate during ventricular filling (Figures 5, 6-left). The oxygenated pulmonary blood from the left atrium enters the cavum arteriosum of the ventricle. The oxygen-depleted systemic blood from the right atrium enters the cavum venosum and then reaches the cavum pulmonale via an opening between the Muskelleiste and bulbuslamelle (Figure 6, left). During ventricular systole, the abutment of the Muskelleiste against the bulbuslamelle effectively separates most of the right atrial blood (which goes to the pulmonary artery and lungs) from that of the left atrium (which goes to the systemic arches) (Figures 5, 6-right). If any blood is left in the cavum venosum after filling of the cavum pulmonale, some mixing of right and left atrial blood would be expected; this mixed blood would leave the heart

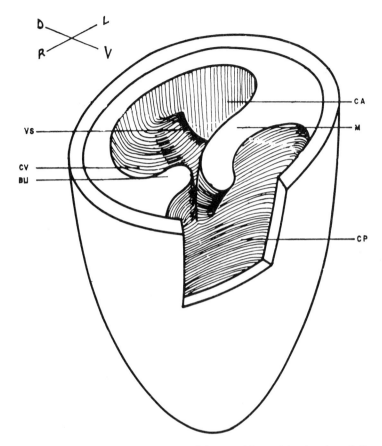

Figure 5. Diagrammatic representation of the varanid ventricle, showing relation of the septa and cava. BU, bulbuslamelle; CA, cavum arteriosum; CP, cavum pulmonale; CV, cavum venosum; M, Muskelleiste; VS, vertical septum; V,D,L, and R refer to ventral, dorsal, left and right, respectively. Modified from Webb et al. (1971).

primarily via the left systemic arch. Consequently, in most cases the systemic (oxygen depleted) blood enters the right atrium, passes to the ventricle and thence to the pulmonary artery (although some may go to the left systemic arch); the oxygenated blood returns to the left atrium from the lungs via the pulmonary vein and goes to the body via the two systemic arches. However, because of the lack of a complete, permanent septal separation of the ventricular cavities, it is not imperative that intracardial routing of the blood remains constant in reptiles (Baker and White, 1970; White, in press). Changes in the relative resistance to blood flow of the pulmonary and systemic circuits can lead to modification of pressure relations within the heart, which in turn alters flow pattern. These changes in pattern of blood flow are known as

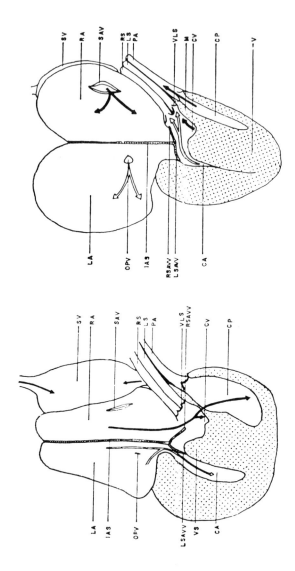

Figure 6.   Diagrammatic longitudinal section through the squamate heart during atrial systole (left) and ventricular systole (right). Dark arrows represent flow of deoxygenated blood, light arrows that of oxygenated blood. CA, cavum arteriosum; CP, cavum pulmonale; CV, cavum cenosum; IAS, interatrial septum; LA, left atrium; LS, left systemic arch; LSVV, left septal atrioventricular valve; SAV, sinatrial aperture; SV, sinus venosus; V, ventricle; VLS, valve of the left systemic arch; VS, vertical septum. Modified from Webb et al. (1971).

shunts. A right-to-left shunt is said to occur when the systemic venous blood tends to bypass the pulmonary circulation and goes selectively to the left systemic arch. A left-to-right shunt is said to occur when blood from the lungs passes through the left atrium to the ventricle, and thence back to the lungs via the pulmonary artery.

Shunting is involved in reptilian thermoregulation and also occurs during diving and apnea (see White, in press). Its significance in diving physiology is discussed below, with presentation of experimental data.

Heart Weight One might expect that sea snakes, because of their presumed need for increased cardiac output at the time of breathing, would have relatively larger hearts than non-diving reptiles. The hearts of a number of sea snakes were weighed and compared with those of land snakes (Table 6). Although some sea snakes did have larger hearts, as a group they were not greatly different from land snakes; many species having relatively smaller hearts

Table 6. Fresh heart weight in percent of body weight (relative heart weight) of some snakes

Species	N[a]	Relative heart weight	
		Mean	Range
Sea snakes			
Aipysurus apraefrontalis	1	0.13	−
Aipysurus duboisii	1	0.14	−
Aipysurus laevis	10	0.24	0.14−0.34
Astrotia stokesii	1	0.26	−
Emydocephalus annulatus	5	0.16	0.14−0.19
Lapemis hardwickii	8	0.23	0.11−0.33
Hydrophis melanocephalus	2	0.18	0.16−0.20
Hydrophis elegans	1	0.18	−
Hydrophis sp.	6	0.20	0.15−0.27
Hydrophis semperi	1	0.19	−
Disteira kingii	2	0.53	0.26−0.79
Sea krait			
Laticauda colubrina	2	0.52	0.42−0.61
File snake			
Acrochordus granulatus	19	0.26	0.17−0.34
Semiaquatic snake			
Natrix natrix[b]	6	0.30	0.26−0.32
Terrestrial snakes			
Morelia spilotes	1	0.43	−
Vipera berus[b]	2	0.26	0.24−0.28

[a]N refers to number of individuals examined.

[b]Values taken from Hesse (1921).

than any of the land snakes studied. Many of the sea snakes fell within the range of relative heart weights of the five species of lizards which have been examined (0.14–0.22% of body weight; Hesse, 1921), and of the two species of land tortoises (*Testudo hermanni* 0.24–0.60; *Testudo gigantea* 0.17–0.32; Hughes et al., 1971). For those species of sea snakes in which five or more individuals were examined, plots of relative heart weight against body weight produced a wide scatter with no discernible trends; thus, relative heart weight does not seem to be size-dependent. In general, it would appear that large heart size is not included among the circulatory adaptations of sea snakes.

Heart Rate All air-breathing, diving vertebrates, including mammals, birds, reptiles, and amphibians, display marked reductions in heart rate during submergence, commonly referred to as "diving bradycardia"; this response may even occur in non-divers, such as man (Andersen, 1966). Among the reptiles which have demonstrated this response are crocodilians, freshwater and marine turtles, terrestrial, semiaquatic, and marine lizards, and terrestrial, freshwater, and marine snakes (Johansen, 1959; Wilber, 1960; Murdaugh and Jackson, 1962; Belkin, 1964; Bartholomew and Lasiewski, 1965; Berkson, 1966; White and Ross, 1966; Pough, 1973b; McDonald, 1974; Wood and Johansen, 1974; Heatwole, in press b, and others). There are fundamental differences between the heart rate responses in sea snakes and those occurring in some other vertebrates.

When sea snakes and file snakes breathe, there is a rapid acceleration of heart rate to a peak (known as the "breathing heart rate") followed by a more gradual decline during periods of apnea (Figure 7). This pattern has been found in all six species of marine snakes which have been examined, including sea kraits (*Laticauda colubrina*), sea snakes (*A. duboisii, A. laevis, H. elegans* and *L. hardwickii*) and the file snake *A. granulatus* (Heatwole, in press b).

There are minor variations in this pattern as influenced by breathing frequency, activity and time of day. When breathing frequency is low, the heart rate during apnea decreases and eventually stabilizes at a low level designated as the "diving heart rate" (Figure 7 B, E). With more frequent breathing, breathing tachycardia occurs before the diving heart rate is achieved and a low, stable level does not occur. Instead, the graph of heart rate against time appears as a succession of peaks and valleys (Figure 7 C).

Activity influences the pattern by accelerating heart rate. When activity is moderate, each group of movements results in a momentary acceleration of heart rate, little difference being apparent between the effect of spontaneous activity and that induced by prodding the animal. Tachycardia arising from activity seldom reaches levels as high as those resulting from breathing. Vigorous activity makes it impossible to distinguish when the animal breathes. However, under such conditions, heart rates are high and erratic.

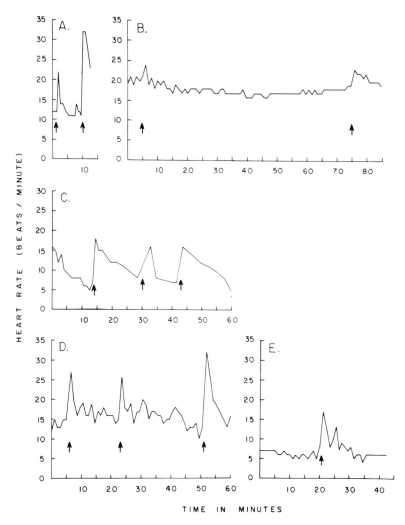

Figure 7. Heart rates of inactive marine snakes. (A) *Aipysurus duboisii*, (B) *Aipysurus laevis*, (C) *Lapemis hardwickii*, (D) *Laticauda colubrina*, (E) *Acrochordus granulatus*. Arrows indicate breaths. From Heatwole (in press b).

The difference between heart rate at rest and at maximal activity (known as heart rate scope) is one measure of the ability of the heart to cope with the increased metabolic demands of exercise. There were several heart rate increments measured in sea snakes that are believed to represent heart rate scope. They are 13.2 beats min^{-1} (*H. elegans*) and 5.9 beats min^{-1} (*A. laevis*).

These values are only one seventh to one fourth those obtained on other reptiles (Gatten, 1974), and it would appear that the capacity for activity in sea snakes is rather limited, both in terms of aerobic metabolic scope (see above) and heart rate scope.

The pattern of heart rate change is influenced by the diel cycle. At comparable levels of activity and breathing frequency, breathing heart rate was lower in *H. elegans* in the evening than during the day, although the heart rate during apnea was not altered.

The magnitude of difference between the breathing and diving heart rates in inactive marine snakes ranges from about 8–19 beats min^{-1}, or a reduction of about 40–75% of the breathing level. Some other diving reptiles have shown reductions greater than this. However, methodological differences may contribute greatly to heart rate changes and interspecific differences may be artifacts arising from different methods. Gaunt and Gans (1969) showed that the mere presence of an investigator in the room may result in both an elevated breathing tachycardia and a lowered diving heart rate, leading to spuriously high heart rate reductions during diving.

The marine snakes reported upon here were unrestrained and free to dive at will; they were in an opaque container and, except for occasional observation periods, were unable to see the investigator. Most previous studies of heart rate during diving have involved forcible submergence of the reptiles, which probably resulted in an overestimate of heart rate reduction during diving. Unfortunately, detailed interspecific comparisons among different groups of reptiles must await application of more refined methods to greater numbers of species.

The changes reported here in heart rate during breathing and apnea in sea snakes probably do not represent true diving bradycardia. Diving bradycardia is known to be (1) insensitive to activity, and (2) usually associated with a syndrome of other physiological changes such as reduction of blood flow to peripheral and splanchnic areas, which consequently respire anaerobically, reserving oxygen supplies for more vital centers such as the brain and heart (Andersen, 1966). Neither of these conditions applies to the observations of sea snakes. The diving heart rate was elevated even by occasional moderate activity (see above) and, at least for the durations of apnea occurring during measurement of heart rate, sea snake metabolism is almost entirely aerobic (see section on blood). Consequently, the diving heart rate should not be considered a true diving bradycardia.

Belkin (1964) has suggested that the diving heart rate in some freshwater turtles is the normal one for the animal (and should not be considered a bradycardia), and that the elevations stimulated by breathing are departures from it, rather than the reverse. He suggested that breathing tachycardia permits rapid equilibration of blood and tissue O_2 and CO_2 tensions with those of lung gas during brief breathing periods. In sea snakes this function is enhanced by breathing tachycardia anticipating the ventilatory cycle. Even in the complete absence of locomotory activity, heart rate begins to increase about 40 seconds before the beginning of the breathing cycle and begins to drop immediately after the breath (Figure 8). Thus, the conditions favoring rapid gaseous exchange in the lung are in operation by the time ventilation is initiated.

Although the use of cutaneous respiration in sea snakes would seem to make peripheral vasoconstriction disadvantageous during diving, true diving bradycardia may possibly occur under some circumstances. Webster (pers. comm.) has recorded heart rates much lower than the diving heart rate during exceptionally prolonged submergences of sea snakes. If this proves to be diving bradycardia, sea snakes would have three heart rate levels: the diving heart rate (base level), from which there are departures upward during breathing (breathing tachycardia), and downward during prolonged submergence (diving bradycardia).

Blood

As an organ of oxygen storage and transport, blood affects the performance of diving vertebrates. It might be assumed a priori that high oxygen-carrying capacity, blood volume, and buffering effectiveness would be of adaptive value in sea snakes. Marine snakes and turtles, being the reptiles most morphologically adapted to life in the water, would be the prime candidates for possessing these adaptations. However, no consistent differences between the bloods of diving and non-diving reptiles have appeared (Wood and Johansen, 1974; Seymour and Webster, 1975).

Hemoglobin Content The average hemoglobin concentration in six Indo-Pacific sea snake species was found to be 9.9 g/100 ml (Seymour and Webster, 1975). This falls within the range in terrestrial reptiles (Dessauer, 1970) but is low by mammalian standards. No measurements of oxygen-carrying capacity are available for sea snakes, and to estimate oxygen capacity from total hemoglobin is dangerous because of potentially high methemoglobin concentration in reptiles. However, the arterial blood in *L. hardwickii*, *H. melanocephalus* and *A. peronii* is never normally saturated, so it is evident that sea snake blood is not specially adapted for oxygen storage. Snyder (1971) showed that transport of oxygen by reptile blood is limited not only by the oxygen capacity (hematocrit) but also by the viscosity, which increases at lower temperatures. Most sea snakes are moderately active animals which apparently do not rely heavily on anaerobic metabolism during voluntary diving (see below), and they have body temperatures generally lower than those of terrestrial reptiles (Graham et al., 1971; Dunson and Ehlert, 1971). Therefore, it seems reasonable that they have reached a compromise between the oxygen transport and storage functions of the blood.

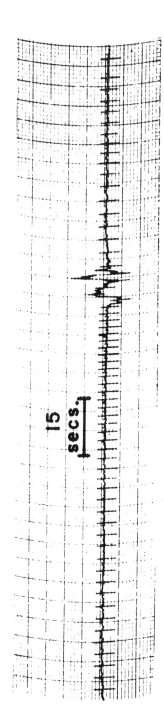

Figure 8. ECG of a *Hydrophis elegans* during breathing and apnea. The disturbance to the trace at the right of center represents a breath. From Heatwole (in press b).

Oxygen Affinity Direct comparison of the affinity of hemoglobin for oxygen is often inhibited by the various effects of temperature, pH, body weight, and experimental technique. However, Pough (1971, and unpublished data) and Seymour and Webster, (1975) obtained oxygen equilibrium curves for several species of land and sea snakes under closely similar conditions. It appears that the oxygen affinity is higher in sea snakes than in land snakes. Nevertheless, except for *Emydocephalus annulatus* and *Hydrophis semperi*, which show high affinity, the values from sea snakes are close to the levels predicted by terrestrial lizards (Table 7, Figure 9).

Johansen and Lenfant (1972) related oxygen affinity to behavior in *Constrictor constrictor* and *Acrochordus javanicus.* The former is a moderately active terrestrial snake with a relatively low affinity and the latter is a sluggish aquatic snake having very high affinity. The data from sea snakes

Table 7. Relationships between body weight and P_{50} in sea snakes, land snakes, and lizards at $25°C$

Species	Mean body weight	P_{50} [a]	Reference
Aipysurus laevis	422	33	Seymour and Webster, 1975
Acalyptophis peronii	230	37	Seymour and Webster, 1975
Emydocephalus annulatus	177	22	Seymour and Webster, 1975
Hydrophis melanocephalus	330	39	Seymour and Webster, 1975
Hydrophis elegans	350	36	Seymour and Webster, 1975
Hydrophis semperi	300	26	Seymour and Webster, 1975
Lapemis hardwickii	430	33	Seymour and Webster, 1975
Constrictor constrictor	3270	41[b]	Johansen and Lenfant, 1972; Galvão et al., 1965
Pituophis melanoleucus	548	44	Greenwald, 1971b
Sauromalus hispidus	574	29	Bennett, 1973
Varanus gouldii	674	27	Bennett, 1973
Heloderma suspectum	1250[c]	38	Edwards and Dill, 1935
Sauromalus obesus	210	32	Dill et al., 1935; Pough, 1973
Iguana iguana	1300[c]	30	Wood and Moberly, 1970
Dipsosaurus dorsalis	45	53	Pough, 1969a
Uma notata	30	56	Pough, 1969a
Sceloporus occidentalis	11	66	Pough, 1969a
Gerrhonotus multicarinatus	25	69	Pough, 1969a

[a]Blood pH was between 7.3 and 7.5 or the P_{CO_2} was 39 mm Hg.
[b]Corrected from 20° to 25°C according to the temperature shifts in P_{50} in *Pituophis, Heloderma,* and *Sauromalus obesus.*
[c]Mean of range.

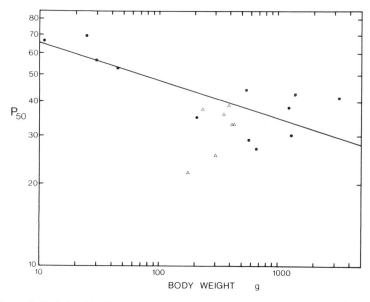

Figure 9. Relationship between body weight and P_{50} in squamates at $25°C$. Circles represent lizards; solid squares, terrestrial snakes; triangles, sea snakes. The line for terrestrial species is described by log P_{50} = 1.95 − 0.14 log B.W.

suggest that activity, rather than diving behavior, can be more closely related to oxygen affinity. Oxygen transport, presumably important in active animals, is best served by a relatively low affinity, whereas oxygen storage, which should be of advantage in snakes spending long periods resting underwater, is best served by a high affinity. It is consistent that, among the sea snakes, *Hydrophis, Acalyptophis, Lapemis,* and *Aipysurus* feed on eels and other fish and are quite active during feeding, while *Emydocephalus* spends considerable time leisurely feeding on fish eggs buried in the sand. Nothing is known about the behavior of *H. semperi,* but it occurs only in Lake Taal (Lake Bombon) in the Philippines and, therefore, probably does not encounter strong currents.

Our studies could not detect appreciable Bohr shifts in sea snake blood. Although the low resolution of the spectrophotometric technique may have obscured small shifts, it is clear that large shifts do not occur in sea snakes. Large Bohr shifts have been thought to be advantageous in diving vertebrates because unloading is favored at relatively higher P_{O_2} (Andersen, 1966). However, because the skin is permeable to oxygen in sea snakes, maintenance of a relatively low arterial P_{O_2} is advantageous since it limits oxygen loss to the sea water.

Buffering Capacity No consistent relationship between diving behavior and blood buffering capacity is evident within any reptile group. The values of non-carbonate buffering capacity in six sea snakes (-9 to -35 mM $HCO_3^-/1/pH$ unit) (Seymour and Webster, 1975) are not significantly different from those in black snakes *Pseudechis porphyriacus* (Seymour, unpublished), or lizards and crocodilians. Similarly, blood bicarbonate levels are typical of terrestrial squamates.

Bennett and others have demonstrated extensive anaerobic metabolism in terrestrial lizards (Moberly, 1968a; Bennett 1972, 1973b; Bennett and Dawson, 1972; Bennett and Licht, 1972). Most reptiles are tolerant of depressions in pH which would be fatal to mammals. Thus sea snakes may be physiologically preadapted for tolerating potential acid-base disturbances resulting from diving. Nevertheless, most of the energy requirements during voluntary dives appear to be met aerobically (see below).

GAS TENSIONS AND ACID-BASE REGULATION DURING DIVING

It is valuable to learn the patterns of physiological changes occurring during natural diving in reptiles. However, it is important to realize that in many experiments the onset and duration of diving depends on the experimenter who forcibly submerges restrained animals in relatively shallow water. Since the animal naturally controls diving, and pressures at depths should increase gas tensions in the lung and blood, the application of forced-dive data to natural conditions must be tentative. In the laboratory, sea snakes respond differently to voluntarily and forcibly extended dives.

Voluntary Breath-Holding

Seymour and Webster (1975) catheterized the dorsal aorta and lung of *A. peronii* and *L. hardwickii.* After recovery from the operations, breathing occurred about every 16.7 min in *A. peronii* and 5.3 min. in *L. hardwickii.* Despite high P_{O_2} in the lung, aortic P_{O_2} never exceeded 57 mm Hg (80% saturation). During the dive, P_{O_2} in the lung and aorta converged until immediately prior to breathing, when the P_{O_2} averaged about 50 mm Hg in the lung and 34 mm Hg in the aorta. Thus only about half of the available oxygen had been used, and the arterial blood remained over 44% saturated. A considerable oxygen reserve may be of value should a snake encounter a prey fish near the end of a dive. Spontaneous breathing also occurs with a considerable oxygen reserve in the turtle, *Chelys fimbriata* (Lenfant et al., 1970), but about 90% of the blood oxygen in the lizard, *Varanus niloticus,* is used during voluntary diving (Wood and Johansen, 1974).

Carbon dioxide tensions remained quite constant and there was only 2.3 mm Hg difference between the pulmonary gas and systemic blood. In sea snakes, CO_2 may be lost cutaneously as fast as it is produced (Graham, 1974; Heatwole and Seymour, 1975), which accounts for the constancy of blood

P_{CO_2} in *L. hardwickii* and *A. peronii*. It appears that CO_2 rapidly moves from the blood carbonate buffer system into the lung gas, which results in little correlation between pulmonary P_{O_2} and P_{CO_2}.

The acid-base picture during a series of voluntary dives has been measured in *L. hardwickii*. Overall blood pH averaged 7.4. During any particular submergence, pH decreased less than 0.1 unit. In contrast to forced dives there was no further decrease in pH following emergence. Blood lactate always remained below 15 mg per 100 ml blood, which indicates that most metabolism during voluntary breath-holding is aerobic. It is important to note that the snakes were only occasionally active during voluntary diving. It is reasonable to assume that, as in terrestrial reptiles, moderate to high levels of activity, even in short bursts, may occasion extensive anaerobic metabolism despite high pulmonary oxygen tension (see Bennett, 1973a).

Forced Diving

When voluntary dives of *L. hardwickii* were artificially extended by preventing the snakes from reaching the water surface, a more or less classical set of responses appeared. Lung and blood P_{O_2} continued to decrease to very low values. Blood pH decreased about 0.4 unit and lactate increased to nearly 100 mg/100 ml blood, the largest deviations occurring after emergence. Coupled with a flood of lactate was a conspicuous elevation of P_{CO_2} and a decrease in bicarbonate. The snakes became very active following the first signs of surface seeking behavior, so it is not known how much the results were affected by activity.

Elevated blood lactate and depressed pH prevailed for over 4 hrs following forced diving. Long recovery periods such as this are typical in reptiles artifically stimulated into activity or submerged (Andersen, 1961; Berkson, 1966; Bennett and Licht, 1972). However, field observations of sea snakes diving repeatedly, after only brief periods on the surface, imply that long recovery is not usually necessary because the dives are accomplished aerobically. The results of voluntary diving support this idea.

Pulmonary Bypass

Simultaneous measurements of P_{O_2} in the lung and aorta of *A. peronii* and *L. hardwickii* were characterized by a marked disparity, particularly at higher P_{O_2}. Also, the arteriovenous oxygen difference averaged only 5.7 mm Hg (1.2 ml O_2/100 ml blood) in *H. melanocephalus*. A large proportion of venous blood fails to equilibrate with lung gas because of either right to left shunting across the incompletely divided ventricle, or incomplete diffusion equilibrium in the lung, or both. Conservative calculations, accounting for potential P_{O_2} differences in the left and right aortic arches, indicate that a minimum of about 50% of the systemic venous blood effectively bypasses the lung. More realistic calculations indicate that this shunt averages about 70% of the systemic flow. In the light of recent evidence for cutaneous gas exchange in snakes (Heatwole and Seymour, 1975; Graham, 1974; Standaert and Johansen, 1974), a value of high shunting appears. Graham (personal communication) showed that cutaneous oxygen uptake in *P. platurus* was more or less directly related to external oxygen pressure, which suggests that the uptake is limited by the rate of diffusion through the skin, rather than the rate of cutaneous blood flow. Therefore, by keeping arterial P_{O_2} low, a high shunt favors cutaneous oxygen uptake when the snake is near the surface of the water, and helps limit oxygen loss to the sea during deep diving when the lung P_{O_2} increases. Additionally, by diluting nitrogen-rich blood from the lung with nitrogen-poor blood returning from the periphery (where equilibration with the sea water occurs), a high shunt reduces arterial and tissue P_{N_2}. This may be valuable in preventing the formation of nitrogen bubbles during decompression, following dives to depths which would otherwise produce caisson disease (Seymour, 1974).

BUOYANCY

Graham et al. (1975) have investigated buoyancy regulation in *P. platurus*. The species has somewhat different buoyancy problems than most sea snakes because of its surface-feeding habits (Klauber, 1935). It floats on the water with its head submerged for long periods, stalking prey. Under these conditions, a high positive buoyancy would be advantageous in that it would conserve energy and permit the animal to float motionlessly. Furthermore, the fact that the lung extends from neck to cloaca (as in most sea snakes) would aid in maintaining a horizontal posture, with just the head and tail submerged; the optimal position for stalking prey and for locomotion by tail-sculling.

However, during diving or prolonged submergence, positive buoyancy would become a disadvantage because it would demand a greater expenditure of energy to move deeper or to maintain position underwater. For snakes that habitually spend most of the time on the bottom and surface primarily to breathe (most species), a negative buoyancy would seem to be advantageous.

Pelamis is able to adjust its buoyancy in relation to its activities. When resting at the surface, starved individuals have air in the lungs amounting to slightly over 11 ml 100 g^{-1} body weight. Fed, and hence heavier, individuals have slightly greater volumes of air (about 13 ml 100 g^{-1}; whereas diving snakes and those resting on the bottom have about 9 and 7–7.5 ml 100 g^{-1}, respectively, and consequently achieve neutral or negative buoyancy. There are two processes involved. One is the physical compression of lung gas with depth, and the other is the use of oxygen from the lung without replacement by CO_2, because of the high rate of cutaneous elimination of the latter gas.

Although other snakes have not been studied to the same extent as *Pelamis*, it is probable that they all share these mechanisms of buoyancy regulation. Seymour and Webster (1975) have demonstrated that a forcibly submerged *L. hardwickii* does not replace CO_2 in its lung proportionately to the depletion of oxygen from it. Furthermore, many species of sea snakes are known to be able to float motionlessly on the surface or to rest quietly on the bottom without twining around coral or other objects (personal observations by senior author), and thus must be able to establish positive or negative buoyancy depending on immediate requirements.

SUMMARY

The surprising fact about sea snakes is that they have few special physiological adaptations for diving. In some ways they even seem to be less adapted for prolonged submergence than some freshwater reptiles. The salient features are the following. (1) Their oxygen consumption is similar to that of land snakes and higher than file snakes (which have an exceptionally low metabolic rate). (2) They share with land snakes and freshwater turtles the capacity for cutaneous gaseous exchange. (3) They voluntarily undergo long periods of apnea. However, alternation of breathing periods with apnea also occurs in some terrestrial lizards (Pough, 1969b) and may be widespread among reptiles, though the periods of apnea are longer in diving species such as crocodilians, turtles and aquatic snakes. (4) They may voluntarily submerge for long periods but are approached, if not overshadowed, in this regard by freshwater turtles and even by the terrestrial lizards which dive into water to escape predators (Moberly, 1968b; Achaval and Langguth, 1973). (5) Their survival time when forcibly submerged (about 5 hrs) is much less than that of most freshwater turtles in complete anoxia (breathing pure nitrogen). When deprived of cutaneous respiration by being subjected to water of low P_{O_2}, their underwater survival may be as low as 21 min (Graham, 1974), which is even shorter than anoxic survival times of most terrestrial lizards and snakes or of crocodilians (Belkin, 1963). (6) Their changes in heart rate during diving are the same or less than those of other reptilian divers, and similar to those of a terrestrial snake when forcibly submerged (McDonald, 1974). (7) Their hematological characteristics such as total hemoglobin, non-carbonate-buffering capacity, and blood carbonate levels are similar to those of land snakes. (8) Oxygen affinity of the blood varies among reptiles, but appears to be correlated with degree of activity of sluggishness rather than with diving habits. Sea snakes do not have large bohr shifts.

It can be concluded that sea snakes do not have any unique physiological characteristics related to their diving habits, but have merely extended some of them to a degree not usually found in their terrestrial relatives. The primary adaptations of sea snakes to their marine existence would seem to be morphological (nostril valves, paddle-shaped tails, reduced gastrosteges) and behavioral (deep diving, mode of feeding) rather than physiological. It would seem that among land snakes physiological potentials for a marine existence are already highly developed, and it is surprising that the evolutionary transition from the land to the sea has occurred so few times.

A final point to be emphasized is the multiple roles in the diving physiology of sea snakes played by skin permeability to the passage of gases. Not only does the skin supplement the lung in oxygen uptake, and surpass it in the elimination of CO_2, but the cutaneous loss of CO_2 aids in buoyancy adjustment. It is probable that outward movement of N_2 through the skin helps prevent deep diving species from suffering the bends (Seymour, 1974).

ACKNOWLEDGMENTS

This work was supported by the National Science Foundation under grant NSF GA 35835 to The Pennsylvania State University and grants NSF GA 34938 and NSF GD 34462 to The Scripps Institution of Oceanography for operation of the *Alpha Helix* Research Program.

REFERENCES

Achaval, F., and A. Langguth. 1973. Nota sobre habitos anfibios de *Tupinambis teguixin teguixin* (L.). (Teiidae, Sauria). Bol. Soc. Zool. Uruguay 2:107.

Aleksiuk, M. 1971. Temperature-dependent shifts in the metabolism of a cool temperate reptile, *Thamnophis sirtalis parietalis*. Comp. Biochem. Physiol. 39A:495–503.

Andersen, H. T. 1961. Physiological adjustments to prolonged diving in the American alligator, *Alligator mississippiensis*. Acta Physiol. Scand. 53:23–45.

Andersen, H. T. 1966. Physiological adaptations in diving vertebrates. Physiol. Rev. 46:212–243.

Baker, L. A., and F. N. White. 1970. Redistribution of cardiac output in response to heating in *Iguana iguana*. Comp. Biochem. Physiol. 35:253–262.

Bal, D. V., and K. V. Navathe. 1949. The circulatory system of *Hydrophis caerulescens* (Shaw). J. Univ. Bombay 17 (new series):1–14.

Barme, M. 1968. Venomous Sea Snakes (Hydrophiidae). Chapter 11 in Venomous Animals and their Venoms (W. Bücherl, E. E. Buckley, and V. Deulofeu, eds.). Vol. 1. pp. 285–308. Academic Press, New York.

Bartholomew, G. A., and R. C. Lasiewski. 1965. Heating and cooling rates, heart rate and simulated diving in the Galapagos marine iguana. Comp. Biochem. Physiol. 16:573–582.

Beddard, F. E. 1904. Contributions to the knowledge of the visceral anatomy of the pelagic serpents *Hydrus platyurus* and *Platyurus colubrinus*. Proc. Zool. Soc. London 2:147–154.

Belkin, D. A. 1963. Anoxia: Tolerance in reptiles. Science 139:492–493.

Belkin, D. A. 1964. Variations in heart rate during voluntary diving in the turtle *Pseudemys concinna*. Copeia:321–330.

Belkin, D. A. 1968. Aquatic respiration and underwater survival of two freshwater turtle species. Respir. Physiol. 4:1–14.

Bellairs, A. 1969. The Life of Reptiles. Vol. 1 Weidenfeld and Nicholson, London. 282 pp.

Bellairs, A. d'A., and G. Underwood. 1951. The origin of snakes. Biol. Rev. Cambridge Philos. Soc. 26:193–237.

Bennett, A. F. 1972. The effect of activity on oxygen consumption, oxygen debt, and heart rate in the lizards *Varanus gouldii* and *Sauromalus hispidus*. J. Comp. Physiol. 79:259–280.

Bennett, A. F. 1973a. Ventilation in two species of lizards during rest and activity. Comp. Biochem. Physiol. 46A:653–671.

Bennett, A. F. 1973b. Blood physiology and oxygen transport during activity in two lizards, *Varanus gouldii* and *Sauromalus hispidus*. Comp. Biochem. Physiol. 46A:673–690.

Bennett, A. F., and W. R. Dawson. 1972. Aerobic and anaerobic metabolism during activity in the lizard *Dipsosaurus dorsalis*. J. Comp. Physiol. 81:289–299.

Bennett, A. F., and P. Licht. 1972. Anaerobic metabolism during activity in lizards. J. Comp. Physiol. 81:277-288.

Berkson, H. 1966. Physiological adjustments to prolonged diving in the Pacific green turtle (*Chelonia mydas agassizi*). Comp. Biochem. Physiol. 18:101–119.

Brattstrom, B. H. 1959. The function of the air sac in snakes. Herpetologica 15:103–104.

Brongersma, L. D. 1958. Les organes de respiration et l'artère pulmonaire chez les serpents. Bull. l'assoc. Anat. No. 97:205–210.

Buikema, A. L. Jr., and K. B. Armitage. 1969. The effect of temperature on the metabolism of the prairie ringneck snake, *Diadophis punctatus arnyi* Kennicott. Herpetologica 25:194–206.

Butler, G. W. 1895. On the complete or partial suppression of the right lung in the Amphisbaenidae and of the left lung in snakes and snake-like lizards and amphibians. Proc. Zool. Soc. London 1895:691–712.

Cantor, T. 1841. Observations upon pelagic serpents. Trans. Zool. Soc. London 2:303–313 plus 2 plates.

Cope, E. D. 1894. On the lungs of the Ophidia. Proc. Amer. Philos. Soc. 33:217–224.

Cope, E. D. 1900. The crocodilians, lizards, and snakes of North America. Report of the U.S. National Museum, U.S. Gov't. Printing Office, Washington.

Dessauer, H. C. 1970. Blood chemistry of reptiles: physiological and evolutionary aspects. In: Biology of the Reptilia Vol. 3 (C. Gans and T. S. Parsons, eds.) Academic Press, New York. pp. 1–72.

Dill, D. B., H. T. Edwards, A. V. Bock, and J. H. Talbott. 1935. Properties of reptilian blood. III. The chuckwalla (*Sauromalus obesus* Baird). J. Cell. Comp. Physiol. 6:37–42.

Dmi'el, R. 1972. Relation of metabolism to body weight in snakes. Copeia 179–181.

Dmi'el, R., and A. Borut. 1972. Thermal behavior, heat exchange, and metabolism in the desert snake *Spalerosophis cliffordi*. Physiol. Zool. 45:78–94.

Doughton, R. (year unspecified) On safari to remote Marion Reef with Ron & Denyse Doughton. Skindiving in Australia 3:4 pp.

Dunson, W. A. 1960. Aquatic respiration in *Trionyx spinifer asper*. Herpetologica 16:277–283.

Dunson, W. A., and G. W. Ehlert. 1971. Effects of temperature, salinity, and surface water flow on distribution of the sea snake, *Pelamis*. Limnology and Oceanography 16:845–853.

Edwards, H. T., and D. B. Dill. 1935. Properties of reptilian blood. II. The gila monster (*Heloderma suspectum* Cope). J. Cell. Comp. Physiol. 6:21–35.

Galvão, P. E., J. Tarasantchi, and P. Guerzenstein. 1965. Heat production of tropical snakes in relation to body weight and body surface. Amer. J. Physiol. 209:501–506.

Gans, C. 1970. Strategy and sequence in the evolution of the external gas exchangers of ectothermal vertebrates. Forma et Functio 3:61–104.

Gatten, R. E. Jr. 1974. Effects of temperature and activity on aerobic and anaerobic metabolism and heart rate in the turtles *Pseudemys scripta* and *Terrapene ornata*. Comp. Biochem. Physiol. 48A:619–648.

Gaunt, A. S., and C. Gans. 1969. Diving bradycardia and withdrawal bradycardia in *Caiman crocodilus*. Nature 223:207–208.

George, J. C., and R. V. Shah. 1956. Comparative morphology of the lung in snakes with remarks on the evolution of the lung in reptiles. J. Anim. Morph. Physiol. 3:1–7.

George, J. C., and R. V. Shah. 1965. Evolution of air sacs in Sauropsida. J. Anim. Morph. Physiol. 12:255–263.

George, J. C., and M. R. Varde. 1941. A note on the modification of the lung and the trachea in some Indian snakes. J. Univ. Bombay 10B:70–73.

Girgis, S. 1961. Aquatic respiration in the common nile turtle, *Trionyx triunguis* (Forskål). Comp. Biochem. Physiol. 3:206–217.

Graham, J. B. 1974. Aquatic respiration in the sea snake *Pelamis platurus*. Respir. Physiol. 21:1–7.

Graham, J. B., J. H. Gee, and F. S. Robison. 1975. Hydrostatic and gas exchange functions of the lung of the sea snake *Pelamis platurus*. Comp. Biochem. Physiol. 50A:477–482.

Graham, J. B., I. Rubinoff, and M. K. Hecht. 1971. Temperature physiology of the sea snake *Pelamis platurus:* an index of its colonization potential in the Atlantic Ocean. Proc. Natl. Acad. Sci. U.S.A. 68:1360–1363.

Greenwald, O. E. 1971a. The effect of body temperature on oxygen consumption and heart rate in the Sonora gopher snake, *Pituophis catenifer affinis* Hallowell. Copeia:98–106.

Greenwald, O. E. 1971b. The effect of temperature on the oxygenation of gopher snake blood. Comp. Biochem. Physiol. 40A:865–870.

Heatwole, H. 1975. Voluntary submergence times of sea snakes and file snakes. J. Mar. Biol. In press a.

Heatwole, H. 1975. Heart rate during breathing and apnea in marine snakes. J. Herpetol. In press b.

Heatwole, H., and R. Seymour. 1975. Pulmonary and cutaneous oxygen uptake in sea snakes and a file snake. Comp. Biochem. Physiol. 51:399–405.

Herre, A. W. C. T. 1942. Notes on Phillipine sea-snakes. Copeia:7—9.

Hesse, R. 1921. Das Herzgewicht der Wirbeltiere. Zool. Jahrb. 38:243—369.

Hughes, G. M. 1973. The Vertebrate Lung. Oxford University Press, London. 16 pp.

Hughes, G. M., R. Gaymer, M. Moore, and A. J. Voakes. 1971. Respiratory exchange and body size in the Aldabra Giant Tortoise. J. Exp. Biol. 55:651—665.

Jacobsen, E. R., and W. G. Whitford. 1970. The effect of acclimation on physiological responses to temperature in the snakes, *Thamnophis proximus* and *Natrix rhombifera*. Comp. Biochem. Physiol. 35:439—449.

Jacobsen, E. R., and W. G. Whitford. 1971. Physiological responses to temperature in the patch-nosed snake, *Salvadora hexalepis*. Herpetologica 27:289—295.

Johansen, K. 1959. Heart activity during experimental diving of snakes. Amer. J. Physiol. 197:604—606.

Johansen, K., and C. Lenfant. 1972. A comparative approach to the adaptability of O_2-Hb affinity. In: The 4th Alfred Benson Symposium: O_2 Affinity of Hemoglobin and Red Cell and Acid-Base Status, edited by P. Astrup and M. Rorth. Copenhagen, Munksgaard, pp. 750—780.

Klauber, L. M. 1935. The feeding habits of a sea snake. Copeia 1935:182.

Krogh, A. 1919. The rate of diffusion of gases through animal tissues, with some remarks on the coefficient of invasion. J. Physiol. 52:391—408.

Lenfant, C., K. Johansen, J. A. Petersen, and K. Schmidt-Nielsen. 1970. Respiration in the fresh water turtle, *Chelys fimbriata*. Respir. Physiol. 8:261—275.

McDonald, H. S. 1959. Respiratory functions of the ophidian air sac. Herpetologica 15:193—198.

McDonald, H. S. 1974. Bradycardia during death-feigning of *Heterodon platyrhinos* Latreille (Serpentes). J. Herpetology 8:157—164.

McDowell, S. B. 1969. Notes on the Australian sea snake *Ephalophis greyi* M. Smith (Serpentes: Elapidae, Hydrophiinae) and the origin and classification of sea snakes. Zool. J. Linn. Soc. 48:333—349.

McDowell, S. B. 1972. The genera of sea-snakes of the *Hydrophis* group (Serpentes: Elapidae). Trans. Zool. Soc. London 32:189—247.

McDowell, S. B. 1974. Additional notes on the rare and primitive sea-snake, *Ephalophis greyi*. J. Herpetology 8:123—128.

Moberly, W. R. 1968a. The metabolic responses of the common iguana, *Iguana iguana*, to activity under restraint. Comp. Biochem. Physiol. 27:1—20.

Moberly, W. R. 1968b. The metabolic responses of the common iguana, *Iguana iguana*, to walking and diving. Comp. Biochem. Physiol. 27:21—32.

Murdaugh, H. V. Jr., and J. E. Jackson. 1962. Heart rate and blood lactic acid concentration during experimental diving of water snakes. Amer. J. Physiol. 202:1163—1165.

Patterson, R. 1973. Why tortoises float. J. Herpetology 7:373—375.

Pickwell, G. V. 1972. The venomous sea snakes. Fauna 4:16—32.

Pough, F. H. 1969a. Environmental adaptations in the blood of lizards. Comp. Biochem. Physiol. 31:885—901.

Pough, F. H. 1969b. Physiological aspects of the burrowing of sand lizards (*Uma*, Iguanidae) and other lizards. Comp. Biochem. Physiol. 31:869—884.

Pough, F. H. 1971. Ontogenetic changes in oxygen-transport properties of blood of garter snakes, *Thamnophis s. sirtalis*. Amer. Zool. 11:657.

Pough, F. H. 1973a. Lizard energetics and diet. Ecology 54:837–844.

Pough, F. H. 1973b. Heart rate, breathing and voluntary diving of the Elephant Trunk Snake, *Acrochordus javanicus*. Comp. Biochem. Physiol. 44A:183–189.

Seymour, R. S. 1974. How sea snakes may avoid the bends. Nature 250:489–490.

Seymour, R. S., and M. E. D. Webster. 1975. Gas transport and blood acid-base balance in diving sea snakes. J. Exp. Zool., 191:169–181.

Shuntov, V. P. 1962. Sea snakes (Hydrophiidae) of the Tonking Bay (Northern Viet-Nam). Zool. Zhur. 41:1203–1209. (In Russian)

Shuntov, V. P. 1966. Distribution of sea snakes in the South China Sea and east Indian Ocean. Zool. Zhur. 45:1882–1886. English translation by Smithsonian Herpetological Information Services (1969).

Shuntov, V. P. 1971. Sea snakes of the north Australian shelf. Ékologiya 4:65–72. English translation by Consultants Bureau (1972).

Snyder, G. K. 1971. Influence of temperature and hematocrit on blood viscosity. Amer. J. Physiol. 220:1667–1672.

Standaert, T., and K. Johansen. 1974. Cutaneous gas exchange in snakes. J. Comp. Physiol. 89:313–320.

Varde, M. R. 1951. The morphology and histology of the lung in snakes. J. Univ. Bombay 19:79–89.

Volsøe, H. 1939. The sea snakes of the Iranian Gulf and the Gulf of Oman. With a summary of the biology of the sea snakes. Danish Scient. Invest. in Iran. Part I:9–45.

Volsøe, H. 1956. Sea snakes. In: The Galathea Deep Sea Expedition 1950–1952. George Allen & Unwin Ltd., London, pp. 87–95.

Webb, G. J. W. 1972. A new hypothesis on the pattern of blood-flow through the squamate heart. Search 3:138–140.

Webb, G., H. Heatwole, and J. de Bavay. 1971. Comparative cardiac anatomy of the Reptilia. I. The chambers and septa of the varanid ventricle. J. Morph. 134:335–350.

Webb, G., H. Heatwole, and J. de Bavay. 1974. Comparative cardiac anatomy of the Reptilia. II. A critique of the literature on the Squamata and Rhynchocephalia. J. Morph. 142:1–20.

White, F. N. 1957. A functional interpretation of integumentary vessels of snakes. Herpetologica 13:127–130.

White, F. N. Circulation. Chapter in: Biology of the Reptilia (C. Gans and T. S. Parsons, Eds.), Academic Press, New York. In press.

White, F. N., and G. Ross. 1966. Circulatory changes during experimental diving in the turtle. Amer. J. Physiology 211:15–18.

Wilber, C. G. 1960. Cardiac responses of *Alligator mississippiensis* to diving. Comp. Biochem. Physiol. 1:164–166.

Wood, S. C., and K. Johansen. 1974. Respiratory adaptations to diving in the Nile Monitor Lizard, *Varanus niloticus*. J. Comp. Physiol. 89:145–158.

Wood, S. C., and W. R. Moberly. 1970. The influence of temperature on the respiratory properties of iguana blood. Respir. Physiol. 10:20–29.

sixteen

Salt and Water Balance in Sea Snakes

William A. Dunson

Of all the marine vertebrates, the fish have achieved the greatest diversity. In the teleosts, special physiological mechanisms (especially in the gills) allow maintenance of a constant electrolyte composition of the body fluids at concentrations considerably below those of the surrounding sea water. The two main problems, that of losing water to the osmotically more concentrated sea and that of gaining salts, must be faced by any animal whose fluids are hypo-osmotic to sea water. Modern-day reptiles have been relatively unsuccessful in colonizing the sea, probably due to difficulties in osmotic regulation. No known reptile is able to excrete ureteral urine more concentrated than its plasma. Considerable water is lost through the respiratory tract, and salts ingested inadvertently or gained by diffusion across the skin have to be excreted in a highly concentrated form to maintain a hypotonic extracellular fluid. Thus all those reptiles highly adapted to the marine environment have developed special salt excreting glands (Dunson, 1969a, 1974). Since the only terrestrial reptiles that have salt glands are lizards, perhaps it is not surprising that separate colonizations of the sea by the turtles and snakes resulted in the convergent evolution of non-homologous salt glands. The evolutionary process leading to development of a pelagic habit in reptiles undoubtedly started by gradual adaptation to life along the shore in salt marshes or mangroves. The diamondback terrapin *(Malaclemys)* is probably the best example of a species which is specialized only for an estuarine life; it does not occur in fresh water and cannot live indefinitely in sea water (Bentley, Bretz and Schmidt-Nielsen, 1967; Dunson, 1970). Yet the terrapin has developed a salt gland and is the only turtle other than the true sea turtles known to have done so. The lachrymal salt gland is identical in position to that found in the true sea turtles (Cheloniidae), but presumably originated independently since the terrapin is in a different family (Emydidae).

There are at least four different families of snakes with marine and estuarine representatives. The true sea snakes (Hydrophiidae) are by far the most successful of these in colonizing the sea. Although they may not have developed from a single primitive marine stock, they all have a sublingual salt gland. The peculiar and highly specialized aquatic file snakes (Acrochordidae) have a marine representative (*Acrochordus granulatus*) with the same sublingual salt gland (Dunson and Dunson, 1973), even though any common evolutionary relationship is remote. New world water snakes of the *Natrix* group have several estuarine subspecies (Conant and Lazell, 1973; Pettus, 1958) but there is as yet no evidence for the presence of a salt gland in these forms. The fourth group, the old world Homalopsine snakes, contains several species that may be almost entirely restricted to estuaries and mangrove swamps, but nothing is known about their mechanisms of salt balance. The literature on reptilian salt glands has been recently reviewed (Templeton, 1972; Dunson, in press), so this discussion will be limited to the special features of salt and water balance in sea snakes.

MAINTAINING BALANCE

Regulation of Plasma Electrolytes

An understanding of the mechanisms of balance requires information on the routes of gain and loss of salts and water. At present data are too fragmentary to allow anything but a qualitative estimate of the importance of the various organs involved. It does appear that sea snakes are capable of maintaining their extracellular fluid at NaCl concentrations considerably below that of sea water. Plasma levels of a large series of wild captured *Pelamis* were 210 mM Na, 167 mM Cl, and 8 mM K (Dunson, Packer and Dunson, 1971). Starvation may lead to dehydration and plasma Na reached 307 mM in one severe case (Dunson, 1968). Five different species of Australian sea snakes (*Aipysurus laevis, Lapemis hardwickii, Hydrophis elegans, Disteira major, H. melanocephalus*) had low plasma electrolyte levels when kept in sea water at 480 mM Na and 576 mM Cl in my lab. Mean values ± SD were 159 ± 16 mM Na and 135 ± 14 mM Cl (N = 8). The hematocrit was 35 ± 3%. Two snakes kept for 3 weeks in fresh water had markedly lower plasma levels, 134 ± 11 mM Na and 106 ± 10 mM Cl. Three NaCl loaded snakes (sea water acclimated) demonstrated a marked elevation in plasma Na to 219 ± 19 mM. These data show that sea snakes can regulate extracellular fluid electrolytes at levels less than half those of sea water. When not exposed to starvation or salt loading, it appears that many species have plasma NaCl concentrations near those of typical terrestrial vertebrates.

Regulation of Body Fluid Volumes

Previous studies have shown that marine turtles tend to have lower total body water contents (measured by dessication), higher extracellular fluid volumes (measured by sucrose dilution), and lower intracellular fluid volumes (calculated by difference) than fresh-water species (Thorson, 1968). Blood and plasma (Evans blue dilution) volumes are higher than those typical of fresh-water species but about the same as those of terrestrial reptiles. All these data are from nembutal anesthetized animals. The only published information on body fluid volumes of a sea snake is a figure of 7.0% body weight for the blood volume of *Pelamis* (measured by exsanguination, Graham, 1973, 1974). This would correspond to a plasma volume of about 4.8% when the hematocrit was 33% (assuming 6% of cell volume as trapped plasma). Somewhat higher values were obtained for plasma volumes of some Australian sea snakes (Dunson and Robinson, unpublished observations). Values of 4.6 and 5.6% were measured in two snakes anesthetized with ether. In nine sea snakes previously anesthetized by cold, plasma volumes measured with Evans blue ranged from 4.0 to 8.7%. It appears that low temperatures may sometimes interfere with the process of equilibration of Evans blue in plasma or perhaps cause an actual increase in plasma volume. The time allowed for equilibration is important, since changes in plasma Evans blue concentrations extrapolated back to zero time during the first hour after injection almost invariably gave the lowest estimated volumes. This is due to the fact that the loss of Evans blue from the plasma was usually most rapid during the first hour and then decreased to a rate that remained relatively constant for as long as 9 hrs. Despite many technical problems with body fluid volume measurements, the available evidence indicates that sea snakes may have larger plasma and blood volumes than any other reptiles. Sea turtles have only slightly smaller volumes (plasma 4.4%, blood 6.6%) (Thorson, 1968).

The trend for marine turtles to have relatively low total body water contents (about 65%; Thorson, 1968) seems not to be true of sea snakes. Eight *Hydrophis melanocephalus* varying in weight from 20 to 888 g were dessicated at 100°C. Four of the eight snakes were newborns weighing about 20 g and they had a high average water content of 81.1 ± 0.7% body weight. The remaining four larger snakes (84 to 880 g) also had a higher total water content (74 ± 4.4%) than expected for marine reptiles (Dunson and Robinson, unpublished observations). These are considerably higher values than those of the two terrestrial snakes (70–71%) studied by Thorson (1968). The higher water content of younger animals observed here seems to be generally true of many vertebrates (Khalil and Abdel-Messeih, 1954).

Tolerance to Fresh Water

The fact that sea snakes are limited mainly to the sea might be explained by their evolutionary history or, perhaps, by competitive interactions with fresh-water snakes of other families. In any case, it seems unlikely that fresh water itself forms a physiological barrier to their movements. Although *Pelamis* has never been found to be a resident in fresh-water habitats, it can be kept in tap water for periods as long as 6 mos. without ill effects (Dunson and Ehlert, 1971). Some Australian species (mainly *Lapemis hardwickii*) that I tested seemed much less tolerant. Of 13 snakes placed in tap water, eight died in 2 to 11 days, one died at 21 days, and four were still alive after periods as long as 11 to 21 days. The exact cause of death under these circumstances is difficult to assess. The presence or absence of compensatory physiological changes associated with exposure to fresh water certainly deserves further study.

Two cases are known in which sea snakes are apparently land-locked in fresh or nearly fresh-water lakes. The best known example is that of *Hydrophis semperi* in Lake Taal, Philippines. Lake Taal is 20 km in diameter and fills a caldera which is drained by the Pansipit River (Moore, Nakamura and Alcaraz, 1966). The river travels less than 10 km before emptying into Balayan Bay. Surface water samples that I took from the lake in December, 1972, were about 12 mM Cl (sea water is 560 mM Cl), showing that the lake surface is, for all practical purposes, fresh. However, *H. semperi* has retained a functional salt gland (Dunson and Dunson, 1974). This raises three main questions. (1) Does this snake migrate to and from the sea? (2) Does Lake Taal become more saline at certain times of the year, at least at certain depths? (3) Has the isolation of this species in the lake been recent enough that no loss of salt gland function has occurred?

The first possibility, that of migration up and down the river, cannot be conclusively answered, but it seems unlikely. The river is swiftly flowing and native fishermen at the Pansipiti fish trap, which blocks most of the river, seem unfamiliar with the snake. Since Lake Taal lies very near sea level, and is reported to be 350 m at its deepest point (P. Ariola, personal communication), the bottom of the lake might be more saline than the surface. Results of a partial hydrological survey carried out in October, 1971, have been made available to me by I. A. Ronquillo, Chief of the Marine Fisheries Biology Division, Philippine Bureau of Fisheries. These data show that the salinity at 40 m is the same as at the surface, but that little oxygen is present at 40 m. Thus although the sea snake might dive to depths greater than 40 m, little food will be present if the water is anoxic. Midwater or bottom salinities at other seasons are unknown. The actual depth at which this snake feeds and the type of food taken are also unknown. A third possible explanation for the presence of a functional salt gland in *Hydrophis semperi* is that isolation in the lake has been relatively recent and that no loss of the gland's ability to secrete has occurred. In ducks (Fletcher, Stainer, and Holmes, 1967) and in diamondback terrapins (Dunson and Dunson, in press), the salt gland decreases in Na-K activated ATPase activity when the animals are transferred from salt water to fresh water. There was no change in the Na-K ATPase content of *Pelamis* salt glands after 48 days in fresh water (Dunson and Dunson, in press). Since *H. semperi* can only be distinguished from the marine *H. cyanocinctus* by its size, coloration, and habitat (Smith, 1926), and Ronquillo (personal communication) reports that the lake was salty as late as the 1600's, recent isolation seems likely. However, a definitive answer to this puzzle must await further research.

Less information is available on the second case of a lake-locked sea snake, in Lake Tegano, Rennell Island (Solomons group). Actually two species of *Laticauda, L. colubrina* and *L. laticaudata crockeri,* are known from the lake, but the latter is more abundant and is subspecifically distinct from the marine form (Wolff, 1969). *L. colubrina* from the lake are identical with marine specimens and are judged to be much more recent migrants into the lake. The lake is brackish $(4-6^o/oo)$ and is connected to the sea by subterranean passages. Sea snakes of the genus *Laticauda* are amphibious in their habits and often are found resting in caves or under bushes on land when not feeding. When more information is available on their life history, their presence in coastal lakes or lagoons may be found to be a common occurrence. Pepys-Cockerell (pers. comm.) reports that unidentified sea snakes (presumably *Laticauda*) occur in Osei Lagoon near Auki, Malaita (Solomons). Genera of more pelagic habits can reach fresh water lakes by swimming up rivers. I have evidence that *Disteira major, Enhydrina schistosa,* and *Hydrophis elegans* occur in some Queensland (Australia) tidal rivers (see Chapter 7), and R. V. Lando (pers. comm.) observed that several species of sea snakes were common in South Vietnamese rivers, even in fresh water. Thus it is not unexpected to find occasional specimens, particularly of coastal species, in fresh-water habitats. One spectacular example is that of an *Enhydrina schistosa* caught in fresh-water Grand Lac (Cambodia), which is connected by the Mekong River to the sea (Bourret, 1934). Present evidence tends to indicate, however, that, aside from the two lakes mentioned, sea snakes do not habitually live in truly fresh-water environments. They may be common in estuaries, which can be quite fresh during the rainy season.

Balancing Intake and Loss

Sources of salt and water intake are (a) food, (b) water that is drunk, and (c) dermal fluxes. Losses occur from (a) the cloaca (kidney and gut), (b) the salt gland, (c) the skin, and (d) the respiratory tract. Our knowledge of the relative importance of each of these organs in partitioning of intake and loss is incomplete, since most studies have been concerned mainly with the salt gland. Recent discoveries of the reduced size of the salt gland in *Hydrophis* (Dunson and Dunson, 1974) and the ability of *Pelamis* to respire aquatically (Graham, 1973, 1974) suggest that the oral epithelium and the integument play a more important role in ion and water balance than previously suspected.

Intake Most sea snakes feed on fish or fish eggs (*Emydocephalus* and *Aipysurus eydouxii* feed solely on eggs) and these sources are relatively low in electrolytes and high in water content. Whole marine fish contain about 77% water and variable amounts of Na and K. Expressed as a concentration in terms of total body water, Na varies from 67 to 277 mM and K from 96 to 135 mM (Holmes and McBean, 1964; Dunson, 1968). Few data are available on the ionic composition of marine teleost eggs, but their salt content seems to be generally less than half that of sea water (Krogh, 1939). In the process of swallowing food, a certain amount of sea water must also be ingested, but this is probably minimized by the elastic esophagus, which closes tightly around the food bolus. Sea water entering the stomach might also be expelled by reverse peristalsis. Although no direct measurements of possible drinking of sea water have been made, voluntary drinking of fresh water has been observed only in *Laticauda* species (Dunson and Taub, 1967) and occasionally in dehydrated *Pelamis*. Thus water is most likely obtained mainly from the food, although there is a possibility that some species drink brackish water from the sea surface after rains.

The mouth and cloaca of most sea snakes are tightly sealed against sea water. There are overlapping labial scales that close the edges of the mouth, rostral openings that allow protrusion of the tongue tips without opening the mouth, and a valve-like arrangment of the cloacal lips that prevents sea water from coming in contact with epithelial membranes. These adaptations seem only natural in an animal that is a hypo-osmotic regulator in sea water. Graham's (1974) observation that substantial cutaneous respiration occurs in *Pelamis* is quite surprising and raises doubts about the presumed low permeability of the sea snake integument. Data are available on the rate of extracloacal (mainly skin) salt loss of snakes placed in distilled water (Dunson and Taub, 1967; Dunson, 1968). The cloaca was cannulated so that renal and intestinal losses were collected separately. Under these conditions, prior to salt loading, sea snakes lose virtually no Na or K to the bath. Pettus (1958) has found that the isolated skin of colubrid water snakes (*Natrix*) from brackish water areas is impermeable to water. The skin of *Pelamis* is well vascularized and the vessels course in a regular polygonal pattern under the scales (Figure 1), as has been observed in terrestrial snakes (White, 1957). The "scales" in *Pelamis* are reduced to knob-like structures; when the skin is stretched considerable inter-scalar space is revealed, especially on the lateral

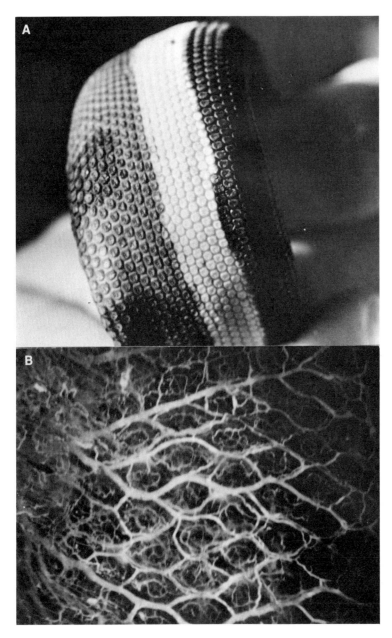

Figure 1. The skin of the yellow-bellied sea snake, *Pelamis platurus*. A. Lateral view showing the reduction of the scales to knobs and the large amount of skin between the scales on the lateral and ventral surfaces. The black dorsal surface is on the right. B. Vascularization of the connective tissue just beneath the skin. An intravascular lead chromate precipitation by Dr. E. Hibbard.

and ventral surfaces. Preliminary studies have demonstrated that *Pelamis* skin is impermeable to sodium (at least just after shedding), and water fluxes are low but measurable (Dunson and Robinson, unpublished observations). The possible relationship between salt gland size and maximum secretory rate, the permeability of the skin to water and salts, and the extent to which aquatic respiration is utilized in different species, deserve further study. Although the current data are limited, it appears likely that sea snake skin has become specialized for the selective passage of oxygen and carbon dioxide and for the selective exclusion of sodium and water. The unknown mechanism by which this preferential transport takes place is of considerable interest.

Loss In reptiles the kidney cannot produce urine hyperosmotic to the plasma. The kidney and cloaca of sea snakes do not seem to have any insoluble urate salts in desert lizards (Minnish, 1970, 1972; Nagy, 1972). The cloaca and, possibly, the lower intestine also serve important roles in salt balance (Templeton, 1972; Junqueira, Malnic, and Monge, 1966). The kidney-cloaca-gut complex probably functions much as it does in birds (Shoemaker, 1972), except that birds can produce urine more concentrated than their plasma. The kidney and cloaca of sea snakes do not seem to have any spectacular capabilities. The cloacal fluid remains osmotically less concentrated than the plasma even after salt loads (Dunson and Taub, 1967; Dunson, 1968). Less than half of the total Na, K and Cl excreted is cloacal (Dunson, 1969a). Only one study (Dunson and Taub, 1967) has attempted to separate the contribution of soluble and bound Na and K in the cloacal fluid of sea snakes. Since the snakes were fasted, it is not surprising that, in most cases, the insoluble ions were not a significant part of the total excretion. However, in a few cases substantial amounts of bound K and Na were detected. In each case, much greater amounts of K were bound, indicating that urate salts may be an important means of renal K excretion in sea snakes. Flow rates of cloacal fluid are considerably less than urine flows measured in fresh water snakes (Dunson and Taub, 1967; Dunson, 1968). The glomerular filtration rate of the sea snake *Laticauda* was also quite low, 0.5 ml/kg hr (Schmidt-Nielsen and Davis, 1968).

Despite the apparent dryness of reptilian skin, large amounts of water can be lost across its surface. In fact, at about 25°C, 64–88% of the total water loss of alligators, turtles, lizards, and snakes is dermal (Bentley and Schmidt-Nielsen, 1966; Prange and Schmidt-Nielsen, 1969). As the temperature increases, respiratory losses may exceed dermal losses considerably. There also seems to be a direct relationship between the rate of cutaneous water loss and the availability of free water in the habitat (Templeton, 1972). At present, there are no measurements available on the net loss of water across sea snake skin or on the partitioning of loss between the skin and the respiratory tract. The intermittent pattern of breathing of diving sea snakes and their possible use of aquatic respiration might be expected to considerably diminish the water loss from the respiratory tract. However, the problem of osmosis across the integument may be made much more severe by the constant immersion in a solution two or three times more concentrated than the body fluids.

Efforts to evaluate the relative roles of the gut, the skin, and the kidney in ion and water balance of sea snakes are severely hampered by the paucity of data. The remaining organ of excretion, the salt gland, has received a great deal more attention since its function in sea snakes was first discovered in 1967 (Dunson and Taub). The actual exocrine gland involved was not found until 1971 (Dunson, Packer and Dunson), and a great deal remains to be learned about the control of gland function by neural and hormonal influences and the mechanism of cellular secretion (see the review by Dunson, in press).

THE SALT GLAND

Size and Structure

Of all known salt glands, the sublingual salt gland of sea snakes is the most peculiar in position. When the ancestral sea snakes were invading brackish water habitats in Southeast Asia or Australia, they probably encountered few other animals competing for a common food source. However, they faced the difficult problem of adjusting to life in high salinity water. This was a unique evolutionary problem since no terrestrial snakes have ever developed salt glands. In birds, lizards, and turtles, nasal and lachrymal glands became specialized for salt secretion. These two options were probably unavailable to the sea snakes since the eye is covered by a transparent "spectacle" of skin, and the nostril is valvular for diving. Thus a serous gland under the tongue developed the ability to concentrate electrolytes. The salt gland secretes into the tongue sheath and the fluid is carried to the outside by extrusion of the tongue (Figure 2). The position of the posterior sublingual salt gland is shown in Figure 3. Although this particular specimen of *Laticauda* is much larger than the *Pelamis,* its gland is considerably smaller. Since *Laticauda* spends much of its time on land, whereas *Pelamis* is pelagic, the relative size of the two glands seems to be related to the degree of adaptation to marine life. However, such a simple relationship between habitat and gland size does not seem to be general. Many fully marine snakes have very small salt glands (Figure 4); e.g., 200-g specimens of *Hydrophis elegans* and *melanocephalus* have relative salt gland weights about one tenth those of similarly sized *Lapemis.* Since the diet of most species is fish, these differences may be related to the permeability of the integument. Those species with larger salt glands also show an inverse relationship between body weight and relative salt gland weight. This presumably is related to the larger relative surface area of

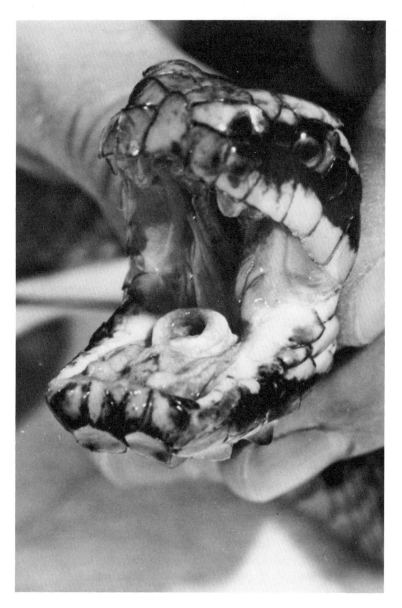

Figure 2. View of the open mouth of *Laticauda colubrina* showing the circular glottis (opening to lung) in the floor of the mouth and the entrance to the tongue sheath immediately in front of it (an inverted "V"). Salt gland fluid is secreted into this sheath and pushed outside by movements of the tongue.

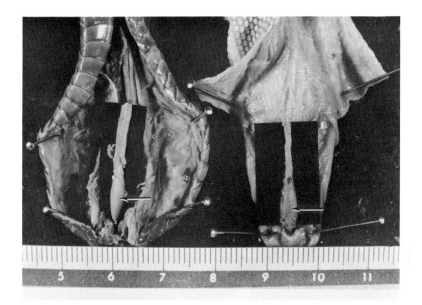

Figure 3. A ventral view of the posterior sublingual salt glands (arrows) of the sea snakes *Laticauda semifasciata* (left) and *Pelamis platurus* (right). Scale in cm.

smaller snakes, which leads to a proportionately greater influx of salts or loss of water across the integument.

It is significant that *H. elegans* shows no change in relative gland weight with decreasing size. Other mechanisms, perhaps a decrease in skin permeability, must assume a more important role in ionic regulation in this species. Two of the species from Figure 4 (*Aipysurus eydouxii, Emydocephalus*) feed exclusively on fish eggs; salt gland weights are high but not exceptionally so, although a tiny (26 g) *A. eydouxii* had the highest relative gland weight yet recorded for a sea snake (0.07%). The little file snake (shown in Figure 4 for comparative purposes) is in a separate family from the true sea snakes, yet it has a sublingual salt gland (Dunson and Dunson, 1973). This is a most interesting case of convergent evolution of homologous glands.

Our knowledge of the gross anatomy and ultrastructure of the posterior sublingual salt gland has been recently summarized (Dunson and Dunson, 1974; Dunson, in press). In some species, the most anterior portion of the gland has basophilic staining properties with hematoxylin and eosin. However, most of the gland is serous with the predominance of one cell type, the principal cell, which is believed to be the site of NaCl transport (Figure 5). This cell is characterized by an enormous elaboration of its lateral surfaces into villi-like evaginations, the presence of numerous mitochondria with dense

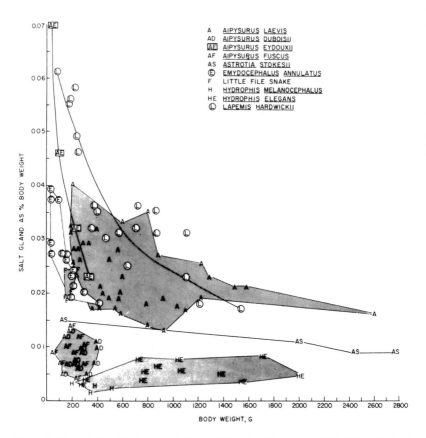

Figure 4. The relationship between body weight and relative wet weight of the salt gland in sea snakes. Hatched or shaded areas represent the total amount of variation observed in one or, in some cases, two closely related species.

granules in the matrix, a minute apical surface, and a subdivision of the basal area of the cell into separate processes. The terminology used for these basal processes poses a problem, because the distinction between basal and lateral surfaces is rather difficult. The important point is that the increased surface area of the principal cells is due to evaginations of the membrane. This is fundamentally different from the basal invaginations of the avian salt gland, the mammalian kidney, and certain other transporting epithelia (Dunson, in press; Pease, 1956). Two less common cell types whose function is unknown are shown in Figures 5B and 5C. One of these (Figure 5B) has simply been called an undifferentiated cell since it has little cytoplasm and few distinguishing features. The other type (Figure 5C) is more specialized, and is characterized by extensive endoplasmic reticulum.

The principal salt gland cells extend from the basement membrane to the lumen (Figure 6). Blood vessels are located outside the basement membrane. Depending on the species, the concentration gradient between the blood plasma and the tubular fluid (as finally secreted) may be as high as five-fold. The numerous lateral evaginations suggest that water or ions (or both) are being absorbed into the cytoplasm. An unanswered anatomical question

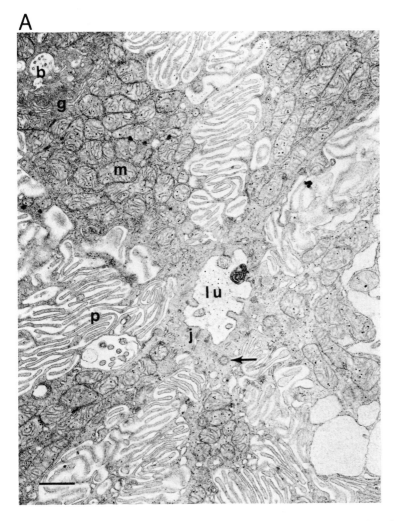

Figure 5. Three cell types in the salt gland of *Aipysurus fuscus*. A. A cross section of a tubule showing the apical ends of five principal cells around the lumen (lu). Mitochondria (m), lateral processes (p), multivesicular body (b), junctional complex (j), centriole (arrow), Golgi apparatus (g). Scale, 1 μ.

B

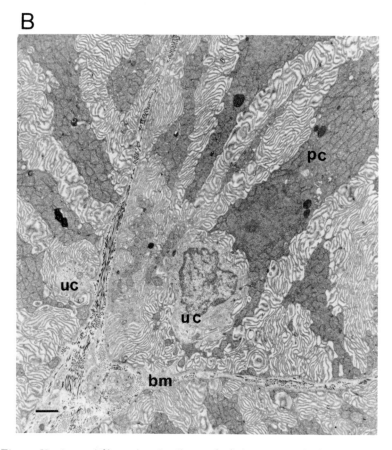

Figure 5B. An undifferentiated cell type (uc) shown near the basement membrane (bm). Scale, 2 μ.

concerns the nature of the apical junctional complexes. If these junctions are functionally open, as they often seem to be in micrographs (Dunson, Packer and Dunson, 1971; Martin and Philpott, 1973), fluid may pass directly into the tubule lumen. A careful study of the junctions found in vertebrate salt glands, using the most modern freeze-fracture techniques (Gilula, 1973), would be invaluable in attempting to understand the process of ion concentration by the salt gland. In bird salt glands the interstitial fluid "channels" actually extend up inside the cells, since the increased surface area is due in larger part to invaginations of the basal cell membrane (Ernst and Ellis, 1969). However, in the early stages of salt gland differentiation in the duck, the cells bear a remarkable resemblance to those of reptilian glands (Ernst and

C

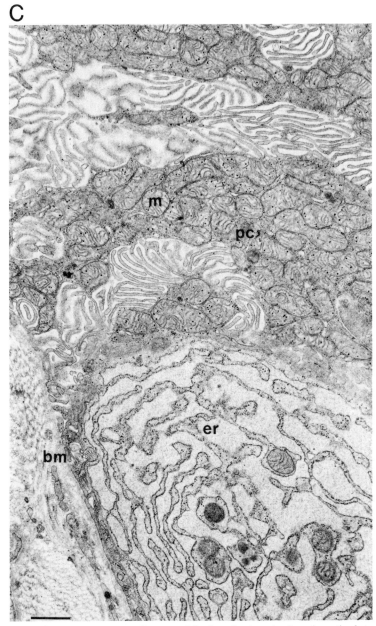

Figure 5C. A specialized cell type with abundant endoplasmic reticulum (er) filled with secretory product. Scale, 1 μ. Basement membrane (bm), mitochondria (m), principal cell (pc). Micrographs prepared by Dr. M. K. Dunson using the procedures of Dunson and Dunson (1974). Snake kept in sea water but not salt loaded.

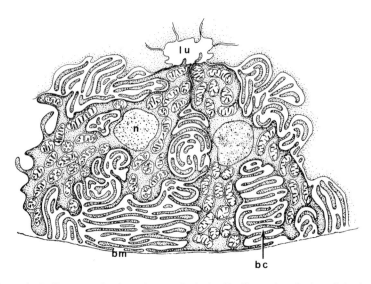

Figure 6. A diagrammatic view of two principal cells, illustrating the interdigitation of lateral processes from adjacent portions of the same cell across the basal cleft (bc). Nucleus (n), lumen (lu), basement membrane (bm). Drawing by Rae Chambers.

Ellis, 1969; Dunson, 1975). In fact, mammalian salivary glands, which are incapable of producing anything but an isosmotic or hypo-osmotic secretion, have many anatomical features in common with reptilian salt glands (Scott and Pease, 1959; Matthews and Martin, 1971). Since both reptilian and avian glands produce fluids of similar electrolyte concentration, the basal invaginations of the avian glands seem to be associated mainly with a much higher flow rate (Dunson and Dunson, 1974).

There are very few ultrastructural differences between the tiny salt glands of some species of sea snakes and the much larger glands of other species, that can be attributed to dissimilarities in secretion rate or concentration. Some sublingual salt glands tend to have reduced interstitial spaces (Dunson and Dunson, 1973), but this might be due to differences in the degree of salt adaptation. A particularly interesting case is that of *Hydrophis semperi* in fresh-water Lake Taal. As previously discussed, this species has a salt gland that seems physiologically active. It should be noted, however, that the salt gland of the marine *H. cyanocinctus*, the closest relative of *H. semperi,* has never been studied. The fine structure of the posterior sublingual gland of *H. semperi* is shown in Figure 7. This tissue sample was taken from the central area of the gland while the gland was still secreting after a salt load. A secretory fluid sample taken 30 min previously was 390 mMCl (earlier maximum was 470 mMCl). Several differences are apparent in a comparison with the gland of *A. fuscus* (Figure 5): the interstitial space is "closed," mitochondria seem less numerous, the surface area is reduced, and the basal area of the principal cells in contact with the basement membrane is increased. Some of these distinctions may be due to the fact that this gland was actively secreting (that shown in Figure 5 was not); but on the whole it seems that the gland of *H. semperi* has several atypical cytological features. Since no studies have been published on the effects of fresh-water acclimation on the

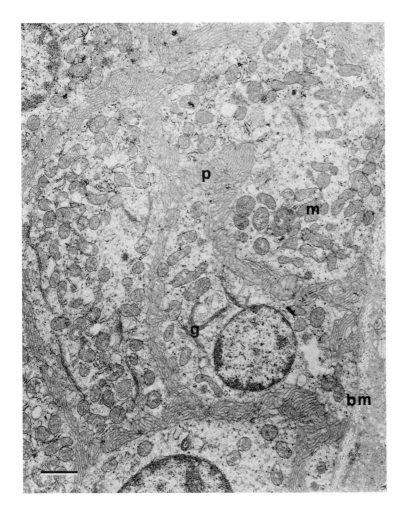

Figure 7. The ultrastructure of the posterior sublingual salt gland of the fresh water Lake Taal "sea" snake *Hydrophis semperi* during salt secretion. Note the closely apposed lateral cell processes (p), the prominent Golgi apparatus (g), the extensive contact of the basal cell surface with the basement membrane (bm), and the numerous mitochondria (m). Scale, 2 μ. Prepared by Dr. M. K. Dunson.

fine structure of reptilian salt glands, further work is needed to evaluate the significance of these findings.

Fluid Concentration and Secretion Rate

An unsuspected diversity among sea snakes in the rate and concentration of salt gland secretion has recently been discovered (Dunson and Dunson, 1974). Mean secretion rates (as measured by a bath technique) vary almost 10-fold. NaCl concentrations of the posterior sublingual salt gland secretion vary almost two-fold (Table 1). Cannulation studies show that the sublingual salt gland can account for most of the extracloacal ion loss measured in a distilled water bath (Dunson and Dunson, 1974). Thus it seems unlikely that glands other than the posterior sublingual are involved in salt excretion, as suggested by Burns and Pickwell (1972). In birds, the degree of adaptation to marine, estuarine, or fresh-water habitats seems closely related to the size of the nasal salt gland and its secretory fluid concentration (Staaland, 1967). The variation in gland size, fluid concentration, or secretory rate among sea snakes (Table 1) seems to be generally unrelated to the ecology of the species, since all but *Laticauda* are fully marine and most feed on fish. It is unlikely that there are significant differences in salt content among fish prey species. Thus, interspecific differences in factors such as renal excretion or skin permeability must be considered possiblities. There is a definite tendency for secretory fluid concentration to remain constant within genera such as *Aipysurus* or *Hydrophis*. Thus, concentration could be considered a conservative factor. Secretory rate, on the other hand, shows considerable variation in each of these same groups. In *Aipysurus,* gland weight is the main determinant of secretory rate. Yet one is left with the inability to explain ecologically why *A. fuscus* or *A. duboisii* possess such small glands in comparison with *A. laevis* or *A. eydouxii.*

Avian salt glands are not generally capable of secreting a more concentrated NaCl solution than sea snakes or other reptiles, yet most marine birds secrete at a much faster rate (Dunson, in press). In the bird order Charadriiformes there seems to be an upper concentration limit between 800–900 mM NaCl. Staaland (1967) speculated that this may be related to the energy requirements of the secretory process. The fact that the upper concentration limit for reptilian glands is approximately the same may be more than a coincidence. Wide differences in secretory fluid concentration in birds appear to be due to the length of the tubules (Staaland, 1967). Since no cytological differences could be discerned between *Aipysurus* and *Hydrophis* (Dunson and Dunson, 1974), a similar relation between tubule length and final secretion concentration may be present in sea snakes.

Among reptiles, the marine iguana seems to have the greatest capacity for extracloacal ion excretion (Dunson, 1969b). Rates of Na excretion may

Table 1. Interspecific differences in electrolyte excretion by the sea snake salt gland (means ±SD)[a]

Species	Maximum rate of Cl excretion, bath data (μmoles/100 g/hr)		Salt gland as % body wt	Fluid concentration (mM)			
	Mean	N		Cl	Na	K	N
Secretory fluid more concentrated than sea water (560 mMCl)							
Aipysurus fuscus	24	1	0.004–0.014	749 ± 97	—	—	2
Aipysurus duboisii	81 ± 12	2	0.005–0.013	813	—	—	1
Aipysurus laevis	157 ± 22	3	0.013–0.040	791 ± 57	798 ± 49	28 ± 6	5
Lapemis hardwickii	162 ± 18	4	0.017–0.061	704 ± 46	676 ± 40	23 ± 2	3
Aipysurus eydouxii	222 ± 25	2	0.023–0.070	749	703	34	1
Secretory fluid similar to or less concentrated than sea water[b]							
Hydrophis melanocephalus[b]	29	1	0.002–0.003	465 ± 33	—	—	3
Hydrophis semperi	32 ± 6	3	—	440	—	—	1
Hydrophis elegans	35 ± 4	2	0.003–0.008	520 ± 30	509 ± 20	20 ± 0.5	3
Disteira major	41 ± 23	2	0.005	453	432	19	1
Acalyptophis peronii	56 ± 1	2	—	514 ± 13	—	—	2
Laticauda semifasciata	68 ± 6	3	—	509	531	9.4	1
Astrotia stokesii	133 ± 6	2	0.009–0.015	520 ± 76	—	—	2
Pelamis platurus	142 ± 28	9	0.034–0.053	594 ± 18	584 ± 29	22.6 ± 9.5	5

[a]From Dunson and Dunson (1974) and unpublished data.

[b]This Ashmore Reef species was called H. belcheri by Dunson and Dunson (1974). Its status is still under review by H. G. Cogger.

exceed 250 μmoles/100g body wt/hr with K losses reaching 50 μmoles/100g hr. Among the sea snakes listed in Table 1, it is apparent that only *Aipysurus eydouxii* (a fish egg eater) has a similarly high rate. Several other species, such as *Pelamis,* may occasionally have an individual rate over 200 μmoles/100 g hr, but these are exceptional cases. Typical fish-eating species have rates of maximum extracloacal loss (salt gland excretion) between 30 and 200 μmoles Cl/100 g hr. The lowest values of salt excretion rate from aquatic birds are about 270 μmoles Na/100 g hr for the Humboldt penguin (Schmidt-Nielsen and Sladen, 1958) and 280 μmoles Cl/100 g hr for the Guam rail (Carpenter and Stafford, 1970). The nasal glands of terrestrial birds probably secrete at considerably lower levels. Thus, there is an overlap in secretory rate of the salt glands of birds and reptiles. However, the maximum secretory capability of the avian gland is about 10-fold greater than that of the reptilian gland.

Mechanism of Secretion

Many important aspects of the physiology of salt secretion remain to be resolved. Most questions revolve around the general concept of ion compartmentalization in tissues. What are the relative electrolyte concentrations of the intracellular and interstitial (extracellular) fluids? Is there a change between inactive and actively secreting states? What are the relative membrane fluxes across the basal, lateral, and apical surfaces of the principal cell? Do the salts destined to be secreted into the tubule lumen move through the cell at all? What subsequent modification of the fluid occurs as it moves down into the collecting ducts? What is the functional significance of the differences in ultrastructure between reptilian and avian salt glands? What is the role of Na-K-activated ATPase in the process of salt secretion?

Although we have very little direct evidence of the pathways through which ions move in the salt gland, a large net flux of NaCl must be occurring between the blood (150 mM Na) and the final tubule fluid (850 mM Na). The reptilian salt gland may be considered as a four-compartment system: (1) the plasma, (2) the interstitial fluid (ISF), (3) the intracellular fluid (ICF), and (4) the luminal fluid in the tubule. We have easy experimental access only to the plasma and the final gland secretion, which may not be the same as the immediate secretory product up in the tubule. Estimates of the ICF concentration are based on the assumption that plasma and ISF are the same. In addition, only inactive glands can be analyzed since there is no way to correct for the luminal fluid concentration. In the usual analysis total tissue salt and water content is measured, and figures for the contribution of plasma and ISF are substracted. Under these conditions most salt glands (including those of sea snakes) have a rather normal Na and K concentration in the ICF (Dunson and Dunson, 1974). These data support the hypothesis that the concentration step for Na occurs across the apical rather than the basal or lateral surfaces. However, the assumptions and conditions inherent to the measurements prevent any definitive conclusions. There is a need for further methods of direct measurement of ICF, ISF, and luminal fluid concentrations. Micropuncture is an obvious possibility, since it could be used on actively secreting glands.

Another approach to this problem is to determine the localization of the presumed transport protein, Na-K ATPase. This might be expected to correspond with the site of the major concentration step between the plasma and the luminal fluid. Histochemical tests for ATPase have given conflicting results. Ballantyne and Wood (1970) reported a predominance of apical enzyme in duck salt gland whereas Ernst (1972) found in the same tissue that it was localized mainly on the lateral and basal surfaces. In the small intestine, a useful approach has been to separate the apical microvilli from the other cell membranes by sucrose gradient centrifugation, and then to carry out biochemical tests on the fractions (Nakao and Nagano, 1972). In this case, Na-K ATPase seems to be present only on the basal and lateral cell membranes. Since the biochemical assay for ATPase is so much more reliable than the histochemical tests and, in addition, provides quantitative rather than qualitative data, it would be worthwhile to attempt separation of an apical membrane fraction from the salt gland. Another interesting technique, applied to the intestine, that would be useful in studying the salt gland is the radioautographic localization of tritiated ouabain (Stirling, 1972).

In considering possible explanations for the interspecific differences in salt gland secretion rate shown in Table 1, gland size rather than ultrastructure seemed to be the most important factor. Another possibility that should be considered is differences in Na-K ATPase content. Since this enzyme is believed to be the sodium pump (Schwartz et al., 1972), it is not surprising that salt glands contain large amounts of it (Hokin et al., 1973). Bonting (1970) found about a fourfold range in Na-K ATPase activities from the elasmobranch rectal salt gland. In the few sea snakes that have been tested, there appear to be few or no differences in Na-K ATPase activities (Dunson and Dunson, 1974). This includes species like *Hydrophis elegans,* with a very low rate of salt secretion, and *Lapemis* that secretes more than four times faster. Similar Na-K ATPase activities were also found in the three nonhomologous reptilian salt glands of turtles, lizards, and snakes (Dunson and Dunson, in press). It would be especially interesting to know the relative ATPase activities of all of the different types of salt glands (avian, reptilian, and elasmobranch). However, slight differences in technique lead to large variations in measured activity, so comparisons between different laboratories are rather difficult at this time. It is clear that avian glands are able to transport far greater amounts of Cl and fluid per mg of gland than either reptilian or elasmobranch glands. A fascinating subject for future study is the question as to whether the avian gland is more "efficient" and requires less ATP to transport a given amount of solute than the reptilian salt gland.

SUMMARY

Aside from three land-locked forms, all sea snakes are marine and consequently show specializations for conservation of water and excretion of excess salts. The kidney is unable to produce a hyperosmotic urine, and apparently has a minor role in excretion of NaC1, in comparison with the salt gland. The sea snake salt gland is the posterior sublingual gland; it secretes a fluid hyperosmotic to sea water into the tongue sheath. When the tongue is extended into the water, the secretions are removed from the body. This salt gland is not homologous with those found in turtles (lachrymal) or lizards and birds (both nasal). Thus, the development of salt glands in reptiles is a remarkable case of convergent evolution. The only fresh-water "sea snake" studied so far, *Hydrophis semperi*, has retained a functional salt gland. A surprising amount of variation in salt gland size and secretory rate occurs among the marine sea snakes. Since this variation seems to be mainly unrelated to diet or to enhanced renal function, it must be assumed that extra-renal and extra-salt gland structures assume a greater role in ion balance in some species. Studies on the role of the kidney-gut complex and the skin are needed to properly assess their overall importance in maintenance of ionic and osmotic balance. There may be a direct relationship between the occurrence of aquatic respiration in some species and the secretory capacity of the salt gland.

ACKNOWLEDGMENTS

These studies were supported by NSF grants GB-16653 and GA-35835 and an Australian Queens Fellowship in Marine Science. Shipboard experiments were supported by NSF under grants GA-34948 and GD-34462 to the Scripps Institution of Oceanography for operation of the *Alpha Helix* Research Program. Dr. C. Burdon Jones and his staff at the James Cook University were of great assistance during a stay in Queensland in 1972–73. Dr. John Minnich kindly reviewed the manuscript.

REFERENCES

Ballantyne, B., and W. G. Wood. 1970. ATPase and Na^+-K^+ transport in the avian nasal gland. Cytobios 2:21—51.
Bentley, P. J., W. L. Bretz, and K. Schmidt-Nielsen. 1967. Osmoregulation in

the diamondback terrapin, *Malaclemys terrapin centrata.* J. Exp. Biol. 46:161–167.

Bentley, P. J., and K. Schmidt-Nielsen. 1966. Cutaneous water loss in reptiles. Science 151:1547–1549.

Bonting, S. L. 1970. Sodium-potassium activated adenosine triphosphatase and cation transport. *In* Membranes and Ion Transport. Vol. 1, J. Wiley & Sons. New York. pp. 257–363.

Bourret, R. 1934. Les Serpents marins de l'Indochine Française. Gouvernement Général de l'Indochine. Hanoi.

Burns, B., and G. V. Pickwell. 1972. Cephalic glands in sea snakes. Copeia 1972:547–559.

Carpenter, R. E., and M. A. Stafford. 1970. The secretory rates and the chemical stimulus for secretion of the nasal salt glands in the Rallidae. Condor 72:316–324.

Conant, R., and J. D. Lazell, Jr. 1973. The Carolina salt marsh snake: A distinct form of *Natrix sipedon.* Breviora No. 400, p. 1–13.

Dunson, W. A. 1968. Salt gland secretion in the pelagic sea snake *Pelamis.* Am. J. Physiol. 215: 1512–1517.

Dunson, W. A. 1969a. Reptilian salt glands. In: *Exocrine Glands.* S. Botelho, F. P. Brooks and W. B. Shelley (eds.), University of Pennsylvania, Philadelphia, p. 83–103.

Dunson, W. A. 1969b. Electrolyte excretion by the salt gland of the Galápagos marine iguana. Am. J. Physiol. 216:995–1002.

Dunson, W. A. 1970. Some aspects of electrolyte and water balance in three estuarine reptiles, the diamondback terrapin, American and "salt water" crocodiles. Comp. Biochem. Physiol. 32:161–174.

Dunson, W. A. Salt glands in reptiles. *In* Biology of the Reptilia. Physiol. A. v. 5 Academic Press, New York. In Press.

Dunson, W. A., and M. K. Dunson. 1973. Convergent evolution of sublingual salt glands in the marine file snake and the true sea snakes. J. Comp. Physiol. 86:193–208.

Dunson, W. A., and M. K. Dunson. 1974. Interspecific differences in fluid concentration and secretion rate of sea snake salt glands. Am. J. Physiol. 227:430–438.

Dunson, M. K., and W. A. Dunson. The relation between plasma Na concentration and salt gland Na-K ATPase content in the diamondback terrapin and the yellow-bellied sea snake. J. Comp. Physiol. In Press.

Dunson, W. A., and G. W. Ehlert. 1971. Effects of temperature, salinity and surface water flow on distribution of the sea snake *Pelamis.* Limnol. and Oceanogr. 16:845–853.

Dunson, W. A., R. K. Packer, and M. K. Dunson. 1971. Sea snakes: An unusual salt gland under the tongue. Science 173:437–441.

Dunson, W. A., and A. Taub. 1967. Extrarenal salt excretion in sea snakes (*Laticauda*). Am. J. Physiol. 213:975–982.

Ernst, S. A. 1972. Transport adenosine triphosphatase cytochemistry. II. Cytochemical localization of ouabain-sensitive, potassium-dependent phosphatase activity in the secretory epithelium of the avian salt gland. J. Histochem. Cytochem. 20:23–38.

Ernst, S. A., and R. A. Ellis. 1969. The development of surface specialization in the secretory epithelium of the avian salt gland in response to osmotic stress. J. Cell. Biol. 40:305–321.

Fletcher, G. L., I. M. Stainer, and W. N. Holmes. 1967. Sequential changes in the adenosine triphosphatase activity and the electrolyte excretory capacity of the nasal glands of the duck (*Anas platyrhynchos*) during the period of adaptation to hypertonic saline. J. Exp. Biol. 47:375–391.

Gilula, N. B. 1973. Development of cell junctions. Amer. Zool. 13:1109–1117.

Graham, J. B. 1973. Aquatic respiration and the physiological responses to submersion of the sea snake *Pelamis platurus*. Amer. Zool. 13:1296 (abst.).

Graham, J. B. 1974. Aquatic respiration in the sea snake *Pelamis platurus*. Resp. Physiol. 21:1–7.

Hokin, L. E., J. L. Dahl, J. D. Deupree, J. F. Dixon, J. F. Hackney, and J. F. Perdue. 1973. Studies on the characterization of the sodium-potassium transport adenosine triphosphatase. X. Purification of the enzyme from the rectal gland of *Squalus acanthias*. J. Biol. Chem. 248:2593–2605.

Holmes, W. N., and R. L. McBean. 1964. Some aspects of electrolyte excretion in the green turtle, *Chelonia mydas mydas*. J. Exp. Biol. 41:81–90.

Junqueira, L. C. U., G. Malnic, and C. Monge. 1966. Reabsorptive function of the ophidian cloaca and large intestine. Physiol. Zool. 39:151–159.

Khalil, F., and G. Abdel-Messeih. 1954. Water content of tissues of some desert reptiles and mammals. J. Exp. Zool. 125:407–14.

Krogh, A. 1939. Osmotic Regulation in Aquatic Animals. Cambridge University Press. Cambridge.

Martin, B. J., and C. W. Philpott. 1973. The adaptive response of the salt glands of adult mallard ducks to a salt water regime: An ultrastructural and tracer study. J. Exp. Zool. 186:111–122.

Matthews, J. L., and J. H. Martin. 1971. Atlas of Human Histology and Ultrastructure. Lea & Febiger. Philadelphia.

Minnich, J. E. 1970. Water and electrolyte balance of the desert iguana, *Dipsosaurus dorsalis*, in its natural habitat. Comp. Biochem. Physiol. 35:921–933.

Minnich, J. E. 1972. Excretion of urate salt by reptiles. Comp. Biochem. Physiol. 41A:535–549.

Moore, J. G., K. Nakamura, and A. Alcaraz. 1966. The 1965 eruption of Taal Volcano. Science 151:955–960.

Nagy, K. A. 1972. Water and electrolyte budgets of a free-living desert lizard, *Sauromalus obesus*. J. Comp. Physiol. 79:39–62.

Nakao, M., and K. Nagano, 1972. Structure and mode of action of Na^+, K^+-ATPase. In: Molecular Mechanisms of Enzyme Action. Y. Ogura, Y. Tonomura and T. Nakamura (eds.). University Park Press. Baltimore. pp. 297–314.

Pease, D. C. 1956. Infolded basal plasma membranes found in epithelia noted for their water transport. J. Biophysic. Biochem. Cytol. 2(Suppl.):203–208.

Pettus, D. 1958. Water relationships in *Natrix sipedon*. Copeia 1958:207–211.

Prange, H. D., and K. Schmidt-Nielsen. 1969. Evaporative water loss in snakes. Comp. Biochem. Physiol. 28:973–975.

Schmidt-Nielsen, B., and L. E. Davis. 1968. Fluid transport and tubular intercellular spaces in reptilian kidneys. Science 159:1105–1108.

Schmidt-Nielsen, K., and W. J. L. Sladen. 1958. Nasal salt secretion in the Humboldt penguin. Nature 181:1217–1218.

Schwartz, A., G. E. Lindenmayer, and J. C. Allen. 1972. The Na^+, K^+-ATPase membrane transport system: Importance in cellular function. *In* Current Topics in Membranes and Transport. F. Bronner and A. Kleinzeller (eds.), vol. 3, p. 1–82. Academic Press. New York.

Scott, B. L., and D. C. Pease. 1959. Electron microscopy of the salivary and lacrimal glands of the rat. Am. J. Anat. 104:115–161.

Shoemaker, V. H. 1972. Osmoregulation and excretion in birds. *In* Avian Biology. D. S. Farner and J. R. King (eds.), vol. 2, p. 527–574. Academic Press. New York.

Smith, M. 1926. Monograph of the Sea-Snakes (*Hydrophiidae*). British Museum of Natural History, London.

Staaland, H. 1967. Anatomical and physiological adaptations of the nasal glands in charadriiformes birds. Comp. Biochem. Physiol. 23:933–944.

Stirling, C. E. 1972. Radioautographic localization of sodium pump sites in rabbit intestine. J. Cell Biol. 53:704–714.

Templeton, J. R. 1972. Salt and water balance in desert lizards. *In* Comparative Physiology of Desert Animals. G. M. O. Maloiy (eds.), Symp. Zool. Soc. Lond. No. 31, p. 61–77.

Thorson, T. B. 1968. Body fluid partitioning in Reptilia. Copeia 1968:592–601.

White, F. N. 1957. A functional interpretation of the integumentary vessels of snakes. Herpetologica 13:127–130.

Wolff, T. 1969. The fauna of Rennell and Bellona, Solomon Islands. Phil. Trans. Roy. Soc. B. 255:321–343.

seventeen

Eyes and Other Sense Organs of Sea Snakes

Emerson Hibbard

Sea snakes have undergone numerous morphological as well as physiological modifications adapting them to their marine environment. In addition to some rather obvious structural differences between them and land-dwelling forms, such as the laterally compressed tail, the loss of ventral scutes, and the presence of narial valves to close the nostrils when diving, sea snakes also possess neural structures which have been modified for a marine existence. These have received little attention, perhaps in part due to the difficulty in obtaining well fixed material for histological study. Often, the material which has been used has been obtained from museum specimens which have been fixed either by immersion in the fixative or by intraperitoneal injection of the fixative.

The *Alpha Helix* Ashmore Reef expedition provided an excellent opportunity to obtain histological preparations of neural tissues from several species of sea snakes, which were fixed by intravascular perfusion using fixatives designed to provide good preservation of neural structures. In this chapter, some of the major sensory structures of sea snakes will be described, with special emphasis being devoted to the visual system; and a few comparisons will be made with other species of sea snakes and with land-dwelling forms.

PREPARATION OF MATERIAL

The histological studies which follow are based primarily on material freshly fixed by perfusion of anesthetized living snakes (through a cannula inserted through the ventricle of the heart into the aorta), first with 200 mM NaCl to flush out the blood, then with fixative. The snakes were anesthetized by Fluothane or ether inhalation, or by injection of Ketalar (ketamine hydrochloride, Parke-Davis) at a dosage of 1 mg/kg body weight.

For silver-stained preparations, perfusion was with Bodian's no. 2 fixative, which was first run rapidly through the vasculature for a period of 5 min, then slowly for 20 min more. The head was then immersed in fixative for an additional 24 hrs before removal of the brain or sense organs. These were later sectioned at 10 μm and stained by Bodian's (1936) protargol method or the Davenport et al. (1939) modification of this technique for finer detail. Perfusion with Bodian's fixative was also used prior to the staining of inner ears with Sudan black B (Rasmussen, 1961).

Whole embryos and fetuses of some species were fixed by immersion in Bodian's fixative, as were the excised eyes of some snakes needed for other purposes which precluded their perfusion. Immersion of eyes in Golgi-Cox fixative (Cox, 1891) for periods of from 6 to 8 weeks was used for Golgi studies.

Tissues prepared for electron microscopic examination were fixed by immersion in cold 2% cacodylate or phosphate-buffered glutaraldehyde and were postfixed in 2% OsO_4 and embedded in Spurr resin (Spurr, 1969).

Species prepared by each of the above methods are listed in Table 1.

OBSERVATIONS AND DISCUSSION

Most of the snakes captured in McCluer Gulf off the northwestern coast of New Guinea were netted from the surface of the sea from whaleboats during daylight hours. Those collected at Ashmore Reef either were captured with snake tongs by divers near the reef or were netted from the fantail of the *Alpha Helix* during early morning hours when they surfaced to breathe. I, assisted by the ship's chief engineer, Mr. G. Trease, was responsible for the capture of most of those taken during the early morning (3:30 to 6:00 A.M.), and I was surprised to find that these consisted almost entirely of snakes belonging to three species: *Astrotia stokesii, Hydrophis melanocephalus,* and *Acalyptophis peronii.* This led to speculation that these species might be nocturnal, and might show appropriate modifications of their visual systems including increased populations of rod-type photoreceptors. Histological examination of their eyes showed that this was not the case, however, and that *Astrotia* appears to lack rods altogether. Although possibly attracted by the ship's light, all are adapted for diurnal vision. The capture of these three species is apparently due to their preference for the deeper water in which the ship was anchored rather than to their nocturnal habits.

Table 1. Species prepared by each of four methods

| Species | Intravascular perfusion with Bodian's fixative | Immersion in Bodian's fixative | | Eyes immersed in glutaraldehyde for electron microscopy | Eyes immersed in Golgi fixative |
		Eyes	Embryos or fetuses		
Aacalyptophis peronii	X		X	X	X
Aipysurus apraefrontalis	X	X	X		
Aipysurus duboisii	X			X	X
Aipysurus foliosquama	X				
Aipysurus fuscus	X	X	X	X	
Aipysurus laevis	X		X	X	
Astrotia stokesii	X	X	X	X	
Emydocephalus annulatus	X	X	X	X	
Hydrophis melanocephalus[a]	X	X	X		X
Hydrophis elegans	X				
Disteira major	X		X		
Hydrophis ornatus	X				
Hydrophis semperi	X			X	
Lapemis hardwickii	X				X
Pelamis platurus	X				

[a]Tentatively assigned by H. G. Cogger to this species. Subsequent revision is expected.

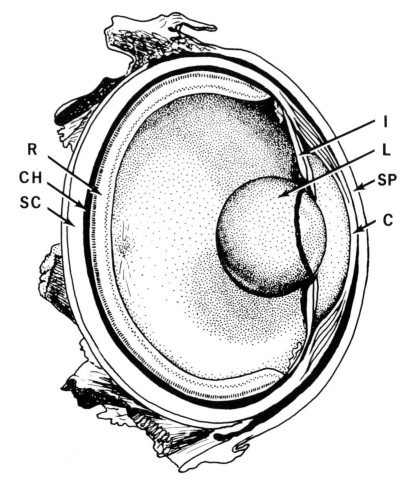

Figure 1. Drawing of the hemisected eye of *Hydrophis melanocephalus* showing retina (R), choroid and pigmented retina (CH), sclera (SC), iris (I), lens (L), spectacle (SP), and cornea (C). × 50.

The Eye

The eyes of sea snakes are nearly spherical and have circular pupils and spherical lenses (Figure 1). Walls (1942) has pointed out that the extreme contraction of the pupil to a pinhole is used by the snake not only in adjusting to variations of brightness, but also in solving the problem of accommodation by an aquatic species which must adjust to viewing objects either in air or in water. The sclerotic coats of the sea snake's eyes are thick and composed of fibrous connective tissue.

A typical sea snake retina, that of *Aipysurus fuscus,* is illustrated in Figure 2. The outer coat of the sclera is compact while the inner part is composed of fibrous connective tissue bundles running in alternate directions. The choroid coat contains large sinuses lying peripheral to the pigmented retina. These sinuses are probably important in the equalization of pressure around the retina during diving. The pigmented layer of the retina is formed from a mosaic of hexagonal cells whose processes project inward between the outer segments of the photoreceptors.

The photoreceptor cells are of four types. In general, they resemble the type A single large cones, type B double cones, type C single small cones, and type D rods described by Underwood (1966) for *Enhydris pakistanica,* an aquatic colubrid snake found in fresh or brackish waters of Asia; but differ from *Enhydris* in having very few rod-type receptors, and very compact myoids.

Examples of the photoreceptor cells of *Aipysurus laevis* are shown in Figures 3 through 8. A type A single large cone having a very large ellipsoid is shown in Figure 3. The nucleus does not project partially through the external limiting membrane as it does in *Enhydris* (Underwood, 1966). Figure 4 illustrates two type B double cones. While the nuclei of the cells are out of the plane of focus in the picture, the outer segments of the axial and

Figure 2. Cross-section through retina, choroid (ch) and sclera (sc) of *Aipysurus fuscus.* X 130.

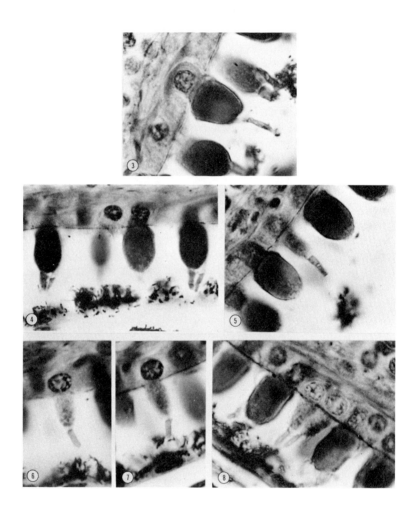

Figures 3–8. Photoreceptor cell types from retina of *Aipysurus laevis.* × 1280. Figure 3: Type A single large cone. Figure 4: Two pairs of Type B double cones. Figure 5: Type D rod. Figures 6 and 7: Thought to be type C small cones. Figure 8: Twin cones.

peripheral cells are clearly shown, in this case being aligned in the same direction beneath the ellipsoid of the axial cell. No regular pattern of alignment of double cones could be found in any of the sea snake retinas, however. The pair of nuclei shown in the center of Figure 4 are also of a pair of double cones; that on the left belonging to a peripheral cell, that on the right to an axial cell. A rod is shown in Figure 5. Unlike that described for *Enhydris*, the nucleus of this cell lies adjacent to the external limiting membrane, apparently because there is little compaction of the photoreceptors in the sea snake retina, so their nuclei lie nearly in the same plane. An exception is those of the peripheral cells of double cone pairs, which are displaced somewhat by the paranuclear body which lies just inside the limitans. The ellipsoid of the rod-type receptor is elongated and narrow. Although they do not differ greatly from the cell described above, I believe the receptors illustrated in Figures 6 and 7 represent small type C cones. They differ from the rods in having larger ellipsoids containing dark globular bodies, and in having rounded outer segments. The dark objects within the ellipsoids probably represent large mitochondria containing inclusion bodies similar to those previously reported for the sea snake *Pelamis platurus* (Hibbard and LaVergne, 1972). In Figure 8, a pair of these cells appear to be fused along the length of the inner segment in much the same manner as the twin cones of a fish retina. Twin cones are said to be related to diurnal activity (Walls, 1942).

Two different cone types are clearly evident in tangential sections shown in Figures 9 through 14, which represent comparable sections of retinas of six species of sea snakes. The difference is particularly apparent in *Aipysurus duboisii* (Figure 9). The retina of *Emydocephalus annulatus* (not illustrated) shows a similar condition. The darkly stained bodies in Figure 9 are the ellipsoids of the large type A cones, while the more lightly stained ones are mostly type C small ones. Double type B cones are not easily distinguishable. *Hydrophis ornatus* (Figure 10) and *A. peronii* (Figure 12) show much more uniformity in staining properties, with a larger proportion of A type cells. In *A. fuscus* (Figure 11) there appears to be a larger percentage of smaller cells, either rods or small cones. In *A. laevis* (Figure 13), whose cell types have been illustrated in Figures 3 through 8, the very narrow myoids of the accessory cells of double cones can be distinguished lying adjacent to the ellipsoids of the axial cells, and the dense bodies within the ellipsoids of the small cells are apparent. The proportions of double to single large cones is high in these snakes, also indicating strong diurnal adaptation (Walls, 1942). The uniform ellipsoids of *A. stokesii* are shown in Figure 14 surrounded by processes from the pigment layer of the retina. Figures 9 through 14 are taken at the same magnification. Although the eyes of these species differ in size, it is clear that the size and packing density of photoreceptor cells vary considerably from species to species.

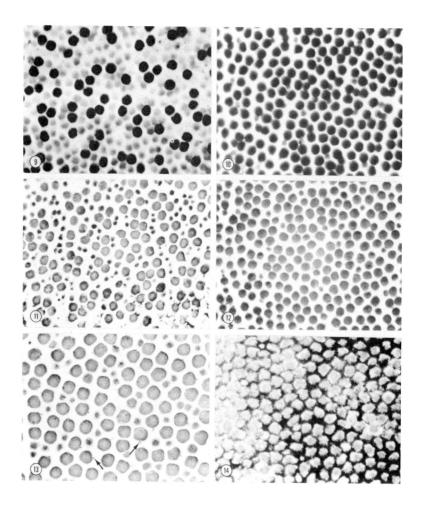

Figures 9–14. Tangential sections through inner segments of photoreceptors of six species. × 50. Figure 9. *Aipysurus duboisii.* Figure 10. *Hydrophis ornatus.* Figure 11. *Aipysurus fuscus.* Figure 12. *Acalyptophis peronii.* Figure 13. *Aipysurus laevis.* Figure 14. *Astrotia stokesii.*

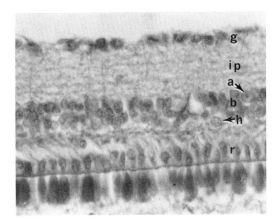

Figure 15. Cross-section of the retina of *Aipysurus duboisii* showing stratification of inner plexiform layer (i.p.). × 50. g, ganglion cell layer; a, amacrine cell nucleus, b, bipolar cell layer; h, horizontal cell nucleus; r, photoreceptor nuclei.

The species in which the larger percentage of small ellipsoids occur, *A. laevis, A. fuscus,* and *A. duboisii,* also show distinct stratification within the inner plexiform layer (Figure 15). These strata represent separate synaptic regions within the inner plexiform layer in which sorting, summation, inhibition, and other information processing occurs before transmission to the brain via the ganglion cells and optic nerve fibers. From a behavioral standpoint, it is interesting that these species are also the ones which seem to be the most visually perceptive and curious about divers in the water.

Efferent fibers have been noted entering the inner plexiform layer of *Astrotia.* Identification was based on the fact that the axons entering the retina branched into two or more processes before disappearing from view in the inner plexiform layer. In fish retinas, such efferent fibers have been found to terminate on amacrine cells, where they serve an inhibitory function (Witkovsky, 1971), but their actual destinations in the snake retina were not determined.

Inclusions, presumably glycogen granules, are present in the ellipsoid mitochondria (Figure 16). Whether the differences in density are the result of changes in state, storage and utilization, or fixation artifact is not clear.

The synaptic pedicles of sea snake photoreceptors are very large and possess features which can be observed under an oil immersion objective with the light microscope. These include fibrils or tubules which radiate from the neck into the pedicle (Figure 17), and have granular structures either within or attached to them. Such structures have been implicated in axonal transport of materials produced within the perikaryon of nerve cells (Kreutzberg, 1969;

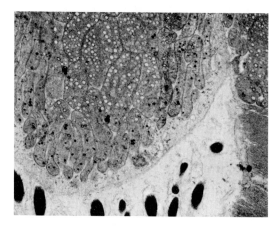

Figure 16. Electron micrograph of ellipsoid of *Hydrophis melanocephalus* showing dense inclusion bodies in peripheral mitochondria and vacuous inclusion bodies in central mitochondria. × 8760.

Schmitt, 1969). In the photoreceptors, they may be involved in the manufacture or transport of the synaptic vesicles which fill the pedicle. Evenly spaced bars can also be discerned in some pedicles (Figure 18); these are probably the synaptic ribbon complexes seen clearly in electron micrographs (Figure 19). Each ribbon is associated with two or more postsynaptic processes belonging to horizontal or bipolar cells. Numerous conventional synapses are present in the same region.

Nuclei of the photoreceptors are distributed in a single or at most two layers, in all the sea snake retinas examined. The inner nuclear layer, which

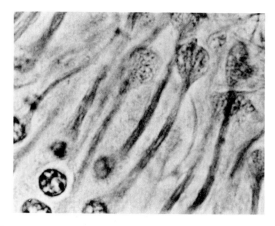

Figure 17. Photoreceptor nuclei and synaptic pedicles of *Aipysurus laevis* showing radiating tubules and granules. × 1280.

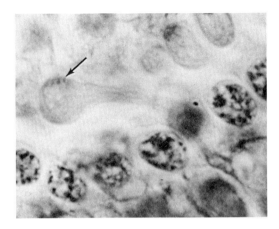

Figure 18. Synaptic pedicle of *Emydocephalus annulatus* viewed under oil immersion. Arrow indicates dense structures probably representing synaptic ribbons. × 1735.

consists of the nuclei of bipolar, horizontal, and amacrine cells, varies from three to seven cells in thickness, while the ganglion cells are distributed in a single layer, sometimes in close proximity to each other but often widely scattered. Optic fibers leave the retina in discrete bundles with a row of glial supporting cells in the center of each bundle (Figure 20).

Golgi preparations of the retina of *H. melanocephalus* (Figures 21 through 27) have provided the information about some of the cellular relationships in the retina which has been used to prepare the stereodiagram shown in Figure 28. In this species, many of the cones appear to bear a

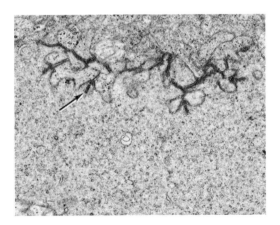

Figure 19. Synaptic ribbons (arrow) in pedicle of *Hydrophis melanocephalus*. × 17,520.

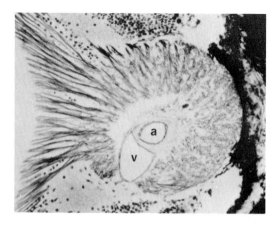

Figure 20. Optic nerve fibers of *Aipysurus duboisii* leaving the retina. Hyaloid artery (a) and vein (v) pass along choroid fissure. × 130.

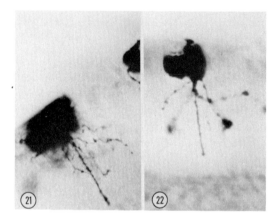

Figures 21 and 22. G1 type of ganglion cells of *Hydrophis melanocephalus*. × 730.

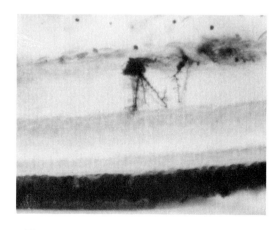

Figure 23. Ganglion cell of *Aipysurus laevis*. × 255.

Figure 24. Bipolar cell (B), cone (C) and Muller cells (M) of *Hydrophis melanocephalus.* × 330.

Figure 25. Amacrine cell (A) of H. *melanocephalus.* × 290.

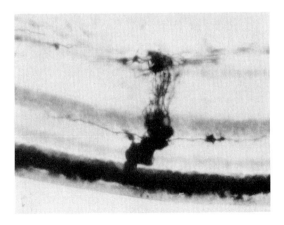

Figure 26. Horizontal cell (H) and processes of H. *melanocephalus.* ×290.

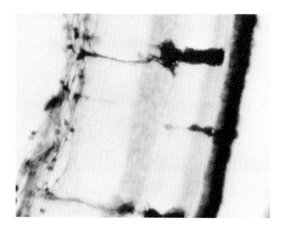

Figure 27. Lateral contact being made in outer plexiform layer with synaptic pedicle of photoreceptor of H. *melanocephalus.* X 365.

one-to-one relationship with the bipolar cells. Two types of bipolar cells and two types of ganglion cells are present. It appears to me that the bipolar cell labeled B1 in the drawing, which has a conspicuous major process projecting into the inner plexiform layer, may transmit information primarily to the G1 type of ganglion cell which has a similar type of process projecting in the opposite direction. Since little summation would be involved, this route probably would carry information involved in pattern perception and visual acuity. Type B2 bipolar cells branch extensively in the inner plexiform layer, as do the dendritic branches of the G2 ganglion cells. These are involved in extensive summation over broad areas of the retina and are probably concerned with brightness discrimination. The horizontal cells (H) and amacrine cells (A) may take part in the summation or lateral inhibition processes in the retina involved in production of border contrast (Dowling and Boycott, 1965). Amacrine cells have been implicated in motion detection in the mudpuppy, *Necturus* (Werblin and Dowling, 1969).

The blood supply to the retina is provided by branches from the hyaloid artery, which enters the retina near the center of the optic nerve. No conus is present in the sea snakes examined. The vessels form a network on the inner surface of the retina and course outward to the ora terminalis, from which blood is returned to the optic nerve via a ventral hyaloid vein.

The Optic Tectum

Although complete serial sections of the brains of several species of these snakes have been prepared, only a few observations about the optic lobes of the brains will be included in the present discussion. Figure 29 illustrates an embryo of *A. peronii* at an early stage of development, indicated by the lack of formation of the spectacle over the eye and by the broad region between the anterior and posterior intestinal portals of the gut. Everted hemipenes can be seen in the photograph. The tectal lobes of the midbrain are large, prominent features which cause a considerable amount of cervical flexure in

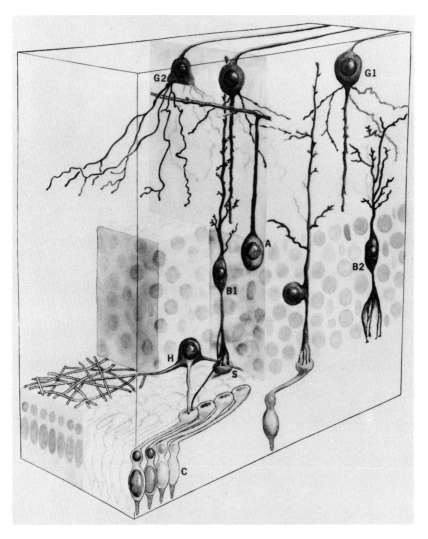

Figure 28. Stereodiagram of cell types seen in Golgi preparations of the retina of *H. melanocephalus.* Approximately × 1120. See text for explanation.

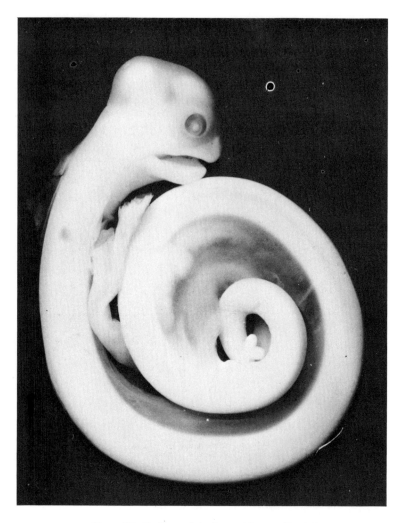

Figure 29. Embryo of *Acalyptophis peronii.* × 4.5.

the embryo. As development proceeds, the forebrain increases rapidly in size while the midbrain lags behind, so that in the adult brain (Figure 30e) the tectal lobes are relatively small and the flexure is lost. Viewed from the dorsal side, the tectal lobes of the various species illustrated appear to be quite similar in size and shape while other parts of the brains vary greatly. The entire brain of a small-headed but large-bodied species such as *H. elegans* (Figures 30, 31a) is elongated and narrow. Its olfactory structures and those of *H. melanocephalus* (Figures 30, 31b) seem to be small and insignificant compared with those of their large-headed cousin *H. ornatus* (Figures 30, 31c). The forebrain of the latter and of *A. foliosquama* (Figures 30, 31d) and *A. peronii* are large and well developed as is that of *E. annulatus*, which closely resembles *A. foliosquama. Emydocephalus* feeds almost exclusively on fish eggs and has a very well developed chemoreceptive system. This special-

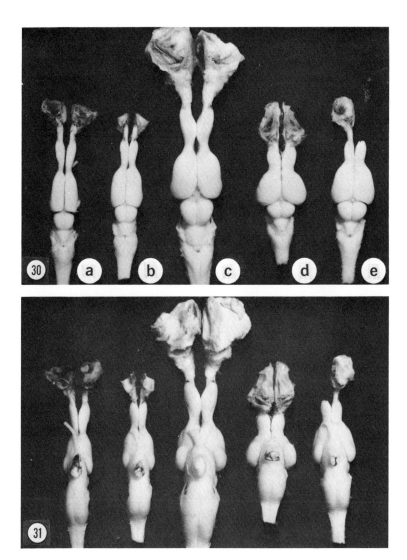

Figures 30 and 31. Dorsal and ventral views of the brains of (a) *Hydrophis elegans*, (b) *Hydrophis melanocephalus*, (c) *Hydrophis ornatus*, (d) *Aipysurus foliosquama*, and (e) *Acalyptophis peronii.* × 2.6.

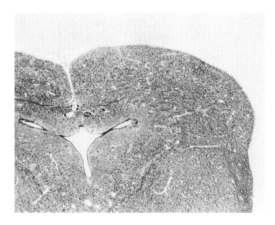

Figure 32. Cross-section through center of the poorly developed tectal lobe of the brain of *Hydrophis elegans.* × 47.

ization has not occurred at the expense of the visual system, which is also highly developed in this species. On the basis of eye structure and size and complexity of the tectal lobes of the brain, the species having the poorest vision is probably *H. elegans,* which has a greatly elongated narrow head, which it pokes into dark crannies for its food. A cross-section of its poorly developed tectal lobes is shown in Figure 32, followed by those of *A. peronii* in Figure 33 and *A. laevis* in Figure 34 for comparison. The vascular supply to the midbrain is rich (Figure 35). During prolonged dives blood is shunted to the brain of mammals from other parts of the body (Angell, James, and Daly, 1972).

Figure 33. Cross-section through center of tectum of *Acalyptophis peronii.* × 47.

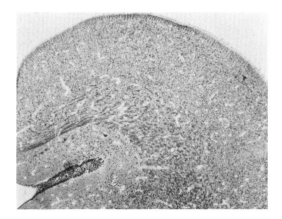

Figure 34. Cross-section through center of tectum of *Aipysurus laevis.* × 47.

Olfactory Organs

Nasal structures of snakes and other reptiles have been extensively reviewed by Katheriner (1900) and Parsons (1959a,b,1970). It has been reported by Katheriner (1900) that Bowman's glands fail to develop in *Hydrophis.* Parsons (1959a,1970) has stated that this is the only reported exception to the rule that these glands are present in all tetrapods except certain neotenous urodeles; and that *Hydrophis* is "the only known reptile with olfactory epithelium and without Bowman's glands." On the basis of structure and

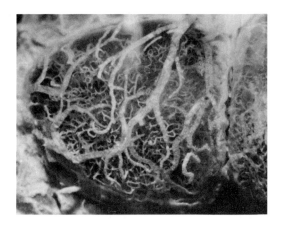

Figure 35. Vasculature of tectal lobe of *Pelamis platurus.* ×25.

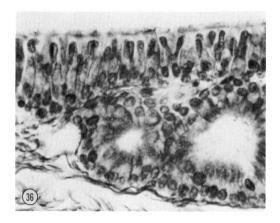

Figure 36. Bowman's glands in olfactory epithelium of *Hydrophis melanocephalus*. ×
510.

position, I have found Bowman's glands in at least three *Hydrophis* species,
H. melanocephalus (Figure 36), *H. ornatus,* and *H. elegans.*

The olfactory epithelium was examined in six species and does not differ
significantly from that described by Parsons (1970) for the nasal cavities of
other reptiles. That portion of the olfactory apparatus used to detect odors of
the contents of the mouth, Jacobson's organ, is very well developed in sea
snakes. Matthes (1934) has pointed out that these organs are immune to the
general reduction of olfactory organs in water snakes. The sea snake's tongue
is used in the same manner as that of land snakes in chemoreception, being
flicked out and in and carrying with it scent particles and olfactory cues in
solution, which are then transferred to Jacobson's organ. There is some
question whether the particles are transferred directly to the duct or lumen of
the organ, or whether they are sucked into it by differential pressure (Bellairs
and Boyd, 1950). The Jacobson's organ of *H. melanocephalus* (Figure 37) is
about half the size of its eye. The mushroom body which projects into the
lumen of the organ from the ventral side is composed of ciliated epithelium
overlying a cartilaginous knob. Parsons (1959a) discusses the columns of cells
which make up the wall of the organ and concurs with Retzius (1894) that
they are made up of sensory and supporting cells. He has noted mitotic
figures near the lumen of the organ during embryonic development. I have
found cells at various stages of mitosis at the basal ends of the columns in
mature snakes, but none near the lumen. Between the basal end of the
column and the lumen, the cells appear to be undergoing some sort of
maturational change. The nucleoli of the cells at the basal ends are also much
enlarged, suggesting that active protein synthesis is occurring in this region.
Since there seems to be no place for the maturing cells to go, these observa-

tions indicate that the overall size of the organ may be increasing, even in the mature snake. With phase contrast objective and oil immersion, one can see the fine olfactory hairs projecting into a coat of mucus lining the lumen of the organ and the long, thick cytoplasmic filaments connecting them with the sensory cell bodies within the columns. Parsons (1959a) could not determine whether nerve fibers run between the columns in Jacobson's organ. In the sea snake material, it is clear that they do, and bundles of nerve fibers can be seen passing along the channels between the columns below the supporting cells near the lumen and leaving the organ from the ventral side.

The Tongue

Moncrieff (1967) has stated that snakes have few taste buds and Bradley (1971) claims they are absent altogether from the tongues of all species of snake so far studied. Burns (1969), however, has described sensory papillae resembling taste buds in the roof and floor of the mouth, which are innervated by maxillary and mandibular branches of the trigeminal nerve in four species of sea snakes (*P. platurus, H. ornatus, H. melanocephalus,* and *Laticauda colubrina*).

Papillae similar to those described by Burns are present in all the species I have examined. They show minor variations in size, shape, and distribution, the most notable being the small, nearly filiform papillae found in *E. annulatus,* the species which feeds on fish eggs.

No taste buds were found on the tongue of *H. melanocephalus,* although large bundles of nerve fibers are present within the tongue. These are primarily motor fibers to the tongue musculature but some fibers form free endings within the epidermis. A curious feature of this tongue is the presence

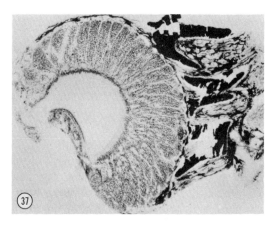

Figure 37. Jacobson's organ of *Hydrophis melanocephalus.* × 58.

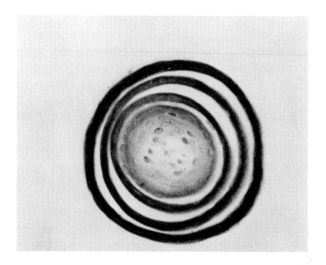

Figure 38. Cross-section through tip of the tongue of *Hydrophis melanocephalus* showing three sheaths of cornified epidermis around it. X 330.

of three separate sheaths of cornified epidermis overlying each fork of its tip (Figure 38). Proximally, the number is reduced first to two and then to one. While their primary purpose may be to protect the tongue both from direct exposure to sea water and from abrasion, perhaps they also may serve a function in mechanoreception whenever the tongue strikes a solid object. They would certainly preclude reception of chemosensory information which might otherwise be obtained from free nerve endings in the tongue tip, even in the absence of taste buds (Tamar, 1972).

The Ear

Detailed histological studies of the ears of sea snakes collected on this expedition have not been made. The membranous labyrinths of several species were dissected out more or less intact, however, and were stained with Sudan black B in order to demonstrate gross structure and innervation. Miller (1968) has studied the cochlear portions of the inner ears of a large number of snakes including seven species of sea snakes. He has noted that, in the hydrophiids, the stapedial footplate is small and there is great reduction in the size of the limbus and basilar papilla, but what the lagenar sacs are enlarged compared to those of terrestrial snakes. The basilar papilla and macula of the lagena make up the sensory epithelia of the cochlea. The basilar papilla is considered to be the reptilian homologue of the organ of Corti of mammals (Wever, 1967). Although nerve fibers from the lagena have been found to enter the acoustic area of the brainstem in a lizard (Hamilton, 1963), the lagena may also serve a vestibular (statoreceptor) function (Schwarzkoff, 1968). The saccular macula may also serve both auditory and vestibular functions in reptiles (Baird, 1970), as it does in lower vertebrates. The utricular macula is a vestibular structure sensing static equilibrium, while the cristae of the semicircular canals are used to detect changes in position. Another sensory structure present in the ear of the sea snake, the macula neglecta, is small and its function is unknown (Baird, 1970).

The basilar papilla lies on a basilar membrane supported by the limbus, which is partially separated from the lagena by a constriction in snakes (Miller, 1968). The limbic portion of the cochlear duct is connected by the ductus reuniens with the cavity of the sacculus (Figure 39). The lagenar macula forms a band of sensory epithelium which extends more than half way around the circumference of the lagenar sac. Figures 40 and 41 illustrate the innervation of the ear of *A. peronii,* which has a short, blunt lagenar sac and a large basilar papilla. The ear of *A. foliosquama* (Figures 42, 43), on the other hand, has an elongated lagenar sac and much reduced basiler papilla, which is more characteristic of sea snake ears. Its lagena resembles that of an elapid snake pictured by Miller (1968), but its basilar papilla is very much smaller. Miller has stated that the auditory performance of snakes is generally considered to be inferior compared with that of other reptiles; and those with smaller basilar papillas probably have poorer auditory capacity than those with larger ones. He has pointed out that comparative studies of sense organs

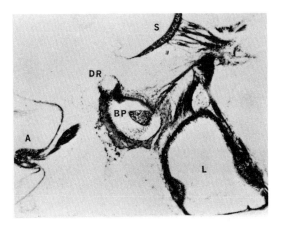

Figure 39. Horizontal section through the inner ear of *Pelamis platurus,* showing the basilar papilla (BP) in the limbic portion of the cochlear duct. The ductus reuniens (DR) joins this part of the duct with the sacculus (S). The crista of the ampulla in the anterior semicircular canal is shown (A) as is the thickened lagenar macula on each side of the lagena (L). × 50.

Figures 40 and 41. Medial and ventral views of the left membranous labyrinth of *Acalyptophis peronii* showing the small lagenar sac and large basilar papilla. × 18.

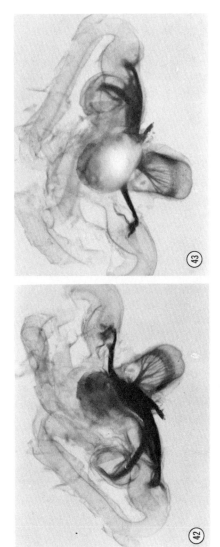

Figures 42 and 43. Medial and lateral views of the left membranous labyrinth of *Aipysurus foliosquama* showing elongated lagenar sac and reduced basilar papilla. × 18.

have contributed to an understanding of taxonomic relationships. The reduction in the size of the limbus and basilar papilla of sea snakes, he considers, may be due to lower transmission of sound stimuli in the environment of an aquatic snake than in that of a burrowing one; but he suggests that the size of the lagena may be related to the size of available space rather than to functional demands. There seems to be some reciprocal relationship between the basilar papilla and lagena, in that reduction in the size of one is accompanied by enlargement of the other, but comparison of the ears of *Acalyptophis* and *Aipysurus* shows no obvious correlations with either their habits or their adaptation for marine existence. *Acalyptophis* is a deep water form and appears to be a more highly specialized sea snake. As was pointed out in the section on vision, the types of photoreceptors and the structure of the retina and tectum of *Aipysurus* indicate that its eyesight may be better than that of *Acalyptophis*. Perhaps it relies less on hearing and therefore has a reduced auditory capacity.

SUMMARY

Histological studies of the retinas of several species of sea snakes indicate that all are highly adapted for diurnal vision. *Astrotia stokesii* appears to have a pure cone retina. *Aipysurus* species have a higher percentage of rod and small cone receptors, more distinct stratification of the inner plexiform layer of the retina, better development of the optic tectum, and probably have generally better vision than other species studied. *Hydrophis elegans* probably has the poorest vision, based upon the state of development of its visual system.

Olfactory and respiratory epithelium of sea snakes does not differ markedly from that of other reptiles, although olfactory structures, with the exception of Jacobson's organ, are somewhat reduced. Bowman's glands appear to be present in some species of *Hydrophis*, contrary to previous reports.

Taste buds are absent from the tongue, but the tongue is an important adjunct to olfaction because of its use in carrying scent particles to Jacobson's organ. It also may be an important mechanoreceptor. Taste buds may be present, however, in the roof and floor of the mouth.

Sea snake ears have well developed sensory epithelia for sensing changes in equilibrium, both static and kinetic, but the cochlear portions serving acoustic functions are poorly developed when compared to those of other reptiles. This is especially true of the basilar papilla, and seems to indicate that sea snakes generally rely more on their visual and olfactory senses than on auditory cues.

ACKNOWLEDGMENTS

This study was supported by National Science Foundation grants GA 35835, GA 34948 and GD 34462 to the Scripps Institution of Oceanography for operation of the *Alpha Helix* Research Program and by grant EY01071-01 from the National Eye Institute, U.S. Public Health Service.

REFERENCES

Angell, J. E., and M de B. Daly. 1972. Some mechanisms involved in the cardiovascular adaptations to diving. *In* S. E. B. Symposia. No. 26. The Effects of Pressure on Living Organisms. (Sleigh and Mac Donald, eds.) Academic Press, New York. pp. 313–341.

Baird, I. L. 1970. The anatomy of the reptilian ear. *In* Biology of the Reptilia. Vol. 2 (C. Gans, ed.). Academic Press, New York. pp. 193–275.

Bellairs, A. d'A., and J. D. Boyd. 1950. The lachrymal apparatus in lizards and snakes. II. The anterior part of the lachrymal duct and its relationship with the palate and with the nasal and vomeronasal organs. Proc. Zool. Soc. Lond. 120:269–310.

Bodian, D. 1936. A new method of staining nerve fibers and nerve endings in mounted paraffin sections. Anat. Rec. 65:89–97.

Bradley, R. M. 1971. Tongue Topography. *In* Handbook of Sensory Physiology. IV. Part 2. Chemical Senses and Taste. (L. M. Beidler, ed.) Springer-Verlag, New York.

Burns, B. 1969. Oral sensory papillae in sea snakes. Copeia 3:617–619.

Cox, W. H. 1891. Inpregnation des centralen Nervensystems mit Quecksilbersalzen. Archiv. fur mikros: Anat. 37:16–21.

Davenport, H. A., J. McArthur, and S. R. Bruesch. 1939. Staining paraffin sections with protargol. Stain Tech. 14:21–26.

Dowling, J. E., and B. B. Boycott. 1965. Neural connections of the retina: Fine structure of the inner plexiform layer. *In* Sensory Receptors. Cold Spring Harbor Symp. Quant. Biol. 30:393–402.

Hamilton, D. W. 1963. Posterior division of the eighth cranial nerve in *Lacerta vivapara.* Nature 200:705–706.

Hibbard, E., and J. LaVergne. 1972. Morphology at the retina of the sea-snake, *Pelamis platurus.* J. Anat. 112:125–136.

Kathariner, L. 1900. Die Nase der im Wasser Lebenden Schlangen als Luftweg und Geruchsorgan. Zool. Jb. Abt. Syst. 13:415–442.

Kreutzberg, G. W. 1969. Neuronal dynamics and axonal flow. IV. Blockage of intraaxonal transport by colchicine. Proc. Nat. Acad. Sci. U.S.A. 62:722–728.

Matthes, E. 1934. Geruchsorgan. *In* Handbuch der vergleichenden Anatomie der Wirbeltiere. Asher. Vol. II:879–948.

Miller, M. R. 1968. The cochlear duct of snakes. Proc. Calif. Acad. Sci. 35:425–475.

Moncrieff, R. W. 1967. The Chemical Senses. Leonard Hill, London.

Parsons, T. S. 1959a. Studies on the comparative embryology of the reptilian nose. Bull. Mus. Comp. Zool. Harvard 120:101–277.

Parsons, T. S. 1959b. Nasal anatomy and the phylogeny of reptiles. Evolution, Lancaster, Pennsylvania 13:175–187.

Parsons, T. S. 1970. The Nose and Jacobson's organ. *In* Biology of the Reptilia. Vol. 2. (C. Gans, ed.) Academic Press, New York pp. 91–191.

Rasmussen, G. L. 1961. A method of staining the statoacoustic nerve in bulk with Sudan Black B. Anat. Rec. 139:465–469.

Retzius, G. 1894. Die Riechzellen der Ophidier in der Reichschleimhaut und im Jacobson'shen Organ. Biol. Untersuchungen, n.s. 6:48–51.

Schmitt, F. O. 1969. Fibrous þroteins-neuronal organelles. Neurosci. Res. Symp. Summ. 3:566–575.

Schwartzkopff, J. 1968. Structure and function of the ear and of the auditory brain areas in birds. *In* Ciba Found. Symp. Hearing Mechanisms in Vertebrates. Little, Brown Co. Boston. pp. 41–63.

Spurr, A. R. 1969. A low-viscosity epoxy resin embedding medium for electron microscopy. J. Ultrastruct. Res. 26:31–43.

Tamar, H. 1972. Principles of Sensory Physiology. Charles C Thomas, Springfield.

Underwood, G. 1966. On the visual-cell pattern of a homalopsine snake. J. Anat. 100:571–575.

Walls, G. L. 1942. The vertebrate eye and its adaptive radiation. Bull. Cranbrook Inst. Sci., Bloomfield Hills.

Werblin, F. S., and J. E. Dowling. 1969. Organization of the retina of the mudpuppy, *Necturus maculosus.* II. Intracellular recording.

Wever, E. G. 1967. The tectorial membrane of the lizard ear: species variations. J. Morph. 123:355–372.

Williams, T. W. Jr. 1948. The visualization of vertebrate capillary beds by intravascular precipitation of lead chromate. Anat. Rec. 100:115–126.

Witkovsky, P. 1971. Synapses made by myelinated fibers running to teleost and elasmobranch retinas. J. Comp. Neurol. 142:205–222.

VENOMOUS NATURE
OF SEA SNAKES

eighteen

Sea Snake Venoms and Toxins

Nobuo Tamiya

The venomous nature of sea snakes is well known among fishermen of the Indo-Pacific area. Many fatal cases of bites by sea snakes caught in fishing nets or encountered unexpectedly have been reported (Reid and Lim, 1957; Reid, 1963; Barme, 1963, 1968; Halstead, 1970). In spite of the extreme potency of the venoms, most species are docile and not aggressive towards man (Barme, 1968; see Chapter 22). Their potent venom is used to paralyze prey fish in a very short time (Chapter 11) or to defend against predators.

Marsden and Reid (1961) reported that the principal signs of sea snake envenomation in man were myalgia and myoglobinuria. Myonecrosis was observed in dogs injected with *Enhydrina schistosa* venom. When one estimates the lethal activity of a sea snake venom or its toxic components in experimental animals, however, the main cause of death is the paralysis of skeletal muscles and resulting respiratory arrest.

Carey and Wright (1960) isolated a neurotoxic component in an immunochemically pure state from *E. schistosa* venom. Tamiya and Arai (1966) crystallized two neurotoxic components, erabutoxins a and b, from *Laticauda semifasciata* venom, which consisted of 62 amino acid residues with molecular weights of 7000. Karlsson, Eaker, and Porath (1966c) and Eaker and Porath (1967) showed that a neurotoxic component, toxin α, of the African cobra, *Naja nigricollis,* was also a basic protein consisting of 61 amino acid residues. The partial amino acid sequence of sea snake erabutoxin b presented by Tamiya and Sato (1966) was very similar to the sequence of cobra toxin α presented by Eaker and Porath (1966). Nearly 40 sea snake and cobra venom components have been isolated and sequenced since then.

LETHAL ACTIVITY OF SEA SNAKE VENOM

The venoms of *L. semifasciata, L. laticaudata, Aipysurus laevis, Astrotia stokesii, Hydrophis melanocephalus, H. elegans, H. ornatus,* and *Lapemis hardwickii* are clear, colorless, viscous solutions and give colorless residues on drying or freeze-drying (130–360 mg/ml, Tamiya and Puffer, 1974). Barme (1968) obtained light yellow flakes on drying the venom. Venom of the above species was ejected along the fang groove into a pipette or a micro-pipette placed over the fang when the snakes bit a piece of tygon tubing held in the mouth. The choice of pipettes depends on the amount of the venom. Reid (1956) obtained venoms by stimulating sea snakes to bite spoons covered with plastic sheets, and Barme (1968) by squeezing the venom gland contents into Pasteur pipettes placed on the fangs.

Sea snake venoms are more toxic than terrestrial snake venoms. The dose-lethality curves of the venoms of the above mentioned species are very steep; all the animals given half LD $_{100}$ survive (Tamiya et al., 1967). The fate of envenomated animals is usually decided in 3 hrs. The lethal dose values for sea snake venoms are summarized in Table 1. Data before 1956 are taken from Reid (1956), and more recent data from Barme (1963, 1968), Halstead (1970) and Tu and Tu (1970). Values vary according to the species of test animals and body weight. Larger animals have smaller values expressed as mg dry venom/kg body weight.

The amount of venom obtained varies with body size, species type and also between individuals (Reid, 1956; Barme, 1958; Tamiya and Puffer, 1974). Large species such as *A. stokesii, A. laevis,* and *H. ornatus* produce as much as 1.16, 0.25, and 0.08 ml of venom, respectively, on the first milking after capture (Table 2). With small species or small-headed species, milking is often difficult and the venom is collected by extracting the excised glands.

Not only the volume, but also the concentration and the lethal activity of the venom vary from one snake to another and from milking to milking (Table 2). This variation in activity is due to the content of neurotoxins.

ISOLATION OF SEA SNAKE TOXINS

Carey and Wright (1960) isolated the toxic component of a sea snake *E. schistosa* venom by CM-cellulose column chromatography at pH 6.6. The component gave a single immunoprecipitation band with the antivenin of the whole venom and accounted for 80–100% of the lethal activity of the whole venom. The venom of the same species was fractionated by Tu and Toom (1971) and Karlsson et al. (1972a). The latter authors obtained several toxic components, of which two have been characterized and sequenced (Fryklund et al., 1972) (Figure 1a, Tables 3 and 4, proteins 6 and 7).

Table 1. Lethal dose of venoms (dry weight)

Sea and terrestrial snakes	Method	Lethal dose (mg/kg)[a]		Reference
		Mouse	Other animals	
Sea Snakes				
Aipysurus laevis	LD$_{50}$ im	0.13		Tamiya and Puffer, 1974
Astrotia stokesii	LD$_{50}$ im	0.64[c]		Tamiya and Puffer, 1974
Enhydrina schistosa	MLD sc	0.1 −0.15		Reid, 1956
	LD$_{100}$ iv		Rabbit 0.026	Reid, 1956, Barme, 1963, 1958
	LD$_{50}$ iv	0.13		Carey and Wright, 1960
	LD$_{50}$ ip	0.04−0.13		Cheymol et al., 1967
	LD$_{50}$ iv	0.35		Tu and Toom, 1971
	LD$_{50}$ im	0.10		Tamiya and Puffer, 1974
Hydrophis melanocephalus[b]	LD$_{50}$ im	0.24		Tamiya and Puffer, 1974
		7×10^{-5} ml/kg[d]	Pigeon 0.5	Reid, 1956
H. cyanocinctus	MLD sc	0.35	Rabbit 0.085	Barme, 1963, 1958
	LD$_{100}$ iv	0.24		Carey and Wright, 1960
	LD$_{50}$ ip	0.67		Cheymol et al., 1967
	LD$_{50}$ iv	0.35−0.70		Tu and Tu, 1970
H. elegans	LD$_{50}$ im	0.12		Tamiya and Puffer 1974
H. fasciatus	LD$_{100}$ iv	0.18		Barme, 1963
H. klossi	LD$_{50}$ ip	0.2 −0.53		Carey and Wright, 1960
H. melanosoma	LD$_{50}$ ip	0.4		Carey and Wright, 1960
H. ornatus	LD$_{50}$ im	0.16		Tamiya and Puffer, 1974
H. spiralis	LD$_{50}$ ip	0.25		Carey and Wright, 1960
Kerilia jerdoni	LD$_{50}$ ip	0.53		Carey and Wright, 1960
Kolpophis annandalei	LD$_{100}$ iv	0.55		Barme, 1963, 1958
Lapemis curtus	MLD sc		Rat 0.6	Reid, 1956
L. hardwickii	LD$_{50}$ ip	0.26−0.29	Rabbit 0.04	Carey and Wright, 1960
	LD$_{100}$ iv	0.2		Barme, 1963, 1958
	LD$_{50}$ iv	0.44		Cheymol et al., 1967
	LD$_{50}$ iv	1.4		Tu and Hong, 1971
Laticauda colubrina	MLD sc	0.25		Reid, 1956

Continued

Table 1. *cont.*

Sea and terrestrial snakes	Method	Lethal dose (mg/kg)[a]		Reference
		Mouse	Other animals	
L. laticaudata	LD$_{50}$	iv	0.42		Tu et al., 1962
	LD$_{50}$	iv	0.18		Tu, 1963
	LD$_{50}$	im	0.3		Arai et al., 1964
L. semifasciata	LD$_{50}$	sc	0.34		Tu, 1959
	LD$_{50}$	im	0.5		Arai et al., 1964
	LD$_{50}$	iv	0.28		Tu et al., 1971
Hydrophis cantoris	MLD	sc		Pigeon 0.5	Reid, 1956
H. gracilis	LD$_{100}$	iv	0.13		Barme, 1963
Pelamis platurus	MLD	sc		Pigeon 0.75	Reid, 1956
	LD$_{100}$	iv	0.5		Barme, 1963
	LD$_{50}$	iv	0.09–0.11		Pickwell, 1974
Praescutata viperina	MLD	sc		Pigeon 0.5	Reid, 1956
Thalassophina viperina	LD$_{100}$	iv	0.35		Barme, 1963
Terrestrial snakes					
Crotalidae					
Trimeresurus flavoviridis	LD$_{50}$	sc	6		
Viperidae					
Vipera russelli	LD$_{50}$	iv	6.2		
Elapidae					
Naja haje	LD$_{50}$	sc	4.0		
Naja naja	LD$_{50}$	iv	0.4		

[a]LD$_{50}$, 50% lethal dose; LD$_{100}$, 100% lethal dose; MLD, minimal lethal dose; sc, subcutaneous injection; im, intramuscular injection; iv, intravenous injection; ip, intraperitoneal injection.

[b]This is the species previously called *H. belcheri* (Tamiya and Puffer, 1974). Its status is currently under review by H. G. Cogger.

[c]Extinction at 280 nm in 1 cm cell, approximately equal to mg.

		Venom volume/head				Venom concentration		LD$_{50}$/g (Mouse)				
								Whole venom				After dialysis
								Intramuscular			Intravenous	Intramuscular
Species	Site of Capture	Body weight (g)	Average (ml)	First milking (ml)	Repeated milking (ml)	A$_{280}$/ml	Dry weight (mg/ml)	A$_{280}$ × 10^{-3}	Dry weight (μg)	ml × 10^{-6}	ml × 10^{-6}	(ml × 10^{-6})
Aipysurus laevis	Ashmore Reef Scott Reef Cartier Island Hibbernia Reef	200–840	0.05	0.06–0.25	0.01–0.08	180 146ᶜ	132ᶜ	0.09 0.14ᶜ	0.13ᶜ	0.50 0.95ᶜ	0.30	0.50
Astrotia stokesii	Ashmore Reef Darwin	2100–3050	0.41	0.26–1.16	0.30–0.58	182		0.64		3.5		
Hydrophis elegans	McCluer Gulf	330	0.02		0.005–0.04	370ᶜ 481ᶜ	277ᶜ 360ᶜ	0.16ᶜ 0.16ᶜ	0.12ᶜ 0.12ᶜ	0.30 0.43ᶜ 0.33ᶜ	0.40	0.75
*Hydrophis melanocephalus*ᵇ	Ashmore Reef	360–520	0.01		0.003–0.02	240ᶜ	244ᶜ	0.24ᶜ	0.24ᶜ	0.07 1.0ᶜ		0.07
Hydrophis ornatus	McCluer Gulf	700	0.05	0.08	0.02–0.08	262 103 314ᶜ	166ᶜ	0.09 0.13 0.30ᶜ		0.35 1.12 0.95ᶜ		0.85
Lapemis hardwickii	McCluer Gulf Ashmore Reef	460–870	0.03	0.07	0.004–0.04	206 244		0.31 0.24		1.5 1.0		

ᵃUnless otherwise indicated, the values were obtained on fresh venoms on the research vessel and give absorption and volume only. It was impossible to weigh small amounts on the floating vessel.

ᵇPreviously referred to as *H. belcheri*. Taxonomic status still under review.

ᶜThe values obtained on freeze-dried venom after three months.

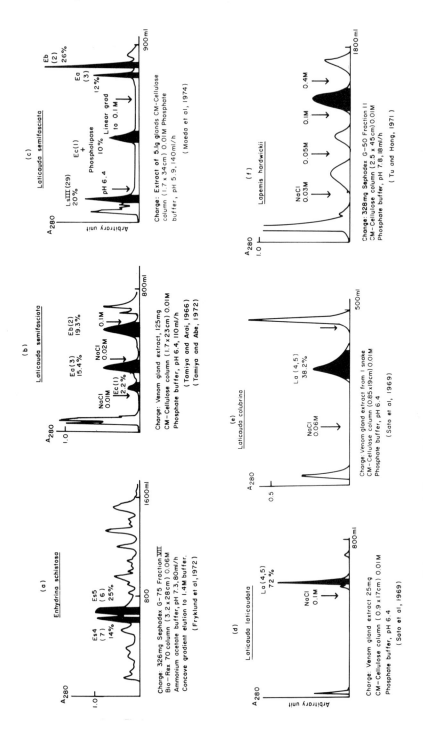

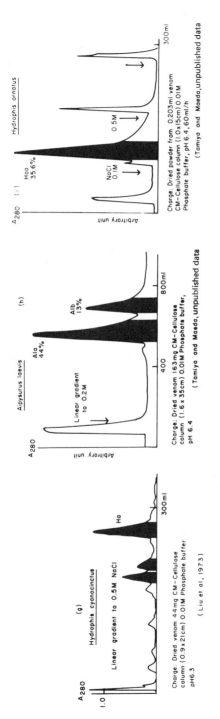

Figure 1.   Separation of the components of sea snake venom by column chromatography.

Table 3. Amino acid composition and lethal dose of Hydrophiidae and Elapidae venom components

Protein number	Hydrophiidae and Elapidae species and venom components	W	K	H	R	D	N	T	S	E	Q	P	G	A	C
1.	*Laticauda semifasciata* Erabutoxin c	1	3	2	3	1	4	5	8	4	4	4	5	0	8
2.	*Laticauda semifasciata* Erabutoxin b	1	4	2	3	1	3	5	8	4	4	4	5	0	8
3.	*Laticauda semifasciata* Erabutoxin a	1	4	1	3	1	4	5	8	4	4	4	5	0	8
4.	*Laticauda laticaudata* Laticotoxin a	1	4	2	5	2	6	5	5	3	6	4	5	0	8
5.	*Laticauda laticaudata* Laticotoxin a'	1	4	2	5	3	6	4	6	2	5	5	5	0	8
6.	Enhydrina schistosa 5	1	5	2	3	1	5	7	6	4	4	2	4	1	9
7.	Enhydrina schistosa 4	1	5	2	3	1	5	7	5	4	4	3	4	1	9
8.	Dendroaspis polylepis α	1	6	3	5	2	3	5	4	3	2	2	5	1	8
9.	Naja nivea β	1	7	2	6	2	3	5	3	2	3	3	6	0	8
10.	Naja nivea δ, Naja haje α	1	6	2	4	2	5	7	4	3	4	4	5	0	8
11.	Naja melanoleuca d	1	6	2	3	2	5	7	4	3	4	4	5	0	8
12.	*Naja nigricollis* Toxin α	1	6	2	3	2	5	8	2	3	3	5	5	0	8
13.	Hemachatus haemachatus II	1	4	2	5	3	6	7	3	2	3	5	5	0	8
14.	Hemachatus haemachatus IV	1	6	2	4	2	3	9	4	3	5	4	5	0	8
15.	*Naja naja atra* Cobrotoxin	1	3	2	6	2	6	8	4	4	3	2	7	0	8
16.	*Bungarus multicinctus* αBungarotoxin	1	6	1	3	2	2	7	6	4	1	8	4	5	10
17.	Dendroaspis polylepis γ	2	9	0	4	5	2	6	4	3	3	4	5	4	10
18.	Dendroaspis polylepis δ	2	10	0	3	3	4	6	4	3	2	4	5	4	10
19.	Ophiophagus hannah A	3	6	0	4	4	3	9	3	3	1	7	4	4	10
20.	Ophiophagus hannah B	2	8	1	3	5	4	9	4	1	1	6	5	3	10
21.	*Naja nivea* Toxin α	1	6	1	6	5	4	5	3	0	1	6	5	3	10
22.	Naja melanoleuca b	1	4	1	5	5	5	8	3	0	1	6	4	4	10
23.	Naja naja siamensis 3	1	5	1	5	6	3	9	3	0	1	6	4	3	10
24.	Naja naja naja 4	1	4	1	6	6	3	9	4	0	1	6	5	2	10
25.	Naja naja naja 3	1	4	1	6	6	3	9	3	0	1	6	5	2	10
26.	*Naja naja* Toxin A	1	4	1	6	8	1	9	3	0	1	6	5	2	10
27.	*Naja naja* Toxin B	1	4	1	6	8	1	9	4	0	1	6	5	2	10
28.	*Naja naja* Toxin C	1	5	1	5	8	1	9	3	0	1	6	4	3	10
29.	Laticauda semifasciata III	2	4	1	2	2	4	6	6	4	2	4	4	4	10
30.	*Naja naja atra* Cardiotoxin	0	9	0	2	2	4	3	2	0	0	5	2	2	8
31.	*Naja naja* Cytotoxin II	0	9	0	2	2	4	3	2	0	0	5	2	2	8
32.	*Naja naja* Cytotoxin I	0	9	0	2	2	6	3	2	1	0	4	2	2	8
33.	Naja nigricollis 14 Cardiotoxin	1	9	0	2	2	4	3	2	0	1	6	2	2	8
34.	*Naja naja* (Cambodia) Cardiotoxin	0	8	0	2	3	5	3	3	0	0	4	2	2	8
35.	Hemachatus haemachatus DLF (12B)	0	12	1	1	2	4	3	3	1	0	5	2	1	8
36.	*Naja haje* Cardiotoxin	1	9	1	1	2	3	4	4	1	0	5	2	1	8
37.	*Naja melanoleuca* Cardiotoxin	0	7	1	2	2	4	3	4	1	1	4	2	2	8
38.	Dendroaspis angusticeps F$_{VII}$	0	4	2	5	3	4	6	5	2	0	5	5	1	8
39.	*Lapemis hardwickii*	1	5	2	3		6	8	6		8	3	4	1	8
40.	*Hydrophis cyanocinctus* Hydrophitoxin	1	6	2	3		6	7	5		8	2	4	1	8

V	M	I	L	Y	F	Net positive charge[b]	Total amino acid	LD(mg/kg) and method, for mouse[c]	Reference
2	0	4	1	1	2	2	62	LD$_{50}$ im 0.13	1. Tamiya and Abe, 1972
2	0	4	1	1	2	3	62	LD$_{50}$ im 0.15	2. Tamiya and Arai, 1966
2	0	4	1	1	2	2.5	62	LD$_{50}$ im 0.15	3. Tamiya and Arai, 1966
1	0	2	1	1	1	5	62	LD$_{50}$ im 0.13	4. Sato et al., 1969
1	0	2	1	1	1	5	62	LD$_{50}$ im 0.13	5. Sato et al., 1969
1	1	2	1	1	0	4	60	LD$_{100}$ iv 0.08	6. Karlsson et al., 1972a
1	1	2	1	1	0	4	60	LD$_{100}$ iv 0.08	7. Karlsson et al., 1972a
2	0	4	0	4	0	7.5	60	LD$_{50}$ sc 0.09	8. Strydom, 1972b
2	1	5	0	2	0	10	61	LD$_{50}$ iv 0.085	9. Botes and Strydom, 1969; Botes et al. 1971
1	0	3	1	1	0	6	61	LD$_{50}$ iv 0.09	10. Botes et al., 1971
2	1	3	0	1	0	5	61		11. Botes, 1972
2	0	3	2	1	0	5	61	LD$_{100}$ iv 0.09	12. Karlsson et al., 1966
1	0	3	2	1	0	5	61	LD$_{50}$ iv 0.11	13. Strydom and Botes, 1971
1	0	1	2	1	0	6	61	LD$_{50}$ iv 0.09	14. Strydom and Botes, 1971
1	0	2	1	2	0	4	62	LD$_{50}$ ip 0.065	15. Yang, 1965
5	1	2	2	2	2	3.5	74	LD$_{50}$ ip 0.15	16. Mebs et al., 1971, 1972
3	0	3	1	1	3	5	72	LD$_{50}$ sc 0.12	17. Strydom, 1972b
3	0	4	1	1	3	7	72		18. Strydom, pers. comm.
5	0	3	1	2	1	3	73	LD$_{50}$ sc 0.30	19. Joubert, 1973
3	0	3	1	2	2	5.5	73	LD$_{50}$ sc 0.35	20. Joubert, 1973
5	2	3	1	1	3	7.5	73	LD$_{50}$ iv 0.081	21. Botes, 1971
5	0	4	1	1	3	4.5	71		22. Botes, 1972
4	0	5	1	1	3	4.5	71	LD$_{100}$ iv 0.10	23. Karlsson et al., 1971
4	0	4	1	1	3	4.5	71	LD$_{100}$ iv 0.10	24. Karlsson et al., 1971
4	0	5	1	1	3	4.5	71	LD$_{100}$ iv 0.10	25. Karlsson et al., 1971
4	0	5	1	1	3	2.5	71	LD$_{50}$ ip 0.15	26. Nakai et al., 1971
4	0	4	1	1	3	2.5	71	LD$_{50}$ ip 0.15	27. Hayashi, pers. comm.
4	0	5	1	1	3	2.5	71	LD$_{50}$ ip 0.15	28. Hayashi, pers. comm.
3	0	2	2	3	1	0.5	66	LD$_{50}$ im 1.24	29. Maeda et al., 1974
7	2	1	6	3	2	9	60		30. Narita and Lee, 1970
7	2	1	6	4	1	9	60	LD$_{50}$ ip 3	31. Hayashi, pers. comm.
5	2	2	6	4	0	8	60	LD$_{50}$ ip 3	32. Hayashi, pers. comm.
3	4	3	5	2	1	9	60		33. Botes, pers. comm.
4	3	4	6	2	1	7	61		34. Botes, pers. comm.
4	3	2	7	1	1	10.5	60		35. Fryklund and Eaker, 1973
8	2	1	4	2	1	7.5	60		36. Botes, pers. comm.
6	2	3	5	3	0	6.5	60		37. Botes, pers. comm.
2	2	1	3	3	0	5	61		38. Viljoen and Botes, 1973
1	1	2	1	1	0		61	LD$_{50}$ iv 0.06	39. Tu and Hong, 1971
1	1	2	1	1	0		59		40. Liu et al., 1973

[a]W, tryptophan; K, lysine; H, histidine; R, arginine; D, aspartic acid; N, asparagine; T, threonine; S, serine; E, glutamic acid; Q, glutamine; P, proline; G, glycine; A, alanine; C, half cystine; V, valine; M, methionine; I, isoleucine; L, leucine; Y, tyrosine; F, phenylalanine.
[b]The positive charge of histidine is counted to be 0.5.
[c]For explanation of abbreviations, see Table 1.

Table 4. Amino acid sequences of Hydrophiidae and Elapidae venom components[a]

Protein number	Species and fraction	Amino acid sequences[b]
1.	*Laticauda semifasciata* Erabutoxin c	R I C F N Q H S S Q P Q T T K T C P S G E S S C Y H K Q W S D F R C S S
2.	*Laticauda semifasciata* Erabutoxin b	R I C F N Q H S S Q P Q T T K T C P S G E S S C Y H K Q W S D F R C S Q
3.	*Laticauda semifasciata* Erabutoxin a	R I C F N Q H S S Q P Q T T K T C P S G E S S C Y N K Q W S D F R C S S
4.	*Laticauda laticaudata* Laticotoxin a	R R C F N H P S S Q P Q T N K S C P P G E N S C Y N K Q W R D H R C S T
5.	*Laticauda laticaudata* Laticotoxin a'	R R C F N H P S S Q P Q T N K S C P P G E N S C Y N K Q W R D H R C G M
6.	*Enhydrina schistosa* 5	M T C C N Q Q S S Q P K T T T N C A E S S C Y K K T W S D H R C A S
7.	*Enhydrina schistosa* 4	M T C C N Q Q S S Q P K T T T N C A E S S C Y K K T W S D H R C S I
8.	*Dendroaspis polylepis* α	M I C Y N H Q S T T R A T T K S C E E N S C Y K K Y W R D H R C S I
9.	*Naja nivea* Toxin β	L Q C H N Q Q S S Q P P T T K T C P G E T N C Y K K R W R D H R C S I
10.	*Naja nivea* Toxin δ, *Naja haje* Toxin α	M E C H N Q Q S S Q P P T T K T C P G E T N C Y K K R W R D H R C S I
11.	*Naja melanoleuca* d	L E C H N Q Q S S Q P P T T K T C P G E T N C Y K K V W R D H R C S I
12.	*Naja nigricollis* Toxin α	L E C H N Q Q S S Q P P T T T C P G D T N C Y K K R W R D H R C S I
13.	*Hemachatus haemachatus* II	L E C H N Q Q S S Q P T T T Q T C P G G E T N C Y K K Q W S D H R C S I
14.	*Hemachatus haemachatus* IV	I V C H N Q Q S S Q P T T T G C S G E T N C Y R K W R W C D A F C S S
15.	*Naja naja atra* Cobrotoxin	T T A I T I P S S A V T L G C P P G E N L C Y R K M W C D A W C S S Q
16.	*Bungarus multicinctus* α Bungarotoxin	R T C I K T F S D Q S K I C P P G E N I C Y T K T W C D A W C S S R
17.	*Dendroaspis polylepis* γ	N K T T F S D Q S K I C P P A G E N I C Y T E T W C D A W C S S R
18.	*Dendroaspis polylepis* δ	T K C Y V T I P D V K S Q T C P A G E N I C Y T K T W C D G F C G R
19.	*Ophiophagus hannah* A	I R C F V T I P D A T S Q T C P D G E N I C Y T K T W C D G F C G R
20.	*Ophiophagus hannah* B	I R C F L T I P D V T S Q I C A D G H V C Y T K T W C D N F C A S
21.	*Naja nivea* Toxin α	I R C F L T I P D V T T S Q D C P N G H V C Y T K T W C D G F C S I
22.	*Naja melanoleuca* b	I R C F L T I P D I T T S K D C P N G H V C Y T K T W C D G F C S I
23.	*Naja naja siamensis* 3	I R C F I T P D I T S K D C P N G H V C Y T K T W C D G F C S I
24.	*Naja naja* 4	I R C F I T P D I T S K D C P N G H V C Y T K T W C D G F C S I
25.	*Naja naja naja* 3	I R C F I T P D I T S K D C P N G H V C Y T K T W C D G F C S I
26.	*Naja naja* Toxin A	I R C F I T P D I T S K D C P N G H V C Y T K T W C D G F C S I
27.	*Naja naja* Toxin B	I R C F I T P D I T S K D C P N G H V C Y T K T W C D G F C S I
28.	*Naja naja* Toxin C	I R C F I T P D I T S K D C P N G H V C Y T K T W C D A F C S I
29.	*Laticauda semifasciata* III	R E C Y L N P H D T Q T C P S G Q E I C Y V K S W C N A W C S S
30.	*Naja naja atra* Cardiotoxin	L K C K L V P L F Y K T C P A G K N L C Y K M F M V A T T
31.	*Naja naja* Cytotoxin II	L K C K L V P L F Y K T C P A G K N L C Y K M Y M V A T
32.	*Naja naja* Cytotoxin I	L K C K L I P L A Y K T C P A G K N L C Y K M Y M V S N
33.	*Naja nigricollis* 14 Cardiotoxin	L K C K Q L I P P F W K T C P A G K N L C Y K M T M R A A
34.	*Naja naja* (Cambodia) Cardiotoxin	L K C K L I P I A S K T C P A G K N L C Y K M F M M S D
35.	*Hemachatus haemachatus* DLF (12B)	L K C K L V P F L S K T C P E G K N L C Y K M F M V S M
36.	*Naja haje* Cardiotoxin	L K C H L V P P V W K T C P E G K N L C Y Q M Y M V S T
37.	*Naja melanoleuca* Cardiotoxin	L E C H K L V P I A H K T C N G E N S C Y R K S R R H P K
38.	*Dendroaspis angusticeps* Fv II	T M C Y S H T T T S R A I L T N G E

#	Total	References
1	62	Tamiya and Abe, 1972
2	62	Sato and Tamiya, 1971
3	62	Sato and Tamiya, 1971
4	62	Sato and Tamiya, unpublished
5	62	Sato and Tamiya, unpublished
6	60	Fryklund et al., 1972
7	60	Fryklund et al., 1972
8	61	Strydom, 1972b
9	61	Botes, 1971
10	61	Botes et al., 1971, 1969
11	61	Botes, 1972
12	61	Eaker and Porath, 1967
13	61	Strydom and Botes, 1971
14	61	Strydom and Botes, 1971
15	62	Yang et al., 1969
16	74	Mebs et al., 1971; 1972
17	72	Strydom, 1972b
18	72	Strydom, pers. comm.
19	73	Joubert, 1973
20	73	Joubert, 1973
21	73	Botes, 1971
22	71	Botes, 1972
23	71	Karlsson, pers. comm.
24	71	Karlsson, pers. comm.
25	71	Karlsson, pers. comm.
26	71	Nakai et al., 1971
27	71	Hayashi, pers. comm.
28	71	Hayashi, pers. comm.
29	66	Maeda and Tamiya, 1974
30	60	Narita and Lee, 1970
31	60	Takechi et al., 1972
32	60	Hayashi et al., 1971
33	60	Botes, pers. comm.
34	60	Botes, pers. comm.
35	61	Fryklund and Eaker, 1973
36	60	Botes, pers. comm.
37	60	Botes, pers. comm.
38	61	Viljoen and Botes, 1973

(Sequence alignment columns are headed by residue positions 40, 45, 50, 55, 60, 65, 70, 75.)

aFrom Maeda and Tamiya (1974).

b1–29, neurotoxins; 30–38, cardiotoxins and other toxins; 1–7, 29, Hydrophiidae; 8–28, 30–38, Elapidae. For explanation of letter abbreviations, see Table 3.

Amino acid residues surrounded by solid lines: Invariant residues among neurotoxins or neuro- and cardiotoxins.

Amino acid residues surrounded by broken lines: Residues with similar properties and common to neurotoxins.

Tamiya and Arai (1966) isolated two neurotoxic proteins, erabutoxins a and b, from *L. semifasciata* venom gland extract in crystalline forms by CM-cellulose column chromatography at pH 6.4 (Figure 1b; Figure 2a,b). The two toxins accounted for 95% of the toxicity of the whole venom. The structures of erabutoxins a and b were elucidated by Sato and Tamiya (1971) and Endo et al. (1971) (Tables 3 and 4, proteins 2 and 3). Tamiya and Abe (1972) and Maeda et al. (1974) isolated two more neurotoxins, namely erabutoxin c and L. semifasciata III, respectively, from the same venom (Figure 1b and c, Figure 2c), and elucidated the sequences (Tamiya and Abe, 1972; Maeda and Tamiya, 1974; proteins 1 and 29, Tables 3 and 4). Erabutoxins a and b were probably obtained from the venom of the same species by Uwatoko et al. (1966), Tu et al. (1971), and Kao et al. (1973). The amino acid compositions of the toxins given by Tu et al. (1971) are a little different from those of erabutoxins a and b, while those given by Kao et al. (1973) were the same.

Sato et al. (1969) crystallized neurotoxic proteins from *L. laticaudata* and *L. colubrina* venom gland extracts (Figure 1d and e, Figure 2d and e). The neurotoxins from the two species had the same amino acid composition and the same disc-electrophoretic mobility. The neurotoxin from *L. laticaudata*, named laticotoxin a, was sequenced (Sato and Tamiya, unpublished data) and proved to be a mixture of at least two very similar proteins, each having 62 amino acid residues (Tables 3 and 4, proteins 4 and 5).

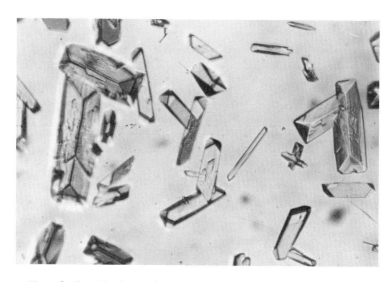

Figure 2. Crystals of sea snake neurotoxins. Figure 2a, Erabutoxin a. ✕ 350.

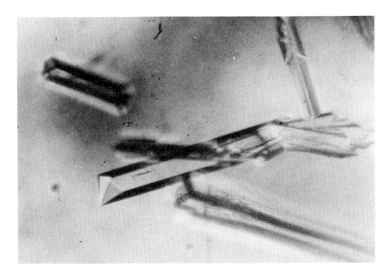

Figure 2b. Erabutoxin b. X 350.

Tu and Hong (1971) fractionated *L. hardwickii* venom gland extract by repeated gel- and CM-cellulose column chromatography and one of the neurotoxic components was crystallized and analyzed for the amino acid composition (Figure 1f, Table 3, protein 39). Liu et al. (1973) chromatographed *Hydrophis cyanocinctus* venom on a CM-cellulose column and ob-

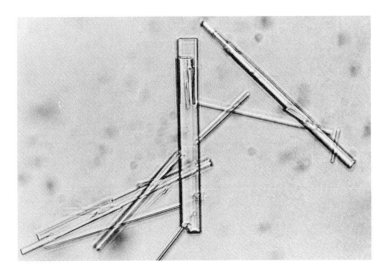

Figure 2c. Erabutoxin c. X 350.

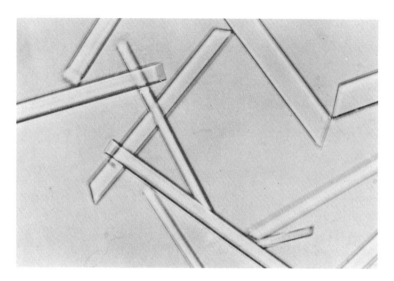

Figure 2d. Laticotoxin a (from *L. laticaudata*). × 1022.

tained three toxic components, one of which was further purified and analyzed for amino acid composition (Figure 1g, Table 3, protein 40). Two neurotoxic components were obtained from *A. laevis* venom, one of which, namely *Aipysurus* a, was crystallized (Figure 1h; Figure 2f). These two toxins accounted for all the toxicity of the original venom (Tamiya and Maeda,

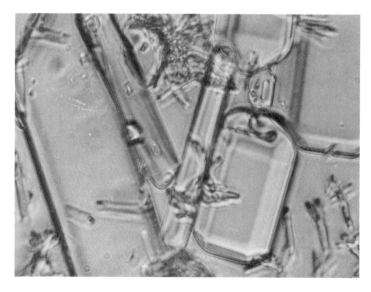

Figure 2e. Laticotoxin a (from *L. colubrina*). × 710.

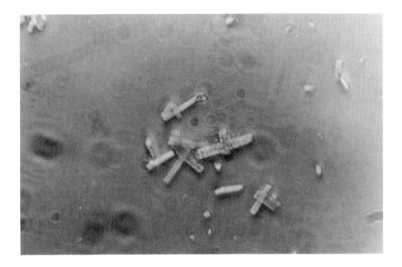

Figure 2f. *Aipysurus laevis* toxin a. × 710.

unpublished). A similar neurotoxic component was obtained also from *H. ornatus* venom (Tamiya and Maeda, unpublished data; Figure 1i). Shepman and Pickwell (1973) chromatographed *Pelamis platurus* venom on a Sephadex G-75-40 column and showed that the main toxic component had a molecular weight of 6000; this value is close to those of other neurotoxins.

All the neurotoxic components of sea snake venoms obtained so far are basic proteins (with a single exception, Laticauda semifasciata III, Tables 3 and 4, protein 29) of low molecular weight. They can be separated from the other components and from each other by column chromatography on carboxyl type ion-exchangers.

STRUCTURE OF SEA SNAKE NEUROTOXINS

The amino acid sequences of the sea snake neurotoxins elucidated so far are very closely related to those of cobra neuro- and cardiotoxins. Amino acid compositions and sequences of the toxins are summarized in Tables 3 and 4. The numbers used for individual proteins and residues in Tables 3 and 4 are referred to in the following discussion. A superimposed structure of sea snake and cobra neurotoxins (proteins 1 to 28) is shown in Figure 3. The common features among the proteins are as follows:

First, all the proteins (except one, protein 29) are basic and of low molecular weight.

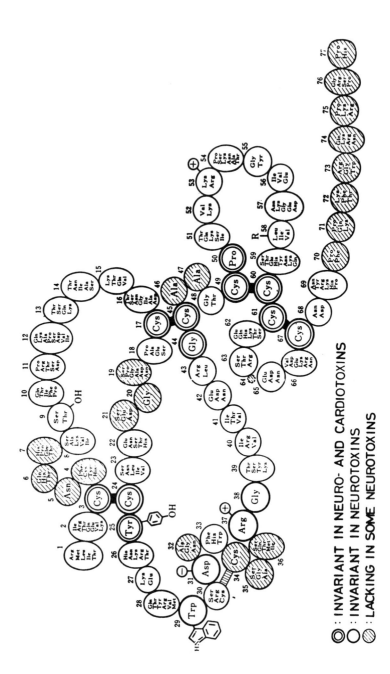

Figure 3.   Superimposed structure of snake neurotoxins (Table 4, proteins 1–28).

Second, the proteins can be classified into three groups namely short-chain toxins with 60–62 amino acid residues and four disulfide bridges (proteins 1 to 15 and 30 to 38), long-chain toxins with 71–74 amino acid residues and five disulfide bridges (proteins 16–28) (Strydom, 1973), and a medium length chain toxin with 66 amino acid residues and five disulfide bridges (Maeda and Tamiya, 1974). No long toxins have been found so far in sea snake venoms.

Third, all the proteins (1 to 38) have identical residues at 11 positions, which are indicated by double circles in Figure 3. Eight positions out of the 11 are occupied by half cystine residues, which form disulfide bridges between the residues 3 and 24, 17 and 45, 49 and 60, and 61 and 67 (protein 15, Yang et al., 1970; protein 3, Endo et al., 1971; protein 21, Botes, 1971; protein 31, Takechi and Hayashi, 1972; protein 27, Ohta and Hayashi, 1973). Other three identical residues are 25-tyrosine, 44-glycine and 50-proline. Rýden et al. (1973) called these identical residues "structurally invariant residues." Two additional half cystine residues, found in common to all the long chain and medium length chain toxins (proteins 16 to 29) at positions 30 and 34, form an additional disulfide bridge (Botes, 1971; Maeda and Tamiya, 1974; Ohta and Hayashi, 1973). The terminal amino and carboxyl groups are not considered to be structurally invariant due to the modification experiments (see below).

The last feature common to the proteins is that all the neurotoxins (proteins 1 to 28) have four more identical residues, namely, 29-tryptophan, 31-aspartic acid, 37-arginine, and 38-glycine. These are indicated by single circles in Figure 3. Rýden et al. (1973) called these residues "functionally invariant residues." There are three more similar groups in all the neurotoxins, namely, a hydroxyl group at residue 9, a plus charge at residue 53, and a large alkyl group at residue 58, which are also indicated in Figure 3. All these seven functionally invariant residues and groups are missing in the proteins 30–38, which are not neurotoxic.

It is of interest to compare the sequences of these proteins and deduce the structure-toxicity and phylogenetic relationships. Protein 29 (L. semifasciata III) is an exception in chain length, and in that it shares four out of seven "functionally invariant residues and groups" with the neurotoxins. It is a weak and easily reversible neurotoxin and not a cardiotoxin (Maeda et al., 1974). The smaller toxicity and the smaller affinity to the receptor site of the protein may be due to its incomplete structure as a neurotoxin (Maeda and Tamiya, 1974). Dayhoff (1972) and Strydom (1972a, 1973) proposed phylogenetic trees by computor analysis of these sequences. Strydom (1973) concluded from the analysis of the sequences of 15 neurotoxins (proteins 2, 3, 8–17, 21, 22, and 26) and a cardiotoxin (protein 30) that the possible ancestor sequence has the same amino acids as the cardiotoxin (30) at 30 positions, namely, at 1, 3, 5, 8, 11, 15–18, 20, 22 to 25, 27, 41, 43, to 45, 49 to 51, 57, 60, 61, 63, and 65–68.

Secondary or tertiary structure of the neurotoxins has been studied by optical rotatory dispersion (ORD) and circular dichromism (CD) of the toxins. Erabutoxin b (protein 2) gives very special ORD and CD curves, which are different from those of ordinary proteins (Sato et al., 1972) and very similar to those of cobrotoxin (protein 15; Yang et al., 1968) and α-bungarotoxin (protein 16; Hamaguchi et al., 1968). Rýden et al. (1973) constructed a model of the *Naja nigricollis* α toxin molecule (protein 12), based mainly on information gained from chemical modification of the toxins. X-ray crystallographic studies are in progress on erabutoxins (proteins 1–3; Low et al., 1971), laticotoxins (proteins 4 and 5; Searl et al., 1973), and cobrotoxin (Wong et al., 1972).

CHEMICAL MODIFICATION OF NEUROTOXINS

Chemical modification studies provide another approach to the structure-function relationships.

Modification of "Structurally Invariant" Residues

The disulfide bridges are essential for toxicity. The toxicity recovers on the reoxidation of inactive reduced cobrotoxin (protein 15, Yang, 1967).

The terminal amino group can be acetylated (*Naja naja siamensis* 3, protein 23, Karlsson et al., 1972b; erabutoxin b, protein 2, Hori and Tamiya, unpublished data), guanidinated (erabutoxin b, protein 2, Hori and Tamiya, unpublished data), carbamylated (*Naja naja siamensis* 3, protein 23, and *Naja naja naja* 3, protein 25: Karlsson et al., 1972b) and trinitrophenylated (cobrotoxin, protein 15: Chang et al., 1971b) while retaining toxicity.

The invariant 25-tyrosine is buried. It is titrated only at pH's above 11.3 (cobrotoxin, protein 15; Chang et al., 1971a; *Naja haje* toxin α, protein 10; Chicheportiche et al., 1972) and not readily nitrated (cobrotoxin, protein 15; Chang et al., 1971a) or iodinated (erabutoxin b, protein 2; Sato and Tamiya, 1970; cobrotoxin, protein 15; Yang et al., 1968). The toxins are inactivated on the nitration of 25-tyrosine (cobrotoxin, protein 15; Chang et al., 1971a; *Naja haje* toxin α, protein 10; Chicheportiche et al., 1972) with concomitant conformational change. Huang et al. (1973) succeeded in iodinating the tyrosine of cobrotoxin (protein 15) with retention of toxicity.

The amidation of the terminal carboxyl group of cobrotoxin (protein 15) does not affect the toxicity (Chang et al., 1971b).

Modification of "Functionally Invariant" Residues

29-Tryptophan seems to be exposed to the surface of the toxin molecule (erabutoxin b, protein 2; Seto et al., 1970; *Naja haje* toxin α, protein 10,

Chicheportiche et al., 1972) and can easily be modified by various reagents (cobrotoxin, protein 15; Chang and Hayashi, 1969, Chang and Yang, 1973; erabutoxins, proteins 2 and 3; Seto et al., 1970, Tu et al., 1971; *Naja haje* toxin α, protein 10; Chicheportiche, 1972; *Lapemis hardwickii* toxin, Table 3, protein 39, sequence not known; Tu and Hong, 1971; *Naja naja siamensis* 3, protein 23, Karlsson and Eaker, 1972). The modified toxins have no lethal activity, although they retain the immunological activity (erabutoxins, proteins 2 and 3; Sato et al., 1970; Tu et al., 1971; Sato et al., 1972; cobrotoxin, protein 15; Chang and Yang, 1973). The tryptophan is functionally invariant.

30-Aspartic acid can be amidated without loss of activity (cobrotoxin, protein 15; Chang et al., 1971b).

Modification of Other Residues

The lysine residues at positions 15 (*Naja naja naja* 3, protein 25), 27 (cobrotoxin, protein 15, *Naja naja siamensis* 3, protein 23, and *Naja naja naja* 3, protein 25), 39 (proteins 23 and 25), 53 (protein 23), and 74 (proteins 23 and 25) can be modified without loss of activity (Karlsson et al., 1972b; Chang et al., 1971b). The inactivation of cobrotoxin on trinitrophenylation of 53-lysine may be due to some other effects (Chang et al., 1971b).

The carboxyl groups at positions 2, 31, 42, 57, and 65 of cobrotoxin (protein 15) can be amidated by glycine methyl ester, retaining the activity (Chang et al., 1971b).

26-Histidine of erabutoxin b (protein 2) can be iodinated (Sato and Tamiya, 1970), and 39-tyrosine of cobrotoxin (protein 15) can be iodinated or nitrated (Chang et al., 1971a), both without loss of the activity.

Chang et al. (1971b) observed the inactivation of cobrotoxin (protein 15) on modification of 21-glutamic acid in the presence of 5M guanidine hydrochloride. The inactivation may be due to conformational change. All the carboxyl groups are amidated in this preparation.

MECHANISM OF ACTION OF SEA SNAKE TOXINS

The action of dried venom of *E. schistosa, H. cyanocinctus,* and *Hydrophis cantoris* was described by Rogers as early as 1903–1904. Fraser and Elliot also described the action of the dried venom of *E. schistosa* and *Lapemis curtus* in 1904–1905. They concluded that the primary action of these snake venoms was on the respiratory center and on the motor endplates. Tu (1959) reported that the venom of *L. semifasciata* and *L. laticaudata* produced marked inhibition of respiration. Carey and Wright (1961) showed that *E. schistosa* venom blocked neuromuscular transmission. The detailed mechanism of neuromuscular blocking by venom from *E. schistosa, H. cyanocinctus, L. hardwickii,* and *L. semifasciata* was described by Cheymol et al. (1967,

1972). They concluded that the venoms irreversibly block nicotinic acetyl-choline receptors of the postsynaptic membrane.

The postsynaptic action of the isolated sea snake toxin preparations was described on erabutoxins a, b, and c (Tamiya and Arai, 1966; Sato et al., 1970; Tamiya and Abe, 1972; Cheymol et al., 1972; Takamizawa, 1970) and laticotoxin a (Sato et al., 1969). The action of the whole venom of *L. semifasciata* can be accounted for by the toxins contained in it (Cheymol et al., 1972). Some typical experiments are shown in Figures 4, 5, and 6. The action of sea snake neurotoxins is similar to that of curare, although not identical.

It is evident from the structural studies that the mode of action of sea snake toxins is almost the same as that of cobra toxins. The specific binding of the neurotoxins to the acetylcholine receptor sites is now accepted as a fact and the toxins are used for the isolation and assay of the receptors (protein 16; Changeux et al., 1970; Bourgois et al., 1971; Raftery et al., 1971; Miledi and Potter, 1971; Barnard et al., 1971; Bosmann, 1972; Fambrough and Hartzell, 1972; Franklin and Potter, 1972; Moody et al., 1973; Schmidt and Raftery, 1973; protein 12; Meunier et al., 1971; Menez et al., 1971; Cohen et al., 1972; Berg et al., 1972; protein 23; Karlsson et al., 1972c; Reiter et al., 1972; Klett et al., 1973; protein 15; Biesecker, 1973).

BIOSYNTHESIS OF SEA SNAKE NEUROTOXINS

The biosynthesis of neurotoxins was studied by injecting ^{14}C-labeled amino acids into the venom glands of *L. laticaudata* (Sato et al., 1969) and *L. semifasciata* (Takeda et al., 1974). Labeled isoleucine injected into the venom glands of *L. semifasciata* was incorporated into the toxin molecules without conversion into other amino acids. Both erabutoxins a and b contain isoleucine residues at positions 2, 40, 41, and 56 (Table 4, proteins 2 and 3). In the first 30 sec after the injection, the labeling appears in the isoleucine at position 56, but not in that at position 2. The labeling at position 2 appears 1 min after the injection, and the labeling pattern of isoleucine residues appears uniform on longer exposure to the labeled isoleucine (Figure 7). The incorporation of amino acids is inhibited by puromycin and cycloheximide. These results indicate that erabutoxins and laticotoxin a are synthesized from the amino-terminal of the molecules by the ordinary protein synthesizing system in about 1 min, although the toxins are relatively small proteins.

The radioactively labeled toxins stay in the venom glands for more than 2 days. The slow turnover of the venom agrees with the observation that the yield of sea snake venom decreases on successive milking on every other day (Tamiya and Puffer, 1974; Table 2).

Individual snakes synthesize erabutoxins a, b, and c in varying ratios (Table 5; Tamiya, 1973). The ratio of the rates of biosynthesis of erabutoxins

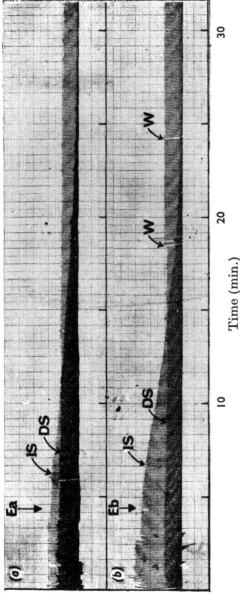

Muscular contraction (arbitrary units)

Time (min.)

Figure 4. Effects of erabutoxins a and b on the contraction of sciatic-nerve-sartorius-muscle preparation of frogs. An isolated sciatic-nerve-sartorius-muscle preparation of a frog (*Rana nigromaculata*) was placed in 4.3 ml of glucose-Ringer solution (9.0 g of NaCl, 0.42 g of KCl, 0.24 g of CaCl₂, 0.5 g of NaHCO₃, and 1.0 g of glucose in 1400 ml of water), which was continuously bubbled with air. The electrical stimulations were given to the preparation either directly to the muscle (DS) or indirectly through the nerve (IS) every 5 sec, and the contractions were recorded by a strain-gauge transducer. The solution of recrystallized erabutoxin a (0.1 ml) was added to the medium at the point marked Ea (final conc. 0.11 μg of Kjeldahl nitrogen/ml of Ringer solution) in (a). The recrystallized erabutoxin b solution (0.1 ml) was added at the point marked Eb (final concn. 0.12 μg of Kjeldahl nitrogen/ml of Ringer solution) in (b). The muscle was washed with the Ringer solution at the points marked W in (b). (From Tamiya and Arai, 1966.)

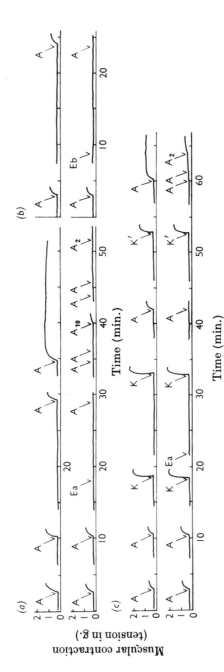

Figure 5.   Effects of erabutoxins a and b on the contraction of isolated frog rectus abdominis muscles stimulated by acetylcholine and by KCI. An isolated muscle from *Rana nigromaculata* was placed in 5 ml of glucose-Ringer solution (6.43 g of NaCl, 0.30 g of KCl, 0.17 g of CaCl$_2$, 0.10 g of NaHCO$_3$ and 0.71 g of glucose in 1000 ml of water), which was continuously bubbled with air. The contraction of the muscle was recorded by a strain-gauge transducer. At the points marked A, A$_2$, and A$_{10}$, acetylcholine solution (0.1 ml) was added to the Ringer solution to give final concentrations of 0.5, 1.0, and 5.0 μg/ml, respectively. At the points marked K and K', KCI solution (0.1 ml) was added to the Ringer solution to give final concentrations of 0.05 M and 0.02 M, respectively. At every interval between the curves, the muscle was washed three times with 5 ml of the Ringer solution and placed in 5 ml of fresh Ringer solution. The right and left muscles of a single individual were used as a pair. Erabutoxin a (0.12 μg of Kjeldahl nitrogen/ml or Ringer solution) and erabutoxin b (the same final concentration as a) were added at the points marked Ea and Eb respectively. (From Tamiya and Arai, 1966.)

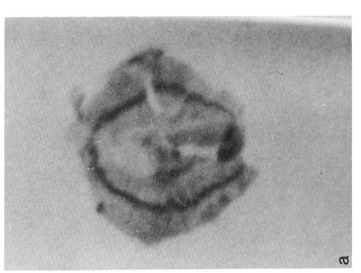

Figure 6. a, Autoradiogram of ^{131}I-labeled erabutoxin b localized in the endplates of the mouse diagram. b, The distribution of endplates of the mouse diagram (stained by Gomori's method). (From Sato et al., 1970).

a and b in *L. semifasciata* is held at a constant value characteristic of an individual snake (Takeda et al., 1974).

The venom glands of sea snakes are a highly specialized tissue, which mainly synthesizes toxins (Table 5 and Figure 1). The observation that the biosynthesis of erabutoxins is not affected by actinomycin D suggests that the mRNAs for the toxin biosynthesis are fairly long-lived (Takeda et al, 1974).

SUMMARY

The lethal activity of the venoms of 23 species of sea snakes has so far been reported.

Several neurotoxic proteins of very similar nature are isolated from the venoms of sea snakes, *L. semifasciata, L. laticaudata, L. colubrina, E. schistosa, L. hardwickii, H. cyanocinctus, A. laevis, H. ornatus,* and *Pelamis platurus.* All of them are basic proteins of low molecular weights and account

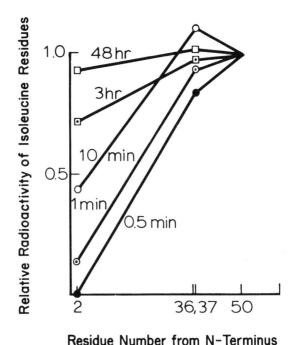

Figure 7. Relative radioactivity of isoleucine residues in the erabutoxin b molecule.

Table 5. Contents of erabutoxins a, b, and c in the venoms of single snakes of *Laticauda semifasciata*[a]

Snake *Laticauda semifasciata*	Total protein extracted (mg)	Erabutoxins (total)		Erabutoxin a		Erabutoxin b		Erabutoxin c	
		mg	%	mg	%	mg	%	mg	%
Very large	85.6	57.1	66.7	13.7	16.2	43.4	50.2		
Very large	65.0	55.6	85.4	9.8	15.1	44.9	68.6	0.9	1.4
Large	71.6	39.0	55.1	8.1	11.5	27.5	38.8	3.4	4.8
Large	41.4	21.2	51.7	6.5	15.9	8.8	21.5	5.9	14.3
Small	29.8	19.8	66.3	5.5	18.3	14.3	48.0		
Medium	11.4	5.9	51.8	2.9	25.1	1.4	12.0	1.7	14.7
Large	5.6	2.3	28.8	1.1	14.0	0.5	6.2	0.7	8.6
Average (70 snakes)	30.3	11.1	36.7	4.55	15.0	6.13	20.2	0.37	1.2
Average (300 snakes)	23.2	9.1	39.0	3.99	17.2	4.54	19.6	0.52	2.2

[a]From Tamiya (1973).

for most of the lethal activities of the original venoms. The toxic proteins are similar to those obtained from cobra venoms.

A comparison of the amino acid sequences and the chemical modification studies of the neurotoxins provide substantial information on the essential structure for the neurotoxicity of these toxins.

The toxins act on the neuromuscular injection at postsynaptic sites, competing with acetylcholine. The toxins are now being used for the studies of neuromuscular physiology and for the isolation of acetylcholine receptor proteins.

The neurotoxic proteins are synthesized from the component amino acids in the venom glands within a minute and last more than 2 days.

REFERENCES

Arai, H., N. Tamiya, S. Toshioka, S. Shinonaga, and R. Kano. 1964. Studies on sea-snake venoms. I. Protein nature of the neurotoxic component. J. Biochem. 56:568–571.

Barnard, E. A., J. Weickouski, and T. H. Chiu. 1971. Cholinergic receptor molecules and cholinesterase molecules at mouse skeletal muscle junctions. Nature 234:207–209.

Barme, M. 1958. Contribution a l'etude des serpents marins venimeux hydrophiidae du Viet Nam. Bull. Soc. Pathol. Exotique 51:258.

Barme, M. 1963. Venomous sea snakes of Vietnam and their venoms. *In* Venomous and Poisonous Animals and Noxious Plants of the Pacific

Region H. L. Keegan and W. V. MacFarlene (eds.) Macmillan Co., New York. pp. 373–378.

Barme, M. 1968. Venomous sea snakes (Hydrophiidae). *In* Venomous Animals and Their Venoms, Vol. I. W. Bücherl, E. Buckley, and V. Deulofeu (eds.) Academic Press, New York. pp. 285–308.

Berg, D. K., R. B. Kelly, P. B. Sargent, P. Williamson, and Z. W. Hall. 1972. Binding of α-bungarotoxin to acetylcholine receptors in mammalian muscle. Proc. Nat. Acad. Sci. 69:147–151.

Biesecker, G. 1973. Molecular properties of the cholinergic receptor purified from *Electrophorus electricus.* Biochem. 12:4403–4409.

Bossman, H. B. 1972. Acetylcholine receptor. I. Identification and biochemical characteristics of a cholinergic receptor of guinea pig cerebral cortex. J. Biol. Chem. 247:130–145.

Botes, D. P. 1971. Snake venom toxins. The amino acid sequences of toxins α and β from *Naja nivea* venom and the disulfide bonds of toxin α. J. Biol. Chem. 246:7383–7391.

Botes, D. P. 1972. Snake venom toxins. The amino acid sequences of toxins b and d from *Naja melanoleuca* venom. J. Biol. Chem. 247:2866–2871.

Botes, D. P., and D. J. Strydom. 1969. A neurotoxin, toxin α, from Egyptian cobra (*Naja haje haje*) venom. J. Biol. Chem. 244:4147–4157.

Botes, D. P., D. J. Strydom, C. G. Anderson, and P. A. Christensen. 1971. Snake venom toxins. Purification and properties of three toxins from *Naja nivea* (Linnaeus) (Cape Cobra) venom. J. Biol. Chem. 246:3132–3139.

Bourgeois, J. P., S. Tsuji, P. Boquet, J. Pillot, A. Rýter, and J. P. Changeux. 1971. Localization of the cholinergic receptor protein by immunofluorescence in eel electroplax. FEBS Lett. 16:92–94.

Carey, J. E., and E. A. Wright. 1960. Isolation of the neurotoxic component of the venom of sea snakes, *Enhydrina schistosa.* Nature 185:103–104.

Carey, J. E., and E. A. Wright. 1961. The site of action of the venom of the sea snake, *Enhydrina schistosa.* Trans. Roy. Soc. Trop. Med. Hyg. 55:153–160.

Chang, C. C., and K. Hayashi. 1969. Chemical modification of the tryptophan residue in cobratoxin. Biochem. Biophys. Res. Comm. 37:841–846.

Chang, C. C. and C. C. Yang. 1973. Immunochemical studies on the tryptophan modified cobrotoxin. Biochim. Biophys. Acta 295:595–604.

Chang, C. C., C. C. Yang, K. Hamaguchi, K. Nakai, and K. Hayashi. 1971a. Studies on the status of tyrosyl residues in cobrotoxin. Biochim. Biophys. Acta 236:164–173.

Chang, C. C., C. C. Yang, K. Nakai, and K. Hayashi. 1971b. Studies on the status of free amino and carboxyl groups in cobrotoxin. Biochim. Biophys. Acta 251:334–344.

Changeux, J. P., M. Kasai, and C. Y. Lee. 1970. Use of a snake venom toxin to characterize the cholinergic receptor protein. Proc. Nat. Acad. Sci. 67:1241–1247.

Cheymol, J., M. Barme, F. Bourillet, and M. Roch-Arveiller. 1967. Action neuromusculaire de trois venin d'Hydrophiides. Toxicon 5:111–119.

Cheymol, J., N. Tamiya, F. Bourillet, and M. Roch-Arveiller. 1972. Action neuromusculaire du venin de serpent marin 'Erabu' (*Laticauda semifasciata*) et des erabutoxins a et b. Toxicon 10:125–131.

Chicheportiche, R., C. Rochat, F. Sampieri, and M. Lazdunski. 1972. Structure-function relationships of neurotoxins isolated from *Naja haje* venom.

Physiochemical properties and identification of the active site. Biochem. 11:1681–1691.

Cohen, J. B., M. Weber, M. Huchet, and J. P. Changeux. 1972. Purification from *Torpedo marmorata* electric tissue of membrane fragments particularly rich in cholinergic receptor protein. FEBS Lett. 26:43–47.

Dayhoff, M. O. 1972. Hormones, active peptides and toxins. *In* Atlas of Protein Sequence and Structure, Vol. 5. National Biomedical Research Foundation. Washington, D.C. pp. D-173–183.

Eaker, D., and J. Porath. 1966. The amino acid sequence of a neurotoxin from *Naja nigricollis* venom. Abstracts, VIIth International Congress of Biochem., Tokyo, pp. 1087–1089.

Eaker, D., and J. Porath. 1967. The amino acid sequence of a neurotoxin from *Naja nigricollis* venom. Japanese J. Microbiol. 11:353–355.

Endo, Y., S. Sato, S. Ishii, and N. Tamiya. 1971. The disulphide bonds of erabutoxin a, a neurotoxic protein of a sea-snake (*Laticauda semifasciata*) venom. Biochem. J. 122:463–467.

Fambrough, D. M., and H. C. Hartzell. 1972. Acetylcholine receptors: Number and distribution at neuromuscular junctions in rat diaphragm. Science 176:189–191.

Franklin, G. I., and L. T. Potter. 1972. Studies of the binding of α-bungarotoxin to membrane bound and detergent-dispersed acetylcholine receptors from *Torpedo* electric tissue. FEBS Lett. 28:101–106.

Fraser, T. R., and R. H. Elliot. 1904. Contribution to the study of sea snake venoms. Proc. Roy. Soc. London 74:104–109.

Fraser, T. R., and R. H. Elliot. 1905. Contribution to the study of the action of sea-snake venoms. Part I. Venoms of the *Enhydrina valakadien* and *Enhydrina curtus*. Phil. Trans. 197:249–279.

Fryklund, L., and D. Eaker. 1973. Complete amino acid sequence of a nonneurotoxic hemolytic protein from the venom of *Hemachatus haemachatus* (African Ringhals Cobra). Biochem. 12:661–667.

Fryklund, L., D. Eaker, and E. Karlsson. 1972. Amino acid sequence of the two principal neurotoxins of *Enhydrina schistosa* Biochem. 11:4633–4640.

Halstead, B. W. 1970. Venomous sea snakes. *In* Poisonous and Venomous Marine Animals of the World, Vol. 3., pp. 627–681. U.S. Government Printing Office, Washington, D.C.

Hamaguchi, K., K. Ikeda, and C. Y. Lee. 1968. Optical rotatory dispersion and circular dichromism of neurotoxins isolated from the venom of *Bungarus multicinctus*. J. Biochem. 64:503–506.

Hayashi, K., M. Takechi, and T. Sasaki. 1971. Amino acid sequence of cytotoxin I from the venom of the Indian Cobra (*Naja naja*). Biochem. Biophys. Res. Comm. 45:1357–1362.

Huang, J. S., S. S. Liu, K. H. Ling, C. C. Chang, and C. C. Yang. 1973. Iodination of cobrotoxins. Toxicon 11:39–45.

Joubert, F. 1973. Snake venom toxins. The amino acid sequences of two toxins from *Ophiophagus hannah* (King Cobra) venom. Biochim. Biophys. Acta 317:85–98.

Kao, C. S., C. S. Liu, and R. Q. Blackwell. 1973. Presence of erabutoxins a and b in venom of the sea snake *Laticauda semifasciata* from Taiwan. Toxicon 11:383–385.

Karlsson, E., H. Arnberg, and D. L. Eaker. 1971. Isolation of the principal neurotoxins of two *Naja naja* subspecies. Eur. J. Biochem. 21:1–16.

Karlsson, E., and D. Eaker. 1972. Chemical modifications of the postsynaptic *Naja naja* neurotoxins. J. Formosan Med. Assoc. 71:358–371.

Karlsson, E., D. Eaker, L. Fryklund, and S. Kadin. 1972a. Chromatographic separation of *Enhydrina schistosa* venom and the characterization of two principal neurotoxins. Biochem. 11:4628–4633.

Karlsson, E., D. Eaker, and G. Ponterius. 1972b. Modification of amino groups in *Naja naja* neurotoxins and the preparation of radioactive derivatives. Biochim. Biophys. Acta 257:235–248.

Karlsson, E., D. L. Eaker, and J. Porath. 1966. Purification of a neurotoxin from the venom of *Naja nigricollis*. Biochim. Biophys. Acta 127:505–520.

Karlsson, E., E. Heilbronn, and L. Widlund. 1972c. Isolation of the nicotinic acetylcholine receptor by biospecific chromatography on insolubilized *Naja naja* neurotoxin. FEBS Lett. 28:107–111.

Klett, R. P., B. W. Fulpius, D. Cooper, M. Smith, E. Reich, and L. D. Possani. 1973. The acetylcholine receptor. I. Purification and characterization of a macromolecule isolated from the *Electrophorus electricus*. J. Biol. Chem. 248:6841–6853.

Liu, C. S., G. S. Huber, C. S. Lin, and R. Q. Blackwell. 1973. Fractionation of toxins from *Hydrophis cyanocinctus* venom and determination of amino acid composition and end groups of Hydrophitoxin a. Toxicon 11:73–79.

Low, B. W., R. Potter, R. B. Jackson, N. Tamiya, and S. Sato. 1971. X-Ray crystallographic study of erabutoxins and of diiodo-derivative. J. Biol. Chem. 246:4366–4368.

Maeda, N., K. Takagi, N. Tamiya, Y. M. Chen, and C. Y. Lee. 1974. Isolation of an easily reversible postsynaptic toxin from the venom of a sea snake, *Laticauda semifasciata*. Biochem. J. 141:383–387.

Maeda, N., and N. Tamiya. 1974. The primary structure of the toxin Laticauda semifasciata III, a weak and reversibly acting neurotoxin from the venom of a sea snake, *Laticauda semifasciata*. Biochem. J. 141:389–400.

Marsden, A. T., and H. A. Reid. 1961. Pathology of sea snake poisoning. Brit. Med. J. 1:1290–1293.

Mebs, D., K. Narita, S. Iwanaga, Y. Samejima, and C. Y. Lee, 1971. Amino acid sequence of α-bungarotoxin from the venom of *Bungarus multicinctus*. Biochem. Biophys. Res. Comm. 44:711–716.

Mebs, D., K. Narita, S. Iwanaga, Y. Samejima, and C. Y. Lee. 1972. Purification, properties and amino acid sequence of α-bungarotoxin from the venom of *Bungarus multicinctus*. Hoppe-Seyler's Z. Physiol. Chem. 353:243–262.

Menez, A., J. L. Morgat, P. Fromageot, A. M. Ronseray, P. Boquet, and J. P. Changeux. 1971. Tritium labelling of the α-neurotoxin of *Naja nigricollis*. FEBS Lett. 17:333–335.

Meunier, J. C., M. Huchet, P. Boquet, and J. P. Changeux. 1971. Séparation de la protéine réceptrice de l'acétylcholine et de l'acétylcholinestérase. C.R. Acad. Sc. Paris 272:117–120.

Meunier, J. C., R. Olsen, A. Menez, P. Fromageot, P. Boquet, and J. P. Changeux. 1972. Some physical properties of the cholinergic receptor protein from *Electrophorus electricus*. Biochem. 11:1200–1210.

Miledi, R., and L. T. Potter. 1971. Acetylcholine receptors in muscle fibres. Nature 233:599–603.

Moody, T., J. Schmidt, and M. A. Raftery. 1973. Binding of acetylcholine and related compounds to purified acetylcholine receptor from *Torpedo californica* electroplax. Biochem. Biophys. Res. Comm. 53:761−772.

Nakai, K., T. Sasaki, and K. Hayashi. 1971. Amino acid sequence of toxin A from the venom of the Indian Cobra (*Naja naja*). Biochem. Biophys. Res. Comm. 44:893−897.

Narita, K., and C. Y. Lee. 1970. The amino acid sequence of cardiotoxin from Formosan Cobra (*Naja naja atra*) venom. Biochem. Biophys. Res. Comm. 41:339−343.

Ohta, M., and K. Hayashi. 1973. Localization of the five disulfide bridges in toxin B from the venom of the Indian Cobra (*Naja naja*). Biochem. Biophys. Res. Comm. 55:431−438.

Pickwell, G. V., J. A. Vick, W. H. Shipman, and M. M. Grenan, 1974. Production, toxicity, and preliminary pharmacology of venom from the sea snake, *Pelamis platurus*. *In* Proc. Third Food-Drugs from the Sea Conf. pp. 247−265. L. R. Worthen, ed. Marine Tech. Soc. Wash., D.C.

Raftery, M. A., J. Schmidt, D. G. Clark, and R. G. Wolcott. 1971. Demonstration of a specific α-bungarotoxin binding component in *Electrophorus electricus* electroplax membranes. Biochem. Biophys. Res. Comm. 45:1622−1629.

Reid, H. A. 1956. Sea snake bite research. Trans. Roy. Soc. Trop. Med. Hyg. 50:517−542.

Reid, H. A. 1963. Snake bite in Malaya. *In* Venomous and Poisonous Animals and Noxious Plants of the Pacific Region. H. L. Keegan and W. V. MacFarlene, eds. Macmillan Co., New York. pp. 355−362.

Reid, H. A., and K. J. Lim. 1957. Sea snake bite. A survey of fishing villages in north-west Malaya. Brit. Med. J. 2:1266−1272.

Reiter, M. J., D. A. Cowburn, J. M. Prives, and A. Karlin. 1972. Affinity labelling of the acetylcholine receptor in the electroplax: electrophoretic separation in sodium dodecyl sulfate. Proc. Nat. Acad. Sci. 69:1168−1172.

Rogers, L. 1903. The physiological action of the venom of sea-snakes. Proc. Roy. Soc. London 71:481−496.

Rogers, L. 1904. The physiological action of the venom of sea-snakes. II. Action on circulation, respiration, and nervous system. Proc. Roy. Soc. London, 72:305−319.

Rýden, L., D. Gabel, and D. Eaker. 1973. A model of the three-dimensional structure of snake venom neurotoxins based on chemical evidence. Internat. J. Peptide Prot. Res. 5:261−273.

Sato, S., T. Abe, and N. Tamiya. 1970. Binding of iodinated erabutoxin b, a sea snake toxin, to the endplates of the mouse diaphragm. Toxicon 8:313−314.

Sato, S., H. Ogahara, and N. Tamiya. 1972. Immunochemistry of erabutoxins. Toxicon 10:239−243.

Sato, S., and N. Tamiya. 1970. Iodination of erabutoxin b: diiodohistidine formation. J. Biochem. 68:867−872.

Sato, S., and N. Tamiya. 1971. The amino acid sequences of erabutoxins, neurotoxic proteins of sea snake (*Laticauda semifasciata*) venom. Biochem. J. 122:453−461.

Sato, S., H. Yoshida, H. Abe, and N. Tamiya. 1969. Properties and biosynthesis of a neurotoxic protein of the venom of sea snakes, *Laticauda laticaudata* and *Laticauda colubrina*. Biochem. J. 115:85−90.

Schmidt, J., and M. A. Raftery. 1973. Purification of acetylcholine receptors from *Torpedo californica* electroplax by affinity chromatography. Biochem. 12:852−856.

Searl, J. E., W. W. Fullerton, and B. W. Low. 1973. X-Ray crystallographic study of laticotoxin a. J. Biol. Chem. 248:6057−6058.

Seto, A., S. Sato, and N. Tamiya. 1970. The properties and modification of tryptophan in a sea snake toxin, erabutoxin a. Biochim. Biophys. Acta 214:483−489.

Shipman, W. H., and G. V. Pickwell. 1973. Venom of the yellow-bellied sea snake (*Pelamis platurus*): some physical and chemical properties. Toxicon 11:375−377.

Strydom, A. J. C., and D. P. Botes. 1971. Snake venom toxins. Purification, properties, and complete amino acid sequence of two toxins from Ringhals (*Hemachatus haemachatus*) venom. J. Biol. Chem. 246:1341−1349.

Strydom, D. J. 1972a. Phylogenetic relationships of proteroglyphae toxins. Toxicon 10:39−45.

Strydom, D. J. 1972b. Snake venom toxins. The amino acid sequences of two toxins from *Dendroaspis polylepis polylepis* (Black Mamba) venom. J. Biol. Chem. 247:4029−4042.

Strydom, D. J. 1973. Snake venom toxin. Structure-function relationships and phylogenetics. Comp. Biochem. Physiol. 44B:269−281.

Takamizawa, T. 1970. Effect of erabutoxin b on the membrane properties of frog sartorius muscle cells. Tohoku J. Exper. Med. 101:339−350.

Takechi, M., and K. Hayashi. 1972. Localization of the four disulfide bridges in Cytotoxin II from the venom of the Indian Cobra (*Naja naja*). Biochem. Biophys. Res. Comm. 49:584−590.

Takechi, M., K. Hayashi, and T. Sasaki. 1972. The amino acid sequence of Cytotoxin II from the venom of the Indian Cobra (*Naja naja*). Mol. Pharm. 8:446−451.

Takeda, M., H. Yoshida, and N. Tamiya. 1974. Biosynthesis of erabutoxins in the sea snake, *Laticauda semifasciata.* Toxicon 12:633−641.

Tamiya, N. 1973. Erabutoxins a, b and c in sea snake *Laticauda semifasciata* venom. Toxicon 11:95−97.

Tamiya, N., and H. Abe. 1972. The amino acid sequence of erabutoxin c, a minor neurotoxic component of a sea snake (*Laticauda semifasciata*) venom. Biochem. J. 130:547−555.

Tamiya, N., and H. Arai. 1966. Studies on sea snake venoms: Crystallization of erabutoxins a and b from *Laticauda semifasciata* venom. Biochem. J. 99:624−630.

Tamiya, N., and H. Arai, and S. Sato. 1967. Studies on sea snake venoms: Crystallization of erabutoxins a and b from *Laticauda semifasciata* venom and of Laticotoxin a from *Laticauda laticaudata* venom. *In* Animal Toxins. F. E. Russell and P. R. Saunders (eds.). Pergamon Press, Oxford. pp. 249−258.

Tamiya, N., and H. Puffer. 1974. Lethality of sea snake venoms. Toxicon 12:85−87.

Tamiya, N. and S. Sato. 1966. Structure and function of crystalline toxins from *Laticaudinae.* Abstracts, VIIth Internat. Cong. of Biochem, Tokyo. pp. 497.

Tu, A. T., and B. S. Hong. 1971. Purification and chemical characterization of a toxin from the venom of *Lapemis hardwickii.* J. Biol. Chem. 246:2772−2779.

Tu, A. T., B. S. Hong, and T. N. Solie. 1971. Characterization and chemical modification of toxins isolated from the venoms of the sea snake, *Laticauda semifasciata* from Philippines. Biochem. 10: 1295–1304.

Tu, A. T., and P. M. Toom. 1971. Isolation and characterization of the toxic component of *Enhydrina schistosa* venom. J. Biol. Chem. 246:1012–1016.

Tu, A. T., and T. Tu. 1970. Sea snakes of southeast Asia and Far East and their venoms. *In* Poisonous and Venomous Marine Animals of the World, Vol. III, pp. 885–903. U.S. Government Printing Office, Washington, D.C.

Tu, T. 1959. Toxicological studies on the venom of a sea snake *Laticauda semifasciata* (Reinwardt) in Formosan waters. J. Formosan Med. Assoc. 58:182–203.

Tu, T. 1963. Toxicological studies on the venom of a sea snake, *Laticauda semifasciata affinis* (Anderson), II. J. Formosan Med. Assoc. 62:87.

Tu, T., M. J. Lin, H. M. Yang, H. J. Lin, and C. N. Chen. 1962. Toxicological studies on the venom of a sea snake *Laticauda colubrina* (Schneider). I. J. Formosan Med. Assoc. 61:1296.

Uwatoko, Y., Y. Nomura, K. Kojima, and F. Obo. 1966. Studies on sea snake venom. Acta Med. Univ. Kagoshima 8:141–156.

Viljoen, C. C., and D. P. Botes, 1973. Snake venom toxins: The purification and amino acid sequence of toxin F_{VII} from *Dendroaspis angusticeps* venom. J. Biol. Chem. VII 248:4915–4919.

Wong, C., T. W. Chan, T. J. Lee, and C. C. Yang. 1972. X-ray crystallographic study of cobrotoxin. J. Biol. Chem. 247:608.

Yang, C. C. 1965. Crystallization and properties of cobrotoxin from Formosan cobra venom. J. Biol. Chem. 240:1616–1618.

Yang, C. C. 1967. The disulfide bonds of cobrotoxin and their relationship to lethality. Biochem. Biophys. Acta 133:346–355.

Yang, C. C., C. C. Chang, K. Hayashi, T. Suzuki, K. Ikeda, and K. Hamaguchi. 1968. Optical rotatory dispersion and circular dichromism of cobrotoxin. Biochim. Biophys. Acta 168:373–376.

Yang, C. C., H. J. Yang, and R. H. C. Chiu. 1970. The position of disulfide bonds of cobrotoxin. Biochim. Biophys. Acta 214:355–365.

Yang, C. C., H. J. Yang, and J. S. Huang. 1969. The Amino Acid Sequence of Cobrotoxin. Biochim. Biophys. Acta 188:65–77.

nineteen

Epidemiology and Clinical Aspects of Sea Snake Bites

H. Alistair Reid

Sea snakes are the most abundant and widely dispersed of the world's venomous reptiles. Sea snake venoms are highly toxic. One "drop" (about 0.03 ml) contains enough venom to kill three adult men; some sea snake species can eject seven to eight such "drops" in a single bite. Around the coastal seas of the Indian and western Pacific oceans, fishermen encounter these sea snakes every day. Fortunately for fishermen sea snakes are not aggressive and, even when they do bite man, rarely inject much of their highly toxic venom. If this were not the case, deaths from sea snake bite would probably stop all sea fishing in many parts of Asia—and in these vast areas fish are a most valuable source of high quality protein.

Not much is known about sea snake bites. Apart from their impact on fishing folk, the effect on the tourist trade can be important. In Malaya, as a result of two bathers being fatally bitten in 1954, there was a serious drop in tourist trade which took several years to recover. This aspect is particularly important in view of the greatly increased tourist traffic to tropical countries where sea snakes are known to occur. What is the danger to a bather in such areas?

In scientific centers throughout the world, venoms are being increasingly recognized as tools for research. In some research fields, venoms are unique because of a highly specific action on vital body processes. Thus, sea snake venom may help to elucidate diseases both of muscles (myopathies) and of nerves (neurological illnesses). Research on snake venoms has already led to improved treatment of human disease such as thrombosis (Reid and Chan, 1968).

EPIDEMIOLOGY OF SEA SNAKE BITES IN MAN

General

Despite the known abundance and toxicity of sea snakes, there are relatively few records in the medical literature of man being bitten by sea snakes. In 1956, my search of the world medical literature revealed only 31 cases mentioned or, less often, recorded from 1825 to 1942. Yet in the early 1950s, Dr. A. A. Wahab in north Malaya succeeded in overcoming the reluctance of many fishing folk to seek hospital treatment, and by 1953–1954, 30 patients with sea snake bite were being admitted to hospital each year from one fishing village alone (Reid, 1956a). It should, of course, be realized that hospital statistics and medical literature can give a very misleading view of the epidemiology of venomous bites and stings. Doctors, like newspapers, tend to note and report only serious or fatal cases; thus medical literature exaggerates the severity of snake bite. Second, people bitten by venomous snakes who do not develop poisoning may never bother to see a doctor. Thus, hospital patients are a selected group and statistics derived from them tend to underestimate the general incidence of venomous bites and stings and tend to overestimate the general severity of poisoning.

World Distribution and Aggressiveness of Sea Snake Species

The distribution of sea snake species can differ very markedly within their vast natural habitat in the Indian and Pacific oceans. Barme (1968) gives a useful table showing the geographical distribution of the different Hydrophiidae species, but admits that it is probably incomplete. He earlier recorded the capture of several thousand sea snakes along the coasts of Vietnam (Barme, 1963); in south Vietnam, *Lapemis hardwickii* represented 75% of the sea snakes captured, whereas in central Vietnam, *Hydrophis fasciatus* was more frequently taken. *H. cyanocinctus* appears to be the commonest species found around Taiwan (Kuntz, 1963) and Hong Kong (Romer, 1972). In the Philippines, large numbers of *H. inornatus* and *L. hardwickii* are caught by fishermen (Herre and Rabor, 1949). *H. cyanocinctus* is also common (Herre, 1942). At Surabaia in northeast Java, Bergman (1943) collected 984 sea snakes; about one-third were *Thalassophis anomalus* and one-third were *L. hardwickii*. *Enhydrina schistosa* has been noted as extremely common in coastal waters of Malaya (Cantor, 1886), India (Day, 1869; Cantor, 1886), Ceylon (Wall, 1921), Pakistan and the Persian Gulf (Blanford, 1876; Knowles, 1921). According to Smith (1926), *E. schistosa* is the most common known sea snake. It abounds in most localities on Asian coasts from the Persian Gulf to Vietnam and north Australia, but it has not been met with in the Philippines. During the three years mid-1960 to mid-1963, a total of 4735 sea snakes were brought alive to the Snake and Venom Research Institute, Penang, northwest Malaya. All these sea snakes were caught in the sea within 10 miles of the coastline of Penang Island. Approximately one-half of these sea snakes were *E. schistosa* and one-quarter were *H. cyanocinctus* (Table 1). Thus species of Hydrophiidae in Malayan and other waters differ from those caught in the *Alpha Helix* expedition. Although species of *Laticauda* are extremely abundant in the Philippines (Herre and Rabor, 1949), I am not aware of any record of man being bitten by Laticaudinae. In the Philippines, Herre (1942) recorded fishermen keeping *Laticauda semifasciata* for eating in large jars into which they thrust their hands with impunity, pulling out live specimens 1–2 m long. But they never handled *H. cyanocinctus* in this way (see Chapter 21).

According to Wall (1921), Smith (1926), and Herre (1942), sea snakes are gentle, inoffensive creatures which bite only under provocation. Cantor (1841) referred to *E. schistosa* and wrote "from my own experience" that sea snakes observed in the Bay of Bengal and the Ganges were very ferocious both in and out of the water. Bright light blinded them, otherwise people would be bitten more often. My own observations of sea snakes in captivity in Malaya indicated marked differences of behavior in different species. Thus, *E. schistosa* is much more aggressive than any other species I have observed. When held, it would start snapping long before the spoon used for venom

Table 1. Sea snake species and venom yields, Snake and Venom Research Institute, Malaysia, 1960–1963

Species	No. of specimens	Venom yield (mg dry weight)	
		Average	Maximum
Enhydrina schistosa	2403	8.5	79
Hydrophis brookii	262	1.1	2
Hydrophis caerulescens	4	—	—
Hydrophis cyanocinctus	1074	8.2	80
Hydrophis klossi	312	1.0	2
Hydrophis melanosoma	4	—	—
Hydrophis spiralis	349	2.1	8
Kerilia jerdoni	188	2.8	5
Lapemis hardwickii	115	1.9	15
Hydrophis gracilis	19	—	—
Pelamis platurus	3	—	—
Praescutata viperina	2	—	—
Total	4735		

collection was within its reach. Having bitten the spoon, the jaws contracted repeatedly with very considerable force. *H. cyanocinctus* would also bite readily as a rule, with less pugnacity but more tenacity, often having to be torn off the spoon or released from my grasp with the spoon still in its mouth. This was in great contrast to specimens of *H. spiralis, H. klossi, H. melanosoma, L. hardwickii,* and *Kerilia jerdoni,* which would rarely bite spontaneously. Often the spoon had to be forced between their teeth; even with this, they sometimes refused to bite. Despite these differences among species—and, for that matter, among individuals of the same species—I agree that, in general, sea snakes are loath to bite man. According to Herre (1942), sea snakes are more aggressive during the breeding season. I have observed at least 40 pregnant *E. schistosa,* and they were no more aggressive than non-pregnant specimens, as judged by venom taking and goading them with fish or a plastic doll.

Survey of Fishing Villages for Sea Snake Bite

Incidence of Sea Snake Bite In 1955–1956, a survey of fishing villages was carried out in northwest Malaya and details of 144 sea snake bites were obtained (Reid and Lim, 1957). In this area, about half the fishermen are Malays and half are Chinese. Because of suspicion and superstition, the fishing folk were most reluctant to talk about any sea snake bites initially, but after several visits, which always included a display of dead sea snakes in a suitable village coffee shop, communication eventually improved markedly. Even so, a retrospective survey such as this can only indicate trends. Apart from a reluctance to talk, a significant number of victims forget about their bites, especially if there was little or no poisoning. Thus, 53 of the 144 bites were received in 1954–1955, the two most recent years of the survey, compared with 49 in 1946–1952 and 42 in or before 1945. It was estimated in the survey report that there was a total of some 150 victims of sea snake bite each year in the villages surveyed. The latter comprised about one-tenth of the Malayan fishing population. Only 18 of the total 144 victims sought orthodox medical help in hospital. This emphasizes the fact that medical statistics do not reflect accurately the general incidence of snake bite.

Species of Sea Snake Asking victims or witnesses (of fatal cases) to identify the sea snake from the collection presented at the survey was successful in 65 cases. The species identified and the number of bites per species were as follows: *E. schistosa* (24), *H. cyanocinctus* (10), *H. klossi* (16), *H. spiralis* (8), *K. jerdoni* (2), *L. hardwickii* (2), and *Hydrophis gracilis* (3). This corresponds well with the frequency with which the various species are caught in the area by fishermen (Table 1). *E. schistosa* caused the most deaths, and this corresponds with experimental findings of venom yield and toxicity (see "Venom yields and lethal toxicity" in this chapter).

Sex, Age, Race, Circumstances As would be expected, 90% of the victims were males, mostly aged 20 years and up, reflecting the groups at risk. The racial incidence among Malays and Chinese was similar except in children. Bites and deaths were more common in Malay children compared with Chinese, probably due to Malay children playing and wading in river-mouths, a habit less favored by the Chinese. Most of these fishing folk were bitten by treading on the snake, and many were bitten in a river-mouth. River-mouths, particularly those with fishing villages, are favorite haunts of sea snakes. Sometimes, sea snakes swim 50–100 miles up rivers (Wall, 1921), and a Malay boy in the survey was fatally bitten in the river edge 5 miles from the sea. Five victims were bitten while swimming in a river-mouth ("swimming" meaning "feet off the river-bed"). One victim felt the snake coiling around his forearm and biting his hand. Trivial poisoning followed. Two severe bites were in the thigh and forearm, respectively, one swimmer was fatally bitten in the hand, and in another fatality the site of the bite was not known. Presumably these five were unlucky enough to hit an oncoming sea snake. Other victims were usually bitten while handling nets or sorting fish, the sea snakes escaping the fishermen's scrutiny despite their customary search for sea snakes as the first action on drawing in their nets.

The number of sea snakes encountered by fishermen varied according to the method of fishing, from nil up to a total of 100 or more each day. The first action on hauling in the catch is to spot sea snakes, pick them up quickly by the tail, and throw them overboard. This responsibility usually rests on one member of the crew, who becomes adept. Malays often used a stick rather than fingers for lifting the snakes. The sea snakes are never killed. Line fishing is not common in the area surveyed, but an average of 20 sea snakes per 300-hook line was quoted by two fishermen using this method in shallow water. Usually they cut off the line concerned, but one victim was bitten trying to disengage a sea snake and thereby save the hook. He had trivial symptoms following the bite, but thereafter conformed to custom, cutting the lines with sea snakes.

As would be expected, sea snakes were very rare in entangling structures (gill nets). They were not numerous in engulfing structures (drive-in nets) and some entrapping structures (palisade traps, lift nets, falling nets). But a gape net, known by the Chinese as *ch't cheh,* invariably caught 10–20 sea snakes each lift. A conical net with the mouth held open by two poles stuck into the sea-bed and the tail raised by floats is used in shallow water, and lifted two or more times daily according to the tide. However, although this net invariably traps large numbers of sea snakes, only four of the 50 victims bitten while handling nets were using this method. The other net in which sea snakes are numerous is a small drag seine called a *kesa* by the Chinese. It is also used in shallow water, being dragged along by two or three fishermen wading in the sea (Figure 1). Of the 50 bitten though handling nets, 27 were handling a

Figure 1. This drag seine, called a *kesa* by Chinese fishermen, is dragged in shallow waters, and it is the most common type of net involved in sea snake bites among Malaysian fishermen.

kesa, 16 (six fatal, five serious, five trivial) being in the sea at the time, and 11 (seven serious, four trivial) in the boat pulling in or sorting the net.

All species of sea snake presented during the survey visits were recognized at one or more villages. *E. schistosa* was considered the most common, and also the most dangerous. But all fishermen agreed that sea snakes never attacked human beings spontaneously. The only exception was one man who claimed to have been chased by an *E. schistosa* while in a fish-trap. However, others present laughingly disbelieved him. Several fishermen recounted sea snakes swimming between their vest and body while they stood in fishing nets; all would be well so long as they kept still. As one fisherman put it, if the sea snakes *were* aggressive, there would be no more fishing.

Site of the Bite About two-thirds were bitten on the lower limb because in one way or another the victim trod on the snake; one-third were bitten on the upper limb through handling the sea snake. In land snake bites in the tropics, more than four-fifths are bitten on the foot, toe or leg (Reid et al., 1963b), whereas in Britain, at least four-fifths are bitten on the finger or hand through foolish attempts to pick up or handle a viper.

Village Treatment About half the victims had a tourniquet applied, though the description of many ligatures suggested a ritual rather than an effective method of delaying absorption. Amputation was never practiced. The fishermen were unanimous that they would rather risk death than lose a finger or toe. My observations during and subsequent to this survey confirmed the good sense of this opinion. The paramount fact about sea snake bites in man became increasingly obvious, namely, that despite the great lethal potential of sea snake venoms, bites of man rarely result in significant envenoming. The site of the bite was excised by seven victims. Judging from the victims' descriptions of the procedures (especially the time it took) and the six scars seen (one victim had died of the bite), it seemed unlikely to me that the excision affected the issue. Experimentally in dogs, a lethal dose from a sea snake bite can be absorbed in under 3 min (Reid, 1956a). There were no instances of incision or suction being attempted.

Subsequent treatment depended on the victim's race. If Chinese, a special herbal brandy made from a variety of herbs in rice wine was taken, and for the next 24 hrs all smoking, talking, and eating were avoided (a sensible measure because if poisoning develops there is usually difficulty in swallowing, which can lead to fatal choking by inhalation of food, vomit, or secretions). Malays, on the other hand, would consult a *bomor* or medicine man who relied mainly on incantations. Malays and Chinese usually disparaged the other's methods and alleged a resulting high mortality, but the survey figures did not support either opinion.

Beliefs and Superstitions All fishermen were well acquainted with the more common symptoms of sea snake poisoning. It was recognized that many victims developed few or none of these symptoms, but this was invariably regarded as being due to the treatment received. Deaths were attributed to disregard of advice or delay in receiving treatment. Land snake bites were much less common in these fishing villages. Offered the alternative of a cobra or a sea snake bite, preference for the former was unanimous. Similarly, they laughed when asked whether they would rather be stung by a catfish, stingray, or jellyfish in preference to a sea snake bite. Anybody who has had the extremely painful and unpleasant experience of these venomous fish stings will realize the significance of the laughter. Fear of sea snakes was admitted by all—"more than anything else," as one fisherman put it. Another fisherman philosophically likened them to war—both the inevitable lot of mankind. Nighttime, and the consequent difficulty in seeing the snakes, were particularly feared although analysis of the survey figures did not suggest this is an important factor in sea snake bite. These fears are prevalent despite the vaunted confidence in their respective treatments.

The reluctance to admit to specific instances of bites was in great contrast to the freedom with which they eventually discussed general aspects of sea snakes. One reason for this reluctance is suspicion. Deaths due to sea snake bite were often reported as "fever" in order to avoid necropsy or delay in burial, both of which conflict with Asian custom; many suspected we intended to make trouble on this account. But the most important factor was superstition. Most Malays admitted frankly to these superstitions, whereas many Chinese scoffed at them. However, we received the impression that the Chinese were in reality just as deeply influenced by superstition as the Malays. Four common superstitions are: (1) Talk about sea snake bites offends the sea snakes and may change their timidity to aggression. (2) If a victim talks about his bite, he will be bitten again. (3) If a pregnant woman hears of a sea snake bite, the victim will die. (4) If fecal droppings of a house lizard fall on a victim, he will die.

The first three discourage the victim from broadcasting his misfortune, and the fourth superstition precludes his being treated in his home. In practice, the victim tells his best friend to fetch the *bomor* (medicine man). If all goes well, no one else in the village is informed of the incident. But as one *bomor* rather cynically admitted to us, if the victim is not satisfied and sends his friend for a second *bomor,* the first *bomor* spreads the news so that a pregnant woman will hear it. The discredit of the inevitable death will then fall on the second *bomor.*

Other common beliefs include: (5) The presence of a *bomor* in the village attracts sea snakes and causes more bites. (6) If fresh lime is taken shortly after a bite, the symptoms will recur and probably be fatal. (7) Drinking blood of a sea snake or eating its tail gives protection against poisoning. A few Chinese fishermen admitted doing this, and others sometimes ate them for general medicinal effect. None ate sea snakes as ordinary food, although one Chinese said his father had been fond of them. Malays believed eating sea snakes would cause shedding of their own skin. (8) Both Chinese and Malays had heard of the *ular belerang,* a sea snake so poisonous that, if it bites the rudder, all in the boat will die. A few claimed to have seen this snake, always far out in deep water of more than 20 fathoms. They described it as about 30 cm long, 2 cm thick, usually a striking yellow color with a longitudinal black stripe (*belerang* is Malay for sulphur). The descriptions suggest a young *Pelamis platurus.*

1957–1964 Penang Hospital Series

General During 1957–1964, a total of 101 patients with unequivocal sea snake bite were observed under my personal care in Malaya. Most were admitted to the Penang General Hospital and all had been bitten in the northwest Malayan area. In this hospital series, poisoning is graded as (1) "nil" when no clinical or laboratory features of poisoning developed; (2) "trivial" when clinical or laboratory evidence of poisoning (a raised serum glutamic oxaloacetic transaminase level is a highly sensitive indicator of sea snake bite poisoning; see "Clinical characteristics of poisoning" in this chapter) lasted only up to 3 days; (3) "serious" when poisoning lasted more than 3 days; and (4) fatal.

Species of Sea Snake Involved: Severity of Poisoning In 10 cases, the biting sea snake was brought and identified by myself: *E. schistosa* (7), *H. cyano-cinctus* (1), *H. spiralis* (1), and *K. jerdoni* (1). In 71 cases, it was reliably identified by the victim from the extensive collection of live sea snakes in the Snake and Venom Research Institute. In 12 cases, the sea snake was seen and reliably recognized as a sea snake (the victims were fishermen, all of whom were only too familiar with sea snakes), but the species could not be satisfactorily identified. In eight cases, the bite was in the sea, the cause not observed; no local pain followed the incident (thereby excluding venomous fish-stings), bite marks were compatible with those of a sea snake, and typical toxemia ensued.

In Table 2 it will be seen that *E. schistosa* was known to cause over half the bites including seven of the eight fatal bites.

Sex, Age, and Race of Patients: Severity of Poisoning As in the survey, over 90% of the victims were male (Table 3). Sex, ages and race reflect the groups at risk, but did not appear to influence the severity of poisoning. The youngest patient was an infant aged 16 months, and the oldest a fisherman aged 70 years.

Occupation of Patients and Circumstances of Bites Of the 101 patients, 80 were fishermen bitten at their jobs, and nine were wives or children of fishermen. Of the latter, eight were bitten washing or bathing near their village. The youngest victim, a 16-month infant, was playing with a tin on the shore unseen by her father who was sorting out the catch nearby; he had earlier spotted an *E. schistosa* and put it into the tin. His daughter was bitten on the wrist. Both the daughter and the sea snake were brought to me. The *E.*

Table 2. 1957–1964 Hospital series; species of sea snake involved and severity of poisoning

Species of sea snake	Severity of Poisoning				
	Nil	Trivial	Serious	Fatal	Total
Enhydrina schistosa	39	4	5	7	55
Hydrophis cyanocinctus	11	2	1	–	14
Hydrophis spiralis	6	3	–	–	9
Kerilia jerdoni	1	–	–	–	1
Lapemis hardwickii	2	–	–		2
Not identified	9	2	8	1	20
Total	68	11	14	8	101

Table 3. 1957–1964 Hospital series; sex, age, race, and severity of poisoning

	Severity of poisoning				
	Nil	Trivial	Serious	Fatal	Total
Sex					
Male	63	11	12	8	94
Female	5	–	2	–	7
Age (years)					
0–9	2	–	2	1	5
10–19	12	2	8	3	25
20–29	18	6	3	1	28
30–39	15	3	–	1	19
40–49	9	–	1	1	11
50 onwards	12	–	–	1	13
Race					
Chinese	41	5	6	2	54
Malay	26	5	8	3	42
Other	1	1	–	3	5

schistosa was a young adult 40 cm long. I "milked" it 2 hrs after the bite and obtained venom which, after drying, weighed 12 mg. The infant weighed 11 kg and the likely lethal dose of *E. schistosa* venom would be 0.5 mg (Reid, 1956a). The venom obtained was therefore equivalent to 24 lethal doses for the patient, who had clear fang marks on the wrist. Fortunately, she developed no poisoning.

Only 12 of the 101 patients were not fishing folk. Eight were bitten while bathing in the sea and two while bathing in a river-mouth. All 10 trod on the sea snake; none were swimming at the time of the bite. One Australian boy was fatally bitten on the seashore where he was "chasing" a sea snake with a knife. The supervisor at the Snake and Venom Research Institute was bitten when milking an *E. schistosa*.

The circumstances of the bites are summarized in Table 4. Sixty-two of the victims were bitten while they tread on the sea snake. This usually occurred in shallow water either in the sea or in a river-mouth. Almost invariably the victim lifted the bitten limb, bringing the sea snake to the surface; and in many cases, the sea snake continued to cling on till torn or shaken off by the victim. In such cases, poisoning was more likely to be serious than in cases in which the sea snake quickly released its bite. Even so, there were several cases in which the snake clung on obstinately, yet no poisoning followed the bite. Handling nets or sorting fish led to bites on the upper limb; the sea snake was not seen until the bite. One fisherman was bitten in a boat when his colleague with the job of finding the sea snakes and throwing them back into the sea, threw a young *E. schistosa* too carelessly, so that it hit the victim at the other end of the boat and promptly bit him on the neck (Figure 2).

Site of the Bite, Repeated Bites, Season, Breeding, and Severity The site of the bite (Table 5) was determined by the circumstances. Treading on the sea snake caused bites on the toe, foot, or leg and resulted in more cases of serious poisoning (17 of 62 cases, or 27%) than finger, hand, or arm bites (five cases of serious poisoning out of 38 cases, or 13%), which were usually caused by handling nets or sorting fish. One patient had been bitten four times, two patients three times, and five patients had been bitten twice; all these previous bites were in fishermen and had occurred before 1957. In three instances, serious poisoning had ensued. When admitted under my care, serious poisoning was observed in only one patient (his third bite; the first caused serious poisoning, the second bite caused only trivial effects). Trivial poisoning occurred in another patient, and in the remaining six patients no poisoning developed. From these limited observations it is not possible to judge whether previous bites affect the resistance of the individual to further bites, but I think this is unlikely for three reasons. First, bites so often occur without envenoming and such bites would have no immunizing effect; second, even if venom is injected, it is very poorly antigenic as judged by reactions in experimental animals (Carey and Wright, 1960); and third, in animals any immunity is short-lived.

The temperature in Malaya varies little and there is no hibernation among land snakes. Monthly incidence of sea snake bite showed little variation; patients were bitten each month throughout the year. One-seventh (14) of the patients were bitten when it was dark, the remaining 87 in the daylight. Severity of poisoning showed no significant variation according to the day,

Table 4. 1957–1964 Hospital series; circumstances of sea snake bites

Activity when bitten	Location when bitten					Total
	In boat	In sea	In river	On shore	Other	
Handling nets	16	1	–	1	–	18
Sorting fish	13	–	–	5	–	18
Trod on while fishing	6	29	9	–	–	44
Trod on while bathing or washing	–	13	5	–	–	18
Other	–	–	–	2	1	3
Total	35	43	14	8	1	101

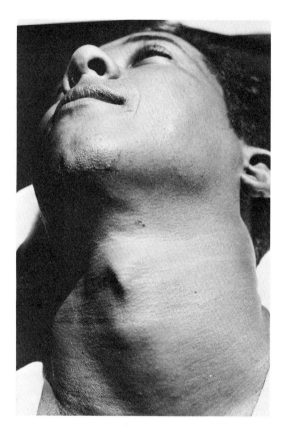

Figure 2. Sea snake bites are inconspicuous, painless, and without swelling. The fang marks are usually circular dots as above but sometimes are mere linear scratch marks. The site of the bite was unusual in the above patient. He was bitten in a boat when his colleague, finding a young *Enhydrina schistosa* in the catch, threw it away too carelessly so that it hit the victim at the other end of the boat and bit him on the neck. Fortunately, no poisoning followed.

the month, or with bites in the dark or light. Observations in the Snake and Venom Research Institute, Penang, suggested that sea snakes in Malayan waters gave birth in May-June, but this appeared to influence neither the frequency nor the severity of bites.

Bite/Hospital Admission Interval, Village Treatment, and Severity The severity in relation to time elapsing between the bite and admission to hospital is summarized in Table 6. Over half the victims were admitted within 4 hrs of the bite. The most rapid admission was that of the supervisor of the Snake and Venom Research Institute, which is on the grounds of the Penang

Table 5. 1957–1964 Hospital series; site of bite and severity of poisoning

Site of bite	Severity of poisoning				Total
	Nil	Trivial	Serious	Fatal	
Toe	8	3	–	–	11
Foot	19	6	5	2	32
Leg	9	–	8	2	19
Finger	25	1	1	2	29
Hand	5	1	–	1	7
Arm	1	–	–	1	2
Neck	1	–	–	–	1

General Hospital. He was accidentally bitten while milking an *E. schistosa*. Fortunately, no poisoning resulted and antivenom did not prove necessary. In the 82 patients coming within 6 hrs of the bite, serious poisoning developed in only 12 cases (about 15%); whereas of the 19 patients coming more than 6 hrs after the bite, 11 or 58% developed serious poisoning–a four-fold increase. This emphasizes the potential fallacy of hospital statistics; the longer the time elapses after a bite, the less likely a victim is to seek medical aid unless poisoning is severe. Thus, hospital statistics underestimate the general incidence of sea snake bite, but overestimate the number of bites with serious poisoning.

Table 6. 1957–1964 Hospital series; bite-admission interval and severity of poisoning

Hours between bite and hospital admission	Severity of poisoning				Total
	Nil	Trivial	Serious	Fatal	
0.5 or less	4	–	–	1	5
0.5–1	6	–	1	1	8
1–2	11	3	1	–	15
2–4	21	2	4	–	27
4–6	19	5	3	–	27
6–10	6	1	1	3	11
Over 10	1	–	4	3	8
Total	68	11	14	8	101

Village treatment for the fishermen or their families was very similar to that recorded in the survey discussed earlier. In no case did it appear to influence the outcome except for involving delay in coming to hospital.

Conclusions on Epidemiology of Sea Snake Bite

The findings of the survey of fishing villages and the 1957–1964 hospital series indicate that sea snake bite is a common occupational hazard to fishing folk in Malayan waters. Both the survey and the hospital series highlight the difficulty in assessing the incidence, the natural morbidity, and natural mortality of these bites; but they effectively show the surprisingly low incidence of serious poisoning in man relative to the lethal potential of sea snake venom in experimental animals (see "Venom Yields and Lethal Toxicity"), even when no effective antivenom is available. The morbidity and mortality in relation to treatment with sea snake antivenom will be considered later. Do these epidemiological features in the Malayan area apply also to other areas of the world where sea snakes abound? I certainly do not think they apply to the African or western coasts of America where the sole naturally occurring species is *Pelamis platurus*. This species does not usually live in the shallow waters such as *E. schistosa* prefers; fishermen are thus less likely to encounter *P. platurus*. Clark (1942) recorded that *P. platurus* was ". . . exceedingly abundant in Panama Bay at some seasons of the year," but that he had never heard of anyone being bitten. So far as I am aware, no sea snake bites have been recorded in the western America area, and I know of only three cases recorded in the African area (Fitzsimmons, 1912). But along Asian coasts, wherever *E. schistosa* is common, I think it is highly likely that fishing folk are often bitten. In the Madras river-mouth in 1815, M'Kenzie (1820) recounted an "epidemic" of sea snake bites. So great was the alarm that the police investigated and confirmed three deaths, all occurring (presumably) in one month. During one month M'Kenzie treated 15 cases with various degrees of poisoning (none fatal). In Vietnam, Barme (1963) records that each year fatal cases are numerous, but actual numbers remain unknown because of superstitions very similar to those found in the Malayan Survey.

What is the risk from sea snakes to bathers? The risk of sea snake bite is certainly much less than the risk of venomous fish stings. During 1957–1959, I observed 13 patients who, while bathing at sea beaches, were bitten by sea snakes (Reid, 1961b), and 140 patients who, while bathing on the same beaches, were stung by catfish, stingrays, or jellyfish. Bathers are occasionally bitten by sea snakes when they inadvertently tread on them. Usually the risk of being bitten is greatly exaggerated. On Penang Island beaches the risk was statistically assessed at one bite per 270,000 man bathing hours. This is in an area where *E. schistosa*, the most dangerous sea snake to man, is commonly found by fishermen. The risk of sea snake bite to bathers is thus low; the risk of death, even without modern treatment, is very much lower owing to the rarity with which sea snakes such as *E. schistosa* inject venom when they bite man. In the hospital series, 58 of the total 101 patients were admitted during 1957–1961 before specific sea snake antivenom was available, and six died. The mortality in this selected group of unequivocal sea snake bites, six deaths out of 58 cases, is 10%. And if the victim *is* envenomed, but receives sea snake antivenom within a few hours of the bite, the mortality should be nil (see "Antivenom," in this chapter). The risk of death from sea snake bite is much less than that of accidental drowning. In 1955–1959, only two bathers in Penang Island waters died from sea snake bite, but 21 bathers from the same beaches died from accidental drowning. The risk of being bitten while swimming is negligible. None of the patients in the 1957–1964 Hospital Series who were bitten while bathing were swimming at the time; they all trod on the sea snake. The risk to bathers of bites by *P. platurus* appears to be even more remote. On one morning, Pickwell (1972) counted 22 stranded specimens of *P. platurus* in half a mile on the Playa del Sol, Puerto Vallarta, in Mexico; great numbers of Mexicans thronged to bathe on these beaches, but sea snake bites were unknown.

PATHOPHYSIOLOGY OF SEA SNAKE BITE POISONING

Venom Yields and Lethal Toxicity

Venom yields of some common species of sea snakes are summarized in Table 1. It should be realized that venom "milking" by pressure over the venom glands, encouraging the snake to bite through a membrane, electrical stimulation, and so on, are all very artificial procedures, and the yields obtained may be extremely capricious, varying significantly from species to species, from specimen to specimen, and from time to time in the same individual specimen. It is quite unknown to what extent these figures represent the amount of venom which the sea snake may or may not inject when they bite prey or when they bite man. At most, the venom yields can give an approximate idea of the amount which different species of sea snakes might inject. Probably more valuable is the amount obtained by milking sea snakes soon after they have bitten human victims; I have obtained large amounts of venom in several such cases where the victim developed little or no poisoning (Reid, 1957). It seems that a defensive bite seldom injects much venom. I think this is the main reason for the low mortality and morbidity in sea snake bite.

The lethal toxicity as judged by animal experiments also varies enormously. Quite apart from differences according to different species of sea snake, the lethal toxicities can vary according to the worker, the method of obtaining the venom, route of injection, types and numbers of animals used, and so on. For example, calculations of LD_{50} for *E. schistosa* venom for mice in μg/kg body weight by various workers are: 107 (Carey and Wright, 1960), 125 (Barme, 1963), 150 (Minton, 1967), and 90 (Tu and Ganthavorn, 1969). In mice and rats, *E. schistosa* venom was twice as toxic as the venom of the tiger snake, *Notechis scutatus,* in rabbits 6 times more toxic, but in cats only half as toxic (Reid, 1956a). Carey and Wright (1960) found *E. schistosa* venom 4 times more toxic than Malayan *Naja naja* venom; venoms of *H. cyanocinctus* and *L. hardwickii* were twice as toxic; venoms of *H. spiralis* and *K. jerdoni* had similar toxicity. Barme (1963) gave minimum lethal doses for mice of venoms from eight species of sea snake, two species of viper, and one species of cobra, evaluated under the same conditions. The doses in μg/kg were as follows:

Species	LD_{50}
E. schistosa	125
H. gracilis	125
H. fasciatus	175
L. hardwickii	200
H. cyanocinctus	350
P. viperina	350
P. platurus	500
Kolpophis annandalei	550
Naja haje	1000
Trimeresurus gramineus	1000
Agkistrodon piscivorus	7500

It is clear from all these findings that sea snake venoms are more toxic than elapid venoms, and much more toxic than viper venoms. But this is countered in many instances by vipers having a more efficient injection apparatus and a greater yield of venom; and elapids are midway between vipers and sea snakes in these two aspects. Rogers (1902–1903) estimated that the minimum lethal dose of *E. schistosa* venom for a 70-kg man would be 3.5 mg or about one-third of the average amount of venom ejected by a fresh adult sea snake. On this basis, the maximum yield of *E. schistosa* venom which I obtained (79 mg) would contain about 22 adult lethal doses.

In summary, I regard *E. schistosa* as the most dangerous sea snake to man on the basis of its abundance, the opinion of fishermen, my own observations on aggressiveness (relative only to that of other sea snake species; *E. schistosa* never bites man unless provoked), venom yields, and lethal toxicities. I would rate other species of sea snakes in descending order of potential danger to man as follows: *H. cyanocinctus, L. hardwickii, H. gracilis, H. spiralis, K. jerdoni, P. platurus,* and *H. klossi.*

Pathophysiology in Experimental Animals

When I investigated the rate of absorption of *E. schistosa* venom in dogs whose tails were bitten by adult specimens of *E. schistosa* (bites involving strong jaw contractions and in all cases resulting in fang marks), I found, by amputating the tail at intervals timed by a stopwatch, that a lethal dose could be absorbed within 3 min or less (Reid, 1956a). I also observed that sea snakes may bite without injecting any significant amounts of venom, even when immediate subsequent milking confirmed the presence of more than enough venom to kill the dogs.

In animals, Rogers (1903a, 1903b), Fraser and Elliott (1905), Kellaway et al. (1932), Carey and Wright (1960, 1961), and Cheymol et al. (1967) considered that sea snake venom was "neurotoxic," acting mainly at the neuromuscular junction. Cheymol et al. (1967) investigated the venoms of *E. schistosa, H. cyanocinctus,* and *L. hardwickii.* Paralysis in preparations from rats, cats, and frogs was peripheral. Nerve fibers did not seem to be affected and muscle fibres were not directly blocked. Specific receptors of the post-synaptic membrane were blocked almost irreversibly. A synergistic action with d-tubocurarine was demonstrated, but neostigmine did not antagonize the paralytic action of the venoms. In doses capable of paralyzing skeletal muscle, the venoms did not affect cardiac contractions in isolated heart preparations from rats and frogs. The authors considered that the action of sea snake venom is practically identical to that of cobra venoms. Lamb and Hunter (1907) injected *E. schistosa* venom subcutaneously into five monkeys and described degenerative changes in the central nervous system and peripheral nerves. Rogers (1903a), Nauch (1929) and Carey and Wright (1960) found little at necropsy. In a later publication, Carey and Wright (1961) reported a direct myotoxic action following injection of *E. schistosa* venom into the femoral artery of rabbits.

In 1959, I injected *E. schistosa* venom subcutaneously into four dogs. Two dogs received the equivalent of 0.1 mg of dried venom per kg body weight; one received fresh venom obtained from two specimens of *E. schistosa* 2 hrs before injection, and the other dog received a solution of dessicated venom reconstituted with distilled water. Both dogs died 1 hr after the injection. Two further dogs received the equivalent of 0.04 mg dried *E. schistosa* venom per kg body weight. One receiving fresh venom died 4 hrs after the injection. The fourth dog receiving reconstituted venom died 3.5 hrs later. Immediately after death, specimens of skeletal muscle were taken from eye, jaw, tongue, intercostal, diaphragm, psoas, forearm, and thigh regions. In all four dogs necrosis was evident in 33%–75% of the muscle fibers from each of the eight regions (Reid and Marsden, unpublished).

Pathophysiology in Man

The clinical paradox of trismus yet flaccid paresis originally stimulated my investigations of sea snake bite (Reid, 1956a). The medical literature then available indicated that sea snake venom was "neurotoxic" and therefore, in two of my fatal cases, tissues of the nervous system were referred to an expert neuropathologist. No histological abnormality was found; at this stage, skeletal muscle was not examined. Experimentally, sea snake venom had been reported as only feebly hemolytic; theoretically, a dose of venom sufficient to cause hemoglobinuria should inevitably be fatal. Yet I knew of patients surviving despite apparent "hemoglobinuria." These anomalies were resolved in 1957 when I realized that the urinary pigment was myoglobin from muscle, and not hemoglobin (Reid, 1961a). This clarified many of the clinical features, and, complementary to the clinical studies, we found the chief pathological lesions of sea snake bite poisoning in man were in skeletal muscle, kidney, and liver (Marsden and Reid, 1961).

In necropsy studies of seven fatal cases and biopsy studies of a patient with very severe nonfatal poisoning, macroscopic changes were deceptively absent, apart from brown or black urine in the bladder. In particular, the color and consistency of skeletal muscles were normal. But, histologically, there were widespread hyaline necroses in skeletal muscles. The toxin picks out individual muscle fibers, leaving a healthy fiber next to a necrosed one, and affects only one or more segments of varying length in a fiber, usually with an abrupt transition to normal muscle. The number of fibers with focal necroses varies from muscle to muscle; in the same patient there may be necroses in 20% or less of the fibers of one muscle, while in another muscle every fiber shows necroses. The affected segment of a muscle fiber first becomes greatly swollen and the sarcoplasm undergoes coagulation necrosis. At this stage, the nuclei and swollen myofibrils can still be distinguished, but the disks of the myofibrils soon lose their differential staining, and both nuclei and myofibrils disappear as they become fused into an amorphous hyaline mass (Figure 3). This necrotic material contracts, leaving an empty space beneath the sarcolemma, which remains intact although it may collapse slightly. Necrotic segments stain more intensely with acid dyes, but this is not conspicuous in routine sections and could easily be overlooked by casual or inexperienced observation. The myonecroses become very obvious with special stains.

Soluble products, notably myoglobin, enzymes and electrolytes, are rapidly absorbed into the blood-stream. Insoluble necrotic fragments are phagocytosed by histiocytes and macrophages. Regeneration and repair begin

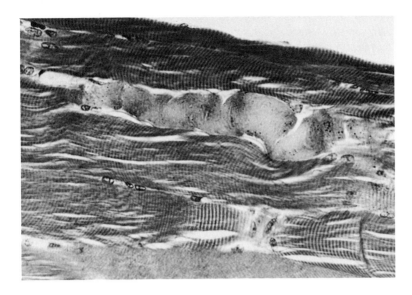

Figure 3. Sea snake venom is primarily myotoxic in man. Muscle biopsy from a patient with severe poisoning shows necrotic fibers which are pale and have no striations. Other fibers retain striations and are apparently healthy.

1—2 weeks after the bite with multiplication of surviving muscle nuclei. The muscle fiber is thus regenerated within its original sarcolemmal sheath and repair is remarkably complete, probably because very few muscle fibers are entirely necrosed. Biopsy 6 months after the bite showed only a little fine scarring.

Renal damage often results from sea snake envenoming as with other types of myonecrosis and other types of envenoming. Distal tubular necrosis was found in all three patients dying more than 48 hrs after the bite. There is extensive necrosis of the epithelium of the loop of Henle, the second convoluted tubule, and the collecting tubules. Desquamated cells with granular and amorphous debris fill the lumen and form casts in the distal and collecting tubules. Pigment giving a positive benzidine reaction is deposited in most of the casts, and even in some of the desquamated cells. The boundary zone is still intensely congested and the interstitial tissue is now edematous, as well as showing both a diffuse and a focal cellular infiltration.

The reactionary or healing stage is not often seen because victims usually die too quickly. Our only example was a patient who died 12 days after the bite. There may be considerable proliferation of the capsular cells of the glomeruli, presumably a reaction to the excreted myoglobin or its breakdown products. The first convoluted tubules appear normal, but, from the loop of

Henle downward, degenerating and regenerating epithelial cells crowd into the lumen, while some of the collecting tubules and excretory ducts are filled with a mass of proliferating cells. The interstitial tissue of the boundary zone and medulla is still edematous and infiltrated with plasma cells, lymphocytes, and histiocytes, but now begins to appear more fibrous. Sitprija et al. (1971) studied two patients with severe poisoning and renal failure. In both patients, biopsies confirmed tubular necrosis in the kidneys and myonecrosis.

In the liver there are no specific changes, but there is usually a centrilobular degeneration with a round- or mixed-cell infiltration of the portal areas. The lungs showed patchy edema, small areas of collapse with compensatory emphysema, and early inflammatory changes in some bronchi were evident, but in no case did it appear likely that the lesions would play an important part in the clinical picture. In cardiac and smooth muscle, no significant lesions have been found.

Apart from the above pathological studies in man, the following clinical observations strongly suggest, in my opinion, that sea snake venom in man is primarily myotoxic rather than neurotoxic:

1. Muscle-movement pains may precede paresis by 3–24 hrs.

2. Initially, much of the paresis is apparent rather than real. The patient may say that he is unable to move his limbs when objectively limb power is normal; the patient is unwilling to move the limbs himself because this is painful.

3. Similarly, the difficulty in opening the mouth is really pseudo-trismus. It differs strikingly from the true trismus of tetanus, which is neurogenic. Sustained pressure on the lower jaw does not increase the gape in tetanus at all, but will do so in sea snake envenoming (though this is very painful for the patient). Second, the jaw-jerk is very brisk in tetanus, but becomes sluggish or absent in sea snake bite poisoning. This suggests that the pseudo-trismus and stiffness in limbs and trunk, in the early stages of poisoning at least, are due to splinting reaction of intact muscle cells protecting injured cells against further damage by stretching.

4. No muscle fibrillation or fasciculation is seen.

5. There is no qualitative change in response to faradic and galvanic stimulation; this is typical of a myopathic lesion (Walker and Adams, 1958). Electromyograms in a patient with severe poisoning also indicated a myopathic disturbance (Sitprija et al., 1971).

6. Myoglobinuria appears before paresis and occurs in minimal poisoning with no paresis.

7. Without antivenom, natural recovery following severe sea snake bite poisoning is slow (months), whereas it is rapid (days) in neurotoxic elapid poisoning.

8. SGOT is greatly raised in minimal poisoning with no myalgia or paresis;

SGOT levels are normal in severe neurotoxic poisoning by Malayan cobra bite.

Myonecrosis can explain the generalized muscle movement pains, hyperkalemia, myoglobinuria, and much of the paresis in severe sea snake bite poisoning. But hyperkalemia and uremia may also contribute to the paresis, since Sitprija et al. (1971) found that hemodialysis produced a rapid improvement of the muscular activity. It is probable that sea snake venom directly attacks the cell membrane of skeletal muscle in human victims. But the patchy distribution of visible damage to skeletal muscles and the absence of lesions in cardiac and smooth muscle are not explained, except that it is increasingly apparent that venoms can be very highly specific in their biological actions; hence they have great value as research tools. In victims dying more than 48 hrs after the bite, acute renal failure appeared to be the immediate cause of death. Experimentally, Bywaters and Stead (1944) showed that myoglobin injected into healthy rabbits caused no renal damage unless the urine was acidified. It is therefore unlikely that the myoglobin released in sea snake poisoning is solely responsible for the renal lesions. Is the venom nephrotoxic? Reid and Jenkins (1948) showed that cobra venom acted directly on the kidney of eviscerated adrenalectomized cats, causing liberation of renin. Early sustained hypertension was observed in two cases; progressive hyperkalemia was the immediate cause of death in another two patients. Renal damage may be mainly responsible for these two features, i.e., a renal pressor factor leading to hypertension, while progressive hyperkalemia arose because diminished renal excretion failed to cope with the extra load from cellular release of potassium.

CLINICAL FEATURES OF SEA SNAKE BITE

Frequency of Poisoning: Fright

The most important clinical fact about sea snake bite is that it is rare for much venom to be injected, and therefore most victims suffer only from the effects of fright. This point requires repeated emphasis because the belief that snake bite in man inevitably means poisoning is still widely held. I have been bitten by a sea snake on two occasions. No poisoning followed a bite by an adult *H. spiralis,* and only slight symptoms of poisoning occurred with a bite by *E. schistosa* (Reid, 1957). In the hospital series of sea snake bites, 58 patients with unequivocal sea snake bite were seen during 1957–1961 before sea snake antivenom became available. In 47 of these bites, trivial or no poisoning followed. Serious poisoning developed in 11 patients, of whom six died. It is therefore notable that, in the minority of cases where serious poisoning does occur, death is likely in about half such cases unless effective antivenom is available. These facts emphasize the importance of distinguishing sea snake bite and sea snake envenoming.

A common symptom in many victims, especially fishermen, regardless of whether venom was injected or not, is a feeling of general coldness. This comes on soon after the initial prick of the bite; no local pain or local swelling occurs in sea snake bite. Thereafter, symptoms due to fright may dominate the clinical picture. These symptoms come on within minutes of the bite and may lead to collapse. The patient may appear semiconscious, with cold, clammy skin, feeble pulse, and rapid, shallow breathing. These symptoms resolve dramatically after a placebo injection.

Sea snake bites are usually inconspicuous, painless, and without swelling. The fang marks are one, two or more small dots which are usually circular as though made by a pin or hypodermic needle (Figure 2); but they can appear as linear scratches. They may be accompanied by teeth marks which are smaller and more likely to be linear. In some cases, there have been no clear fang marks, just an odd "scratch" mark, and yet serious poisoning has occurred.

Clinical Characteristics of Poisoning

The latent period from bite to the onset of poisoning symptoms varied from 0.5 to 3.5 hrs in the hospital series. In serious poisoning, the latent period never exceeded 2 hrs. Usually, the first symptom is muscle aches, pains, and stiffness on movement in the neck, throat, tongue, shoulders, trunk, or limbs. In a few cases these myalgic symptoms have been preceded by giddiness, a dry feeling in the throat, vomiting or general weakness. The aching stiffness becomes generalized within half an hour. Initially it is like the muscle soreness after unaccustomed exercise (when I developed mild poisoning following the *E. schistosa* bite, the aching pains were just like the results following the first training at the start of a football season). Swallowing and speaking become increasingly difficult. Examination 1 to 2 hrs after the bite reveals moderate or severe pain on *passive movement* of arm, thigh, neck, or trunk muscles (Figure 4). Muscles may be tender on pressure such as squeezing a limb, but this feature, unlike pain with *passive movement*, is often absent or unimpressive. On neurological examination, findings, including power and tendon reflexes, will be normal at this stage. The patient is unable (or unwilling owing to the pain) to sit up unaided or open the mouth fully. Involvement of jaw muscles by the myotoxic sea snake venom leads to pseudo-trismus—a splinting effect of intact muscles protecting the damaged ones. Other early features are headache, thick feeling of the tongue, constant thirst, episodic sweating, and vomiting. In rare cases, the patient denies muscle pains and stiffness, complaining only of weakness; however, on

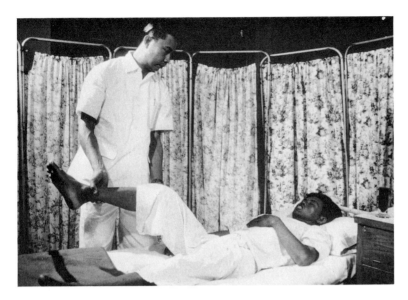

Figure 4. In sea snake bite poisoning, generalized muscle pains on movement start within two hrs of the bite. Passive movement of neck, trunk, and limbs–bending as here–becomes very painful.

examination, passive movement is painful. Myoglobinuria becomes evident on inspection 3–6 hrs after the bite; a dusky yellow color and positive protein and occult blood tests precede by an hour or so the red-brown color of spectroscopically positive myoglobinuria (Figure 5). In most cases, the blood pressure is normal. Sometimes there is early hypertension. Hypertension on admission is often due to fright but this quickly resolves. When early hypertension is sustained, it is possibly secondary to nephrotoxic effects. Usually hypertension is a late development of asphyxial origin.

After some hours, true paresis of peripheral type may ensue, and, later still, tendon reflexes become depressed, then absent. The paresis becomes flaccid; ptosis, ophthalmoplegia, inability to protrude the tongue or swallow, "broken neck syndrome" (from paresis of neck muscles), and inability to sit up result. But even at a late stage in some patients, active limb movement may be notably preserved. Ptosis may be mistaken for drowsiness; however, the patient is usually mentally alert until respiratory failure is far advanced. There is no clinical evidence of cerebral, cerebellar, or extrapyramidal involvement and sphincter disturbance is unusual. The combination of glossopharyngeal palsy with inhalation of vomit or secretions or both can precipitate early respiratory failure which, if not dealt with promptly, can be rapidly fatal. Respiratory failure from muscle weakness may supervene within a few hours

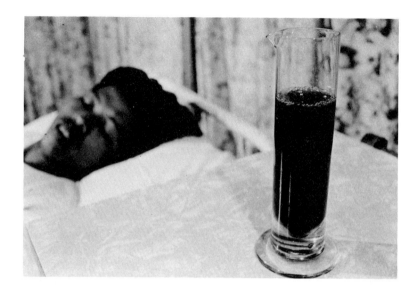

Figure 5. A few hours after sea snake bite urine is brown or red with myoglobin (pigment from damaged muscles). The patient also shows ptosis and pseudotrismus. Difficulty and pain in opening the mouth are due to a spasm of the undamaged jaw muscles protecting injured muscles against further damage by stretching.

of a bite, or as long as 60 hrs after the bite. Breathing becomes shallow, the blood pressure rises, and there is increased sweating. The subject becomes drowsy, then comatose. Pupils dilate and their reaction to light fails shortly before death. Other patients succumb from hyperkalemic cardiac arrest, or (later) from acute renal failure. Three-quarters of the victims dying do so within 24 hrs of the bite. The most rapid death recorded is 2.5 hrs after the bite (Fitzsimmons, 1912); the longest period between bite and death is 24 days (Karunaratne and Panabokke, 1972). Death 48 hrs or more after the bite is usually due to acute renal failure.

If significant toxemia follows a sea snake bite, moderate leucocytosis is invariable. The degree and duration correlate approximately with the severity of the toxemia. Eosinophils have not been increased. No evidence of abnormal hemolysis or coagulation defect has been found. Reticulocytes, platelets, saline fragility of red blood cells, serum bilirubin, urinary urobilinogen, bleeding-time, coagulation time, one-stage prothrombin time, direct Coombs, Schumm's, Donath-Landsteiner, and Kahn tests were always normal. Myoglobinuria is easily overlooked or mistaken for hemoglobinuria. The simplest distinction is observation of the plasma color, which is normal with myoglobinuria (because the myoglobin molecule is much smaller than hemoglobin and is rapidly excreted); with hemoglobinuria the plasma is pink or red during the phase of acute hemolysis. Other confirmatory tests of myoglobinuria include spectroscopy (preferably after conversion to carboxymyoglobin), electrophoretic mobility (Whishnant et al., 1959), and immunoassay (Farmer et al., 1961). The most sensitive test of sea snake envenoming is the serum glutamic oxalocetic transaminase (SGOT). The marked elevation of SGOT is due to release of the enzyme from damaged muscle and similar changes have been recorded in idiopathic myoglobinuria (Pearson et al., 1957). SGOT has been grossly raised in a patient with very trivial myalgic symptoms and no abnormal clinical signs; it is thus a very sensitive confirmary test of sea snake bite poisoning, but the level does not necessarily reflect the severity of the lesions. The serum glutamic pyruvic transaminase (SGPT) may also be raised if there is liver dysfunction. Lumbar puncture has revealed normal cerebrospinal fluid.

Protein, numerous granular casts, and some erythrocytes in early urine specimens indicate serious kidney damage, which may explain early sustained hypertension. Plasma urea, creatinine, and potassium are usually raised in severe poisoning, and become progressively raised in the terminal stages of fatal cases. The electrocardiogram (ECG) is particularly useful for detecting and monitoring hyperkalemia (Figure 6). Apart from changes due to hyperkalemia, ECG abnormalities, specially in the right chest leads, are common in severe poisoning (Reid, 1961a), although clinical, radiological, and pathological evidence of direct cardiovascular damage is conspicuously absent.

Diagnosis

The clinician has to answer two main questions, namely, is it a sea snake bite, and, more important, is there significant poisoning? Fish-stings are much more common than sea snake bites, especially among bathers. Severe local pain follows; its presence excludes the possibility of a sea snake bite, which, after the initial prick, is painless. The appearance of the fang and teeth marks at the site of the bite is of little diagnostic help—one or more circular dots as though made by a hypodermic needle. There is no local swelling unless it is caused by a tight tourniquet. Sometimes there are just a few scratch marks. The inconspicuous local features of a sea snake bite can be deceptive. In one patient the doctor thought that "it could not be a sea snake bite since there were no fang marks." This led to a fatal delay in admitting the patient. Fangs and teeth may break off and remain embedded in the skin. Fishermen quite often draw a hair over the site to extract teeth, thereby confirming that a bite has been made. But personally, I never found this succeeded by the time the patient reached hospital. A sea snake bite may be diagnosed when the

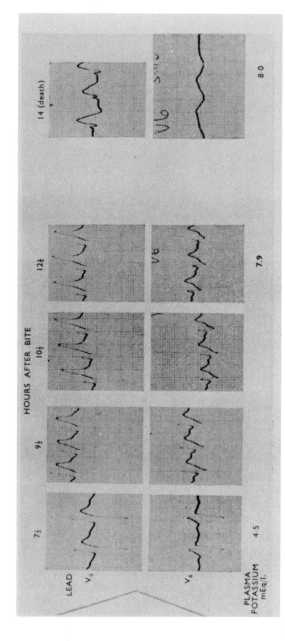

Figure 6. The electrocardiogram in this fatal case shows the typical tall, peaked T-waves of hyperkalemia progressing to cardiac arrest. The excess potassium is released from damaged skeletal muscles. The electrocardiograph is very useful clinically in detecting and monitoring hyperkalemia for prognostic and therapeutic purposes.

opportunity for contact with a sea snake has been clearly established, by absence of pain, and by marks compatible with those made by sea snake fangs.

Significant envenoming is shown by the history of myalgic pains and "weakness;" examination 1 to 2 hrs after the bite reveals moderate or severe pain on passively moving the patient's arm, thigh, trunk, or neck muscles. Proteinuria, followed by red-brown color indicating myoglobinuria, confirms the diagnosis of serious poisoning. A high SGOT is a sensitive sign of envenoming, but it is unlikely the result would be received in time to influence treatment.

If a patient should come to a doctor within 1 hr of being bitten, before symptoms of poisoning might have started (an uncommon event), judgment must be reserved. But if 2 hrs have elapsed since the bite and there are no "remote" pains on muscle movement, serious poisoning can be excluded. The only exception to this "2-hour clearance" rule would be when a victim applies an effective tourniquet within a minute or so of the bite and keeps it on until he reaches medical aid.

Prognosis: Natural Recovery Course in Poisoning

Multiple bite marks suggest a high venom dose, though single marks do not necessarily indicate a small dose. Vomiting, ptosis, weakness of external eye muscles, dilation of pupils with a sluggish light reaction, and a leucocytosis exceeding 20,000 are all sinister signs. The remaining early clinical features are equally common in patients who subsequently recover (without anti-venom), but the tempo is quicker in the potentially fatal cases—a matter of hours rather than days (Figure 7). Signs of respiratory insufficiency with hypertension and cyanosis indicate the end is near. If an ECG is available, serial records are the most practical means of revealing hyperkalemia for prognostic and therapeutic purposes. Tall, peaked T-waves in chest leads V2, V3, and V4 are a danger sign (Figure 6). After the first 3 or 4 days following the bite, renal failure is the chief hazard, and may cause death with remarkably few warning symptoms. A "fixed" specific gravity of 1.010–1.013, together with a low urine volume output and progressively rising blood urea, indicates the need for urgent treatment.

In severe poisoning, when the patient has not received effective anti-venom, recovery may take up to 6 months (Figure 8). Myalgia and myoglobinuria reach a peak during the first week and recede in the second week. Paresis becomes more complete during this week. Improvement in power starts slowly during the 3rd week. Tendon reflexes return during the 3rd or 4th week. The patient is now able to lift his head off the bed and sits up by rolling onto his side and helping himself up with his arms. For the next month, the clinical resemblance to muscular dystrophy is striking; the patient

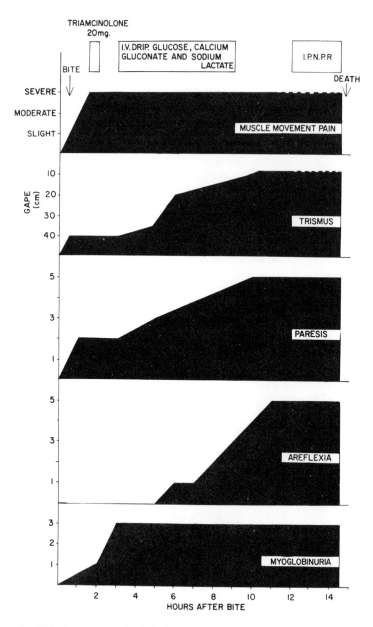

Figure 7. Clinical course to death before sea snake antivenom was available. Paresis follows muscle-movement pains; death occurred despite adequate artificial respiration.

I.P.N.P.R., intermittent positive/negative-pressure artificial respiration. Paresis: 5 = respiratory failure; 4 = unable to lift one or more limbs; 3 = unable to lift head; 2 = unable to sit up spontaneously; 1 = objective weakness less than 2. Areflexia: 5 = 7–8 tendon reflexes absent; 4 = 5–6 absent; 3 = 3–4 absent; 2 = 1–2 absent; 1 = present but weak. Myoglobinuria: 3 = dark brown, red, or black, spectroscopically positive; 2 = light brown or dark yellow, spectroscopically positive; 1 = benzidine-positive, spectroscopically negative.

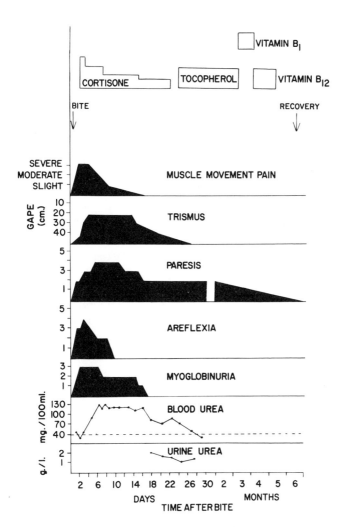

Figure 8. Natural course of recovery in severe poisoning. Muscle movement pains recede before paresis, which takes 6 months for full recovery. Tendon reflexes become normal within 2 weeks. Raised blood urea with low urinary urea reflects renal damage.
Notation as in Figure 7.

"climbs up himself." During the next few months, hand-grip, "press ups," and sitting up spontaneously from the lying position slowly return to normal. The best guide to the rate of recovery is the duration of myoglobinuria—each day myoglobin is visible on inspecting the urine means approximately 1 week of illness. Full recovery occurs in 3 to 4 weeks in moderate cases and within a few days in trivial poisoning.

Permanent renal damage can result from sea snake bite poisoning and some muscle weakness has still been detectable 1.5 years after the bite. But none of these long-term effects should occur if the patient receives effective antivenom. No evidence of long-term liver damage has been found.

MANAGEMENT AND TREATMENT OF SEA SNAKE BITE

First-aid Measures

First-aid comprises the measures taken by the victim or associates before receiving medical treatment. A firm ligature should be applied at the base of the toe or finger, or, if the bite is higher up, around the thigh or arm. The purpose of the ligature is to compress the underlying tissues and thus delay absorption of venom *if* venom has been injected. (As will be seen from the above, this is an unlikely event, but there is no reliable way of knowing, shortly after the bite, whether venom has in fact been injected or not.) The tourniquet should not be so tight that the arterial pulses are obliterated, and it should be left on until the patient reaches medical aid. If the victim is able to reach a hospital or a medical center holding effective antivenom within an hour, there is no point in applying a tourniquet. Incision and suction are ineffective and not recommended. The victim should go to hospital as quickly as possible. Experimentally, muscle movements entailed by walking and so on can accelerate absorption of venom (again, *if* venom is injected); because of this, some writers have advised that all exertion must be avoided. Such advice, in my opinion, is ill-founded because it is quite impracticable, and if attempted would be highly likely to increase emotional reactions of fear. Experiments have also shown that amputation of a bitten part, if performed within 3 min of a bite, could effectively prevent poisoning. It might be possible to do this in the case of a toe or finger bite; but almost certainly the toe or finger would be sacrificed unnecessarily.

On rare occasions the sea snake has been killed, and in that event it should be taken to hospital (for scientific identification and investigations). Otherwise, no attempt should be made to recover the sea snake; I know of three instances when associates of the victim tried to catch the sea snake and another bite resulted.

Antivenom should play no part in first-aid treatment. It is strictly medical treatment and, if wrongly used, can be more dangerous than the sea snake bite. Antivenom is only needed in a small proportion of sea snake bites and to be effective has to be given by intravenous infusion under expert medical supervision. The only exception to this important matter might be a sophisticated expedition with no hospital available within 5–6 hrs of the bite. Provided the expedition included a doctor or a medical assistant specially trained in the administration of antivenom, it might be sensible to carry antivenom. But even in such exceptional circumstances, antivenom administration would constitute a medical and not a first-aid procedure.

Medical Treatment

General Measures When first seen by a doctor, the majority of patients with sea snake bite will pass the "2-hour clearance test" and require only reassurance, which is best achieved by a prompt injection of a placebo such as vitamin B complex. Any ligature that has been applied should be promptly released. If the doctor has any doubt about poisoning subsequently developing (for example, if the victim has presented very shortly after the bite, or has applied a tourniquet which could delay absorption of venom), the patient should be detained for several hours and frequently observed for signs of poisoning. If these develop, or are already present when the patient is first seen, then antivenom is indicated. If symptoms do not develop within a few hours, the patient can be discharged.

As soon as significant toxemia is apparent, antivenom should be given and general supportive measures adopted. Removal of sea snake venom from the site of the bite by incision, suction, and so on, would not be as effective as hospital treatment. It is not known whether appreciable venom is excreted by the kidneys in man. When I injected into animals urine from patients with severe sea snake envenoming the results were equivocal. But it is rational to promote a diuresis, both to encourage excretion of venom and secondary toxic products, and to minimize renal damage. The patient should drink a liter of water as quickly as possible, or be given a rapid intravenous infusion of a liter of a mixture of 25% glucose, 10% calcium gluconate, and molar sodium lactate. Postural treatment is vital to prevent inhalation of vomit or secretions, or both; the patient should be kept off his back so that gravity will assist tracheal drainage of chest secretions; infection and lung collapse are thus prevented. Physical rest is important in severe poisoning, to avoid tearing the fragile sarcolemmal sheaths that normally guide the regenerating muscle fibers. I used to give steroid therapy as a nonspecific, antitoxemic drug, as a muscle strengthener, and as a means of increasing potassium excretion by the kidneys (Reid, 1961b); but this was before effective antivenom became available. In practice, it was not notably successful and I would no longer recommend its use except for delayed antivenom reactions. I also tried neostigmine in five patients in the hope that it might "unblock" the myoneural junctions; no discernible improvement resulted. Tracheostomy and artificial respiration may still be needed if patients present late and are already in respiratory failure. But this supportive measure should no longer be needed provided effective antivenom can be given in adequate doses. Hyperkalemia sometimes improves with insulin, and if this does not succeed in shifting the potassium back into the cells, a potassium-removing ion-exchange resin should be given by gastric tube. In this type of case, where the ECG shows the tall peaked T-waves of hyperkalemia, hemodialysis can be dramatically successful (Sitprija et al., 1971). Peritoneal dialysis has also been tried (Karunaratne and Panabokke, 1972); the patient improved temporarily but eventually died 24 days after the bite. However, the dialysis was not started until 10 days after the bite and was done under adverse conditions. Effective antivenom was not available for these patients.

Antivenom Specific antivenom is the most important therapeutic agent available for the effective treatment of systemic snake bite poisoning. If it is used correctly it can be effective even though it is not given until hours or sometimes days after the bite.

The two main disadvantages of antivenom are cost and adverse reactions. Adequate antivenom treatment is expensive, and this is particularly important in those parts of the world where snake bite is a major medical problem, in the developing areas of the tropics. Five ampoules of sea snake antivenom, which may be needed for adequate treatment of a patient with very severe sea snake envenoming, may cost the equivalent of 200 U.S. dollars. With un-refined antivenom, the overall incidence of adverse serum reactions is about 30%. Severe immediate reactions are, of course, less common, perhaps about 3%. Three therapeutic antivenoms have been shown to be effective for sea snake bite poisoning—*Enhydrina schistosa* antivenom (Reid, 1962) and *Notechis scutatus* antivenom from the Commonwealth Serum Laboratories, Melbourne, Australia, and *Lapemis hardwickii* antivenom made in Vietnam (Barme et al., 1962). The latter antivenom is no longer available. The two Australian antivenoms are available commercially and both are refined so that adverse serum reactions are much less likely to occur than with unrefined antivenoms. Nevertheless, anaphylactic reactions can occur and may be fatal (Reid, 1957; Lancet editorial, 1957). In other words, antivenom can be lethal.

We have already seen that only a small minority of human beings bitten by sea snakes do in fact develop poisoning (only about one-third of the patients coming to Penang Hospital in 1962–1964). It should therefore be obvious that at least two-thirds do *not* require antivenom. And yet the idea unfortunately still persists for many people, including doctors, that antivenom automatically should be injected in every single case of sea snake bite, or even in cases where sea snake bite is merely suspected. Indiscriminate use of sea snake (or other) antivenom can easily bring it into disrepute, first, by unnecessarily increasing the number of serum reactions; second, by encouraging inadequate dosage in the few patients who really could benefit from antivenom; and third, by the unnecessary, even harmful, waste of money.

A controlled trial of specific antivenom in patients with Malayan viper envenoming showed highly significant benefit in systemic poisoning (Reid et al., 1963a). Disappointingly, the antivenom did not appear to benefit the *local* effects of envenoming, especially local necrosis. In land snake bite, the adequate treatment of local necrosis remains a major problem. Fortunately this problem does not arise in sea snake bites because local effects are negligible. Thus, the only indication for giving effective antivenom in sea snake bites is *clinically evident systemic poisoning.*

The first refined therapeutic sea snake antivenom to be made has been produced at the Commonwealth Serum Laboratories (CSL) by hyperimmunizing horses with *E. schistosa* venom supplied from the Snake and Venom Research Institute, Penang. Hyperimmunization is carried out by a series of injections of increasing doses of *E. schistosa* venom over a period of 2–6 months, followed by maintenance "booster" doses. The horse develops immunity and its serum is removed and purified–a process for separating the antitoxic immunoglobulins from unwanted proteins. The incidence of allergic reactions in human beings is thus reduced from 30% (with unpurified antivenom) to about 10%. The CSL sea snake antivenom is in liquid form, each ampoule containing 1000 units (sufficient to neutralize 10 mg *E. schistosa* venom by in vitro tests). The volume may vary but is usually 37 ml per ampoule. If it is kept in an ordinary refrigerator at 4°C, loss of potency is negligible, even though the ampoule is marked with a two year "expiry date" (stored at 5–15°C, loss of potency is under 3% per annum; at 20°C under 5% per annum; at 37°C, 10–20% per annum). It should therefore be realized that antivenom does not become useless immediately the expiry date is passed. Provided the solution is clear on inspection, it is safe to use; but if it has become cloudy or opaque, the antivenom should be discarded since there will then be a much greater danger of unwanted reactions.

Shortly after I first received this CSL sea snake antivenom in Penang, I was able to use it to treat two victims with severe poisoning (Reid, 1962). In at least one of them (Figure 9), the poisoning was likely, by comparison with previous cases, to have been fatal. Without antivenom, severely poisoned victims have invariably taken weeks or months to recover (Reid, 1961a). The improvement following antivenom in these two subjects was by comparison dramatic; clinical recovery took only 6 days and 3 days, respectively. A third patient seen at this time with moderate poisoning was not given antivenom because the supply was then so severely restricted. He took 2 weeks to recover (Figure 10). During 1962 to early 1964, I treated 10 patients with serious sea snake envenoming by the CSL antivenom. Seven received either 1000 or 2000 units and responded dramatically, recovering completely in a few days. One patient was admitted moribund 45 hrs after the bite. The delay in admission was mainly due to a doctor dismissing the possibility of sea snake bite because he could not make out definite fang marks. The patient received 2000 units of antivenom and temporarily improved, but he died 59 hrs after the bite. Another patient, admitted 8 hrs after the bite in advanced poisoning, received 5000 units of antivenom and greatly improved so far as the myotoxic signs were concerned. But he developed increasing hyperkalemia which did not respond to insulin, and he died 19 hrs after the bite. The 10th patient was admitted with severe poisoning 46 hrs after the bite. He was given 5000 units of antivenom. He steadily improved and had fully recovered 25 days after the bite. In all 10 cases, the antivenom was given solely by intravenous infusion. A mild urticarial skin eruption occurred in

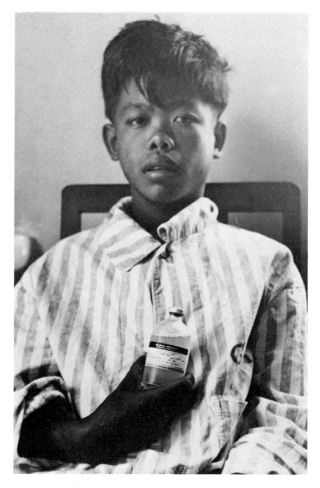

Figure 9. This young fisherman had extremely severe sea snake bite poisoning when he came to hospital 6 hrs after the bite. But improvement with sea snake antivenom was dramatic and recovery was complete within a week.

four patients, but quickly responded to antihistamine treatment. No hypotensive serum reactions occurred. In Table 7 it is shown that in 1957–1961, before sea snake antivenom was available, six of 11 patients with serious poisoning died. In 1962–1964, 10 of the 11 patients with serious poisoning were given antivenom and only two died. If more antivenom had been available, it is more than likely that the two deaths would have been prevented and that recovery in the 10th patient would have been much more rapid.

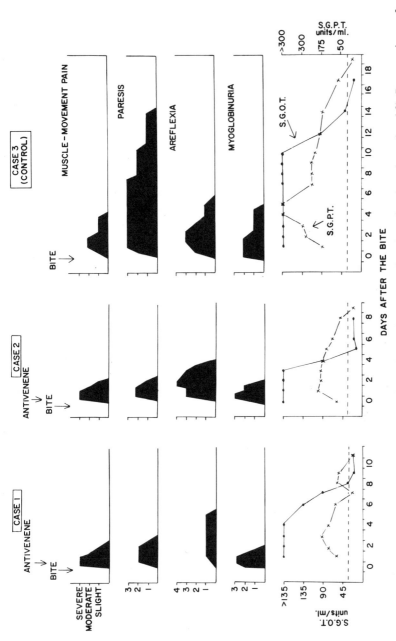

Figure 10. Rapid recovery after administration of sea snake antivenom in two severely poisoned patients (cases 1 and 2). Recovery in case 3 with only moderate poisoning and no antivenom (because supply was very restricted) is, by comparison, much delayed. Notation as in Figure 7.

451

Table 7. 1957–1964 Hospital series; severity of poisoning before and after sea snake antivenom became available

	Severity of poisoning				
	Nil	Trivial	Serious	Fatal	Total
1957–1961 (no antivenom)	41	6	5	6	58
1962–1964 (specific antivenom available)	27	5	9	2	43

One of the most important aspects of these cases is the fact that antivenom was successful although not given until up to 2 days after the bite (the earliest it was given was 3 hrs after the bite). It is therefore not only safe but very desirable to wait until there is clear evidence of poisoning before giving sea snake antivenom. For example, if a victim is seen within 1 hr of being bitten, before symptoms may have developed, or if the patient presents with an effective tourniquet applied, a placebo injection should be given and the patient kept under observation, the tourniquet having been removed in the latter case. If significant poisoning symptoms do not ensue during the next hour, antivenom is *not* indicated. In the minority needing antivenom, the intravenous route is mandatory. It is much more effective than other parenteral routes; it is also safer because, if serum reactions occur, administration can be slowed or stopped; whereas the whole dose is already in the patient with an intramuscular or subcutaneous injection. In sea snake bite poisoning, it is safe to delay administration for 30 min after a subcutaneous test dose of 0.2 ml antivenom to exclude sensitivity. Furthermore, if the sensitivity test is positive, it should be possible to desensitize the patient by graded-dose technique, culminating in an effective intravenous neutralizing dose.

The intravenous infusion is started slowly (15 drops per min). If a reaction occurs (and reactions can occur although the sensitivity test is negative), the drip should be temporarily stopped and 0.5 ml adrenaline 1:1000 solution should be injected subcutaneously. If adrenaline is injected at the first sign of anaphylaxis, it is quickly effective and usually the drip can be cautiously re-started. In the 10 cases recorded above no patient developed hypotensive anaphylactic reactions, whereas, in treating patients with land snake envenoming by unrefined antivenom, anaphylactic reactions were fairly common. I found adrenaline (if given promptly) much more effective than steroids or antihistamine drugs for this type of reaction. In some cases, several injections of adrenaline are needed. In early or moderate cases of poisoning, 1000 units of antivenom should suffice; in later or more severe cases 3000–

10,000 units would be more suitable. The speed of administration is progressively increased so that the infusion is completed within about an hour. If by then there has been little significant improvement, further antivenom should be given. The myotoxic symptoms will quickly resolve in successful treatment but, for the next few days, the possibility of hyperkalemia and renal failure should be constantly monitored by ECG, renal output, and blood urea estimations. Late serum reactions may also occur up to 2 weeks after the bite and are best treated by steroids (Reid, 1957).

The CSL sea snake antivenom is made by using *E. schistosa* venom as antigen. By in vitro tests, Carey and Wright (1960) found that *E. schistosa* antivenom significantly neutralized venoms of *H. cyanocinctus* and *H. spiralis;* similarly, Tu and Ganthavorn (1969) found it neutralized venoms of *H. cyanocinctus, L. hardwickii,* and *P. platurus.* Minton (1967) found that *N. scutatus* (tiger snake) antivenom, also from CSL, neutralized *E. schistosa* venom as effectively as the specific antivenom. More recently, Baxter and Gallichio (1974) studied in vitro neutralization of venoms of *Aipysurus laevis, Astrotia stokesii, E. schistosa, H. cyanocinctus, H. elegans, Disteira major, H. spiralis, L. hardwickii, L. semifasciata,* and *N. scutatus* by *E. schistosa* antivenom and *N. scutatus* antivenom. Both antivenoms neutralized all these venoms and *N. scutatus* was usually more effective. But the cost of *N. scutatus* antivenom sufficient to neutralize 10 mg *E. schistosa* venom would be twice that of *E. schistosa* antivenom; the volumes would be similar for each antivenom because *N. scutatus* antivenom is more concentrated (380 units per ml) than the *E. schistosa* antivenom (27.3 units per ml). The amount of antivenom needed to neutralize 10 mg venom would be cheaper with *E. schistosa* antivenom for venoms of *E. schistosa, Disteira major,* and *L. hardwickii;* and cheaper with *N. scutatus* antivenom for venoms of *A. laevis, A. stokesii, H. cyanocinctus, H. elegans, H. spiralis, L. semifasciata,* and *N. scutatus.*

These important studies require clinical confirmation but they suggest to me that *E. schistosa* antivenom remains the antivenom of choice for the regions where *E. schistosa* or *L. hardwickii* are the most common species encountered by man; this area stretches from the Gulf of Iran to Vietnam and as far as Indonesia. For the western Pacific coastal regions, *N. scutatus* antivenom would be preferable for treating sea snake bite poisoning.

PREVENTION OF SEA SNAKE BITE AND POISONING

Since fishermen are at special risk of sea snake bite, active immunization was suggested (Reid, 1956b). But later, I realized that snake venoms are poor antigens, although many snake handlers mistakenly regard themselves as immune because they are frequently bitten without symptoms of poisoning (they do not realize that this is because the snake has not injected venom). Animals require many inoculations before resistance develops, some individual animals never acquire immunity, and immunity when acquired lasts only a few months (Kuwajima, 1953; Carey and Wright, 1960). To immunize fishing folk effectively against sea snake bite poisoning would involve an initial course of about six injections each month and then booster doses 2 or 3 times a year for the rest of their fishing lives. Such a program is completely impracticable; enormous quantities of sea snake venom would be needed, the cost would be fantastic, and even if it were offered to fishing folk, I do not think they would accept more than one or two injections.

Fishermen might reduce the risk of sea snake bite by being more careful how they handle nets, sort fish, and so on. But they are well aware of this without advice from outsiders. They are also aware that when walking in the sea or river-mouth, one should shuffle along in order to warn off sea snakes. Amateur fishermen of course should be advised to treat sea snakes with great care. Although sea snakes may seem docile most of the time, it would be extremely foolish to rely on their reluctance to bite man, as I myself once found (Reid, 1957). In some regions, sea snakes may be caught by amateur fishermen using a line and hook. The line should be cut and the sea snake dropped into the water, without handling. If a sea snake finds its way by net or line into a boat, no attempt should be made to kill it. It should be lifted sharply by the tail, held at arm's length with regular shaking of the hand (this is most effective in keeping the sea snake vertical and stopping it "climbing up itself" to bite the hand), and then thrown into the sea. This procedure was used by most of the Malaysian fishermen I saw at their work.

Bathers in regions where sea snakes can occur should follow the example of fishermen and shuffle, rather than walk, on the sea bed. Bathers are quite safe swimming in the sea, if their feet do not touch the sea bed, and therefore should keep swimming as far as possible. River-mouths should also be avoided, but, generally speaking, the river-mouths where sea snakes occur are dirty, muddy regions that no tourist or visiting bather would find attractive.

If sea snake antivenom is available in local hospitals (as it should be), education is often needed to persuade fishing folk that they should go to the hospital as soon as possible after a sea snake bite and not delay matters with village treatment. In many areas it would take only one or two cases successfully treated in hospital to change their habits from reluctance to eagerness in seeking modern medical treatment in hospital.

GENERAL COMMENTS AND CONCLUSIONS

A survey of fishing villages in northwest Malaya confirmed that fishing folk are often bitten by sea snakes. It was estimated that some 1500 victims were bitten each year among the Malayan fishing population, but very few indeed sought orthodox medical help in hospitals. Thus medical statistics cannot accurately reflect the incidence of sea snake bite. Furthermore, victims developing severe poisoning are more likely to go to hospital than those developing slight or no poisoning. Hospital statistics, therefore, tend to underestimate the true incidence of sea snake bite and overestimate the number of cases with severe poisoning.

The survey confirmed that sea snake bite is an occupational hazard, 90% of the victims being bitten through treading on a sea snake or handling a sea snake while fishing. Fishermen may encounter up to 100 or more sea snakes a day depending on the method of fishing. The most common method leading to sea snake bite was using a small drag seine pulled along by two or three fishermen in shallow water. Village treatment differs according to racial customs. Details are outlined; the fishing folk have great faith in this treatment, but they admitted that they would be very happy if hospitals had a "special injection" for sea snake bite (the survey was carried out before sea snake antivenom became available). Fishermen are well informed about sea snakes but have numerous superstitions which tend to conceal sea snake bites, for instance, that talking about sea snake bites offends the sea snakes and may change their timidity to aggressiveness or that talking about sea snake bites will lead to further bites.

During 1957–1964, a total of 101 patients with unequivocal sea snake bite were personally observed. Epidemiological features in this hospital series are reviewed. *Enhydrina schistosa* was identified as causing over half the bites, including seven of the eight fatal bites. Sex, age, and race of the victims, the time of day, and the season of the year did not appear to influence the severity of poisoning. The youngest victim was aged 16 months. She was bitten by an *E. schistosa,* which I milked 2 hrs after the bite and obtained venom equivalent to 24 lethal doses for the patient (who had clear fang marks on her wrist). Fortunately, she developed no poisoning. Only 12 of the 101 patients were not fishing folk, and 10 of these 12 were bitten while bathing through treading on the sea snake. No bathers were bitten while swimming. Over 90% of the victims were male and 80 of the 101 patients were fishermen bitten at their jobs. Most victims were bitten on the lower limb through treading on the snake, and this resulted in more cases of serious poisoning (18 of 62 cases, or 29%) than upper limb bites (five cases of serious poisoning out of 38 cases, or 13%). Bites on the upper limb were caused through handling nets, and sorting fish among which the sea snake was overlooked. Over half the patients were admitted within 4 hrs of the bite. In the 82 patients coming within 6 hrs of the bite, serious poisoning developed in only 15%, whereas 58% of the 19 patients coming more than 6 hrs after the bite showed serious poisoning—a four-fold increase indicating that, as time elapses after the bite, the victim is less likely to seek medical help unless poisoning is severe.

This hospital series confirmed the relatively low mortality of sea snake bite in man—a very low mortality considering the high lethal toxicity of sea snake venom to experimental animals. Thus, in 58 patients with unequivocal sea snake bite seen during 1957–1961 before sea snake antivenom became available, the mortality rate was only 10%. Trivial or no poisoning followed in 80% of the bites. On the other hand, of the 11 patients (20%) with serious poisoning, over half (six patients) died. These facts emphasize the importance of distinguishing sea snake bite and sea snake envenoming.

These epidemiological features observed in Malaya probably apply to most fishing folk along Asian coastlines where sea snakes abound. In this vast area, sea snake bite must be a common hazard, a hazard generally feared by millions of fishing folk, and a common cause of illness and death. But it is most unlikely that the extent of this problem will be revealed to orthodox medicine for many decades to come because most fishing villages are far from medical centers; and even if hospitals or medical centers are available, fishing folk are usually reluctant to attend them. Only one species of sea snake, *Pelamis platurus,* extends to the east coasts of Africa and west coasts of the tropical Americas, but for various reasons this species does not appear to constitute much of a hazard to fishing folk in these areas.

Quite apart from the risks to individuals, the risk of sea snake bite to bathers is important because of its effects on the tourist trade. In Malaya, as a result of two bathers being fatally bitten in 1954, there was a serious drop in tourist trade that took several years to recover. Although bathers are occasionally bitten along Asian coasts, when they inadvertently tread on a sea snake, the risk of a fatal sea snake bite in this area is extremely low; the risk of death from accidental drowning to bathers using these beaches is more than ten times higher. The risk of bathers being bitten while swimming is negligible. Since a highly effective sea snake antivenom is now available, if a bather were unfortunate enough to be bitten and, even more remotely, serious poisoning ensue, death should not occur provided adequate medical treatment is given within a few hours of the bite.

On the basis of its abundance, the opinion of fishermen, my own observations on its aggressiveness relative to that of other sea snakes, venom yields and lethal toxicities, and my observations on victims, I regard *Enhydrina schistosa* as much the most dangerous sea snake to man. I would rate other species of sea snakes in descending order of potential danger to man as follows: *Hydrophis cyanocinctus, Lapemis hardwickii, Hydrophis gracilis, Hydrophis spiralis, Kerilia jerdoni, Pelamis platurus,* and *Hydrophis klossi.*

Experimentally in animals a lethal dose can be absorbed within 3 min or less of the bite. The effects in animals have been observed to be "neurotoxic," acting mainly at the neuromuscular junction. However, in dogs injected with *Enhydrina schistosa* venom, myotoxic effects have been observed. In man, both pathological and clinical observations clearly show that sea snake venom is primarily myotoxic. In fatal cases, there is widespread necrosis of skeletal muscle and the changes are described in detail. Renal damage, specially tubular necrosis, is common. The liver shows non-specific changes. In cardiac and smooth muscles, there is a notable absence of lesions.

The rarity of serious poisoning is again emphasized. This is most important because the belief that snake bite in man inevitably means poisoning is still widely held. Thus, most human victims of sea snake bite suffer only from the effects of fright. Symptoms of fright may dominate the clinical picture if the patient knows of the existence of sea snakes—in fishing folk, for example. Bite marks are inconspicuous, painless (unlike venomous fish stings), and without swelling. Fang marks are usually circular dots but may appear as linear scratch marks.

In the minority of victims who develop serious poisoning, the latent period between the bite and onset of the first symptoms of envenoming never exceeded 1.5 hrs. A characteristic generalized myalgia starts usually 0.5 to 1 hr after the bite. Aches, pains, and stiffness occur on moving limb, neck, tongue, or trunk muscles. Pseudotrismus is also characteristic—"pseudo" because, unlike the trismus of tetanus, the jaw *can* be depressed if force is used, and this is very painful. The red-brown color of myoglobin, the muscle pigment, becomes visible in the urine in serious poisoning a few hours after the bite. True flaccid paresis follows later and especially involves the eyes, lids, tongue, swallowing, neck, and breathing muscles. Respiratory failure can occur early from a combination of paresis of tongue and throat with inhalation of vomit or secretions. In severe poisoning, respiratory failure from muscle weakness may supervene within a few hours of the bite, or as long as 60 hrs after the bite. In fatal cases, most victims die 12–24 hrs after the bite, either from respiratory failure or from high blood potassium (released from damaged muscles) stopping the heart, or a combination of these features. If the victim survives 48 hrs he may still die from acute renal failure. The longest period recorded between bite and death is 24 days (life was prolonged by artificial kidney treatment). The laboratory features of serious poisoning are reviewed. The most sensitive laboratory test of sea snake envenoming is marked elevation of the SGOT, an enzyme released from damaged muscle. The SGOT is raised even in very slight poisoning.

The diagnosis of significant poisoning is very important as it will determine suitable treatment, especially the need for antivenom. Significant poisoning is shown by the pain revealed on passively moving the patient's arm, thigh, neck, and trunk muscles. Protein in the urine followed by the red-brown color of myoglobin confirms the diagnosis of serious poisoning. If a patient is seen within 1 hr of being bitten, before symptoms of poisoning might have started, he should be continually observed. But if 2 hrs have elapsed since the bite or since the release of an effective tourniquet, serious poisoning can be excluded.

The important clinical prognostic signs are considered. An electrocardiogram is very useful for detecting high blood potassium. In severe poisoning, renal function must be carefully monitored. In severe poisoning, when the patient has not received effective antivenom, full recovery may take up to 6 months. During this recovery the clinical picture strongly resembles that of muscular dystrophy.

First-aid treatment comprises the measures taken by the victim or associates before receiving medical treatment. A firm ligature or tourniquet should be applied. The object is to compress the tissues and thus delay absorption of venom, provided that venom has been injected. Although it is unlikely that venom will be injected, there is no reliable way of knowing shortly after the bite whether venom has, in fact, been injected or not. But if within an hour the victim is able to reach a medical center which has effective antivenom, there is no point in applying a tourniquet. Incision and suction are not effective and are not recommended. The victim should go to hospital as quickly as possible. On the rare occasions when the sea snake has been killed, it should be taken to hospital. Antivenom is medical treatment and, generally speaking, should play no part in first-aid treatment.

Regarding medical treatment, it should be remembered that in most cases significant poisoning does not ensue and the patient requires only reassurance. But if there is *any* doubt about envenoming, the patient should be detained for several hours (a minimum of 2 hrs after release of any tourniquets applied) and should be frequently observed for signs of poisoning.

As soon as significant toxemia is apparent (in most cases it will already be apparent when the patient presents himself, if he is one of the unfortunate few with envenoming), effective antivenom should be given. A test for serum sensitivity is done and, if negative, the full therapeutic dose of 2000–10,000 units sea snake antivenom should be given by intravenous infusion. If the serum sensitivity test is positive, there should be time for temporary desensitization of the patient by graded dose technique enabling the administration of a full therapeutic dose 1–2 hrs later. Adrenaline must be immediately available for serum reactions, which can occur even though the preceding sensitivity test is negative. The sea snake antivenom is made at the Commonwealth Serum Laboratories, Australia, using *Enhydrina schistosa* venom as antigen. Experimentally, the antivenom effectively neutralizes venom of 10 other sea snake species. Clinically, the antivenom proved very successful in Malaya. In 1957–1961, before it became available, six of 11 patients with serious poisoning died despite hospital supportive treatment. In 1962–1964, 10 patients with serious poisoning were treated with the antivenom. Seven recovered dramatically within a few days. One patient, admitted moribund 45 hrs after the bite, temporarily improved but died 59 hrs after the bite. Another patient temporarily improved, but died from hyperkalemia. If more attention and hemodialysis had been available, these two patients probably would have recovered. The 10th patient was admitted with severe poisoning 46 hrs after the bite. He steadily improved with antivenom and had fully recovered 25 days after the bite. Experimentally, antivenom made by using as antigen the venom of *Notechis scutatus,* the Australian tiger snake, is very effective in neutralizing sea snake antivenoms. If clinical studies confirm these finds, this should become a very useful alternative antivenom for sea snake bite in the western Pacific coastal regions.

Supportive medical treatment in serious envenoming includes promoting a diuresis to encourage excretion of venom and secondary toxic products and to minimize renal damage; physical rest to avoid tearing the fragile muscle fiber sheaths which guide regenerating damaged fibers; tracheostomy and artificial respiration in patients presenting late and already in respiratory failure; reversal of high blood potassium with insulin and exchange resins; and dialysis for renal failure.

In the prevention of sea snake bite and poisoning, I have considered active immunization on a communal scale for fishing folk since they are at such special risk; but for various reasons I conclude that such a project is not practicable. Amateur fishermen should be advised to treat sea snakes with great care; in particular, they should be warned against relying on the apparent docility of sea snakes. Bathers in regions where sea snakes occur should avoid river-mouths, should shuffle rather than walk on the sea bed, and should keep swimming as far as possible.

In conclusion, it is fortunate for fishermen that sea snakes are not usually aggressive. It is even more fortunate that, when sea snakes do bite man, it is unusual to inject their highly toxic venom. Otherwise, deaths from sea snake bite would probably stop all sea fishing in many parts of Asia. The nutritional and economic implications of such an eventuality would be catastrophic. Again, fortunately, a highly effective sea snake antivenom is now available so that, even in the rare cases of serious sea snake bite poisoning, death should not occur if the victim receives adequate medical treatment within a few hours of the bite.

REFERENCES

Barme, M. 1963. Venomous sea snakes of Viet Nam and their venoms. *In* Venomous and Poisonous Animals and Noxious Plants of the Pacific Ocean. (H. L. Keegan and W. V. Macfarlane, eds.). Macmillan Co., New York. pp. 373–378.

Barme, M. 1968. Venomous sea snakes (Hydrophiidae). *In* Venomous Animals and their Venoms. (W. Bucherl, E. Buckley, and V. Deulofeu, eds.). Academic Press, New York. Vol. I, pp. 285–308.

Barme, M., M. Huard, and X. M. Nguyen. 1962. Preparation d'un serum anti-venin d'Hydrophiides. Premiers essais therapeutiques. Ann. Inst. Pasteur. 102:497–500.

Baxter, E. H., and H. A. Gallichio. 1974. Cross neutralisation by tiger snake (*Notechis scutatus*) antivenene and sea snake (*Enhydrina schistosa*) antivenene against several sea snake venoms. Toxicon 12:273—278.

Bergman, A. M. 1943. The breeding habits of sea snakes. Copeia 3:156—160.

Blanford, W. T. 1876. Zoology and geology. *In* F. J. Goldsmid et al. (eds.), Eastern Persia: An Account of the Journeys of the Persian Boundary Commission, 1870—1872. Vol. 2. Macmillan Co., London. p. 427.

Bywaters, E. G. L., and J. K. Stead. 1944. The production of renal failure following injection of solutions containing myohemoglobin. Quart. J. Exp. Physiol. 33:53—70.

Cantor, T. 1841. On pelagic serpents. Trans. Zool. Soc. 2:303—311.

Cantor, T. 1886. Miscellaneous papers relating to Indo-China. Vol. 2. Triebner & Co., London. p. 237.

Carey, J. E., and E. A. Wright. 1960. The toxicity and immunological properties of some sea snake venoms with particular reference to that of *Enhydrina schistosa*. Trans. Roy. Soc. Trop. Med. Hyg. 54:50—67.

Carey, J. E., and E. A. Wright. 1961. The site of action of the venom of the sea snake *Enhydrina schistosa*. Trans. Roy. Soc. Trop. Med. Hyg. 55:153—160.

Cheymol, J., M. Barme, F. Bourillet, and M. Roch-Arveiller. 1967. Action neuromusculaire de trois venins d'Hydrophiides. Toxicon. 5:111—119.

Clark, H. C. 1942. Venomous snakes. Some Central American records: incidence of snake-bite accidents. Amer. J. Trop. Med. 22:37—39.

Day, F. 1869. On the bite of the sea-snake. Ind. Med. Gaz. 4:92.

Farmer, T. A., W. J. Hammack, and W. B. Frommeyer, Jr. 1961. Idiopathic recurrent rhabdomyolysis associated with myoglobinuria. Report of a case. New Eng. J. Med. 264:60—66.

Fitzsimmons, F. W. 1912. The Snakes of South Africa. T. Maskew Miller, Cape Town. pp. 159—160.

Fraser, T. R., and R. H. Elliott. 1905. Contributions to the study of the action of sea snake venoms. Part I: Venoms of *Enhydrina curtus*. Phil. Trans. Roy. Soc. B. 197:249—279.

Herre, A. W. C. T. 1942. Notes on Philippine sea-snakes. Copeia 1:7—9.

Herre, A. W. C. T., and D. S. Rabor. 1949. Notes on Philippine sea snakes of the genus Laticauda. Copeia 4:282—284.

Karunaratne, K. E. S., and R. G. Panabokke. 1972. Sea snake poisoning. Case report. J. Trop. Med. Hyg. 75:91—94.

Kellaway, C. H., R. O. Cherry, and F. E. Williams. 1932. The peripheral action of the Australian snake venoms. II. The curare-like action in mammals. Australian J. Exp. Biol. Med. Sci. 10:181—194.

Knowles, R. 1921. The mechanism and treatment of snake-bite in India. Trans. Roy. Soc. Trop. Med. Hyg. 15:72—92.

Kuntz, R. E. 1963. Snakes of Taiwan. U. S. Naval Med. Res. Unit No. 2. Taipei, Taiwan.

Kuwajima, Y. 1953. Immunological researches on the main Formosan poisonous snakes, especially on the venoms. IV. Production of polyvalent antivenin and expiration of antivenins. Japan. J. Exp. Med. 23:299—304.

Lamb, G., and W. K. Hunter. 1907. On the action of venoms of different species of poisonous snakes on the nervous system. VI. Venom of *Enhydrina valakadien*. Lancet 2:1017—1019.

Lancet editorial. 1957. Death after adder-bite. Lancet 1:1095.

Marsden, A. T. H., and H. A. Reid. 1961. Pathology of sea-snake poisoning. Brit. Med. J. 1:1290–1293.

M'Kenzie. 1820. An account of venomous sea snakes on the coast of Madras. Asiatic Res. 13:329–336.

Minton, S. A. 1967. Paraspecific protection by elapid and sea snake antivenins. Toxicon 5:47–55.

Nauck, E. G. 1929. Untersuchungen uber das gift einer seeschlange (*Hydrus platurus*) des Pazifischen Ozeans. Arch. f. Schiffts. v. Trop. Hyg. 33:167–170.

Pearson, C. M., W. S. Beck, and W. H. Bland. 1957. Idiopathic paroxysmal myoglobinuria; detailed study of a case including radioisotope and serum enzyme evaluations. Arch. Int. Med. 99:376–389.

Pickwell, G. V. 1972. The venomous sea snakes. Fauna 4:17–32.

Reid, G., and Jenkins, G. 1948. The liberation of renin from the kidney by tissue injury with cobra venom. Aust. J. Exp. Biol. Med. Sci. 26:215–222.

Reid, H. A. 1956a. Sea-snake bite research. Trans. Roy. Soc. Trop. Med. Hyg. 50:517–542.

Reid, H. A. 1956b. Sea-snake bites. Brit. Med. J. 2:73–78.

Reid, H. A. 1957. Antivenene reaction following accidental sea-snake bite. Brit. Med. J. 2:26–29.

Reid, H. A. 1961a. Myoglobinuria and sea-snake bite poisoning. Brit. Med. J. 1:1284–1289.

Reid, H. A. 1961b. Diagnosis, prognosis and treatment of sea-snake bite. Lancet 2:399–402.

Reid, H. A. 1962. Sea-snake antivenene: successful trial. Brit. Med. J. 2:576–579.

Reid, H. A., and K. J. Lim. 1957. Sea-snake bite: a survey of fishing villages in north-west Malaya. Brit. Med. J. 2:1266–1272.

Reid, H. A., P. C. Thean, and W. J. Martin. 1963a. Specific antivenene and prednisone in viper-bite poisoning: controlled trial. Brit. Med. J. 2:1378–1380.

Reid, H. A., P. C. Thean, and W. J. Martin. 1963b. Epidemiology of snakebite in north Malaya. Brit. Med. J. 1:992–997.

Reid, H. A., and K. E. Chan. 1968. The paradox in therapeutic defibrination. Lancet 1:485–486.

Rogers, L. 1903a. The physiological action of the venom of sea snakes. Proc. Roy. Soc. 71:481–496.

Rogers, L. 1903b. Physiological action of the venom of sea snakes. II. Action on circulation, respiration, and nervous system. Proc. Roy. Soc. 72:305–310.

Romer, J. D. 1972. Illustrated Guide to the Venomous Snakes of Hong Kong. Government Press, Hong Kong.

Sitprija, V., R. Sribhibhadh, and C. Benyajatl. 1971. Haemodialysis in poisoning by sea-snake venom. Brit. Med. J. 3:218–219.

Smith, M. A. 1926. Monograph of the Sea Snakes (Hydrophiidae). British Museum (Natural History), London.

Tu, A. T., and S. Ganthavorn. 1969. Immunological properties and neutralization of sea-snake venoms from southeast Asia. Am. J. Trop. Med. Hyg. 18:151–154.

Wall, F. 1921. The Snakes of Ceylon. H. R. Cottle, Colombo, Ceylon. p. 518.

Walton, J. N., and R. D. Adams. 1958. Polymyositis. Livingstone, Edinburgh, p. 18.

Whishnant, C. L., R. H. Owings, C. G. Cantrell, and G. R. Cooper. 1959. Primary idiopathic myoglobinuria in a Negro female: its implications and a new method of laboratory diagnosis. Ann. Int. Med. 51:140–150.

twenty

Sea Snake Antivenin and Experimental Envenomation Therapy

James A. Vick,
Jurgen von Bredow,
Marie M. Grenan,
and George M. Pickwell

Each year unknown but significant numbers of persons die from sea snake bite. Reid and Lim (1957) conducted the first survey of the incidence of sea snake bite and concluded that, in the area of their survey in coastal northwestern Malaysia, about 150 people were bitten each year. In 125 cases of sea snake bite investigated, 22 were fatal and 48 others were considered severe.

More recently Sawai et al. (1972), in a survey of snake bite throughout southeast Asia, reported deaths or severe poisoning from sea snake bite in West Malaysia (11% of all poisonous snake bites), East Malaysia, Thailand, and the Phillippines. Areas where sea snakes abound but have not yet been surveyed include coastal Pakistan, India, Sri Lanka, Bangladesh, Burma, the entire Indo-Australian Archipelago, and the more primitive regions of costal

The work described in this report was authorized under Project/Task No. 1W762710AD25-02, Medical Defense Against Chemical Agents, Prophylaxis & Therapy for Lethal Agents (U). This work was started in July 1971 and completed in September 1974.

In conducting the research described in this report, the investigators adhered to the "Guide for the Care and Use of Laboratory Animals" as promulgated by the Committee on Revision of the Guide for Laboratory Animals Facilities and Care of the Institute of Laboratory Animal Resources, National Research Council.

A portion of this research was funded by the United States Navy Bureau of Medicine and Surgery.

northern and western Australia and Queensland. In all such areas there is a substantial population of native people at risk, many of whom must make their living in and on the costal waters, where contact with sea snakes is an eventual certainty.

In 1962, Reid reported the first successful use of an antivenin specific for sea snake bite that was made at the Commonwealth Serum Laboratories, Australia, by hyperimmunization of horses with venom from the common, or beaked, sea snake, *Enhydrina schistosa.* Today, this antivenin remains the only commercially available therapeutic antidote for sea snake envenomation.

We here report on the effectiveness of this antivenin against three sea snake venoms as yet not thoroughly tested in vivo; on the antidotal effectiveness of samples of antivenin held for periods up to 8 years; on the comparative therapeutic value of artificial respiration with and without sea snake antivenin in experimental primates; on the effect of respiratory stimulants (curare antagonists) in sea-snake-envenomated primates; on the effect of sea snake venom on consciousness and central nervous system activity in primates; and finally on the morphological site of sea snake toxin neuromuscular blockade. We hope that these results contribute to a more thorough understanding of sea snake venom and its effects on animals, and ultimately lead to an increased effectiveness in treating human sea snake bite victims.

MOUSE ANTIVENIN ASSAYS

Materials and Methods

Our venom samples were obtained either directly from the sea snakes by milking with subsequent lyophilization (*Pelamis platurus*), or obtained from dealers as a lyophilized or desiccated preparation (*Laticauda semifasciata* and *Laticauda laticaudata,* respectively). Intravenous venom toxicities were determined in statistically valid numbers of mice by probit analysis (Finney, 1971) and by the graphical method of Miller and Tainter (1944). The test mice were all albino females of the Walter Reed randomly bred ICR strain, 9–10 weeks old, weighing 25–30 g.

Five lots of sea snake antivenin, batch numbers 549–009 (1964), 011–1 (1967), 020–1 (1969), 23–1 (1970), and 25–1 (1972), were stored at 5°C from time of receipt until time of testing, a period of 9 months to 8 years. Each batch of the antivenin was originally tested by the manufacturer against the venom of *E. schistosa,* and the volumes of each vial or ampule were adjusted so that the contents of one ampule would be effective in neutralizing 10 mg of that toxin. As a consequence, volumes ranged from as little as 22.3 ml (1964) to 43.4 ml (1970). In our experiments each lot of antivenin was tested for potency against the venoms of *L. laticaudata, L. semifasciata,* and *P. platurus.*

On each day of assay the venom was prepared fresh in a stock solution of cold physiological saline solution (pH 6.5). Aliquots of each antivenin were removed from the ampules, kept cold, and shielded from light until just prior to injection. Before each test, 0.2 ml of each antivenin was injected intravenously into mouse control groups to determine sensitivity to the horse serum. Of the five lots of antivenin, only batch number 25−1 (1972) showed any adverse effect. In one of five test mice, the serum produced swelling of the face, irritation of the nares, and a generalized condition of depression for about 1 hr. In the assay, the antivenin (0.1 or 0.2 ml) was injected into the dorsal tail vein within 5 secs after intravenous injection of the venom. The individually marked mice were observed for signs and survival for 48 hrs.

The venom doses used were those that would kill 100% of an unprotected test population. Preliminary tests showed that the antivenin protected the mice at doses exceeding 5 to 7 times the LD_{50} of the venom. Mice dying during the first 30 secs after antivenin injection were assumed to have died from the venom effects before the antivenin could exert an effect. Only those mice surviving a minimum of 5 min were considered in the assays. For each assay, 10 mice were used per point, except at the lower doses when five mice per point were used for each antivenin assay, depending on how sharply denoted the LD_{50} and LD_{99} points appeared. Statistical analysis was by the same methods mentioned above for venom toxicity determination.

Results

Pelamis platurus In our female mice the LD_{50} was 0.11 mg/kg while the minimum dose required to kill 99% of the test mice was 0.15 mg/kg. The principal signs noted in the envenomated mice were rapid and labored respirations, mydriasis, increased heart rate, prostration, and loss of the body righting reflex.

Mice given the antivenin showed essentially the same signs. They became prostrate at 2−5 min and showed severe mydriasis and increased respirations. They also exhibited a perceptible vasodilation of the ears and tail, in contrast to the paleness of the unprotected mice. At 2−2.5 hrs postinjection, depending on the doses of venom used, the protected mice began to recover, and by 4 hrs postinjection they were essentially normal. No deaths occurred beyond 4 hrs. The results showed that all lots of the antivenin were effective against *P. platurus* venom to a rather similar degree (Table 1).

Laticauda laticaudata Toxicity tests of *L. laticaudata* venom yielded an LD_{50} of 0.16 mg/kg and an LD_{99} of 0.26 mg/kg. The principal signs noted in envenomated mice were the same as those observed after *P. platurus* envenomation. The cause of death seemed to be respiratory failure. As the venom doses exceeded the LD_{99}, the survival times decreased rapidly, and at the doses used in the antivenin assays, the mice died in 2−4 min. The mice

Table 1. Effectiveness of sea snake antivenin[a] against the venom of three heterologous sea snake species

| Species | Date of tests | Venom LD_{50} (mg/kg) | Venom LD_{99} (mg/kg) | Venom neutralized by | | | | |
				Venom LD_{50} (mg/kg)	Potency factor[b]	1 ml AV (mg)	1 unit AV (mg)	Antivenin batch, Strength (units[c]/ml); batch no.
Pelamis platurus	Sep 72	0.11	0.15	1.06	9.6	0.1	0.004	Feb 72; 26.6 units/ml; #25–1
				1.20	10.8	0.1	0.004	Jun 70; 27.5 units/ml; #23–1
				1.12	10.1	0.1	0.004	Mar 69; 23.1 units/ml; #020–1
				1.48	13.3	0.1	0.002	26 Jun 67; 44.8 units/ml; #011–1
				1.17	10.5	0.1	0.003	24 Nov 64; 34.4 units/ml; #549–009
Laticauda laticaudata	Dec 72–Jan 73	0.16	0.26	1.31	8.2	0.3	0.011	Feb 72
				1.03	6.4	0.2	0.007	Jun 70
				1.10	6.9	0.3	0.013	Mar 69
				0.90	5.6	0.2	0.004	26 Jun 67
				0.65	4.1	0.2	0.006	24 Nov 64
Laticauda semifasciata	Apr 73–May 73	0.30	0.48	1.90	6.3	0.4	0.015	Feb 72
				1.70	5.7	0.4	0.014	Jun 70
				1.65	5.5	0.4	0.017	Mar 69
				1.30	4.3	0.3	0.007	26 Jun 67
				1.20	4.0	0.3	0.009	24 Nov 64

[a]Commonwealth Serum Laboratories, Australia: equine, liquid, sea snake antivenin (AV) produced from the venom of the common sea snake, *Enhydrina schistosa*; five batches of varying age; all injections were intravenous, in mice.
[b]Potency factor = LD_{50} AV + venom/LD_{50} venom only

receiving venom and antivenin showed essentially the same signs described above, depending on the dose of venom used. If the antivenin was effective, the mice showed a slight depression with increased respirations. At 4 hrs, surviving mice had recovered fully and no deaths were observed beyond this time. In general all antivenin lots were effective against *L. laticaudata* venom, but the respective potencies of the lots varied (Table 1). The newest antivenin batch (1972) exhibited the highest potency, and the oldest (1964) showed the lowest potency, as might be expected.

Laticauda semifasciata Toxicity studies on *L. semifasciata* venom showed that the LD_{50} was 0.30 mg/kg and the LD_{99} was 0.48 mg/kg. The major signs of envenomation were the same as those noted for the other sea snake venoms. If the toxic effects of the venom were completely neutralized by the antivenin, the mice showed only a mild depression with increased respiratory rate. If the antivenin failed to protect, the mice were severely depressed and respired rapidly for a long time after injection. Before death, respiration became slower and more shallow. No deaths occurred beyond 3 hrs. All lots of the antivenin were antidotal to some degree, with the most recent appearing to be the most potent (Table 1).

Discussion

Toxicities of Venoms Our study shows higher toxicity to mice for *Pelamis* than toxicities reported by others for this species (Barme, 1963, 1968; Tu and Ganthavorn, 1969; Bolanos, 1972), but lower for *L. laticaudata* and *L. semifasciata* that those reported earlier by Vick (1970). On the other hand, our value for the LD_{50} of *L. laticaudata* venom is almost identical to that of Tamiya et al. (1967) and T. Tu (1967) for this species. Furthermore, our present value for *L. semifasciata* is similar to that obtained by several previous workers. (T. Tu, 1959; Tamiya et al., 1967; Tu, Hong and Solie, 1971; Tu and Salafranca, 1974).

Assuming that all venom injections were intravenous, two probable causes of these discrepancies are the variation in mouse strains and gender used in the venom assays, and the condition of the venom employed. In addition to milking, techniques employed by others include dissection of venom glands and subsequent extraction and purification of the venom. Conceivably, some loss of toxicity results from such operations.

Potencies of Antivenin These studies indicate that the Commonwealth Serum Laboratories liquid equine antivenin for sea snake envenomation was effective in counteracting the lethal effects of the venom from *P. platurus, L. laticaudata,* and *L. semifasciata.* An interesting observation was the approximate equivalency of potency exhibited by the older batches of antivenin (1964, 1967) compared to the more recent batches (1969–1972) when employed against *Pelamis* venom. With the *Laticauda* venoms, however, antivenin potencies declined with age to a predictable degree, but even the 8-year-old batch still retained considerable protective capability (Table 1).

Our method of injecting antivenin immediately after venom injection might be thought to result in apparent lower potencies of the antivenin, compared to results obtained from the more standard procedure of injecting venom and antivenin (premixed) simultaneously. However, comparison with recent work of others where the premixing procedure was followed indicates no consistent differences (Table 2).

The results of our in vivo experiments using commercially available antivenin against the venom of the amphibious sea snakes, *L. laticaudata* and *L. semifasciata,* and the single truly pelagic form, *P. platurus,* confirm to some extent the recent in vitro tests on the same species reported by Tu and Salafranca (1974). Our values are for *L. semifasciata.* We are in close agreement with Tu and Salafranca for *L. laticaudata,* and are somewhat lower than the results of Tu and Ganthavorn (1969), but substantially below the results of Tu and Salafranca for *P. platurus* (Table 2).

We do not know the cause or causes for the discrepencies between our results and those of others. Particularly perplexing are the differences between our work with the Commonwealth Serum Laboratories antivenin for February 1972 and that of Tu and Salafranca (1974) using antivenin from the same lot. Differences may be expected to arise from experiments employing different strains of mice, different sexes—ours were all females, theirs, males— and perhaps venoms of varying qualities obtained by different means. In the *Pelamis* experiments, where the discrepancies are greatest, we believe that our method of obtaining pure venom by milking with capillary tubes produces a substance resulting in a more reliable LD_{50} value (Pickwell et al., 1972).

Regardless of these differences, it is clear that commercial equine sea snake antivenin is a powerful antidote to the venoms of *P. platurus, L. laticaudata,* and *L. semifasciata.* These species may be now added to the list of sea snakes whose venom is effectively countered by *E. schistosa* antivenin. Those presently include—in addition to *E. schistosa—Hydrophis cyanocinctus, Hydrophis major, Hydrophis elegans, Hydrophis spiralis, Lapemis hardwickii, Astrotia stokesii,* and *Aipysurus laevis* (Baxter and Gallichio 1974).

Finally, it is important to mention the findings of Minton (1967), lately confirmed and expanded by Baxter and Gallichio (1974), that monovalent antivenin for Australian tiger snake venom (*Notechis scutatus*) possesses powerful antidotal capabilities against the venom of all sea snakes tested thus far (nine species). In all cases except the homologous *E. schistosa,* the *Notechis* antivenin was more effective than *Enhydrina* antivenin. This discovery holds the promise of valuable insights to be gained in the area of comparative immunochemistry, and the possibility of more effective envenomation therapy through the use of monovalent, but broadly paraspecific, antivenin.

Table 2. Neutralization of sea snake venom by commercial antivenin: results of this study compared with previous work

Species	LD_{50} (mg/kg)	Venom neutralized by 1 ml commercial antivenin (mg)	Venom neutralized by 1 unit antivenin[a] (mg)	Reference
Pelamis platurus	0.11	0.1	0.004	Present study; Pickwell et al., 1972
	0.18	0.6	–	Tu and Ganthavorn, 1969
	0.43	2.2	0.084	Tu and Salafranca, 1974
Laticauda laticaudata	0.16	0.3	0.011	Present study
	0.16	0.4	0.013	Tu and Salafranca, 1974
Laticauda semifasciata	0.30	0.4	0.015	Present study
	0.38	0.8	0.029	Tu and Salafranca, 1974
	–	0.1	0.004–0.007	Baxter and Gallichio, 1974

[a] 1 unit of this commercial antivenin is defined as that quantity of a given batch that neutralizes 0.01 mg of *Enhydrina schistosa* venom.

Extrapolation to Man By extrapolation from our mouse assays (Table 1), we have estimated LD_{50} values for man together with the quantities of commercial sea snake antivenin required for neutralization (Table 3). In these estimates only values from the 1972 antivenin batch have been used.

EFFECTIVENESS OF ARTIFICIAL RESPIRATION, ANTIVENIN, AND OTHER DRUGS ON SEA SNAKE ENVENOMATION IN THE MONKEY

Poisoning by sea snake venom, if severe enough, may lead to respiratory paralysis and death (Reid, 1956). With the onset of respiratory paralysis, it is possible to support the victim on artificial respiration and thereby prolong life. If no permanent damage is done to the neuromuscular junction by the presence of the venom, it should be possible to support the victim until the venom has been neutralized by the body and the neuromuscular junction has had sufficient time to recover. This concept of therapy was investigated in rhesus monkeys.

Materials and Methods

Adult rhesus monkeys weighing from 5–10 kg were used in this section of the study. The unanesthetized monkeys were placed in restraining cages and followed for changes in vital physiological functions. Each monkey was given 0.3 mg/kg of *L. semifasciata* venom intramuscularly. At the time of severe signs (drooping of the eyelids, loss of coordination, and respiratory distress), the monkeys were immediately intubated and placed on artificial respiration. Under local anesthesia (lidocaine), the right femoral vein was cannulated for drug administration and venous blood sample collection, and the left carotid artery was cannulated for blood pressure monitoring and collection of arterial blood samples. The respirator was adjusted to maintain proper P_{CO_2} and P_{O_2} levels in the arterial and venous blood. Dextrose, saline solution, and Ringer's

Table 3. Hypothetical sea snake venom toxicities for a 70-kg human[a]

Species	LD_{50} (mg)	Antivenin required for neutralization (ml)	LD_{99} (mg)	Antivenin required for neutralization (ml)
Pelamis platurus	7.7	77.0	10.5	105.0
Laticauda laticaudata	11.2	37.3	18.2	60.7
Laticauda semifasciata	21.0	52.5	33.6	84.0

[a]Values based on mouse assays are summarized in Table 1; antivenin figures based on commercial batch from February 1972.

lactate were administered for fluid support and to maintain kidney function. These basic supportive techniques have proved adequate to maintain monkeys paralyzed with curare for more than 72 hrs (Vick, 1970).

The experimental variations were as follows.

1. Five monkeys were given venom and supported by artificial respiration. One of these animals was also given physostigmine, Anectine chloride (succinylcholine chloride), neostigmine, and dimethylphenyl piperazine (DMPP) separately as a pilot study to ascertain whether the venom could be displaced from the receptors.

2. Two monkeys were given Flaxedil (gallamine triethiodide) before injection of the venom and supported with artificial respiration in an attempt to ascertain whether the receptor could be protected.

3. Two monkeys were given venom, supported by artificial respiration, and treated with antivenin.

Results

For a period of 20–25 min after the injection of venom, the animals showed no effect; however, once signs began to appear they progressed rapidly. At 25–28 min, the animals became noticably anxious and frightened; weakness began with a drooping of the eyelids, followed by a loss of coordination, which caused them to stagger awkwardly about the cage. Within 5 min of the onset of signs the animals fell to the bottom of the cage, completely paralyzed. The monkeys were then intubated and placed on artificial respiration (AR).

The monkeys remained completely paralyzed for 12–15 hrs, exhibiting no visible response to any form of sound or tactile stimulus. Although no movement was evident, there was often a momentary increase in blood pressure during periods of stimulation, suggesting that the animal was aware of the stimulus but not able to respond to it. Twelve to fifteen hours after the onset of complete paralysis, there was slight recovery of some muscle function, usually only a flicker of an eyelid, then a movement of the eyeball itself. Upon painful stimulation of a major muscle group, a twitch sometimes was elicited. From these initial movements the animals made a slow but steady recovery. There was never any evidence of a sudden reversal or sudden recovery of responses, only a slow progressive return of function. At 18–20 hrs, respiration began to recover. Determining when the animals should be allowed to breathe on their own depended on their ability to maintain proper blood P_{O_2} and P_{CO_2} values. Upon adequate recovery of the respiratory parameters (19–23 hrs), the annulas were removed and the animals were returned to their holding cages. Although the monkeys thereafter were concious and their vital signs were adequate, they remained in a weak and lethargic condition until the following day, when they appeared normal in all respects.

The relatively rapid recovery of the neuromuscular junction from the effects of sea snake venom indicated that the binding of the venom to the receptors was reversible. Although it is possible to postulate the synthesis of new receptors, this process takes considerably longer than the time required for complete recovery of the animal. If the venom binding was reversible, we believed that the venom might act competitively with another compound having a high affinity for the same receptor. If a competitive compound could be found that could displace the venom from the receptor, recovery of the neuromuscular junction might be somewhat faster.

Compounds that show significant stimulation of the receptors usually have a high affinity for the receptor. It therefore seemed possible that these compounds might force competitive blockers from the receptor. Several receptor stimulants were tested in an attempt to reverse the sea snake venom receptor binding. Five hours after a 5-kg monkey was completely paralyzed with sea snake venom, 0.5 mg/kg of physostigmine was injected intravenously. This compound allows acetylcholine to accumulate at the nerve-muscle endplate, where an excess ultimately should remove a competitive compound from the receptor. In our experiment, however, no effect from the physostigmine was observed.

Six hours after the onset of paralysis, 500 mg of Anectine chloride were infused intravenously into the monkey. This compound also causes accumulation of acetylcholine and is capable of stimulating the receptor directly. Again we met with no success; no effect on the animal was discernible.

In a third attempt, we used neostigmine bromide, a compound similar to Anectine, but longer acting. Neostigmine (30 mg) was infused into the monkey but did not reverse the paralysis.

Since the above compounds had no effect on the paralysis of the animal, we next decided to attempt a very potent nicotinic stimulant, DMPP. This compound has a very high affinity for the receptor of the neuromuscular junction. Upon intravenous infusion of 8 µg/kg, there was a marked increase in blood pressure, but no reversal of paralysis.

The lack of any effect from these stimulants indicates that the block was not competitive, yet with supportive care the receptor-venom complex was spontaneously reversible. Conceivably, the venom may simply diffuse from the receptor, or it may be degraded by means of an enzyme system.

Since we were unsuccessful in removing the venom from the receptor once paralysis had occurred, we attempted to learn whether it might be possible to prevent the venom binding to the receptor by using a reversible blocker of the neuromuscular junction (i.e., curare-like compounds). Intravenous administration of 5 mg/kg of Flaxedil is known to cause complete paralysis lasting 2.5–3 hrs in monkeys. We reasoned that the Flaxedil might protect the receptor from attack by the sea snake venom, thus allowing recovery in approximately that period of time. In our experiments testing this approach, two monkeys paralyzed with Flaxedil and given 0.3 mg/kg of venom required about the same amount of time for recovery as those treated with venom alone. Thus, this powerful curare-like agent was apparently displaced by the venom, or Flaxedil acted at a different site.

Prevention of the onset of venom receptor blockade in mice by injection of an antivenin immediately after envenomation has been discussed above. Experimental removal of the venom from the receptor after the occurrence of a complete blockade has not yet been reported, although this clearly takes place in successful clinical situations (Reid, 1962).

In order to explore this aspect of nerve-muscle blockade, two monkeys were paralyzed with sea snake venom and supported on AR as already described. Thirty minutes after the onset of complete paralysis, 40 ml of sea snake antivenin were administered by slow intravenous infusion. No immediate reversal of the paralysis was observed, but signs of recovery were noticeable within 4–5 hrs, and complete recovery took place in 5–6 hrs. Although the effects were not immediate, the dramatic reduction in recovery time compared to AR alone indicated that the antivenin was apparently able to remove the venom from the receptor. These experiments are summarized in Table 4.

Discussion

More than 70 years ago, Rogers (1903) employed artificial respiration on cats envenomated with *E. schistosa* venom. However, the purpose of his experiments employing AR was to evaluate the effect of venom on the heart, and in these he showed that AR following respiratory arrest could restore normal cardiac function. He thus correctly demonstrated the apparent lack of direct action of sea snake venom on cardiac tissue, subsequently confirmed for *Pelamis* venom by Pickwell et al. (1972).

Still earlier, Richards (1873, cited in Rogers, 1903) kept a dog bitten by *E. schistosa* alive for 24.5 hrs after respiratory failure by employing artificial

Table 4. Recovery of monkeys from sea snake envenomation

Test animal	Form of treatment	Oneset of recovery (hrs)	Time of recovery (hrs)
1, 2, 3, 4	Paralyze with venom, support with artificial respiration (AR)	12–15	19–23
1, 2	Inject with Flaxedil, paralyze with sea snake venom, support with AR	12–14	18
3, 4	Paralyze with venom, support with AR, treat with antivenin	4–5	5–6

respiration, and only lost the animal upon the accidental shutdown of his AR system.

Reid (1956) reported a case of sea snake envenomation in man where artificial respiration failed to save the victim. He nonetheless recommended a tank respirator for sea snake bite victims suffering respiratory insufficiency (Reid, 1961).

Recently, Murai and Ogura (1974) employed AR on rabbits envenomated with erabutoxin, and neurotoxin isolated from *L. semifasciata* venom. In results comparable to those reported here (Table 4), they found that a period of 14–18 hrs was required for the animal to regain spontaneous respiration. These authors further reported that the erabutoxin-induced dyspnea was not antagonized by simultaneous administration of stimulants such as neostigmine. Our work with monkeys thus confirms these findings.

In all of our experiments with artificial respiration, the animals recovered fully from a potentially lethal challenge of *L. semifasciata* venom (Table 4). The dramatic reduction in recovery time when antivenin was employed with AR serves to emphasize the efficacy of its use as a chemotherapeutic agent in cases of sea snake envenomation. Artificial respiration alone, however, may still be effective in treating bite victims.

EFFECT OF SEA SNAKE VENOM ON LEVEL OF CONSCIOUSNESS IN A MONKEY

Since the monkey that had been poisoned and then treated with DMPP, in the study described earlier, responded with an increase in blood pressure, it was decided to test the level of consciousness during the onset and recovery from the venom-induced respiratory paralysis.

Methods and Results

A monkey was prepared with permanently implanted electrodes to determine the activity of the cortex and the midbrain. The animal was anesthetized with the short-acting anesthetic, Brevital, to facilitate intubation and the cannulation of an artery and a vein for monitoring of blood pressure, fluid administration, and the taking of blood samples. When the monkey was able to breathe spontaneously, respiration was monitored by means of a flowmeter. The animal was allowed to recover from the anesthetic for 2 hrs, at which time it was alert and exhibited a normal awake EEG pattern. An intramuscular injection of 0.30 mg/kg of *L. semifasciata* venom led to a depression and halt in respiration within 30 min. The respiratory halt was indicated by a lack of rhythmic respiration in the flowmeter pattern (Figure 1A, B). The resulting anoxia caused unconsciousness at all levels of the central nervous

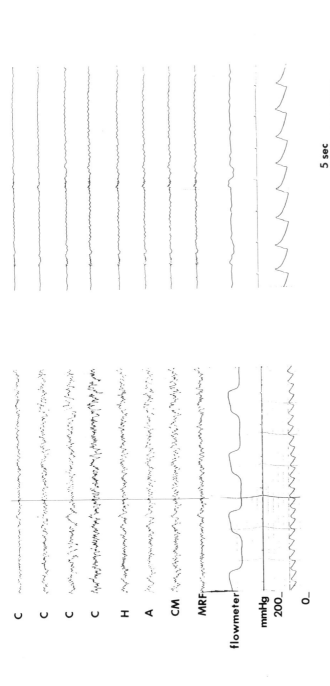

Figure 1. Effect of sea snake venom on the EEG of a concious monkey. A, The parameters recorded during the control period before intramuscular administration of the sea snake venom: C, cortex; H, hippocampus; A, amygdala; CM, central median of the thalamus; MRF, mesocephalic reticular formation. The flowmeter was connected to a tracheal cannula. Blood pressure shown at bottom. B, The effect of anoxia induced by complete respiratory paralysis which occurred within 30 min following experimental envenomation. C, Return of normal EEG patterns upon institution of artificial respiration. D, Return of normal spontaneous breathing in 22 hrs after the start of intensive support.

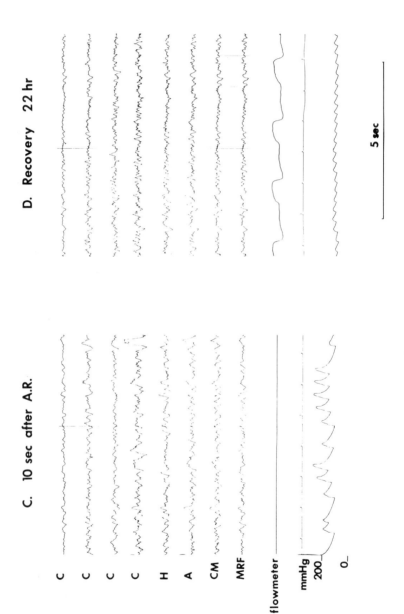

Figure 1 C and D.

system (CNS), as indicated by the characteristic lack of activity or flattening of the EEG pattern (Figure 1B). The anoxia also induced profound brady-cardia, as would be expected. As soon as the EEG trace flattened, the animal was put on AR, whereupon the EEG pattern immediately returned to normal (Figure 1C). This response of the CNS to AR was faster than the recovery of the cardiac tissue, as indicated by the continued bradycardia for 10 sec after initiation of AR. After 22 hrs of intensive support, the animal was able to breathe without assistance, as indicated by the flowmeter tracing (Figure 1D).

Except for the momentary flattening of the EEG trace because of anoxia, the pattern remained normal even though the respiratory musculature was paralyzed for more than 20 hrs. Consciousness therefore, was maintained during the paralysis.

Discussion

Based on the unchanged EEG wave forms of an animal undergoing sea snake envenomation (Figure 1), we think that no direct effect on the CNS from sea snake venom is likely to be demonstrated under ordinary circumstances. Rogers (1903) employed relatively massive doses of *E. schistosa* venom in cats and rabbits (1–4 mg/kg), but found that respiratory paralysis was complete before any reflex functions of the spinal cord became impaired. In contrast, Vick et al. (1964) found that cobra venom had a very rapid and severely depressant effect on the anesthetized dog. Cessation of EEG wave patterns occurred before cerebral hypoxia could have developed, indicating that some component of cobra venom does attack the CNS.

SITE OF RESPIRATORY PARALYSIS

Effect of Sea Snake Venom on Central and Peripheral Respiration of an Anesthetized Cat

The fact that consciousness was unaffected during the sea snake venom intoxication suggests that respiratory paralysis occurrs exclusively at the level of the neuromuscular junction. Paralysis of respiration can occur at either a central site by poisoning of the brain stem (e.g., by an overdose of barbitu-rates or heroin) or by paralyzing the peripheral respiratory muscles with curare or botulinum toxins. It is also possible to poison both the central and peripheral sites with anticholinesterase poisons. Identification of the site of paralysis would be useful in developing better therapy for treatment of envenomation.

Materials and Methods The central component of respiration can be monitored by the electrical activity of the phrenic nerve, and a peripheral record of respiration can be obtained by means of a flowmeter connected to a tracheal cannula. Recording of the electrical activity of the phrenic nerve for our purposes was most readily accomplished in the cat (Figure 2). It is the neuronal drive of the CNS mediated by the phrenic nerve that activates the diaphragm. Every inhalation shown in Figure 2 (bottom trace) is correlated with a burst of electrical activity traveling along the phrenic nerve (center trace).

Results and Discussion Upon intramuscular administration of 1 mg/kg of *L. semifasciata* venom, there was a slow but steady blockade of the neuromuscular junction (Figure 2B). The first indication of malfunction of the respiratory muscles was the increased stimulus required to drive the muscles to an extent that was sufficient for the maintenance of respiration. This was manifested by an increased amplitude in the integrated activity of the phrenic nerve without any increase in the amplitude of the respiratory air flow (Figure 2B).

At 30 min after envenomation, the respiratory excursion began to decrease even though the CNS respiratory drive was far greater than it was during the control phase (Figure 2C). The peripheral respiratory activity continued to decrease in the presence of maintained central activity until finally respiration was blocked to the extent that it could not support life (Figure 2D). Cardiac irregularities induced by anoxia led to a depression in circulation and ultimately a depression of CNS respiration, as indicated by a decrease in phrenic nerve activity (Figure 2D). At this point the animal was supported by AR in order to allow recovery of the vital functions.

When the cat was removed from the respirator a short time later, it was totally unable to breathe (Figure 3A). This resulted in an accumulation of CO_2, which in turn induced a brief increase in blood pressure and phrenic nerve traffic. The concomitant anoxia soon led to cardiac and CNS depression, resulting in a reduced phrenic nerve output. The recovery of marginal respiratory function occurred 2 hrs after the start of the experiment. A maximal central respiratory stimulus was required to drive the peripheral respiration at that time (Figure 3B). This experiment indicates that sea snake venom intoxication in the cat is entirely peripheral. The CNS was functional and transmitting respiratory impulses to the diaphragm, but the diaphragm could not respond.

The Site and Reversibility of Respiratory Blockade

As early as 1903, Rogers had determined experimentally that *E. schistosa* venom was primarily a respiratory toxin that acted upon the phrenic nerve endplates. While be believed that all neuromuscular junctions were eventually

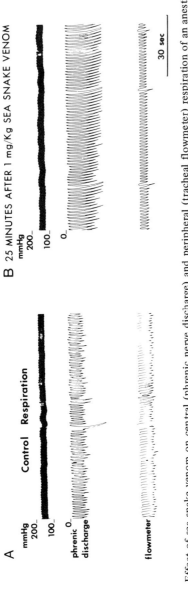

Figure 2. Effect of sea snake venom on central (phrenic nerve discharge) and peripheral (tracheal flowmeter) respiration of an anesthetized cat. Blood pressure shown at the top. A, control; B, onset of effects after 25 min; C, development of blockade at 28 min; D, respiratory blockade complete after 31 min.

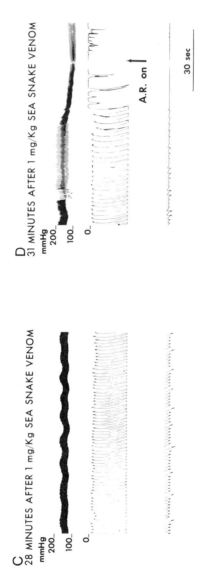

Figure 2 C and D.

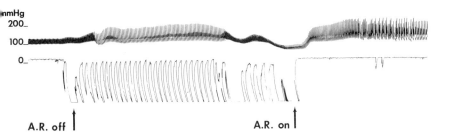

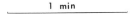

CONNECT ARTIFICIAL RESPIRATION 20 MINUTES AFTER ONSET OF COMPLETE PARALYSIS

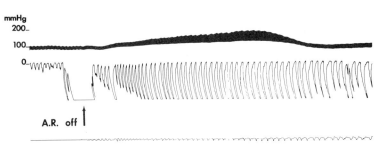

DISCONNECT ARTIFICIAL RESPIRATION 2 HOURS AFTER ONSET OF COMPLETE PARALYSIS

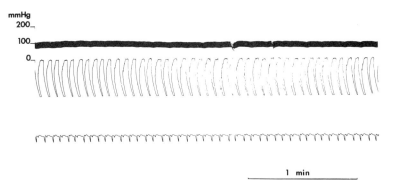

Figure 3. Effect of sea snake venom on central and peripheral respiration of an anesthetized cat (continued from Fig. 2). Blood pressure (upper) phrenic nerve discharge (middle) and tracheal flowmeter (lower). A, Complete peripheral respiratory blockade 20 minutes after onset of paralysis. The central nervous system remains functional.
Figure 3B, (Lower two traces). Begin recovery of peripheral respiration 2 hours after start of experiment. Central nervous system respiration remains functional.

paralyzed, he noted that the venom did not seem to affect the nerve cell directly.

Subsequently, Carey and Wright (1961) clearly showed the paralyzing action of *Enhydrina* venom on the isolated rat phrenic nerve-diaphragm preparation. Thus, sea snake venom exerts its neurotoxic effect by pheripheral respiratory paralysis. Tamiya and Arai (1966) showed that erabutoxin produced a postsynaptic neuromuscular blockade in the frog sciatic-sartorius preparation in a manner similar to that of cobra venom and curare. Cheymol and colleagues (1967) tested the neuromuscular blocking properties of the sea snakes *E. schistosa, H. cyanocinctus,* and *L. hardwickii,* and found that receptors of the postsynaptic membrane were blocked almost irreversibly, but neither nerve or muscle fibers were directly affected. Later Cheymol et al. (1972) using *L. semifasciata* venom (erabutoxins a and b) supplied by Tamiya, confirmed the peripheral action of the venom in blocking the motor endplates in the rat diaphragm preparation. This was still further confirmed by Ogura and Murai (1974), using the same preparation. Moreover, they found that the action of erabutoxin was not antagonized by anticurare agents. Work in Tamiya's laboratory, using iodinated erabutoxin in the mouse diaphrahm preparation, demonstrated the localization of the toxin on the endplates (Sato et al., 1970).

The very interesting work of Lee et al. (1972)—in which the action of erabutoxin b was compared with that of α-bungarotoxin, toxin A, and cobrotoxin on the rat phrenic nerve diaphragm preparation, among other preparations—demonstrated that the neuromuscular blockade of erabutoxin b or cobrotoxin could be slowly reversed using either neostigmine or repeated washing. The blockade by α-bungarotoxin was entirely irreversible, however, and that of toxin A only slowly reversible in some preparations. In the chick biventer cervicis nerve-muscle preparation, all four toxins produced irreversible neuromuscular blockade. Thus, there is a suggestion of a difference in results to be found depending on the preparation employed and also depending to a very important extent on whether intact animal preparations are used.

Our results with intact monkeys and those of Ogura and Murai (1974) from rabbits indicate that *L. semifasciata* venom produces a neuromuscular blockade that does not respond readily to stimulants such as neostigmine. In our work, the block was slowly reversed when the animal was supported on artificial respiration (Table 4). Considering the differences in the procedures and preparations, we do not think that these results necessarily contradict those of Lee et al. (1972).

Our experiments with the intact cat phrenic nerve test (Figures 2 and 3) provide in vivo confirmation of the results discussed above. Therefore, the cause of respiratory failure from sea snake envenomation is, most probably, neuromuscular blockade between the phrenic nerve and the diaphragm. The specific cholinergic receptors in the neuromuscular junction, to which the powerful sea snake neurotoxins bind, have yet to be identified, but the toxins themselves provide perhaps the most directly useful tool for continuing these investigations (see Lee, 1971 and Tu, 1973, for useful summary reviews).

SUMMARY

1. Commercially prepared *E. schistosa* antivenom is effective in mice against poisoning by the venoms of *L. laticaudata, L. semifasciata,* and *P. platurus.* The antivenin retains good potency up to 8 years.
2. The use of the antivenin in combination with AR reduces respiratory paralysis in poisoned monkeys from 18–24 hrs to 5–6 hrs.
3. Blockade of neuromuscular transmission by sea snake venom is not reversed by anticurare drugs.
4. Sea snake venom is a peripheral toxin; there seems to be no component affecting the CNS.

REFERENCES

Barme, M. 1963. Venomous sea snakes of Viet Nam and their venoms. *In* Venomous And Poisonous Animals And Noxious Plants of the Pacific Region. H. L. Keegan and W. V. Macfarlane, eds. Pergamon (Macmillan), New York. pp. 373–378.

Barme, M. 1968. Venomous sea snakes (Hydrophiidae). *In* Venomous Animals And Their Venoms. Vol. I. Venomous Vertebrates. W. Bucherl, E. E. Buckley and V. Deulofeu, eds. Academic Press, New York. pp. 285–308.

Baxter, E. H., and H. A. Gallichio. 1974. Cross-neutralization by Tiger Snake (*Notechis scutatus*) antivenene and sea snake (*Enhydrina schistosa*) antivenene against several sea snake venoms. Toxicon 12:273–278.

Bolaños, R. 1972. Toxicity of Costa Rican snake venoms for the white mouse. Am. J. Trop. Med. Hyg. 21:360–363.

Carey, J. E., and E. A. Wright. 1961. The site of the venom of the sea snake *Enhydrina schistosa.* Trans. Roy. Soc. Trop. Med. Hyg. 55:153.

Cheymol, J., M. Barme, F. Bourillet, and M. Roch-Arveiller. 1967. Action neuromusculaire de trois venis d'Hydrophiides. Toxicon 5:111–119.

Cheymol, J., F. Bourillet and M. Roch-Arveiller. 1972. Actions neuromusculaire de fractions isolees de venins de serpents. In Toxins Of Animals And Plant Origin. Vol. 2. A. deVries and E. Kochva, eds., Gordon and Breach, New York. pp. 655–666.

Finney, D. J. 1971. Probit Analysis. 3rd ed. Cambridge University Press. 333pp.

Lee, C. Y. 1972. Chemistry and pharmacology of polypeptide toxins in snake venoms. Ann. Rev. Pharm. 12:265–286.

Lee, C. Y., C. C. Chang, and Y. M. Chen. 1972. Reversibility of neuromuscular blockade by neurotoxins from elapid and sea snake venoms. J. Formosan Med. Assoc. 71:344–349.

Miller, L. C., and M. L. Tainter. 1944. Estimation of the ED50 and its error by means of logarithmic-probit graph paper. Proc. Soc. Exp. Biol. Med. 57:261–264.

Minton, S. A., Jr. 1967. Paraspecific protection by elapid and sea snake antivenins. Toxicon 5:47–55.

Murai, S., and Y. Ogura. 1974. Pharmacological studies on erabutoxin. II. Effects on the circulatory and respiratory system of rabbits. Japanese J. Pharm. 24 (suppl.):114.

Ogura, Y., and S. Murai. 1974. Pharmacological studies on erabutoxin. (1) On the isolated phrenic nerve-diaphragm preparation of the rat. Japanese J. Pharm. 24(suppl.):114.

Pickwell, G. V., J. A. Vick, W. H. Shipman, and M. M. Grenan. 1972. Production, toxicity and preliminary pharmacology of venom from the sea snake, *Pelamis platurus.* pp 247–265. Food-Drugs From the Sea. Proc., L. R. Worthen, ed. Marine Technology Society, Washington, D. C.

Reid, H. A. 1956. Sea-Snake bites. Brit. Med. J. 2:73–86.

Reid, H. A. 1961. Diagnosis, prognosis, and treatment of sea-snake bite. Lancet: 399–402.

Reid, H. A. 1962. Sea-snake antivenene: successful trial. Brit. Med. J. 2:576–579.

Reid, H. A., and K. J. Lim. 1957. Sea-snake bite. A survey of fishing villages in northwest Malaya. Brit. Med. J. 2:1266–1272.

Rogers, L. 1903. On the physiological action of the poison of the Hydrophidae. Part II. Action on the circulatory, respiratory, and nervous system. Proc. Roy. Soc. Lond. 72:305–319.

Sato, S., T. Abe, and N. Tamiya. 1970. Binding of iodinated erabutoxin b, a sea snake toxin, to the endplates of the mouse diaphragm. Toxicon 8:313–314.

Sawai, Y., K. Koba, T. Okonogi, S. Mishima, Y. Kawamura, H. Chinzei, A. Bakar, T. Devaraj, S. Phong-Aksara, C. Puranananda, E. Salafranca, J. S. Sumpaico, C. S. Tseng, J. F. Taylor, C.-S. Wu, and T.-P. Kuo. 1972. An epidemiological study of snake-bites in southeast Asia. Japanese J. Exp. Med. 42:283–307.

Tamiya, N. and H. Arai. 1966. Studies on sea-snake venoms. Crystallization of erabutoxins a and b from *Laticauda semifasciata* venom. Biochem. J. 99:624–630.

Tamiya, N., H. Arai and S. Sato. 1967. Studies on sea snake venoms: Crystallization of erabutoxins "a" and "b" from *Laticauda semifasciata* and of laticotoxin "a" from *Laticauda laticaudata. In* Animal Toxins. F. E. Russell and P. R. Saunders, eds. Pergamon Press, London. pp. 249–258.

Tu, A. T. 1973. Neurotoxins of animal venoms: snakes. Ann. Rev. Biochem. 42:235–258.

Tu, A. T., and S. Ganthavorn. 1969. Immunological properties and neutralization of sea-snake venoms from southeast Asia. Am. J. Trop. Med. Hyg. 18:151–154.

Tu, A. T., B. Hong and T. N. Solie. 1971. Characterization and chemical modifications of toxins isolated from the venoms of the sea snake, *Laticauda semifasciata,* from the Philippines. Biochemistry 10:1295–1304.

Tu, A. T. and E. S. Salafranca. 1974. Immunological properties and neutralization of sea snake venoms (II). Am. J. Trop. Med. Hyg. 23:135–138.

Tu, T. 1959. Toxicological studies on the venom of a sea snake, *Laticauda semifasciata* (Reinwardt) in Formosan waters. J. Formosan Med. Assoc. 58:182–203.

Tu, T. 1967. Toxicological studies on the venom of the sea snake *Laticauda laticaudata* affinis. *In* Animal Toxins, F. E. Russell and P. R. Saunders, eds. Pergamon Press, London. pp. 245–248.

Vick, J. A. 1970. Venomous sea snakes. *In* Poisonous and Venomous Marine Animals of the World. Vol. 3. Vertebrates continued. B. W. Halstead. U.S. Government Printing Office, Washington, D.C. pp. 974–975.

Vick, J. A., H. P. Ciuchta, and E. H. Polley. 1964. The effect of endotoxin and snake venom on cortical electrical activity. Nature 203:1387–1389.

RELATIONSHIPS
TO MAN

twenty-one

Commercial Sea Snake Fisheries in the Philippines

Emmanuel Y. Punay

It is only in the Philippines that sea snakes are commercially exploited on a large scale (Punay, 1972). This sea snake industry is a diversified economic activity, and the bulk of it is for export. The industry involves three phases: 1) snake gathering; 2) preservation, processing and tanning; and 3) manufacturing into finished products. The particular products are treated in the latter portions of this paper, although the main product is sea snake skins.

Only three species of true sea snakes (Hydrophiidae) in the Philippines are of major export value: *Laticauda semifasciata, L. laticaudata,* and *Hydrophis inornatus. Laticauda colubrina* and *Hydrophis belcheri* are considerably less common, but are occasionally included in the commercial catch. The Lake Taal sea snake, *Hydrophis semperi,* is almost unexploited. The file snake, *Acrochordus* (not a true sea snake but in the family Acrochordidae) is considered a predator in fish ponds and is chopped up, dried, and used in animal feed. The skins of big file snakes (3-inch skin width) are stripped off, vegetable-tanned, and manufactured into cheap leathercrafts that are sold in some tourist shops in Manila.

Commercial sea snake activities in the Philippines were started about 1934 on Gato Island, north of Cebu, by the Japanese. Initial processing plants were set up in Barrio Tapilon, Municipality of Daanbantayan, Province of Cebu. There, the Japanese taught the local fishermen to catch snakes, to use alcohol as an antidote for sea snake bites, and to skin, scrape, salt, and package the product. The skins were then shipped to Japan, and it was only in 1971 that we, in the Philippines, learned that they were then exported to Europe as "Japanese sea snake leather." The Japanese should receive credit for being the first to realize that sea snake skins offer a good substitute for other reptile skins since they could be easily caught in the tens of thousands in the Philippines. However, they have also been responsible for the subsequent over-exploitation of the fishery. There is an urgent need at present for implementation of a plan for conservation so that the fishery can continue on a sustained yield basis.

COMMERCIALLY IMPORTANT SPECIES OF SEA SNAKES IN THE PHILIPPINES

Laticauda

L. laticaudata and *L. semifasciata* up to 3.6 m long have been reported, although the most common sizes utilized in the industry are those measuring 1.5–1.8 m long (live measurement, because they change in length during the tanning process). These two species are the most commonly utilized, due mainly to their large circumference which results in a wide area of finished leather. A 15 cm wide by 1.5 m long raw hide of these species stretches to 1.8 m long after "chrome tanning." On the other hand, the leather tends to shrink under the "alum process."

L. laticaudata and *L. semifasciata* are the most common species on Gato Island. They are marked with 40–50 black bands on a grayish blue (in freshly shed individuals) to greenish brown background. These two species are believed to become sexually mature when about 3 years old. A snake of this age would be about 1.5 m long and females would lay from five to seven eggs. *L. colubrina* is usually found on small islets (Figures 1,2) and is believed to mature sexually at a length of only 1.2 m. The maximum length attained is about 2 m. All of the *Laticauda* species are locally called "Balingkasaw." Smith (1926) and Taylor (1922) should be consulted for details on identification of the species.

The eggs of *Laticauda* are laid in crevices of islets or coral reefs (see also Herre, 1942, and Herre and Rabor, 1949). Since the eggs are not buoyant, but sink to the bottom, it may be possible that they can hatch underwater. Eggs have been found in caves above the water line and underwater at 5–7 fathoms. Water temperatures observed were as low as 15°C. The incubation time is not known. The smallest snakes ever caught were about 20 cm long. Since sea turtle eggs become inviable if exposed to sea water (Witham, 1971), it would be most interesting and quite surprising if *Laticauda* eggs not only survive exposure to sea water, but can actually hatch underwater.

Aside from their search for snake eels as food in coral reefs, it seems that breeding is the main reason for the migration of *Laticauda* to certain islands. This is indicated by the presence of immature snakes in the open sea, whereas

Figure 1. *Laticauda colubrina* coiled up on a rocky islet about 5 m from the sea (photo by W. Dunson).

mature snakes are found on the reefs. The congregation of snakes on islets occurs between the end of June and late September. However, even as early as March, adult sea snakes have been observed in great numbers at sea, permitting an efficient harvesting by "patrol-diving" before the snakes reach the islets.

Although breeding seems to be seasonal in *Laticauda,* sea snakes can still be gathered on Gato Island between October and March. The number present is lower during these months, and the snakes caught are mostly males and smaller than those caught in the summer. Saint Girons (1964) also found a preponderance of males in a large sample of *L. colubrina* taken from an islet off New Caledonia. It is obvious that long-term ecological studies on these interesting breeding aggregations are needed for a rigorous understanding of *Laticauda* population dynamics. However, there is no reason to dispute the

Figure 2. Catching sea snakes (*Laticauda colubrina*) on an islet near Port Moresby, New Guinea. Alan Decker is holding the snake and Roger Seymour is looking on (photo by W. Dunson).

assertion that the snakes are moving to certain islands during the summer and subsequently dispersing. Exceptionally heavy collecting of snakes on Gato Island in the first half of 1971 (during a peak demand for skins) greatly depleted the number of snakes. Yet the area was repopulated with mature snakes within a few weeks when oversupply caused the demand to collapse.

Hydrophis

The habits of *H. belcheri* differ considerably from those of the *Laticauda* group. *H. belcheri* is a completely aquatic snake. It bears its young alive at sea and never comes ashore. Although it may reach 2.1 m in length, it has a narrow body with a very long neck and tiny head. Its local name is *walo-walo* and several fishermen have reportedly died from its bite. In contrast the bites of *Laticauda* species do not appear to be fatal.

The *duhol*, *H. inornatus*, is common along sandy bottoms on the eastern coast of Luzon. It has a robust body (up to 15 cm in circumference) even though the head is relatively small and total length rarely exceeds 1.2 m. It is believed to mature at a length of about 0.8 m.

H. semperi is most unusual since it lives in fresh water in Lake Taal on Luzon Island. It is also called *duhol* and is considered a delicacy by some orientals due to the presence of fatty tissue.

SEA SNAKE FISHING GROUNDS IN THE PHILIPPINES

The Philippines are probably one of the richest fishing grounds for sea snakes in the world. There have been no scientific surveys of this resource, however, and the extent of the fishery is unknown.

Although the Japanese have concentrated their efforts on Gato Island (north of Cebu), there are undoubtedly many other localities that are equally productive. A careful analysis of coastal maps could reveal many potential sites for subsequent examination by actual survey. Generally, sea snakes abound on islands and islets with caves or crevices which are surrounded by moderately deep water, and which are far away from the mainland or from human disturbance. There are many such places in the Philippines, but the most likely spot is in the Cuyo Islands in Palawan Province. Other spots which would justify surveys are the southwestern coast of Masbate Island, the Gigantes Islands of Iloilo Province, Torres Islands west of Catbalogan (Samar), Sorsogon and the Bicol Peninsula, Batangas Bay, Lubang Island (Mindoro), and Zamboanga and Sulu Provinces.

METHODS OF CATCHING SEA SNAKES

Sea snakes are often gathered by hand. The body and the neck are grabbed and the snakes are put in a sack. The *Laticauda* species are inoffensive and tend to shy away from a capturing hand. Many fishermen even claim that "they don't bite." But when excited by rough handling, sudden changes in the environmental temperature, or pain, they do react by striking. Snake divers in the Philippines use rubber bands made out of motorcycle tubes to tie as many as seven sea snakes together; they often get bitten. The bite and subsequent effects are painful but not usually fatal. *Hydrophis belcheri* are much more dangerous. They resist capture by vigorous biting.

Fishermen occasionally catch sea snakes on their hooks and lines, *basnigs* (bagnets), and trawls. Whenever fishermen operate near coral reefs and rocky shelves, they invariably catch sea snakes which are after the fish that the men are catching. Blast fishermen encounter these creatures feeding on dead and stupefied fish. When blast fishing was seemingly a hopeless problem in this country in 1971, not a few fishermen in the Visayan Sea fished for sea snakes instead of food fish. This was at the height of the demand of sea snake skins from Japan and Okinawa, a time of good prices. These fishermen used to blast a school of fish in coral reefs, wantonly destroying even the beautiful corals around them, just to attract sea snakes. Of course, this is basically a chumming method of fishing for sea snakes. The fishermen made more money on sea snakes than on fishing for food. But they were so indiscriminate in catching even the undersized ones that the buyers eventually refused them.

Laticauda species can generally be found under overhanging ledges or inside islet caves with underwater entrances. Divers strap underwater flashlights to one arm to search these areas. *L. colubrina* is often easier to gather since it coils on top of rocks on islets where conditions are cool and damp.

The *Hydrophis* species are mostly gathered by chumming in the open sea above coral reefs. Fishermen usually spread a good quantity of bait fish into the sea and wait for sea snakes to come and feed on them. As soon as a sufficient number have come, the fishermen dive and catch them by hand. A scoop net with bait fish is also left on the bottom at a depth of 5–7 fathoms. After a few minutes, sea snakes enter the scoop net, begin feeding, and can be captured. For each dive, a good catcher can bring up six snakes, three in each hand. One man aboard the motor boat receives the snakes and secures them in a sack to prevent escape. In this manner, an average of 40 snakes could be gathered by each man in a night or in a day of snake fishing. Since sea snakes feed at night, more snakes can be caught then.

Another method of catching sea snakes is "patrol-diving." The fishermen "patrol" around coral reefs where sea snakes may have been previously sighted. The boats go on and on until they spot a snake breathing at the surface. Then they dive for it, using weights to catch up with the diving snake, and grab it. Often, they can find several more coiled at the bottom. This is a very tiresome method but still effective.

ECONOMIC EXPLOITATION

Sea Snakes as Aphrodisiacs

Wild animals make exotic foods. They are, of course, nutritious, but many people in addition attribute "magical" properties to them. In Manila there is a restaurant that serves sea snakes, taken alive and fresh from an aquarium to your table. Its name is *Mariposa de Vida,* and it is said to be one of the few "aphrodisiac" restaurants in the world. Orientals are the main customers for sea snake dishes. At one time, some Japanese tourist customers ordered a live sea snake to be brought to their table. With a knife, they slit the snake's throat and drank the blood. Then they chopped the wriggling snake into small pieces, and ate it raw soaked in soy sauce! A more typical recipe is that of sea snake *adobo,* my own personal favorite. The snake meat is chopped into slices and soaked first in vinegar, and then in toyo mixed with garlic and pimiento for 15 min. The meat is next boiled for 30 min in soda, drained, fried, and seasoned with onions, tomatoes, and pickles.

Sea Snake Meat

At first only sea snake skins were in demand, and there seemed to be no use for the meat and internal organs. The fishermen's families complained of foul odors from the beaches, caused by the decaying viscera and meat. So they started to find ways of utilizing them. They fed the meat to their home-raised hogs with good results. The snake meat is now being used in poultry and hog feeds in ground form. Actually, sea snake meat has a much higher protein (68+%) and vitamin A content than many meats. Since it is also suitable for human consumption, some fishermen believe that some canned fish, especially those which are packed round, are sea snakes. However, there is no canned snake being produced.

At times, usually during winter, the Japanese have ordered smoked sea snakes. The fishermen actually broiled these under gable roofs. Small or immature sea snakes had their skins left on; the mature ones were stripped as the skins could still be sold. In all cases, the visceral organs and the heads were removed.

Use of the Viscera

The gall bladder is especially prized by Orientals for medicinal purposes. The Chinese are especially keen about this for stomach trouble, skin diseases, and as an aphrodisiac. It is also said to remove body impurities. The bile fluids are extracted from the gall bladder just after skinning (otherwise the gall bladder is easily ruptured). Three fresh gall bladders in a glass of wine, or three dried gall bladders boiled in coffee, are considered an aphrodisiac.

Next in importance to the gall bladder is the snake fat. Fat is found as lobules in the posterior part of the snake's abdominal cavity. For a sexually mature snake, the amount of fat varies from 200–300 g, and upon cooking may yield about 100 cc of oil. Sea snake oil is thought to contain high amounts of vitamin A and is good for margarines or butter. It also has been found valuable for industrial uses. The first step in processing it is to treat it with sulfonates to eliminate the rancid odor.

Processing Sea Snake Skins

Stripping Sea snakes are brought ashore alive inside sacks. At the beaches, fishermen have S-shaped hooks hung on a pole or tree. The snakes are hooked through the upper jaw as a base for pulling off the skins, or alternatively, a loop of rope is tied around the neck and the other end tied to an anchorage. The skin around the neck is cut and, depending on the customer's choice, the skins will be slit on the dorsal or ventral surface. The skin is easily pulled down to the cloaca, where the tail starts to flatten. Here the muscles have to be freed from the skin with a knife. The tail is shaped like a scoop net after stripping, and it has to be opened with a knife to align or flatten it with the rest of the skin. Lazy fishermen simply cut the skin at the cloaca, but the tail is usable for watch straps or shoe bands.

The snake's blood is drained out and the meat is exposed white. The viscera and the eggs, if the snake is a female, are exposed and these are removed. The eggs taste like an incubated chicken egg after boiling, except that the white and yellow portions are homogenous, like fish roe.

The meat is dried without salt for 3 days under the sun, if intended for use in animal feeds. It is also broiled or smoked for human consumption, usually as an export item for Japan, China, and Okinawa.

Scraping The skin always retains some flesh on it after stripping, especially near the neck and tail. To meet the standard set by foreign buyers, the skin is scraped with a dull axe-like tool before salting. Sometimes, if scraping is delayed for more than 12 hrs, the skins have to be salted to prevent the attack of bacteria which causes perforation of the skins. The salt also enhances the discharge of lactic acid from the skin tissues and delays putrefaction. For skins that are to be subjected to chrome tanning, some flesh should be left on, in order to add to the skin's tensile strength after tanning. However, leathercraft manufacturers have a scraping machine (sieve) to attain uniform thickness.

Salting Salting standards dictate that fresh skins, whether scraped or not, should be salted sufficiently. This means that the salt, if in crystalline form, should completely cover the flesh side; if in ground form it should be about 3 mm thick. A 1.8 m long skin should use up about 400 g of salt. The skins are then rolled up either immediately or gradually while salting.

It is easy to detect an undersalted skin. A 1.8 m long skin ought to attain a diameter of about 9 cm. Smaller rolls denote undersalting and must be resalted at once if they are to keep in good condition.

Storing, Drying, and Packing Rolled skins should not be exposed to moisture, or the salt melts and bacterial or fungal attack occurs. This is characterized by reddening of the flesh side of the salted skin. A buyer of sea snake rawhide should know that, in such a condition, perforations on the leather will appear after tanning.

Salted sea snake rawhide should be allowed to drip without exposure to humidity. To prolong the life of the cured skins, it is preferable to allow the lactic acid to drip for at least 48 hrs. The best way to store the skins is in plastic bags with a drain hole at the bottom. In this state, the skins may last for a year without deterioration before tanning. However, for exporting of rawhides, the salted skins are air-dried or cured to decrease their weight. Direct sun-drying makes them brittle. This is called an "irreversible chemical reaction" in leather chemistry.

In shipping sea snake rawhides for export, the skins are individually packed and sealed in cellophane, crated, and properly labeled. This is often required by foreign buyers in order to avoid complications with foreign customs or health laws. Other foreign buyers require a preliminary tanning for the skins. The most common state is the "pickled" and mordanted skin. It is a way of preserving the quality and strength of the skins before tanning, and of eliminating the slimy odor. Others prefer tanned, but prefinished snake leather.

Tanning Tanning is the intricate chemical process of "cooking" rawhides into finished leather for manufacture. Dried rawhide, no matter how strong it may seem, is subject to decomposition. Tanning not only preserves the skin, but also modifies it in many ways. The tanning process actually strengthens and softens the rawhides, so as to attain form for desired leathercrafts. It is only through tanning that desired color, texture or finish can be attained, as we see in beautiful finished leathercrafts. For instance, belt leather is crisp. Glove leather must be soft. Shoe upper leather must be stretchable. In any case, it must be strong.

Tanning processes take no less than 7 days to complete. There are several methods of tanning sea snake skins. One is the alum process and another is the chrome process. The first allows natural colors to show, but the tensile strength is not improved. The second thickens and strengthens the rawhide and allows more effective coloring or application of pigmentation. In both processes, the softness is affected by the amount and quality of industrial oil used in the later stages of tanning. Sea snake oil made from the fat has been used with good results by some tanneries. The finishing step for the tanned sea snake skins is the application of a top coat. For utmost luster, the "wet look" spray is applied. In this case, the skin must pass through a pressing machine so that rough surfaces can be smoothed out. Soft leathers with lacquer are not pressed, but glazed, and they exude a genuine snake leather look. The details of the tanning process remain a trade secret.

Snake skin leather and other snake designs have been popular for their beauty and exotic quality. People use snake-design shoes, handbags, wallets, belts, and even clothes (Figure 3). Unfortunately, those that seemingly dazzle the eyes with their luster are usually just imitations; they are leatherettes. The test of a real skin is made by burning a portion of it. Leatherettes smell like rubber when they burn. Genuine skins do not actually burn and they smell like broiled meat. Designs on some other leathercrafts are merely embossed

Figure 3. The author being interviewed on a Manila television station; he is holding a *Laticauda semifasciata*. Note that his coat, bow tie, shoes, and belt are tailored from sea snake leather.

498

on cow or carabao (water buffalo) leather. Real reptile skins, when properly tanned, are exceptionally beautiful and command good prices.

Since reptile skins are hard to obtain, there are still less than a handful of dealers supplying them. Now that sea snake skins have been "discovered" as a good substitute source for quantity production of reptile skins, the supply should increase. Filipinos are now capable of tanning good quality reptile skins, and have the manufacturing expertise to export sea snake leather products to world markets.

CATCH STATISTICS

There are no reliable catch statistics that can be offered in this paper, only some estimates. The official Fisheries Statistics issued by the Philippine Bureau of Fisheries considerably underestimate the trade. This is due to inadequate reporting by the Regional Offices of the Bureau of Fisheries, probably because sea snakes are classified only as a "minor fishery product." Consequently, much tariff has been missed by the government, as little interest has been given to this "minor product."

In the light of these circumstances, the best data can be gathered directly from those involved in the sea snake industry. Even these figures will probably be underestimates to some degree since it is a tendency of business-men to underdeclare their actual figures. The volume presently reported is less than 50,000 snakes per month, and this fluctuates considerably depending on the demand.

Rawhides

In the first half of 1971, Japan received about 200,000 sea snake rawhides consisting of the three species of *Laticauda, Hydrophis inornatus,* and *H. belcheri.* In the second half, there were no shipments. In 1972, about 180,000 sea snake rawhides of the same assortment were exported, mainly to Japan. In 1973, about 180,000 skins were exported. In 1974 the trade will probably reach 450,000 skins because there is a marked upswing in demand, owing to the promotions that I have conducted here and abroad. I have estimated that the Philippine waters have a future potential production of 100,000 mature sea snakes per month. Half of these could be gathered from presently known areas.

Leather

Since 1930, various snake leathercrafts have been produced in the Philippines from *Acrochordus granulatus* (file snake) skins. In 1959 utilization of *Lati-*

cauda species was started. These have been sold in tourist shops in Manila. The Filipino market for sea snake leathercraft was initiated only in 1973 by the author. It is only the beginning of the effort to promote these products among Filipinos. Sales on tanned sea snake leather are still negligible. The producers of these items rarely sell them for further processing, since they are mostly vegetable or alum tanned, and therefore are usually unacceptable to foreign buyers. Most buyers prefer to manufacture the tanned skins into various leathercrafts in their own factories. The only Philippine producer of good quality sea snake leather sells most of its goods locally. The locally tanned leather amounts to about 2000 pieces of file snakes, 5000 pieces of assorted *Laticauda* species, and 1500 pieces of assorted *Hydrophis* species monthly.

Dried Meat

It takes about seven to 10 pieces of dried sea snake meat (11% moisture content) to make one kilo. I estimate that the amount of dried meat ground for hog and poultry feeds is 4000–5000 kg monthly.

CONSERVATION

Heavy commercial exploitation of sea snakes is unusual, and it is believed that the Philippines are supplying most of the world markets. Fisheries Administrative Orders 69 and 69-1 provide a set of rules for the legal exploitation of "minor" fishery products such as sea snakes. Unfortunately, they do not provide for conservation, or measures against over-exploitation. Practically anyone can possess, kill, process, or sell sea snake products. The Fisheries Administrative Orders also do not provide for protection of concessionaires' rights. Thus, the extent of exploitation is determined mainly by the market demand. In recent years leather has become more and more valuable and there have been temporary booms in demand due to the dictates of fashion. One such period of heavy demand occurred in 1971, when hundreds of thousands of rawhides were shipped to Japan, tanned and processed, and exported to Europe as Japanese snake leather. At the present time, there is again an acute shortage of leather world-wide and the demand for sea snake skins is high. It is not surprising that Philippine businessmen want to regain control over all phases of the industry, so that they may share in the greater profits associated with sales of the finished product rather than the rawhides. The future development of the industry also depends on the recognition of the Philippines as the source of the hides.

The lack of regulations has led to the gathering of young snakes, of females before they lay their eggs, and to the catching of more snakes than can be considered a sustained yield from any one area. Although there are few data on which to base population projections, it seems likely that continued unrestricted collecting can only lead to a decline in production and perhaps even a catastrophic collapse. This result would, of course, benefit no one in the long run. The survival of the commercial fishery up until the present time can mainly be attributed to the seasonal nature of the catching process and to occasional periods of lessened demand.

The future of the Philippine sea snake fishery and the industries associated with processing of the various products depends on implementation of the following points:

1. Government enforcement of catch limits, minimum sizes, and seasons in order to maintain a sustained yield.

2. Development of local industries that handle the complete process of gathering, processing, manufacturing, and marketing. These companies are more likely than overseas concerns to appreciate the value of conserving a limited resource, especially if they are granted a concession over a certain area.

3. Initiation of a program for scientific investigation of the sea snake resources of the Philippines, and especially of population dynamics in those areas currently being intensively exploited.

SUMMARY

Sea snakes are fished commercially in the Philippines, mainly for export as rawhides to Japan. *Laticauda semifasciata, L. laticaudata,* and *Hydrophis inornatus* make up most of the catch. *Laticauda* species are caught in great numbers on or near isolated islets and reefs where they congregate to breed between June and September. Tiny Gato Island, north of Cebu Island, has been exploited in this way for at least 40 years. Recently, a local industry has developed which is tanning the skins and attempting to develop markets for the finished products. Aside from the skin leather, sea snakes furnish meat for human and animal consumption (ground up for feeds), oil, and exotic foods such as bile from the gall bladder for mystical purposes (i.e., as an aphrodisiac). There is a great demand for sea snake leather at the present time and conservation practices imposed by the Philippine Government will be necessary to ensure a sustained yield in the future. Surveys of potential new fishing grounds are needed, as are basic studies on the population dynamics of the huge breeding aggregations of *Laticauda.*

REFERENCES

Herre, A. W. C. T. 1942. Notes on Philippine sea-snakes. Copeia 1:7–9.

Herre, A. W. C. T., and D. S. Rabor. 1949. Notes on Philippine sea snakes of the genus *Laticauda*. Copeia 4:282–284.

Punay, E. Y. 1972. Sea snake fishing–soon, a booming industry. Philippine Fishing J. 10:4–8.

Saint Girons, H. 1964. Notes sur l'ecologie et la structure des populations des Laticaudinae (Serpents, Hydrophiidae) en Nouvelle Caledonie. Terre et la Vie 111:185–214.

Smith, M. 1926. Monograph of the Sea-snakes (*Hydrophiidae*). Wheldon & Wesley, London.

Taylor, E. H. 1922. Herpetology of the Philippine Islands. V. 2. The Snakes of the Philippine Islands. Bureau of Printing, Manila.

Witham, R. 1971. Breeding of a pair of pen-reared green turtles. Quart. J. Fla. Acad. Sci. 33(4):288–290.

twenty-two

Attacks by Sea Snakes on Divers

Harold Heatwole

The aggressiveness of sea snakes is a subject upon which there has been much divergence of opinion but little careful systematic observation. Various authorities have used terms ranging from "vicious" and "ferocious" to "docile," "gentle," and "inoffensive." Halstead (1970) has reviewed this largely anecdotal literature and it will not be treated in detail here. Little can be gleaned from it except that herpetologists have disagreed widely on the temperament of sea snakes.

As with many other behavioral traits, temperament shows considerable interspecific differences (Herre, 1942). Conflicting views on sea snake aggressiveness can be attributed in part to overgeneralization on the group as a whole, based on a few encounters with only one or two species. Persons who would not presume to generalize about the behavior of a family of terrestrial snakes from observations of a few representatives, have been content to make sweeping statements about the temperament of sea snakes, with almost no first-hand experience with live members of the group. Herpetologists have been understandably terrestrial in their habits, and until recently none were trained as divers. In addition, herpetologists and sea snakes are largely allopatric, the former being concentrated in Europe and America, the latter in Indo-Australasian waters. Consequently, for information on sea snake aggressiveness, most scientists have had to rely on second-hand accounts of varying accuracy by fishermen, sportsmen, and other persons not trained in scientific observation. Such accounts are subject to the usual lack of objectivity of most humans in regard to ophidian behavior, and the tendency to interpret almost any overt movement by a snake as aggressive. Deliberate exaggeration sometimes may have been involved, in an attempt to dramatize experiences for personal or financial reasons. Often, the specific identity of the snake involved was in question. Even more confusing are the honest differences of opinion expressed by highly experienced divers regarding the same species of sea snake—views ranging from belief in malicious aggressiveness to conviction that the snakes were merely passively curious (e.g., see accounts by Doughton, Bisson, Harding and Deas, years unspecified). On several occasions, I found that my field observations did not correspond to those reported by very able, veteran underwater photographers. In order to resolve these differences and to record aggressive behavior on film, several expeditions to Queensland reefs were made in collaboration with Ben and Eva Cropp. A systematic study of aggressive behavior was carried out on these expeditions. Although supplemented by other field work and literature accounts, that study forms the backbone of the present report.

The study included only a few species from a few reefs, primarily Saumarez Reef and the Swain's Reefs, and consequently does not provide general answers to the question of sea snake aggressiveness. However, certain features do emerge which (1) resolve the opposite conclusions previously reached by the participants of the expedition; (2) indicate some of the variables influencing aggressiveness in one species; (3) permit an assessment of some interspecific differences in temperament; and (4) provide a comparative basis for future observations.

From the literature and clinical data it is clear that sea snakes do bite humans and that fatalities sometimes result (see Chapter 23). What is not clear is the extent to which these bites are inflicted defensively (e.g., when the snake is captured in a net or stepped upon by a wading fisherman), as opposed to attack (bite from a free-swimming snake which could just as easily escape without biting). From the practical viewpoint, it has been felt necessary to put nets around some bathing beaches in an attempt to keep out sea snakes, or to post signs warning bathers (Pickwell, 1972b).

DEFENSIVE BITING

A great number of vertebrates will attempt to bite a molester when captured, cornered, or persistently disturbed. This is such a generalized defensive pattern that it is not surprising that many sea snakes employ it. Pickwell (1972b) has cautioned against the erroneous belief that the small-headed species cannot get a sufficient gape to cause a dangerous bite on a finger or other appendage.

The prevalence of defensive biting varies greatly among species. This is well illustrated by those with which I have had the most field experience.

Figure 1. The author with a captured *Aipysurus laevis* at Swain's Reefs. (Photograph by Ben Cropp).

When captured with a snake tongs or noose, *Aipysurus laevis, Aipysurus fuscus, Astrotia stokesii,* and *Lapemis hardwickii* almost invariably turn and repeatedly bite the object restraining them (Figure 1), unless grasped just behind the head. These same species (with the possible exception of *A. fuscus,* which I've never caught in a trawl), as well as *Hydrophis elegans,* often bite ropes and fish captured in a trawl net. *A. laevis* and especially *A. stokesii* are vigorous defensive biters, often biting objects lying within reach when placed on the deck of a boat. The latter frequently opens its mouth wide and attempts to bite the flat deck surface. All of these species should be considered defensive biters. *Aipysurus duboisii* is less prone to bite but will do so.

By contrast *Acalyptophis peronii* and *Hydrophis melanocephalus* must be subjected to severe treatment before they can be induced to bite. They were rarely observed to attempt biting either during capture or subsequent handling in the laboratory. None of the *Emydocephalus annulatus,* from either the Coral Sea or Ashmore Reef, ever attempted to bite upon capture, nor did any subsequently do so when subjected to various experimental treatments in the laboratory. It is doubtful if biting is part of the usual defensive behavioral repertoire of these species.

My experience with *Laticauda* is limited to less than a dozen individuals and consequently my impressions may be erroneous. However, none ever attempted to bite. At Wari Island, Louisiade Archipelago, Papua-New Guinea, small children were observed to fearlessly catch and handle live *Laticauda colubrina* to the total unconcern of nearby adults. Gail and Rageau (1958) report similar observations from New Caledonia. It appears that this genus should be listed among the docile ones, although the danger of premature generalization is exemplified by the report (Woodland, pers. comm.) that although the Fijians are not usually afraid of *Laticauda*, they avoid them in the breeding season because they believe the males to be prone to bite at that time.

Enhydrina schistosa is probably a ready biter, at least defensively, since the few individuals I've had experience with had ugly dispositions; and this species' record of human fatalities is impressive. Many additional species probably also are prone to bite as they are important in inflicting casualties on humans (see Chapter 19); Halstead (1970) lists 14 species known to have caused human envenomation. Pickwell (1972a) reports that *Pelamis platurus*, the most widespread of sea snakes, frequently bites and locks onto a net or even their own bodies when captured.

After a few days, or in some cases, only a few hours of captivity, even some pugnacious species such as *A. laevis, L. hardwickii,* and *A. stokesii* do not attempt to bite if gently handled. However, this "taming" should not be relied upon. In one case an *L. hardwickii* which had been in captivity a number of weeks and handled nearly daily without displaying any aggressive tendencies, suddenly attempted to bite, fortunately succeeding in envenomating a respirometer rather than the investigator's hand. Nevertheless, with caution some normally aggressive species can be rather easily used in laboratory work after a short period in captivity.

ATTACKS

The distinction between defensive biting and attack has been made above. There are, in turn, two categories of attack, provoked and unprovoked. Provocation is here arbitrarily considered to mean direct contact with a snake, vigorous movement in its immediate vicinity, or disturbing it by removing cover, such as coral, from above it. An unprovoked attack is defined as one originating without the application of the above-mentioned stimuli. The semantic argument that mere presence of a human in the water within the snake's sensory range constitutes provocation is rejected, as it would require any attack to be a provoked one by definition, and would obscure real differences in degree of aggressive behavior among individuals or species.

One must carefully distinguish between real and imagined attacks. Snakes will often approach and follow divers, either on the surface or beneath the water (Pickwell, 1972b). An unsolicited approach by a large, highly venomous snake toward a person can understandably induce a frame of mind not conducive to detached observation of snake behavior. Consequently, such approaches may often be considered an "attack," without the diver lingering to see whether the snake would indeed attempt to bite, once it reached its destination. Also, an inappropriate response by an approached diver may induce an attack which would not otherwise occur.

During underwater observation of a dense population of *A. laevis* at Cato Island, I was occasionally approached by snakes that either changed course or left cover and came directly toward me, sometimes from distances of up to about 10 m. Their slow, deliberate locomotion suggested purposefulness yet did not convey the impression of aggressive intent. Consequently, rather than flee, I remained immobile and allowed the snakes to approach. They established contact, moving slowly along beside me, repeatedly sticking out their tongues against my wet suit. The duration of this behavior ranged from a few momentary investigations to longer ones of perhaps 10 sec. Subsequently, at other localities in the Coral Sea, I habitually employed this technique whenever snakes approached; after a brief investigation they usually returned to their previous activities.

The snake tongue is involved in chemoreception and the observed behavior was clearly related to sensory investigation of the diver. If one is permitted to use a somewhat teleological term for descriptive purposes, such snakes appeared to be "curious." The stimuli inducing the initial approach are unknown but are probably either visual or arise from vibrations made by the diver's movements. Only a few of the many snakes encountered displayed approach and investigative behavior; most completely ignored a diver, even when he swam along beside them at only a meter's distance.

My experience made me skeptical of reports of sea snake attacks, particularly since some non-scientist divers also considered the snakes' behavior to express curiosity rather than aggression. Further study has indicated that for *A. laevis*, at least, the truth lies somewhere between the two extreme views. This species does attack under some circumstances, and part of the differences in opinion held by different persons familiar with its behavior arose from different methods of treatment of the snakes. My previous approach had been to observe as unobtrusively as possible, or if it were desirable to capture one, to do so with the most minimal disturbance possible. In the latter case, snakes were caught and taken immediately to a boat. Ben Cropp, who favored the view that sea snakes were aggressive and who had filmed a number of attacks, used a totally different procedure. For filming purposes action was important and snakes were molested, with the result that there were frequent attacks. When we worked together, my treatment resulted in only rare attacks, his in frequent ones. In some cases, a third diver was used to induce attacks which I could observe and Ben could film. Part of this study has been embodied in the television release *Sea Snakes of the Coral Sea*. Two important aspects of the study were the identification of attack characteristics, and an assessment of some of the stimuli inducing attack.

Characteristics of Attack

In contrast to the slow, leisurely way a curious snake approaches a diver, an attacking snake moves with astonishing rapidity; the graceful undulations of ordinary locomotion give way to a rather jerky movement (perhaps simply a function of increased swimming speed), which gives the impression that the head is darting back and forth. The most characteristic feature of attacking snakes is their persistence. They chase fleeing divers for long distances and repeatedly return to the attack after being violently kicked with flippers or pushed aside by a spear gun or snake tongs. Escaping or fending off an attacking snake can be an exhausting experience, especially for the uninitiated. In one instance a snake bit the diver (protected by a wet suit) four times before giving up the attack.

The behavioral differences between a curious snake and an attacking one are striking; the latter leaves no doubt in the mind of the recipient as to the aggressive nature of the action. Once one has experienced or seen an attack, it is subsequently easy to distinguish between the approaches of curious and aggressive snakes.

Stimuli Inducing Attack

The stimuli inducing attack are not clearly understood, since some individuals will attack under the same conditions that cause others merely to attempt escape. One important factor seems to be the stage of the reproductive cycle (Herre, 1942; Pickwell, 1972b); *A. laevis* seems to be much more prone to attack in the mating season than at other times.

During expeditions to the Swain's Reefs (October, November, December, January) when mating activity is low or nonexistent (no courtship observed), few attacks could be induced. On the *Alpha Helix* expedition to Ashmore Reef (December, January), large numbers of *A. laevis* were captured or observed, and attempts were made on several occasions to induce attacks, yet only one abortive and one doubtful attack occurred. In the former, the snake had been grasped by snake tongs but escaped; instead of fleeing as did most *A. laevis* under similar conditions during that expedition, it moved toward its would-be captor in typical attack style but did not bite. Instead it turned away when a few centimeters from the person, and returned to the bottom and sought cover under coral.

The doubtful attack has been described by the recipient (McCosker, pers. comm.): "While doing so [attempting to free a fish trap] I felt a snake swim along my right thigh and side, and then wrap a loose coil along my extended right arm. With this realization, I frantically swam to the surface, shaking my right arm, and released the snake. I did not observe it attempt to bite me, but it did follow me to the surface, where I catapulted into the boat." Deas (year unspecified) has similarly mentioned that while absorbed in underwater photography he would suddenly find a sea snake (almost certainly *A. laevis*) wrapped around a leg.

In contrast to the paucity of attacks mentioned above, during visits to the Coral Sea in the months of May, June, and July when *A. laevis* courtship was frequently observed, attacks were easily induced. Interruption of the activities of courting pairs (see Figure 2), or close approach to them, nearly invariably resulted in an attack.

To study this further, I passed a nylon line through the upper and lower lips of a dead *A. laevis,* tied it securely, and attached a small sinker to the bottom of the line about 40 cm below the snake's head. In this way, I could snorkel on the surface while pulling the dead snake along near the bottom. By

Figure 2. A courting pair of *Emydocephalus annulatus* at Ashmore Reef, January 1972. The male is the upper melanistic individual. Photograph by the author.

towing it at an appropriate speed, it moved in a sinuous lifelike manner, and when brought in the vicinity of some other snakes it induced courtship. The courting partner never mated with the dead snake, presumably because of the absence of an appropriate behavioral response by the latter. A courting snake would follow a towed one for extended periods of time. If the experiment continued until it had to surface to breathe, it often sighted the investigator and usually attacked without being subjected to further stimulation.

The facts that (1) attacks are more easily induced in the mating season than at other times, and that (2) snakes actively courting or mating are more prone to attack than those engaged in other activities, suggest that the reproductive condition in *A. laevis* is related to aggressiveness.

Given the paucity of information on reproductive cycles in sea snakes, it is premature to generalize about the aggressiveness of most other species. One could classify an aggressive species as docile simply through lack of underwater experience with it during the mating season, or conversely overestimate the aggressiveness of a rather docile one by having encounters only during the mating season. With this limitation in mind, several observations on other species can be cited.

There is one record of an attack by an *Aipysurus duboisii*, similar in all respects to those of *A. laevis*. My field notes (Saumarez Reef, July 2, 1971, 1145 hrs) of that attack read: "Another one [*A. duboisii*] came up for air, swam about 30 cm on the surface, then started down, stopped, looked in my direction, came rapidly toward me with a jerky side-to-side head motion and went for my leg. I gently pushed it away [with snake tongs] and it came again. I caught it in the tongs."

One other species which I have observed in considerable numbers both during the mating and non-mating season is *E. annulatus*. Despite frequent interruption of courting pairs, no attacks were sustained and it seems to be a genuinely docile species at all seasons.

It is probable that species which readily bite defensively also readily attack in the mating season, and that species docile in defense are docile in all contexts. However, I have had insufficient experience with other species over wide enough seasonal ranges to verify this hypothesis. I have been reluctant to test the tendency of *A. stokesii* to attack, because of my findings that the fangs of this large species can readily penetrate a wet suit. The most important species in terms of human fatalities, *E. schistosa*, has not been studied. However, it occurs mostly in muddy estuarine waters and, although constituting a significant health hazard to fishermen of southeast Asia, is of less importance to divers, who seldom invade their domain. Although *P. platurus* has been reported to suddenly attack a clam diver (Halstead, 1970), Pickwell (1972a) noted that two individuals of this species avoided a diver investigating them.

Bearing in mind that ease of inducement of attack varies seasonally, one can examine the type of stimuli that are operative, at least at certain times of the year. Except for courting snakes, or other rare exceptions, *A. laevis* can be approached closely without inducing attack. As long as the diver's movements are slow and smooth, most snakes ignore him. Rapid, vigorous movements or direct contact with the snake result either in the reptile swimming away or attacking. Severe treatment such as violently kicking it with a flipper is especially effective in inducing attack. One incident illustrating this point took place in the Swain's Reefs. Two other divers and I spent 10–15 min observing a foraging *A. laevis* at close range (occasionally approaching with the face-plate 25 cm from it, to observe closely its investigation of crevices in the coral). The snake showed no overt response. After this period, one diver kicked the snake smartly with a flipper. There was an immediate flurry of activity (some of which was recorded on film), the snake persistently attacking each of us in turn; when kicked away by a flipper it would attack the nearest diver, repeatedly pressing home the attack. This dramatic change in behavior clearly illustrates the role of the diver's behavior in determining whether or not a snake will attack.

Unprovoked Attacks

Unprovoked attacks are rare but they do occur. I know of only three unquestionable cases. One consisted of an *A. laevis* coming from a number of meters away and attacking a swimmer (Eva Cropp) at the water's surface and pursuing her some distance. The previous activity of this snake is unknown, and the possibility exists that it had come to the surface for air following courtship activity. Preceding the attack, Eva was swimming at an angle to the snake's path of movement, not directly toward it.

The second case was also an attack by *A. laevis*. Two divers had been observing and filming the snake near the bottom for a considerable time. It had displayed no previous overt response before suddenly attacking (photograph in MacLeish, 1972). The third case is the attack by *A. duboisii* mentioned above.

Deas (year unspecified) provides accounts which are suggestive of unprovoked attacks (Saumarez and Kenn Reefs, and almost certainly referring to *A. laevis* which he shows in an underwater photograph). He states: "One scuba diver was chased from 80 ft. and then across the surface before reaching the safety of the boat" and later in the article indicates that others "would zoom up from the bottom, and dodge every attempt to keep them at bay, but the majority were docile." A number of other accounts in the popular skin-diving literature describe attacks, some of which appear to be unprovoked, although usually descriptions of the actual events are not sufficiently detailed for an assessment to be made.

Preventing or Fending Off Attack

Despite the possibility of unpleasant exceptions to the above generalizations, experience does indicate some behavioral guidelines for divers. Clearly, the objectives of most divers will be the opposite of mine during the above study; i.e., to prevent rather than to induce attack. Snorkelers or swimmers are less subject to contact with sea snakes, because most snakes that inhabit waters in which people swim usually stay near the bottom except when surfacing to breathe. (Note, however, that two of the unprovoked attacks occurred at the surface.) Unless there is some special reason for diving in waters where sea snakes are known to be abundant, the easiest way to avoid attack is to dive elsewhere. Since this may not always be possible or desirable, the second-best procedure is to wear protective clothing. I have presented 6 mm wet suit Neoprene (enveloping soap or other material which would retain fang marks if penetrated) to sea snakes and, after it was bitten, have examined the material inside. To date, only *A. stokesii* and exceptionally large *A. laevis* have been able to penetrate wet suits; they should therefore be treated with caution. In most cases, however, a full wet suit with hood, gloves, boots, etc., covering as much skin as possible, is good protection. In Viet Nam, two divers were inspecting the bottom of a boat when one (without a wet suit) was bitten by a sea snake (and subsequently became incapacitated). The second (with a wet suit) came to his aid and was also bitten but without ill effect, the wet suit affording complete protection (Pickwell, 1972b).

If approached by a sea snake which is moving slowly, there are two prescribed procedures. One is to remain as motionless as possible and permit the snake to investigate and leave. Vigorous swimming movements, unless one has a good head start and is a strong swimmer, are ill advised, because they may induce a curious snake to attack. A second method is effective after a bit of practice. If a curious snake approaches, gently interposing the flat face of a flipper between the snake and yourself will often result in the snake investigating the flipper and leaving without subjecting more vulnerable areas to examination. Occasionally this method will stop an attacking snake in apparent confusion, but is seldom effective because of the speed and persistence of the attacker. In any event, kicking the snake with a flipper or hitting it with a spear gun is contraindicated, except as a last resort to keep an attacking snake from reaching exposed areas. The procedure of throwing things at sea snakes approaching on the surface, as advocated by Pickwell (1972b), although sometimes effective in scaring away a snake, is just as apt to induce attack and is not advised. Even during an attack, restraint of a snake or blocking its advances should be as gentle as the situation allows.

Sexually stimulated snakes show little discrimination in their courting and will court ropes hanging over the side of a boat, and persistently direct their behavior toward anchor chains, etc. This observation suggested a technique which has occasionally (though not invariably) proved effective in diverting attacks. Persons diving during the mating season where sea snakes are numerous are advised to carry a short length of dark rope. If attacked, the rope can be dropped; sometimes the snake's attention is diverted to the rope and it is followed as it sinks to the bottom, permitting the diver to make a leisurely retreat.

CATCHING SEA SNAKES

For divers interested in catching live sea snakes in good condition for scientific study or for display in zoos or aquaria, there are two paramount considerations: safety for the diver and safety for the snake. Sea snakes are easily injured by rough handling, and initial high mortality among captive animals often results. Netting with hand nets at the surface prevents injury but does not often yield many snakes except in exceptionally rich areas. Noosing is not advisable, because it not only is the method most likely to injure the snake, but it often results in misses which could provoke attack. Capture by snake tongs* (Figure 1) is a relatively safe method for both snake and diver in the hands of experienced snake catchers, and is probably the best compromise between the two safety factors mentioned above. With a little practice one quickly learns to apply sufficient force to prevent escapes, yet not injure the snake. However, the best underwater way to capture a snake without injuring it, is to rapidly grasp it immediately behind the head with one hand and then quickly grab it near mid-body with the other (before it has opportunity to wrap around the first hand and apply leverage to free the head). This permits a firm grip without unduly squeezing vital organs such as the heart, and it permits the captor to move the two hands in conformity to the snake's bodily movements, thereby preventing parting of the rather fragile vertebral column (one of the most common injuries sustained by sea snakes during capture; Limpus, pers. comm.). This method places the inexperienced snake catcher under a greater risk of being bitten, especially if capture of an active snake is attempted. Novices should practice on small, docile, relatively weakly toxic species resting on the bottom, before pursuing more dangerous animals. A combination of snake tongs and hand capture, especially if performed jointly by two persons, is effective. The snake is gently grasped

*Pillstrom snake tongs, Fort Smith, Arkansas, U. S. A. For use in sea water, daily rinsing in fresh water followed by spraying with a de-moisturizing lubricant is essential maintenance.

with snake tongs and, when it has its mouth occupied biting them, it can be grasped behind the head, and carefully unwound from the tongs. This prevents skeletal injuries sometimes sustained as a result of the snake wrapping around the tongs, contracting its body muscles in an attempt to free itself and thereby parting its vertebrae. This source of injury is especially prevalent if snakes must be carried in tongs for long distances. The time that a snake is restrained by tongs should be minimized, either by taking it from the tongs as described above before swimming back to a boat, or by having a boat with containers of sea water available near the snake catchers at all times. Tom Allen, a member of an underwater filming team, captured sea snakes with a nylon diver's bag. He put his hand into the bag, swam up to a snake and by gently holding the animal, turned the bag right-side-out over it (Harding, year unspecified). That expedition encountered no aggressiveness and the method would appear to be the safest one available for the snake. Its use would be inadvisable in the face of any aggression by the snake. I have not tried this method personally.

In any method involving hand capture, each person must decide whether the advantage of gloves (reducing the chances of envenomation from a bite) outweighs their disadvantage (restricting manual dexterity, thereby increasing the probability of being bitten).

In choosing a method one has to consider whether to minimize risk to the snake or to the diver. Common, aggressive, highly venomous species are best captured in large numbers by a method safe to the diver, in hopes that a sufficient number will survive the rough treatment. Rare, relatively less venomous or docile species may warrant a method protecting the snake against injury but making the diver more vulnerable. Inevitably such decisions must be personal ones and cannot be dictated by a manual. Availability of antivenins or other medical aids may be an important influential factor.

Any form of recklessness or exhibitionism in handling sea snakes constitutes unwarranted risk to the diver and his underwater companions and should be avoided. The practice of capturing sea snakes by the tail, towing them rapidly backwards and flipping them into a dinghy at the surface, as employed by a few divers, constitutes unjustified, irresponsible theatrics, and has, in several instances I have observed, nearly resulted in serious consequences. This method is not only foolish but also injures the snakes.

SUMMARY

Sea snakes vary greatly in aggressiveness, some species almost always attempting to bite when captured, others seldom if ever doing so. Few species have been studied in detail and generalizations about the group as a whole are premature. However, *A. laevis,* one of the more aggressive species, will ordinarily ignore a diver even if approached quite closely, or will merely investigate him and leave without any aggressive behavior. During the mating season, this species is more prone to attack when molested than at other times of the year, when escape is the prevalent response. Even in the mating season, vigorous movements in its vicinity, or physical maltreatment, are usually required to induce attack; if the animal is actually or has recently been courting, it is especially sensitive to disturbance and attack may assume a more spontaneous aspect. Unprovoked attacks, though extremely rare, do occur. Attacks are characterized by rapid, jerky movements easily distinguished from the more graceful, leisurely approach of "curious" snakes.

The best way to avoid attack is not to molest snakes and, if approached, to refrain from vigorous activity, especially striking the animal. Attacks can sometimes be diverted by dropping a rope in front of an attacking snake. Wet suits are good protection against most species.

ACKNOWLEDGMENTS

I am greatly indebted to a number of divers without whose assistance, underwater expertise, familiarity with Queensland reefs, and/or first-hand experience with sea snakes and knowledge of good localities, my underwater work would have been much more difficult. They are Ron and Valerie Taylor, Wally Muller, Ron Isobel, Walter Schneider, Sherman Minton and especially Ben and Eva Cropp, David Krassoff and Vic Martin, who participated in the systematic study of aggressiveness reported in this chapter and who shared considerable personal risks in the interest of better understanding of snake behavior. The Cropps and the Taylors are also gratefully acknowledged for making available movie films and still pictures of sea snakes for my use. This work was supported in part by the National Science Foundation under grant NSF GA 35835 to the Pennsylvania State University and grants NSF GA 34948 and NSF GD 34462 to The Scripps Institution of Oceanography for operation of the *Alpha Helix* Research Program.

REFERENCES

Bisson, R. (Year unspecified) Skindiving safari to the Kenn Reefs. Fathom 1:6 pp.
Deas, W. (Year unspecified) Sea snakes. Skindiving in Australia 2:26.
Doughton, R. (Year unspecified) On safari to remote Marion Reef with Ron & Denyse Doughton. Skindiving in Australia 3:4 pp.
Gail, R., and J. Rageau. 1958. Introduction a l'etude des serpents marins (Ophidiens Hydrophiidae) en Nouvelle-Calédonie. Bull. Soc. Path. Exotique Paris 51:448–459.
Halstead, B. W. 1970. Poisonous and Venomous Marine Animals of the World, Vol. 3, Vertebrates, continued. U.S. Govt. Printing Office, Washington, D.C., 1006 pp.

Harding, J. (Year unspecified) A closer look at sea snakes. Fathom 1:20—24.

Herre, A. W. C. T. 1942. Notes on Phillipine sea-snakes. Copeia 1942:7—9.

MacLeish, K. 1972. Diving with sea snakes. National Geographic 141:564—578.

Pickwell, G. V. 1972a. The venomous sea snakes. Fauna 4:16—32.

Pickwell, G. V. 1972b. Sea snakes of Viet Nam and southeast Asia. *In* Handbook of Dangerous Animals for Field Personnel (G.V. Pickwell and W.E. Evans, Eds.). Naval Undersea Center, San Diego, Publication TP 324, pp. 5—25.

twenty-three

Sea Snakes and the Sea Level Canal Controversy

William A. Dunson

The Panama Canal is too small for many modern ships, and it will soon be utilized to its maximal carrying capacity. In conjunction with the demands of the Panamanian government for a renegotiation of the original treaty, this size problem has stimulated studies on the feasibility of the construction of a sea level canal. Some idea of the emotionally charged atmosphere in which these events have developed may be gained by an examination of various congressional speeches and hearings concerned with the canal (U.S. Gov't., 1970 a,b; Flood, 1966).

The final report of the Atlantic-Pacific Interoceanic Canal Study Commission appointed by President Johnson was submitted on December 1, 1970. It recommended that Panama was the most suitable site for a sea level canal, that nuclear excavation not be used, and that the risk of adverse ecological effects was acceptable (U.S. Gov't., 1971). The ecological conclusions were based on a rather subjective evaluation of very meager data. Yet Batelle Memorial Institute, which was in charge of the limited studies that were made, stated that "It is highly improbable that blue-water species like the sea snake and the crown-of-thorns starfish could get through the canal except under the most unusual circumstances." The National Academy of Sciences was asked in 1969 by the Commission to recommend a program of studies to monitor ecological changes in the event that the sea level canal were built. The Committee of Ecological Research for the Interoceanic Canal (CERIC) that was formed, was unfortunately not asked to consider the more important question of whether the canal should be built at all (Newman, 1972; Boffey, 1971). In fact, CERIC's final report was virtually ignored by the Commission, presumably since CERIC disputed the idea that ecological effects would be relatively harmless.

This controversy between the "environmentalists" urging restraint and further study and the "engineers" who seem unconcerned about ecological effects is only to be expected in a project of the magnitude of the sea level canal. However, three additional elements seem unique to this case: (1) for most species too few data are available for any definitive scientific arguments to be marshaled in favor of either side; (2) the champions of U.S. sovereignty over the Canal Zone find the claims of possible ecological damage, regardless of their intrinsic merits, useful for their cause; (3) the course of political relations between the U.S. and Panama is being used to force the U.S. to relinquish control of the present canal and accept the sea level canal as a face-saving alternative. Thus it should be obvious that the whole issue is very complex and subjective. The present discussion will be limited to a consideration of the possible migration of the yellow-bellied sea snake (*Pelamis*) through the proposed canal. Although the question of snake movements excites the public imagination, it is likely that any of a thousand other migrants could be much more damaging to the ecology of the Caribbean. The sea snake case is useful to consider because the public is concerned about it, and because enough data are now available to predict the likely consequences of introduction of this species into the Atlantic Ocean.

The general biological problems associated with mixing of ocean fauna and the introduction of alien species have been considered in numerous publications (Laycock, 1966; Rubinoff, 1968; Rubinoff and Rubinoff, 1968; Topp, 1969; Aron and Smith, 1971; Jones and Manning, 1971; Por, 1971; Jones, 1972; Zaret and Paine, 1973). Although these authors differ considerably in their points of view, the general conclusion that rather drastic changes in the balance of an ecosystem can follow the introduction of a single species is inescapable. In a few cases, one might debate the desirability of these changes. In some instances (such as lampreys in the Great Lakes), irreparable damage has been done. Thus biologists tend to be leary of any proposed ocean mixing because of the unpredictable outcome.

I first became involved in this issue because of my work on the distribution of *Pelamis* in relation to temperature and salinity. Field work along the Pacific coast of Mexico in the Summer of 1970, and between San Diego and Panama on board the R/V *Alpha Helix* in the Fall of 1970, convinced me that views on the distribution of *Pelamis* expressed by the Batelle Memorial Institute and published in the Commission report in December, 1970, were incorrect. The following account summarizes our present knowledge of the factòrs controlling the distribution of *Pelamis*.

The yellow-bellied sea snake is the only sea snake found in our hemisphere and is the most widely distributed member of the sea snake family. It is present in all tropical seas that it has been able to reach (Dunson and Ehlert, 1971; Graham et al., 1971). In a way, only an accident of geography has prevented it from reaching the Atlantic Ocean and the Caribbean. This snake probably migrated to the Pacific coast of the Americas after the Central American land bridge came up out of the sea for the last time (4 million years ago). Movement across the isthmus was therefore impossible. Movement around the tips of either South America or Africa was blocked just as effectively by cold surface waters (Figure 1). The only other possible entry to the Atlantic would be via the Suez canal. However, conditions in the Red Sea are unsuitable for sea snakes, possibly due to the high salinity and high surface temperatures during the summer. Winter temperatures in the Mediterranean Sea are much too low to allow survival of sea snakes anyway, so it would not be possible for the snakes to reach the tropical Atlantic even if they did penetrate the Suez region.

The tropical Atlantic Ocean seems to be a suitable habitat for sea snakes, and only a series of barriers in various parts of the world have prevented colonization in the past. Based on a study of the present ranges of *Pelamis* and sea surface temperatures, it appears that this snake could colonize an area of the Atlantic extending from the North Carolina–Virginia line to southern Brazil. In this area, mean monthly sea surface temperatures never go below 20°C. If one is convinced that the snakes actually would reproduce and spread in the Atlantic, the next logical question is whether or not they could actually pass through the proposed sea level canal. They apparently have not been successful in crossing through the present canal, due probably to the multiple locks, the sinuous coastline of Gatun Lake which would divert them from the main channel, and the fresh water of the whole system. These sea snakes can live for weeks and probably years in fresh water, so simple survival is not a problem. Like most marine animals, however, sea snakes probably choose to avoid low salinity estuarine waters.

More importantly, the snakes would actually have to swim into the present canal, whereas tidal currents in the proposed canal could carry the snakes in. A striking result of recent studies is the finding that these sea snakes do very little swimming, but drift passively with surface currents (Kropach, 1971; Dunson and Ehlert, 1971). Under certain conditions, when surface water flows are converging, the snakes are concentrated into slicks by the hundreds and thousands. It was previously thought that these pelagic or "blue water" snakes were found too far from the coast to possibly enter a canal. On the 1970 cruise of the R/V *Alpha Helix,* we found snakes between 200 yards and 50 miles off the coast. Most of the snakes seem to be within 1–10 miles of the coast. We also talked to natives who reported that, at certain times of the year, snakes were washed up on the beaches while still alive. This stranding phenomenon has also been reported in Panama Bay by Kropach (see Chapter 10). Thus it appears rather likely that some snakes will be able to pass through the proposed canal.

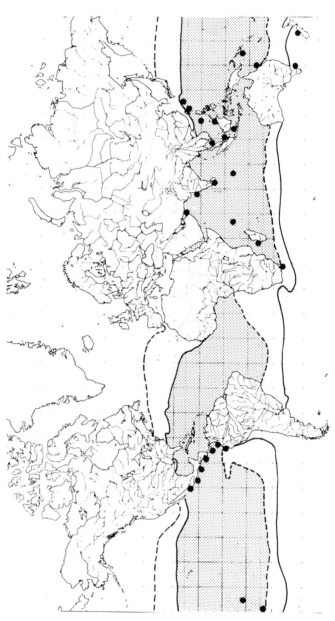

Figure 1. Distribution of *Pelamis platurus* (black dots) in relation to the 20°C mean surface sea water isotherms in August (dashed line) and February (solid line). The stippled portion, representing an area in which the monthly mean is always 20°C or above, closely corresponds to the best present estimates of the *Pelamis* breeding range (excluding the Atlantic Ocean and Red Sea, which have no sea snakes). (From Dunson and Ehlert, 1971; reprinted by permission of the American Society of Limnology and Oceanography, Inc.).

The major factor inhibiting the spread of *Pelamis,* if it is introduced into the Atlantic Ocean, will be predation. None of the Pacific predatory fish tested by Rubinoff and Kropach (1970) would attack or eat *Pelamis.* This recognition by the potential predator is probably visual (Figure 2) and gustatory, and perhaps olfactory. Atlantic fish readily attacked and ate *Pelamis;* 35 attacks resulted in three deaths of the predator. Several *Pelamis* were regurgitated by a predator that subsequently died. An intense selection pressure against *Pelamis* predators in the Atlantic eventually would lead to recognition of this prey as dangerous, and to avoidance by predators. In the meantime, the colonization of the Atlantic by *Pelamis* would be slowed by the death of individuals eaten by "naive" predators (Rubinoff and Kropach, 1970).

There now seems to be general agreement with my original postulate (Dunson, 1971; Sullivan, 1970; Bailey, 1970) that *Pelamis* would pass through the sea level canal, if it were built without barriers, and become established in the Atlantic Ocean. Pickwell et al. (1972) and Kropach (1972) both stress that little danger to humans is to be expected even if colonization is successful. This does not differ from my point of view as originally expressed, or as restated before a hearing of the subcommittee of the Committee on Merchant Marine and Fisheries, House of Representatives on December 10, 1971 (U.S. Gov't., 1972). I have always maintained that the menace is mainly psychological and similar to that of the Portuguese man-of-war, which prevents swimming at Caribbean beaches from time to time. What various authors seem to overlook is that the threat of possible death, even if only slight, can be a powerful economic force in the tourist industry. The facts that *Pelamis* is relatively common on the Pacific coast of Mexico, that few if any deaths result, and that tourists are not deterred, are not useful arguments against the potential danger of *Pelamis* in the Caribbean for several reasons: (1) bathing beaches at the major Mexican resort of Acapulco are mainly inside the bay, where snakes are rarely found; (2) few tourists at Puerto Vallarta, where *Pelamis* is sometimes found next to and actually on the bathing beaches, realize that these snakes are dangerously venomous; and (3) Mexican fishermen on the Pacific coast work mainly in lagoons or bays due to the heavy surf on exposed beaches, and do not usually encounter *Pelamis* except as moribund beach specimens. Kropach (1972) has been bitten six times by *Pelamis,* apparently without envenomation or any ill effect.

Yet this is hardly evidence that *Pelamis* is to be considered relatively harmless, since Rubinoff and Kropach (1970) found that about 9% of the attacks by Atlantic fish on *Pelamis* in aquaria led to death of the predator. Since *Pelamis* appears to use its venom primarily for protection against predators, a fairly low rate of envenomation imposes a rather high selection pressure against attacks. I suggest that most people would be reluctant to swim with this snake, even if it is only likely to inject a lethal dose of venom every 11th bite.

Figure 2. An underwater or fish's eye view of *Pelamis* floating at the surface. Note the conspicuous coloration of the tail. This and the bright yellow ventral surface are probably a warning to potential predators. (Photograph by Dave Hamilton, Pennsylvania Mirror).

SUMMARY

Despite environmental differences between the Caribbean Sea and Panama Bay, major faunal movements through the proposed Panama sea level canal are likely. The probability that the yellow-bellied sea snake (*Pelamis*) would successfully transit the canal (built without physical or chemical barriers) and colonize the Atlantic is judged to be high. This prediction is based on the surface feeding and drifting habits of the snake and its presence along the shores of Panama Bay. The long-term consequences of this migration are less predictable. *Pelamis* appears to have characteristics that would make it a good colonizer in a habitat like the Atlantic, where competition is limited. Thus a gradual spread throughout the tropical and subtropical regions of the Atlantic would be expected. The speed of colonization of this venomous snake could be slowed by the predation of carnivorous fish. Although *Pelamis* is a dangerously venomous snake which could prove to be a nuisance in tourist areas, it is not likely to cause major ecological disruption. Much more serious effects could be caused by coral predators, or by diseases or parasites against which the Atlantic fauna and flora have little protection.

REFERENCES

Aron, W. I., and S. H. Smith. 1971. Ship canals and aquatic ecosystems. Science 174:13—20.

Bailey, D. 1970. A thermal barrier for snakes. Biomedical News Dec.:14.

Boffey, P. M. 1971. Sea-level canal: How the Academy's voice was muted. Science 171:355—358.

Dunson, W. A., and G. W. Ehlert. 1971. Effects of temperature, salinity, and surface water flow on distribution of the sea snake *Pelamis*. Limnol. Oceanog. 16:845—853.

Dunson, W. A. 1971. The sea snakes are coming. Nat. Hist. 58:52—61.

Flood, D. J. 1966. Isthmian canal policy questions. U. S. Gov't. Print. Off., Wash. D.C. 67—843. House Document No. 474 (89th Congress, 2nd session).

Graham, J. B., I. Rubinoff, and M. K. Hecht. 1971. Temperature physiology of the sea snake *Pelamis platurus:* An index of its colonization potential in the Atlantic Ocean. Proc. Nat. Acad. Sci. USA 68:1360—1363.

Kropach, C. 1971. Sea snake (*Pelamis platurus*) aggregations on slicks in Panama. Herpetologica 27:131—135.

Kropach, C. 1972. *Pelamis platurus* as a potential colonizer of the Caribbean Sea. Bull, Biol. Soc. Wash. 2:267—269.

Laycock, G. 1966. The Alien Animals. Ballantine Books, New York.

Newman, W. A. 1972. The National Academy of Science Committee on the Ecology of the Interoceanic Canal. Bull. Biol. Soc. Wash. 2: 247—259.

Pickwell, G. V., J. A. Vick, W. H. Shipman, and M. M. Grenan. 1972. Production, toxicity, and preliminary pharmacology of venom from the sea snake *Pelamis platurus. In* Food-Drugs from the Sea. Proc. 3rd Conf. L. R. Worthen (ed.). Marine Technology Soc. Wash. D.C. p. 247—65.

Por, F. D. 1971. One hundred years of Suez canal—A century of Lessepsian migration: Retrospect and viewpoints. Syst. Zool. 20: 138–159.

Jones, M. L. (ed.). 1972. The Panamic Biota: Some observations prior to a sea-level canal. Bull. Biol. Soc. Wash. No.2:1–269.

Jones, M. L., and R. B. Manning. 1971. A two-ocean bouillabaisse can result if and when sea-level canal is dug. Smithsonian 2:12–21.

Rubinoff, I. 1968. Central American sea-level canal: Possible biological effects. Science 161:857–861.

Rubinoff, R. W., and I. Rubinoff. 1968. Interoceanic colonization of a marine goby through the Panama canal. Nature 217:476–478.

Rubinoff, I., and C. Kropach. 1970. Differential reactions of Atlantic and Pacific predators to sea snakes. Nature 228:1288–1290.

Sullivan, W. 1970. What if snakes and starfish change oceans? New York Times, Dec. 13. Section 4:12.

Topp, F. W. 1969. Interoceanic sea-level canal: Effects on the fish faunas. Science 165:1324–1327.

U. S. Gov't Print. Off. 1970a. Report on the problems concerning the Panama canal. 91st Congress. 2nd Session. Committee Print. #52–584. 96 pp. Wash. D.C.

U. S. Gov't Print. Off. 1970b. Cuba and the Caribbean. 91st Congress. 2nd Session. #47–893. pp. 204–231. Wash. D.C.

U. S. Gov't Print. Off. 1971. Interoceanic canal studies. 1970. Atlantic-Pacific Interoceanic Canal Study Commission. #0–410–974. Chp. VI. Environmental Considerations. pp. 59–62. Wash. D.C.

U. S. Gov't Print. Off. 1972. Panama Canal treaty negotiations. 92nd Congress #84–659. Serial No. 92–30. pp. 229–238. Wash. D.C.

Zaret, T. M., and R. T. Paine. 1973. Species introduction in a tropical lake. Science 182:449–455.

Index